THE ULTIMATE

ENCYCLOPEDIA OF THE
MOVIES

This is a Carlton Book

Text copyright © 1995 Derek Winnert/Carlton Books Limited
Design copyright © 1995 Carlton Books Limited
MOMI is a trademark and © of the Museum of the Moving Image

First published in 1995 by Carlton Books Limited

10 9 8 7 6 5 4 3 2 1

A CIP catalogue record for this book is available from the
British Library

ISBN 1-85868-079-4

Project editor – Martin Corteel
Project art direction – Russell Porter
Design – Paul Cooper
Production – Garry Lewis
Picture research – Liz Heasman
Editorial Assistant – David Ballheimer

Printed and bound in Spain

General Editor

Derek Winnert saw his first film from his grandmother's arms at the
Grand Cinema, Edinburgh – it was the Boris Karloff Frankenstein – but
he was fully ensnared in the magic of the movies when his mother took
him to *The Ladykillers* at the age of 10. His school actually screened films
and surprisingly for those days taught the theory of film. While
studying at Oxford, he spent too many evenings watching movies. His
first job was at the Western *Morning News* in Plymouth where he soon
found himself working as film reviewer. In London he came to work for
The Times as chief sub-editor at the age of 25, a job that gave him plenty
of time to visit the Electric, the Scala, the Everyman, which showed
double and often treble bills, and of course the National Film Theatre,
where he saw seasons of movies in their entirety. At *The Times* he helped
to found *Preview*, Britain's first newspaper listings magazine, and wrote
film stories for it. He was also film and video editor at the *Radio Times*,
and he is now a freelance writer and film reviewer.

Other Contributors

Carol Allen is a writer and broadcaster, who reviews the movies for
Singled Out, contributes arts features to *The Times* and other
publications, and broadcasts on the movies and theatre for BBC and
Independent radio. She was the movie critic/correspondent for LBC
Radio and has reviewed for *Chic, New Woman* and *The People*.

Gary Amphlett is a screenwriter and broadcast journalist. He co-
wrote and was assistant director on the film *L'Angleterre Underground*, a
Channel 4/European co-production, and has another screenplay
currently under option. Previously a film critic with *Good Times*, he has
taught video production at Westminster University, works as a sports
commentator in radio and was Director of Tottenham Hotspur
Television.

Xan Brooks served as assistant director on movie productions in
London and the United States, and studied the movies at Manchester
University and Amherst College, Massachusetts. He is the movie editor
at *The Big Issue* magazine.

Paul Sussman was educated at Cambridge University, since when
he has worked variously as a builder, grave-digger, dish-washer, private
detective, stand-up comedian and actor. He owned his own theatre
company – TAD Theatre – in Liverpool, has performed in numerous
plays and films, but now earns his keep as a columnist and
commissioning editor on *The Big Issue* magazine. He is two-ninths of the
way through his first screenplay.

George Watson is an artist, designer and writer, who has exhibited
his sculpture and painting in London and Europe. He was concept
designer for the first Pavlova Dance Festival in London and designs
merchandising for the Royal Opera House and the English National Ballet.

THE **ULTIMATE**

ENCYCLOPEDIA OF THE

MOVIES

General Editor

DEREK WINNERT

THE DEFINITIVE ILLUSTRATED GUIDE TO THE MOVIES

In association with

MUSEUM *of the moving image*

Foreword by

BARRY NORMAN

CARLTON

The Museum of the Moving Image

MOMI is the world's most exciting museum of film and television. Operated by the British Film Institute and located on London's South Bank, next to the National Film Theatre, MOMI tells the story of the moving image from the magic of shadow puppets and optical toys to the multimedia and satellite world of today.

The story of the moving image is shown as a technical development, a cultural and artistic record and one of the most powerful social phenomena of the twentieth century. The Victorian world of photography and magic lantern shows leads to the earliest film and rapid technical development. The museum shows the visitor the birth of Hollywood and the excitement of the silent era, including a ride on a Russian Agit Prop train.

The many facets of film are covered, from animation and documentary to sound and newsreels. Cinema is shown from all over the world, but the centrepieces of the museum are the Hollywood studio and the re-creation of a British Odeon cinema of the 1940s.

Television grows from its pre-war beginnings, through the fondly remembered programmes of the growth of the BBC and ITV, up to the high technology of today's television studios.

The museum's displays include wide collections of technical equipment, props and costumes from films and studios, advertising material an memorabilia. Its famous real exhibits include Marilyn Monroe's "shimmy" dress from *Some Like It Hot*, Frankenstein's monster and Muffin the Mule.

MOMI is no ordinary museum – it shares its story by showing visitors over 800 moving images, by having actors in period costume and style explain the displays, by showing films in its own cinema, by having exhibits to do and enjoy as well as see and hear. At MOMI visitors can make their own cartoons, act in a Hollywood film, see an animator at work, read the television news or fly like Superman.

Contents

Robin Williams: *Greeting the new day in* Good Morning Vietnam *(1987)*

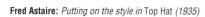

Fred Astaire: *Putting on the style in* Top Hat *(1935)*

Foreword
by Barry Norman

I have a strong personal involvement with MOMI. My programme, then *Film '88*, was on hand to record its opening and returned later to celebrate its tenth anniversary. In the meantime and thereafter my (younger) self on video has been among the exhibits, interviewing anyone interested and – so I am informed, though the enormity of it strains credulity – sometimes being roundly insulted by uncouth young interviewees. What, one asks oneself, is the younger generation coming to?

Well, let us graciously gloss over all that. Let us instead turn our attention to the very latest developments because to MOMI's other treasures is now added this book, a welcome and encyclopedic tome that combines biographical notes about the stars with film reviews, background information on, for instance, the amazing special effects in *Jurassic Park* and a crisp résumé of the evolution of the cinema over the past 100 years.

You wish to be reminded of the key films of each era? They are here. You want to know why Monroe wiggled or Schwarzenegger looks so blank? The answers lie within. Was Lassie a canine drag artiste? Who won which Oscar when and for what? Seek no further, for the following pages will satisfy your curiosity.

There are, God knows, more film reference books than you could shake a stick at. Some of them are even pretty good. But this one is unlike any other in that it refuses to conform to this category or that. It may not have all the information you seek, but it has an awful lot more than you will find in any other single volume. Movie books are my lifeline; I need them to do my job and the MOMI Encyclopedia, believe me, will have a very prominent place on my shelves.

Barry Norman
April 1995

Introduction

Whittling away the thousands of worthy challengers for our two lists of key artists and landmark movies of film's first century from all around the world into just 500 names and 270 movies has proved a vexatious business. But it's also been a fun parlour game for us – and we hope all our readers too. Yet the end result should not be looked on as a kind of "Schindler's List", a Noah's Ark where they come in one by one excluding all but the chosen few.

Rather, this collection provides a series of signposts to map the history of cinema. In the end the two lists, however informed and "historical", are personal and prejudiced: it's our list. You'll have your own favourites and your own choices. We hope most of them will be here, but inevitably you might not agree with many of our final choices or you might take issue with what has been written about your favourites, and that's part of the fun.

Though we've taken it seriously, it's just a game, or, as Hitchcock said to his star Bergman: "It's only a movie, Ingrid." Even so we hope you will agree that the names and movies which follow represent the cream of the crop of the movie industry – names and movies which have left an indelible mark on our century's culture, extended the boundaries of cinema or set new standards of excellence.

How do the people and films qualify for the two lists? The qualifications are based on a combination of impact, longevity and track record. Don't expect a hatchet job: we've come to celebrate the cinema's first 100 years, to praise Caesar not to bury him. So we've tried to be analytical and informative, but non-judgmental. The Who's Who profiles, though they're unashamedly peppered with informed opinions and prejudices, are an appraisal and appreciation of people we like. The Landmark Movies are a mixture of films we like and movies that we simply cannot ignore. A reader wrote to me recently that *Citizen Kane* (1941) was boring, murky and unwatchable – a "critics' film", they scoffed. Well, even if it was never a popular success and the critics liked it more than the public, it's perhaps the most famous film of all time, one it would be a crime to ignore, and you'll find it here. Conversely *The Rocky Horror Picture Show* (1975) may not be the best film of all time, but it's here partly just because we like it and partly because it's a great example of its kind of film. We know our readers are fans out there, and so are we.

The book's opening section is an attempt to gain a historical perspective by taking cinema's first 100 years a decade at a time, looking for themes and concerns through 10-year periods. A decade is, of course, an entirely arbitrary period of time, an attempt to impose rational order on an industry or art-form that's as chaotic as the universe it represents. The sections on genres, or types of films, are on safer ground, and we've tried to whisk through the main themes and films of thrillers, musicals or westerns, and throw in a few provocative ideas along the way.

This book is the work of half a dozen very different people, with varying backgrounds, experiences and views as the writers' profiles suggest. But as I've been editing all the work, I've come to realize that this is its strength – an assembly of the diverse, coming together as an entertaining, thought-provoking, informative whole. I hope you'll enjoy it and learn things from it, as we've done. Good reading and happy cinema-going!

The History of the Movies

This century people across the globe have grown up with the movies – the world's most popular form of entertainment. Countless millions still thrill to the excitement of a night out at the flicks. Popcorn in the foyer and ice-cream during the intermission are the perfect accompaniment to the on-screen menu: witty one-liners, lingering kisses, high-speed car chases and mind-blowing special effects, plus, of course, Keanu and Winona or Arnie and Meryl.

The Myth and the Magic

Today, after 100 years of film-going, we may think we're more sophisticated, but we're still just the same, simply satisfied sensation-seekers our great-grandparents were: eager searchers for a good time, an unusual experience, or just bright lights and a fun night out. The thrill 1931 audiences got from *Frankenstein* is exactly mirrored in 1993's *Jurassic Park*.

Some wit once called the cinema "a womb with a view". There's no doubting the primeval attraction of watching films with a disparate bunch of strangers united only by the common experience of sitting in the dark, looking at and being aroused by the stars and the emotions they, the scriptwriters and directors are conjuring up. It's a wonderful feeling, this communal shared laughter or fear evoked by a great comedy or thriller. Certainly there's no experience like sitting in one of the surviving mega-cinemas enveloped in a big screen with wraparound sound.

The experience of watching films on video or television has clearly made the magic of the movies available to all, more than at any time in history, but it isn't the same experience at all. Oddly,

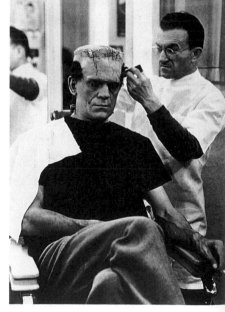

Frankenstein: *Jack Pierce makes up Boris Karloff*

though, some films, especially those with lots of close-ups, talking heads and intimate scenes can play better on television, with its concentrated images. Now many so-called "cinema" films are being made for television and video screening, using narrower ratios, with definite scene breaks so advertisers can screen their wares during a movie, and a natural break halfway, so the movie can be split over two nights or either side of the news.

Among all the arts, the cinema creates a unique illusion of reality. Time isn't real time. Shorthand and elisions are used. Acting is a mere representation of the truth and sometimes it's deliberately theatrical or stylized. Movie stories are a distorting mirror, and they may be symbolical, metaphorical or set out to promote a certain prejudiced viewpoint. The film talks in a language of its own we all recognize and respond to: the wipe, the fade-out, the close-up and so on.

The Power to Persuade

US President Woodrow Wilson called the cinema's first great full-length epic *The Birth of a Nation* (1915) "like history written in lightning". Its director, D. W. Griffith, had invented all the necessary language and grammar of the cinema, and had seen the power of the movies as propaganda. The film, with its apologia for the Ku Klux Klan, is considered so potent that 80 years on people are still trying to suppress it. From the moment of its release, the movies were seen as an enormous influence for good or evil, which is why from the very start they've come under the scrutiny of the world's "moral watchdogs" or even political guardians.

Films have been held responsible for every manner of social and moral problem, for example street riots with *Do the Right Thing*, (1989), moral decay with *The Killing of Sister George* (1968), causing violence through *Pulp Fiction* (1994), or serial killing with *Natural Born Killers* (1994) and so on. *The Silence of the Lambs* (1992) was attacked for anti-gay stereotyping, then accused of glorifying killing. Martin Scorsese's deeply religious *Last Temptation of Christ* (1988) was lambasted for blasphemy, along with Monty Python's absurdist farce *Life of Brian* (1979).

Campaigns are regularly held to ban films, invariably on the most foolish, spurious and wrong-headed grounds. Often this is sheer prejudice, the equivalent of the book-burners of earlier times. Dr Josef Goebbels, Nazi propaganda minister from 1933 to 1945, saw the power of the cinema to influence whole populations and encouraged

films of Nazi propaganda, extolling Aryan virtues and Teutonic heroes. Goebbels promoted Leni Riefenstahl's documentary on the 1934 Nuremberg rally, as powerful a piece of propaganda as the cinema has yet achieved. In Russia *Battleship Potemkin* (1925) was certainly made as propaganda, though director Sergei Eisenstein extended it way beyond that into the realm of popular, everlasting art. But it was banned in Britain as encouraging revolution, and it turned out to be Britain's longest ban, apart from that imposed on Tod Browning's American horror film *Freaks* (1932), banned simply for reasons of taste, for being too poisonous and evil-toned. The British censor didn't care for the wicked influence of Marlon Brando's leather-clad gang in *The Wild One* (1954) either, though when it was finally unleashed in 1968, it seemed more kitsch and silly than "dangerous".

Escapist Rubbish?

At the other end of the scale, some parents complain that Hollywood's constant diet of sentimental, easy-viewing, escapist films is mind-rotting for their children – indeed many adults might say the same for

The Last Temptation of Christ: *Protestors lambasted it as 'blasphemous'*

a lot of the grown-up output. It all depends on your point of view. Everyone is a film critic with an opinion and a prejudice. Everyone is a moralist with a point of view and line to draw. The movies never stood a chance of a quiet life and now they wouldn't want it. Controversy sells tickets, though it's always going to be a fine line. You can't sell seats for a banned movie.

Nevertheless, the movies still possess a unique magic, and one

the publicists are naturally keen to protect. As the world is perceived to have grown darker and more complex, there seems to be more and more need for the kind of glamour and escapism purveyed by the big studios in the 1930s. It's all more tentative now, more knowing, less innocent, but it's still there in spadefuls. There's been a full-circle return to the glamour of an evening out in bright lights with a large bucket of popcorn at a plush "picture palace". The Hollywood studio system may have long gone, but the studios remain, albeit mostly in non-American hands, still churning out the costly, escapist blockbusters for an international public eager for entertainment. Give us a good comedy or adventure and we're out in our millions.

Films like *Jurassic Park* (1993) and *Forrest Gump* (1994) are as big as anything from the Hollywood golden age, and twice as welcome, because such indisputable blockbusters are rarer now. Fewer film-makers seem to possess the Midas touch, but the people who do, like Steven Spielberg, Oliver Stone or Quentin Tarantino, are the toast of our culture.

Natural Born Killers: *Attacked for its violence*

The First Steps
The image is everything

The discovery of cinema has all the elements of a detective story. All the clues were there, waiting for someone to notice them and then put them together for the "grand dénouement": the solution to a problem we had subconsciously been working on since the dawn of art – how to capture an image of an ongoing sequence of time, preserve it and reproduce it.

Magic lantern: The camera obscura principle

From the earliest cave paintings we have attempted to reproduce the moving images seen by our eyes and preserve them. But painting and sculpture are dealing with one frozen moment in an image's lifetime. The earliest example of artificially created moving images is found in the art of the shadow puppets, which appear to have originated in Java and India and were a feature of oriental life for several thousand years. A typical example is the Javanese Wayang Purwar shadow plays, which used virtually two-dimensional figures made of stiff leather, articulated at the joints and operated by rods.

Lens, Light and Image

Meanwhile, in another part of the forest as it were, the study of optics was developing. Simple lenses were known in classical Greece and an early study of the principles of lenses was made by the Arab mathematician Al Hazan while Europe was still deep in the Dark Ages. Another development in the focusing of light and images was the "camera obscura", based on the observation that light passing through a small hole into a darkened room forms an upside-down image of the scene outside – a device which was used in several variations as an artist's aid,

until being incorporated into the development of the camera in the 19th century.

But before then came the Magic Lantern, which used the "camera obscura" principle of an image, illuminated by a light source and projected through a lens on to a screen, and turned it into popular entertainment. An interesting application of the Magic Lantern was the Fantasmagorie, developed in 1790s Paris by Belgian show-man Etienne-Gaspard Robert, known as Robertson. His Fantascope was mounted on a wheeled carriage so it could be moved toward and away from the screen, giving the effect of tracking and zooming, but controlled from the projec-

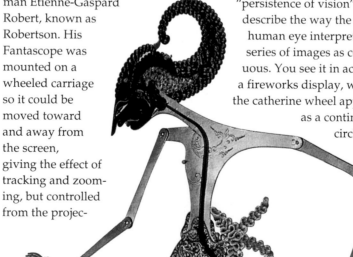

tor. Audiences were treated to an early "horror movie" of grotesque and macabre images projected on to gauze and smoke, which changed size, appeared and disappeared and even changed form, showing for example a human form dissolving into a skeleton.

Persistence of Vision

An important observation now comes into the picture, the phenomenon originally known as "persistence of vision", to describe the way the human eye interprets a series of images as continuous. You see it in action at a fireworks display, where the catherine wheel appears as a continuous circle and you

can "draw" patterns in the air with a sparkler. It is caused by the split second it takes for the image from the eye to get to the brain and be processed. If the images are received below the "perceptual threshold", as is the case with projected film, where the brain has to process 24 images (frames) a second, the action appears to be continuous.

The Birth of Photography

At the same time the last element of the soon-to-be-born cinema was coming into focus with the development of photography throughout the 19th century. In France in the 1820s Joseph Nicéphore Niépce fixed an eight-hour exposed image on to a silver compound, the first stage in the glass daguerreotype that he developed with Louis Daguerre. William Fox Talbot used a related process to fix an image on sensitized paper, which was then refined by Frederick Scott in the 1850s, using the new collodion or wet plate process, which improved the quality and sparked off interest in commercial photography. Then in 1888 George Eastman developed the Kodak camera, using rolls of paper negative film, quickly

Shadowy past: A Javanese puppet

Arrivée d'un Train à la Gare de Vincennes (**1896**)*: An early cinematic treat for train spotters*

The brothers Lumière had opened the door to a new storytelling medium and a new industry. French showman Georges Méliès, who had been using magic lanterns in his magic and illusion presentations for years, was in the audience of the Lumières' cinema world première. He seized on the new medium with enthusiasm, incorporating Edison shorts into his stage show, then experimenting with his own films. In 1896 he built Europe's first film studio at Montreuil and became totally immersed in film-making. He was particularly fascinated by fantasy, for which he discovered many innovative optical and special effects techniques, and Méliès' films such as *A Trip to the Moon* and *The Conquest of the Pole* are still capable of amusing and fascinating audiences today.

Meanwhile in America new film-makers were more interested in realistic story telling. In 1903 Edwin S. Porter created the first western in the story of *The Great Train Robbery*, featuring Broncho Billy Anderson. Anderson was an early example of the "film star", a new profession which was to provide major icons for the 20th century.

superseded by celluloid.

The new technique made it possible to reproduce the real image, as opposed to the artist's impression, and provided an invaluable tool for those interested in the analysis of movement. Foremost among them was an Englishman, Eadweard Muybridge, regarded by many as the "father of cinema" for his work on what was effectively early stop-motion photography. Commissioned initially to settle a bet about whether all four feet of a running horse were ever off the ground at the same time, Muybridge rigged up a battery of cameras activated by trip wires as the horse galloped by, giving him a sequence of photographs.

Thomas Edison, inventor of the light bulb and the phonograph, was quick to spot the entertainment potential of these developments. With his assistant W. K. L. Dickson, using Eastman's celluloid film, he developed his own camera, the Kinetograph, to shoot short, continuous-loop, moving films, usually of popular vaudeville entertainers doing their act. These films were held in place by sprockets, moved along an electric motor and viewed inside the enclosed Kinetoscope cabinet.

The Problem is Solved

All that remained was to pull everything together for the denouement – the projection of

moving film. French showman Emile Reynaud came close with his Praxinoscope à Projections, which projected images painted on celluloid film mounted on a movable sprocket system via a combination of lenses, mirrors and magic lantern.

Two brothers, Auguste and Louis Lumière, experimenting with the idea of making films for Edison's Kinetoscope, combined the principle of the camera with that of the sewing machine, moving the film along on its sprockets, pausing for the shutter to open and

either expose the film or project the image, closing the shutter while the "sewing machine" moved the film on a frame, then repeating the whole process – the principle on which movie cameras and projectors still operate today. They patented their combined camera, processor and projector as the

Cinématographe, started shooting little one-minute films on such subjects as *Workers Leaving the Lumière Factory* and, on 28 December 1895, presented their first show to the public in the basement of the Grand Café in Paris. The new entertainment was an immediate "box-office hit" and cinema was born.

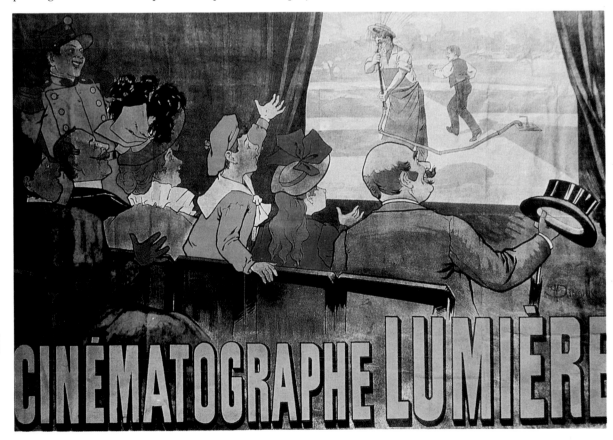

Lumière Cinématographe: A box office hit

The 1910s:
The age of innocence

Historically the 1910s are closer to the Crimean War than they are to us in the 1990s. And yet they were the key years in the development not just of the cinematic art, but of just about everything we have come to associate with cinema – when film for the first time became a widely recognized artistic medium. The feature film and the cartoon, the war film and the costume epic, the slapstick comedy and the adventure serial all appeared at this time, as did the close-up, the dissolve, the crosscut, the fade, parallel editing, and a host of other cinematic techniques that are today taken for granted.

It was America's decade, in which Hollywood was born, and with it the studio system and the millionaire film star. Though Italy produced the first ever epic feature, *Cabiria*, in 1914, and German expressionism made its appearance around 1918–19, with the onset of World War One the film industries of Europe went into cold storage, leaving the field clear for United States domination. Only Scandinavia produced anything approaching the same number or quality of films as America, and by the end of the decade most Scandinavian stars and directors were themselves haemorrhaging away to the Land of the Free.

It was also the decade of great individuals: towering, innovative personalities who transformed the embryonic film industry with their artistry and foresight. Greatest of all was David Wark Griffith, the "Father of Film" and the man generally credited with either discovering or developing the essential grammar of modern cinema (see feature opposite).

The American Pioneers

But Griffith was not the only innovator. Thomas Harper Ince, another Biograph protégé, had established his own studio at Inceville, California, in 1914, thereafter directing and producing some of the decade's most popular westerns. It was Ince who launched the careers of Frank Borzage, William S. Hart and Henry King, and who established the streamlined, highly efficient system of film production that has influenced Hollywood ever since.

Mack Sennett was also hugely influential, joining with Ince and Griffith in 1915 to form Triangle Productions. He, too, had started at Biograph, but in 1912 moved west to California and founded the Keystone Studio, developing a raucous, irreverent, anarchic strain of slapstick humour that took the world by storm and did much to establish American commercial domination of the cinema.

Frank Capra started his career as a Sennett gag writer, and a whole generation of directors and performers owed him their success – George Stevens, Gloria Swanson, "Fatty" Arbuckle, Carole Lombard, Marie Dressler, Harold Lloyd, Wallace Beery, Mabel Normand, Ben Turpin and, most notably, Charlie Chaplin.

Although Florence Lawrence – the "Biograph Girl" – was the first performer to boast her name above the title of her films, and Mary Pickford – "Little Mary" – predated him in popularity, Chaplin was the first truly great film star, a universal icon who, within a year of his arrival at Keystone in 1913, was feted the world over. His humour was subtler than Sennett's, and his lovable tramp character, which first appeared in his second film, *Kid Auto Races at Venice*

Nickelodeons: *Cheap and cheerful picture houses*

Charlie Chaplin: The first truly great film star

(1914), was an everyman stereotype that bridged all boundaries of age, race, class or nationality. After a few months, he was directing his own films, improvisatory masterworks such as *The Tramp* (1915), *The Bank* (1915) and *Easy Street* (1917).

The achievements of Chaplin and Griffith, Sennett and Ince existed within a wider framework of change and evolution within the film industry. The focus of production moved from the east coast to California, where the climate and light were better and the tax laws less restrictive. A host of small, independent film companies sprang up, several of which were later to develop into the great studios of Hollywood's Golden Era. Producers such as the Warner Brothers, Samuel Goldwyn, Louis B. Mayer, Carl Laemmle, William Fox and Adolph Zukor all entered films at this time, and by the end of the decade the movie business had assumed its definitive form.

The length of films increased from one or two to five or seven reels, and so did cost – from $500 for a two-reeler in 1912 to $20,000 for a five-reeler in 1915. The great studio publicity machines were created, specially built picture houses began to replace the old

nickelodeons, and audiences changed as the middle-classes began flocking to cinemas.

Early European Cinema

Although it was a decade of American primacy, film-making was certainly not an exclusively American business. In France, Louis Feuillade produced an endless stream of high-quality adventure serials such as *Fantomas* (1913–14) and *Les Vampires* (1915); while in Germany popular costume epics such as *Madame Dubarry* (1919) were giving way to a new cinematic expressionism, as exemplified by Robert Wiene's *Cabinet of Dr Caligari* (1920).

Only in Scandinavia, however, was there growth comparable to that in the States. In Sweden, under the guidance of Charles Magnusson at the Svenska Bio studio, Victor Sjöström and Mauritz Stiller emerged as world-class directors, with Sjöström's *The Sons of Ingmar* (1919), and Stiller's *Herr Arne's Treasure* (1919) among the greatest films of the early silent cinema. In Denmark, meanwhile, the Nordisk Film Company nurtured a wealth of talent, including actress Asta Nielsen and writer/director Carl Dreyer, and wowed Europe with its high production values and risqué choice of subjects. It also produced, with works such as *Atlantis* (1913) and *The Sky Ship* (1916), some of the earliest sci-fi pictures.

For all the burgeoning health and inventiveness of the Scandinavian film industry, however, its output was still negligible compared to that of America. It was here that the fundamental elements of screen technique were being developed at this time; here that the world's most popular films were being produced; here that cinema's new gods made their home; and here, above all, that the seemingly limitless possibilities of film were being harnessed and driven forward.

The Father of Film

The importance of David Wark Griffith was twofold. Firstly, he was the cinema's first consummate storyteller. In the 500 shorts he directed for the Biograph film studio between 1908 and 1914, as well as in his later epic features, he raised the art of screen narrative to new and unimagined heights. Secondly, he was the man who liberated film from the conventions of theatre, expanding both the expressive and technical scope of the medium and moulding it into an art form all of its own.

Before Griffith, directors had treated film as merely an extension of the stage, placing their camera directly in front of

the action and filming their stories scene by scene. Griffith, however, began cutting his scenes into small fragments, editing them together in such a way as to heighten tension and enhance the narrative.

It was Griffith who first brought depth and definition to film, experimented with the use of light and shade, developed the possibilities of close-ups and extreme long shots, and, with *The Birth of a Nation* (1915), created the first American epic feature film.

The latter's unprecedented length, visual daring and narrative scope caused a worldwide sensation – "Like

history written in lightning," said US President Woodrow Wilson – making it the most influential, and certainly one of the most profitable films of all time. Together with later Griffith features such as *Intolerance* (1916), *Hearts of the World* (1918) and *Broken Blossoms* (1919) it demonstrated once and for all the grace, majesty and infinite possibility of cinema, laying the foundations for everything that was to follow and establishing Griffith as the single most important filmmaker in history. "The task I am trying to achieve is above all to make people see," was the master's own assessment of his role.

The 1920s:
The age of the flapper

The 1920s was an immensely fertile period for cinema, with film-makers everywhere spreading their wings and trying to extend the boundaries of the form established by the pioneers in the previous decade. Films got even bigger, costlier – and better.

Hollywood spent the Jazz Age largely eschewing realism in favour of escapist melodramas and historical extravaganzas. The "flapper" did, however, make a belated appearance on the silver screen with Cecil B. DeMille's *Manslaughter* (1923) starring Leatrice Joy. In world cinema terms, America led the pack, but European cinema dogged its tracks with many great works, particularly among German, French and Swedish films.

America at the Forefront

America's new production company United Artists, formed in 1919, found Douglas Fairbanks Sr making ever more confident and graceful swashbucklers: *The Mark of Zorro* (1920), *The Three Musketeers* (1921), *Robin Hood* (1922), *The Thief of Bagdad* (1924), *Don Q* (1925), *The Black Pirate* (1926), *The Gaucho* (1927) and *The Iron Mask* (1928). Fairbanks's new wife, Mary Pickford, was the world's sweetheart, with a series

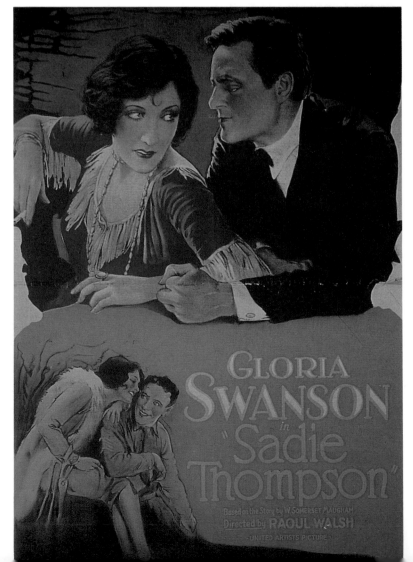

of sentimental melodramas with titles like *Pollyanna* (1919), *Suds* (1920), *Little Lord Fauntleroy* (1921 – as mother and son!), *Tess of the Storm Country* (1922) and *Coquette* (1929) for which she won an Oscar. But their only film together, 1929's *The Taming of the Shrew* ("by William Shakespeare with additional dialogue by Sam Taylor") failed, marking the end of their box-office ascendancy.

Pickford's main rival, Gloria Swanson, hit her stride with *The*

Glorious Gloria: Swanson was Mary Pickford's main rival

Affairs of Anatol (1921), *Manhandled* (1924) and *Sadie Thompson* (1928). Although MGM boss Louis B. Mayer sneered "In America men don't like fat women", "the Swedish Sphinx" Greta Garbo nevertheless became a silent superstar in *The Torrent* (1926), *The Temptress* (1926), *Flesh and the Devil* (1926), *Love* (1927), and *The Divine Woman* (1928).

The Fairbankses' United Artists partners, Charles Chaplin and D. W. Griffith, came up with an unbroken run of successes. Chaplin delivered his first feature *The Kid* (1921), a winning combination of knockabout comedy and pathos that made a child star of

Douglas Fairbanks Sr: Great and graceful swashbuckler

Jackie Coogan, following it with *The Pilgrim* (1923), *A Woman of Paris* (1923), *The Gold Rush* (1924 – his masterpiece of the decade) and *The Circus* (1928). Griffith's big years were 1921, with *Way Down East* and *Orphans of the Storm*, and 1926, with *Sally of the Sawdust* and *The Sorrows of Satan*, though after that his career was in decline.

Rudolph Valentino became a major attraction with exotic romantic pictures like *The Sheik* (1921), *The Four Horsemen of the Apocalypse* (1921), *Blood and Sand* (1923) and *Son of the Sheik*, released after his sudden death from peritonitis on August 23, 1926. Lon Chaney Sr ("Man of a Thousand Faces") was seen at his best as Quasimodo in *The Hunchback of Notre Dame* (1923), *The Phantom of the Opera* (1925), *The Unholy Three* (1925) and *London After Midnight* (1927). The great Austrian director Erich Von Stroheim burst on to the American scene with *Foolish Wives* (1922), *Greed* (1924), *The Merry Widow* (1925) and *The Wedding March* (1927) before the absurd extravagances of the unfinished *Queen Kelly* (1928) killed his career. The western came of age with James Cruze's *The Covered Wagon* (1923), John Ford's *The Iron Horse* (1924), *Riders of the Purple Sage* (1925) with Tom Mix and *In Old Arizona* (1929), the first all-sound oater.

Sherlock Junior: *Buster Keaton, probably the closest rival to Charlie Chaplin, was at his best in this 1926 comedy*

Europe in Hot Pursuit

German movies were in the first full flush of creativity, with a highly imaginative series of expressionist fantasy masterworks such as Paul Wegener's *The Golem* (1920), Robert Wiene's *The Cabinet of Dr Caligari* (1920) and *The Hands of Orlac* (1924), F. W. Murnau's *Nosferatu* (1921) and *Faust* (1926), Paul Leni's *Waxworks* (1924). These were crowned by the work of the great Fritz Lang – *Destiny* (1921), *Dr Mabuse* (1922), *Die Nibelungen* (1924), the sci-fi classic *Metropolis*

(1926) and *Spies* (1928). G. W. Pabst provided notable work in *Joyless Street* (1925), *Secrets of a Soul* (1926), *Pandora's Box* (1928) and *Diary of a Lost Girl* (1929), the last two with the vibrant American import Louise Brooks.

In Sweden, Victor Sjöström showed he was a world master with *Masterman* (1920), *Ordet* ("The Word") and *The Phantom Carriage* (both 1921) before making a career in America with *He Who Gets Slapped* (1924), apparently MGM's first production, starring Lon Chaney, Norma Shearer and

John Gilbert. Fellow Swede Mauritz Stiller proved his worth with *Erotikon* (1920) and the highly popular *Gösta Berlings Saga* (1924), the latter launching Greta Garbo, whom he accompanied to America, though *his* career failed to prosper. In Russia, film-making giant Sergei Eisenstein made his debut with *Strike* and *The Battleship Potemkin* in 1925, following them with *October* (1926) and *The General Line* (1928).

The year 1924 was an important one for France: René Clair served up his debut with *Paris Qui Dort* and Jean Renoir made his with *La Fille de l'Eau*. These were to prove the two big names of French 1920s and 1930s cinema. The 1920s also saw Jacques Feyder starting a notable career with *L'Atlantide* (1921), *Crainquebille* (1922), *Carmen* (1926), *Thérèse Raquin* (1928) and *Les Nouveaux Messieurs* (1929).

The 1920s roared out on some of the decade's finest, most mature films, such as René Clair's *An Italian Straw Hat* (1928) and Luis Buñuel's debut with *Un Chien Andalou* (1928), while in Hollywood King Vidor made *The Crowd* (1928) and Sjöström *The*

Wind (1928). William Wellman's air corps romantic drama *Wings* (1927), with its breathtaking aerial and trench-warfare sequences, was the first film to win the Oscar for Best Picture at the newly established Academy Awards. The Oscars themselves were an indication that the movies were taking themselves seriously and that the new 20th-century art-form was definitely coming of age.

Roaring with Laughter

The decade was known as the Roaring Twenties, and in the movie houses the audiences were roaring with laughter. Indeed, chroniclers of the cinema later also called it the Laughing Twenties – a label attached to a 1960s compilation of Laurel and Hardy's great short comedies of 1926 onwards. Stan and Ollie carved out a masterly niche in character-based slapstick, which performed the rare trick of being remarkably subtle at the same time as silly. *Battle of the Century* (1927), *You're Darn Tootin'* (1928), *Two Tars* (1928), *Big Business* (1929), *Perfect Day* (1929) and *Men o' War* (1929) show them at their wittiest. Buster Keaton countered his great rival Chaplin with *Our Hospitality* (1923), *The Three Ages* (1923), *Sherlock Junior* (1924), *The Navigator* (1924) and *Go West* (1925), and capped them all with his masterpiece, *The General* (1928). The other great silent comic, the perenially scared and bespectacled Harold Lloyd, kicked off with *A Sailor-Made Man* (1921), and topped it with *Safety Last* (1923), *Why Worry?* (1923), *The Freshman* (1925), *The Kid Brother* (1927) and *Feet First* (1930).

Speakeasy:
"You ain't heard nothin' yet!"

To call non-sound-synchronized cinema silent gives a false impression. The silent cinema was never truly silent; it was from the outset an experience with sound – organs, gramophone discs and even full-scale orchestras in accompaniment to the images. There was always an aural element, so the move towards the talkies was part of a natural progression towards dramatic unity, and music played a large part in this shift.

It's interesting, though, that this new development wasn't initially considered necessary or permanent and, at the beginning, it was seen as a novelty that many people, including the shrewdest movie moguls of the day, predicted wouldn't catch on.

The First Words

It was *The Jazz Singer* that changed all that in 1927 when audiences first heard and saw Al Jolson singing. The truly magical quality of fully synchronized sound took them by storm – they really hadn't "heard nothin' yet". The race was on to fit all the major Hollywood studios with expensive new sound stages – and an entirely new film genre was born: the musical.

Warner Bros started making *The Jazz Singer* as a silent in the usual way with scenes interrupted by rather ponderous inter-titles, which now raise a smile or two, like: "God made her a woman and love made her a mother." But they also recorded some dialogue, improvised by Jolson and co-performer Eugenie Besserer who plays his mother. Jolson speaks only 280 words in the film, and

Besserer has only a few more, but just imagine the impact on audiences of the day when the first celluloid mouths actually poured out words they could hear. What a step forward in terms of realism and developing the film medium! *The Jazz Singer* now provides a valuable record of Jolson's audi-

ence-grabbing style of performance in the 1920s, and here he is in the all-new talking pictures, singing Irving Berlin's "Blue Skies", his own "Mother I Still Have You", Gus Kahn's "Toot Toot Tootsie Goodbye" and naturally "My Mammy". He was dubbed "the world's greatest entertainer" and *The Jazz Singer* allows us to see why.

The huge box-office success of the movie showed that the Warner studio had guessed the public mood correctly, and they began making talkies as quickly as possible, a move that turned them into Hollywood's third most powerful studio. Just 12 months earlier, in 1926, the then financially rocky

little studio had taken a risk by joining Western Electric in the Vitaphone Company, and that same year had screened a number of showcase shorts to accompany their John Barrymore feature *Don Juan*. Although the results were shaky technically, the public success of these presentation shorts encouraged Warners to take a do-or-die plunge into the new medium. For Warners and Hollywood, the talkies turned out to be the fairy-tale magic potion that revived the movies' fortunes to live happily ever after.

Though they are called "talkies", it was the synchronization of music and pictures already present as part of the entertain-

My Mammy: *Al Jolson and Eugenie Besserer in* The Jazz Singer, *the first talkie*

The Kinetoscope: Thomas Edison's milestone

ment that popularized the new development rather than the verbalization of the drama.

Early Experiments

Technically, sound was first synchronized in a clumsy, unreliable way on cylinders and phonograph records, following the actors' mouth patterns. In 1889 Thomas Edison demonstrated his Kinetophonograph, his Kinetoscope linked to a gramophone. Various refinements of this were launched: in the 1910s the French developed a Chronophone and in America inventors came up with the Cinephone. The breakthrough in recording a soundtrack was a combined effort between a German and an American system, called respectively the Tri-Ergon and the Phonofilm, the latter invented in 1923 by Lee De Forest. The US public wasn't particularly impressed when it was unveiled in selected cinemas. But the American studio Fox persisted in developing it and launched the

first successful experiment as Movietone in 1926. Astonishingly, given the march of progress, this continues to form the basic process for today's soundtrack recording.

In Britain Alfred Hitchcock provided the first British part-talkie by secretly filming some sequences of *Blackmail* (1928) in sound, unbeknownst to his studio bosses. The picture was released in both silent and sound versions, because most cinemas hadn't yet invested in the expensive new technology required to show it in sound form. Indeed many exhibitors were unconvinced about the long-term future of the talkies and were reluctant to make the investment, thereby temporarily holding back the development of the new medium.

Blackmail starred German actress Anny Ondra, who spoke little English, and when she tried to record her part as a London girl called Annie White, she spoke in an unacceptably broken English accent. There was no post-dubbing then, so Hitchcock hired English actress Joan Barry to speak the dialogue into her own mike while naturally crouching out of view of the camera, as Ondra mimed her words. The result was crude but effective enough.

Britain's first all-talkie wasn't made till 1930, a would-be spectacular called *Titanic* – which, as its title might suggest, now seems a disaster, since the huge new sound cameras were unable to be moved around and were virtually static, so this new breed of film

looked like a filmed play. Also the sound quality and voice reproduction were remarkably poor, with the actors mouthing the words at a snail's pace. Still, it was a start, and the technology developed remarkably quickly, with sophisticated sound cameras and sophisticated films on screens everywhere in a matter of a couple of years. America got going fast and the rest of the world had to catch up just as pronto.

Music, Maestro, Please

Of course, sound meant musical scores and with them great music and famous film composers. Among those score-meisters who would be on most moviegoers' list

***Alfred Hitchcock films Britain's first part-talkie* Blackmail:** *German star Anny Ondra had to mime her words*

of favourites are Erich Wolfgang Korngold (*The Adventures of Robin Hood* (1938), *The Sea Hawk* (1940), *King's Row* (1941)), Dmitri Tiomkin (*High Noon* (1952), *Giant* (1956), *Gunfight at the OK Corral* (1957), and John Barry (*From Russia with Love* (1963), *Out of Africa* (1985), *Dances with Wolves* (1990)). Many directors, too, had their favourites and used them over and over again: Alfred Hitchcock's was Bernard Herrmann (*Vertigo* (1958), *North by*

Northwest (1959), *Psycho* (1960)). John Huston's was Alex North (*The Misfits* (1961), *Wise Blood* (1979), *Under the Volcano* (1984)). Steven Spielberg's is John Williams, who provided the music for all his hits – *Jaws* (1976), *Close Encounters of the Third Kind* (1977), *Raiders of the Lost Ark,* (1981) *E.T.* (1982), *Empire of the Sun* (1987) and *Jurassic Park* (1993).

The arrival of sound was the most significant development in the history of the cinema, at least during its first century. Since the initial revolution, successive technical advances in each new generation have really only been refinements of quality not changes of form. There have of course been continual enhancements in quality like stereophonic sound, Sensurround, surround-sound, quadraphonic sound and, more recently, George Lucas's TFX sound, but there has been no comparable revolutionary advance in the cinematic form itself – it's just become bigger, louder, larger, more colourful and more engulfing. For the next revolution we must wait for the marriage of sound, light and sensation. And for that, we must look towards the developing area of virtual reality.

Silent Ending:
Stars fade, stars rise

"Sound didn't do any more to the industry than turn it upside down and shake the entire bag of tricks from its pocket," said *Variety* magazine in 1929. The coming of the talkies indeed precipitated the greatest upheaval in the history of the motion picture industry.

Warner Brothers, who had sparked the revolution with *The Jazz Singer* in 1927, were, in the words of *Variety*, "advanced from the last place amongst the film companies to first in the league". Fox, too, had hopped on the sound bandwagon early, becoming inestimably richer and more powerful in the process, while RKO, one of the key players of the 1930s studio system, was created specifically to take advantage of the talkie revolution. If the big companies thrived, dozens of smaller ones went to the wall. The arrival of sound necessitated enormous investment in new equipment, research and studios, and many, possibly most, of the less wealthy businesses were unable to bear the financial burden.

For those that could meet the new requirements, however, the benefits were enormous, with US cinema attendance shooting upwards from 57 million in 1927 to 110 million in 1930. The structure of Golden Age Hollywood, with production dominated by just five major studios – Loew-MGM, Fox, Warners, RKO and Paramount – was due in no small part to the skill deployed by those studios in exploiting the talkies.

Painful Transition

If the advent of the talkies had major financial, technical and industrial repercussions, however, their effect was particularly evident on a human level. Sound made careers, and sound broke

them, with the period 1927–30 seeing an unprecedented turnover of Hollywood personnel.

The most oft-quoted example of a career ruined by the coming of sound was that of John Gilbert (see box), the suave, silent-screen lover who in 1927 was earning $250,000 per picture, yet whose career was washed up by the early 1930s. His downfall was caused partly by his voice, which came across as high-pitched on the rudimentary sound-systems of the day and seemed ludicrously out of keeping with his image as the swashbuckling macho-man of silent film. He was also enormously costly to employ, an expense the studios could ill afford as they were already up to their eyes in debt funding the changeover to sound. Part of the appeal of the new generation of actors such as Clark Gable was that they were a lot cheaper than those they were supplanting.

Cost, then, and voice, but above all image was what ruined John Gilbert and with him a host of other silent stars. Mary Pickford, Tom Mix, Douglas Fairbanks Sr, Ramon Novarro, Gloria Swanson, Clara Bow, Louise Brooks and Lillian Gish were among the many icons of the silent cinema whose careers faltered with the coming of talkies, not necessarily because they sounded wrong, but because, at a time of renewal, they were emblematic of a bygone age.

All Change

Heaviest hit were silent comedy performers such as Harold Lloyd, Harry Langdon and Buster

Keaton. The latter was MGM's highest-paid comedian at the end of the 1920s, yet, like Gilbert, his career was effectively over within five years of the arrival of sound. The humour of Keaton and others was quintessentially silent humour, dependent for its effect on physical gags and visual clowning. The talkies, however, demanded verbal humour, and

The Great Dictator (1940): *Charles Chaplin waited 13 years to make a talkie*

with it a whole new cast of faces – W. C. Fields, Eddie Cantor, Mae West, Jack Benny, The Marx Brothers, Jimmy Durante, Will Rogers and Bob Hope were among the many New York stage comics drafted into Hollywood at this time. Laurel and Hardy, meanwhile, were the exact opposite of Keaton, for they had struggled in silent cinema but, with the coming of talkies, found their niche and were suddenly propelled into the front rank of screen comedians.

One of the few silent comics not to be ruined by sound was Charlie Chaplin, who survived by the simple ploy of remaining resolutely silent. His first film of the sound era, *City Lights* (1931), opened to rave reviews despite its lack of dialogue, and his next, *Modern Times* (1936), was also hugely popular and silent (though it did include the odd sound effect). Only in *The Great Dictator* (1940), 13 years after the advent of talkies, did he speak for the first time, and then only at the end of the film. Significantly, it was his last truly popular movie.

If Chaplin survived by ignoring sound, other silent stars embraced it and prospered. Marie Dressler, Norma Shearer, Ronald Colman, Janet Gaynor, William Powell and the Barrymores all worked successfully in the new medium, as did Greta Garbo, despite MGM's fears that audiences wouldn't take to her thick Scandinavian accent. Such had been the case with Emil Jannings, Vilma Banky and Pola Negri, but Garbo's husky, deep-toned drawl merely added to her allure, and when she finally did make her sound debut, in *Anna Christie* (1930), her impact was immense.

A surprising number of important silent directors also enjoyed a painless transition to sound. D. W. Griffith and Mack Sennett didn't make it, but their careers were already in decline before 1927 and talkies merely hastened the process. Cecil B. DeMille crossed over

Garbo talks in **Anna Christie (1930):** *"Gimme a viskey, ginger ale on the side, and don't be stingy, baby"*

happily enough, however, as did Lewis Milestone, Howard Hawks, John Ford, Frank Capra, Fritz Lang, Ernst Lubitsch, Raoul Walsh, King Vidor and Alfred Hitchcock. Walt Disney brought out his first speaking cartoon – *Steamboat Willie* – in 1928 and thereafter contributed much to the fledgling medium with his *Silly Symphonies* series.

A New Generation

Stars faded, then, and stars survived; but with the coming of sound stars also appeared. A whole new generation of actors and directors came to Hollywood at this time, plucked in the main from the theatre world where the spoken word was paramount. Directors George Cukor, Preston Sturges, John Cromwell and Rouben Mamoulian all started their careers on Broadway before coming to film in the late 1920s and early 1930s, as did choreographer Busby Berkeley and actors Fred Astaire, Fredric March, Clark Gable, George Arliss, Leslie

Howard, Paul Muni, Edward G. Robinson, James Cagney, Katharine Hepburn and Spencer Tracy.

For some the beauty of the silent cinema could never be replaced. Jacques Tati refused dialogue, while Mel Brooks revived visual comedy with *Silent Movie* (1976). They are in a minority, how-

ever. The talkies swept aside those who could not let go of the silent era and installed a new society in their stead. "It would have been more logical if silent pictures had grown out of the talkie instead of the other way around," said Mary Pickford. It didn't happen like that, however, and Pickford and her generation fell because of it.

A toast to the silents: (left to right) *Dom DeLuise, Marty Feldman and Mel Brooks in* Silent Movie *(1976)*

19

The 1930s:
The age of glamour

The sound era had opened with a musical, *The Jazz Singer* (1927), and the 1930s started with a series of popular musical entertainments to cash in on the sound experience. This was not only Hollywood's reaction to the arrival of sound, but also its response to the Depression: give the public some expensively made, mass-produced, cheap-to-see entertainment to take their cares away.

Among the best of these musicals were the Warner backstage shows like *Dames* (1934) and *42nd Street* (1933), whose accent was on smell-of-the-greasepaint realism. This mood reflected the house style at Warners – tough and gritty – where they embarked on a controversial series of violent, quick-stepping gangster movies like *Little Caesar* (1930) and *Public Enemy* (1931) for sensation-seekers, leading to a moral-majority backlash that was as loud as the ringing at the box-office cash-register.

Starry Heights

But the main accent was on glamour and the studio that provided it was Metro-Goldwyn-Mayer, the biggest of them all. MGM, under tyrannical boss Louis B. Mayer, boasted more stars than there are in the heavens, and these included the king and queen of Hollywood, Clark Gable and Joan Crawford. Mayer favoured simple films of the *Andy Hardy*, *Lassie*, *Dr Kildare* "family values" variety, but gradually 1930s films became more sophisticated with witty comedy thrillers like the *Thin Man* series and the arrival of the screwball comedy (see feature, right).

It Happened One Night (1934) swept the board at the 1934 Oscars

and its director Frank Capra, memorable maker of *Mr Deeds Goes to Town* (1936) and *You Can't Take It with You* (1938), guided the movies towards being more populist and homespun. At their peak the American studios were producing an amazing 800 movies a year of every kind, and exhibiting a remarkable robustness and naturalism that makes them stand up well today. Acting and directing styles were noticeably realistic, and the pace was firecracker. Despite all the censorship and emphasis on family entertainment, the bulk of movies were remarkably mature and intelligent.

Technically, too, movies were improving. Colour started to gain hold when director Rouben Mamoulian and his cinematographer Ray Rennahan filmed *Becky Sharp* (1935) in eye-smacking, full three-tone Technicolor, an important advance on the early two-strip system or previous attempts to tint films. The important films of the latter period of the 1930s were expensively made in colour – *The Wizard of Oz* (1939) and *Gone with the Wind* (1939) for example.

In one way, though, things were getting worse. In 1930 the Hays Production Code was established, imposing strict standards of so-called "morality" on American

movies. This had the obvious effect of gagging creative work – everything from gangster pictures to Mae West comedies felt the chill – and films became more cosy and conservative as the world headed toward rearmament and warfare. The code gagged movies until 1966 when it was finally revised under pressure from courts and civil liberties groups.

French Polish

The 1930s were a great period for French cinema, in particular Jean Gabin became the big star of the day in masterworks like *La Belle Equipe* (1936), *Pépé le Moko* (1937),

La Grande Illusion (1937) and *La Bête Humaine* (1938). It was a golden age for French film directors, too, such as Jean Vigo, exponent of experimental poetic realism (*L'Atalante*, 1934), social comic commentator René Clair (*A Nous la Liberté*, 1931), Jean Renoir (*La*

Bête Humaine, 1938, and *La Règle du Jeu*, 1939), and the *Marius* trilogy of provincial-life chronicler Marcel Pagnol.

Marcel Carné and his dramatist Jacques Prévert invented the *film noir* with *Quai des Brumes* (1938), *Hôtel du Nord* (1938) and *Le Jour se Lève* (1939), mixing gangsters and poetry in imaginative tales of frustrated love and doomed lives.

In Germany, Adolf Hitler's assumption of power led to the Nazi Minister of Propaganda, Dr Goebbels, controlling the film medium, encouraging escapist entertainments and blatant propaganda pieces, the most impor-

Screwball Comedy

Screwball comedy, or madcap farce, blending the wacky with the sophisticated, was the vehicle for the clever, refined Hollywood wit of the 1930s. It reached its apogee in films like *The Awful Truth* (1937) and *Mr Blandings Builds His Dream House* (1948), both with Cary Grant, the cinema's suavest and most stylish exponent of the double- and triple-take. When Grant was paired with the mistress of screwball style, Katharine Hepburn, as he was in *Holiday* (1938), *Bringing Up Baby* (1938) and *The Philadelphia Story* (1940), the result was faultless.

The screwball form follows a loose but defined series of rules, usually with an initially incompatible hero and heroine thrown together in a ridiculous but plausibly plotted situation. Although the premise may be farcical, the development of the story and the acting are taken entirely seriously, and out of the melting-pot of the farce general truths about life, love, the social order, politics and human relationships emerge. The surface of the comedy is foolish but it masks acute human observation. Happily this still much-admired form continues to attract film-makers in movies like Peter Bogdanovich's *What's Up Doc? (1972)*, the Tom Hanks pic *The Money Pit (1986)* and *Overboard (1987)* starring Kurt Russell and Goldie Hawn.

tant of which was *Triumph of the Will* (1935), Leni Riefenstahl's record of the 1934 Nuremberg Rally. More happily, European talent, such as Ernst Lubitsch, Fritz Lang and Billy Wilder, fleeing from Nazism, brought a major boost to Hollywood.

The British in Hollywood

Across the Channel in Britain, *The Private Life of Henry VIII* (1933) became Britain's first worldwide hit, turning Oscar-winning Charles Laughton into an international star and putting British films on the map. It spurred its maker Sir Alexander Korda into building Denham Studios in 1936 with help from the Prudential Assurance Company, as an attempt at a British Hollywood ("Hollywood on the Thames").

Alfred Hitchcock's *The 39 Steps* (1935) and *The Lady Vanishes* (1938) turned him into Britain's best-known director, but Hollywood beckoned and, by the end of the 1930s, he was lost to the British film industry. British films created many popular stars – Robert Donat, Laurence Olivier, Vivien Leigh – but Hollywood claimed the best of them, sapping the strength of the home industry.

The end of the decade saw Hollywood at its most expansive, ebullient and distinguished. Just as the world was about to

embark on a crippling war, 1939 brought ten or so of Hollywood's greatest movies of all different kinds – *The Wizard of Oz*, *Gone with the Wind*, *Stagecoach*, *Mr Smith Goes to Washington*, *The Hunchback of Notre Dame*, *Wuthering Heights*, *Dark Victory*, *The Private Lives of Elizabeth and Essex*, *Ninotchka* and *Goodbye Mr Chips*. Such films exhibit a mesmerizing pizzazz and unshakeable confidence, which are rare in today's movie-making and confirm the rightness of the label given to this period. The 1930s were indeed the Golden Age of Hollywood.

Bringing Up Baby: *Screwball stars Katharine Hepburn and Cary Grant*

The Hollywood Studios: The product of the Dream Factory

Physically Hollywood is a place in Los Angeles, christened by a Kansas property-dealer's wife, Deida Wilcox, when they settled there in 1886. They sold up in 1903, just as the East Coast-based movie industry was looking for sunny sites in California to make films.

The first regular producer of films in Los Angeles was Colonel William Selig, who created the region's first major studio in 1909. When Cecil B. DeMille started the Jesse L. Lasky Feature Play Company in 1913 with Lasky and Sam Goldwyn, the Hollywood studio system was born. The greatest of the studios were United Artists (formed by Charles Chaplin, Douglas Fairbanks, Mary Pickford and D. W. Griffith), Metro-Goldwyn-Mayer (inaugurated by bosses Louis B. Mayer and Sam Goldwyn in 1924), Warner, Paramount (originally Famous Players), Fox (which later became Twentieth Century-Fox), Universal, Columbia and later Disney. RKO (founded in 1921) was the king of the smaller studios, which also included Allied Artists, its subsidiary Monogram, and Republic (begun in 1935).

Movie-making Monsters

These movie moguls were among the most colourful of all Hollywood's legendary characters. Most were benign monsters, some just monsters. Goldwyn (1882–1974) made his way into the public's affection with his "Goldwynisms" – "include me out", "anyone who goes to a psychiatrist should have his head examined", and "a verbal contract isn't worth the paper it's written

The lion roars: *The world-famous voice of Metro-Goldwyn-Mayer*

Sam Goldwyn: *"Include me out!"*

Hollywood Legend

As a movie-making capital, Hollywood soon spread out physically beyond its original perimeters as studios sprang up over a wide area of LA. But, much more than that, "Hollywood" developed into a self-created myth and legend, the way in which America, a country without royalty and with a comparatively short history, defines itself. Hollywood's never-ending fairy tale is virtually the story of the 20th century, and most of western culture has been affected by its influence (with the notable exception of France in particular which has resisted strongly, and its own cinema industry has remained more powerful, influential and independent as a result). But no culture in the world has been unaffected by the all-embracing Hollywood animal, the mouthpiece of America.

This seemingly benign and innocent beast is actually a rather dangerous animal that is in the vanguard of America's cultural imperialism, constantly reaffirming and spreading the nation's values and products.

Falling Stars

In another respect, too, the animal is dangerous. It's a hungry fame machine that chews up the people involved with it and spits them out the moment it's done with them. For every star who survives the system, there are ten who are destroyed by it, plus sad thousands who never make it at all. The Hollywood conveyor belt makes untold riches, fame and godlike status look easily attainable, utterly desirable and deceptively simple, but of course they are not. Even the greatest became casualties. Among the mightiest of stars, Katharine Hepburn was named "box-office poison" in the 1930s when her films flopped one after another (even "classics" like *Bringing Up Baby*, 1938); Joan Crawford was distraught when she was fired by her MGM boss Louis B. Mayer and when her daughter wrote a wounding bestseller about her; Bette Davis had to advertise for work in the 1960s and her daughter too turned on her in print. In the 1990s after a non-stop run of success in the 1980s, Arnold Schwarzenegger (paid in percentages and jet planes for *Terminator 2*, in 1991) was reviled for making just one movie, *The Last Action Hero* (1993), that was less than a mega-hit.

Hollywood exists at its brightest as an image and an image constructor. People throughout the world are committed to it, hanging on its every word, as we get excited about who's nominated for Oscars, how much this or that picture took in its opening weekend in America, who will play which character in which movie, who's getting married to whom or sleeping with whom, and so on. This gossip-column trivia has now become important worldwide news, often ending up on the front page of newspapers rather than in just their showbiz sections.

Virtually everybody is affected by Hollywood; we all grew up on it and are now the product of it. Few people the world over haven't seen *Gone with the Wind* (1939), *Snow White and the Seven Dwarfs* (1937), *The Wizard of Oz* (1939), *Star Wars* (1977) or *Jurassic Park* (1993). For better or worse, this cultural unifier is bringing the world closer together, making us think and behave alike – so we had better ensure that the voice it speaks with is the one we want to be heard.

on". Among the other memorables, Zukor (1873–1976) went on to notch up his century, still Paramount chairman in his 100s; Mayer (1885–1957), known as the "czar of all the rushes", ran MGM with an iron fist in a velvet glove; while reclusive millionaire and eccentric movie-buff Howard Hughes (1905–76) bought up RKO studios in the 1940s and ran it eccentrically.

The Star System

The star system, which enjoyed its heady heyday in the 1930s, was basically a glamour package where even the male stars were promoted in the main for their sexual allure and good looks. Most leading actors were chosen for their charisma in close-up rather than their acting prowess, though there were mould-breaking exceptions like Spencer Tracy, James Cagney or Fred Astaire whom the public was encouraged to admire for their special talent to entertain. The pack was led by a man who, though he could certainly act, was essentially a good-looking hunk. Clark Gable, nicknamed the King of Hollywood, was the only natural choice for Rhett Butler in *Gone with the Wind* (1939), otherwise the public frankly wouldn't have given a damn about the movie.

But the main focus of the star system was the gorgeous gals, those powdered, painted, primped beauties of the silver screen, copied by shop and factory girls the world over. Joan Crawford's shoulder pads changed the female outline forever, Veronica Lake's hairstyle adorned many a spotty adolescent, outrageously betrousered women became Katharine Hepburn dress-alikes, cigarettes were smoked in Bette Davis puffs, while many an eyebrow was plucked into the famous Dietrich arch.

All studios cultivated a rollcall of contract artists they could call on for the usually stereotyped roles they played, but MGM in particular maintained a huge roster of stars. Studio boss Louis B. Mayer adopted his players as a kind of extended family, with his favourite actor, Lionel Barrymore (the studio's longest-serving player), at its head. The family of course had children – Elizabeth Taylor, Judy Garland, Mickey Rooney and Roddy McDowall – and even a dog, Lassie. Mayer was a kindly tyrant: when he fell out with one of his "family", he behaved ruthlessly, ultimately even dispensing with the Queen of Hollywood, Joan Crawford.

Hooray for Hollywood: *Ernst Lubitsch calls the shots*

Hollywood at War:
Fighting the good fight

Laugh with Hope: *Comedian Bob Hope entertaining the troops*

It is one of the greater paradoxes of the 20th century that an industry which has done so much to fictionalize warfare should itself have been so involved in the real thing. Whether as combatants, fund-raisers, propagandists, documentary-makers, morale-boosters or educators, the American film fraternity has, from Chaplin's fund-raising tours of World War One to Cher's 1994 visit to war-torn Bosnia, contributed something to just about every major conflict of modern times.

The Great War 1914–18

That contribution started with The Great War of 1914–18. As the world's leading communications medium it was inevitable that cinema would play a significant role as a propaganda tool. After America entered the conflict in 1917, the war effort was bolstered by a stream of morale-boosting, flag-waving anti-German pictures, with Mary Pickford's *The Little American* (1917), Griffith's *Hearts of the World* (1918), Chaplin's *Shoulder Arms* (1918) and Winsor McCay's epic cartoon *The Sinking of the Lusitania* (1918) all doing their bit to emphasize the supposed moral superiority of the Allied cause.

Animator John Bray produced a newsreel series aimed at educating the public on the issues involved in the war, while cartoonist Max Fleischer – creator of *Betty Boop* and *Popeye* – was commissioned to work on army training films at Fort Sill, Oklahoma.

Basil Rathbone, Nigel Bruce, Ronald Colman and Walter Brennan were among the many Hollywood legends who actually fought in the war, although they only came to acting at the end of the war and no major Hollywood figure actually fought in Europe.

Epic Conflict 1939–45

Hollywood's involvement in World War One was negligible compared with its massive contribution to World War Two (1939–45). The sheer enormity of this conflict, coupled with a sense that it was a righteous struggle and strong government encouragement of film industry participation, galvanized Tinseltown in a way that had never happened before.

From the outset an extraordinary number of film personnel abandoned their jobs and enlisted to fight. David Niven and Leslie Howard were among the first, the

Betty Grable: *The most popular of all World War Two pin-ups*

latter being shot down and killed in 1943 while returning from a government mission to Lisbon. James Stewart and Clark Gable joined the US Air Force, Laurence Olivier and Robert Newton the Royal Navy, and Audie Murphy, the greatest B-western star of the post-war period, was America's most decorated soldier of the war.

The creation in 1942 of the Office of War Information saw a glittering array of screen talent pressed into service, making training and information films. As chief of the Field Photographic Branch of the Office of Strategic Services, John Ford made a number of top-secret military training films with intriguing titles such as *How to Operate Behind Enemy Lines* and *How to Interrogate Enemy Prisoners*, while Disney pitched in with a series of public information cartoons such as *The New Spirit* (1942), urging people to pay their income tax on time.

The most significant contribution to the Office of War Information came from director Frank Capra. His 20-minute weekly armed forces entertainment show – *The Army-Navy Screen Magazine* – was hugely popular, as was his *Know Your Allies – Know Your Enemies* series. His most significant work, however, was the seven-film *Why We Fight* series, a masterful compilation of cartoon, voice-over and documentary footage which, in Capra's own words, "not only stated, but in many instances actually created and nailed down American and world pro-war policy."

Elsewhere big-name stars such as John Garfield, Bette Davis, Bob Hope and Betty Grable were entertaining troops behind the lines (two million Grable photos were dispatched to Europe), selling war bonds or working in the Hollywood Canteen. The latter, founded in 1942 with Bette Davis as its first president, was a club open to military personnel in which stars would mingle with servicemen, perform and serve food.

Hollywood's most lasting contribution came from a small group of directors who captured first-hand documentary footage of the war. George Stevens travelled across Europe filming US troops in action, while Lewis Milestone's *Our Russian Front* (1942), William Wyler's *The Memphis Belle* (1944)

James Stewart (left) and Clark Gable: Two of many stars from Hollywood who enlisted in World War Two

and John Ford's *Battle of Midway* (1942) all recorded, in dramatic fashion, aspects of the conflict on land, at sea and in the air. Most oustanding of all was the work of John Huston, whose *Battle of San Pietro* (1945), about American troops fighting in Italy, and *Let There be Light* (1946), a study of mentally disturbed soldiers, are amongst the finest pieces of non-fiction filmmaking ever. *Let There be Light* was deemed so subversive that it was not released until 1986.

Television Takes Over

The American film industry's involvement in the Korean War (1950–51) was cursory, limited to gung-ho fictional narratives and,

although Marilyn Monroe and Bob Hope flew out to entertain the troops, there was little sense of the moral urgency that had defined the 1939–45 conflict.

By the time of Vietnam in the 1960s, television had taken over from film as the basic medium of mass communication, thereby depriving Hollywood of its unique position as a supplier of propaganda and information. As one critic put it, "Vietnam was a television war."

Industry veterans John Wayne and John Ford did their bit to support the war effort, with Wayne producing *The Green Berets* (1968) and Ford directing *Vietnam, Vietnam* (1971) for the United States Information Agency. But

there was a feeling in Hollywood that this was not a morally just war; and its leading lights conspicuously failed to swing behind the government as they had done in World War Two.

In fact, high-profile stars such

LIVE FAST – DIE YOUNG

CAROLE LOMBARD

Carole Lombard, bubbly blonde comedienne and wife of Clark Gable, was Hollywood's first significant casualty of World War Two. She had sent President Roosevelt a telegram the day after Pearl Harbor offering her services to the state, as a result of which she was despatched on a bond-selling tour in January 1942. On the way home her plane crashed near Las Vegas with the loss of all lives. Her death at 34 was a huge shock to America, greater even than that of Monroe 20 years later. Fittingly her last and greatest role was alongside Jack Benny in Lubitsch's brilliant anti-Nazi black comedy *To Be or Not To Be* (1942).

as Donald Sutherland and Jane Fonda used their celebrity status to campaign against the conflict. Fonda left the Government in no doubt as to what she thought of its policy with her film *FTA* (*F*** the Army*) (1973), while Robert Altman's *M*A*S*H* (1970) and Dalton Trumbo's *Johnny Got His Gun* (1971) can both be read as tacit criticisms of the war. Director Oliver Stone – Hollywood's only significant Vietnam combatant – has devoted much of his career to publicizing and condemning the horror, confusion and dreadful human wastage of the conflict.

The tub-thumping militarism of John Wayne has given way to the anti-Gulf War campaigning of Steve Martin and Emma Thompson. It is unlikely that the US film industry could or would ever again contribute to the extent it did during World War Two. Hollywood's fighting days, it seems, are over.

The 1940s:
The age of upheaval

The 1940s found the age of Hollywood at its most golden, with a grip on the public's hearts and minds as yet unchallenged by the rise of television. Capitalizing on the optimism and economic upturn of the post-war years, the American motion picture industry embarked on a frenzy of productivity that all but smothered the efforts made by other nations.

British cinema enjoyed a healthy period, buoyed up by the work of Carol Reed, David Lean and Powell and Pressburger, while France, missing the genius of the absent Jean Renoir, found solace in the burgeoning talents of Jacques Tati and Jean Cocteau. Most significant for European cinema was the emergence in war-torn Italy of the neo-realist strain spearheaded by directors Vittorio De Sica and Roberto Rossellini. But, for the most part, the decade belonged to the stars-and-stripes.

The Feel-good Factor

In 1946 the Hollywood film industry enjoyed its most successful year to date, evidence of a public sick of wartime worry and desperate for a little light entertainment. Mainstream Hollywood duly responded with a diet of home-spun reassurance and feel-good escapism. It was the 1940s that witnessed the rise of the MGM musical, that most traditionally warm-hearted and uncomplicated of genres. Perhaps most representative of this new trend was the bright 'n' breezy Gene Kelly-Frank Sinatra outing *On the Town* (1949), a film that effectively transformed soundstage Manhattan into a glistening new frontier, a lively, benevolent kingdom ripe for the

adventures of our sailors-on-leave heroes. Similarly, the decade's most successful film series – the globe-hopping *Road* pictures of Bob Hope and Bing Crosby – provided heady evidence of the nation's new-found optimism. Kicking off with 1940's *Road to Singapore*, the films offered a winning mix of bickering repartee, croonable tunes and knockabout slapstick, viewing the world's once alien and forbidding four corners through the carefree, deprecating gaze of its comic leads. The nervy mood of American isolationism was clearly at an end.

While it's tempting to regard such relentless bonhomie as a "ding dong the witch is dead" response to the end of World War Two, the prevalent tone actually seemed firmly established during the decade's early years. Even in the war's most turbulent days, Hollywood was intent on raising

the spirits, either with escapist "entertainments" or patriotic tub-thumpers like *The Purple Heart* (1944) or John Ford's *They Were Expendable* (1945) and this trend appeared to merge smoothly both with the later homecoming celebrations and the nation's mammoth economic boom.

But, for good or ill, these were times of change for the American people, and even many of the decade's most outwardly conservative pictures seemed to subtly address the implications of this trumping march of progress. Vincente Minnelli's gleaming 1944 musical *Meet Me in St Louis* poignantly evoked the lost years of 1900s America, the Oscar-laden *The Best Years of Our Lives* (1946) spotlighted a veteran's troubled re-adjustment to civilian life and Frank Capra's *It's a Wonderful Life* (1946) revealed US everyman-hero Jimmy Stewart to be riddled with anxieties, snapping at his picture-

The Best Years of Our Lives: *The GI (Dana Andrews) comes home to an uncertain future*

Italian Neo-Realism

Rising phoenix-like from the ashes of war-ravaged Italy, neo-realism signalled a new direction and vitality for European cinema. While its lifespan was short – wedged between the fall of Mussolini and the new censorship and the economic upswing and censorship clampdown during the late 1940s – its influence proved monumental, with echoes in the French New Wave and in the output of Martin Scorsese and Robert Altman. With the political climate in turmoil and the major studios wrecked by bombing, a wealth of small independent production companies sprang up across the nation. Suddenly liberated, directors like Luchino Visconti, Roberto Rossellini and Vittorio De Sica began shooting with skeleton crews on outdoor locations, using natural light, non-professional actors and begged, borrowed and stolen film stock.

The picture generally acknowledged as the beginning of neo-realism is Visconti's *Ossessione* (1942), banned by the Fascist regime for its harsh, unsentimentalized portrait of conditions in smalltown Italy. Three years on and the stylistic and thematic properties of Visconti's blueprint were allowed greater expression, most notably in Rossellini's *Rome, Open City* (1945) and De Sica's *Shoeshine* (1946). Fuelled by Italy's depressed economic backdrop, neo-realist narratives were typically naturalistic in spirit, returning to the folk-tale tradition in their affectionate but unpatronizing view of the nation's rank and file. But, in keeping with the movement's ragged, documentary-style realism, these plots were also free-flowing and open-ended, reflecting the new uncertainty of their post-war milieu. This invigorating blend of the innovative and the age-old reached its peak in De Sica's 1948 Oscar-winner *Bicycle Thieves*, a simple, beautifully wrought working-class fable that still stands as a landmark of European cinema.

postcard family and ultimately attempting suicide. In the meantime Orson Welles had followed his epoch-making *Citizen Kane* (1941) with *The Magnificent Ambersons* (1942). Despite being mangled by some recutting in RKO studios, it's arguably the more resonant achievement – a low-key, quietly heart-wrenching farewell to an innocent world of serene, tree-lined streets and pony-traps, before the coming of the motor-car.

Film Noir

Over on the Hollywood flipside, one strain of movie proved more nakedly critical. Speaking years later about his 1941 directorial debut, the great John Huston recalled: "The actors were all in their places, looking at me expectantly. I'd no idea what was required. Finally my assistant whispered 'Say action!' I did so and *The Maltese Falcon* was under way." *The Maltese Falcon* was the film generally credited as the pioneer of a genre ingenuously billed by studio publicity as "romantic melodramas" but later re-christened *film noir* by critics in France. A shotgun-wedding of German expressionism and the 1930s gangster flick, *film noir* was the decade's most distinctive and satisfying brainchild – a hard-bitten but weirdly honest antidote to the productions of the Hollywood mainstream. In a series of vintage crime thrillers – most notably 1944's *Laura* and *Double Indemnity* and 1946's *The Big Sleep* and *The Postman Always Rings Twice* – *film noir* effectively redesigned the movie landscape and evoked a precarious, shadowy realm trudged through by world-weary, fallen-angel heroes.

Film noir had no time for the soft-centred reassurances which were offered by other movies. Reeling from bust, depression, world war and the arrival of the atomic bomb, the genre positively luxuriated in its chaotic new

world order. The current boom, it seemed to say, is only lining the pockets of the crooks, while women – who had been drawn into the workplace while their husbands were away fighting – have grown into rapacious, all-powerful *femmes fatales*.

These pictures showed us the underbelly of the American Dream and their cynical world-view served up a tangy foretaste of the decade that followed, as the once-reliable western slid into insecure self-reflection and the merciless McCarthyite purges tore deep into the industry's deep-rooted liberal faction.

The 1950s: The age of TV and teenagers

In the period of post-war blues, young people, tired of middle-aged cinema, wanted something new and exciting. Since they had money, the movie moguls were ready and willing to pander to them. What they served up were rebels. Marlon Brando roared on to the scene mounted on a Harley, dressed head to foot in leather in *The Wild One* (1954), and with James Dean the first American teenager was born, complete with a full set of angst and attitude to spare in *East of Eden* (1955).

Along with the American teenager, there came also a new kind of music with the shocking rise of rock 'n' roll. Hard to believe today that the avuncular Bill Haley in *Rock around* the *Clock* (1956) upset half a nation the size of the USA, but then this was "the devil's music"! Elvis Presley inherited the baton, embarking on an impressively long series of movies which lasted through the next decade, doing notable acting work in three early dramas – *Love Me Tender* (1956), *Loving You* (1957) and *Flaming Star* (1960). Among the new stars none burned brighter than Marilyn Monroe in films like *The Seven Year Itch* (1955) and the faultless *Some Like It Hot* (1959). The western grew up and went psychological with John Wayne in *The Searchers* (1956) and Paul Newman in *The Left-Handed Gun* (1958). Top directors were attracted to the form – Anthony Mann, Nicholas Ray, Budd Boetticher, Don Siegel and Sam Fuller.

LIVE FAST – DIE YOUNG

JAYNE MANSFIELD

Jayne Mansfield was a spunky blonde with big boobs and a small talent for self-parody who tried hard to succeed and be taken seriously as an actress but never quite ceased to be what her detractors called her – "an ersatz Monroe". After a couple of good roles, as a gangster's moll (above) in *The Girl Can't Help It* (1956) and a film sexpot in *Will Success Spoil Rock Hunter?* (1957), it emerged that she'd already shown the best of herself and, despite vast quantities of self-publicity, her career was in nose-dive by 1960. She died in a horrific car accident in 1967, aged 34, driving to a television appearance. Her head was severed and the story goes that they first identified her body by the bust measurement.

The Western goes psychological: *John Wayne starred in John Ford's masterpiece* The Searchers

Television Triumphs

Television became an affordable commodity. It soon became a permanent feature in most people's homes, an integral part of the living space, and the television culture was born. Its huge potential for advertising made it financially powerful and its enormous turnover of material made it an ideal spawning ground for up-and-coming writers, directors and actors. Soon TV talent arrived on the big screen with luminaries like director Sidney Lumet (*Twelve Angry Men* (1957)) and writer Paddy Chayefsky (*Marty* (1955), *The Bachelor Party* (1957)).

Movies laughed at television in comedies, but in private the producers were worried. To combat the threat of the small screen, the movies got big, then bigger. First CinemaScope with *The Robe* (1953), then Cinerama for *The Wonderful World of the Brothers Grimm* (1962), and *It's a Mad Mad Mad World* (1963).

Gimmicks like 3D were employed in horror films (*House of Wax*, 1953), thrillers (*Dial M for Murder*, 1954) and even musicals (*Kiss Me Kate*, 1953), while there was an accent on stronger material of the kind audiences couldn't see on television, like chillers and films dealing with hitherto taboo subjects. Otto Preminger paved the way with *The Man with the Golden Arm* (1955, drugs) and *Anatomy of a Murder* (1959, rape). In an age of black-and-white television, the movies used colour as a lure. By the late 1950s, instead of colour being a rare luxury for just the most important roadshow movies, virtually all Hollywood's important films were made expensively in colour.

Studios Collapse

The mid-1950s also saw the major Hollywood studios' grip relax, as the studio system collapsed and the studios themselves raced to get into television. Warners, for example, started producing television

series of westerns like *Maverick*, *Cheyenne* and *Tenderfoot* and thrillers such as *77 Sunset Strip* and *Hawaiian Eye*, though their very success made films in these genres that much more difficult to market.

With the loosening of the studios' stranglehold, many of the major stars began to go freelance: even Clark Gable left MGM, and got paid more on an individual film basis, starting the trend towards the mammoth salaries of stars in the 1990s. Stars like James Stewart became their own producer, when he embarked on a profitable, career-revitalizing series of westerns with *Winchester 73* (1950). Other stars such as Burt Lancaster and Kirk Douglas set up their own powerful production companies, producing respectively *Sweet Smell of Success* (1957) and *Spartacus* (1960)

The McCarthy witch-hunts and the Un-American Activities Committee sent talented left-wing American film-makers either to jail or to England, enriching the British cinema with the arrival there of Joseph Losey and Carl Foreman. But the American cinema was for a time in the first half of the 1950s paralysed with fear and conservatism in the most uncreative of climates.

Japanese Realism

In the post-war recovery of the Japanese cinema it was, as so often, the success of one film that paved the way for the others. Akira Kurosawa's 1950 film *Rashomon* (1950) won the best film first prize at the 1951 Venice Film Festival, smoothing the path for its success in cinemas worldwide. Kurosawa embarked on one of world cinema's most distinguished careers, joining earlier masters Yasujiro Ozu and Kenji Mizoguchi in the hall of Japanese fame, as at last western audiences came to see the masterworks of the nation's cinema previously denied to them. Kurosawa's masterpieces of this period include *The Seven Samurai* (1954), *Throne of Blood* (1956) and *The Hidden Fortress* (1958).

Ozu made some of his greatest films in the 1950s, among them *Early Summer* (1951), *Tokyo Story* (1953), *Early Spring* (1956), and *Late Autumn* (1960). His films are true artworks – patient, quietly passionate, eternally longing, humanistic dramas, made with a heightened realism that's realistic but with a deeper poetic dimension. In this period, too, Mizoguchi shot his two great masterworks, *The Life of O-Haru* (1952) and *Ugetsu Monogatari* (1953), in a poetic realist style. Thematically, he probed the Japanese female's psyche and her ambiguous position in a changing, modernizing nation.

A New Wave in France

In France, another development was punching nails in the old Hollywood coffin, the French New Wave (*Nouvelle Vague*). This was ironic because the movement's founding fathers, critics-turned-film-makers Godard, Truffaut and Chabrol, were great admirers of Hollywood craftsmen like Hitchcock, Ford and Hawks.

Hollywood in Britain:
The unfulfilled dream

The story of the British studios and the British film industry itself is one of struggle and considerable achievement against the odds. A series of largely unsympathetic governments and a severely limited domestic market, too small to compete successfully with America, are just two of the reasons why the dream of creating a Hollywood in Britain has never been realized. From time to time, films such as *Gandhi* (1982) *Four Weddings and a Funeral* (1994) and *The Madness of King George* (1995) elicit the cry "The British are coming", but this is more by way of a swansong than a battle yell.

The early days of cinema had the appearance of a "level playing field". In Britain, small studios were springing up anywhere there was space and light, rather in the manner of fringe theatres in the 1960s. The earliest studio appears to have been that founded by American E. B. Koopman in 1897 behind the Tivoli in London's Strand to provide pictures for the Mutoscope slot machines.

One of the most successful pioneers was Cecil Hepworth, who set up a 10-by-6-foot studio in his back garden at Walton-on-Thames, keeping costs low by using members of his own family in his films. His *Rescued by Rover* (1904) was a big hit for its time. With a budget of £7 13s 9d (£7.69), it sold 395 prints. Hepworth was also one of the few pioneers to survive into the 1920s.

By then cinema had moved out of the variety halls and fairgrounds into film theatres and the early circuits were emerging, later to develop into the big three – Associated British Picture Corporation, Odeon and Gaumont British. The last of these was absorbed by Rank's Odeon in the early 1940s, creating the duopoly which still largely controls cinema exhibition in the UK today.

What were to become the major film studios were being built. W. G. Barker opened up at Ealing in 1909 and filmed stage actor Sir Herbert Tree as *Henry VIII*. Hard on Ealing's heels came Twickenham in 1913, then Worton Hill studios in Isleworth and Lime Grove at Shepherd's Bush. In the early 1920s

Michael Balcon went into production at Islington, forming Gainsborough Pictures, where he and his German partner Erich Pommer nurtured the talents of new young director Alfred Hitchcock. Balcon expanded his sphere of production in 1932, when recruited to run the new Gaumont British Pictures operation at Lime Grove. An early studio at Elstree foundered in 1920, but the site was given new cinematic life in 1927 when John Maxwell founded British International Pictures in the new studio complex just completed by American J. D. Williams, where he was first off the British mark with the new talkies.

Pinewood is part of the story of Methodist flour-mill owner J. Arthur Rank, while Shepperton, also founded in the 1930s, later became a production centre for Alexander Korda.

The Consolidation Years

Alexander Korda, a film critic and producer from Hungary, arrived in England in 1931, and founded his own company, London Films, initially making "quota quickies" – low-budget, quick-turnaround films to meet the demands of the newly introduced British quota system. He moved into the bigger league with the financially successful and prestigious *The Private Life of Henry VIII* (1933) starring Charles Laughton, as a result of which he raised the money to build his own studios at Denham.

The next major player entered the game in the mid-1930s. J. Arthur Rank was a wealthy and ardent Methodist, whose ideas about the moral responsibility of entertainment had much in common with those of the BBC's John Reith. After his first production *The Turn of the*

Denham Studios: Alexander Korda's dream

Classic Ealing comedy: Lab assistant Alec Guinness invents an everlasting fibre in The Man in the White Suit

Tide (1935) suffered from limited release, he turned his hard-headed Yorkshire business sense toward creating a sound basis for his new venture, acquiring distribution interests and the newly built Pinewood studios. Despite a financial crisis in the industry in the late 1930s, Rank weathered the storm and, by the end of 1941, he controlled Elstree as well as Pinewood plus two of the major exhibition circuits, and his growing empire was set to finance the bulk of the decade's most prestigious films.

Two of his main producers were Transylvanian Gabriel Pascal and Italian Filippo Del Giudice. Pascal won the confidence of playwright George Bernard Shaw, bringing *Pygmalion* (1938) to the screen, but he came a cropper with the over-budget *Caesar and Cleopatra* (1945). Del Giudice, who was behind David Lean's *In Which We Serve* (1942), brought Lean, Carol Reed and Anthony Asquith into the Rank fold for such classics as *Great Expectations* (1946) and *Oliver Twist* (1948), *The Third Man* (1949) and *The Browning Version* (1950). Other talent he recruited included the Boulting Brothers (*Brighton Rock*, 1947) and Laurence Olivier (*Henry V*, 1945). In 1941 Gainsborough came under Rank control, producing films popular

The Boulting brothers: An innovative force

with the wartime female filmgoer, such as *The Man in Grey* (1943), *The Seventh Veil* (1945) and *The Wicked Lady* (1945).

In the late 1940s, Rank ran into financial difficulties, and although his empire survives to this day, the aim of a "British Hollywood" at Pinewood was finished.

Meanwhile Michael Balcon, who had taken over production at Ealing Studios in 1938, was working with his team of directors towards a "house style" which was to be particularly British – the

Ealing comedy exemplified by *Passport to Pimlico* (1949), *The Man in the White Suit* (1951) and *The Ladykillers* (1952).

Another important post-war development was the buying-out of British Lion distributors by Korda, who was then able to add Shepperton to the studio space already under his control at Denham and Isleworth.

Meanwhile Elstree, the nearest there was to a British Hollywood, had stayed in continuous production apart from a period of closure during the war. A minor but important addition to the scene in the 1950s was Hammer, who found their feet with *The Quatermass Experiment* (1955) and churned out Frankenstein, vampire and other movies of the genre for the next 20 years. Regarded at the time as just cheap and fearful, the "Hammer House of Horror" is now revered as a significant part of the British Gothic tradition.

American money and a flowering of new home-grown talent kept the studios fully employed

throughout the 1960s, but trouble loomed when the American money went home. EMI, who took over Elstree in 1969, attempted to plug the gap with the appointment of film-maker Bryan Forbes as their head of production and the announcement of an ambitious programme of films, including *The Railway Children* and *The Go-Between* (both 1970).

A False Dawn

Throughout the 1970s, 1980s and 1990s the British film industry has laboured under a gathering cloud of gloom and lack of confidence, brightened with occasional bursts of success from Oscar winners like *Chariots of Fire* (1981) and *Gandhi* (1982).

These films and others hinted at a renaissance in the 1980s with a burst of optimism and the flag-waving of British Film Year (1985), but the euphoric bubble was burst by the harsh realities of recession. As Britain is being pulled economically and politically towards Europe, it is conversely increasingly dominated by America in terms of cinematic and even television culture, while the wealth of up-and-coming talent strains to please the elusive transatlantic market and is starved of an effective way of telling its own truth.

Governments continue to pay mere lip-service to the twin truths that a flourishing film industry not only makes economic sense, but also, as a major mass communications medium, has a vital role to play in creating both the British image on the world stage and the self-image and self-esteem of its citizens. While this attitude still prevails, Michael Balcon's ambition of "building up a native industry with its roots firmly planted in the soil of this country" will remain only a partially realized and now fading dream.

The 1960s:
The age of Aquarius

The 1960s was a decade of fun, fashion and far-reaching social change, all of which were reflected by the cinema. It was also a period of more internationalism in film-making and movie-watching, with an increased awareness of cinema on a world basis and a growing interchange of creative talent.

The British New Wave

The wind of change was particularly strong in British cinema in the early 1960s. Though influenced by the French New Wave, the British move toward a more realistic and gritty style and the exploration of working-class subjects had its national roots in the last years of the previous decade and the ideas of the so-called "angry young men" – writers such as John Osborne and John Braine and directors like Lindsay Anderson, Karel Reisz and Tony Richardson, all co-founders of the Free Cinema movement.

Reisz kicked off the decade with the groundbreaking *Saturday Night and Sunday Morning* (1960) and produced Anderson's debut feature film *This Sporting Life* (1963), both of which featured working-class heroes rebelling against the limitations of their birth and background. Richardson, with the forerunner of these, *Look Back in Anger* (1959), already under his directorial belt, went on to translate another theatre groundbreaker *A Taste of Honey* (1961) to the screen, along with *The Loneliness of the Long Distance Runner* (1962) and the very different, bawdy costume comedy *Tom Jones* (1963).

"Hollywood, England"

The ready availability of American money, either backing British product or using British studios as an economically advantageous production base, made it a boom time for the UK industry, helping to fund big-budget productions such as *Becket* (1964), *The Lion in Winter* (1968) and the high production values and literary excellence of director David Lean working with writer Robert Bolt. At the other end of the scale, a steady money-earner throughout was the basic and bawdy humour of the *Carry On* films.

Some of the most important British cinema of the time was created by Americans working in England: Joseph Losey, Stanley Kubrick and Richard Lester.

Big-budget boom: Peter O'Toole in Becket

The French New Wave

The directors of the *Nouvelle Vague*, like the British new wave that it influenced, had its roots in the 1950s in the group of young critics/ embryo film-makers who wrote for André Bazin's journal *Cahiers du Cinéma*. Rejecting what they saw as the moribund traditions of French cinema, they formulated the more personal *auteur* approach, influenced by their love of *film noir* and, particularly in the case of François Truffaut, Claude Chabrol and Eric Rohmer, their admiration for Alfred Hitchcock. They started to put what was to be a revolution in French cinema into practice in the late 1950s: Truffaut with *The Four Hundred Blows/Les Quatre Cent Coups* (1959), Chabrol with *Le Beau Serge* (1958) and *Les Cousins* (1959), and Jean-Luc Godard with *A Bout de Souffle* (1960), to which Truffaut and Chabrol made a creative contribution, and which caused a worldwide sensation among the cinema-going public for its revolutionary approach.

An International Screen

Meanwhile other talents were crossing borders. East European cinema was gaining a wider audience. While Andrzej Wajda remained in his native land, fellow Polish film-maker Roman Polanski, after the success of *Knife in the Water* (1962), turned to the west, making *Repulsion* (1965) and *Cul-De-Sac* (1966) in England, then moving to America for *Rosemary's Baby* (1968). Czech cinema was causing waves in the work of Jan Kadar and Elmar Klos (*The Shop on the High Street*, 1965), Ivan Passer (*Intimate Lighting*, 1965) and Milos Forman (*The Firemen's Ball*, 1967). Soviet films, too, were reaching Western eyes – Grigori Chukrai's affecting *Ballad of a Soldier* (1959) pleased audiences in the early 1960s, as did Andrei Tarkovsky's *Ivan's Childhood* (1962). And the films of Ingmar Bergman had become a "must see" for film buffs.

In West Germany new funding assistance supported the work of innovative new talents such as Volker Schlöndorff, Wim Wenders, Rainer Werner Fassbinder and Werner Herzog. Veteran Spanish director Luis Buñuel moved into his greatest

England swings: The Beatles in Richard Lester's A Hard Day's Night

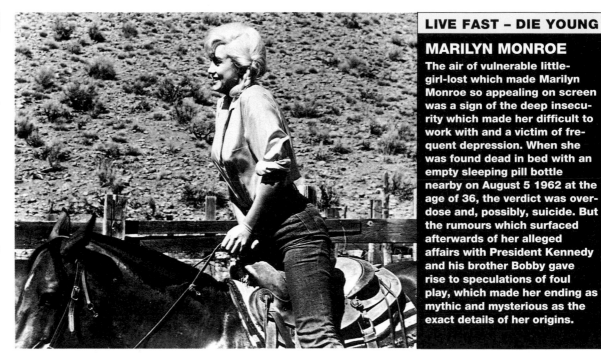

period with *Exterminating Angel* (1962) and *Belle de Jour* (1967). The Bengali films of Satyajit Ray were winning festival prizes and the delightful *Shakespeare Wallah* (1965) introduced the team of James Ivory, Ismail Merchant and Ruth Prawer Jhabvala to the wider world. While Italian masters such as Federico Fellini, Pier Paolo Pasolini and Michelangelo Antonioni were broadening the art-house audience, fellow countryman Sergio Leone took the western genre along a new and more violent route with *A Fistful of Dollars* (1964).

The Mainstream Scene

Musicals were still a viable proposition, though usually the film of the hit show as opposed to the original cineplays of the 1940s and 1950s. Barbra Streisand made her film debut in the role she had made her own on Broadway, *Funny Girl* (1968), then going on, despite her youth, to play the Ethel Merman role in *Hello, Dolly!* (1969), and there were even two British musicals: *Oliver!* (1968) and *Oh! What a Lovely War* (1969). Landmark films of the decade included *Bonnie and Clyde* (1967) and *Butch Cassidy and the Sundance Kid* (1969). Mike Nichols emerged as a major new director with *Who's Afraid of Virginia Woolf?* (1966) and *The Graduate* (1967), Roger Corman created a cult out of low-budget horror movies, many of them based on stories by Edgar Allan Poe, and Woody Allen was beginning to spread his wings.

British stars launched themselves into American films: Sean Connery was made bankable by James Bond, Julie Christie by *Darling* (1965) and Michael Caine by *Alfie* (1966). Ken Russell made his international mark with *Women in Love* (1969), moving on to bigger-budget, British-made extravaganzas in the 1970s. But as fellow Brit John Schlesinger was casting his eye over New York in the Oscar-winning *Midnight Cowboy* (1969), the economic conditions which had caused the Americans to come to the UK were changing and British film-makers were soon found themselves revisited by their age-old problem, lack of finance.

The 1970s:
The age of uncertainties

Lending credence to the view that an anxious, troubled society produces the greatest art, the 1970s arguably saw the creative high-point of the US film industry. The decade found this previously questing nation looking suddenly exhausted and directionless, plagued by political corruption and looming bankruptcy; its morale sapped by a growing energy crisis.

The Utopian hopes of John Kennedy's New Frontier and Lyndon Johnson's Great Society had come a cropper with the Vietnam War and the Watergate scandal which toppled Richard Nixon from the presidency in 1974. Opinion polls recorded galloping disillusion among the public and a lack of faith in all institutions, with inward-turning narcissism replacing 1960s social activism. And yet this angst-ridden decade gave rise to some of the finest pictures ever made.

Turbulent Times

This creative flowering was partly due to the counter-culture's influence belatedly percolating through to Hollywood's money-men and partly due to the industry's depressed state, which prompted studios to take risks on more alternative, untried film-makers. New directors like Martin Scorsese, Michael Cimino, Robert Altman, Francis Ford Coppola, Peter Bogdanovich, George Lucas and Steven Spielberg brought distinctive, personal visions to their projects, producing work that was a captivating mix of the personal and political, holding a mirror up to their own turbulent times.

The Vietnam catastrophe was duly probed – implicitly at first in films like Altman's *M*A*S*H*

(1970), later more overtly in Cimino's *The Deer Hunter* (1978) and Coppola's hallucinatory *Apocalypse Now* (1979). The same director's 1974 picture *The Conversation* offered an unnervingly prescient commentary on Watergate-era wire-tapping, while traditional genres found themselves turned audaciously upside down. Altman rustled up a fine revisionist western in *McCabe and Mrs Miller* (1971), while his *Thieves Like Us* (1974) – along with Sidney Lumet's brilliant *Dog Day Afternoon* (1975) – rang bewildering changes on the reliable crime thriller. Most significantly, Coppola's mighty double-header *The Godfather* (1972) and *The Godfather Part II* (1974) turned the gangster flick into an overpowering parable of the American Dream, cross-cutting the young Don Vito's (Robert De Niro) ascent with his son Michael's (Al Pacino) modern-day slide into ruin and corruption.

It was *The Godfather*, too, that won a deserved second Academy Award for wayward superstar Marlon Brando though, in keeping with the era's contemptuous rejection of the nation's most sacred institutions, the actor shunned the Oscar ceremony, sending in his stead a Native American envoy to protest against Hollywood's misrepresentation of the American Indian. Five years later, confrimed Manhattanite Woody Allen would also fail to col-

lect his Best Picture award for 1977's *Annie Hall*, preferring to spend the night playing clarinet at his favourite New York jazz haunt.

While pictures critical of American culture traditionally came from the artistic left wing, more conservative responses were also evident, lashing out at what they saw as the moral decay caused by the 1960s sexual and social revolution. Michael Winner's *Death Wish* (1974) and the Clint Eastwood star vehicle *Dirty Harry* (1971) were rabble-rousing updates of the old western formula of a solitary engine of justice dishing out law 'n' order to shifty, contaminating evil-doers. In contrast, the decade's most notorious vigilante picture, Scorsese's brutal *Taxi Driver* (1976), drew on influences from both sides of the political spectrum, indulging the notion of its avenging protagonist as some Fascistic superman while at the same time savaging the warped, upside-down culture that celebrates such men as heroes.

Fascistic superman: Robert De Niro in Taxi Driver

pion, Ronald Reagan – in short, a no-nonsense, pistol-packing clean-up man.

Further afield matters were less tangled. The New German Cinema movement was the decade's key European trend, eclipsing the output of post-Free Cinema Britain and post-New Wave France, though 1960s Gallic icon Jean-Paul Belmondo slid into the movie main-stream with a series of hugely profitable cops-and-robbers outings. Most heartening was the development of the Australian New Wave in that nation's previously dormant film industry. Led by such directors as Peter Weir and Fred Schepisi, the movement introduced a new elegance and lyricism to the art-form, with pictures like *Picnic at Hanging Rock* (1975) and *The Chant of Jimmy Blacksmith* (1978) turning the vast Australian interior into a new frontier, an untamed territory ripe for movie exploitation.

Return to Fantasy

But perhaps film-goers could only take so much merciless scab-picking. The second half of the decade saw a swing back to more populist escapism, old-style yarns given a revitalizing new lick of paint. *Wunderkind* Spielberg stunned audiences with two perfectly crafted pictures in *Jaws* (1975) and *Close Encounters of the Third Kind* (1977), while buddy George Lucas, formerly an assistant to Coppola, notched up history's most profitable movie in 1977 with the dazzling sci-fi swashbuckler *Star Wars*. On a wider cultural level, the American people seemed to be pining for some reassurance, an end to self-doubt and – in the words of the independent candidate of Altman's *Nashville* (1975) – "new roots for the nation". The 1980 presidential elections saw them flocking to the banner of a former B-movie actor, good guy cowboy-star and New Right cham-

New German Cinema

While the *Nouvelle Vague* was busy electrifying France in the early 1960s, it seemed inconceivable that a similar renaissance could ever take place in Germany. The film industry had been a shambles since the Third Reich's collapse, with the nation split down the middle and any defining national character fractured and overrun by the East-West occupying forces. Young directors found themselves hamstrung by both lack of finance and a largely barren cultural heritage. The expressionist exuberance of the inter-war years was lost in the mists of time, while a veil had been discreetly drawn across the propagandist output of the Nazi era. But by the late 1960s, aided by interest-free government loans and transmission deals with the nation's state-run TV networks, new directors finally began to find their way to the fore. The early 1970s saw this renaissance gaining strength. Wim Wenders's debut feature *The Goalkeeper's Fear of the Penalty* (1971) heralded a mighty new talent, Fassbinder's *The Merchant of the Four Seasons* (1971) had critics in raptures and Werner Herzog's 1972 epic *Aguirre, Wrath of God* proved the movement's powerhouse international breakthrough.

The term "New German Cinema" never referred to a stylistic or thematic revolution. Rather, the label threw a convenient canopy over the groundswell of diverse young directors who rose up together to become revered names on the international movie circuit. The movement's high-tide mark came in the mid- to late 1970s, with Fassbinder's *Fear Eats the Soul* (1974), which won the Cannes Palme D'Or, and Volker Schlöndorff's *The Tin Drum* (1979), left, which scooped the Best Foreign Film Oscar.

The 1980s:
The age of the brat

The 1980s were the period of the Reaganization or con-servatization of the movies, as the industry swung politi-cally to the right. American films enjoyed golden ages in the 1930s and 1970s, but the average US film of the 1980s seemed to be aimed at moronic teenagers, with *My Science Project* (1985), *The Invisible Kid* (1988) and *Bill and Ted's Excellent Adventure* (1989) being greeted by enormous box-office and even critical favour.

Most of the films of the era seemed to be espousing back-ward-looking, retrograde values and promoting cosy, unreal views of the family and marriage, with a leaning towards themes that were success- and money-oriented.

ooze out through the 1990s.

The era of money-worship was best represented by Oliver Stone's liberal-thinking *Wall Street* (1987), where Oscar-winning Michael Douglas's awful, rapacious Gordon Gecco character somehow became the film's hero. Stone also provided a pair of highly popular movies that reinvented history and finally allowed Americans to come to terms with the Vietnam war, *Platoon* (1986) and *Born on the Fourth of July* (1989). Sylvester Stallone continued his right-wing *Rambo* and *Rocky* cycles, while a bodybuilder with a thick Austrian accent, Arnold Schwarzenegger, became the biggest, most highly paid draw in the history of the movies, as films moved into ultra-costly, leave-your-mind-in-neutral actioners, sci-fi pics and horror

flicks, accompanied by a steady, controversial advance in the depiction of violence.

After the innovations of the 1970s, the 1980s' films represented a period of disappointment. Of course there were outstanding films and outstanding directors, but, as film budgets rocketed and big business took control of the movies, there was little experi-ment and little real excitement. However, there were encouraging developments like the resurgence of the French cinema, partly due to the extraordinary international success of *Jean de Florette* (1986) and its sequel *Manon des Sources* (1986), plus *Cyrano de Bergerac* (1990), though it did sometimes seem that Gérard Depardieu had turned himself into a one-man film industry. Thoughtful, intelli-gent films were still being made abroad, even strange austere pic-tures like the Cannes-winning

Yuppies Rule OK

Michael J. Fox is the era's yuppie star *par excellence*. An unthreaten-ing 20-something adult usually playing a kid, he starred in *The Secret of My Success* (1987), a non-threatening werewolf movie, *Teen Wolf* (1985), and especially in Spielberg's *Back to the Future* trilogy – cosy, comfortable sci-fi for the 1980s. Francis Coppola also con-tributed to this comforting cycle with *Peggy Sue Got Married* (1986), a *Back to the Future* for the older crowd, sending middle-aged Kathleen Turner back to her school prom to try to right the decisions she made then that have made her present life rotten.

Romance was back in fashion, as Norman Jewison's *Moonstruck* (1987) plainly proved. Among other 20-somethings playing kids, Keanu Reeves hit the jackpot with *Bill and Ted's Excellent Adventure* (1989), the spearhead of a wave of nerdy, easygoing, crowd-pleasing acne-comedies that continued to

Crafty Fox: *The era's yuppie star par excellence was Michael J. Fox, star of the* Back to the Future *trilogy*

LIVE FAST – DIE YOUNG

JOHN BELUSHI

The great comic anti-hero of his generation, John Belushi, drank too deeply of life's pleasures and fell victim to the classic twin temptations of alcohol and drugs, unable to handle becoming a star overnight through his Emmy-award-winning work on the NBC network's *Saturday Night Live*. After making seven films, from his notable debut in *National Lampoon's Animal House* (1978) to *Neighbors* in 1981, he died aged only 33 in a Los Angeles hotel as a result of a massive intake of heroin and cocaine.

Under Satan's Sun (1987). Spain's Pedro Almodóvar (*Women on the Verge of a Nervous Breakdown*, 1988) and Finland's Aki Kaurismaki (*Hamlet Goes Business*, 1987) became names to conjure with, at least among the cine-literate.

Independent Initiative

In Britain, with mainstream cinema having fallen asleep or into the hands of the nostalgists (*Chariots of Fire* (1981), *Gandhi* (1982), *A Room with a View* (1985)), the mavericks were also providing the most interesting work – Derek Jarman, Peter Greenaway, Mike Leigh, Stephen Frears and Ken Loach. Many of the top British directors were in fact working in America, including such talents as Ridley and Tony Scott, Adrian Lyne and Alan Parker.

Cannes was also the showcase for a few adventurous American films, some of which won the Palme D'Or – Steven Soderbergh's *sex, lies and videotape* (1989) and *Wild at Heart* (1990) – showing that America was after all still making films for adults. The country's independent sector gave world cinema the greatest hope for the future with directors like Jim Jarmusch, the Coen Brothers, Steven Soderbergh, Hal Hartley

and Gus van Sant. One or two 1970s maverick, left-of-field directors beavered on through thick and thin. Robert Altman continued to be busy in a variable output, though *Come Back to the Five and Dime , Jimmy Dean, Jimmy Dean* (1982), *Streamers* (1983) and *Tanner 88* (1988) were among his best work. David Lynch scored a notable *succès de scandale* with *Blue Velvet* (1986) and Barry Levinson notched a personal triumph with his debut *Diner* (1982), reflecting

on young lives in his Baltimore hometown, and he moved to mainstream success with *Good Morning, Vietnam* (1987) and *Rain Man* (1988). Steven Spielberg turned to serious dramas to prove his credentials – *The Color Purple* (1985) and *Empire of the Sun* (1987).

Gay cinema finally escaped from the closet and came of age, albeit partly as a response to the threat of AIDS, with films like Bill Sherwood's *Parting Glances* (1986), Norman René's *Longtime*

Companion (1990) and Derek Jarman's *Caravaggio* (1986). Donna Deitch's *Desert Hearts* (1985) proved to be a notable milestone in the history of lesbian cinema.

Young, gifted and black filmmaker Spike Lee made the breakthrough with *She's Gotta Have It* (1986), *School Daze* (1988) and *Do the Right Thing* (1989), spearheading the rise of black cinema that, along with the work of the other notable independents, takes the cinema story into the 1990s.

The Brat Pack

SAINT ELMO'S BAR

The 1980s was the decade of the Brat Pack and the yuppie movies, began by Francis Ford Coppola's two films of S. E. Hinton's stories of disaffected youth, *The Outsiders* (1983) and *Rumble Fish* (1983) – the parent films of the Brat Pack. *The Outsiders* assembled the mighty Packers for the first time and, though the film wasn't a success at the box-office, it was tremendously influential on the decade thanks to the press who coined the "Brat Pack" and helped promote their young careers. There's a formidable line-up of

talent in *The Outsiders*: Rob Lowe, Patrick Swayze, Ralph Macchio, C. Thomas Howell, Matt Dillon, Emilio Estevez, Leif Garrett, Diane Lane and Tom Cruise, of whom only the last now seems destined for real longevity and superstardom. Lowe and Estevez reteamed for the hit *St Elmo's Fire* (above) in 1985.

The Brat Pack torch was taken up, polished and successfully marketed by John Hughes with his *The Breakfast Club* (1985) and *Pretty in Pink* (1986). He then turned his teen pictures

into kiddie pix, finally to hit the jackpot with *Home Alone* (1990). Almost all of Hughes's films are, in fact, variations on the same theme: enterprising youngsters get up to and enjoy some kind of fairly innocent mayhem, before authority returns and the social order is re-established. *Ferris Bueller's Day Off* (1986), with Matthew Broderick and chums plotting a day of truancy from school in Chicago, only to stage a panic return to please the adults, is a prime example of this kind of film.

The 1990s:
Cinema comes of age

Halfway through the 1990s things are looking promising. Cinema attendances are up; more films are being made; and greater attention is being paid than ever before to the work of non-English-speaking directors. Minority issues are, for the first time, gaining broad acknowledgement in mainstream cinema.

Not the least encouraging of signs has been Hollywood's attempt to tackle "serious" topics in a serious way. AIDS, homelessness, the Holocaust, feminism and racism have all been treated with minimal glitz and maximum dignity.

America Leads the Way

As ever, America has dominated the market. Steven Spielberg directed the highest-grossing movie of all time, *Jurassic Park* (1993), knocking himself from the top spot he had occupied since *E.T.* phoned home in 1982. Almost as popular, however, has been the cutesy cartoon epic *The Lion King* (1994), which, along with *Beauty and the Beast* (1991) and *Aladdin* (1992), has signalled a remarkable upturn in the Disney studio's flagging fortunes.

Against such undoubtedly enjoyable but essentially escapist fodder must be set a number of American films that have attempted to confront more profound issues. *Falling Down* (1992), with Michael Douglas, provided a disturbing insight into the racial and social tensions of America's inner cities; Jonathan Demme's *Philadelphia* (1993) was Hollywood's first mainstream attempt to deal with AIDS, *Forrest Gump* (1994) re-evaluated the 60s and Vietnam, while Kevin Costner's *Dances with Wolves*

(1990) and Walter Hill's *Geronimo* (1994) retell the story of the Wild West from the Native American perspective. Most significant of all has been Spielberg's *Schindler's List* (1994), an Oscar-winning, three-and-a-half-hour Holocaust epic that ranks as one of the finest and most edifying films of the last quarter century.

It is a decade that has seen a revival in fortunes for many of Hollywood's more established film-makers. Martin Scorsese's career didn't need reviving in the first place, but with *Goodfellas* (1990), *Cape Fear* (1991) and *The Age of Innocence* (1993) he again demonstrated both the diversity of his talent and his ability to produce popular mainstream pictures. Robert Altman, perennial Hollywood outsider, came up with two coruscating studies of modern-day Los Angeles society – *The Player* (1992) and *Short Cuts* (1994) – and grizzled living-legend Clint Eastwood brought the western back to life with his darkly complex *Unforgiven* (1993).

If old-timers have again been flexing their artistic muscles, the 1990s have also been a good decade for new and independent

dent directors. Quentin Tarantino announced himself as the most exciting film-maker of his generation with his stunning debut movie, *Reservoir Dogs* (1993), consolidating his position with 1994's *Pulp Fiction* and scripting *Natural Born Killers* (1994), Oliver Stone's controversial take on the modern-day serial killer. The Coen Brothers, meanwhile, have established themselves as the decade's most idiosyncratic visual stylists with *Barton Fink* (1991) and *The Hudsucker Proxy* (1994), while Hal Hartley, Steven Soderbergh, Abel Ferrara and Whit Stillman are among the many other independents who have immeasurably added to the richness of 1990s cinema.

Mainstream Acceptance

It has been an important decade for minority film, too. Tom Kalin's *Swoon* (1992), Rose Troche's *Go Fish* (1994) and Gus Van Sant's *My Own Private Idaho* (1991) all brought gay cinema to a wider audience. Likewise, high-octane tales of the black urban ghetto such as John Singleton's *Boyz 'N' the Hood* (1991), Mario Van Peebles's *New Jack City* (1991) and The Hughes Brothers' *Menace II Society* (1993) have all achieved an unheard-of level of popularity for black cinema. Spike Lee, prickly guru of Afro-American film-makers, staked a strong claim to mainstream acceptance with his sweeping biopic *Malcolm X* (1993). Women film-makers have also been making slow inroads into what is still an alarmingly male-dominated medium. Penny Marshall's *Awakenings* (1990) and *A League of Their Own* (1992) were both enormously popular, while Julie

On the edge: Michael Douglas in Falling Down

Oriental Cinema

The 1990s have, for the first time, seen Oriental film breaking into the western mainstream. In the vanguard have been China's Fifth Generation directors – so called because they were the fifth class to graduate from the Beijing Film Academy – who reject traditional narrative structures and infuriate the Chinese authorities by tackling themes that have not been officially sanctioned.

Pre-eminent among this new wave have been Chen Kaige and Zhang Yimou. It was Kaige's *Yellow Earth* (1985) that first put modern Chinese cinema on the map, while his *Farewell My Concubine* (1993), a sweeping, sumptuous epic based around the Peking Opera, is possibly the finest Chinese film ever made. Zhang Yimou has also attracted huge critical acclaim in the west with such visually sumptuous works as *Red Sorghum* (1988), *Raise the Red Lantern* (1991) and *The Story of Qui Ju* (1992).

Taiwan has matched the artistry if not the productivity of Chinese cinema with such delicate, idiosyncratic works as Hou Hsiao-Hsien's *A City of Sadness* (1989), and Ang Lee's *The Wedding Banquet* (1993) and *Eat Drink Man Woman* (1995). Tran Anh Hung's *The Scent of Green Papaya* (1993) was the first Vietnamese film to win a major western award (Cannes Best First Film).

Hong Kong and Japan have tended towards a more violent, Americanized cinema than that of other Eastern countries. Modern Japanese cinema, like much of its culture, is based on a loose fusion of sci-fi, cartoon and hardcore rock music, with the Manga video series, Katsuhiro Otomo's *Akira* (1987) and Sinya Tsukamoto's *Tetsuo* (1990) and *Tetsuo 2* (1992) fairly representative of the whole. 'Beat' Takeshi's elegaic gangster thrillers temper violence with intelligent plotlines and innovative camerawork. Hong Kong, likewise, has gravitated towards the action end of the market, although directors such as John Woo have brought an impressive level of artistry to their violence.

Chinese cinema, however, is the one to watch out for. It has a rich, intelligent, epic quality to it and, despite persistent state repression and censorship, should grow in influence and popularity as the millennium approaches.

"Stupid is as stupid does": Homely Gump wisdom

Dash was the first Afro-American female director to gain commercial theatrical distribution with her *Daughters of the Dust* (1992). Most important of all has been the work of New Zealander Jane Campion, who first gained widespread attention with *Sweetie* (1989) and *An Angel at My Table* (1990), then went on to direct one of the great films of the decade so far in *The Piano* (1994).

European Scene

Britain achieved its biggest-ever commercial money-spinner with Mike Newell's upper-crust romantic comedy *Four Weddings and a Funeral* (1993), although Ken Loach's searing IRA thriller *Hidden Agenda* (1990) and Mike Leigh's savage inner-city odyssey *Naked* (1993) both presented a somewhat less rosy picture of life in modern-day England. The most popular British movies, however, remain those beautifully shot, perfectly acted period pieces so beloved of American audiences, with Merchant Ivory's *Howards End* (1992) and *The Remains of the Day* (1993) and Richard Attenborough's *Shadowlands* (1993) being the obvious, and best, examples.

The French film industry, meanwhile, buoyed up by generous government subsidies, remains one of the most active outside America, producing an enviable stream of intelligent, challenging, high-quality pictures. From the costumed magnificence of *Cyrano de Bergerac* (1990) to subtler, more contemplative works such as *La Belle Noiseuse* (1991) and *Un Coeur en Hiver* (1993), French film-makers have proved themselves second to none in their ability to portray the inner workings of their characters.

LIVE FAST – DIE YOUNG

RIVER PHOENIX

Talented, haunting youngster River Phoenix was a tragic victim of the 1990s cult of personality. A product of the hippy early 1970s, Phoenix was soon on a collision course because of his conflicting images of beatific, other-worldly boy and hip LA sex symbol.

He died at 22 in the public gaze on the sidewalk outside Johnny Depp's Hollywood Boulevard nightclub, the Viper Room. After the worldwide shock of his death faded, Phoenix's image looked tarnished because he had posed as the young generation's Mr Clean, attacking drug abuse, while running in Hollywood's fast lane and indulging in "speedballing", imbibing a deadly cocktail of cocaine and amphetamines.

Lights, Cameras, Action

The history of cinema is not only one of artistic advance and popular culture, but also one of technological and scientific progress. In this section we look at the state of the art in special effects and animation, as well as examining other essential off-screen aspects of movie-making such as the role of the director, publicity and censorship.

The Great Directors:
An indelible imprint

In all this century's landmark pictures it's invariably the director who is considered to be of paramount importance and is ultimately credited with a project's success or failure. But while it's hard to underestimate a director's influence, such a view can at times be too simplistic.

Film production is, as the old adage informs us, a collaborative process, whose outcome is dependent on a wealth of factors: writers, directors, technicians, set designers, editors, actors, studio money-men. Playwright-director David Mamet (*Glengarry Glen Ross*, 1992), sick of seeing his original vision compromised by outside forces, suggests an amendment to the adage: "Film is a collaborative process – bend over."

The pre-eminence of the film director in the creative process was not always as entrenched as it is today. Back in the 1930s and 1940s the industry was star-driven

and, though several film-makers – Griffith, Renoir, Eisenstein, Lang – were recognized as artists of talent, the general perception of the director was as an efficient craftsman, a trained studio envoy whose role it was to keep the story moving smoothly and showcase its featured stars. Furthermore, popular films were widely dismissed by highbrow cultural critics as mass-produced commodities. Any movie that came out of the Hollywood system, they argued, was inherently compromised and preconditioned, and therefore invalid as "art".

The Director as Artist

This perception was exploded by the arrival of the *auteur* theory, evolved in the 1950s through the critical writings in the Parisian film journal *Cahiers du Cinéma*. Developed by such future master-directors as François Truffaut and Jean-Luc Godard and later expanded by critic Andrew Sarris,

Calling the shots: François Truffaut (seated)

this approach argued that certain film-makers were able to overcome studio constraints and imbue the finished work with their own distinctive vision. With this in mind, Truffaut drew up his *politique des auteurs*, listing those directors who could truly be termed *auteurs*: from France Jean Renoir, Jacques Tati, Jean Vigo, and from Hollywood Alfred Hitchcock, John Ford, Orson Welles, Howard Hawks. The pictures of these *auteurs*, Truffaut argued, were immediately recognizable thanks to a recurrence of thematic properties, pictorially conveyed, and it was this quality that raised them above the anonymous industry "hacks". This ground-breaking new approach proved bewildering, not just for contemporary critics but for many of the lauded individuals themselves. Hitch and Welles accepted the notion easily enough, but Ford was forever uncomfortable with his role as a highbrow icon. "I make westerns," he stated flatly.

But if we are to chart the development of the film's art-form through the work of the key directors, Ford would be an unforgivable omission. So, too, would D. W. Griffith, now reviled for his sentimental story-telling and overt bigotry, but whose development of film language – parallel editing,

John Ford: "I make westerns"

cross-cutting – effectively made him the father of narrative cinema. After Griffith came the bravura expressionist imagery of Fritz Lang, the revolutionary montages of Sergei Eisenstein and the fervent surrealism of movie wizard Luis Buñuel. The onset of sound made room for a new kind of *auteur* with the rise of such masters of plot and dialogue as Ernst Lubitsch, Howard Hawks, Frank Capra, Preston Sturges and Elia Kazan. Hitchcock's polished, Freudian-tinged suspense thrillers, with their self-consciously voyeuristic use of the camera, spawned a host of imitators, while 1940s and 1950s Hollywood also saw Ford and John Huston's muscular directorial styles exploring male American values. Across the Atlantic, cultural imperatives gave rise to different but equally spellbinding oeuvres, from the stark humanistic fables of Robert Bresson, Pier Paolo Pasolini and the mighty Ingmar Bergman through to the flamboyant artistry of Federico Fellini, Luchino Visconti and the French *Nouvelle Vague*. Further afield, Oriental film showed its pedigree with the monumental art-works of Akira Kurosawa and Yasujiro Ozu, while Satyajit Ray found himself positioned at the cutting edge of Asian cinema.

The 1950s and 1960s witnessed the flowering of the British "Free Cinema" movement, the dark wit of Roman Polanski and Stanley Kubrick and the weighted, stylized operatics of spaghetti-western guru Sergio Leone. Meanwhile the cultural avant-garde found their ways through into film production in the parodic exuberance of Andy Warhol, the low-budget ingenuity of John Cassavetes and the gleeful pop-culture assemblages of Kenneth Anger.

American cinema enjoyed a glorious high point in the 1970s, thanks to the rise of Francis Ford Coppola and Steven Spielberg,

Battleship Potemkin: The incandescent Odessa Steps sequence

All of film's contemporary directors owe a debt to the greats of the past. Echoes of the *Nouvelle Vague*'s jump-cutting exuberance can be seen in the work of Martin Scorsese, while Steven Spielberg's eye-catching spectaculars betray more than a passing resemblance to the epics of David Lean. But recent years have witnessed a new phenomenon – the development of the "homage", a self-conscious appropriation of admired scenes and styles. Not plagiarism, you understand – "homages". Though possessed of his own distinctive vision, Quentin Tarantino's work is peppered with backward glances to classic movies, and the Coen Brothers raided both the screwball and expressionist styles of the 1930s for their 1994 retro-comedy *The Hudsucker Proxy*. Most audaciously, talented writer-director Brian De Palma, usually under the influence of Alfred Hitchcock, cannibalized the landmark "Odessa Steps" section from Eisenstein's *Battleship Potemkin* (1925), using it tellingly at the climax of *The Untouchables* (1987) and then resurrecting and plundering it again for his underrated crime thriller *Carlito's Way* (1993). While such shrewd cinematic "cover versions" may enrage purists, their sheer thrill value is undeniable.

the loose-jointed ease of Robert Altman and the visceral, meticulously-wrought shot construction of Martin Scorsese. More recently, audiences have thrilled to the weird and wonderful visions of David Lynch, Quentin Tarantino and controversial Chinese *auteur* Zhang Yimou. But this roster of names – glittering as they may be – is inevitably confined by contemporary critical perceptions and in years to come other directors of the past, currently languishing in the doldrums, will no doubt be reappraised. Just look at British visionary Michael Powell: feted in the 1940s, reviled in the 1960s and 1970s and now restored to

his rightful place among the century's movie greats.

New Voices

Also notable in most lists of all-time greats is the general absence of both ethnic minority and women directors. Despite its hugely creative output, the film industry has traditionally been a preserve of white middle-class males, though thankfully this too seems to be changing, with the arrival of such skilled new artists like Spike Lee and New Zealand director Jane Campion. The rise of such diverse new talents can only enhance the movie scene, hinting at great things still to come.

Cinematography:
Making a big impression

Cinema, in the memorable judgment of director John Boorman, is the process of turning money into light. Film creates the illusion of reality in motion and this art of illumination – the balance of light and shadow, the play of colours on the screen, the placement and movement of the camera – to a large extent decides a film's success or failure.

While the director is generally credited as the defining force behind a movie, it is his director of photography – or cinematographer – who is largely responsible for the nuts-and-bolts look of a picture.

Cinematography, quite literally, means "writing in movement" and throughout movie history a number of cinematographers have marked the century's key films with their own unique play of light and shadow.

Sound and Light

Even in the earliest days of silent cinema – from the epic canvases of D. W. Griffith to the deep-shadowed interiors of the German expressionist school – certain aesthetic styles were already in place. But the headlong rush of creativity evident in the best silent pictures floundered with the arrival of sound. The weighty new technology hampered the fluidity of early film. Cameras were locked in place, films became studio-bound

and actors were rooted in place beside concealed microphones. But while the film camera took years to free itself from the constraints of its new recording equipment, the development in lighting technique continued to blossom. The 1930s saw the full flowering of individual studio looks, with contracted cinematographers shunted from project to project, their primary role being to light the stars as alluringly as possible. William Daniels is widely hailed as creating the Greta Garbo "look", director Joseph von Sternberg evolved the stark illuminations that accentuated Marlene Dietrich's sculpted features and respected cinematographer Charles B. Lang recalls studio chiefs telling him: "Put your shadows anywhere, but don't put 'em on their faces."

Certain camera craftsmen began experimenting further with black-and-white imagery. Greg Toland's high-contrast visuals proved massively influential, bringing a scuffed documentary authenticity to John Ford's *The Grapes of Wrath* (1940) and conjuring up a ground-breaking display of deep-space pyrotechnics in Orson Welles's masterful *Citizen Kane* (1941).

The stripped-down peak of this film-making style came with the onset of *film noir*. Cinematographers like Ernest Haller (1957's *The Tall T*), John Alton (1955's *The Big Combo*) and James Wong Howe honed their skills to a Spartan art-form, etching in the barest visual contours and leaving the rest of the frame brooding and unreadable. Directors like John Huston and Fritz Lang may be seen as the kings of the *film noir* genre, but the influence of these artists in the shadows can never be overlooked.

Colour

The arrival of colour forced cinematographers to rethink their most basic assumptions. Colour film-making evolved in fits and starts, from the hand-painted prints of *Intolerance* (1916), through the two-tone Technicolor of 1933's *Mystery of the Wax Museum*, the landmark three-strip technique of *Becky Sharp* (1935) to the glistening vistas of *The Wizard of Oz* (1939) and *Gone with the Wind* (1939).

As the use of colour spread like wildfire through the medium, cinematographers began to explore the painterly

Citizen Kane: *Cinematographer Greg Toland's spellbinding jigsaw of deep-space light and shade*

Technicolor triumph: *Vast vista of the Atlanta wounded in* Gone with the Wind

potential of the full spectrum. Filters – slivers of glass or gelatin – began to give the film stock new tints and textures. Vilmos Zsigmond fogged and flashed the stock to give Altman's *McCabe and Mrs Miller* (1971) the ghostly look of an old photograph. The legendary Vittorio Storaro's exquisite colour combinations turned *The Conformist* (1970), *The Last Emperor* (1987) and *Apocalypse Now* (1979) – with Marlon Brando's domed orange head emerging from the darkness – into full-blooded feasts for the senses. Coppola's *Godfather* pictures were given extra dimension by Gordon Willis's risky experiments in underexposing, while Nestor Almendros's equally

daring use of natural twilight brought a special kind of magic to Terrence Malick's *Days of Heaven* (1978), visually one of the most beautiful movies ever made.

Fortunately black-and-white film-making continues to be a viable alternative, too. Gordon Willis brought Woody Allen's *Manhattan* (1979) to vibrant life, Michael Chapman's razor-sharp tones put the final polish on Martin Scorsese's boxing biopic *Raging Bull* (1980), while Haskell Wexler won an Oscar for his stark, probing treatment of Richard Burton and Elizabeth Taylor in 1966's *Who's Afraid of Virginia Woolf* – a candid approach that had Burton fretting about the unflattering depiction of his acne

scars. More recently, Steven Spielberg leaned heavily on the monochrome artistry of Janusz Kaminski when crafting his Oscar-laden Holocaust drama *Schindler's List* (1993).

Tricks and Techniques

Throughout the years other upheavals and developments have had their own effects on the film-maker's art. With cinema facing increasing competition from television, the 1950s witnessed a Pandora's Box-worth of screening devices intended to entice viewers to the local drive-in or picture-house: Cinerama, VistaVision, CinemaScope and 3D. The eye-opening but error-prone Cinerama required the use of three 35mm projectors to throw jigsaw sections of footage on to a gargantuan concave screen, while mogul Sam

Goldwyn testily dismissed the more popular CinemaScope technique as "making a bad picture twice as bad". But, although widescreen movie-making remains a problematic and infrequently used approach, there's little doubting its impact when used to its full potential; just feast your eyes on the Monument Valley splendour of *The Searchers* (1956) or the billowing yellow sandscapes of Bertolucci's *The Sheltering Sky* (1990) and David Lean's *Lawrence of Arabia* (1962).

Be it square, rounded, a distended oblong, or even three-dimensional, the cinema screen has held audiences spellbound for generations. Provided there are artists to fill these shifting canvases of light with their own distinctive visions, the future of film looks safe and sound.

Lighting an icon: *Marlon Brando in* Apocalypse Now

Technological Advances in the Cinema

For such a young art-form, cinema has gone through a dizzying set of shifts and upheavals over the past century. Forever trying to anticipate and satisfy the cravings of the great cinema-going public, the industry pioneers have applied a series of innovations to a skeletal art-form. Some – sound, colour, movable cameras – quickly became an inseparable part of the cinema experience. Others, like Cinerama, Odorama, 3D and the electrified cinema seats that accompanied William Castle's *The Tingler* (1959), are now dismissed as gimmicky curios. What's certain, though, is that there is too much money involved in film production for the industry ever to rest on its laurels. The computer-generated imagery of films like *Terminator 2* (1991), the multi-media burst of Oliver Stone's *Natural Born Killers* (1994) and the creeping influence of interactive film and video systems point the way of things to come.

Sets, Costumes and Make-up:
The theatrical illusion

While wise film-makers quickly realized that film and theatre were very different media, both of them tell a story through drama and aim to create the temporary illusion that the story is real. The work of the set and costume designers and the make-up artists, whose arts are common to both media, is a vital part of the final on-screen effect.

The earliest film designers were scene painters from the theatre, creating crude theatrical backdrops for the silent movies. This was in the days when daylight was essential for film-making. Studios were glass-roofed, open to the air and even revolving, to catch as much sunlight as possible, and many films were shot in the open air.

For *Quo Vadis?* (1912) Italian director Enrico Guazzini, a former painter and decorator who designed his own sets and costumes, created the biggest sets yet constructed, while the opulent settings for Pastrone's *Cabiria* (1914) were influential on Walter L. Hall's giant Babylonian sets for *Intolerance* (1916), which in turn were developed further in terms of scale by Wilfred Buckland's enormous castle, which cost a quarter of the budget of Douglas Fairbanks's *Robin Hood* (1922).

Expressionism and other European styles

The most important stylistic development in early cinema was the expressionist movement, which first appeared in German painting

of fate, madness and the supernatural. Prominent among the set designers of the movement was director/designer Paul Leni, whose work in particular gave the art director a new importance in expressionism.

The dominant European influ-

Design for the dance: Hein Heckroth's set designs influenced choreography and direction on The Red Shoes

and theatre around 1905. It was influenced by a variety of factors, including primitive art, medieval woodcuts, the painting of Van Gogh and Freudian psychology. Expressionism made itself felt in the cinema in *The Cabinet of Dr Caligari* (1919), and its hallmarks were extreme stylization of acting, sharply angled and grossly distorted sets, vivid lighting and menacing shadows, with the object of giving "objective expression to inner experience" in stories

ence in the 1930s was the poetic realism of the French cinema. This, too, used distorted perspectives but in a very different way, emphasizing the unusual detail of streets and rooftops in studio-built cityscapes which combined documentary realism with fantasy, all totally under the designer's control. Leading design lights of the movement were Lazare Meerson, Eugène Louriée and Alexandre Trauner.

In Britain the grandiose theatrical sets of Vincent Korda,

former painter and brother of Alexander, stood out from the discreetly understated drawing rooms of his contemporaries, who were taking their cue from the theatre of the day. Michael Powell and Emeric Pressburger held the contribution made to their films by design in high esteem, with Powell describing the designer as "the creator of those miraculous images on the big screen", needing the skills of painter, architect and engineer combined. The men he had particularly in mind were Alfred Junge (*Black Narcissus*, 1947) and the ballet designer Hein Heckroth (*The Red Shoes*, 1948).

The Hollywood style

To achieve the look of Hollywood films in the 1920s and 1930s a whole army of visual creators – designers, builders, modelmakers, carpenters, backdrop and matte painters – toiled under the leadership of the heads of art departments, who got most of the credit. The most famous was Cedric Gibbons, designer of the Oscar statuette, many of which he collected on behalf of his team in his 32 years at MGM. The studio's visual style was frequently influenced by Art Deco, as was that of RKO's Fred Astaire/Ginger Rogers vehicles under the eye of Van Nest Polglase. Anton Grot brought the expressionist look to his work at Warners, as did UFA veteran Hans Dreier to Paramount, where he also developed a talent

The Cook, The Thief, His Wife and Her Lover: Sumptuous set design

for glamour and elegance. Richard Day designed Erich von Stroheim's films in the silent days, then moved on to the major studios.

William Cameron Menzies was a legend in the Hollywood art departments. A stickler for detail and control, he storyboarded shots of his sets and was said to bully his directors on camera angles and how his creations should be lit. His finest hour came with *Gone with the Wind* (1939), where he was the constant creative factor through three directors and numerous cameramen. He even directed some sequences himself uncredited, and made the film one of the first fully to recognize the role of the production designer.

In the 1940s tighter budgets and the development of portable equipment made location work more popular, giving the designer the added challenge of dressing a "real" venue and ensuring that it harmonized with studio scenes. Reflecting the change, the Oscar design award, originally for "Interior Decoration", was changed in 1947 to one for Art and Set Decoration.

Dressing the Actors

An important contribution to the "house styles" of the 1930s was made by the costume departments, who became as influential as the fashion houses in dictating what the public wore. Foremost among them was Edith Head at Paramount, who was variously responsible for projecting the glamour image of the major stars and

dressing large casts of players and extras in historically researched period costumes. Two important figures at MGM were Adrian, who created fashion gowns for Garbo, Shearer and Crawford, and Helen Rose, an Oscar-winner of the 1950s, who also designed Princess Grace Kelly's wedding gown.

In the 1960s, when British fashion was attracting world interest, costumiers Julie Harris and Phyllis Dalton won Oscars for *Darling* (1965) and *Doctor Zhivago* (1965) respectively, as did Anthony Powell for *Death on the Nile* (1978) and *Tess* (1979), and Cecil Beaton for *Gigi* (1958) and *My Fair Lady* (1964). As a result of the climate of increased internationalism that developed then, UK production designers have since become world stars of their profession, in particular John Box (*Oliver!*, 1968), Ken Adam (*Dr Strangelove*, 1964) and Anton Furst (*Batman*, 1989).

Previous experience in visuals shows in the work of several

prominent directors: Luchino Visconti, once a costume designer for Jean Renoir; Vincente Minnelli, initially a set and costume designer on Broadway; and Derek Jarman, who designed *The Devils* (1971) for Ken Russell. While film has always been a team effort, it is even more so in today's art departments, as designers have to incorporate the work of special effects wizards and computer technologists into the look of their films, along with all the other elements of design.

But whatever the style of the film, they are all there to serve cinemagoers' demands: tell me a story, take me into a different world and convince me this illusion is real.

A Change of Face: The Art of Make-up

One of the purposes of make-up has always been to make the stars look good. Studio make-up pioneer Max Factor, who developed Pan-Cake for Technicolor, also built a vast cosmetics empire on the desire of ordinary women to look beautiful. George Westmore, a British immigrant to Hollywood in 1917, founded a three-generation dynasty of make-up artists.

Even in the early days, there was another demand on the make-up department: to make the stars look bad, in terms of blood, scars, ageing and deformity. George's son Wally created Fredric March's Mr Hyde make-up in 1932, while Boris Karloff had been transformed into the monster in *Frankenstein* by Jack Pierce a year earlier. More recently,

Chris Walas and Stephan Dupuis gave Jeff Goldblum a spectacular and uncomfortable transformation in *The Fly* (1986); an example of the increasing dedication required by make-up artists and actors in this area.

Surprisingly, the first Oscar for Make-up was not awarded until 1981, to Rick Baker for *An American Werewolf in London* (1981).

A Midsummer's Night Dream: A bewitched Bottom gives the make-up artist plenty of scope

Special Effects:
Tricks and techniques

To a great extent the history of special effects is the history of the fantasy genres. Though cinema itself can be said to have started as a special effect and its development since closely linked to ever more novel and startling representations, nowhere has the art of making the impossible appear to happen found a more fruitful development than in horror, sci-fi and fantasy.

To a great extent the history of special effects is the history of the fantasy genres. Though cinema itself can be said to have started as a special effect and its development since closely linked to ever-more novel and startling representations, nowhere has the art of making the impossible appear to happen found a more fruitful development than in horror, sci-fi and fantasy.

It all started 100 years ago in Paris with Georges Méliès, the founding father of the fantasy film. Méliès copied Lumière in recording commonplace occurrences like the train's arrival in *Arrival of a Train at a Paris Terminal* (*Arrivée d'un Train à la Gare de Vincennes* – 1896) but it was the technical possibilities of the new medium that fascinated him most. The story goes that Méliès first discovered the possibilities of trick photography by accident, when his film stuck momentarily in the middle of recording the Parisian public moving about, creating the illusion of people disappearing and reappearing.

Fantasy Takes Flight

In 1896 he created the first European movie studios, with indoor stages and artificial light, where his output included trick documentaries and films with special effects like the 1901 *The Dream of Christmas*, using faked snow and day-for-night. His pioneering 1902 fantasy film, *A Trip to the Moon* (*Le Voyage dans la Lune*), ensured his place in cinema history and established the fantasy genre artistically. Even now it seems exciting and astoundingly inventive, so it's hardly surprising that it caught the public imagination worldwide – especially in America, prompting the Americans to plan their own fantasy films. By 1924, Hollywood was producing an outstanding, highly sophisticated example of the form, both technically and artistically, in Douglas Fairbanks's *The Thief of Bagdad*, where the hero takes off on a special effects magic-carpet ride. Hollywood hasn't looked back since.

When the big studios ruled in Hollywood, each had its own special effects unit, but after the 1950s this increasingly important area of film-making fell into the hands of the independents. Today's leading exponent is George Lucas's Industrial Light and Magic, first established to invent the spectacular trickery for *Star Wars* in 1977. Stanley Kubrick's pioneering film *2001: A Space Odyssey* (1968), with its still amazing spacecraft shots (courtesy British SF/X wizard Douglas Trumbull) and the monkey make-up, may have been the spark but *Star Wars* was the tinder for Hollywood's hugely profitable, high-profile, and continuing cycle of special effects-led fantasy films like *Close Encounters of the Third Kind* (1977), *E.T.: The Extra Terrestrial* (1982), the *Back to the Future* trilogy and the revolutionary *Alien* (1979). And since the special effects in themselves excited the public so much, they were increasingly used for other types of film – comedies like

Mighty Kong: *Willis O'Brien's magic trickery*

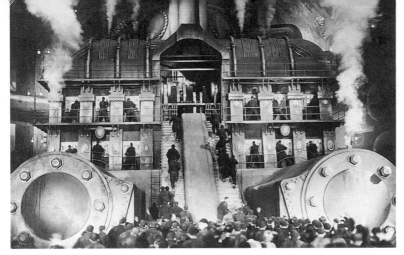

Marvellous Metropolis: *The breathtaking set design for Fritz Lang's silent classic*

InnerSpace (1987) and children's films like *The Never Ending Story* (1984). The reawakened interest in the sci-fi genre during the 1980s sparked a parallel rekindling of the horror genre and created a significant overlap which also took full advantage of the increasingly sophisticated possibilities for cinema trickery.

Wizards and Wonders

Among the many special effects wizards, six names stand out: John Dykstra, who received an Oscar for his pioneering computer-controlled-camera special effects on *Star Wars* (1977); visual effects expert Dennis Muren, winner of Oscars for *The Empire Strikes Back* (1980), *E.T.* (1982) and *InnerSpace* (1987); Stan Winston who took an Oscar for Best Visual Effects for *Aliens* (1986); Rick Baker, the recipient of Best Make-Up Oscars for *An American Werewolf in*

London (1981) and *Harry and the Hendersons* (1987); Rob Bottin, Oscar-winner for *Total Recall* (1990); and Carlo Rambaldi, who was awarded his Oscars for *E.T.* (1982) and for *Alien* (1979) (based on the fantastical designs of H. R. Giger with whom he shared the award).

Superman: *You'll believe a man can fly*

Special effects fall into two main categories: those achieved by camera or film trickery and those made with actual constructed props, machines and prosthetics. Among the visual technical trickery used by the film-makers are Matte shots (dropping an alien

image into a shot by means of masking off part of the original footage and later adding the extra element in the space left for it), optical printers (a projector and a camera rolled into one), the blue-screen process (another kind of screening mechanism, largely used for adding backgrounds) and, of course, good old back-projection. Mechanical effects such as exploding blood pellets producing fake gun impacts, miniatures and model work are all part of the armoury of trick cinema.

From the flashing electronic pseudo-science of *Frankenstein* (1931), through the transformation

in *Dr Jekyll and Mr Hyde* (1932) and the seminal *King Kong* (1933), with its stop-motion animation and over-sized animatronics, to the marvellous model work and painted back-projections of *War of the Worlds* (1953) and *Forbidden Planet* (1956), right up to the computer animations of *Tron* (1982), *The Abyss* (1989) and the two

Terminator films (1984 and 1991), and of course *Jurassic Park*'s realer-than-real computer-generated dinosaurs (1993), the history of FX has been one of pushing human visual ingenuity to its utmost –and, in so doing, employing ever more up-to-the-minute technologies.

Reality – Who Needs It?

Computers can have seemingly paradoxical uses. On the one hand they allow the removal of the tell-tale wires and props the film-makers used, as in *Superman* (1978) where, as the movie poster said, you really believe a man can fly, while also allowing you to add "unreal" elements on to the film,

for example snow, rain, fire or 30-foot dinosaurs that were never actually on the set. More than this, computers can now doctor original film footage: for example on *Zelig* (1983) Woody Allen was integrated with Hitler and others, and on *Forrest Gump* (1994) Tom Hanks appeared together with John Kennedy, Richard Nixon and John Lennon. Computers can now generate an entire scene and in this way trickery has become so seamless you can no longer that believe anything you see on the screen ever actually existed, making it an even more powerful and potentially dangerous tool.

By the mid-1990s mainstream cinema was flirting with the idea of virtual reality in a technofear film like *Disclosure* (1995), so can the (un)reality be far away? As the millennium dawns and the computer becomes ultra-sophisticated, will we see the day when real actors and sets are unnecessary? Scary!

Terminator 2: Judgment Day

James Cameron's spectacular-looking sci-fi film's $100,000,000 budget was seemingly largely shared between the human star Arnold Schwarzenegger and the real stars of the movie, Stan Winston and Dennis Muren's Oscar-winning state-of-the-art visual effects.

These effects mostly concern Arnie's foe, the second cyborg, a new improved model T-1000, composed of a mercury-like liquid metal which can metamorphose into any shape or form in the most spectacular way. Technically these computer-generated images are an advance on similar techniques used in *The Abyss* (1989) and among the most spectacular shape-shifting sequences are when T-1000 develops metal spears for arms, or turns into a black-and-white tiled floor which later reassumes its apparently human form. But the film's most breathtaking moment is when T-1000 oozes through prison bars to reconstitute on the other side.

Animation:
Cartoon fun on the big screen

Animators John Halas and Joy Batchelor have described their profession thus: "If it is the live action film's job to present physical reality, animated film is concerned with metaphysical reality – not how things look, but what they mean."

From the earliest days of film – earlier, indeed, since the principles of graphic animation were inherent in Plateau's Phenakistiscope (1832), Horner's Zoetrope (1834) and Reynaud's Praxinoscope (1876) – animation has transported audiences from the confines of the known world into a magical place beyond, a place where accepted laws of reality are suspended and anything goes.

There can be few people in the western world who haven't, at some point, seen a Disney cartoon, or an entertainment based on moving puppets. There would have been no *King Kong* (1933), *Star Wars* (1977) or *Jurassic Park* (1993) without the principles of graphic animation; half the adverts we see on television wouldn't exist; and a generation of children is now emerging for whom the animated narrative is the fomative cultural experience.

Mixed Media

The boundaries of the animated art are almost limitless. If the most popular applications have always been the cartoon and stop-motion puppet manipulation, it has nonetheless manifested itself in countless other artistic forms. The first animated feature, Lotte Reiniger's *Die Abenteuer des Prinz Achmets* (1926), was based on silhouetted cut-outs, as were Terry Gilliam's hugely popular *Monty Python* cartoons, and George Dunning's Beatles feature *Yellow Submarine* (1968).

Since 1941 Alexandre Alexeieff has, in association with Claire Parker, constructed complex narratives around the shadows thrown by pins on a board, while as early as 1921 Walter Ruttman was exploring abstract animation in his *Light Play Opus 1*, a striking series of polymorphous images moving to a synchronized musical score. Most significant for the recent history of cinema has been the development, since the early 1960s, of computer animation. Early pioneers included John and James Whitney and Stan Vanderbeek, and computerized graphics are now an integral part of the Hollywood special effects tool box.

For all its multifarious applications, however, the art of animation will always be most closely associated with the cartoon and, to a lesser extent, the puppet film. The cinema cartoon first developed at the turn of the century, early examples being J. Stuart Blackton's *Humorous Phases of Funny Faces* (1906) and Emile Cohl's *Fantasmagorie* (1908).

Cartoon Pioneers

The key figure in the genre's early genesis was Winsor McCay, whose *Gertie the Dinosaur* series (1910–19) was the first real cartoon blockbuster. McCay was later to bemoan the bastardization of his art – "Animation should be an art, but you fellows have turned it into a trade," he told a gathering of animators in 1920 – but his influence was still immense, spawning such legendary cartoonists as Otto Messmer and Pat Sullivan, responsible for *Felix the Cat*; Max and Dave Fleischer, begetters of the *Out of the Inkwell* series of the 1910s and *Betty Boop* in the late 1920s; John R. Bray, Raoul Barre, Albert Hurter and, most significant of all, Walt Disney.

Disney is the jewel in the crown of the cartoon. Contemporaries considered him as important a film-maker as Chaplin and Griffith, and his name has become synonymous with a whole genre of popular culture. It was Disney who produced the first American sound cartoon, *Steamboat Willie* (1928); the first three-strip Technicolor cartoon, *Flowers and Trees* (1932); and the first American feature cartoon, *Snow White and the Seven Dwarfs* (1937). His characters – Mickey Mouse, Donald Duck, Pluto, Goofy – have become part of popular iconography; his theme parks the biggest tourist attractions in America; and, although his cine-

Betty Boop: *Luscious cartoon sex-bomb*

Pussy galore: *Felix the Cat, the first popular cartoon icon*

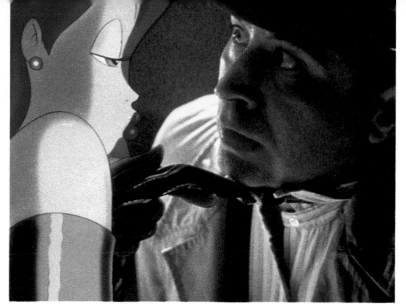

Who Framed Roger Rabbit: *Bob Hoskins*

with the puppet work of Jiri Trnka in the 1950s (see box). Notable also were Russians Alexander Ptushko and Ladislas Starevitch, whose *Story of the Fox* (1938) stands as one of the masterpieces of the genre.

In the States stop-motion animation has been employed primarily in the field of special effects. From Willis O'Brien's trailblazing *King Kong* (1933), via Ray Harryhausen's fantasy monsters and George Pal's sci-fi creations of the 1950s, through to modern day extravaganzas such as the *Star Wars* trilogy and Spielberg's *Jurassic Park* (1993), stop-motion has brought life to a dazzling assortment of objects and characters, making the impossible possible and rendering the outlandish commonplace. In Britain, working for the BBC, Nick Park won two Oscars for his stop-motion animations *Creature Comforts* (1990) and *The Wrong Trousers* (1993).

The whole genre has lately been lifted to new heights by Tim Burton's remarkable fantasy *The Nightmare before Christmas* (1994), two years in the making and the most advanced application of stop-motion techniques to date. The power of animation to thrill and transcend, inherent since the first tentative sketches of Blackton and Cohl, is clearly as strong and vibrant as ever.

Czech Animation

Although it has long produced some of the world's most stylistically daring animators – Jiri Brdecka, Eduard Hoffman, Karel Dodal and Karel Zeman to name but a handful – Czechoslovakia would have remained a cinematic backwater had it not been for the work of Jiri Trnka. "He was the master," said Brdecka, "the first to show us that animation could be an art-form." Based in Prague, Trnka, a former puppeteer and cartoonist, raised the art of stop-motion puppet animation to unsurpassed heights, imbuing his creations with a vivacity and fluency of movement that have rarely, if ever, been matched. His work was rooted in Czech folklore, and with masterpieces such as *The Czech Year* (1947), *The Emperor's Nightingale* (1947), *Old Czech Legends* (1957) and *A Midsummer Night's Dream* (1959) he revolutionized his art and propelled Czechoslovakia to the forefront of world animation.

matic influence waned towards the end of the 1950s, modern Disney features such as *Beauty and The Beast* (1991), *Aladdin* (1992) and *The Lion King* (1994) continue to delight audiences and breathe life into a genre that has struggled for the last 20 years to find a market.

Disney has dominated but by no means monopolized the popular cartoon. Non-Disney animators such as Tex Avery, Paul Terry, Bill Hanna and Joe Barbera enjoyed massive followings, while United Productions of America, founded in 1945 by disgruntled Disney employees, brought a new absurdity to the form with its *Mr Magoo* series and the *Gerald McBoing Boing* illustrations of Robert Cannon. Robert Zemeckis's *Who Framed Roger Rabbit* (1988) marked a watershed in the fusion of live and animated action, and was, until the Disney revival of the 1990s, the most popular cartoon of all time.

In Britain John Halas and Joy Batchelor have long produced high-quality animations – including *Animal Farm* (1954), the first British feature cartoon – while some of the most striking British animation of recent years has come from the studio of George Dunning, including the Oscar-winning *The Snowman* (1982) and *When the Wind Blows* (1987). Eastern Europe, too, has advanced the cartoon art, notably with the work of the Zagreb school in Yugoslavia, and the disturbing graphics of Poland's Jan Lenica and Walerian Borowczyk.

Stop-motion

Stop-motion puppet animation – the manipulation of a mannequin, frame by frame, to create the illusion of movement – is another widely popular application of the animator's art, although its time-consuming nature has made it less prolific than the animated cartoon. The puppet tradition has always been stonger in Europe than America, and it was in Czechoslovakia that the stop-motion genre reached its apogee

Puppet romance: *Tim Burton's surreal* The Nightmare Before Christmas *(1994)*

Publicity:
Packaging people

The golden days of Hollywood in the 1930s and 1940s were the apex of film publicity. Never before nor since has it been raised to such an art-form. Today it's run like a smoothly oiled, highly controlled corporate business, with everything that appears about a star – their photographs, their interviews and stories about them – carefully regulated by the agents and personal publicists. But in these democratic times they are presented as real people, very similar to the members of the audience: stars now will be photographed unshaven, hair unwashed, wearing tatty jeans.

Greta Garbo: *A face with no bad angles*

Back then, movie stars were painted, packaged and presented as perfect, unreal, unattainable, god-like creatures – shining, beautifully crafted objects of desire with the mythical quality of characters from legend come to life. Names, characters and whole lives were created for them by the studios' powerful publicity machines.

The Hollywood publicity treatment was as much a part of the showbiz make-believe as the films. There existed a strange complicity between the studios, the fanzines, newspapers and the public. It was like a game they all entered into and the counters in this game were the actors and actresses.

The Camera Never Lies?

High among the key studio publicity personnel were the photographers, the unsung heroes at the studios. Their work was sprayed and doctored until the photographs were as much painting as anything else. Clarence Sinclair Bull and George Hurrell were the leading lights in the publicity department of the biggest studio of all – MGM. Sinclair Bull was entrusted with the most sacred job of all, photographing the screen goddess to end all goddesses, Greta Garbo – the face that launched a thousand publicity photos. "It was a face with no bad side and no bad angles," according to Sinclair Bull, who made the star look ethereal and brought out hidden depths in this great face, helping to sell a million tickets to her wildly romantic, escapist films.

Press pack: *Feeding fantasies for film fans*

Both the movies and the Sinclair Bull photographs have stood the test of time far beyond their original purely commercial purpose. No one was making pictures, still or moving, for posterity. It wasn't until the 1960s that the quality of the publicity photographers' work was properly recognized as having a lasting artistic merit, and they have since been the subject of many exhibitions.

Everybody the world over is familiar with trailers, lobby cards and movie posters as effective means of conveying information, but today we look upon some of the best examples as an art-form – Warner's black-and-white poster for *The Jazz Singer* (1927), for example, the beautiful posters for Ealing Studios, the stylish output of London's Academy Cinemas. Notably, Howard Hart Benton was hired for *The Grapes of Wrath* (1940) poster and Henry Clive for glamour portrayals of the great stars, but one designer stands out, the Italian-born Batiste Madalena, whose poster paintings for George Eastman between 1924 and 1929 reached the level of art.

Advertising

At the beginning of the movies, the phenomenon of film itself was sufficient lure for a public enthralled by the novelty of the new medium, and initially studios didn't name actors at all. Stars would simply be known as, for example, "the Biograph girl", and the canny early producers did this so as not to have to pay them too much. But quickly the public was eager to know more about their favourites, and of course the nameless stars were clamouring for proper recognition. Producer Carl Laemmle became the first to accede to the growing demand for biographical detail when he named "the Biograph girl" as Florence Lawrence, whom he'd bought for his own company. From this simple act everything else followed and from the early 1910s film stars became the main item in selling the product. The star system was born and Mary Pickford and Charles Chaplin become the first superstars.

Howard Strickling, the publicity director at MGM, the biggest Hollywood studio in the 1930s, was a trusted intimate of studio boss Louis B. Mayer. He followed the boss's paternalistic attitude towards the contract artistes, taking care of their personal needs as well as their professional lives and ensuring that the stories the studio put out were based on at least a semblance of the reality, unlike some of the lesser studios' publicists who would invent lives wholesale for their stars.

But the main movie information consisted of direct, up-front announcements of new releases, which had started in the 1920s. Expenditure on advertising rocketed from the 1960s onwards when the movies used their main competitor, television, for their campaigns. In the 1980s and 1990s it became entirely common for the advertising budget of a new movie to exceed the production costs, even on an expensive picture like *Alien* (1979).

Advertising is backed up by the industrious efforts of the publicists, always trying to find an angle on a film, a new star or an issue to get their picture or artiste in the papers or magazines. In the 1980s it was the American press who created the entirely spurious notion of the "Brat Pack" (a clever journalistic label based on the 1960s term "Rat Pack" for Frank

Holy megabucks, Batman!: Tim Burton's 1989 film about the Gotham City crime-fighter was a toy and merchandizing spinoff bonanza

Sinatra's showbiz buddies).

In one of the cinema's most famous publicity stunts, producer David O. Selznick launched a campaign to find the actress to play Scarlett O'Hara in *Gone with the Wind* (1939). The nationwide search was conducted in the fullest glare of publicity and so were the screen tests of all the available stars. Selznick then ignored all his own brouhaha and imported an English actress, Vivien Leigh, for the part, thus ensuring that her casting was such big news that she made the cover of *Time* magazine.

Merchandising

Batman was the hit of its year (1989) but the toy and record spin-offs produced an even greater cash-register bonanza. You can hardly see a movie now without some form of product placement. *The Flintstones* (1993) was linked with a well-known hamburger chain, with the restaurant appearing in the movie and the real-life

diners advertising the picture with offers of spin-off products.

Today most popular blockbuster movies seek to incorporate a hit single or an entire soundtrack by a well known performer, such as Prince in *Batman* – or popular works such as Mozart's greatest hits on the soundtrack of *Amadeus*

(1984). *Star Wars*-related goods, sweets, children's games, video games, and the like, and various books of the film flooded world markets during the period of the three films (1977–83), making the main characters familiar icons which have been absorbed into our culture.

Jane Russell Outlawed

Producer Howard Hughes showcased his discovery Jane Russell in his controversial sexed-up western *The Outlaw*, a version of the Billy the Kid–Doc Holliday story. It was filmed in 1941, but the American Production Code refused to give it a Seal of Approval. By the time it received a proper release in 1948 under the auspices of RKO, the studio Hughes had just bought, the film was minus such torrid scenes as the one where a thrusting-topped Russell stripped for bed to warm up the ailing hero. Nevertheless, the film was publicized on the strength of its sexiness and notoriety.

Censorship: Cut!

All art, created by an individual or by a small group for consumption by the masses, sooner or later comes up against censorship. As the most populist and widely accessible of all art-forms, film has traditionally faced the most interference, its contents forever scrutinized and deemed "acceptable" or "unacceptable". The form of the medium also counts against it. The cinema is regarded as the most realistic and immediate art-form, even presenting a kind of "heightened reality" in its use of emotive music, artificial effects and attention-grabbing camera shots.

Coupled with this is drama's natural role in detailing the development and resolution of conflict, be it through fiery debate, physical combat or sex. Throughout its lifespan, film has constantly been reined in and regulated by a society nervous of its impact, projected in glowing larger-than-life detail on to the delicate sensibilities of the populace.

Age of Innocence

Only in its fledgling, formative years did cinema enjoy a period of comparative freedom, with bare breasts visible in D. W. Griffith's *Intolerance* (1916) and a nude bathing scene spicing up 1933's *Ecstasy*. But this "age of innocence" was ended, in America at any rate, by the arrival of the regulatory Hays Office in 1930, its aim being the "establishment and maintenance of the highest moral and artistic standards in motion picture production". The Hays Office oversaw the development of Hollywood studio scripts and in 1938 drew up a list of stars whose work was judged to be morally suspect.

Top of the list was brazenly sexual, but always tongue-in-cheek Mae West, whose film shoots were traditionally overseen by the Hays Office watchdogs. "I'd be insulted if a picture I was in didn't get an X-rating," she reflected years later. "Don't forget, honey, I *invented* censorship."

Looking back, it's significant to note how many of the cinema's milestone movies suffered at the hands of contemporary censors. F.W. Murnau's *Nosferatu* (1921) was banned in the UK on its initial release, while Fritz Lang's sci-fi masterwork *Metropolis* (1926) only escaped after heavy cuts. Most notorious was the treatment meted out to Sergei Eisenstein's *Battleship Potemkin* (1925). Unnerved, in the wake of the 1926 General Strike, by the film's rabble-rousing tale of a successful uprising against the powers-that-be, the British authorities withdrew the picture from public exhibition until 1954 – the second longest ban in UK history after the 1932–63 block imposed on Tod Browning's searing circus shocker *Freaks* (1932). Similarly banned in the UK (until 1967) was Marlon Brando's leather-clad biker turn in *The Wild One* (1954), while the 1950s also saw censors hack 16 minutes from Henri-Georges Clouzot's white-knuckle *The Wages of Fear* (1953) and Max Ophüls's seductive *La Ronde* (1950), tried for obscenity in the United States.

Sex and Violence

The social and sexual upheavals of the 1960s inevitably found their reflection in western cinemas, with censors taxed by Sam Fuller's hard-

Hell for leather: *Biker Marlon Brando shook up Middle America in the British-censored* The Wild One

hitting asylum exposé *Shock Corridor* (1963) and Roger Corman's lurid counter-culture biker opus *The Wild Angels* (1967). The late 1960s and early 1970s witnessed a sudden rise in explicit on-screen violence. Arthur Penn's *Bonnie and Clyde* (1967) and Sam Peckinpah's *The Wild Bunch* (1969) ushered in a new depiction of movie carnage, shot in loving slow motion that turned death and destruction into a kind of poetic abstract art.

Most notorious of this new breed of shocker was Stanley Kubrick's future-world fable *A Clockwork Orange* (1972). While fiercely anti-violence, Kubrick's picture was claimed to have triggered off a spate of real-life attacks and the ensuing controversy prompted the director to withdraw the film from British release – a ban that stands to this day.

The 1960s and 1970s also saw a new frankness in cinema's depiction of sex. Only Luis Buñuel's pedigree as one of the movie greats smuggled his unflinching *Belle de Jour* (1967) past the gaze of western censors, while Oliver Reed and Alan Bates's infamous fireside wrestling scene in 1969's *Women in Love* set a new precedent in male nudity. Robert Aldrich spiced up his *The Killing of Sister George* (1969) with a lesbian love scene and jittery censors took the scissors to much of the gender-bending *ménage à trois* woven throughout

the 1970's counter-culture fable *Performance*. Marlon Brando and Maria Schneider's butter-smearing session in *Last Tango in Paris* (1972) ensured the picture's place in the movie hall of infamy, followed four years later by the highly explicit Japanese erotic art-pic *In the Realm of the Senses* (1976), banned in the UK until 1991. But the key picture in the rise of sex in the cinema is 1974's *Emmanuelle*, starring Sylvia Kristel as a young bride on a globe-hopping voyage of discovery. With its plethora of prettily lit, soft-focus heaving, *Emmanuelle* dragged what had previously been the preserve of the "adult cinema" into the movie mainstream, showcasing it for public consumption.

The Power to Corrupt?

Censors were further tested in the 1980s by the explosion of the home-video market and the arrival of so-called "video nasties" like *Driller Killer* (1980) and *I Spit on Your Grave* (1981). Video nasties, easily accessible and with the possibility of repeated viewings in the privacy of your own home, were thought to wield an influence that was profoundly corrupting – always the primary motivating concern of film censors. In the 1990s Oliver Stone's tabloid-style, serial-killer satire *Natural Born Killers* (1994) was thought to have

Pure titillation: Sylvia Kristel poses in a wicker chair in one of the quieter moments in Emmanuelle IV

prompted a set of copycat crimes in France and the US, leading its British cinema release to be delayed for six months. The cinema watchdogs are forever out to protect the public's interest.

Censorship is arguably the most volatile topic affecting cinema today. Purporting to be clear-cut and clinical, its implementation is invariably haphazard, fired by individual perceptions and prejudices and varying from nation to nation, where differing cultural taboos or political agendas all play their part. Crucially, for censorship to remain justified, it must respond with a fine-tuned empathy to the work in question. Certain directors, after all, can

tackle the most contentious topics in the most direct of ways without any tell-tale taint of exploitation. John Trevelyan, one-time chief of the British Board of Film Censors, claimed that hacking footage from the work of recognizably great film-makers was "the equivalent of taking a first-rate painting and saying 'cut out three square inches on the right-hand side, four-and-a-half inches down'. I don't think one should do that."

Director John Huston had his own opinion. "Censorship hurts pictures," he said. "It damages them. The only form of censorship that's at all significant is what the French do – burn the theatre down."

Pornography

"Film is not a gun," insists director Claude Chabrol, striking at the heart of the debate on the pros and cons of censorship – the impact of film art/entertainment on the subsequent consciousness and actions of its recipient. What seems unarguable is that part of cinema's enduring appeal lies in its ability to titillate and stir the blood, be it with a *film noir* thriller or a glowing close-up of Marilyn Monroe. Sex-appeal and the excitement provoked by cathartic violence have always been endemic components of film. Taken to its extremes, this jaded craving for ever-more outlandish thrills leads us into the illegal twilight fringe of pornographic cinema. Filmed acts of unsimulated sex and violence (the hard-core flick, the snuff movie) bear no comparison to the structured artistry of narrative cinema, but they nonetheless have their roots in many of the same basic human urges. To ignore the root causes of film pornography propagates ignorance as to its role and effect – whether corrosive or a valuable safety-valve – on the people that use it.

Who's Who in the Movies

In its heyday, Metro Goldwyn Mayer's motto was that it had "more stars than there are in the heavens". This celestial boast, though typical Hollywood hyperbole, was a testimony to the fundamental importance of the film star to the movies' enduring appeal. What follows is an A to Z guide to 500 of the most influential actors and actresses, directors and producers from the first hundred years of world cinema. By luck, fate, natural-born talent or sheer hard-driving ability, each of these men and women has left their mark on twentieth-century popular culture, and most have to a greater or lesser degree pushed cinema into exciting new areas or at the very least been superlative at what they do. From Culkin to Coppola, from Gable to Grable, these are the markers round which the history of cinema can be mapped.

Abbott and Costello

Comics

Born: WILLIAM (BUD) ABBOTT, *Asbury Park, NJ, October 2, 1895*
Died: *April 24, 1974*
Born: LOUIS CRISTILLO (COSTELLO), *Paterson, NJ, March 6, 1906*
Died: *February 26, 1959*

Creeping up on an unaware public through burlesque and radio success, odd-couple comics Bud Abbott and Lou Costello became Universal's top box-office pull, raucous morale-boosters during the blackest days of World War Two. A film debut of the undercard of *One Night in the Tropics* (1940) set the stage for a hit vehicle in *Buck Privates* (1941), with the duo's tussles with army life accompanied by breezy Oscar-nominated tunes from the Andrews Sisters. Abbott and Costello's respective characters were unchanging and clearly delineated. Bud, 11 years older, played the aggressive straight man, barking orders while shrill, podgy "bad boy" Lou nabbed all the laughs. Forged by years in vaudeville, their best routines were pared down, rat-tat-tat exchanges marked by skewed logic and spiralling confusion. Their huge success prompted Universal to lavish funds on these production-line outings, inserting major musical and dramatic stars and later roping in a host of horror players for a series of comedy creepers, kicking off with 1948's *Abbott and Costello Meet Frankenstein*. Such diverse notables as Ella Fitzgerald, Boris Karloff, Lucille Ball, Lon Chaney Jnr, Charles Laughton, the Inkspots and Bela Lugosi have all, at one time or another, plied their trade in an Abbott and Costello picture. In the 1950s the boys moved on to TV work, but Costello's death in 1959, worn out at 52, left Abbott with no one to bully. Poignantly, his last job was voicing his own character in an Abbott and Costello cartoon spin-off syndicated on American TV in 1966.

Alan Alda

Actor, writer, director

Born: *New York, NY, January 28, 1936*

"I didn't want to be famous, I just wanted to make a living and be very good at what I do," says Alda, and for a while it looked as though he'd get his wish. For, even though he was the son of popular actor Robert Alda, he had to struggle to become a success and his first movies didn't do well. But his role as Hawkeye in TV's *M*A*S*H* (1972–83) changed all that, giving him the chance to hone his acting, write and direct episodes, while becoming internationally renowned. In the wake of *M*A*S*H* came a string of hit movies, including *Same Time Next Year* (1978), *California Suite* (1978) and *The Seduction of Joe Tynan* (1979) with Meryl Streep, which he also wrote, pointing to a new phase in his career. With *M*A*S*H*'s extraordinary 11-year run coming to an end in 1983, Alda wrote, directed and starred in the acclaimed *The Four Seasons* (1981) with Carol Burnett, *Sweet Liberty* (1986) with Michael Caine, *A New Life* (1987) with Ann-Margret and *Betsy's Wedding* (1990) as a man who decides to throw the world's most expensive wedding for his daughter Molly Ringwald. The films shared the same warm sense of humour and generous nature towards the world, representing the humanist, liberal, middle-class values of their creator. More recently he's worked profitably twice for Woody Allen in *Crimes and Misdemeanors* (1989) and *Manhattan Murder Mystery* (1993).

Woody Allen

Actor, comic, director, writer
Born: ALLEN STEWART
KONIGSBERG, *New York, NY,*
December 1, 1935

The bespectacled comedian, philosopher and chronicler of the neuroses of our time, with the permanently worried look and fly-away hair, has dominated American humour since the mid-1960s in nightclubs, books, plays and movies. Allen is the great American director-writer-star of the 1970s and 1980s. After writing gags for TV, newspapers and theatre, he started performing self-penned scripts in 1961 in Greenwich Village venues, graduated to TV chat shows and launched into movies with his script for Peter Sellers's *What's*

Woody Allen: Chronicler of our neuroses

New Pussycat? (1965) in which he also appeared. He made his directorial debut in *Take the Money and Run* (1969) and his initial silly, popular films like *Sleeper* (1973) gave way to posher films with serious intent and a formal beauty behind the jokes. Some, like *Interiors* (1978) and *September* (1987), could hardly be termed comedies at all. His most popular picture remains *Annie Hall* (1977), which won him three Oscars, though in the 1980s it was rivalled by *Hannah and Her Sisters* (1986). But his finest film is arguably *Manhattan* (1979), a thrilling ode to

his home town. He's famously obsessed with himself, his health and beautiful women, and his three companions, Louise Lasser, Diane Keaton and Mia Farrow, have all acted with him. Farrow in particular was outstanding in a dozen of his pictures until a family scandal split them in 1992.

Pedro Almodóvar

Director, writer
Born: *Calzada de Calatrava, Spain,*
September 25, 1951

Pedro Almodóvar is the gender-bending *enfant terrible* of modern Spanish cinema. Cult, camp, kitsch and outrageous, he has consistently challenged the perceptions of post-Franco Spain with a battery of witty, socially perceptive screwball melodramas. Films such as *Women on the Verge of a Nervous Breakdown* (1988) are not merely frenzied, multi-layered analyses of a country in social and emotional turmoil, but have become the flagships for a generation kicking against the austere conformity of the Franco years. He had worked as an actor, writer, cartoonist and rock musician before turning to film with a series of self-funded shorts. *Pepi, Lucy, Bom and Other Girls Like Mom* (1980), a slapstick punk sex comedy, was his first full-length feature, introducing the riotous disorganization, sexual ambivalence and social awareness that was to define all his future work, and with *Women on the Verge of a Nervous Breakdown*, about 48 hours in the lives of a series of madcap women, and *Tie Me Up! Tie Me Down!* (1990), the story of a psychotic young stud (Antonio Banderas), he became a director of international importance. His most recent film, *Kika* (1994), introduced a surprisingly dark and brutal element into his work, and it is this ability to do the unexpected and explore new styles which continues to keep him at the cutting edge of Spanish cinema.

Robert Altman

Director, writer
Born: *Kansas City, Mo.,*
February 20, 1925

A true original, Robert Altman arrived at the front rank of American directors late in life, with a highly distinctive style that continues alternately to beguile and enrage the Hollywood establishment. He made his feature debut in 1955 with *The Delinquents*, but first seized widespread attention when he helmed 1970's *M*A*S*H* (already rejected by a dozen directors), an exuberant army farce that while nominally set in Korea, implicitly spotlighted the surreal horrors of the contemporary Vietnam struggle. He followed up this worldwide hit with the unfocused *Brewster McCloud* (1970), rustled up a shrewd "anti-western" in *McCabe and Mrs Miller* (1971), a febrile *film noir* with *The Long Goodbye* (1973) and a goofy heist thriller with 1974's *Thieves Like Us*. Altman's featherlight directorial approach ("It's as if he's not on the set," claims Robert Duvall) coupled with his unsentimental debunking of sacred cows inevitably throw up flops and creative follies such as 1976's *Buffalo Bill and the Indians*, the intense but unloved *Secret Honor* (1984) or the undervalued kids' fantasy *Popeye* (1980). But in his rejection of conventional narrative structure and innovative use of multitrack sound, Altman can be viewed as the most intrinsically American of film *auteurs*, an artist whose work grapples with the disparate voices, facets and impulses of a jumbled, emergent culture. Significantly, his greatest movies are free-flowing panoramas – the filmworld satire *The Player* (1992), the Los Angeles odyssey *Short Cuts* (1993) and his epic 1975 masterwork *Nashville*. After a decade in the doldrums, the 1990s found this white-bearded old maverick right back in vogue.

Don Ameche

Actor
Born: DOMINIC FELIX AMICI,
Kenosha, Wis., May 31, 1908
Died: *December 6, 1993*

Ameche showed a talent to amuse in a career that spanned seven decades beginning in 1928 with a stage production of George Bernard Shaw's Th*e Devil's Disciple* and ending on the last day of filming *Corrina Corrina* in 1993. His first screen appearances in *Sins of Man* and *Ramona* (1936) prompted Fox to sign him to a long-term contract, where he made many lighthearted entertainments, among them a number of musicals with Alice Faye, including *In Old Chicago* (1938), and *That Night in Rio* (1941). He was a delightful D'Artagnan in the 1939 musical of *The Three Musketeers*, became known as the man who invented the telephone when he played the title role in *The Story of Alexander Graham Bell* (1939), and received critical acclaim for what's probably his finest performance in Ernst Lubitsch's fantasy *Heaven Can Wait* (1943). Out of fashion with the post-war mood, Ameche hit the TV trail, hosting *International Showtime*. But in the 1980s he scored a notable cinema comeback in John Landis's *Trading Places* (1983) and in 1985 won Best Supporting Actor Oscar in Ron Howard's sci-fi heartwarmer *Cocoon*. A busy old age followed with *Harry and the Hendersons* (1987), David Mamet's *Things Change* (1988) and *Folks!* (1992). Few performers gave such sheer uncomplicated pleasure.

Lindsay Anderson

Director, critic, writer
Born: *Bangalore, India,*
April 17, 1923
Died: *30 August, 1994*

An angry idealist and advocate of the Free Cinema movement, exploring the artistic significance of mundanity and working-class experience, Anderson was co-founder (with Karel Reisz and Tony Richardson) of the radical film periodical *Sequence* in 1947. While still writing about film, he became a documentary film-maker himself in 1948, winning an Oscar in 1954 for *Thursday's Children*. In 1957 he became direc-tor of London's Royal Court Theatre and directed his first fea-ture film in 1963: *This Sporting Life*, adapted from David Storey's novel about a bitter and troubled

'The Sound of Music': *Julie Andrews with a few of her favourite children*

working-class rugby star. In 1968 Anderson examined the other side of the class picture in *If...*, an anar-chic and scathing portrait of the public school system as a metaphor for English society, which became the first of a trilogy taking apart establishment hierar-chies in a similar if less successful way – *O Lucky Man!* (1973) and *Britannia Hospital* (1982). *The Whales of August* (1988), a loving study of old age featuring veter-ans Bette Davis and Lillian Gish, marked a change to a much softer style, though *Glory! Glory!* (1989), a television film about televange-lists, has echoes of the angrier and unreserved Anderson of the 1950s and 1960s. An admirer of John Ford's work, which influenced his early affinity for the poetic aspects of cinema, Anderson published a critical appreciation *About John Ford* in 1981. He died suddenly while on holiday in France.

Julie Andrews

Actress, singer
Born: JULIA ELIZABETH WELLS, *Walton-on-Thames, England, October 1, 1935*

Behind Julie Andrews's girl-next-door charm and thoroughly English niceness and good sense lies the iron discipline of her the-atrical background. The daughter of showbiz parents, Andrews toured the British music halls as a child and her freak, four-octave voice stunned audiences at her London revue debut aged 12. While playing *Cinderella* at the London Palladium in 1953, she was offered the lead in the Broadway production of the mock-1920s musical *The Boyfriend* and became the toast of New York. More acclaim followed for her Eliza in *My Fair Lady*, but while appearing in another Lerner and Loewe musical *Camelot*, spe-cially written for her, she learned she had lost the *My Fair Lady* (1964) film role to Audrey Hepburn. Ironically she then won an Oscar for her film debut as *Mary Poppins* (1964) in competition with Hepburn. *The Sound of Music* (1965) became one of the most popular film musicals ever, fol-lowed by *Thoroughly Modern Millie* (1967) and the less successful *Star!* (1968). Attempting to change her image from goody goody musical heroine to adult woman, she co-starred with Paul Newman in

Hitchcock's *Torn Curtain* (1966) but it was through her husband, director Blake Edwards, that she finally made the transition with *The Tamarind Seed* (1974), *10* (1979), the self-satire of *S.O.B.* (1981) and the excellent drag musical *Victor/Victoria* (1982). Later films have failed to match these, though the star image and public affection are undiminished.

Kenneth Anger

Director, writer
Born: *Santa Monica, Calif., 1930*

Kenneth Anger stands as the key figure of the American avant-garde, a writer (*Hollywood Babylon*) and film-maker who has stead-fastly stuck to the artistic fringes, pursuing his own subversive agenda. His debut at 17, the con-troversial homoerotic fairytale *Fireworks* (1947), was followed by the gentler *Rabbit's Moon* (1950), while the beguiling *Eaux d'Artifice* (1958) led a measured jaunt through the fountain gardens at Tivoli. Anger's most significant works are stitched-together film collages, embracing ancient mythology and the dark mysti-cism of Aleister Crowley, shot through with the symbols and semiotics of American popular culture. His most renowned piece, 1963's *Scorpio Rising*, proves an outlandish homage to the biker image pioneered by Marlon Brando in *The Wild One*. During the 1960s Anger became increas-ingly aligned to the wilder aspects of the counter-culture. His *Kustom Kar Kommandos* (1965) production was abandoned after the death of its lead protagonist while the only print of his notorious *Lucifer Rising* was stolen by a member of Charles Manson's "family" who buried it – legend has it – in the deserts of Death Valley. Following this mishap – a typically Angeresque mix of the tragic, comic and the maddening – Anger announced his retirement, return-ing in 1969 with the cobbled-

together *Invocation of My Demon Brother*, underpinned by a mantra-like Mick Jagger score. Two lengthy re-cut and re-shot versions of *Lucifer Rising* appeared in 1974 and 1980.

Ann-Margret

Actress, singer, dancer
Born: ANN-MARGRET OLSSON, *Valsjobyn, Sweden, April 28, 1941*

Red-haired Ann-Margret has everything except a surname. She mixes a meltingly vulnerable Scandinavian beauty with a formidable talent as an actress, nightclub singer and dancer. And she's one of showbiz's great sur-vivors. Discovered performing in cabaret by George Burns, she became a swinging-60s sexpot, typecasting with a short shelf life. But she survived the 1960s – debuting as Bette Davis's daugh-ter in 1961's *Pocketful of Miracles*, co-starring with Elvis in *Viva Las Vegas* (1964) and Steve McQueen in *The Cincinnati Kid* (1965), and languishing in the *Stagecoach* (1966) remake. Her sexy, Oscar-nominated role as Jack Nicholson's mistress in *Carnal Knowledge* (1971) put her right back on the map, leading to other good parts in British movies like *Tommy* (1975), nominated again after Ken Russell submerged her in baked beans. But American cinema doesn't seem to know what to do with her and the 1980s brought her a lot of bad luck. Neil Simon's *I Ought To Be in Pictures* (1982), Elmore Leonard's *52 Pick-Up* (1986) and Alan Alda's *A New Life* (1988) were all grade-A pro-jects that just didn't make the box-office breakthrough. TV helped her out: *Who Will Love My Children?* and her Emmy-winning performance in *A Streetcar Named Desire* showed just how good she can be in the right material. 1994 saw her back on the big screen, her beauty undiminished at 53, romancing Matthau and Lemmon in *Grumpy Old Men*.

Michelangelo Antonioni
Director, writer
Born: *Ferrara, Italy, September 29, 1912*

Highly praised for his bleak minimalism and lingering, leisurely-paced shooting style, Antonioni experienced a long and difficult struggle to gain his place in the film industry, not making his first feature film *Story of a Love Affair* (1950) until he was 38. As a student he wrote some film reviews, then worked in a bank and on a provincial newspaper, until going as a penniless film student to Rome, where he eventually found screenwriting work with Roberto Rossellini. His first film *Gente del Po*, a documentary about fishermen, started in 1943, was not completed until 1947 because of the war. Antonioni made his mark on the international scene with *L'Avventura* (1960), which with *La Notte* (1961) and *L'Eclisse* (1962) forms a pessimistic trilogy, exploring barren eroticism and the popular 1960s theme of non-communication. *The Red Desert* (1964), his fourth and last collaboration with actress Monica Vitti, is notable for its use of colour to express the helpless despair of his characters in a barren technological wasteland. His first English-speaking film, the highly successful *Blow Up* (1966), set in the nervously hip world of "swinging" London, led to Hollywood and *Zabriskie Point* (1970), a confused hymn to hippiedom. Antonioni returned to his familiar enigmatic form with the popular Jack Nicholson thriller *The Passenger* in 1975.

Fatty Arbuckle
Actor, director
Born: ROSCOE ARBUCKLE, *Smith Centre, Kan., March 24, 1887*
Died: *June 29, 1933*

It speaks volumes for the diminished interest in the slapstick silent that Roscoe "Fatty" Arbuckle is now remembered more for an infamous Hollywood vice case than for the comic artistry that lit up early cinema and inspired apprentice Buster Keaton. Bright-eyed and blimp-like, he graduated from vaudeville stage work to success as one of Mack Sennett's Keystone Kops and as the star and sometime director of a wealth of production-line one- and two-reelers – 47 in 1913 alone. At his peak he was second only to Chaplin in popularity, trading on his screen image as a game, bumbling oaf, thwarted in his pursuit of bob-haired bathing beauties by his own fussy ineptitude. Highspots among a mammoth film roster include *The Butcher Boy* (1917), *Out West* (1920) and *Fatty and Mabel Adrift* (1916), with regular co-star Mabel Normand. In the 1920s Arbuckle moved more into features with starring roles in *The Travelling Salesman* (1920) and *Brewster's Millions* (1920). But his career was wrecked when he was accused of the rape and murder of starlet Virginia Rappe at a Hollywood party – a charge he was acquitted of in January 1921. Subsequently banned from many picture-houses and relegated to walk-on roles, Arbuckle concentrated on work behind the camera, filming a number of shorts and in 1927 directing his first feature, *The Red Mill*. A gradual rehabilitation as an actor was cut short by his death in 1933.

Jean Arthur
Actress
Born: GLADYS GEORGIANNA GREENE, *New York, NY, October 17, 1905*
Died: *June 19, 1991*

Hiding behind the independent working girl image and blond husky-voiced sexiness of this talented comedienne was a timid brunette, who hated the palaver and publicity that went with being a star – arguably the reason behind her reputation for being "difficult". The daughter of a New York photographer, she began modelling as a schoolgirl and was spotted by Hollywood. After a good supporting role in the John Ford film *Cameo Kirby* (1923), she spent ten years playing unmemorable small parts, until in 1931 she announced her retirement from films, returning to New York to do stage work. Although persuaded back in 1933, her mature comedic talent remained undiscovered until John Ford used her once more and made her a star, casting her opposite Edward G. Robinson in *The Whole Town's Talking* (1935). She did some of her best work for Frank Capra – *Mr Deeds Goes to Town* (1936), *You Can't Take It With You* (1938) and *Mr Smith Goes to Washington* (1939). Other notable films include Howard Hawks's aviation drama *Only Angels Have Wings* (1939) and two George Stevens comedies *The Talk of the Town* (1942) and *The More the Merrier* (1943). In 1944 she retired from the limelight to study philosophy, emerging to do two last films – *A Foreign Affair* (1948) for Billy Wilder and the classic western *Shane* (1953).

Fred Astaire
Actor, singer, dancer, choreographer
Born: FREDERICK AUSTERLITZ, *Omaha, Nebr., May 10, 1899*
Died: *June 22, 1987*

The finest screen dancer of all time twinkled with unmatched elegance through most of the best musical comedies of his legendary time, and as a singer introduced more hit songs than any other movie star in history. His partnership with Ginger Rogers was one of the most successful showbusiness pairings ever. Aged 7 he was touring the vaudeville circuit with his sister Adele as his dancing partner, graduating to Broadway and then Hollywood. His screen debut was opposite Joan Crawford in *Dancing Lady* (1933), having sur-

Fred Astaire: "Can dance a little"

vived the studio verdict, "Can't act, slightly bald. Can dance a little". His partnership with Rogers began in *Flying Down To Rio* (1933), for which he thought she was miscast, and despite a tetchy relationship they went on to make 10 films together, including *Top Hat* (1935), *Swing Time* (1936) and *Shall we Dance* (1937), he classy, she sexy. Other partners included Rita Hayworth in *You'll Never Get Rich* (1941), Cyd Charisse in *Silk Stockings* (1957) and his successor, Gene Kelly, in *Ziegfeld Follies* (1945), whom he always named as his favourite dance partner to avoid embarrassing his female counterparts. He retired from dance for a second time, aged 60, turning to dramatic roles, and was Oscar-nominated for *The Towering Inferno* (1974). His only previous Academy Award recognition was a special Oscar in 1949 for "raising the standard of musicals", an undeniable truth.

Mary Astor
Actress
Born: LUCILLE VASCONCELLOS LANGEHANKE, *Quincy, Ill., May 3, 1906*
Died: *September 25, 1987*

The handsome, aristocratic Astor had a long run in the movies from silent stardom in 1921 to character parts in the 1960s. It was a career of ups and downs, partly because she preferred to be a character actress rather than a star, and partly because acting wasn't the be-all of her life ("I didn't like the work and I hated Hollywood"). She appeared in over 100 movies, but her fame rests on a handful of parts in which her acting touched greatness. Among them is *The Great Lie* (1941) in which she unthinkably outbitched Bette Davis ("If I didn't think you meant so well I'd feel like slapping your face"), winning an Oscar for it. The evil-tongued society beauty became one of her stock characters. Warners rewarded her with *The Maltese Falcon* (1941) in which her *femme fatale* was a perfect foil for Bogart. She made a lucrative deal with MGM but they unsuitably plunged her into playing "mothers for Metro," though she gamely made this role her own too in films such as *Thousands Cheer* (1943) and *Meet Me in St Louis* (1944) as Judy Garland's mom. The 1930s were tough for her when her diaries were blazoned in the press and the 1950s were hard too because of a drink problem. She retired after *Hush... Hush, Sweet Charlotte* in 1965 and took up writing.

Sir Richard Attenborough

Director, producer, actor

Born: *Cambridge, England, August 29, 1923*

The original "luvvie", his boyish persona ripe for parody, Attenborough is a survivor of over 50 years in the business, latterly as an Oscar-winning director. The son of a college administrator, he grew up in Leicester, turned to acting early and, while still at RADA, was offered his first film role in Coward's *In Which We Serve* (1942). Frequently a screen coward, he broke free of typecasting, making his name in *Brighton Rock* (1947) as the psychotic Pinkie, after which he was popular on both sides of the Atlantic.

Frustrated with the British film industry, he set up his own production company, producing *The Angry Silence* (1959), *Whistle Down The Wind* (1961) and *The L-Shaped Room* (1962), before making his directorial debut with *Oh! What A Lovely War* (1969), a saccharine but popular version of the original by Joan Littlewood. *A Bridge Too Far* (1977) followed a knighthood, but the best was still to come. "Everything I've directed has been a sort of training. I didn't want to direct *per se*, I wanted to make *Gandhi* (1982)." Thus a 20-year obsession was realized when he director-produced his way to a suitably epic Oscar-winning speech. Attenborough tackled apartheid in *Cry Freedom* (1987), and, acting again after a long gap, battled tyrannosaurus rex and a torrid Celtic accent in *Jurassic Park* (1993). As the highest-profile defender of the British film industry, he continues to lobby tirelessly where others have given up.

Tex Avery

Animator

Born: *FRED AVERY, Dallas, Tex., February 26, 1907*
Died: *August 26, 1980*

Director of some of Hollywood's finest 1940s and 1950s cartoons and creator of *Chilly Willy*, *Droopy* and *Lucky Ducky*, Avery started in movies in 1930 with the *Aesop's Fables* series, then went to Universal where he directed *Oswald the Rabbit* cartoons – he was later one of the creators of *Bugs Bunny*. In the 1940s he produced a new kind of cartoon, more violent and surreal than had so far been seen, distinguishing his work from that of his contemporaries Friz Freleng and Chuck Jones, which was much sweeter-toned but soon showed the influence of this new, harder-edged approach. Though Avery's characters are overtly for children, the action and story lines are very adultly handled and soft names

like *Chilly Willy* conceal an undercurrent of anarchy and violence. His work influenced cartooning up to the present day, and this, for the 1940s, very modern style of toughness and cynicism quickly became the main driving force in popular animation, with the exception of Disney's far softer approach. From the late 1950s, TV took over the making of cartoons and Avery moved into the lucrative field of animated commercials. The new breed of cartoon became a pale reflection of his early work and mainstream animation has seen few major developments since.

Dan Aykroyd

Comedian, actor

Born: *Ottawa, Canada, July 1, 1951*

The tall, free-wheeling, appealingly vague comic Aykroyd was discovered by John Belushi, with whom he teamed up in a Toronto revue, and they were in at the beginning of America's *Saturday Night Live* late-night TV show in 1975 – a crucible for young alternative comic talent. Their routines included the Blues Brothers, Jake and Elwood, the black-suited, quasi-criminal rhythm 'n' blues bruisers brought unforgettably to the screen in 1980. Though they collaborated on two other films – Spielberg's *1941* (1979) and *Neighbors* (1981), *The Blues Brothers* remains their best work on film together. Belushi's sudden death in 1982 badly affected Aykroyd and he stopped working for a time, bouncing back for *Trading Places* (1983) with a cast including another *Saturday Night Live* alumnus, Eddie Murphy. 1984 was a good year when he was one of the four zanies in the smash hit *Ghostbusters* and enjoyed a cameo in *Indiana Jones and the Temple of Doom* (1984). A stream of hits in broad comedies followed including *Spies Like Us* (1985) where he and Chevy Chase play unwitting decoys in an espionage plot. But in 1989, switching gear and abandon-

ing his comic persona completely, he was Oscar-nominated as Best Supporting Actor for his skilled dramatic performance as Jessica Tandy's son in *Driving Miss Daisy*. He went on to score hits in another straight character role as the mortician dad of the *My Girl* films (1991, 1994).

Lauren Bacall

Actress, singer

Born: *BETTY JOAN PERSKE, New York, NY, September 16, 1924*

The gravel-voiced siren with the tough talk and the tomboy grin was first spotted modelling on the cover of *Harper's Bazaar* magazine by director Howard Hawks, who promptly signed her to a seven-year contract. At the tender age of 20 she was cast in her first screen role in *To Have and Have Not* (1944) opposite the great and, by then, well-established Humphrey Bogart, whom she married the following year and remained with until his death in 1957. Their sizzling screen chemistry produced some of her most memorable performances, especially in *The Big Sleep* (1946), *Dark Passage* (1947) and *Key Largo* (1948), during which period she developed her screen persona as the cool wisecracking blonde who was more than a match for any tough guy. Married to actor Jason Robards from 1961 to 1973, she saw a lull in her film career in the latter half of this period, though she had great success on Broadway with *Cactus*

Lauren Bacall: *Sultry siren with a tough edge*

Flower in 1967 and her Tony-award-winning *Applause*; a musical version of *All About Eve*, in 1970. She re-emerged on screen in 1974 with *Murder on the Orient Express* followed by *The Shootist* (1976) with John Wayne. Now a rich and varied artist, Bacall will always be best remembered for her lady-baritone voice, her silky toughness and some of the most provocative eyebrow acting in cinema history.

Lucille Ball

Actress

Born: LUCILLE DESIRÉE BALL (*aka* LUCY MONTANA *and* DIANE BELMONT), *Jamestown, NY, August 6, 1911*
Died: *April 26, 1989*

With her clownish, exaggerated gestures and large expressive mouth and eyes, energetic red-head Lucille Ball appeared in over 50 films but is best known as perhaps the most successful television comedienne of all time. At 15 she headed for New York City, fared badly at drama school and was unsuccessful as a chorus-line girl, but moved into bit parts in scores of films, beginning with *Roman Scandals* (1933). She got her first credit for *Carnival* (1935), but Hollywood failed to match her comic talent with suitable roles. She had a single line in *Top Hat* (1935), but by *Having Wonderful Time* (1938) was second lead to Ginger Rogers, and snatched top billing as a spoiled heiress in *Too Many Girls* (1940). Ball once claimed that her only film she liked was *The Big Street* (1942), but her association with her male equivalent, Bob Hope, worked well. After *Sorrowful Jones* (1949) he specifically requested her for *Fancy Pants* (1950). But *The Magic Carpet* (1951) was a low point and, together with husband, Cuban bandleader Desi Arnaz, she switched to television, setting one of the most successful comedy series ever in motion. She enjoyed

tremendous control over *I Love Lucy* (1951–1961) and its follow-up, *The Lucy Show* (1962–74), which turned her into a national heroine with a megastardom undreamt of in her movie days. How satisfying it must have been for the former 1930s minor contract artist at RKO to end up owning the studio! She had one last try at cinema glory with the musical *Mame* in 1974, but left filming it too late.

Anne Bancroft

Actress

Born: ANNA MARIA LOUISA ITALIANO, *Bronx, NY, September, 17, 1931*

A woman of hawkish beauty and a finely-tuned actress with screen presence of considerable weight, Bancroft never had the career she

***Anne Bancroft:** Here's to you, Mrs Robinson*

deserved, nor, especially in the early years, the respect and acclaim from Hollywood her prodigious talent should have commanded. Her first screen role was Richard Widmark's club singer girlfriend in *Don't Bother to Knock* (1952), a small appearance leading to a succession of similar parts of widely varying quality through the 1950s until *The Restless Breed* (1957), where she played a half-Indian girl besotted with a vengeful cowboy. Exasperated by the poor material she was offered and Hollywood's indifference to her talent, she

returned to New York, winning two Tony awards for her stage work. She had great success in *Two for the See Saw* (1958) opposite Henry Fonda but it was *The Miracle Worker* (1960) which brought her back to films and made her a star, re-creating the role in the 1962 screen version that brought her an Oscar. Firmly established for some time now, with characters as widely varying as Mary Magdalene in Zeffirelli's *Jesus of Nazareth* (1976) and the Victorian actress Dame Madge Kendal in *The Elephant Man* (1980), Bancroft is perhaps best known for her portrayal of the sexually ravenous Mrs Robinson in *The Graduate* (1967) with Dustin Hoffman. She has been married to comedian Mel Brooks since 1964, but made only one film with him, *To Be or Not to Be* (1983).

Theda Bara

Actress

Born: THEODOSIA GOODMAN, *Cincinnati, Oh., July 29, 1890*
Died: *April 7, 1955*

Bara was the first ever screen sex goddess. Few of her films have survived, but looking back across almost three-quarters of a century at those that do it's hard to see what all the fuss was about – a pale plump face, heavy pre-Raphaelite body and little obvious acting ability hold scant appeal for today's audiences. Her success was a testament to the skill of imaginative publicists, who cast her as an exotic temptress with

***Theda Bara:** Exotic temptress of the silent screen*

occult powers and an endless capacity to drive men wild with desire. It worked, and for five years she was an enormous and unparalleled sensation. The lack of acting ability hardly mattered. She made her first big splash on screen as a heartless vamp in *A Fool There Was* (1914). Over the next four years she was in 39 films, cast almost exclusively as powerful and manipulative sex goddesses – *The Devil's Daughter* (1914) as a vengeful vampire; *The Serpent* (1916) as a vengeful Russian peasant; *Romeo and Juliet* (1916); *Cleopatra* (1917); *Madame Du Barry* (1918) and *Salome* (1918). She always projected a certain overwrought power and intensity, but became a victim of her own fame and marketing, and by 1920 her career was effectively over. She attempted the odd unsuccessful comeback, making her last film in 1926 (*The Dancer of Paris*), and died of cancer in 1955.

Brigitte Bardot

Actress

Born: CAMILLE JAVAL, *Paris, France, September 28, 1934*

The original sex-kitten, Bardot was the first non-Hollywood world star, and her pouting, eager sexiness was the international language that took the continental "X" film into the major movie theatres of the USA and Britain. Born into a wealthy family, Bardot studied ballet as a child but was encouraged by a photographer to model, under the name Bébé. At 15 she attracted the attention of the then assistant director, Roger Vadim, whom she was later to marry. Her screen debut was *Crazy For Love* (1952), and by 1956 she was starring in *The Light Across the Street*. The real breakthrough, though, came in Vadim's first film as director, *... And God Created Woman* (1956). Her sun-tanned nudity combined with her apparent availability – the press were encouraged to believe the on-screen sex

And God created … *Brigitte Bardot*

was the real thing – made her a sensation, a new kind of sex symbol: a playful, uninhibited man-trap. After divorcing Vadim, she married Jacques Charrier, her co-star in *Babette Goes to War* (1959), survived a suicide attempt on her 26th birthday, and worked with Cocteau (*The Testament of Orpheus*, 1960), Malle (*A Very Private Affair*, 1961) and Godard (*Contempt*, 1964), before retiring from the screen in 1973. She continues to arouse passions, even as a recluse preferring the company of the animals in her sanctuary in the south of France.

Drew Barrymore

Actress

Born: ANDREW BARRYMORE, *Los Angeles, Calif., May 22, 1975*

The little girl who taught ET to talk starred in what was the largest grossing film in history,

Drew Barrymore: *Pistol-packin' bad girl*

aged seven, but as an adult the Shirley Temple of her day has struggled to live up to such a precocious start. Grand-daughter of John, daughter of John Drew and Ildiko Jaid, Drew was born into Hollywood's "Royal Family" of the early half of the century, made her acting debut aged 11 months in a dog food commercial, and at five, after uttering the immortal line, "Mommy, I want to be in the movies, and I want to do it now", made her first feature, *Altered States* (1980). Steven Spielberg's *E.T.The Extra-Terrestrial* (1982) secured her place in screen history as pigtailed Gertie, loyal friend to the button-nosed alien, but Spielberg's claim that "she'll be the next Meryl Streep" has not yet been substantiated. She was effectively brattish, suing her parents, in *Irreconcilable Differences* (1984), but Barrymore thereafter did her best work at self-destruction, taking up alcohol aged nine, and cocaine at 12. At 13 she was barred from pestering film star Bruce Willis, and at 14 attempted suicide. In 1990 she penned her autobiography, *Little Girl Lost*, and returned to the screen in *The Amy Fisher Story* (1990) but found quality parts hard to come by. She was on form in *Guncrazy* (1992) and *Bad Girls* (1994) and is still young enough to become an adult star if only she can win the roles.

John Barrymore

Actor

Born: JOHN BLYTHE, *Philadelphia, Pa., February 15, 1882*
Died: *May 29, 1942*

Brilliant but self-destructive, John Barrymore echoes down the years as a great boozer and womanizer and a great actor in both Shakespeare and light comedy. Born to actor parents and younger brother to fellow actors Ethel and Lionel, John Barrymore at first bucked the family tradition by becoming a cartoonist, but turned to the stage in 1903, where his charismatic good looks and magnificent voice quickly earned him a matinee idol following and the epithet of "The Great Profile". He turned to films in 1913, where the public liked him best playing the great lover, as in *Don Juan* (1926) whereas Barrymore's preference was for more tortured roles, such as *Dr Jekyll and Mr Hyde* (1920). The talkies came too late to make full use of the famous voice and Shakespearean talent, and his Mercutio in *Romeo and Juliet* (1936) was described variously as "in the true Shakespearean tradition" and "overcooked ham". *Grand Hotel* and *A Bill of Divorcement* (both 1932) were big hits, but by the time he co-starred with brother Lionel as a fading matinée idol hooked on drink in *Dinner at Eight* (1933) real life was taking its toll in terms of fading memory and reliance on cue cards. Later performances, often self-parodying, veered between brilliant and disastrous, and he died penniless, a veteran of four marriages, countless liaisons and empty bottles.

Lionel Barrymore

Actor, director

Born: LIONEL BLYTHE, *Philadelphia, Pa., April 28, 1878*
Died: *November 15, 1954*

Elder brother of John and Ethel, Lionel enjoyed a career stretching back to the dawn of the cinema in *Friends* (1909) and the Griffith short *The Battle* (1911). His career took off in 1926 with a contract at MGM, where he was still employed at the time of his death. The highlight of his silent period was *Sadie Thompson* (1928), but he came into his own with the coming of sound, appearing in his first talkie, *Alias Jimmy Valentine*, in 1929, then directing several films like *Confession* (1929) and *Madame X* (1929) before winning an Oscar for his performance in *A Free Soul* (1931) as a drunken attorney, after which he abandoned directing altogether. The early 1930s were a golden period, producing classics like *Arsène Lupin* (1932), *Grand Hotel* (1932) and *Rasputin and the Empress* (1932) – notable as the only film all three Barrymores made together. Working on, despite debilitating arthritis, even performing in a wheelchair in the last decade of his career, he moved from playing handsome leading men to crusty fathers to grumpy grandpas, later mixing appearances in major classics like *It's a Wonderful Life* (1946) and *Duel in the Sun* (1946) with the popular long-running *Dr Kildare* series as the truculent Dr Gillespie. He was still a beloved star right through to his death at 76, and if anyone doubts his versatility as an actor they need only see *The Devil-Doll* (1936) where he played a crotchety grandma!

Kim Basinger

Actress

Born: *Athens, Ga., December 8, 1953*

Statuesque blonde Basinger was primarily famous for her blatant sex appeal in a series of hot femme fatale roles until she was sued into bankruptcy after backing out of *Boxing Helena* because of its "graphic and gratuitous" nudity in 1993. Of Cherokee ancestry, Basinger was a model, a singer, and a *Playboy* centrefold before her film debut in *Hard Country* (1981).

Never Say Never Again (1983) gave her exposure, and Robert Altman gave her credibility (*Fool For Love*, 1985), but she really became a name to be reckoned with as the compulsive masochist in the soft-porn romp *Nine and a Half Weeks* (1986) alongside Mickey Rourke. She was dragged through a swamp by Richard Gere in *No Mercy* (1986), was glamorously extra-terrestrial in *My Stepmother Is an Alien* (1988), and took *Batman*'s fancy in 1989, by which time she had accrued enough wealth to buy a whole town in her native Georgia. Her decision to pull out of *Boxing Helena* just four weeks before shooting was due to begin in 1991 caused Main Line Pictures to sue for damages. Basinger was unhappy that the nudity was graphic without being "artistic", but her earlier career-stripping counted against her, and she was ordered to pay around £5 million. She succeeded in reversing the judgment on appeal, but has yet to recoup her earlier box office success, despite appearing with husband Alec Baldwin in *The Getaway* (1994).

Alan Bates

Actor
Born: ARTHUR BATES, *Allestree, England, February 19, 1934*

Alongside Albert Finney, the hardy, mop-haired Alan Bates was the premier player of England's kitchen-sink era – fittingly both were to make their debuts as brothers in Tony Richardson's seaside showfolk exposé *The Entertainer* (1960). Bates's first three roles were to establish him as a major talent, following his enviable debut with a lead role as the hounded fugitive taken for Christ in *Whistle Down the Wind* (1961) and a grand turn as a northern draughtsman wrestling with wife and mother-in-law headaches in John Schlesinger's acclaimed *A Kind of Loving* (1962). Demonstrating deceptive weight

and versatility, he finished the decade with show-stealing performances in high-profile efforts like *The Go-Between* (1970), *Far from the Madding Crowd* (1967) and *Women in Love* (1969), while his anguished portrait of a persecuted Russian Jew in John Frankenheimer's *The Fixer* (1968) earned an Academy Award nomination. Since the 1960s, the barnstorming Bates performance has been less in evidence, despite his continued high standing as an actor. He gave a forceful turn in Lindsay Anderson's *In Celebration* (1976) and brought a compelling restraint to his role as a shell-shocked World War One veteran in 1982's *The Return of the Hero*. More recently, Bates – now working more on British television – proved the dignified saving grace in two intriguing but mishandled psycho-dramas, Dennis Potter's *Secret Friends* (1991) and Claude Chabrol's *Dr M* (1990).

Ned Beatty

Actor
Born: *Louisville, Ky., July 6, 1937*

A plump and jovial star character actor whose work ranges from the comic to the villainous, genial professional Ned Beatty will try his hand at anything and can make even the poorest material sparkle. Beatty was an esteemed actor of the American stage with vast experience before John Boorman cast him in *Deliverance* (1972) alongside Burt Reynolds, with whom he formed a regular partnership during the 1970s and 1980s in movies like *White Lightning* (1973), *W.W. and the Dixie Dancekings* (1975), *Physical Evidence* (1988) and *Switching Channels* (1988). One way or another there's no way filmgoers can miss him with his consistently showy parts in high-profile movies like *Nashville* (1975), *All the President's Men* (1976), *Exorcist II* (1977) and *The Big Easy* (1987). He has worked in Britain a couple of

times in *Restless Natives* (1985), making up for that poor comedy with *Hear My Song* (1991) as the Irish opera star Josef Locke, but perhaps his biggest audience is the TV millions who watch *Roseanne* where he makes frequent and welcome appearances as John Goodman's dad. He was Oscar-nominated for his delightfully sweaty performance as the evil boss of the American conglomerate who acquires the TV station in *Network* (1976), and scored a big personal hit in the *Superman* movies as villain Gene Hackman's sidekick Otis. Beatty has remained a major movie player since 1972 and continues to move freely between films and TV.

Warren Beatty

Actor, director, producer, writer
Born: HENRY WARREN BEATY, *Richmond, Va., March 30, 1937*

The good looks and liaisons with some of the film world's most eligible actresses have sometimes overshadowed Beatty's genuine acting talent and the strong personality of a man determined to make his own choices. Younger brother to Shirley MacLaine, he started his career in radio, television and the theatre. Noticed by writer William Inge and cast in his screenplay for *Splendor in the Grass* (1961), Beatty was an immediate hit with younger audiences, going on to play the Italian gigolo opposite Vivien Leigh in *The Roman*

Warren Beatty: Hollywood Rennaisance man

Spring of Mrs Stone (1961). After a handful of forgettable movies, he turned producer as well as star for the Depression bank-robber story *Bonnie and Clyde* (1967). Initially rejected in America, hailed as a masterpiece in Britain and then taken up in his home country, it gave Beatty muscle in the film world, and the power to pick and choose – choices which included Altman's western *McCabe and Mrs Miller* (1971), Pakula's thriller *The Parallax View* (1974) and the sharp comedy *Shampoo* (1975). In 1978 he went for co-operative total power, starring in, co-directing, co-producing and co-writing the return-from-death fantasy *Heaven Can Wait* – something of a training for taking the same roles solo with *Reds* (1981), a very personal project about American Communist John Reed and the Russian Revolution and unmatched by later films – the costly megaflop *Ishtar* (1987), *Dick Tracy* (1990) and *Bugsy* (1991).

Jean-Paul Belmondo

Actor
Born: *Neuilly, France, April 9, 1933*

It seemed the insolently charismatic Belmondo would be consigned to a bit-part career playing hoods and heavies until the New Wave adopted him as their own. Much of the thanks for his sudden ascent goes to Jean-Luc Godard who saw in the raw ex-boxer the potential for a modern-day leading man for a new kind of French cinema. Belmondo's role as the doomed anti-hero in *Breathless* (1959), sliding from petty crook to hounded killer in his self-conscious aping of Hollywood's gangster stars, stands as the sublime symbol of the movement's heady objectives. It led to two more significant collaborations with Godard in *Une Femme est une Femme* (1961) and the landmark thriller *Pierrot le Fou* (1965). The New Wave's beat-up, chain-smoking muse gained further notoriety with Jean-Pierre Melville's *Leon*

Jean-Paul Belmondo: *Cigarette'n'shades cool*

Morin, Priest (1961) and *Docteur Popaul* (1972), a controversial black comedy from Claude Chabrol. Throughout the 1970s Belmondo's career took on a noticeably more populist slant. His eight outings with director Henri Verneuil zipped his tough-guy persona into a trim action-movie premise, many of these films scoring major box-office hits. He was a crook on the run from Omar Sharif in *The Burglars* (1971) and a cop stalking a telephone killer in the wildly popular *Night Caller* (1975). In the 1980s and 1990s Belmondo's film career appeared to stagnate, though the old devil-may-care charm was still in evidence in the 1985 heist caper *Hold Up*.

John Belushi

Comedian, actor
Born: *Chicago, Ill., January 24, 1949*
Died: *March 5, 1982*

The late, lamented king, now patron saint, of the slob comedians, Belushi started out, like several of his contemporaries, on America's *Saturday Night Live* TV show – a seminal showcase for alternative comedy that brought to light many now famous talents including Eddie Murphy, Chevy Chase and his comedy partner Dan Aykroyd. Built like a tank, large unshaven features rippling with gleeful menace, he specialized in creating characters of terminal hedonism and almost apocalyptic disregard for social nicety. Typical among these was the

crazed, indestructible college fraternity drunk Bluto in *National Lampoon's Animal House* (1978), a modified version of which he employed in Spielberg's wacky *1941* (1979). Belushi's larger-than-life performances mixed liberal doses of grossness, damaged charm and express-train energy with a talent for facial pantomime that might have been the envy of many a silent screen star. Privately never a settled individual, his taste for hard living and his prodigious appetites for drink and drugs earned him a reputation for hell-raising; in the words of Dan Aykroyd, he was a good friend but a bad guy. Though his career

John Belushi (right): *King of the kamikaze comics*

was cut short by his death from a drug overdose at 33, for many, his performance as the anarchic, rhythm 'n' blues-loving ex-con Jake in *The Blues Brothers* (1980) is enough by itself to ensure his place as a major icon of kamikaze comedy.

Tom Berenger

Actor
Born: *Chicago, Ill., May 31, 1950*

A handsome, thinking-person's action hero in the style of Harrison Ford, Berenger made an inauspicious debut in the horror flick *The Sentinel* (1977) when his main scene was cut from the release print. Then he nearly became a star, playing a psychopath in his first leading role in *Looking for Mr Goodbar* (1977), followed by the

sexy *In Praise of Older Women* (1978), and taking over Paul Newman's old part in the prequel *Butch and Sundance: The Early Days* (1979). He had to wait until 1986 for real success as the evil GI in Oliver Stone's *Platoon*, and he was terrific again in Ridley Scott's keythriller *Someone to Watch Over Me* (1987) as the good cop and as the white supremacist in Costa-Gavras's *Betrayed* (1988), showing he can swap effortlessly between goodie and baddie roles. Established as a major Hollywood player, he made some unlucky choices in big movies with top directors that were artistic and box office flops, like Hector Babenco's *At Play in the Fields of the Lord* (1991). An actor who can impress in the most basic action material like the war picture *Sniper* (1993), Berenger's ability to portray good or bad was exploited in Sharon Stone's thriller *Sliver* (1993), where we think he's the killer. If he gave up trying to be a big star he could easily have a good career as a video action hero. Will he carry on though? "I don't have ambition like I used to... If they don't want me, I don't care."

Ingmar Bergman

Director, writer
Born: *Uppsala, Sweden, July 14, 1918*

Ingmar Bergman is one of world cinema's most influential and distinctive artists. Theatrically trained, he has a style notable for its lyrical language, stark imagery (often in collaboration with cinematographer Sven Nykvist) and immaculate handling of a troupe of regular players. The art-house successes of 1952's *Summer with Monika* and *Smiles of a Summer Night* (1955) were followed in 1957 by a forceful double bill of contrasting classics in the bittersweet *Wild Strawberries* and *The Seventh Seal*, an allegorical odyssey that cemented Bergman's place among the greats. His most typical works

are searing, high-minded essays on mankind's role in an alienating universe. These grand concerns reached their apogee with his trio of religious pictures – the Oscar-winning *Through a Glass Darkly* (1961), 1962's *Winter Light* and the lesbian-tinged, censor-taxing *The Silence* (1963) – later dismissed as "bogus" by their creator, who turned to more intimate, penetrative studies with *Persona* (1966) and *Cries and Whispers* (1971). But to label Bergman as a gloom-monger is to ignore the sweeping artistry and flamboyance of his finest movies. Nowhere is this better shown than in his captivatimg TV-filmed fairytale *Fanny and Alexander* (1982). This six-hour saga heralded Bergman's public "retirement" as a film-maker, though he continues to write for the screen, penning the autobiographical *The Best Intentions* (1991), which won the Cannes Palme d'Or in 1992.

Ingrid Bergman

Actress
Born: *Stockholm, Sweden, August 29, 1915*
Died: *August 29, 1982*

A soulful, statuesque beauty, Ingrid Bergman remains one of cinema's most enduring icons. While she was sceptical about her abilities – advising daughter Isabella Rossellini to "keep it simple, make a blank face and the music will fill it in" – Bergman was able to communicate a luminous vulnerability that brought resonance to even her weakest roles. Homegrown film success in her native Sweden brought her to Hollywood where, even during her charmed early years, she pushed against her assigned sex symbol pigeonhole, tackling the role of a cockney tart in 1941's *Dr Jekyll and Mr Hyde* and winning an Oscar for her portrayal of a menaced wife in *Gaslight* (1944). She was achingly convincing in *Casablanca* (1942), and in *Notorious*

Ingrid Bergman: 'Keeping it simple' in Notorious

(1946), the best of her three collaborations with Alfred Hitchcock, revealed impressive depth and nuance as the wounded good-time girl used as a pawn by secret-service man Cary Grant. But Bergman's scandalous affair with director – and eventual husband – Roberto Rossellini tarnished her on-screen image. Dubbed "a powerful force for evil" by an American senator, she spent seven years in effective exile in Italy where she featured in five Rossellini-directed features, beginning in 1950's *Stromboli*. Their marriage annulled, she made a triumphant return to Hollywood, winning an Oscar as *Anastasia* (1956). In later years she took another Oscar for *Murder on the Orient Express* (1974) and returned to Sweden for her acclaimed final role, as a concert pianist in Ingmar Bergman's *Autumn Sonata* (1978).

Busby Berkeley

Director, choreographer
Born: WILLIAM BERKELEY ENOS, *Los Angeles, Calif., November 29, 1895*
Died: *March 14, 1976*

The choreographer who freed dance from its theatrical conventions and made it a cinematic art, Berkeley conducted trick parade drills of up to 1,200 men and trained as an aerial observer in World War One. This influenced his cinema work in the "Busby top shots" for which he was known to bore holes in the studio roof, and in the military precision and kaleidoscopic symmetry of his routines. As a successful Broadway choreographer after the war, he was invited to Hollywood to work on Eddie Cantor's *Whoopee!* (1930). The influence of contemporary fine art shows in his most important work for Warners in the 1930s – the surreal dancing skyscrapers of *42nd Street* (1933), the 56 white pianos in *Gold Diggers of 1935* and the cubist technique of breaking up the real world, as in the jigsaw puzzle of Ruby Keeler's face on the backs of the chorus in *Dames* (1934). He also touched on serious issues with the Depression marchers in *Gold Diggers of l933* and, in the same film, the chorus girls clad only in large coins for

Chorus of approval: Busby Berkeley's dancers

We're in the Money – images which, combined with his objectification of women as mere elements in a pattern, have led to contemporary accusations of sexism, but can equally be seen as comment on sexist attitudes of the time. Married six times, Berkeley slipped into retirement in the 1950s.

Bernardo Bertolucci

Director, writer
Born: *Parma, Italy, March 16, 1940*

The controversial *Last Tango in Paris* (1972), which gave a whole new sensual dimension to butter and extended the limits of cinematic sexual frankness, is Bertolucci's least typical film. As a teenager, he made his own amateur films, before becoming Pasolini's assistant on *Accatone* (1961). At 22 he directed the sombre *The Grim Reaper* (1962), which flopped, but his second film, *Before the Revolution* (1964), the story of a young man torn between his upper-class background and his ideals, was widely praised in Europe and America. 1970 was marked by two highly accomplished films, *The Spider's Stratagem* and *The Conformist*, of which the latter – polished, stylish and arguably Bertolucci's best work – makes an intriguing connection between sexual repression and Italian Fascism of the 1930s, encapsulated in its dominating visual image of the two central female characters dancing the tango together. In 1976 he returned to his Northern Italian roots for the epic personal and historical saga *1900*, a rich (for some over-rich) account of Italian social and political history told through the story of two men from different ends of the social spectrum. The epic scale continued in his Oscar-winning *The Last Emperor* (1987) – visually stunning but intellectually and emotionally unsatisfying; qualities which were exacerbated in the remainder of his "oriental trilogy"– *The Sheltering Sky* (1990) and *Little Buddha* (1994).

Jacqueline Bisset

Actress
Born: JACQUELINE FRASER-BISSET, *Weybridge, England, September 13, 1944*

Though doctor's daughter Bisset once said "A movie star? I sure as hell don't feel like one", she has always seemed to enjoy being a star. She's had plenty of practice. A former model, she made her debut in the mid-1960s in sex-kitten cameos in landmark British films like *The Knack* (1965) and *Cul-de-Sac* (1966), but it was in Hollywood that she made her name when Steve McQueen picked her for *Bullitt* (1968). Back then there was a suspicion that although she was beautiful, she couldn't actually act. There were glimmerings of things to come in *The Grasshopper* (1970) and *The Thief Who Came to Dinner* (1973), but it was François Truffaut who revealed her as a real actress – convincing and delightful in French for his *Day for Night* (1974). Since then she's enjoyed a profitable career in international movies like *Murder on the Orient Express (1974)*, *The Deep* (1977) and *The Greek Tycoon (1978)*. In the 1980s her best moments were bitching with Candice Bergen in *Rich and Famous* (1981) and the Rob Lowe romp *Class* (1983), playing a sexy older woman. As the Rhodes romance *High Season* (1987) showed, she stayed stunningly attractive in her forties, with just a hint of vulnerability beneath the polished exterior. And when she gets a decent vehicle to display it, her acting, as evidenced in John Huston's *Under the Volcano* (1984), remains impeccable.

Dirk Bogarde

Actor, author
Born: DEREK NIVEN VAN DEN BOGAERDE, *London, England, March 28, 1921*

Throughout the 1940s and 1950s Bogarde seemed simply a handsome, well-packaged product of

Dirk Bogarde: Flawless in Death in Venice

the Rank Organization's charm school. Certainly his studio didn't know what to do with him or show any realization of his special talent as an actor, though that crept through in films like *Quartet* (1948), *The Spanish Gardener* (1956) and *A Tale of Two Cities* (1958). They were happiest with him as young doctor Simon Sparrow in the hugely popular comedy series spawned by *Doctor in the House* (1954). In 1954 he started his crucial association with American director Joseph Losey in *The Sleeping Tiger*, but it was his role as a blackmailed homosexual in Basil Dearden's groundbreaking *Victim* (1961) that changed his career overnight, losing him his young fans while gaining him a new niche in adult cinema. He teamed with Losey again for *The Servant* (1963) as a depraved butler, *King and Country* (1964), *Modesty Blaise* (1966) and *Accident* (1967), giving notable, varied performances. Finding another sympathetic director in Luchino Visconti, he was superb as the Nazi tycoon in *The Damned* (1969) and as the anguished author in *Death in Venice* (1971). After this he concentrated mainly on writing books, though he enjoyed memorable work in Europe with Renais's *Providence* (1977), Fassbinder's *Despair* (1978) and Tavernier's *Daddy Nostalgia* (1990).

Humphrey Bogart

Actor

Born: HUMPHREY DEFOREST BOGART, *New York, NY, January 23, 1899*
Died: *January 14, 1957*

Bogart is one of the century's greatest icons, up there with Monroe, Dean and Gable. Woody Allen lionized him and turned his supposed catchphrase into a play and film title, *Play It Again Sam* (1972). An actor makes an entire career out of impersonating him: no redundancies in that job. But Bogey wasn't like the other leg-

ends. For a start he wasn't beautiful or even conventionally handsome. By the time he came into his own with *High Sierra* in 1941 he was in middle age and looked crumpled and bruised by life. But after a 12-year apprenticeship, he had perfected his art – that of playing the role of Humphrey Bogart. He was attractive because of the paradox of his persona – a unique

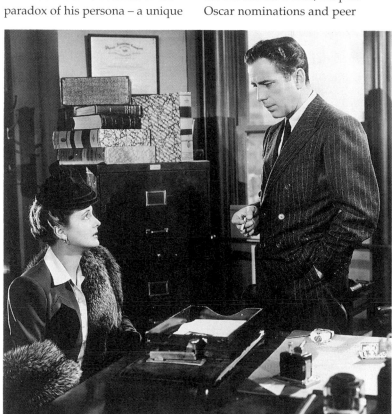

The Maltese Falcon: Humphrey Bogart as gumshoe Sam Spade with treacherous client Mary Astor

mixture of toughness and sensitivity, cynicism and romance, pessimism and humour. The man who liked drinking and hard living took his acting very seriously too. And above all there was the voice, that impassioned lisping growl that people love to imitate. He was a hero or anti-hero for all ages because everyone can find in him some quality to admire. Hard to choose the best of Bogey, but his Oscar-nominated *Casablanca* (1942), *The Caine Mutiny* (1954), *The Maltese Falcon* (1941), *To Have and Have Not* (1944), *The Big Sleep* (1946) and *The African Queen* (1951), for which he won an Oscar, are all contenders.

John Boorman
Director, writer

Born: *Shepperton, England, January 18, 1933*

An ambitious, some say pretentious, British director whose best work has been in Hollywood, Boorman has struggled to make the movies he wants, despite Oscar nominations and peer approval. The son of a pub landlord, the young Boorman had set up a thriving dry-cleaning business before being called up into the army, then becoming a film critic and documentary maker. His feature debut starring the Dave Clark Five, *Catch Us If You Can* (1965), was a poor imitation of The Beatles' films, but he moved to the USA where *Point Blank* (1967) made his reputation as an innovative story-teller. The uneasy revenge thriller's remorseless paranoia was to become a regular theme of his. He again cast Lee Marvin in the near-silent *Hell in the Pacific* (1968), returned to

Britain for *Leo the Last* (1970), which earned him the Best Director's Award at Cannes and, back in the US, was Oscar-nominated for the backwoods nightmare *Deliverance* (1972). Thereafter he lost his way. *Exorcist 2: The Heretic* (1977) wasn't as bad as some said but its failure to replicate its predecessor's success slowed his career. Mythology reared its head in the majestic *Excalibur* (1981) and the grand eco-protest movie *The Emerald Forest* (1985), starring his son Charley. As writer, producer and director his most recent success has been *Hope and Glory* (1987); semi-autobiographical, it won him Oscar nominations for Best Picture and Director.

Ernest Borgnine
Actor

Born: ERMES EFFRON BORGNINO, *Hamden, Conn., January 24, 1915*

With broad dark features equally capable of genuine warmth or blood-chilling stares, Borgnine came late to Hollywood at 36, after stage and TV work, in his first film *China Corsair* (1951) and for the next five years, although typecast as various villains, appeared in some important movies, notably *From Here to Eternity* (1953) and *Bad Day at Black Rock* (1954). Finally cast against his stereotype as the shy lovelorn butcher in *Marty* (1955), he won Best Actor Oscar and a British Film Academy Award. It looked like things might change, but Hollywood, not knowing what else to do with him, reverted to his old action image in films like *The Vikings* (1958). In 1960, his career struggling, he turned to TV and European films. The hit series *McHale's Navy* (1962–65), and the movie in 1964, re-established his star status. Then able to do big films like *The Dirty Dozen* (1967) and *The Wild Bunch* (1969), he worked consistently between movies and TV, trying his hand at a dizzying array of westerns, war films costume dramas, even sci-fi, plus two more TV series – *Future Cop* (1976) and *Airwolf* (1984–86) – the sequel *The Dirty Dozen: The Next Mission* (1985) and some big movies like *The Poseidon Adventure* (1972) and *Jesus of Nazareth* (1976). A popular figure, he is still a busy star in his seventies.

Frank Borzage

Director
Born: *Salt Lake City, Utah, April 23, 1893*
Died: *June 19, 1962*

Frank Borzage went from silent screen extra to film-maker of consistent skill and sensitivity in the early years of sound cinema. As Jazz Age extravagances gave way to 1930s Depression, he kept America honest with his affecting and humane vision of society's underbelly, winning Oscars for both *Seventh Heaven* (1927), his silent melodrama on Parisian waifs, and the sound picture *Bad Girls* (1931), spotlighting poverty-row Manhattan. While drawn to tales of high drama and consuming passions, Borzage's naturalistic style, coupled with a sympathetic handling of society's ills, kept his films heartfelt and rooted in reality. These qualities stood him in good stead for his 1932 version of *A Farewell to Arms*, Hemingway's sweeping romance set in World War One Italy, one of the most precisely crafted adaptations of the author's work to date. Margaret Sullavan proved an ideal vehicle for the director's distinctive style, giving resonant turns in two socially critical studies of Nazi Germany, *Little Man, What Now?* (1934) and *The Mortal Storm* (1940), but Borzage was not always so serious. With 1936's *Desire*, pairing Marlene Dietrich with Gary Cooper, he demonstrated a flair for quick-paced comedy while the shipboard caper *History Is Made at Night* (1936) showed the director at the peak of

his confident powers, before the onset of the slow steady decline that marred his post-war career.

Jean-Christophe Bouvet

Actor, director, writer
Born: *Paris, France, March 24, 1947*

Talented French character actor Jean-Christophe Bouvet moves easily from serious roles on either side of the law (as police inspector or murderer) to subversive film jester challenging accepted values in French society. It was this gleefully unclassifiable quality that made him the ideal choice to play Satan opposite Gérard Depardieu in Maurice Pialat's 1987 Cannes Palme d'Or winner *Under Satan's Sun*. Bouvet's exuberant, show-stealing turn ranks among his best work. Bouvet established his reputation in four films by director Paul Vecchiali – *Change Pas de Main* (1975), *La Machine* (1977), *C'est la Vie* (1980) and *Archipel des Amours* (1982). *La Machine,* an urgent and poignant cry against the suddenly reinstated death penalty, gave him his first starring role as a young man facing the guillotine and Bouvet had a hand in the fact-based script, which was drawn from the transcripts of a controversial trial. He has also been associated with the challenging films of Jean-Claude Biette, most notably *Loin de Manhattan* (1981) and *Le Complexe de Toulon* (1994), worked on Cyril Collard's only film, the acclaimed César-winning AIDS drama *Savage Nights* (1992), and has enjoyed a series of collaborations with André Téchiné, appearing in his *J'embrasse pas* (1991). Also in 1994 he scored a substantial commercial success with *La Cité de la Peur*, playing a serial killer. On the other side of the camera, Bouvet, who once served as assistant to the eminent Claude Chabrol, has produced two highly acclaimed directorial ventures in *Les Dents de Ma Mère* (1991) and *La Verve de Mon Père* (1994).

Kenneth Branagh

Actor, director
Born: *Belfast, Northern Ireland, December 10, 1960*

Kenneth Branagh is a throwback to the days of the great actor-manager-directors, so it is no surprise that he has been widely hailed as the new Olivier. A man of boundless energy, he has become a virtual one-man British film industry, involving himself in every aspect of film production – acting, directing, writing and producing – and creating, in the process, a number of extremely enjoyable if faintly middle-of-the-road populist movies. Having worked extensively on stage, Branagh's first notable screen performance came as a World War One veteran in *A Month in the Country* (1987). He made a bravura directorial debut with a gritty, energetic adaptation of Shakespeare's *Henry V* (1989), in which he also starred; and while it lacked the power and finesse of Olivier's 1944 version, it nonetheless brought Branagh and his Renaissance Company to international attention. It also marked his first big-screen pairing with wife Emma Thompson, who starred with him in his next three films: *Dead Again* (1991); *Peter's Friends* (1992); and the Tuscany-set colourful Shakespearian romp *Much Ado About Nothing* (1993). His big-budget 1994 offering, *Mary Shelley's Frankenstein*, saw him displaying a new maturity as both performer and director; and it seems inconceivable that one who has achieved so much at such an early age will not go on to become one of the key figures in British movie history.

Klaus Maria Brandauer

Actor, director
Born: *Bad Aussee, Austria, June 22, 1944*

German-speaking Brandauer has broken through the language barrier into a successful international

career and in the 1980s was often named as one of the world's greatest film actors up there with De Niro and Depardieu. His reputation is securely based on three

Klaus Maria Brandauer: One of the world's greatest

films about German Fascism made for director Istvan Szabo – *Mephisto* (1981), *Colonel Redl* (1984) and *Hanussen* (1988). Making his mark indelibly on world cinema in the Oscar-winning *Mephisto*, Brandauer is dazzling as the acclaimed actor Hendrik Hofgen (based on real-life Gustav Grundgens), famed portrayer of Mephistopheles, who sells out to the Nazis. He's equally magnetic in *Colonel Redl* as the Jewish bisexual head of military intelligence to the Austro-Hungarian Empire and as the clairvoyant Klaus Schneider in *Hanussen*. Brandauer was Oscar-nominated for his portrayal of author Karen Blixen's husband in *Out of Africa* (1985), effortlessly upstaging Hollywood stars Streep and Redford. A clearly impressed Sean Connery called for him to enliven his comeback as James Bond in *Never Say Never Again* (1983) and again for his John Le Carré Moscow spy shenanigans *The Russia House* (1990). Brandauer's other English-speaking films include Andrew Birkin's underestimated study of childhood, *Burning Secret* (1988), from the Stefan Zweig tale, and the Jack London children's story *White Fang* (1991). He directed *Georg Elser* (1989), *Seven Minutes* (1989) and *Mario and the Magician* (1992).

Marlon Brando

Actor, producer, director, Godfather
Born: *Omaha, Nebr., 3 April, 1924*

The legendary Method actor made his Broadway debut in *I Remember Mama* in 1944, after military academy and acting classes. Playing Stanley Kowalski in Tennessee Williams's masterpiece *A Streetcar Named Desire* (1951) turned him into a stage star, then a sweaty T-shirted film icon. While his co-star Vivien Leigh won an Oscar, Brando had to settle for a nomination, followed by two more for *Viva Zapata!* (1952) and his Mark Antony in Shakespeare's *Julius Caesar* (1953). But he won an Oscar for *On the Waterfront* (1954) and bagged another for his magnificent mumbling as *The Godfather* (1972), though he declined the statuette, protesting at his country's ill-treatment of the American Indians. Often named as the pre-eminent post-war American film actor, he was typed as a rough 1950s rebel, but his quintessential leather-clad biker in *The Wild One* (1954) has worn badly. He boldly, or foolhardily, attempted many parts at odds with his Method

Wild one: *An actor named Brando*

style and the attempt to widen his range led to him being miscast in the musical *Guys and Dolls* (1955), as Napoleon in *Desirée* (1954) and as Fletcher Christian in *Mutiny on the Bounty* (1962). He launched into directing with the bracing revenge western *One-Eyed Jacks* (1961), but, though he was busy, the 1960s were a disappointing decade for him. Despite a few effective cameos such as his Oscar-nominated attorney in *A Dry White Season* (1989), he's done no work of substance since *Last Tango in Paris* (1972) though the Brando mystique continues unabated.

Walter Brennan

Actor
Born: *Swampscott, Mass., July 25, 1894*
Died: *September 21, 1974*

Brennan's tough, leathery face has enlivened so many classic movies that it is a mystery why he is not better known than he actually is. A supreme character actor, he exercised a 25-year monopoly on the portrayal of cantankerous, grumpy old men. His greatest moments were in westerns and if you've ever watched a Howard Hawks or John Wayne movie, chances are you've seen Brennan. The name might not be immediately familiar, but the face is unmistakeable.He went into movies in 1923 as a stuntman. After bit parts and small roles, he first made an impression as "Old Atrocity" in Hawks's brilliant *Barbary Coast* (1935), and then won the first-ever Oscar for Best Supporting Actor for his performance in the lumberjack drama *Come and Get It* (1936). He received the award twice more – for *Kentucky* (1938) and *The Westerner* (1940) – and throughout the 1940s and 1950s appeared in, and enriched, an extraordinary array of Hollywood classics: *Sergeant York* (1941); *To Have and Have Not* (1944); *My Darling Clementine* (1946); *Red River* (1948); *The Far Country* (1954); *Bad Day at Black Rock* (1955); and *Rio Bravo* (1959), in which he produced one of the screen's great character performances as Stumpy. As one would suspect of such a tough and determined old-timer, Brennan worked consistently right up to his death in 1974.

Jeff Bridges

Actor
Born: *Los Angeles, Calif., December 4, 1949*

With his father Lloyd Bridges and older brother Beau as actors, Jeff began acting at an early age, making his debut as a baby in *The Company She Keeps* (1950), appearing on his father's 1950s TV show *Sea Hunt* and later working on stage. After a couple of TV films and his adult movie debut in *Halls of Anger* (1970), he scored a huge hit and Oscar nomination in *The Last Picture Show* (1971), building on his success throughout the 1970s with films like *Thunderbolt and Lightfoot* (1974), *Hearts of the West* (1975), *Stay Hungry* and *King Kong* (1976). But Bridges hit a bad patch in the early 1980s with flops like *Cutter's Way* (1981) and Disney's computer caper *Tron* (1982). Box-office favour returned to him in the mid-1980s with the thriller *Against All Odds* (1983), his Oscar-nominated performance in *Starman* (1984) and the 1985 thriller *Jagged Edge*. His talent and popularity have since been confirmed by his performances in Coppola's *Tucker* (1988), *The Fabulous Baker Boys* (1989) and 1990's *Texasville*, Bogdanovich's *Last Picture Show* sequel, though the status of bankable star has eluded him. Some projects like *American Heart* (1993) just seem over the public's head, while thrillers like *Blown Away* (1994) seem to show he hasn't got the popular touch. In the 1990s he remains a superb screen actor, one of Hollywood's finest. Just look at him in *The Fisher King* (1991).

Charles Bronson

Actor
Born: CHARLES BUNCHINSKY, (*aka* BUCHINSKI *and* BUCHINSKY), *Ehrenfeld, Pa., November 3, 1921*

Dour and hatchet-faced ("I guess I look like a rock quarry that someone has dynamited"), Bronson was a massive star in the 1970s, most famously as the brutal, lone avenger of the *Death Wish* series. The ninth of 15 children of a Lithuanian coalminer in Pennsylvania, Bronson was the only one to finish high school, but at 16 joined his brothers in the mine. An army gunner during World War Two, he determined not to return, and instead studied art before heading for Hollywood. From his debut, *You're in the Navy Now* (1951) to his first hits, *The Magnificent Seven* (1960), *The Great Escape* (1963) and *The Dirty Dozen* (1967), he played demented villains until his departure for Europe, where he became a box-office giant. Sergio Leone's *Once Upon a Time in the West* (1968) signalled a character departure from surly men of few words and much violence, to *heroic* men of few words and much violence, and in late middle age he found himself less a father figure more an international sex symbol. He starred opposite his late wife Jill Ireland in *The Family* (1970) and 14 other films, and his collaborations with British director Michael Winner have proved memorable. The theme of ruthless avenger was honed for *Death Wish* (1974), and three sequels followed, together with accusations of Bronson's misanthropy. By *Death Wish 4* (1987), Bronson insisted on a different director, judging the third film to be too violent.

Louise Brooks

Actress
Born: *Cherryvale, Kan., November 14, 1906*
Died: *August 8, 1985*

A programme note for a season of Brooks's films in Paris once declared: "Like the statues of antiquity, she is outside time. It is sufficient to see her to believe in beauty, in life, in the reality of human beings." Although she made few films of any note, Brooks – with her pale white face,

Louise Brooks: *Consummate screen siren*

huge eyes, lush mouth and brilliant black bob of shining ebony hair – will always be one of the greatest and most alluring of screen sirens. She came to Hollywood as a dancer in the Ziegfeld Follies and made her name in a series of not particularly good flapper-age comedies: *Love 'em and Leave 'em* (1926); *The City Gone Wild* (1927); and *A Girl in Every Port* (1928). At the height of her fame, she decamped to Germany, where she starred in two ground-breaking studies of female sexuality by G.W. Pabst: *Pandora's Box* (1929) and *Diary of a Lost Girl* (1929). Her performances were incandescent, but 20 years ahead of their time, and when she returned to America her career nosedived. She went bankrupt and ended up working as a sales assistant before becoming a virtual recluse in 1948. She later wrote one of the most perceptive books ever on Hollywood (*Lulu in Hollywood*), and was rediscovered by a new generation of filmgoers alive to her immortal beauty and consummate acting skill.

Mel Brooks

Director, actor, writer, producer

Born: MELVIN KAMINSKY, *Brooklyn, NY, June 29, 1926*

Brooks is a true original, a blissfully funny artist in an era when they're thin on the ground. Considered second only to Woody Allen among sound cinema's writer/director/comics, he's a scattergun talent, peppering films with as many missed jokes as hits, but when they're funny they're very funny ("In eroticism they use a feather, in pornography they use the whole chicken"). He progressed from club comic to TV gag writer, then grabbed his film breakthrough directing Gene Wilder in the hilarious bad-taste musical comedy *The Producers* (1967), scooping the Oscar for best screenplay. This established the breathlessly wacky mood and freewheeling style that became Brooks's trademark. His best films, the hysterical, affectionate genre spoofs *Blazing Saddles* and *Young Frankenstein* (both 1974), remain all-time comedy classics though he enjoyed similar success parodying film styles in *Silent Movie* (1976) and 1977's *High Anxiety*. The 1980s brought a falling-off with *History of the World –Part 1* (1981) and *Spaceballs* (1987), but a marked improvement in the 1990s with *Life Stinks* (1991) and *Robin Hood: Men in Tights* (1993) ensures his continued place among the greats. Brooks is married to Anne Bancroft, his co-star in *To Be or Not To Be* (1983). His company Brooksfilms produced *The Elephant Man* (1980), *Frances* (1982), *The Fly* (1986) and *84 Charing Cross Road* (1987).

Yul Brynner

Actor

Born: TAIDJE KHAN, *Siberia, Russia, July 12, 1915*
Died: *October 10, 1985*

In common with that other Hollywood brooder Burt Lancaster, Brynner spent some of his pre-movie career as a circus performer, though unlike big Burt he never brought these talents to his movies. His second screen appearance as the King of Siam in *The King and I* (1956) brought him an Oscar and established him as a box office draw – it was a part he had played on Broadway with Gertrude Lawrence to great acclaim and one that followed him throughout his career. His next role as the Pharaoh in DeMille's *The Ten Commandments* (1956) also pleased the public, even if the film did not please the critics, and there followed a succession of pirates, spies, chieftains and other exotic roles befitting his looks and pronounced but undefinable accent. Moviegoers never liked him with hair and those few movies where he sported it, like *The Buccaneer* (1958), were never as successful. Though he quickly became a familiar and popular movie figure, it was not until 1960 that his most definitive image was created in *The Magnificent Seven* (1960), a classic westernized

Yul Brynner: *Bald but sexy*

remake of Kurosawa's great *Seven Samurai* (1954), where, bald, brooding and dressed in black he portrayed a gunman with a sense of honour which crystallized him forever in the public imagination – a part he all but lampooned 13 years later in the sci-fi actioner *Westworld* (1973).

Geneviève Bujold

Actress

Born: *Montreal, Canada, July 1, 1942*

Alluring, exceptionally talented French-Canadian star Bujold, who mixes the fruits of Quebec Conservatory classical drama training with a natural bubbly charisma, has several times looked like making the break into the major league. But failing to achieve a consistent body of work, she has settled for giving a sporadic series of impressive, versatile performances when she's given half the chance. After a stage career and some Canadian films, Bujold gained widespread attention in Philippe De Broca's American cult hit *King of Hearts* (1966). But it was her spirited, Oscar-nominated performance as Anne Boleyn in *Anne of the Thousand Days* (1969) opposite Burton's Henry VIII that made her a world star. Her hold on that stardom was always shaky, but throughout the 1970s and 1980s she notched up some notable performances in between more than her fair share of drossy movies. Brian De Palma used her sensuality teasingly for his thriller *Obsession* (1976), she was ideal as the lady in peril in Michael Crichton's sci-fi mystery *Coma* (1978), and Clint Eastwood called her for his dark-toned cop outing *Tightrope* (1984). More recently some of her best opportunities have come in Alan Rudolph's cult films, gracing *Choose Me* (1984), *Trouble in Mind* (1985) and *The Moderns* (1988). She also impressed as the object of twin Jeremy Irons's desire in David Cronenberg's *Dead Ringers* (1988).

Luis Buñuel

Director, writer, producer, actor

Born: *Calanda, Spain, February 22, 1900*
Died: *July 29, 1983*

Never did anyone utter a truer piece of self-analysis than Buñuel's statement: "Religious education and surrealism have marked me for life" – the Catholic Church, bourgeois culture and Fascism being his prime targets, and surrealism his weapon. As a young man in Paris he collaborated with student friend Salvador Dali on the famous short *Un Chien*

Andalou (1928), with its shocking images, such as the razor blade and eye sequence, followed by *L'Age d'or* (1932), largely Buñuel's work, and his first cinema assault on his lifelong targets. *Land Without Bread* (1932), a powerful documentary about peasant poverty, was his last as director for 15 years, during which he produced minor Spanish films and compiled pro-Republican documentaries. Stranded in America by Franco's victory, he scraped a living until moving to Mexico in 1947, where he resumed directing. In 1961 he made *Viridiana* in Spain with the blessing of the Spanish government, who failed to recognize its subtle assault on Catholicism and Fascism until its acclaim at the Cannes Film Festival. His subsequent films, made mainly in France and satirizing bourgeois conventions – *Belle de Jour* (1967), *The Discreet Charm of the Bourgeoisie* (1972) and *Phantom of Liberty* (1974) – struck a nerve with the 1960s generation's rebellion against their parents' values. These dazzling products of Buñuel's fruitful old age are world cinema masterworks, showing the director still true to his scurrilous, surrealist youth.

Richard Burton

Actor

Born: RICHARD WALTER JENKINS, *Pontrhydfen, South Wales, November 10, 1925*
Died: *August 5, 1984*

Despite a dazzling rollercoaster of a life and a glittering movie career which earned him seven Oscar nominations, Richard Burton never quite achieved the recognition he sought as Britain's premier actor. His ruggedly handsome Celtic looks and early success on stage weren't enough to make him an instant hit in films, struggling through 14 years of only moderate success with a few highlights such as *My Cousin Rachel* (1952), *Alexander the Great* (1956) and *Look*

Back in Anger (1959). His career altered forever in 1962 when he met Elizabeth Taylor for *Cleopatra* and an on/off love affair kept them both on the front page until his death. During their heyday they did hit the heights and *Who's Afraid of Virginia Woolf?* (1966) and *The Taming of the Shrew* (1967)

Richard Burton: *Surplus of talent*

showed what they could achieve together, prompting fans to forgive *The Sandpiper* (1965) and *Boom* (1966). Solo, Burton had three golden moments with *Becket* (1964), *The Night of the Iguana* (1964) and *The Spy Who Came In From The Cold* (1965). But the couple drank too deep of life's pleasures and from 1970 both their careers were catalogues of failures in unambitious projects. Just a couple of times in 15 years – when he re-created his stage role in *Equus* (1977) and in his last film *1984* (1984) – did the hugely talented, mesmerically voiced Burton give a taste of the way things might have been.

James Caan

Actor

Born: *New York, NY, March 26, 1939*

James Caan's place among the current acting hierarchy is hard to pinpoint. Despite once looking the brightest of America's rising stars, flawed choices and awkward behaviour have left him sadly overlooked and underused. At the

peak of his Hollywood power he appeared to make two calamitous decisions – rejecting the lead roles in *One Flew Over the Cuckoo's Nest* (1975) and *Kramer vs Kramer* (1979), both eventual Oscar-winners for their respective stars. Instead of serving as a springboard, Caan's potent turn as Mafia princeling Sonny in Francis Coppola's *The Godfather* (1972) has proved a rare high point amid an erratic film canon. Caan gained attention with two effective turns for Howard Hawks, first in the racetrack yarn *Red Line 7000* (1965) and the next year cast alongside John Wayne in *El Dorado* (1966). Karel Reisz's *The Gambler* (1974) was raised a notch by Caan's portrayal of an anguished professor, he made an admirable action hero in the sci-fi thriller *Rollerball* (1975) and was reunited with Coppola for the neglected *Gardens of Stone* (1987). Between these minor gems there were too many mediocre outings unworthy of his talents. "It's impossible to be good in a bad movie," Caan once observed. In 1990, he returned grandly to form, playing the terrorized writer in the gruelling *Misery*, but his subsequent screen foray, the sprawling *For the Boys* (1991), revealed this foolhardy, uncompromising performer right back to his maddening old ways.

James Cagney

Actor, singer, dancer, producer

Born: *New York, NY, July 17, 1899*
Died: *March 30, 1986*

Few actors can claim to have put as much raw energy on celluloid or influenced their genre as profoundly as Cagney. The feisty little tough guy with the machine-gun staccato from New York's Lower East Side started out in vaudeville revues. On Broadway in 1930 he got his first film role when Warner Bros bought the rights to the show *Penny Arcade*, employing the two stars, Cagney and Joan Blondell, to

film it as *Sinner's Holiday* (1930). Star status came with *The Public Enemy* (1931), a morality tale of the downward spiral of a life spent in crime, followed by vintage performances in films like *Little Caesar* (1931) and *A Midsummer Night's Dream* (1935), as Bottom, until 1938 when he made the classic *Angels with Dirty Faces*. Not the shape or style of a modern singer/dancer, Cagney was a hoofer in the old vaudeville tradition and he could tap with the best, as he showed in the film biography of the Broadway impresario George M. Cohan, *Yankee Doodle Dandy* (1942), winning an Oscar for Best Actor. In 1949, he reached the pinnacle of

James Cagney: *"You doidy rat"*

his bad-guy film career in *White Heat*, which had a seminal influence on the gangster genre. The cinema of the 1930s and 1940s in particular would have been a great deal poorer without the work of this incandescent little man.

Michael Caine

Actor

Born: MAURICE JOSEPH MICKLEWHITE, *London, England, March 14, 1933*

Caine, one of Britain's tiny band of international stars, possesses the secret known only to the greats – how to be very good in very bad films. His long, ubiquitous career, beginning in 1956 with *A Hill in Korea* and encompassing over 75 films, includes more than its fair share of turkeys. He's made a shrewd decision to handle himself like a vintage Hollywood star, sometimes appearing in five films a year and seeming to accept every part he is offered. In the 1960s he broke the mould of what a star should be, making virtues out of being bespectacled, cockney-accented and unconventionally handsome. After years of struggle, he attracted widespread attention cast against type as a British officer in *Zulu* (1964), but it was playing *Alfie* (1966), the cockney Casanova, that turned him into a star and fixed his sharp-suited wideboy image in the public consciousness. Among the turkeys, Caine has proved that he is an accomplished

British citizen Caine: Plums and turkeys

actor in some highly regarded films. After being rewarded with Oscar nominations for *Alfie*, *Sleuth* (1972) and *Educating Rita* (1983), he finally won an Oscar for Best Supporting Actor for his layered performance as Meryl Streep's husband in Woody Allen's *Hannah and her Sisters* (1986). He has shrewdly moved in and out of genres, and he is equally adept at comedy and drama. Now in his sixties, this British national institution has retained his popular touch despite his millionaire status.

Jane Campion
Director, writer
Born: *Waikanae, New Zealand, 1954*

New Zealand-born Jane Campion is the most prized female film-maker of the 1990s, bringing a distinctive and distinctly feminine flavour to a traditionally male-dominated arena. After studying at the Australian Film School, she seized the critics' attention when her programme of short films won the 1986 Cannes Palme d'Or. These pictures' quirky concerns and stylistic hallmarks – off-centre compositions, crisp colours, spiky editing – found full expression in her feature debut, *Sweetie* (1989), a blackly funny look at an oddball family in meltdown. This proved a dynamic calling-card, but Campion was still busy honing her craft. Her second effort, 1990's *An Angel at My Table*, originally filmed for New Zealand television, displayed a new-found grace and precision. Weaving the poignant, biographical saga of tortured novelist Janet Frame, the film entranced viewers with its unsentimental mood and exquisite attention to the intricacies of a life on the edge. Campion's third feature proved more ambitious still. *The Piano* (1993) puts a feminist slant on a standard, star-crossed lovers plotline, rooting the tale in the sea-buffeted wilds of 19th-century New Zealand. This emotional *tour de force*, lyrically directed and driven by the performances of Harvey Keitel and Oscar-winning Holly Hunter, scooped the 1993 Palme d'Or at Cannes, becoming the year's high-brow art-house sensation. Campion's star continues to rise.

John Candy
Comic, actor
Born: *Toronto, Canada, October 30, 1950*
Died: *March 4, 1994*

The 18-stone comic from Toronto bit by bit edged his way to stardom through an ability audiences prize above all others – making them laugh. He got his break in Chicago's Second City improvisational theatre company in 1972 and back in Canada he began appearing in films like the Elliott Gould thriller *The Silent Partner* (1978). In 1979 he made the transition to American movies in Spielberg's *1941*, reuniting with Dan Aykroyd for *The Blues Brothers* (1980). But he really made

The Candyman: Cool comedy running

his mark playing a series of side-kicks: opposite Tom Hanks in *Splash!* (1984) and *Volunteers* (1985), with Richard Pryor in *Brewster's Millions* (1985), and Mel Brooks in *Spaceballs* (1987). In 1984 he landed his first starring role in *Summer Rental* (1985) and his obnoxious salesman pestering Steve Martin in *Planes, Trains and Automobiles* (1987) was a career high spot. Laughter turned to tears and *The Great Outdoors* (1988) went to video, while *Who's Harry Crumb?* (1989), which he produced, promptly vanished. Nevertheless Candy stayed hot, getting nearly red hot, with a few hits like *Uncle Buck* (1989) and *Only the Lonely* (1991) but a long line of flops like *Nothing but Trouble* (1991), *Delirious* (1991) and *Once upon a Crime* (1992). He died suddenly of a heart attack aged 44 when the best was yet to come. The public showed their affection by rushing out to make a huge hit of his last completed picture, *Cool Runnings* (1994), where he plays the coach of a Jamaican bobsleigh team.

Frank Capra
Director, writer
Born: *Sicily, May 18, 1897*
Died: *September 3, 1991*

A youthful immigrant to LA from Sicily, the life of Frank Capra – one of the world's best-loved directors – mirrors the American ideals his pictures so roundly celebrated. Although his career as a director began in the silent era, he's best known for his homespun, sparklingly scripted social fables of the 1930s and 1940s. Clark Gable and Claudette Colbert may have made a firecracker pairing in the multi-Oscar-winning *It Happened One Night* (1934), but Capra's finest interpreters were players like Gary Cooper, the incorruptible out-of-towner hero of *Mr Deeds Goes to Town* (1936), or James Stewart as the political pawn turned champion in *Mr Smith Goes to Washington* (1939). A fall from favour following World War Two sent Capra's career into decline, with critics sniping at what they saw as his "Capracorn" style – sentimental, naive, unquestioning patriotism. But while he never truly probed the nature of American democracy – painting his villains as bad men in a basically decent system – his finest work contains a heart and honesty that touches a core in all but the most cynical viewer. *It's a Wonderful Life* (1946) remains the cream of Capracorn, a timeless ode to the common American with a heart-tugging turn from Stewart as the discouraged small-town saint. It was Capra's own favourite, the film he played for his own family each Christmas until his death.

Marcel Carné
Director, writer, critic
Born: *Paris, France, August 18, 1909 (aka* ALBERT CRANCHE*)*

Carné captured perfectly the mood of his time – the World War Two years and those just prior –

with the pessimistic fatalism of his bittersweet romantic dramas about characters caught in an inevitable tragic destiny, living out their stories among the cluttered rooftops, narrow cobbled streets, waterfront cafés and shabby lodgings created by designer Alexander Trauner. The son of a Paris cabinet-maker, Carné became assistant and protégé to director Jacques Feyder, who was instrumental in getting him his first feature *Jenny* (1937), where he demonstrated his talent for drawing first-class performances from actors. This also marked the beginning of Carné's long and successful collaboration with screenwriter Jacques Prévert, with whom he made *Drôle de Drame* (1937), *Quai des Brumes* (1938) and *Le Jour se Lève* (1939). During the occupation the Carné/Prévert team continued to work together, with the clandestine assistance of Trauner and composer Joseph Kosma, who were both Jewish, producing the subversive historical allegory *Les Visiteurs du Soir* (1942). Their dazzling masterpiece *Les Enfants du Paradis* (1945), a tale of love and theatre life in nineteenth-century Paris, was shot during the occupation and released post-liberation. With the coming of the New Wave, Carné's style became unfashionable, but the cinematic world he created remains in the public mind as epitomizing one aspect of the French soul.

John Cassavetes

Actor, director, writer, producer

Born: *New York, NY, December 9, 1929*
Died: *February 3, 1989*

Cassavetes carved a unique career as a maverick star and director. A broding, incisive actor, he was certainly a name among discerning film-goers, though never achieved the status of movie star of the first rank. As a director committed to

making films as an art from, he made a notable, idiosyncratic contribution to American cinema in the sixties and seventies, but he ended his career on a run of disappointments; and even in his best films, the quality was variable. He made his name on TV as the detective-pianist in the cult show *Johnny Staccato* (1959), then in major movies such as *The Dirty Dozen* (1967) and *Rosemary's Baby* (1968) as well as a long line of humbler but intriguing efforts like *The Killers* (1964), *Two Minute Warning* (1976) and *The Fury* (1978). It was work such as this that helped him finance his "real" career – as highly influential director of experimental movies made very much out of the Hollywood mainstream, most notably *Shadows* (1960), *Faces* (1968), *Husbands* (1970) and *Gloria* (1980). He combined *cinéma vérité* techniques – hand-held camera, abrupt editing, grainy prints – with improvised acting to create a magical world of his own, peopled by a small, select band of gifted actors: Peter Falk, Ben Gazzara, Seymour Cassel and his wife, Gena Rowlands. Depending on your mood and taste, these movies are either wonderful, infuriating or both, proving an inspiration for the Coppola-Scorsese movie-brat generation of film-makers.

Claude Chabrol

Director, writer, producer, critic

Born: *Paris, France June 24, 1930*

Instrumental in the creation of the French New Wave and the concept of *auteur*, Chabrol has been compared to Hitchcock, about whom he co-authored a book with Eric Rohmer in 1957. He abandoned plans to enter the family pharmacy business in favour of writing film criticism, until an inheritance through his first wife enabled him to finance his first film *Le Beau Serge* (1958), which he wrote and produced as well as directed. This was immediately followed by *Les Cousins* (1959), an

ironic tale of youthful conflict and destruction, whose success enabled him to form his own production company and help launch the careers of other New Wave colleagues such as Rohmer, Jacques Rivette and Philippe de Broca. The expensive failure of *Landru* (1962) set him back, but his "golden age" came in the mid-1960s with a string of highly acclaimed studies on his recurrent themes of obsession and compulsion, including the love triangle of *Les Biches* (1968), *La Femme Infidèle* (1968), *Que La Bête Meure* and *Le Boucher* (both 1969), three of which starred his then wife, Stéphane Audran, who also featured in his 1978 success *Violette Nozière*. In the 1980s he made the intriguingly titled *Poulet au Vinaigre/Cop au Vin* (1984) – more Simenon than Hitchcock and also featuring Audran – and the highly praised *Une Affaire des Femmes/The Story of Women* (1988).

Lon Chaney Sr

Actor

Born: ALONSO CHANEY, *Colorado Springs, Colo., April 1, 1883*
Died: *August 26, 1930*

The first Hollywood horror star, Chaney was publicized as the 'man of a thousand faces', title of the 1957 biopic with James Cagney from which most modern awareness of his work stems. Chaney was most popular for his genius in disguise and his incredible creativity with make-up – a contemporary review said his undisguised appearance in *Tell It to the Marines* (1926) "didn't look quite natural" – and is best remembered for his grotesques. Yet his importance to the genre has a lot more to do with his sensitivity as an actor in showing the tortured soul behind the monstrous exterior, setting the standard for the best movie monsters of later generations. He started in Hollywood in 1912 in a variety of small character roles usually as villains, often in west-

erns, but his career only gained momentum after *The Wicked Darling* (1919) which started a long association with the pioneering horror director Tod Browning, in a period before Browning's crystallization of the modern horror genre with the Lugosi *Dracula* (1931). Chaney's was a long and prolific career but alas the films have not worn well, and his reputation is in eclipse apart from *The Hunchback of Notre Dame* (1923) and *Phantom of the Opera* (1925), still considered two milestones of the silent cinema. His other, though lesser known, key role was the vampire in *London After Midnight* (1927).

Lon Chaney Jr

Actor

Born: CREIGHTON CHANEY, *Oklahoma City, Okla., February 10, 1906*
Died: *July 12, 1973*

Following in father's footsteps, Lon Jr took up a career in the movies, splitting his time mostly between horror films and westerns, though he was only ever a star in the former. Jr was not nearly as important a cinematic figure as his father but, ironically, he is now by far the better remembered of the Chaneys, largely due to lack of interest in even the classics of the silent era and television's penchant for filling late night schedules with creaky old 1940s and 1950s horror flicks. A huge man with a doleful face and haunted eyes, he specialized in portraying confused, doomed victims of some terrible curse as in *The Wolf Man* (1941) for which he is now best remembered. Of the 150-plus films he made, those most often seen today are *Man Made Monster*, *The Mummy's Tomb* (1942), the first of a series he made "under wraps", including *The Mummy's Curse* and *The Mummy's Ghost* (both 1944), *Frankenstein Meets the Wolf Man* (1943) and the farcical *Abbott and Costello Meet*

Frankenstein (1948). There were notable non-horror performances in the Bob Hope movie *My Favourite Brunette* (1947) and as the marshal in *High Noon* (1952), though by far his best performance was as the pathetic Lenny in the first screen version of Steinbeck's novel *Of Mice and Men* (1939).

Sir Charles Chaplin

Actor, director, writer
Born: CHARLES SPENCER
CHAPLIN, *London, England,*
April 16, 1889
Died: *December 25, 1977*

The little man from South London with the bowler hat, silly moustache and baggy trousers is, and will probably remain, the greatest, best-loved and most-feted icon the cinema has ever produced. He grew up in crushing poverty, toured with Fred Karno's music-hall troupe, and ended up working on one- and two-reelers for Mack Sennett's Keystone Film company. By 1915 he was already being billed as the world's greatest comedian and, over the next 25

Charlie Chaplin: *Little tramp, big star*

years, acted in and directed a string of classic films, deftly weaving tragedy with comedy, and pathos with slapstick: *The Tramp* (1916); *The Cure* (1917); *The Immigrant* (1917); *The Kid* (1921); *The Gold Rush* (1925); *City Lights* (1931); *Modern Times* (1936). These

were the works of a master satirist and storyteller, and perfectly reflected the strengths and weaknesses, likes and dislikes of a film-going generation. His searing lampoon of Hitler – *The Great Dictator* (1940) – was, however, the last truly popular film he made. The sublime *Monsieur Verdoux* (1947), a comedy about a mass murderer, was way ahead of its time and, although *Limelight* (1952) saw some of his popularity restored, his reputation declined rapidly after the war. He was awarded a belated special Oscar in 1972, acknowledging his pivotal role in the development of film, and was knighted in 1975.

Chevy Chase

Actor, comedian
Born: CORNELIUS CRANE CHASE,
New York City, NY, October 8, 1943

The first of the "alternative" American comedians to move into feature films, invariably as a smug, stumbling fall-guy, Chase has consistently been moderately successful at the box office, but often in mediocre, slapstick fare. The son of a publishing executive and a plumbing heiress, he grew up in privileged, upper-middle-class New York, developing his satirical edge as an artist on *Mad* magazine while writing and performing on *The National Lampoon Radio Hour*. He hankered to appear on camera, though, and was tremendously popular as the abrasive frontman on television's *Saturday Night Live*, the show that also made John Belushi and Dan Aykroyd. His aggressive style and bafflingly obvious catch-phrase, "I'm Chevy Chase and you're not", won him two Emmy awards and took him to Hollywood ahead of his co-stars, although he had already made a big-screen debut in *The Groove Tube* (1974). In *Foul Play* (1978) he was impressively straight-faced alongside Goldie Hawn, and *Caddyshack* (1980) was followed by *National Lampoon's*

Vacation (1983), the first of a series of less than hilarious ventures. Successes with *Fletch* (1984), *Spies Like Us* (1985), *Three Amigos!* (1986) and *The Couch Trip* (1987) enabled him to host the 1988 Academy Awards ceremony, but he needs to inject some of his notorious, off-the-cuff eloquence and wit if he is to be remembered as a truly remarkable screen presence, or an enduring comedian.

Cher

Actress, singer
Born: CHERILYN SARKISIAN LA
PIERRE, *El Centro, Calif.,*
May 20, 1946

Cher has enjoyed three careers so far. First as a 1960s singer with husband Sonny Bono, second as a talk show celebrity and third as an Oscar-winning actress of considerable talent. Her film debut was *Wild on the Beach* (1965), followed by *Good Times* (1967) and *Chastity* (1969) with Bono. But it wasn't until 1982, divorced and with a solo music hit career, that she made her debut proper in Robert

Cher: *"I got you babe"*

Altman's film of *Come Back to the Five and Dime, Jimmy Dean, Jimmy Dean*, re-creating her off-Broadway stage role. Mike Nichols liked it and cast her as Meryl Streep's lesbian friend in *Silkwood* (1983), for which she was Oscar-nominated. Cher was a hot property, with her role as the mother of a disfigured teenager in Bogdanovich's *Mask* (1985) scoop-

ing Best Actress prize at Cannes. She had a series of flashy roles in high-profile pictures – *The Witches of Eastwick* (1987) opposite Jack Nicholson and *Suspect* (1987) with Dennis Quaid – before hitting pay-dirt with *Moonstruck* (1987), which won her an Oscar as a romantic New Yorker who changes from frumpy to gorgeous to win Nicholas Cage. Now a big star, she did *Mermaids* (1990) as Winona Rider's hippyish mom. Given the quality of her performances, it's a thin film roster, though she's still young and popular enough to have a major career if she so decides.

Maurice Chevalier

Actor, singer
Born: *Paris, France,*
September 12, 1888
Died: *January 1, 1972*

The debonair, quintessentially French chanteur with the twin trademarks of straw hat and irrepressible grin charmed the world in a career that spanned five decades, taking him from early-1930s films which were among the first great Hollywood musicals to the scene-stealing grand old Frenchman of "*Sank Eavens for Leetle Girls*" and Disney comedies of the 1960s. Born in Paris, the ninth of 10 children, he began entertaining in cafés at 12 and appeared in his first film *Trop Crédule* as far back as 1908. He learnt English as a prisoner of war in Germany and in the early 1920s formed his own company which produced five films. Paramount signed him in 1928, fitting him into several now-classic musicals with a winning combination of wit, exuberance and lilting light-as-air music, including *The Love Parade* (1929), *Love Me Tonight* (1932), *One Hour Wth You* (1932) and *The Merry Widow* (1934), all with Jeanette MacDonald. His reputation was damaged by accusations of collaboration in World War Two. Despite being cleared of all charges, he was shunned by Hollywood until 1958 when his performance in *Gigi* was a hit and he was welcomed back with a special Oscar. Chevalier then enjoyed a renaissance, enchanting a new generation as priests, grandfathers and avuncular charmers, but unable to work in later years he grew depressed and died a recluse aged 83.

Julie Christie

Actress

Born: JULIE FRANCES CHRISTIE, *Assam, India, April 14, 1941*

Wide-mouthed, with a radiant smile, this English actress's sunny screen personality was the embodiment of the spirit of the swinging 60s, sexually liberated, independent and unreserved. Born on her father's tea plantation, Christie was educated in Brighton, until she moved to Paris to study art, aged 16. She returned to Britain to study acting, breaking into television in 1960. By 1962 she was debuting on the big screen in *Crooks Anonymous*, where she was spotted by director John Schlesinger, who cast her as *Billy Liar*'s free-spirited love object in 1962. Schlesinger's *Darling* (1965) was a darker story of destructive beauty, written for her and winning her not only an Oscar but also international stardom. Her beauty distracted from her acting, though, and the critics turned on her for *Doctor Zhivago* (1965) and *Fahrenheit 451* (1966), deserting her until she attempted to reject glamour (impossible with her looks) for *McCabe and Mrs Miller* (1971), where she played opposite her long-time lover, Warren Beatty, and was again Oscar-nominated. Nicolas Roeg's nightmarish *Don't Look Now* (1974) was followed by a cameo role in *Nashville* (1975), and more bedroom and bathroom romps with Beatty in *Shampoo* (1975), before he directed her to great effect in *Heaven Can Wait* (1975). Shedding her star image,

Julie Christie: Never plain Mrs Miller

she returned to India for *Heat and Dust* (1983), and continued to globetrot her way through a series of films picked for their political liberalism rather than and great commercial value in the 1980s and 1990s.

René Clair

Director, writer, actor, author

Born: RENÉ-LUCIEN CHOMETTE, *Paris, France, November 11, 1898*
Died: *March 15, 1981*

Perhaps because of Clair's childhood in the market district of Paris, his films show a respect and love for ordinary people. His delightful comic fantasies revived and revitalized the French comedy tradition for cinema. A brief stint as a silent film actor awakened Clair's interest in the medium. He completed his first film, the comic science fiction fantasy *Paris Qui Dort* (1924), in only three weeks, followed by the Dadaist *Entr'acte* (1924), a series of further fantasy works, which included *Le Voyage Imaginaire* (1926), and an updated version of the Labiche-Michel play *Un Chapeau de Paille d'Italie/The Italian Straw Hat* (1927). Despite his initial opposition to the talkies, in his first sound film, *Sous Les Toits de Paris* (1930), Clair used the everyday sounds of Paris to great atmospheric effect, then going on to show his mastery of comic timing in *Le Million* and *A Nous la Liberté* (both 1931). In England he made *The Ghost Goes West* (1935)

with Robert Donat, and a wartime move to Hollywood proved fruitful with such films as *I Married a Witch* (1942) and *It Happened Tomorrow* (1944). Back in France after the war, he turned to more serious themes and his popularity declined. Apart from screenplays, he wrote three novels, the French version of the play *Born Yesterday*, two collections of film criticism and numerous unpublished poems from his youth.

Montgomery Clift

Actor

Born: EDWARD MONTGOMERY CLIFT, *Omaha, Nebr., October 17, 1920*
Died: *July 23, 1966*

Intensely sensitive, with exquisitely chiselled features and an edge of real madness, Clift was the first of a new breed of "rebel stars" in the early 1950s, until a car smash warped his haunting good looks. A professional actor at 14, he rejected Hollywood until finding the scripts he liked. The first film he shot was *Red River* (1948), but a delayed release meant that *The Search* (1948) was shown first, for which he immediately received an Oscar nomination. "Monty's" brooding, naturalistic style earned

Montgomery Clift: Eternally entertaining

him further nominations for *A Place in the Sun* (1951) and *From Here to Eternity* (1953), but he turned to drink and drugs, apparently suffering from chronic guilt at his concealed homosexuality, and during the making of *Raintree*

County (1957) survived a horrific car crash, his life being saved by long-time friend and co-star Elizabeth Taylor. Physically, Clift was disfigured, and his personality never fully recovered. He struggled on to make *The Misfits* (1961) with Marilyn Monroe, who claimed, "he's the only person I know worse off than me", was sued for his on-set behaviour during *Freud* (1962), but earned his fourth Oscar nomination for an emotionally charged, seven-minute performance in *Judgment at Nuremberg* (1961), which he worked on for free. His last film was *The Defector* (1966), the year that he died of a heart attack, almost certainly related to his earlier accident.

Glenn Close

Actress

Born: *Greenwich, Conn., March 19, 1947*

The powerful, intense Close is a strong contender for America's best film actress of the 1980s, the only serious rival to Meryl Streep and winner of five Oscar nominations, starting with her movie debut, *The World According to Garp* (1982). She won a Tony award for Tom Stoppard's *The Real Thing* on Broadway and an Emmy nomination for the first-rate TV movie *Something about Amelia* (1984). It's already a glittering career but the top prizes of Oscar and box-office gold have so far just eluded her, and it's taken another stage appearance, in Andrew Lloyd Webber's musical *Sunset Blvd*, to provide the showbiz glitz she needs. Her other Oscar nomination highlights came with *The Big Chill* (1983), Robert Redford's *The Natural* (1984), *Fatal Attraction* (1987) and her knife-edge performance as the vengeful lover in 1988's *Dangerous Liaisons*, her best show of acting so far. She became a top Hollywood player with the thrillers *Jagged Edge* (1985) and especially *Fatal Attraction* (1987) as

Scorsese, Robert Altman and Steven Spielberg were his only serious rivals. Inspired by an apprenticeship with Roger Corman, he made his feature debut with the B-movie shocker *Dementia 13* (1963), following it up with a handful of low-key but admired pictures, most notably 1969's feminist road movie *The Rain People*. All the while this multi-talented *enfant terrible* was scripting – *Reflections in a Golden Eye* (1967), *The Great Gatsby* (1974), the Oscar-winning *Patton* (1970) – and producing (1973's *American Graffiti*) too. Coppola hit paydirt with the Oscar-winning *The Godfather 1* and *2* (1972 and 1974), a modern American epic of familial ties and cultural corruption which he followed with a nightmarish miniaturist thriller in *The Conversation* (1974). The remainder of the decade saw Coppola labouring on his *tour de force* – the phantasmagoric Vietnam odyssey *Apocalypse Now* (1979). But Coppola's grandiose dreams of an independent studio came a cropper when the lavish, old-style musical *One from the Heart* (1982) bankrupted his American Zoetrope company. The director retaliated with two low-budget gems in *The Outsiders* and *Rumble Fish* (both 1983) but has since seemed handcuffed by his enforced role as a hired hand. Fortunately the old verve was still in evidence in *Tucker* (1988), *Bram Stoker's Dracula* (1992) and his long-awaited series closer, *The Godfather 3* (1990) .

Roger Corman

Director, writer, producer
Born: *Los Angeles, Calif., April 5, 1926*

Roger Corman is a film phenomenon – the acknowledged master of the low-budget exploiter who boasts that none of his 200-plus movies has failed to take a profit. He broke into the film business as a messenger boy, then a screenwriter, making his directorial debut with the bargain-basement oater *5 Guns West* (1955). Working outside the studio system, Corman's output jumped between genres with indiscriminate zeal, hopping from drama (1958's *I, Mobster*) to sci-fi (1956's *It Conquered the World*) to monster movie (1957's *Attack of the Crab Monsters*) to mobster movie (1970's *Bloody Mama*) to beatnik horror spoof (1959's cult favourite *Bucket of Blood*). Invariably shot on nickel 'n' dime budgets in frenzied five- to 10-day schedules, Corman's pictures are marked by their wacky characters, offbeat plots and wry political savvy. In the early 1960s he impressed critics with his run of dark screenic interpretations of Edgar Allen Poe. But Corman was nothing if not daring. The decade's end found him at the forefront of counter-culture cinema, directing proto-hippie pictures *The Trip* (1967), *The Wild Angels* (1966) and *Gas-s-s-s* (1970) – with music courtesy of Country Joe and the Fish. Corman may well go down in history as tutor-cum-father-figure to some of America's brightest talent. Jack Nicholson, Francis Coppola, Martin Scorsese and Robert De Niro all served an apprenticeship with Corman on their way to screen immortality.

Kevin Costner

Actor, director, producer
Born: *Los Angeles, Calif., January 18, 1955*

Costner is a disappointment for those who think movie stars should be superhuman: like a latterday James Stewart, he's made being a good-looking ordinary Joe into a world-beating turn. It took him a long time to get established. His 1981 debut was inauspicious enough; support roles in two obscure films, *Shadows Run Black* and *Sizzle Beach USA*. An eighth-billed part in Ron Howard's excellent 1982 comedy *Night Shift* led to his first lead role, the B-movie *Winning Streak*. Then came two setbacks: his parts in *Frances* (1982) and Lawrence Kasdan's *The Big Chill* (1983) ended up on the cutting room floor, while *Fandango* and *American Flyers* (both 1985) were unexpected flops. Suddenly his luck turned. Kasdan made

Kevin Costner: Good-looking ordinary Joe

amends by casting him in his western *Silverado* (1985), and his Mr Nice Guy role as FBI agent Eliot Ness in Brian De Palma's huge hit *The Untouchables* (1987) made him a star. The tense thriller *No Way Out* (1987), the sexy baseball movie *Bull Durham* (1988) and the enchanting *Field of Dreams* (1989) proved that Costner had arrived. But it was his 1990 Oscar-winning western, *Dances with Wolves* (which he also directed and produced), that turned him into a superstar and major Hollywood player, a status which was confirmed by the huge success of *Robin Hood: Prince of Thieves* (1991), *JFK* (1991), *The Bodyguard* (1992) and *Wyatt Earp* (1994). He does have a range and power as an actor but it's within narrow parameters. Carefully chosen roles have kept the ambitious, tenacious Costner at the top of the Hollywood tree.

Joseph Cotten

Actor
Born: *Petersburg, Va., May 15, 1905*
Died: *February 6, 1994*

Urbane and handsome, Joseph Cotten gained notoriety as an actor even before his movie debut, teaming with friend Orson Welles for their infamous *War of the Worlds* radio broadcast. It was Welles, too, who gave Cotten many of his choicest film opportunities, with his assured turn in *Citizen Kane* (1941) marking the first of six collaborations running though to 1975's pseudo-documentary *F for Fake*. Due to his determinedly low-key, unshowy style, Cotten was never regarded as a major Hollywood icon but as an actor his skills were second to none. He proved particularly adept at playing flawed modern-day heroes, the basically decent but often powerless protagonist epitomized by his portrayal of dimestore hack Holly Martins in *The Third Man* (1949). Typically, perhaps, it was Alfred Hitchcock who cast him against type in 1943's *Shadow of a Doubt*, with Cotten turning in a performance of icy wickedness as Uncle Charlie, the debonair, charming, utterly deranged "merry widow strangler". Though increasingly constricted in bland, big-budget movies, Cotten impressed on Michael Cimino's maligned *Heaven's Gate* (1980) and as a scheming southerner in

Joseph Cotten: Resting on his laurels

Hush....Hush, Sweet Charlotte (1966) and seemed well pleased with his career. "Orson Welles lists *Citizen Kane* as his best film, Hitchcock opts for *Shadow of a Doubt* and Sir Carol Reed chose *The Third Man*," he once reflected. "And I'm in all of them!"

Sir Noel Coward

Playwright, writer, actor, director, producer, composer
Born: NOEL PIERCE COWARD, *Teddington, England, December 16, 1899*
Died: *March 26, 1973*

The man who made dressing-gowns and cigarette holders fashionable is best known as a stage playwright, but his flippant, elegant wit and clipped delivery transferred easily to the screen, and made him one of the most enduring entertainment celebrities of the century. The son of a music publisher, he had little formal education but was on stage aged 10. Multi-talented, he made his screen debut (in two roles) in D. W. Griffith's *Hearts of the World* (1917). He also penned songs, including *Mad Dogs and Englishmen*, earned his first screenwriter's credit for *The Queen Was In The Parlour* (1927), and had three of his phenomenally successful stage plays made into silent films by 1931. In 1942 he co-directed the wartime propaganda film that won him a Special Academy Award, *In Which We Serve*, and so began the partnership with David Lean that spawned his best screen work. It included *Blithe Spirit* (1945) and culminated in the classic romance *Brief Encounter* (1946), a movingly straight account which Coward co-produced and scripted from his own play. Thereafter, he largely stuck to acting, a profession he once described as "just saying the lines and trying not to bump into the furniture". His last film was *The Italian Job* (1969), shortly before he was knighted. Despite

his claim only to have "a talent to amuse", his comedy of insincerity was smart, incisive and that proved enduring.

Joan Crawford

Actress
Born: BILLIE CASSIN (*aka* LUCILLE FAY LeSUEUR), *San Antonio, Tex., March 23, 1904*
Died: *May 10, 1977*

The eyes, the mouth, the shoulder pads. These were the weapons in Crawford's armoury and they flashed, gashed and thrashed their way across the screen through more than 40 years as a star. She was far less an actress than a screen phenomenon and more than anything an out-and-out survivor. Opinions on her

Crawford: *The eyes, the mouth, the shoulder pads!*

talent varied as did opinions on her personality – "As a human being, Miss Crawford is a very great actress" said Nicholas Ray, her director in *Johnny Guitar* (1954). But whether it was her frenetic flapper in the silent *Our Dancing Daughters (1928)*, which established her career, the ambitious, flirtatious stenographer in *Grand Hotel* (1932), which the fanzines said she stole from Garbo, or any one of the dozens of shopgirls-making-good that became the staple of her mid-career, there could never be any doubt that she filled the screen. The quintessential Crawfords like *A Woman's Face* (1941), *Mildred Pierce* (1945), which won her an

Oscar, *Humoresque* (1946), her legendary feud with Bette Davis culminating in the classic *What Ever Happened to Baby Jane?* (1962) and even her late career in horror screamers like *Strait Jacket* (1964), *Berserk* (1967) and the endearingly awful *Trog* (1970) – still played with utter conviction – secure her place in the old Hollywood pantheon, way back when movie stars were creatures much larger than life.

David Cronenberg

Director, writer, actor
Born: *Toronto, Canada, March 15, 1941*

Bespectacled, cultivated Cronenberg is an ordinary, studious-looking, normal sort of chap. But the mild, quiet exterior belies the colourful imagination capable of conceiving such grisly movies as *Shivers* (1975), his first major film, in which parasites turn the residents of a high-rise block into sex-crazed zombies. In *Rabid* (1977) Montreal is hit by a plague spread by a growth in a porno star's armpit and most famously in *Scanners* (1981) Cronenberg served up the cinema's original exploding head. By the time of *The Dead Zone* (1983) he's ambitiously trying to spread his wings, leaving behind disgusting special effects and exploitation movies in favour of even more frightening horror that's classier, more stylish and more thoughtful. This encouraging development has continued through 1986's *The Fly* (the film's motto "Be afraid, be very afraid" could be Cronenberg's catch-phrase) in which Jeff Goldblum movingly mutates into a monster, and 1988's brilliant psycho-thriller *Dead Ringers* with Jeremy Irons chilling as disturbed twin gynaecologists. Moving on further, Cronenberg convincingly took a starring role in Clive Barker's horror movie *Nightbreed* (1990), then tried the impossible in filming William Burroughs's *The Naked*

Lunch (1991). If that was a noble failure, his stage-to-screen transfer of the Broadway play *M Butterfly* (1994), reuniting him with Irons, was just a failure. For a man immersed in horror films, both were too literal and too ordinary by half.

Bing Crosby

Actor, crooner, golfer
Born: HARRY LILLIS CROSBY, *Tacoma, Wash., May 2, 1904*
Died: *October 14, 1977*

A revered band singer, light comedian and American institution, forever associated with his *Road* movie buddy Bob Hope, Crosby enjoyed a well-cultivated screen image of easy-going charm in contrast to his reputation as a man of relentless ambition and posthumous revelations of cruelty as a father. His Christmas Day TV specials made him a member of everybody's family in the States. From 1943 he was the biggest box-office draw for five consecutive years. As a law student he played drums and sang, and after joining forces with Al Rinker was taken on by the Paul Whiteman Orchestra. They first appeared in *The King of Jazz* (1930) and in 1931 Crosby became an overnight star on his own radio show. Having made musical shorts with Mack Sennett, he was launched to stardom on the back of a five-picture deal with Paramount. He developed a flair for comedy and in 1940 starred

Bing Crosby: *Vintage crooner*

77

alongside Hope and Dorothy Lamour in *Road to Singapore*, the first of a vastly popular series in which he continued to feature as late as 1962. The Irving Berlin musical *Holiday Inn* (1942), in which he starred with Fred Astaire, was a huge hit and the featured song *White Christmas* sold a phenomenal 30 million copies. Crosby won an Oscar as Father O'Malley in the sentimental *Going My Way* (1945) and when he stopped filming after *Stagecoach* in 1966 he still appeared regularly on TV and stage.

Tom Cruise

Actor

Born: THOMAS CRUISE MAPOTHER IV, *Syracuse, NY, July 3, 1962*

Who would have guessed while watching the chubby teenaged military cadet in *Taps* (1981) that they were looking at the beginning of one of the most successful movie careers of recent years. One of the few survivors, and certainly the most successful member, of the "Brat Pack", Cruise has capitalized on his boyish charm and clean-cut good looks to become the heart-throb and hero of millions, whether in the ecstatic dance in his underpants in *Risky Business* (1983) or the jaw-clenching man-gotta-do of *Top Gun* (1986). His career moved from rites-of-passage

Tom Cruise: *Born on the third of July*

movies to boys'-own-adventure films until the more challenging *Rain Man* (1988), where he held his own opposite no less a scene stealer than Dustin Hoffman, and *Born on the Fourth of July* (1989), as the wheelchairbound Vietnam War veteran – easily his best performance to date, for which he was Oscar-nominated. Though his acting has gained depth and range since his teen movies, doubtless benefiting from working with his many illustrious co-stars, like Paul Newman in *The Color of Money* (1986) and Robert Duvall in *Days of Thunder* (1990), Cruise's appeal lies in his open-faced freshness, his evident charm and not a little in his matinée idol looks. His breathtaking bisexual bloodsucker Lestat in *Interview with the Vampire* (1994) shows Cruise is deterfminted his looks won't hinder the development of his career.

George Cukor

Director

Born: GEORGE DEWEY CUKOR, *New York, NY, July 7, 1899*
Died: *January 24, 1983*

Cukor's early experience directing for theatre taught him the art of handling actors and though he was known as a "woman's director", male stars too flourished under his direction. His first Hollywood work was coaching male actors in their dialogue for *All Quiet on the Western Front*. The "woman's director" label began with Constance Bennett and *What Price Hollywood?* (1932), which he later remade as the musical *A Star Is Born* (1954), drawing a superb performance from Judy Garland and an equally good one from the much less difficult James Mason. The most famous film he never made, being sacked ten days into production, was *Gone with the Wind* (1939), although the scenes he shot were used in the final version. His long and successful collaboration with Katharine Hepburn, which began with her first film *A Bill of*

Divorcement (1933), included *Little Women* (1935), *The Philadelphia Story* (1940), *Adam's Rib* (1949) and *Pat and Mike* (1957); again, Spencer Tracy was pretty evident in the latter two! But actresses certainly did good work with Cukor; Garbo – *Camille* (1937), Judy Holliday – *Born Yesterday* (1950), Candice Bergen and Jacqueline Bisset in Cukor's much-maligned comeback film *Rich and Famous* (1981). Audrey Hepburn was regarded as a disappointment in his only Oscar-winner *My Fair Lady* (1964), to some extent because so many people thought the role should have gone to Julie Andrews.

Macaulay Culkin

Actor

Born: *New York City, NY, August 26, 1980*

The winsome blond Culkin is the world's most successful child star since Shirley Temple. His reward is a huge earning capacity, negotiated by his manager father, who has also got siblings Kieran and Quinn into movies. Culkin began performing on stage at the age of four and made his first movie at seven, *Rocket Gibraltar* (1988) with Burt Lancaster, followed by *See*

Macaulay Culkin: *Richest boy in the world?*

You in the Morning (1989) and *Jacob's Ladder* (1990). His particular brand of obstreperous cuteness made itself evident in *Uncle Buck* (1989) and *Only the Lonely* (1991), both with John Candy. Culkin shot

into the big time with John Hughes's comedy hit *Home Alone* (1990) as the child left behind in Chicago by his vacationing family. *Home Alone 2: Lost in New York* (1992) repeated virtually the same story, only in New York. Ironically, while the child's throwaway violent treatment of the comic crooks in those films raised not an eyebrow, *The Good Son* (1993), in which he plays a *Bad Seed*-style child murderer, was temporarily refused a UK release because of the story's similarity to a notorious murder case. His other films are the popular *My Girl* (1990), where he was stung to death by bees, the uneven *Getting Even with Dad* (1994), and a part-animated child's fantasy *The Pagemaster* (1994). He was then seen as *Richie Rich* (1995) the richest boy in the world – which he must virtually be for real.

Tony Curtis

Actor

Born: BERNARD SCHWARTZ, *Bronx, New York, NY, June 3, 1925*

When asked recently who was the most attractive person with whom he had ever acted, Tony Curtis responded without a blink: "I am". His answer is indicative both of the humour and absolute self-assurance that have carried him from the Bronx to dapper, ageless, yarn-spinning Hollywood legend. Never one of the screen's finest actors, he is without doubt one of its greatest characters – and yes, that cute, cherubic face *is* one of the most attractive things ever to have appeared in CinemaScope. His career started with a seven-year contract at Universal. Most of his early movies are eminently forgettable, excepting the fun swashbuckler *The Prince Who Was a Thief* (1951), but things came together in the latter half of the 1950s with a dizzying succession of classic films: *Trapeze* (1956); *Sweet Smell of Success* (1957); *The Defiant Ones* (1958); and *Some Like It Hot* (1959).

Tony Curtis: *Prime Hollywood beefcake in drag*

The 1960s started well with the toga-epic *Spartacus* (1960), but, with the exception of his ferocious performances in *The Boston Strangler* (1968) and as a McCarthy-esque senator in *Insignificance* (1985), he has hardly done a worthwhile film for the last three decades. It doesn't really matter. He is one of Hollywood's great personalities and, if not a great actor, his presence will always make the direst films just a little less dire.

Michael Curtiz

Director
Born: MIHALY KERTESZ, *Budapest, Hungary, December 24, 1888*
Died: *April 10, 1962*

Curtiz was not merely one of the most prolific directors in film history – well over 160 movies in a 50-year career – but also one of the most popular. Although best remembered as the creator of the legendary *Casablanca* (1942), he was an artist of extraordinary breadth, versatility and vision, equally adept at turning out rollicking action adventures (1938's *The Adventures of Robin Hood*) as he was at producing atmospheric social dramas (1945's *Mildred Pierce*). Born in Hungary, he made his screen debut – as both actor and director – in 1912, thereafter making some 60 European movies before relocating to America in the mid-1920s to churn out a series of

silents for Warners. His biblical epic *Noah's Ark* (1929) brought huge acclaim and introduced the dramatic set pieces, rousing action sequences and sensitive, multi-dimensional handling of characters that, over the next 30 years, he was to use in a host of classic movies – *The Adventures of Robin Hood*; *Yankee Doodle Dandy* (1942); *Passage to Marseille* (1944); *Flamingo Road* (1949); *White Christmas* (1954); *We're No Angels* (1955). He won an Oscar for *Casablanca*, and on the strength of that film alone deserves a special place in the Cinema Hall of Fame. As it was, he left a host of other classics, bolstering his reputation as one of the finest and most imaginative directors who worked within the Hollywood studio system.

Peter Cushing

Actor
Born: *May 26, 1913*
Died: *August 11, 1994*

An actor of considerable elegance and style, Cushing had, in common with that other great master of horror Boris Karloff, the ability to build enormous screen tension, not just to frighten, but to

Peter Cushing: *The gentlest of gentlemen*

create the expectation of fear. A man with finely wrought, striking features and capable of a wide range from genuine warmth to the

most glacial coldness, he appeared on both sides of the screen battle between good and evil, from the best Sherlock Holmes since Rathbone in *The Hound of the Baskervilles* (1959) and his classic Van Helsing in *Horror of Dracula* (1958), through his inspired but misguided genius in *The Curse of Frankenstein* (1957) – the first of six Frankenstein movies – to the insidious malevolence of Dr Schreck in *Dr Terror's House of Horrors* (1964). In real life the gentlest of gentlemen, he was a key figure in the development of British horror films, along with Christopher Lee with whom his career was closely linked, making more than 20 films together between 1957 and 1973. One of the most refined and meticulous performers of the genre, always acting with total commitment and making credible, figures of sometimes improbable fantasy, he had a long and varied career including early screen appearances in Laurel and Hardy's *A Chump at Oxford* (1939), Olivier's *Hamlet* (1948) and British television's landmark *1984* (1954). The current renaissance of interest in Hammer Studios' output should ensure Cushing's artistry the attention it deserves.

Zbigniew Cybulski

Actor
Born: *Ukraine, USSR, November 3, 1927*
Died: *January 8, 1967*

Cybulski, with his trademark tinted glasses, is the only star of Eastern bloc cinema ever to have made much of an impression on western audiences. He was a national icon in his own lifetime, and has been likened to a Polish James Dean, an analogy based as much upon his tragic early death (at 40, falling off a train) as his ability to convey the confusion and hopelessness of a young, post-war generation. He trained as a journalist, formed his own avant-garde theatre company and

appeared in a number of films – notably *The End of the Night* (1957) and *The Eighth Day of the Week* (1957) – before his portrayal of a disillusioned post-war resistance worker in Wajda's *Ashes and Diamonds* (1958) brought him international recognition. His performance perfectly mirrored the mood of contemporary Poland, and over the next 10 years – despite drink and discipline problems – he turned in a handful of equally profound characterizations: as a theatre director in *See You Tomorrow* (1960); a bored, vodka-swilling young man in *Innocent Sorcerers* (1960); a war hero in *L'Amour à Vingt Ans* (*Love at Twenty*) (1962); and a fraudulent hero in *How to Be Loved* (1963). Following his gruesome death, he was the subject of a film homage by Wajda – *Everything for Sale* (1968) – and remains one of the few Polish actors to be widely appreciated internationally.

Willem Dafoe

Actor
Born: *Appleton, Wis., July 22, 1955*

Trained in New York's fringe theatre, Dafoe made his film debut in *Heaven's Gate* (1980), leading to a starring role as a biker in *The Loveless* (1981) directed by Kathryn Bigelow. There followed a series of striking roles in offbeat movies like *The Hunger* (1983), *Streets of Fire* (1984), *Road House 66* (1984) and *To Live and Die in L.A.* (1985) until his Oscar-nominated performance in Oliver Stone's *Platoon* (1986) as Sgt Elias turned him into a star. His new status was confirmed by his other two memorable performances, both in 1988, as Jesus in Scorsese's *The Last Temptation of Christ* and the righteous FBI agent of Alan Parker's *Mississippi Burning*. Instead of fulfilling his promise of becoming a major star in the 1990s he stepped back into his previous persona of cult figure, often seeming to make wilfully wayward choices. Not cast in a romantic hero mould, he has appeared in supporting roles in two more Oliver Stone pictures, *Born on the Fourth of July* (1989) and *The Doors* (1991). He starred memorably in a pre-*Schindler* concentration camp film, *Triumph of the Spirit* (1989), but it received scant attention, while good work in Paul Schrader's *Light Sleeper* (1991), *White Sands* (1992) and the Madonna farrago *Body of Evidence* (1992) also went for little. His action role in the Harrison Ford adventure *Clear and Present Danger* (1994) was just the kind of part he needs to play to win back a popular audience.

Bette Davis

Actress
Born: RUTH ELIZABETH DAVIS, *Lowell, Mass., April 5, 1908*
Died: *October 6, 1989*

Saucer-eyed, staccato-speaking, cigarette-puffing Davis was truly the greatest of the Hollywood female stars, outstripping her nearest rival Joan Crawford, whom she hated in a bizarre life-long feud. Her reign lasted nearly 60 years and she made 100 films, bowing out on a major role with Lindsay Anderson's *The Whales of August* (1987). Davis won two Oscars, for *Dangerous* (1935) and *Jezebel* (1938), and received 10 nominations, including *Dark Victory* (1939), *The Letter* (1940), *The Little Foxes* (1941) and *Mr Skeffington* (1944). She was inclined to give mannered, artificial performances, but this didn't stop them being truthful and it only added to her films' appeal and their longevity. Her run at the very top lasted only a decade, from *Of Human Bondage* (1934) to *The Corn Is Green* (1945), but there were many other high spots during the next 40 years, *All about Eve* (1950) and *What Ever Happened to Baby Jane?* (1962) among them. Davis is remembered not only for her extravagant acting but also as a tenacious fighter – for better parts, for a better deal for women, for freedom from studio slavery, to recover from a stroke, and to win back the love of her daughter who'd written a hurtful book about her. The woman who was nicknamed "Mother Goddam" came across as a brave, emotional powerhouse, and despite her formidable toughness, Davis often seemed touchingly vulnerable and was just as stalwart a friend as an enemy.

Bette Davis: *Eyes the prize (here her fourth husband, actor Gary Merrill)*

Doris Day

Actress, singer
Born: DORIS VON KAPPELHOFF, *Cincinnati, Oh., April 3, 1924*

The perennially bubbly Doris ended a 20-year reign in the movies in 1968 after *With Six You Get Eggroll* and little has been seen of her on TV since *The Doris Day Show* ended in 1973. The former dance-band singer became an immediate success aged 24 when she stood in for Betty Hutton in the shipboard musical *Romance on the High Seas* (*It's Magic*). She soon established herself as America's favourite musicals star in *Calamity Jane* (1953), *Young at Heart* (1954) and *The Pajama Game* (1957) while making hit thrillers like *Storm Warning* (1951) and Hitchcock's *The Man Who Knew Too Much* (1956). These were the best of her films, but too often her talents were squandered on inferior romances and unconvincing biopics. In the late 1950s, she switched to her own brand of sexless sex comedies, usually with Rock Hudson. *Pillow Talk* (1959) (for which she was Oscar-nominated), *Lover Come Back* (1961), *That Touch of Mink* (1962) and *Send Me No Flowers* (1964) made her top box-office attraction on four occasions between 1959 and 1966. Though Day was engulfed in the tide of sexual permissiveness in the late 1960s, she is today a heroine for both feminists and fun-seekers alike. If you want a measure of her talent, listen to the soundtrack of *The Pajama Game* and watch her skilled acting against James Cagney in *Love Me or Leave Me* (1955).

Daniel Day-Lewis

Actor
Born: *London, England, April 29, 1957*

Aquiline and handsome, British actor Daniel Day-Lewis has glided smoothly from homegrown art-house acclaim to Hollywood superstardom. This son of poet-laureate C. Day-Lewis made his film debut as a teenage tearaway in 1971's *Sunday Bloody Sunday* but it was not until 1985 that he gained widespread attention with powerhouse turns in the year's two key British pictures. His contrasting performances – as the monocled, buttoned-up Cecil in Merchant-Ivory's costumer *A Room with a View* and as a gritty, gay street punk in the urban drama *My Beautiful Laundrette* – impressed audiences and marked Day-Lewis out as a performer of singular talent and versatility. His role as a philandering neurosurgeon in 1987's elegant *The Unbearable Lightness of Being* paved the way for his Oscar-winning *tour de force*, twisted and tortured as paralysed writer Christy Brown in *My Left Foot* (1989). While this gruelling role drained its interpreter – Day-Lewis suffered a mini-breakdown during the National Theatre's production of *Hamlet* the following year – it also set him up for mainstream movie success. He dutifully hit the big time as the po-faced, intrepid hero of the bland *The Last of the Mohicans* (1992) and in the lead role of Martin Scorsese's *The Age of Innocence* (1993). Neither part, however, carried the same charge and emotional weight as the actor's performance in the controversial IRA drama *In the Name of the Father* (1994).

Cecil B. DeMille

Director, producer, writer
Born: CECIL BLOUNT DEMILLE, *Ashfield, Mass., August 12, 1881*
Died: *January 21, 1959*

The founder of Hollywood, Cecil B. DeMille produced and directed 70 films, pioneered the development of movies' classic narrative style, and with jackboots, riding crop and outsized megaphone was the archetypal dictatorial director of public perception. The son of a lay preacher, he acted in and managed his mother's theatre troupe.

Forming a film company with Jesse L. Lasky and Samuel Goldwyn (then Goldfish), he set off to shoot in Flagstaff, Arizona, but ended up in the then sleepy village of Hollywood where he made the town's first-ever feature, *The Squaw Man* (1914), a commercial and critical success. Establishing Paramount Pictures, he ploughed money into sets rather than stars, instigated the switch to features and became associated with biblical epics and the "cast of thousands". DeMille earned Oscar nominations for *The Ten Commandments* (1923) and its spectacular remake (1956), but didn't win the statuette until a special award in 1949, followed by another for *The Greatest Show on Earth* (1952). It was around this time that DeMille's self-celebrated autocracy was again exhibited in his leading role in the anti-Communist witch-hunt of the era. He once said, "Every time I make a picture, the critics' estimation of the American public goes down 10%", but by the time of his death his pictures had grossed a staggering $750 million, and Hollywood had become the film capital of the world.

Robert De Niro

Actor, director
Born: *New York, NY, August 17, 1943*

De Niro is the Method actor's actor. Widely regarded as the finest performer of his generation, he immerses himself in his roles, putting on 60 pounds to play boxer Jake La Motta in Scorsese's seminal *Raging Bull* (1980) and wearing period silk boxer shorts to get into the role of Al Capone in *The Untouchables* (1987). He studied acting with Stella Adler, and made his first big cinema splash as a fatally ill baseball player in *Bang the Drum Slowly* (1973). *Mean Streets* (1973) marked the start of his collaboration with Scorsese, and together they have produced

some of the richest and most disturbing studies in anti-heroism ever to hit the screen: *Taxi Driver* (1976); *Raging Bull* (1980); *The King of Comedy* (1983) and *Cape Fear* (1991). His list of credits spans

Robert De Niro: *Fearfully fine in* Cape Fear

some of the most influential films of the past two decades – *The Godfather Part Two* (1974), for which he won his first Oscar (he got another for *Raging Bull*); *The Deer Hunter* (1978); *Goodfellas* (1990) – while he has recently turned his hand to directing with *A Bronx Tale* (1993). There are few actors who can match De Niro's intensity and involvement, although he is not as natural, and hence not as easy to watch, as Newman or Nicholson. Great actor, but not the sort of guy you want to take home to meet mum.

Vittorio De Sica

Director, actor
Born: *Sora, Italy, July 7, 1901*
Died: *November 11, 1974*

Renowned film-maker De Sica directed around 25 films from *Teresa Venerdi* (1941) onwards, garnering praise from critics and public throughout the world, and picking up many awards, including a remarkable four Oscars for Best Foreign Film. His realist works are among the best examples of their Italian post-war kind,

spearheading a new, influential school of film-making, and his *Shoeshine* (1946), *Bicycle Thieves* (1948), *Miracle in Milan* (1950) and *Umberto D* (1952) are considered among the all-time greats. After making his film acting debut in 1918 in *The Clemenceau Affair*, he was a polished heart-throb in Italian movies of the 1920s and 1930s, and he continued his acting after World War Two to finance his films, appearing in *Madame de* (1952), *Bread, Love and Dreams* (1953), *A Farewell to Arms* (1957) and *The Shoes of the Fisherman* (1968). As director, he lost his way in the 1960s, struggling on such international pictures as the Peter Sellers comedy *After the Fox* (1966) and *A Place for Lovers* (1969), though several collaborations with the two big Italian stars Sophia Loren and Marcello Mastroianni brought fame and fortune – and an Oscar for *Yesterday, Today and Tomorrow* (1964). He also encouraged Loren to Oscar-winning peak in *Two Women* (1961). In old age he returned to form with the acclaimed *The Garden of the Finzi-Continis* (1971) which won him his fourth Best Foreign Film Oscar.

Danny De Vito

Actor, director
Born: *Asbury, New Jersey, November 17, 1944*

Diminutive, chubby and vitriolic, De Vito has become one of the cinema's most unlikely stars. He made his film debut in the forgotten *Dreams of Glass* (1968) and despite his memorable appearance in *One Flew Over the Cuckoo's Nest* (1975), produced by his erstwhile room-mate Michael Douglas, we might never have heard much more of him but for his starring role as the malignant cab company boss Louis in the classic TV comedy series *Taxi* (1978–83). During the run he did two more films with *Cuckoo's Nest* star Jack Nicholson, *Goin' South* (1978) and *Terms of Endearment* (1983). But it

was after the series that his film career really got going, when Douglas cast him as the comic relief in his comedy thriller *Romancing the Stone* (1984) and its sequel *The Jewel of the Nile* (1985). De Vito stole the show. *Ruthless People* (1986) with Bette Midler saw him on top form and by this time he was so popular that the money men allowed him to direct himself in the Hitchcock parody *Throw Momma from the Train* (1987). The films moved noticeably upmarket without losing touch with his popular audience. He quarrelled with Richard Dreyfuss in *Tin Men* (1987), manipulated Arnold Schwarzenegger in the hugely popular *Twins* (1988) and was a vintage villain as the Penguin in *Batman Returns* (1992). He continues to be Hollywood's favourite nasty little man.

James Dean

Actor
Born: *Marion, Ind., February 8, 1931*
Died: *September 30, 1955*

Anguished adonis Dean enjoyed the shortest, most meteoric career in film history. In just three films, made in the 14 months before his death, this intense, inarticulate innocent-seeming kid became a giant screen legend as the representative of the postwar generation of frustrated young people – the first American teenager. He was more than just a pretty face like Jeffrey Hunter, less of an actor than his idol Marlon Brando, whose Method acting he favoured. Dean was something else; a phenomenon, the manifestiation in the public eye of his movie *Rebel Without a Cause* (1955). His was a fast run up the ladder, moving in three years from college to TV commercials, to a clutch of bit movie roles to a brace of plays on Broadway. Returning to Hollywood in 1954, he landed the Oscar-nominated star role as mixed-up kid Cal in Steinbeck's *East of Eden* (1955), desperate for his father's love. Only one day after he completed another Oscar-nominated part in George Stevens's legendary *Giant* (1956) opposite Rock Hudson and

James Dean: *The first American teenager*

Elizabeth Taylor, Dean ran into another car in his new Porsche on the way to Salinas to take part in a race. Thousands of grief-stricken fans simply would not believe he'd been killed. Dean had died but the legend was born and his poster still hangs on bedroom walls across the world.

Alain Delon

Actor

Born: *Sceaux, France, November 8, 1935*

Delon has taken a little talent and stretched it a very long way. He is one of the major stars of French cinema and, despite his continued protestations to the contrary, essentially owes his success to his sinister good looks. His own exotic lifestyle – alleged underworld connections, and murder scandals – added to his dangerous on-screen allure, and it is no coincidence that he is at his best, and most popular, in hard-edged gangster flicks. After serving in the French marines he landed a small part in *Quand La Femme s'en Mêle* (1958). His first real success was as a murdering imposter in *Plein Soleil* (1959), after which he enjoyed a run of prestige

films with big directors: Visconti's *Rocco and his Brothers* (1960) and *The Leopard* (1963); and Antonioni's *Eclipse* (1962). His first big gangster movie was *Mélodie en Sous-Sol* (1963), and it was within this genre that he was happiest, making some grand, exciting films over the next decade: *Le Samourai* (1967); *The Sicilian Clan* (1969); *The Red Circle* (1970); *Borsalino* (1970); *Dirty Money* (1972) and *Scorpio* (1972). He was underrated as a Paris art-dealer in Losey's *Mr Klein* (1976), but, except for *Swann in Love* (1984), playing against type as a camp aristocrat, his star has been on the wane since the mid-1970s.

Catherine Deneuve

Actress

Born: CATHÉRINE DORLÉAC, *Paris, France, October 22, 1943*

In an earlier, more innocent age Cathérine Deneuve might have played saintly, imperilled heroines. As it turned out, feted by such directors as Roman Polanski, Luis Buñuel and Robert Aldrich, she became a symbol of modern-day disillusion, playing characters whose serene, luminous exterior masked a sullied, possibly deviant centre. After an inauspicious film debut aged 12 and several misguided outings with her then husband, director Roger Vadim, Deneuve struck just the right note as a pregnant shopgirl in Jacques Demy's bewitching *The Umbrellas of Cherbourg* (1964) and rose to wider fame as the unstable manicurist in swinging 1960s London in Polanski's *Repulsion* (1964). But it was film maverick Luis Buñuel who provided her with her most lasting role as the respectable wife-ornament turned hooker heroine of *Belle de Jour* (1967), collaborating with her again on his surrealistic black comedy *Tristana* (1970). These defining roles painted Deneuve as an oddly subversive sex symbol, a passive object of male possession who nevertheless remained somehow

remote and impregnable and could thus never quite be "had" in traditional terms. Performances in a similar vein sparked up Robert Aldrich's thriller *Hustle* (1975) and the alluring vampire outing *The Hunger (1982)*. Moving into elegant middle age, Deneuve gave a grand turn as a rubber plantation matriarch in 1991's *Indochine*, and brought class to 1994's *Ma Saison Préférée*. She is clearly still a force to be reckoned with.

Gérard Depardieu

Actor

Born: *Chateauroux, France, December 27, 1948*

A huge, broad-framed Gallic bear, Depardieu is both a one-man French film industry and a screen actor of unparalleled power and

Depardieu: *Large gestures and boundless energy*

range. He is a masterful, intuitive performer, a man of large gestures and boundless energy, whose oversized exterior belies his sensitivity and emotional depth. The son of an illiterate metalworker, he dabbled in petty crime before studying acting in Paris. His extraordinary rawness and magnetism soon won him small parts on television and in film, usually as a minor hoodlum, his big breakthrough coming as a petty crook in Blier's anarchic *Les Valseuses* (1973). This heralded two decades of frenetic activity, making up to five films a year, most of them eminently forgettable but all enriched by

Depardieu's commanding, charismatic presence. He was majestic in two costume dramas, *The Return of Martin Guerre* (1982) and *Danton* (1983), then earned a massive international hit with *Jean de Florette* (1986). His portrayal of a struggling, hunchbacked farmer was a glorious characterization, matched only by his flamboyant and moving performance as *Cyrano de Bergerac* (1990). The huge popularity of the latter launched him into American films, where he enjoyed worldwide success with Peter Weir's *Green Card* (1991). Quintessentially Gallic, down to owning his own vineyard, he is a vital life force at the heart of world cinema.

Marlene Dietrich

Actress, singer

Born: MARIE MAGDALENE VON LOSCH, *Berlin, Germany, December 27, 1901*
Died: *May 6, 1992*

Far more than just a film star, Dietrich was both a consummate all-round entertainer and one of the great cultural icons of the 20th century. With her peroxide hair, huge eyes, rich German voice and soulful face she radiated a magnetism and erotic grandeur that left the public spellbound and made her a living legend. Born in Berlin, she worked in cabaret

Marlene Dietrich: *Cultural icon*

before becoming an international star as Lola, the sensual nightclub singer in *The Blue Angel* (1930). Her purring voice and blatant eroticism struck a chord, and she was rushed to Hollywood for a series of unforgettable Paramount movies – *Morocco* (1930); *Dishonoured* (1931); *Shanghai Express* (1932); *Blond Venus* (1932); *The Scarlet Empress* (1934); and *The Devil Is a Woman* (1935) – all directed by her obsessive Svengali Josef von Sternberg. But her star was already waning when she broke with von Sternberg in 1935, and by 1939 she was sending up her own image in the spoof western *Destry Rides Again*. Thereafter most of her film work was in character parts, notably in Billy Wilder's *A Foreign Affair* (1948) and Fritz Lang's *Rancho Notorious* (1952), and although she continued to pop up in films throughout the 1950s and 1960s, she concentrated increasingly on a singing career. She remained mysterious, ambiguous and utterly beguiling to the end, a transcendent sorceress and a byword for sophisticated screen sexuality.

Matt Dillon

Actor
Born: *Rochelle, NY, February 18, 1964*

Dillon, the improbably named movie star who developed from "Cocteau-esque faun" to mean and moody James Dean-heir apparent, found himself in his

Matt Dillon: *A talent to impress*

twenties outstripped by his fellow brat-packer Tom Cruise. As he hit 30 in 1994, the looks and talent were there but the movies weren't.

He was just 14 when director Jonathan Kaplan plucked him from the corridors of his New York high school to co-star in his rebels without causes tale *Over the Edge* (1979). Although still a child, he showed astonishing star quality. Disney gave him top billing in *Tex* (1982), the first film of S.E. Hinton's troubled youth stories, but his stardom was sealed the following year when Francis Coppola signed him for two more Hinton tales, *The Outsiders* and *Rumble Fish* (both 1983). Coppola uses him as an icon, but the kid can act too. He showed flair for comedy in another 1960s piece *The Flamingo Kid* (1984), as a Brooklyn beach boy, and scored a mainstream hit as Gene Hackman's son in *Target* (1985). Rescue from a late-1980s rut came with his much-acclaimed mature performance as a drug addict on the run in Gus Van Sant's *Drugstore Cowboy* (1989), but the terrible thriller *A Kiss Before Dying* (1991) sent his career back into the doldrums. In the 1990s he still looks as though he has the legs for longevity, but he may need a hit of *Top Gun* proportions if he's to stay the course.

Walt Disney

Producer, animator, director
Born: *Chicago, Ill., December 5, 1901*
Died: *December 15, 1966*

Walt Disney was an artist who became an institution; a jobbing animator who made himself a part of American heritage and head of a worldwide multi-million-dollar industry. He served his apprenticeship as a commercial artist, then as a studio animator, before setting up Walt Disney Productions in 1928. The rest is history. An uncanny combination of artistic visionary, technical wizard and consummate businessman, Disney came to dominate the world of animation. He produced the first sound cartoon with Mickey Mouse's *Steamboat Willie* (1928)

and the first cartoon to win an Oscar with the pioneering Technicolor outing *Flowers and Trees* (1932). In the world's first animation feature, *Snow White and the Seven Dwarfs* (1937), Disney evolved cutting-edge camera techniques to turn previously flat images fluid and three-dimensional. The enduring appeal of this and subsequent Disney outings rests on age-old fairytale structures allied to dazzling visuals and a host of immortal characters. But Disney refused to rest with this phenomenally successful formula, branching into live-action features with *20,000 Leagues Under the Sea* (1954), television shows and epic theme parks with Disneyland, established in California in 1955. Disney may have died in 1966, but so clear-cut and comprehensive were the guidelines he set down that he lives on through his company's output, the inspiration behind Disney World, EuroDisney and blockbusters like *The Little Mermaid* (1989), *Beauty and the Beast* (1991), *Aladdin* (1992) and *The Lion King* (1994).

Robert Donat

Actor
Born: *Manchester, England, March 18, 1905*
Died: *June 9, 1958*

A popular leading man of 1930s and 1940s British film, Robert Donat's acting career was hampered and ultimately cut short by illness. With his resonant delivery and poetic good looks, he established a glowing reputation on the London stage before signing a movie contract with Alexander Korda. He proved effective in support opposite Charles Laughton and Merle Oberon in Korda's *The Private Life of Henry VIII* (1933) and made an attractive, swashbuckling hero in the title role of 1934's *The Count of Monte Cristo*, his only US outing. But America could not fail to note the professionalism of this most English of players. In 1939

Donat's place among acting luminaries was sealed with an Oscar for his generation-hopping role as the beloved schoolteacher in the antique classic *Goodbye Mr Chips*. In the infrequent film appearances which followed he gave memorable lead turns in Carol Reed's costume drama *TheYoung Mr Pitt* (1942) and as a committed barrister in the screen adaptation of Terence Rattigan's stage play *The Winslow Boy* (1948). Donat's most enduring role, though, remains that of the quick-thinking innocent on the run in 1935's *The Thirty-Nine Steps*, arguably the best-crafted, most entertaining of Alfred Hitchcock's British thrillers. It stands as a fitting peak to a film career that ended with the actor's affecting swansong as a Christian convert in *The Inn of the Sixth Happiness (1958)*, released after his death.

Kirk Douglas

Actor
Born: ISSUR DANIELOVITCH DEMSKY, *Amsterdam, NY, December 9, 1916*

That little hole in Kirk Douglas's chin has become as central a part of film iconography as Chaplin's bowler and Clint's cheroot. It has

Kirk Douglas: *Ruthless, dimpled anti-hero*

dimpled its way through an assortment of memorable films, as well as plenty of forgettable ones. Off-screen he has a reputation for being arrogant, inflexible, and intolerant of criticism – not surprising, perhaps, for a man who was brought up in abject poverty, the son of a Russian Jewish immigrant rag and bone man, who battled his way to the top against all the odds. Such toughness of character has certainly informed his greatest roles, most of which have been heroes shot through with a not altogether attractive ruthlessness and simmering discontent: the unscrupulous pugilist in Stanley Kramer's boxing flick *Champion* (1949); the cold-hearted journalist in Wilder's *Ace in the Hole* (1951); the aggressive movie producer in Vincente Minnelli's *The Bad and The Beautiful* (1952); Van Gogh in *Lust for Life* (1956); the tubercular Doc Holliday in *Gunfight at the OK Corral* (1957); the idealistic World War One French army officer in Kubrick's masterful *Paths of Glory* (1957); and the Roman slave leader in *Spartacus* (1960). Although extraordinarily effective in the right vehicle, he has scored little of note since the 1960s, and his star has now been well and truly eclipsed his son Michael's.

Michael Douglas

Actor, producer
Born: *New Brunswick, NJ, September 25, 1944*

It is much to credit of Michael Douglas, the eldest son of movie legend Kirk, that he has deliberately avoided riding on the back of his father's fame, carving instead his own considerable niche in the film industry both as an actor and highly successful producer. In the process he has proved himself to be a cannier businessman than his illustrious predecessor and, by some accounts, a better performer as well. Born in 1944, he served a long television apprenticeship in the classic 1970s series *The Streets of San Francisco*, starring his dad's pal Karl Malden. During this period he also started dabbling in movie production, scoring huge hits with *One Flew Over the*

Michael Douglas: *Carving a niche*

Cuckoo's Nest (1975) and *The China Syndrome* (1979), in which he also starred. The 1980s and 1990s saw his irresistible rise to the top of the Hollywood actors' pile, with a string of blockbuster successes including: *Romancing the Stone* (1984), *Fatal Attraction* (1987); *Wall Street* (1987); for which he won the Best Actor Oscar that had always eluded his father; *Black Rain* (1989); *Basic Instinct* (1992); and *Falling Down* (1993). Like his father he is at his best in dark, anti-heroic roles that combine guts and sex appeal with amoral ruthlessness; and it seems likely that he will remain a key component in the Hollywood dream machine for many years to come.

Richard Dreyfuss

Actor
Born: *Brooklyn, NY, October 29, 1947*

In a long career Dreyfuss has become a big star – twice. After walk-ons in *Valley of the Dolls* and *The Graduate* in 1967, George Lucas picked him to be one of the leads in *American Graffiti* (1973). When Lucas's friend Spielberg cast Dreyfuss in two of the biggest successes of all time, *Jaws* (1975) and *Close Encounters of the Third Kind* (1977), he responded by showing he could command a big-budget hit and handle straight drama as a charismatic leading man. But comedy is his forte and he won an Oscar for Neil Simon's *The Goodbye Girl* (1977) and

enlivened the black comedy *Whose Life Is It Anyway?* (1981). Suddenly everything went wrong when in 1982 he was arrested on a drugs charge. He got help to conquer his dependency, remarried and after a long lay-off rocketed back to the top in *Down and Out in Beverly Hills* (1986), with a triumphantly funny performance. He had a run of four hits in two years: *Tin Men* (1987) with Danny De Vito, as Streisand's lawyer in *Nuts* (1987), the comedy cop thriller *Stakeout* (1987) and a double role as an actor/dictator in *Moon over Parador* (1988). But the now white-haired star found success hard to hold on to. His reunion with Spielberg, *Always* (1989), was a flop, heralding a period in the 1990s when he has struggled to find a hit vehicle for his classy comedy skills.

Faye Dunaway

Actress
Born: DOROTHY FAYE DUNAWAY, *Bascom, Fla., January 14, 1941*

Brilliant at being ruthless and voracious, Dunaway machine-gunned her way to 1960s' stardom, her icy glamour set off by razor cheekbones and a dazzlingly ironic smile. Born to military par-

Faye Dunaway: *Enigmatically sexy in* Chinatown

ents, during her childhood she shifted between the US and Germany but found success easily in Hollywood shortly after her debut in *The Happening* (1967). She

was literally shot to stardom and won an Oscar nomination as the determinedly restless southern gal turned romantic outlaw, chomping cigars alongside Warren Beatty in *Bonnie and Clyde* (1967), a role already rejected by many of Hollywood's leading women. A mixed bag of roles followed, from western (1970's *Little Big Man*), swordplay (1973's *The Three Musketeers*), to disaster movie (1974's *The Towering Inferno*), but Bonnie apart she is most memorable as Mrs Evelyn Mulwray in Roman Polanski's *Chinatown* (1974). Her lack of screen warmth was exploited to the full, winning her a second Oscar nomination, but the director judged her a "gigantic pain in the ass" for her perfectionism, adding "she demonstrated certifiable proof of insanity". Nevertheless her highly strung, power-hungry TV executive earned her an Oscar for *Network* (1976), and a camped-up portrayal of Joan Crawford in *Mommie Dearest* (1981) won surprise cult favour, inviting comparison with her steely predecessor. She was over the top again in *Supergirl* (1984) but, though her alcoholic *Barfly* (1987) won substantial critical approval, a more enduring comeback was not on the cards.

Irene Dunne

Actress
Born: *Louisville, Ky., December 1, 1901*
Died: *September 4, 1990*

One of the most captivating stars of the 1930s and 1940s, Dunne trained as a singer, but sparkled in a broad spectrum of roles spanning musicals, screwball comedy, soap opera and serious drama. Very much the lady, but modern, independent and witty, she charmed audiences with her beauty, grace and passion. *Cimarron* (1931), only her second picture, began a run of five Oscar nominations, which also included

Theodora Goes Wild (1936), *The Awful Truth* (1937), *Love Affair* (1939) and *I Remember Mama* (1948). Among her other films of consequence were the classy weepies *Back Street* (1932) and *Magnificent Obsession* (1935), and the top musicals *Roberta* (1935) and *Show Boat* (1936). After a dull patch following *My Favorite Wife* (1940), happily teamed as so often with Cary Grant, she had two big post-war hits, as the governess in 1946's *Anna and the King of Siam* (the non-musical precursor of *The King and I*) and in *Life with Father* (1947). Dunne retired in 1952, shortly after playing Queen Victoria, rather convincingly too, in *The Mudlark* (1952), though the British public was less than pleased at an American star impersonating Victoria the year before Elizabeth II's coronation. She quit the screen far too early and lived to a ripe old age, spending so long in retirement that most people asked "who's Irene Dunne?" when she died in 1990.

Deanna Durbin

Actress
Born: EDNA MAE DURBIN, *Winnipeg, Canada, December 4, 1921*

Durbin was one of cinema's key child stars and most successful musical actresses. With her fresh, open face, generous nature and beautiful singing voice, she was Hollywood's own Cinderella, helping audiences to escape into a fairytale world of decent people, nice songs and happy endings. She was spotted early by MGM talent scouts and cast with Judy Garland in *Every Sunday* (1936). She was then taken up by Universal producer Joe Pasternak, who featured her in *Three Smart Girls* (1936). The combination of sugary-sweet story – little girl gets her warring parents back together – and popular songs proved an immense hit, and supplied the template for all her most successful films: *One Hundred Men and a*

Girl (1937); *Mad about Music* (1938); *That Certain Age* (1938); *Three Smart Girls Grow Up* (1939); *First Love* (1939); *It's a Date* (1940). She made the transition from teenage to adult actress with little apparent difficulty, and her performance as a New Orleans nightclub singer in *Christmas Holiday* (1944) suggested that she could have gone on to be a considerable acting force. However, the public refused to accept her as anything other than the sweet-faced little songstress, and in 1949 – aged 27 – she retired. Unlike many child stars, Durbin's fairy tale story has an upbeat ending – she married, moved to France with her husband and lived happily ever after.

Robert Duvall

Actor
Born: *San Diego, Calif., January 5, 1931*

The weatherbeaten, gimlet-eyed Robert Duvall is one of America's finest actors, a larger-than-life figure who nevertheless remains flexible and skilled enough to mesh with any chosen role without constricting "star persona" baggage. "Being a star is an agent's dream," he says, "not an actor's." Acclaimed stage work was followed by a haunting film

Robert Duvall: Gimlet-eyed actor par-excellence

debut as the mysterious Boo Radley in 1962's *To Kill a Mockingbird* and a hilarious turn as a buttoned-up major in Robert

Altman's *M*A*S*H* (1970). Top-league success arrived with Francis Coppola's *The Godfather I and II* (1972 and 1974), where his performance as the trusty family lawyer stood up well against the more flashy star turns of Marlon Brando, Al Pacino and Robert De Niro. He also scored with a creepy unbilled cameo in Coppola's *The Conversation* (1974) and teamed with the director again for a grandstand turn as the surf-loving Kilgore in the epic Vietnam odyssey *Apocalypse Now* (1979). Now entering old age, Duvall looks at his creative peak, after peppering the past two decades with a clutch of high-charged performances. He earned a Best Actor Oscar for the 1982 country-western gem *Tender Mercies* and gave a gritty turn as a veteran cop in Dennis Hopper's *Colors* (1988), while his support turn as a grizzled Indian killer sparked up Walter Hill's *Geronimo* (1994).

Clint Eastwood

Actor, director, producer
Born: *San Francisco, Calif., May 31, 1930*

The lean, mean "man with no name" is by far the biggest and most enduring movie star of the last 30 years. From *A Fistful of Dollars* (1964) to *Unforgiven* (1992), Eastwood rarely failed to fill villains with lead, and cinemas with audiences. A child of the Depression he trailed his itinerant father around the West Coast, before himself becoming a lumberjack, steelworker, swimming instructor and honky-tonk pianist. His screen debut was in *Revenge of the Creature* (1955), before television, with its tight schedules, helped shape his minimalist acting style. Unable to afford James Coburn, Sergio Leone offered Eastwood the "spaghetti western" *A Fistful Of Dollars*, in which he portrayed the coldest killer ever seen on screen. Eastwood was a giant success and went on to make *For A*

Clint Eastwood: Making our day

Few Dollars More (1965) and *The Good, The Bad and The Ugly* (1966) before returning to Hollywood. He teamed up with Don Siegel to be just as dangerous and even more unhinged in *Dirty Harry* (1971), the psycho-cop with the "go ahead, make my day" attitude problem. *Magnum Force* (1973) and other sequels kept the money coming in, but meanwhile Eastwood had turned to comedy (*Every Which Way But Loose*, 1978) and directing. His debut as director was *Play Misty for Me* (1971), and directorial credits include *High Plains Drifter* (1972), *Bird* (1988), and *Unforgiven*, a script he had waited 10 years to "age into", winning him overdue Oscars for Best Film and Director.

Blake Edwards

Director, writer
Born: WILLIAM BLAKE McEDWARDS, *Tulsa, Okla., July 26, 1922*

Blake Edwards is one of the most versatile and enduring forces in American cinema. Although best known for his broad comedies – *Breakfast at Tiffany's* (1961), *10* (1979), *Blind Date* (1987) – he has, over the past 40 years, proved himself equally at home directing thrillers, musicals, dramas and romances. He started out as an actor and scriptwriter, before making his directorial debut with the musical *Bring Your Smile Along*

(1955), thereafter gaining widespread recognition with the World War Two farce *Operation Petticoat* (1959) and the frothy romantic comedy *Breakfast at Tiffany's*. There followed an eclectic string of hits, ranging from the sustained drama of *Days of Wine and Roses* (1962), one of cinema's most disturbing portraits of alcoholism, to the delightful absurdity of *The Pink Panther* (1964). He suffered a multi-million-dollar flop with *Darling Lili* (1970), but bounced right back with the complex romance *The Tamarind Seed* (1974), starring wife Julie Andrews, and *The Return of The Pink Panther* (1974). The wacky sex comedy *10* was a huge hit and has set the tone for all his best work since – *S.O.B.* (1981); *Victor/Victoria* (1982) and *Blind Date*. A true screen maverick, Edwards is impossible to categorize, and it is perhaps this lack of definition which has denied him the consistent popularity his films seem to warrant.

Sergei Eisenstein

Director, writer, film theoretician

Born: *Riga, Latvia, January 23, 1898*
Died: *February 11, 1948*

Arguably the most important figure in the history of cinema, Eisenstein pioneered framing and editing techniques which are still frequently imitated today. He grew up in a comfortable, bourgeois home, and by the age of 10 was fluent in four languages. He enlisted in the Red Army in 1918, then moved into *agitprop* theatre but, convinced of its limitations, set to work on his debut feature, *Strike* (1925). *Pravda* commended it as "the first revolutionary creation of our cinema", and he was commissioned to make *Battleship Potemkin* (1925), one of the most remarkable films ever (see Landmark Movies). But his hostility to "socialist realism" led to

increasing criticism at home. For *Ten Days That Shook the World* (1928), all Leningrad was put at his disposal, but Trotsky's expulsion forced him to make changes, some under the personal supervision of Stalin. In the 1930s Eisenstein visited the USA where he was revered, but when promised offers failed to materialize he headed south. *Que Viva Mexico!* (1932) was over-budget and never completed, and he retreated to the USSR, where he was discredited and forced to condemn the "formalism" of his own work. He continued to make fine films, but died of a heart attack during the second part of the planned trilogy *Ivan The Terrible* (1939 and 1945). Sergei Eisenstein accelerated the artistry of film-making. Every clashing montage, subjective camera angle and slow-motion sequence has its roots in the language of his cinema.

Douglas Fairbanks Sr

Actor

Born: DOUGLAS ELTON ULMAN, *Denver, Colo., May 23, 1883*
Died: *December 12, 1939*

Dashing, Broadway-trained Fairbanks became a key silent swashbuckling hero of his day. In

Douglas Fairbanks Sr: *Archetypal buckle swasher*

the two decades from 1915 he brought his acrobatic prowess and *joie de vivre* to a series of much-loved action-adventure films, some of which remain cinema classics, including *The Mark of Zorro* (1920), *The Three Musketeers*

(1921) and *The Thief of Bagdad* (1923). Looking at pictures of this broad-built, heavy-jawed man, his status as a romantic hero might seem surprising to modern audiences, but it's well worth seeing some of his famous, and much-copied, action sequences to appreciate his startling strength and grace in movement. He might have photographed like somebody's dad but on screen he was like a cat, and his films are among the few from this era apart from silent comedies that still delight. Also a luminary of Hollywood society, he was married to the equally famous silent star Mary Pickford with whom he founded the United Artists film studio along with D. W. Griffith and Charles Chaplin in 1919. They lived in great style at their fairy-tale mansion "Pickfair" and their lives were a matter of avid public interest. His films embodied a spirit of eternal optimism which became unfashionable with the Depression, and the more cynical mood of the 1930s meant that audiences turned away from his films toward material with a sharper edge.

Douglas Fairbanks Jr

Actor

Born: DOUGLAS ELTON ULMAN FAIRBANKS, *New York, NY, December 9, 1909*

Son of the great Douglas Fairbanks Sr and actress Anna Beth Sully, Doug Jr had a considerable head start, entering films as a star at the age of 13 and, just as his father's career waned at the time of the Depression, his began to flower. Always an actor of considerably lighter touch than his father, he displayed a sense of self-mockery that the more cynical 1930s and 1940s found highly attractive. Mixing with the young Hollywood set exemplified by Joan Crawford, his wife from 1929 to 1933, helped him forge a more popular, modern style. By the

mid-1930s adventure had come back into fashion, and Jr mixed action movies like *Gunga Din* (1939) and *The Exile* (1947), ironically just the kind of films which had stopped being successful for Sr, with sophisticated comedies like *The Rage of Paris* (1938) and *Joy of Living*. He established himself as an honorary Englishman, spending lots of time both personally and professionally in Britain where he worked in 1934 on *Catherine the Great*, even being appointed honorary Knight of the British Empire in 1949. In the 1940s he became a significant film producer but around the early 1950s seemed to tire of movies, acting in films only rarely after *Mr Drake's Duck* (1951). Later he worked as a TV producer and for a time continued to perform on stage internationally.

Mia Farrow

Actress

Born: MARIA DE LOURDES VILLIERS FARROW, *Los Angeles, Calif., February 9, 1945*

Despite her enduring image as wide-eyed and vulnerable, Farrow has courted controversy off-screen, notably in her very public separations from Frank Sinatra, André Previn and, most notoriously, Woody Allen. Daughter of director John Farrow and Tarzan's

Mia Farrow: *Cutting-edge talent*

Jane, Maureen O' Sullivan, she made her debut in *John Paul Jones* (1959), and was a major hit on TV in *Peyton Place* and as Polanski's devil-victim in *Rosemary's Baby* (1968). Her 1966 marriage to Frank Sinatra, 30 years her senior, was followed two years later by divorce, with Farrow receiving an arsenic cake from an outraged fan. She went on to partner Robert Redford as the doomed Daisy Buchanan in *The Great Gatsby* (1974), but will forever be associated with Woody Allen and his films. The first of 12 such collaborations as Woody's muse began with *A Midsummer Night's Sex Comedy* (1981), included *The Purple Rose of Cairo* (1985), *Hannah and Her Sisters* (1985) and culminated with the title role in *Alice* (1991), said largely to be based on her real self. But in 1992 the most acrimonious of splits severed the seemingly perfect partnership. Allen was having an affair with her adopted daughter, and Farrow accused him of abusing another (one of seven adopted and four biological children of Farrow's). The court case generated sensational publicity, with as many psychiatrists as lawyers involved. Allen was cleared of abuse, Farrow got custody of the children, but her career's most productive period looked to be over.

Rainer Werner Fassbinder

Director, writer, actor, producer, playwright
Born: *Bad Wörishofen, Germany, May 31, 1946 (aka FRANZ FASSBINDER)*
Died: *June 10, 1982*

A leading light of the new German cinema, created a body of work wallowing in decadence and despair. His prolific output of films, stage and television in the 1970s suggests an almost manic energy. His parents divorced in 1951 and Fassbinder described his childhood as "lonely and lacking in love and affection". In the 1960s, while directing an avant-garde theatre company and experimenting with short films, he met the actors, such as Hanna Schygulla, and the technicians, who became the basis of his film "repertory company". His films, shot on low budgets and minimalist sets, were marked by static camera work, mannered dialogue and an air of ambiguity, while his choice of themes seemed designed to shock – mass murder, lesbianism, homosexuality, and in the case of *Ali: Fear Eats the Soul* (1974), the film which brought him international recognition, the socially defiant relationship between an ageing cleaning woman and a young Moroccan immigrant. At home his film themes and open homosexuality provoked hostility and charges of anti-Semitism, anti-Communism and anti-feminism, until *The Marriage of Maria Braun* (1978), which dealt with the moral cost of Germany's post-war economic recovery. Later work includes the epic television serial *Berlin-Alexanderplatz* (1980), the big-budget *Lili Marleen* (1981) and his last film, the theatrically imaginative but spiritually bankrupt *Querelle* (1982). He died in his Munich apartment of sleeping pills and cocaine.

Alice Faye

Actress, singer, dancer
Born: ALICE JEANNE LEPPERT, *New York, NY, May 5, 1912*

Plump, blonde, cute and cuddly, with large eyes and a sweet temperament, Faye was the delightful, effervescent star of a string of enjoyable 1930s musicals. An entertaining comedienne, she had a beautiful contralto voice, was highly regarded by the likes of Irving Berlin and Cole Porter, and when it came to projecting a song on screen few could match her. She worked as chorus girl before making her film debut as the lead in *George White's Scandals* (1934). Audiences immediately took to her appealing voice and amiable nature, and she was soon established as a major musical star. She was particularly effective in period movies, with bright costumes and sentimental songs, scoring notable successes with *In Old Chicago* (1938); *Alexander's Ragtime Band* (1938); *Little Old New York* (1940); *Lillian Russell* (1940); and *Hello Frisco Hello* (1943). She worked well with Carmen Miranda in *That Night in Rio* (1941) and *Weekend in Havana* (1941), and was surprisingly good as a wealthy spinster in the straight murder mystery *Fallen Angel* (1945). However, in the mid-1940s she fell out with her studio, Fox, who were reluctant to cast her out of musicals, and she showed few regrets about quitting movies to spend more time with her family. She was tempted back only twice in intervals between a busy stage and recording career – for *State Fair* (1962) and *The Magic of Lassie* (1978).

Federico Fellini

Director, writer, actor
Born: *Rimini, Italy, January 20, 1920*
Died: *October 31, 1993*

One of the giants of the Italian cinema, Fellini has moved progressively away from narrative storytelling towards the surreal, image-led style of dreams and nightmares. Details of Felllini's early life were embellished by his imagination, as many of them became grist to his creative mill. At 17 he took to an aimless truant street life – the subject of his first success *I Vitelloni* (1953). He worked as a cartoonist, for a theatre troupe – the inspiration for his first film *Variety Lights* (1951) – and eventually got into films assisting Rossellini. The success of *I Vitelloni* was followed by *La Strada* (1954), with Fellini's wife, Giulietta Masina, star of many of his films, as the waif who is bought but never owned by Anthony Quinn's bewildered bully. That and *Le Notti di Cabiria* (1957) won Oscars, and *La Dolce Vita* (1960) won sensational headlines and young admirers for its picture of the decadent sweet life of the Via Veneto idle rich. The dreamlike aspects of that became more evident in subsequent work – the fantasy and self-analysis of *8½* (1963), the Freudian *Juliet of the Spirits* (1965), the surreal connections of *Satyricon* (1969), distorted memories of *Amarcord* (1973) and the eccentricity of Donald Sutherland's performance as *Casanova* (1976), offset by the surprisingly accessible, nostalgic and much underrated *Ginger and Fred* (1984).

Fernandel

Actor
Born: FERNAND JOSEPH DÉSIRÉ CONSTANDIN/CONTANDIN, *Marseilles, France, May 8, 1903*
Died: *February 26, 1971*

With his horse-like face, huge white teeth and bubble eyes, Fernandel was one of France's most popular and prolific stars. He made over 150 films in a career spanning 40 years and, while best known for his comic characterizations, proved the consummate all-round actor, giving some of his finest performances in straight roles. He was a comic singer before landing his first screen role as a messenger boy in *Le Blanc et Le Noir* (1930). There followed a series of farces, including Jean Renoir's first talkie – *On Purge Bébé* (1931) – before he gained widespread recognition in *Le Rosier de Madame Husson* (1932). As a kind-hearted village idiot, he was at once poignant, comical, ridiculous and lovable, and never significantly deviated from those characteristics in future work. He was unforgettable as a cuckolded knife-grinder in Pagnol's *Harvest* (1937); as a jeweller's assistant in *Fric Frac* (1939); and as an irascible village priest in *The Little World of*

Don Camillo (1952), and though the disappointments were plentiful he never lost his capacity to produce an unexpected *tour de force*, notably as an escaped prisoner of war in *The Cow and I* (1959). One of the most loved of French stars, Fernandel worked right up until his death, with his many creative flops overlooked by a tolerant moviegoing public.

Sally Field

Actress, producer
Born: SALLY FIELD MAHONEY, *Pasadena, Calif., November 6, 1946*

A petite actress with a strong talent for both comedy and drama, she transformed herself from cute and wholesome television juvenile to a big-screen star of note, confounding those who dismissed her career as finished in the mid-1970s. The daughter of acting parents, she starred in two popular television series in the 1960s and a number of TV movies but made her dramatic mark winning an Emmy as the fragmented personality *Sybil* (1977). She gained international attention as union organizer *Norma Rae* (1979), won Oscars for that and her role as the plucky widow in *Places in the Heart* (1981), shone as the investigative reporter opposite Paul Newman in *Absence of Malice* (1981) and was touching as James Garner's young lover in *Murphy's Romance* (1987). She turned producer for *Punchline* (1989), mixing comedy and drama as a housewife determined to be a stand-up comic. She played another of her "tough and tiny women" roles in the underrated *Not Without My Daughter* (1991) and the soap queen in the critically dismissed satirical comedy *Soapdish* (1991). She was good, if just a little young-looking, as Julia Roberts's mother in *Steel Magnolias* (1989), though ironically has since shown herself quite at ease with her middle years, playing Robin Williams's estranged wife in *Mrs*

Doubtfire (1993) without benefit of glamorous make-up and Tom Hanks's mother in *Forrest Gump* (1994).

Dame Gracie Fields

Actress, singer, comedienne
Born: GRACE STANSFIELD, *Rochdale, England, January 9, 1898*
Died: *September 27, 1979*

"Our Gracie", the chirpy Lancashire lass, won the hearts of the British public with her comic songs, ballads and spirited working-class heroines, but never quite translated her colloquial talents overseas. Born above a fish-and-chip shop, she was hugely popular

Our Gracie: *Singing for England*

as a music-hall entertainer, made her first sound recording in 1928, and became a radio star of such importance that Parliament once adjourned to listen to her show. Coming to the screen in her thirties she quickly became Britain's highest-paid, and best-loved film star. Her cheery spirit was just what the British public wanted during the Depression years, and from her debut *Sally In Our Alley* (1931) to *Sing As We Go* (1934) she generated a string of hits. In *Look Up And Laugh* (1935) she played middle class for the first time, but to less effect, and *Queen Of Hearts* (1936) was directed by Monty Banks, the former silent comic who was later to become her second husband. Despite US backing in the late 1930s, she remained a mystery across the Atlantic, until

she controversially moved there during the war. Banks was Italian-born and threatened with internment by the British authorities, but Gracie's departure seemed like betrayal and her popularity at home waned. Fields was made a Dame in 1979, and returned to open the Rochdale theatre named after her, before dying of a heart attack.

W. C. Fields

Actor, comedian, juggler, misanthropist, child-hater
Born: WILLIAM CLAUDE DUKINFIELD, *Philadelphia, Pa., February 10, 1879*
Died: *December 25, 1946*

The bulbous-nosed, boozy vaudevillian became one of Hollywood's most inimitable star comedians, exponent of the complaining but good-hearted reprobate, the eternally optimistic victim in a malicious world full of babies and mothers-in-law. Renowned for his deadpan delivery and perfect timing, his cynical attitudes ensure he has always retained a big cult following. At 11 he became a runaway and lived on the streets for three years. He started in vaudeville at 14 with a comic juggling act, which he later tried to include in every movie role. After a spell in the Ziegfeld Follies, Fields acted in both stage and screen versions of the musical *Poppy*, and Paramount signed him up. His career took off with the

Fresh Fields: *W.C. spies a child*

arrival of the talkies and he was soon writing and improvising his own films. His Micawber in *David Copperfield* (1935) was a great success, despite a juggling routine Dickens forgot. He drank hard and was taken ill during the remake of *Poppy* (1936) and it was finished without him. But some of his best work was to follow, notably *The Bank Dick* (1940) and *Never Give a Sucker an Even Break* (1941). A casting agent's dream came off when he was paired with the equally eccentric Mae West in *My Little Chickadee* (1940). Diagnosed with polyneuritis in 1942, he continued to drink and work, dying on Christmas Day 1946.

Peter Finch

Actor
Born: WILLIAM MITCHELL, *London, England, September 28, 1916*
Died: *January 14, 1977*

Finch had good looks, star presence and acting talent – at least when the roles were right. His were the kind of craggy, matinée idol looks that, like Cary Grant's, got better with age. He was adept at nice, honourable, middle-class, Trevor Howard sort of people – doctors, administrators, authors – and was at his best conveying intelligence and thought. Though Finch never quite became a Hollywood star, he had a long and honourable career in England, thanks in part to a long-term contract with the Rank Organization. This proved a mixed blessing: Rank kept him in work but there were a lot of feeble movies as well as several huge hits. When the contract ended in 1961, his films became more adventurous and his career blossomed. The work kept coming, quality work with respected directors, and he didn't have to escape to Europe to find it. Cast against type, he was remarkably sensitive as Oscar Wilde in *The Trials of Oscar Wilde* (1960) and as a gay doctor in Schlesinger's

Sunday, Bloody Sunday (1971) Finch won the British Film Academy Best Actor award five times, the last as the "mad as hell" TV anchorman in *Network* (1976), for which he also made history as the first player to win a posthumous Oscar. He died at the highest point of his career, just at the moment he might have cracked Hollywood's major league.

Albert Finney

Actor, director

Born: *Salford, England, May 9, 1936*

When Finney's definitive working-class hero burst onto the screen in 1960, all virility, swagger and youthful sex appeal, in the influential *Saturday Night and Sunday Morning*, he became British cinema's hottest property. Three years later *Tom Jones* was even more successful, turning him into an international star and millionaire. Since then he's retained his position as major star, moving easily between film and theatre, and finding work in America, thanks partly to having perfected an acceptable American accent. But Finney has made too few movies and not all have reached the highest standards. He's not at his best in light entertainments such as *Two for the Road* (1967), the musicals *Scrooge* (1970) and *Annie* (1982), or as Poirot in *Murder on the Orient Express* (1974). But when he's given really meaty roles, like *Charlie Bubbles* (1968), the tough thriller *Gumshoe* (1971), *Shoot the Moon* (1982) opposite Diane Keaton, *The Dresser* (1983) or John Huston's *Under the Volcano* (1984), he can do little wrong. In his fifties he's still full of energy and youthful hunger for further peaks to climb. He was terrific in *Orphans* (1987), as an Irish mobster in *Miller's Crossing* (1990), as the frustrated older Irishman in *The Playboys* (1992) and as Terence Rattigan's crusty schoolteacher in *The Browning Version* (1994). He

may yet achieve the destiny predicted for him as "the new Olivier".

Errol Flynn

Actor

Born: *Hobart, Tasmania, June 20, 1909*
Died: *October 14, 1959*

With legs up to his armpits and cheekbones sharp enough to cut diamonds on, Errol Flynn was *the* swashbuckling sex bomb of Hollywood in the 1930s and early 1940s, starring in some of the most memorable romantic adventure movies of all time. He spent his early years knocking around the South Seas before making his screen debut as a corpse in *The Case of the Curious Bride* (1935). He was given the lead in the swash-

Errol Flynn: *Insouciant tongue-in-cheek-heroism*

buckling adventure yarn *Captain Blood* (1935), and thereafter enlivened a host of adventure classics with his laid-back, insouciant, tongue-in-cheek heroism: *The Charge of the Light Brigade* (1936); *The Adventures of Robin Hood* (1938); *The Dawn Patrol* (1938); and *They Died with Their Boots On* (1941). These established him, if not as a great actor, at least as one of the cinema's great romantic leads. However, he was drinking

increasingly heavily, and his career tailed off through the 1940s and early 1950s. It was only in his bloated and ravaged final years, portraying an alcoholic wastrel in *The Sun Also Rises* (1957) and the alcoholic John Barrymore in *Too Much Too Soon* (1958), that he showed once again some of the magnetism and charisma that had informed his earlier work. He died in Vancouver in 1959.

Bridget Fonda

Actress

Born: *Los Angeles, Calif., January 27, 1964*

Grand-daughter of Henry and daughter of Peter. Blessed with good looks and a bubbly personality, she seems to have inherited a lot of the family talent. When given a good script she shines, and she has also enlivened some indifferent films. She made her debut in the Franc Roddam segment of the opera film *Aria* (1987) in a non-singing role, and continued for a while working in British films. She was one of the ensemble cast of Zelda Barron's affectionately nostalgic youth film *Shag* (1987), and then gave a memorably perky performance as Mandy Rice-Davies in Michael Caton Jones's *Scandal* (1989), about the Christine Keeler affair which shook Britain in the 1960s, following that up with her role as Blair Brown's sluttish younger sister in David Hare's *Strapless* (1989). She returned to America to play the young journalist in *The Godfather: Part Three* (1990) and appeared in *Singles* (1992), a genuinely charming variation on the theme of the youthful mating game. The same year she was terrorized by roommate Jennifer Jason Leigh in Barbet Schroeder's thriller *Single White Female* (1992) and then chose a dud with *The Assassin* (1993), John Badham's misconceived remake of Besson's *Nikita*. She fared better in the comedy *It Could Happen to You* (1994), sharing a big lottery win and a romance with Nicholas Cage.

Henry Fonda

Actor

Born: HENRY JAYNES FONDA, *Grand Island, Nebr., May 16, 1905*
Died: *August 12, 1982*

His good looks, slow-spoken sincerity and overall manner of gentle reliability embodied all the qualities Americans saw as being best in their national character. A descendant of early Dutch settlers,

Henry Fonda: *Fine-grained American institution*

Fonda was a founder member of a theatre company which included his first wife, Margaret Sullavan, and James Stewart. He scored a success on Broadway in *The*

Farmer Takes a Wife, then went to Hollywood to repeat the role on film (1935). Within two years he was an established star. Twin peaks of his early career were two John Ford movies, *Young Mr Lincoln* (1939) and *The Grapes of Wrath* (1940). After his navy service in the Pacific, critics detected a new maturity in his post-war performances, such as *My Darling Clementine* (1946) and his first unsympathetic role *Fort Apache* (1948), also the year of his Broadway comeback as *Mister Roberts*. He did not return to Hollywood until 1955 to make the film version. Thereafter he divided his time between stage and screen. Later film roles include Pierre in *War and Peace* (1956), the patient juror who saves a man's life in *Twelve Angry Men* (1957) and a succession of ageing sheriffs, politicians, police chiefs and other public officials. His Best Actor Oscar came for his final performance as the querulous and outspoken old man in *On Golden Pond* (1981), although a year earlier he had been given an honorary Academy Award.

Jane Fonda

Actress
Born: *New York, NY, December 21, 1937*

It's hard to imagine a more varied and eventful life than that experi-

Jane Fonda: Out-of-this-world sex symbol

enced by the flame-headed, self-possessed Jane Fonda. Born into the Hollywood aristocracy, the daughter of actor Henry, she went from catwalk model to leading lady, was christened "Hanoi Jane", reviled for her opposition to the Vietnam War, pocketed a fortune from her much-hyped fitness videos and is now perceived as an impregnable queen of the US establishment; happily hitched to media tycoon Ted Turner. At her film-making peak in the late 1960s and early 1970s, Fonda was box-office aphrodisiac, a shapely hybrid of Hollywood and the hippie culture. Her featherlight touch let her run rings around co-star Robert Redford in Neil Simon's vogueish romantic soufflé *Barefoot in the Park* (1967), while husband Roger Vadim, capitalizing on her tomboyish sexuality, cast her as the bikini-clad *Barbarella* (1968), a kitsch pop-culture assemblage that combined comic-book fantasy with 1960s hedonism. But as the counter-culture's exuberance gave way to self-reflecting cynicism, so Fonda's work took on a notably darker hue. She was heartfelt and affecting in *They Shoot Horses, Don't They?* (1969) and won an Oscar for her portrait of a high-class prostitute in Alan Pakula's majestic thriller *Klute* (1971). Over the past two decades Fonda has limited her film work, while significant roles have been thinner on the ground, despite an acclaimed turn in the fact-based *Julia* (1977) and a sensitive performance opposite Robert De Niro in the socially conscious *Stanley and Iris* (1989).

Glenn Ford

Actor
Born: GWYLLYN SAMUEL NEWTON, *Quebec, Canada, May 1, 1916*

Ford is the all-but-forgotten star. Other than *Gilda* (1946), the *film noir* with Rita Hayworth which made his name, it's hard to recall

more than a handful of notable roles: his ex-cop in Fritz Lang's *The Big Heat* (1953), his harassed teacher in *The Blackboard Jungle* (1955), his villain in Delmer Davies's western *3.10 to Yuma* (1957), and his two outings with Bette Davis, *A Stolen Life* (1946) and *A Pocketful of Miracles* (1962). Born in Quebec in 1916, Ford was a product of the studio system, signed up by Columbia Pictures in the late 1930s after theatre work in California. He married actress Eleanor Powell in 1943 and served as a marine in World War Two. *Gilda* was his reward, and for 15 years his career blossomed. Ford was busy and popular with the public, and indeed in 1958 he was the box office's top-rated star. By the 1960s the public had begun to tire of his solid, dependable, regular-guy persona. Ford spent most of the decade making westerns and in 1971–72 had a successful TV cowboy series in *Cade's County*. But westerns went out of fashion and, apart from the odd cameo appearance such as Clark Kent's dad in *Superman* (1978), and a few TV movies, he slid into happy retirement.

Harrison Ford

Actor
Born: *Chicago, Ill., July 13, 1942*

Rugged and good-looking, with a Bogartian sneer and an action-man scar on his chin, Ford personifies America's cherished ideal of the courageous, intelligent, self-deprecating frontiersman. It is this identification with a national self-image that has made him *the* action-adventure film superstar of the 1980s and early 1990s. He landed a seven-year contract with Columbia at the age of 24, but was then humiliatingly dropped after a few minor parts in minor films: "You ain't got it, kid," one studio executive dourly informed him. He gave up acting in favour of carpentry, but was soon back on screen in a series of roles, culmi-

nating in his breakthrough movie, *Star Wars* (1977). The arrogant, egocentric, sneering good-guy Han Solo set the tone for his cre-

Harrison Ford: "He's got it, kid"

ations in a series of comic-strip mega-blockbusters: *Raiders of the Lost Ark* (1981); *Blade Runner* (1982); *Witness* (1985); *Indiana Jones and the Last Crusade* (1989); and *The Fugitive* (1993). Though forays into light comedy (*Working Girl*, 1988) and nervous breakdown (*The Mosquito Coast*, 1986) suggest untapped acting reserves, his range is not particularly broad. Still, if there's a woman to be saved or justice to be done then Harrison's the man for the job.

John Ford

Director, writer
Born: SEAN O'FEENEY, *Cape Elizabeth, Me., February 1, 1895*
Died: *August 31, 1973*

John Ford is the bigger-than-life colossus of American screen, a man whose life and art are woven into the fabric of US history. Born into the last years of the Wild West, he was to return to this epoch throughout a 60-year career, constantly re-examining and celebrating the events by which his nation was born. Shooting 1946's *My Darling Clementine*, his dramatization of the gunfight at the OK Corral, Ford had no doubts of the film's authenticity: "I knew Wyatt and he told me all about it ... We did it exactly the way it had been." His pictures' politics might now look reactionary yet this was no dubious hindsight romanticism but a vision governed by the sensibilities of the Old West – the sanctity of church and family, the base wickedness of the Red Indian. For although Ford often tussled effectively with contemporary settings – most impressively with the Depression odyssey *The Grapes of Wrath* (1940) – it is with the western that he remains inextricably linked. Despite viewing himself as no more than a proficient craftsman, he was lionized by *auteur-theorist* critics who hailed his muscular, lyrical style and the consistency of his concerns. In later years Ford's work became subtler and more reflective, with *The Man Who Shot Liberty Valance* (1962) and his *tour de force The Searchers* (1956) revealing new understanding of the darker, more complex implications of the frontier legend his film-making skill had largely helped create.

Milos Forman

Director, writer

Born: *Caslav, Czechoslovakia, February 18, 1932*

Milos Forman was Czechoslovakia's premier filmmaker, a modern product of Eastern Europe's folk-tale tradition who struggled to adapt his delicate style to a broader canvas, following his 1968 move to the US. His best early work, *Loves of a Blonde* (1965) or *The Fireman's Ball* (1968) used amateur performers and part-improvised dialogue to paint idiosyncratic portraits of working-class life, but a similar approach in his first American effort, the clever but unloved *Taking Off* (1971) worked less well. "My English was still very poor," Forman confesses. "In scenes where I encouraged improvisation, very often I didn't understand a word the actors were saying." By 1975 Forman was confident enough with the new culture to tackle a screen adaptation

of one of its finest contemporary novels, Ken Kesey's *One Flew Over the Cuckoo's Nest*. A savagely staged study of rebellion and conformity, it swept the Oscar board picking up six awards including Best Picture, Director and Actor (for Jack Nicholson's high-fuelled central turn). Since that triumph, Forman's career has been patchy. He scored big popular success with the inventive *Amadeus* (1984), but a 1979 screen version of hippie musical *Hair* arrived about a decade too late, while an adaptation of E.L. Doctorow's multilevelled *Ragtime* (1981) looked shapeless and ill-conceived. At the end of the 1980s *Valmont* (1989), his finely fashioned tale of sexual shenanigans in imperial France, was sadly overlooked in favour of Stephen Frears's *Dangerous Liaisons* (1988).

George Formby

Comic, singer

Born: GEORGE BOOTH, *Wigan, England, May 26, 1904*
Died: *March 6, 1961*

The Lancashire music-hall comedian with the cheeky charm and ever-ready ukulele was just what 1930s audiences wanted. He was a hit in Empire countries and Europe too, though he never cracked America. Son of a north-country comic, he tried his hand as a jockey, but took to the boards at 16 and was soon topping the bill. He toured Britain both solo and as a double act with his wife Beryl, who managed his career purposefully. After success as a record and radio star, he jumped on to the movie bandwagon with a series of 16 films from 1934 to 1947, the first, *Boots Boots* (1933) being made in a converted garage for £3,000. A bigger-budget outing, *Off the Dole* (1935), followed, leading to a contract with Ealing studios. The films of this period are attractive and jolly with broad satirical swipes at easy targets such as bus conductors, ice-skaters, policemen and

spies (*Let George Do It*). Ealing's talented writers knew how to create successful vehicles for him, but after he left for Columbia-British in 1942 his films struggled to match the winning formula. The post-war mood brought a total change in taste that abruptly ended Formby's career, as the British public rejected the light, homely comedy of the 1930s. Formby returned to the theatre and at the time of his death his career was on the up and up again.

Jodie Foster

Actress, director

Born: ALICIA CHRISTIAN FOSTER, *Los Angeles, Calif., November 19, 1962*

Few child stars become successful adult stars, but just one film did the trick for Foster, *The Accused* (1988), winning 1989's Best Actress Oscar for her powerful performance in a controversial film about sexual responsibility. As the lustful Sexy Sadi gang-raped in a bar, Foster again shows her ability to play the vamp, first displayed when she played the

Jodie Foster: *The world at her feet*

torch singer Tallulah in *Bugsy Malone* (1976), when she was only 12 but she seemed completely grown up. That quality landed her another tricky role – as a teenage prostitute in *Taxi Driver* (1976) – bringing a blaze of controversy, and she returned to making films

with Disney, *Candleshoe* (1977) and *Freaky Friday* (1977). But she burst on to world headlines again in 1981 when John Hinkley said he'd shot President Reagan to prove his love for her. Wisely she worked at her studies, gaining a literature degree from Yale. Back in the movies, she fought her way to the top as an adult in oddball films like *Hotel New Hampshire* (1984) and *Five Corners* (1987). Her second Oscar as the FBI officer stalking Hannibal "the Cannibal" Lecter in *The Silence of the Lambs* (1991) confirmed her place at the top of the Hollywood pile. She made a low-key directing debut with *Little Man Tate* (1991) before emerging a confident leading lady in mainstream pictures like *Sommersby* (1992) and *Maverick* (1994); a beautiful, stylish woman with the world at her feet.

Michael J. Fox

Actor

Born: *Edmonton, Canada, June 9, 1961*

Despite limitations as an actor, Fox may well be remembered as the most representational film star of 1980s America. Twinkly-eyed and baby-faced, he was a teen icon in the Donny Osmond mould – sexually unthreatening, perpetually pubescent. At 17 he played a 10-year-old on Canadian television and nearing his 30th birthday was still acting the teenager in *Back to the Future III* (1990). Fox's screen persona made him the movie symbol of yuppie USA. After rising to fame as the Reaganite nipper in the TV sitcom *Family Ties*, he scored with audiences as a high-school loser turned canine winner in 1985's *Teen Wolf*. Stratospheric success greeted his next film outing, *Back to the Future* (1985), starring as the skateboarding whiz sent back to the 1950s to match-make his mismatched parents. But the most significant Fox role remains his turn as the bright-as-a-button mailroom clerk who thrusts his way to corporate stardom in the lightweight yuppie manual *The Secret of My Success* (1987). As the decade wore on Fox's film image looked increasingly outmoded and a brave move into "serious acting" floundered with the misconceived *Bright Lights, Big City* (1988). In the 1990s his appearances have carried less popular impact, despite a neat turn in the Capra-esque *Doc Hollywood* (1991) and a valiant stab at black comedy with 1994's *Greedy*.

John Frankenheimer

Director

Born: *New York, NY, February 19, 1930*

For a brief period in the 1960s John Frankenheimer was perhaps America's most powerful, provocative film director. A master craftsman in monochrome, his shadowy black and white studies brilliantly caught the essence of a nation stricken with cold-war paranoia. After early work in television, he flexed his film-making muscles with the claustrophobic yet ultimately liberating *Birdman of Alcatraz* (1962), spotlighting Burt Lancaster's Oscar-nominated turn as the Job-like prisoner Robert Stroud. But it was with the political suspenser that Frankenheimer really excelled, again casting Lancaster as a rebelling US general in the tautly crafted *Seven Days in May* (1964). Frankenheimer's undoubted film-making peak came with the banned 1962 picture *The Manchurian Candidate*, a work of feverish, sustained ferocity, packed with tangled psychology and bravura setpieces and anchored by a career-best turn from a battle-worn Frank Sinatra. Resonant and disturbing, it ranks with the finest political thrillers ever made. From the mid-1960s John Frankenheimer seemed gradually to lose the white-hot skill that typified his early work. While his inventive handling was still

apparent in efforts like the gripping *Seconds* (1966) or *The French Connection II* (1975), the great pictures were fewer and farther between. Maybe Frankenheimer has been too much a product of his time, the voice of a cold-war USA both mistrustful of outside attack and suspicious of internal manipulation.

Sam Fuller

Director, writer

Born: *Worcester, Mass., August 12, 1911*

Sam Fuller's early experiences as a crime reporter and soldier during World War Two obviously shaped the hard-bitten cynicism that underpins the bulk of his films as writer and director. Long dismissed in Hollywood as a disreputable manipulator, his rough-edged, choppy film-making style and tough handling of taboo topics proved a major influence on the rising talent of the 1960s, particularly the French New Wave. In later years, Fuller made guest appearances in Godard's *Pierrot le Fou* (1965) and Dennis Hopper's phantasmagoric *The Last Movie* (1971). Fuller fashions his greatest films around the tensions between the individual and a social group, defiantly breaking down conventional notions of good and evil. In *Pickup on South Street* (1953) a cramped subway carriage becomes a microcosm for an alienating, acquisitive world, while the controversial *The Naked Kiss* (1964) spotlights a woman's emerging awareness that her eminently respectable, golden-boy fiancé is also a child-molester. Fuller's tough, modern-day sensibility breathed new life and urgency into such tried-and-tested action genres as the western *Run of the Arrow*, (1957), gangster thriller *Underworld U.S.A.* (1961) or war picture *The Big Red One* (1980). His most memorable works, though, remain his most provocative, unclassifiable ones – *Shock Corridor*

(1963), a nightmarish study in mental breakdown or *White Dog* (1982), a much-maligned, hugely unsettling exploration of urban racism.

Jean Gabin

Actor

Born: JEAN-ALEXIS MONCORGÉ, *Meriel, France, May 17, 1904*
Died: *November 15, 1976*

Jean Gabin, with his broad, sad features and thin-lipped mouth, was one of the greatest and most-lauded icons of French cinema. A stoical, Gauloise-puffing, anti-heroic outsider, he personified the pre-war mood of his native country and, although the 1930s period contained his finest films, was still being voted France's most popular star as late as 1970. The son of music-hall entertainers, he made

Jean Gabin: Sad-eyed maverick of French cinema

his film debut in *Chacun sa Chance* (1930), thereafter starring in an extraordinary array of landmark French movies: as a pick-pocket in *Les Bas-Fonds* (1936); a master-crook in *Pépé Le Moko* (1937); and a prisoner of war in *La Grande Illusion* (1937). He finished the decade with his three greatest films – Jean Renoir's *Quai des Brumes* (1938) and *La Bête Humaine* (1938); and Carné's *Le Jour se Lève* (1939). The last, as a murderer holed up in a hotel waiting to be arrested, was probably the most memorable embodiment of the Gabin image – resigned, tired-of-life, dissolute. After the war Gabin

reinvented himself as a solid, faintly conservative authority figure, and spent the latter half of his career playing an array of gangsters, patriarchs and detectives, most notably in *Maigret Tend un Piège* (1958), *Les Grandes Familles* (1958), and *Mélodie en Sous-sol* (1963). But, although this later work was often effective, it is mainly for his extraordinary, iconographic creations of pre-war France that Gabin will be best remembered.

Clark Gable

Actor

Born: WILLIAM CLARK GABLE, *Cadiz, Ohio, February 1, 1901*
Died: *November 16, 1960*

Craggy and jug-eared, Clark Gable may initially have appeared an unlikely sex symbol, looking – as one contemporary wag observed – like a taxicab with its doors open. But, with his trademark pencil moustache and devil-may-care charm, he came to represent the essence of masculinity to 1930s filmgoers, decimating the underwear industry when he stripped to the waist in *It Happened One Night* (1934) and enraging America's moral guardians when he cussed out his tiresome love interest at the climax of 1939's *Gone with the Wind*: "Frankly my dear, I don't give a damn." Gable effectively came to rule popular 1930s cinema with star roles in *Red Dust* (1932),

Clark Gable: Damn fine actor

Mutiny on the Bounty (1935) and *Gone With the Wind*, his most legendary movie outing. His enduring strength stemmed from a fixed, well-defined screen persona. He was the perennial likeable rogue; the more wild half of a buddy duo with solid sometime co-star Spencer Tracy, the no-nonsense tamer of feisty film sirens Jean Harlow, Claudette Colbert and Vivien Leigh. After wartime military service and the plane-crash death of wife Carole Lombard, Gable resumed a lighter film schedule. Only in the 1950s did his box-office appeal look to be waning, though he left on a high note – powerfully cast opposite Marilyn Monroe in the elegiac western *The Misfits* (1961).

Abel Gance

Director, writer, playwright, actor

Born: ABEL PERETHON, *Paris, France, October 25, 1889*
Died: *November 10, 1981*

Innovative director of epic films, Gance was a great pioneer of cinema techniques. In the early 1980s the restoration of Gance's masterpiece *Napoléon* (1927) by British documentary director Kevin Brownlow finally brought about the overdue acknowledgement of his place in cinema history. An actor/writer from 1909, Gance made some unsuccessful shorts, but was more interested in theatre, until the outbreak of World War One, when he turned his full attention to films. By 1917 he was a big audience draw but unpopular with the "front office" who disapproved of his experimentation, which included his use of distorting mirrors and lenses for fantasy sequences in *La Folie du DrTube* (1915); the creation of Polyvision for *Napoléon* – a spectacular triple screen process which predated Cinerama by 25 years; Perspective Sonore, a forerunner of stereo, for the sound remake *Napoléon Bonaparte* (1934); and per-

haps most importantly his use of rapid editing and innovative camera movement, particularly for action sequences, where he placed his camera where none had gone before – trucks, horses, pendulums, even hand-held. Through those techniques he told powerful stories: *J'Accuse* (1918), a strong anti-war statement, using newsreel-style filming of real soldiers under fire; *La Roue* (1921), a tale of incestuous passion; and *Napoléon*, arguably the greatest epic of the silent screen. The coming of sound, combined with Gance's combative relationship with production controllers, confined him thereafter to largely unimpressive commercial films.

Bruno Ganz

Actor, director

Born: *Zurich, Switzerland, March 24, 1941*

A reliable actor with an engagingly boyish continental charm, Bruno Ganz made his mark on the international screen in his middle years. After military service, Ganz began his career in West German theatre and made his feature film debut in *Chikita* (1961). He was co-founder with director Peter Stein of the radical Schaubühne Theatre in Berlin, where he stayed for five years, returning in 1982 to play Hamlet. He first major film role was in Eric Rohmer's *The Marquise of O...* (1976). Some of his best-known work has been for Wim Wenders – *The American Friend* (1977), *Nosferatu – The Vampire* (1978) and as the angel longing to be human in *Wings of Desire* (1987), a role he reprised for Wenders in *Faraway, So Close* (1993). He was also memorable as the war correspondent suffering a crisis of conscience in Schlöndorff's *Circle of Deceit* (1981), actually filmed in war-torn Beirut. He had a supporting role in *The Boys from Brazil* (1978), and played the romantic lead as Blair Brown's charming but feckless

lover in the British film *Strapless* (1989). In 1991 he went to Australia to work on Gillian Armstrong's *The Last Days of Chez Nous*, where he was wryly sympathetic as a Frenchman whose marriage to an Australian woman is falling apart. He made his directorial debut in 1982 as co-director of *Gedächtnis*, which won several prizes in Germany.

Greta Garbo

Actress, goddess

Born: GRETA LOUISA GUSTAFSSON, *Stockholm, Sweden, September 18, 1905*
Died: *April 15, 1990*

Hard to imagine tall, ungainly, remote Garbo being a star today. Indeed would she have been a star at all had there not been silent movies? Her asexual, supercool Nordic beauty and extraordinary ability to convey extremes of emotion without words and with economy of gesture marked her out in

Greta Garbo: *Standing alone at the top*

the silent 1920s and remained her hallmarks in 1930s talkies. Unlike many contemporaries, she survived the transition to sound with a hit version of *Anna Christie* (1930) advertised as "Garbo Talks!" Her odd, throaty speaking voice worked in her favour, becoming a famous trademark as did her immortal catchphrase "I want to be alone", uttered in her 1932 hit *Grand Hotel*. Garbo's films may creak a bit now but the best still exert a powerful pull, and she

still shines as brightly as ever in them. Who looks at John Gilbert in *Queen Christina* (1933), Fredric March in *Anna Karenina* (1935) or Robert Taylor in *Camille* (1937) when she's stealing every scene? She's ideally cast as these three nobly suffering tragic heroines, and they've lasted better than her other pictures, though we still laugh with her in her long-awaited comedy *Ninotchka* (1939). Her sudden retirement at her peak in 1941 after *Two-Faced Woman* was a great loss to the movies, though it ensured her immortality. She avoided publicity and throughout her long life largely achieved her ambition to be left alone.

Ava Gardner

Actress

Born: *Grabton, NC, November 24, 1922*
Died: *January 25, 1990*

Gardner survived being voted "the world's most beautiful woman" and went on to become a considerable actress of great allure, making some memorable appearances during the 1950s. The former secretary landed an MGM contract in 1941 on the strength of her brother-in-law's photos, making a walk-on in *We Were Dancing* (1942) and her first featured appearance in her second *Dr Gillespie* movie *Three Men in White* (1944). Marriages to Mickey Rooney (1942), Artie Shaw (1945) and Frank Sinatra (1951) increased her profile, but it was playing the floozie who betrays Burt Lancaster in *The Killers* (1946) that made her a star. MGM cast her effectively as tragic Julie in *Show Boat* (1951), then opposite Gable in *Mogambo* (1953), bringing her sole Oscar nomination. She was Guinevere in *Knights of the Round Table* (1953), a gypsy dancer in *The Barefoot Contessa* (1954) and was perfectly cast in two Hemingway outings, *The Snows of Kilimanjaro* (1952) and *The Sun Also Rises* (1957). Her MGM contract ended in 1958 and with it the best phase of her career. In the 1960s, looking older but no less beautiful, she was compulsive in John Huston's *Night of the Iguana* (1964), and she also did *The Bible*

***Ava Gardner:** The world's most beautiful woman*

(1966) and *Judge Roy Bean* (1972) for him. Roles became increasingly difficult to find, and she made her final film, the D. H. Lawrence biopic *Priest of Love*, in 1981.

John Garfield

Actor

Born: JULIUS GARFINKLE, *New York, NY, March 4, 1913*
Died: *May 21, 1952*

Handsome, strong-featured and dark-haired, Garfield might have become a major star had his career not been ruined by the McCarthy witch-hunts of the early 1950s. In many ways he proved the direct precursor of Brando and Dean – an aggressive, tortured loner from the wrong side of the tracks, victimized by the world but always struggling to improve his lot, a persona made all the more powerful because he himself had grown up amidst the slums and street-gangs of downtown New York. Having worked in theatre, he made his film debut as a poor boy in love with one of four sisters in *Four Daughters* (1938). There followed a series of powerful, rebellious performances, usually as a troubled outsider: *They Made Me a Criminal* (1939); *The Sea Wolf* (1941); *Air Force* (1943); *Pride of the Marines* (1945); *The Postman Always Rings Twice* (1946). He gave three

of his greatest performances in the late 1940s: as a boxer in *Body and Soul* (1947); a victimized Jewish soldier in Kazan's *Gentleman's Agreement* (1947); and a racketeer in *Force of Evil* (1948). He was compelling as a smuggler in *The Breaking Point* (1950), but thereafter found it increasingly difficult to obtain work because of his supposed left-wing sympathies. Eventually blacklisted, he died of a heart attack in 1952.

Judy Garland

Singer, actress

Born: FRANCES ETHEL GUMM, *Grand Rapids, Minn., June 10, 1922*
Died: *June 22, 1969*

The little songbird with the big eyes and the voice that could take you to the end of the rainbow was born in a trunk, the daughter of vaudeville artistes. Garland first appeared on stage aged three, was a practised performer at five, and at 14 signed a seven-year MGM contract. She was cast opposite Mickey Rooney in a hit partnership that lasted seven movies, including *Babes in Arms* (1939) and *Strike Up the Band* (1940). But it was as Dorothy in *The Wizard of*

***Judy Garland:** As American as Gumm*

Oz (1939), taking over from Shirley Temple and singing a song that was nearly cut, the heartrending *Over the Rainbow*, that the Garland legend was born. She was already hooked on pills as a teenager, first for weight prob-

lems, then stress. At 20 she was consulting psychiatrists, and in 1941, her unhapppy marriage to the first of five husbands began a series of personal unhappinesses that undermined a supposedly fairytale career. Between suicide attempts, lawsuits, nervous breakdowns and dismissal by MGM, there were priceless high spots like *Meet Me in St Louis* (1944), *Easter Parade* (1948) and *A Star Is Born* (1954). She died in London in 1969 of an overdose, during a comeback bid. At the funeral, New York was blocked with adoring mourners and the Garland cult was born. In 1945, she married director Vincente Minnelli, and their daughter Liza carries on her musical tradition.

James Garner

Actor

Born: JAMES SCOTT BAUMGARNER, *Norman, Okla., April 7, 1928*

The man who did much to popularize telephone answering machines in television's *The Rockford Files* (1974–80) is eminently watchable with his handsome grin, laid-back charm and nice line in comic delivery, and was a top movie star of the 1960s before turning to television in the 1970s. He dropped out of school to enlist in the marines as soon as he was 16, and saw action in Korea where he was wounded and received the Purple Heart. Returning to Oklahoma, he tried university and a variety of odd jobs before being offered a stage role by an old friend. Garner's genial warmth transferred easily to his screen debut, *Toward the Unknown* (1956), and led to him starring in the television western series *Maverick* (1957–62), revived in cinemas in 1994 with Garner and Mel Gibson. Back on the big screen he replaced a disaffected Charlton Heston in *Darby's Rangers* (1958), and was a great success as the cheerful con-man in *The Great Escape* (1963).

After sparring with Doris Day in *Thrill of It All* (1963) and *Move Over Darling* (1963), he survived *Grand Prix* (1966), got meaner for *Duel at Diablo* (1966), and funnier for *Support Your Local Sheriff*, which he also produced. Despite a physique good enough to model swimming trunks in his early days, his appeal is in his wit rather than his brawn, and he was finally nominated for an Oscar, wooing Sally Field in *Murphy's Romance* (1985).

Greer Garson

Actress

Born: *County Down, Northern Ireland, September 29, 1914*

The undisputed queen of the 1940s weepie, Garson always exuded a faintly middle-aged air, even in the early days of her career. Possessed of a strong character and homely, sexless beauty, she slotted ideally into the role of Hollywood's favourite suffering wife and matriarch. She won an Oscar (giving the longest-ever acceptance speech) for her part in *Mrs Miniver* (1942), as the coura-

***Greer Garson:** Hollywood's favourite matriarch*

geous, strong-hearted mother of an English family trying to cope with the war, and played much the same character – dependable, noble, suffering – for the rest of her career. Born in Northern Ireland, she worked on the London stage before making her screen debut in *Goodbye Mr Chips* (1939).

She was perfect as the dependable, determined Elizabeth Bennett opposite Olivier in *Pride and Prejudice* (1940), excellent if sentimental as the founder of an orphanage in *Blossoms in the Dust* (1941), and outstanding in *Mrs Miniver*. This heralded a number of fine roles, notably as the wife of an amnesiac in *Random Harvest* (1942) and as the scientific heroine in *Madame Curie* (1943). However, as the 1950s dawned the type of hanky-clenching tearjerker with which she was associated started to go out of fashion, and her career tailed off. She gamely attempted other types of role and TV work, but never again touched that sentimental chord that had once made her so popular.

Janet Gaynor

Actress
Born: LAURA GAINOR, *Philadelphia, Pa., October 6, 1906*
Died: *September 14, 1984*

Janet Gaynor was the first actress to win an Academy Award. She received the honour not so much for her acting ability, which was nothing out of the ordinary, but because people adored her tiny body, little-girl face and huge, bush-baby eyes. She was the embodiment of innocent, helpless waifdom, and her success says a lot more about the sentimentality of pre-war America than her own acting skills. She started as a film extra and got her break in the early disaster movie *The Johnstown Flood* (1926). John Ford starred her in *The Blue Eagle* (1926), which was followed by the three films for which she won her Oscar – *Sunrise* (1927), *Seventh Heaven* (1927) and *Street Angel* (1928). She laid it on pretty thick as the suffering waif, and she and co-star Charles Farrell – with whom she was to star in 12 further pictures – entered popular folklore as "America's Favourite Lovebirds". Meanwhile Winfield Sheehan, chief executive of Fox, took her under his wing, promoting

her in a series of gooey smash hits – *Four Devils* (1929); *Daddy Long Legs* (1931); *Tess of The Storm Country* (1932). She then went to Selznick and made two of her finest films – *A Star is Born* (1937) and *The Young in Heart* (1938) – but her career was waning and in 1938 she decided to quit on a high note and retired.

Richard Gere

Actor
Born: *Philadelphia, Pa., August 29, 1949*

"I will not become a piece of meat just so some jerk will pay $5 to look at an image on a screen," says Gere. "I think people can be educated from negative cheap-thrill movies to great movies." Yet Gere has traded heavily on his good looks, and his films have contained more than their fair share of nude scenes, with some of his best acting coming in strictly commercial movies like *An Officer and a Gentleman* (1982), *No Mercy* (1986) and *Pretty Woman* (1990). His search for cinema as art has led him out of his depth into movies like *Days of Heaven* (1978) and *The Cotton Club* (1984), where he was outclassed by Sam Shepard and Bob Hoskins respectively. Two arthouse performances stand out, however: Paul Schrader's *American Gigolo* (1980) as a male prostitute and *Breathless* (1983) as a small-time gangster. In them, he appears as a Brando-style character, a mixture of pent-up sexuality, aggression and sensitivity. They remain the most satisfying manifestations of the Gere persona, but both pictures floundered at the box office. In 1990 two contrasting films suddenly turned his career round and made him a hot star again – *Pretty Woman*, in which he romances hooker Julia Roberts, and the tough thriller *Internal Affairs*. He's had his ups and downs since, but a romantic film with Jodie Foster like *Sommersby* (1993) shows that even in greying middle age he still has box-office pull.

Mel Gibson

Actor, director
Born: *Peekskill, NY, January 3, 1956*

Antipodean macho heart-throb Gibson was actually born in the USA, moved to Australia at 12, attended acting school and started in the State Theatre of New South Wales in Sydney. After his debut in *Summer City* (1977), he gave a delicate performance as the simple but sexy gardener in Colleen McCullough's *Tim* in 1978, but soon shot to international stardom as the daredevil futuristic desert

Mel Gibson: Aussie heart-throb

warrior of the *Mad Max* trilogy (1979–85). Upmarket wartime adventure films *Gallipoli* (1981) and *The Year of Living Dangerously* (1983) (with Sigourney Weaver) confirmed his allure, but when Hollywood swooped with contracts, they put him in posh films where he was out of his depth – *The River* (1984) and *Mrs Soffel* (1984). It was the paybox bonanza of *Lethal Weapon* (1987) and its two sequels, playing the jokey, offbeat cop Martin Riggs, that took him to the top of the Hollywood tree, where he has stayed, despite wobbly movies like *Tequila Sunrise* (1988) and *Air America* (1990). His courageous attempts to vary the pace of his career by playing Shakespeare in Zeffirelli's *Hamlet* (1990) and by directing himself in *The Man without a Face* (1993) have been respectfully if unexcitedly received. He was on much safer

ground with the popular fantasy romance *Forever Young* (1993) and a comedy western, *Maverick* (1994), both of which exactly judged his popular appeal and the extent of his limited but genial range.

Sir John Gielgud

Actor
Born: *London, England, April 14, 1904*

With his patrician features, unflappable demeanour and sing-song voice, Gielgud is one of the delights of world cinema. Primarily a theatre man, his film career divides into two halves. In the early 1930s he played a number of straight lead roles, notably a sinister spy in Hitchcock's *The Secret Agent* (1936), and Disraeli in *The Prime Minister* (1940). He was always enjoyable, but it was only in the 1950s and 1960s, when he started to adopt more eccentric character roles, that he really started to look at home on screen. Having gained widespread renown in theatre, he made his film debut as a member of a travelling music troupe in *The Good Companions* (1932). Following *The Prime Minister*, he concentrated on stage work for a decade before returning to film as Cassius in Joseph Mankiewicz's *Julius Caesar* (1953), the first in an

John Gielgud: The best of Britain

extraordinary series of crisp, idiosyncratic and perfectly judged character turns: Henry IV in Welles' *Chimes At Midnight* (1966); a vindictive writer in *Providence* (1977); a doctor in *The Elephant Man* (1980); a wonderfully stiff-upper-lipped butler in *Arthur* (1981), for which he won a Best Supporting Actor Oscar; and an aristocrat in *The Shooting Party* (1984). Undimmed by advancing years, he gave one of his finest performances, aged 87, as the lead in Peter Greenaway's *Prospero's Books* (1991), fulfilling a long-stated ambition to play Shakespeare's exiled duke.

Lillian Gish

Actress
Born: LILLIAN DE GUICHE, *Springfield, Oh., October 14, 1893*
Died: *February 27, 1993*

Wraith-like, innocent and frail, with huge almond eyes, Gish was the personification of the silent-screen heroine. She was also an extraordinary film actress – a charismatic, transcendent artist who pushed forward the accepted boundaries of film performance and was as magnetic in her later cameo roles as she had been at the beginning of her career 40 years previously. She started making

Gish: Personification of the silent-screen heroine

films for D. W. Griffith at Biograph in 1912, and for the next 10 years worked for virtually no other director. She hit the big time as female lead Elsie Stoneham in

the epoch-making *Birth of a Nation* (1915), and went on to make a succession of classic features – *Intolerance* (1916); *Hearts of the World* (1918); *Broken Blossoms* (1919); *True Heart Susie* (1919); *Way Down East* (1920); *Orphans of the Storm* (1922). After leaving Griffith, she worked in Italy on *The White Sister* (1923) and *Romola* (1924), and then gave two extraordinary performances for Victor Sjöström in *The Scarlet Letter* (1926) and *The Wind* (1927). However, with the coming of sound, the studios wanted new faces, and her career petered out. She continued to pop up to notable effect in films throughout her long life, especially *Duel in the Sun* (1946), *The Night of the Hunter* (1955), Robert Altman's *A Wedding* (1978) and Lindsay Anderson's *The Whales of August* (1987), made when she was 94. She was given a special Oscar in 1971. Her sister Dorothy was also a Griffith silent star.

Jean-Luc Godard

Director, writer, producer, actor, critic
Born: *Paris, France, December 3, 1930*

Jean-Luc Godard was the anarchic king of the French New Wave, the film-maker who best epitomized the movement's ideals in their purest yet most elusive essence. A critic on the magazine *Cahiers du Cinéma*, he rustled up a bravura film debut with *A Bout de Souffle* (1959), an intoxicating hand-held, jump-cutting trip through both Paris and the semiotics of the American gangster picture. He followed this innovative cinema blueprint with a vibrant romance in *Une Femme Est Une Femme* (1961), a sci-fi fable with *Alphaville* (1965) and the audacious chase thriller *Pierrot le Fou* (1965), all featuring then-wife Anna Karina. Each picture was a masterwork of spontaniety, free-flowing and open-ended, deliberately taking alternative routes out from con-

ventional narrative structures. The savage *Weekend* (1967) heralded a more overtly political stance for Godard's work as his subsequent

Godard: Chainsmoking New Wave visionary

films took on more radical forms, avoiding what he saw as the compromising effect of conventional storylines. He has flirted occasionally with a more commercial style – 1972's elegant *Tout Va Bien*, 1980's *Slow Motion* and *Prénom: Carmen* (1984) – but seems generally content to pursue his own uncompromising, often excluding agenda, working principally on video. Fellow director Henri-Georges Clouzot once asked the errant genius if he agreed that each movie should have a beginning, a middle and an end. "Certainly," replied Godard. "But not necessarily in that order."

Whoopi Goldberg

Actress, comedian
Born: CARYN JOHNSON, *New York, NY, November 13, 1949*

The hilarious Goldberg has the stand-up comedian's precise talent to aim a laugh and time a joke, but her film career has been impeded by a lack of strong vehicles or steady direction. She started performing aged eight in New York, and by 1975 was appearing in repertory theatre. A solo show led to her Broadway debut in 1983 which was seen by Steven Spielberg who cast her in *The Color Purple* (1985), winning her Best Actress Golden Globe and an

Oscar nomination. A run of star roles in rotten movies followed. Who remembers *Jumpin' Jack Flash* (1986), *Burglar* (1987), *Fatal Beauty* (1987), *Clara's Heart* (1988) or *The Telephone* (1988)? In a remarkable turnaround, her Oscar-winning support performance as the fake medium in *Ghost* (1990) and her exuberant turn as a phony nun on the run in *Sister Act* (1992) took her to the top of the Hollywood pile. She put herself on the line by playing a serious role as a troubled South African teacher in the anti-apartheid musical *Sarafina!* (1991) and gained enormous attention when there were rumours of a love affair with married Ted Danson, her co-star in the dismayingly silly comedy *Made in America* (1993). Whoopi has worked extensively on TV, including a 1990 flop series based on the film *Bagdad Café* and as Guinan in *Star Trek: The Next Generation*, and in 1994 won her biggest audience so far as Oscar ceremony compere.

Sam Goldwyn

Producer
Born: SAMUEL GOLDFISH, *Warsaw, Poland, August 27, 1882*
Died: *January 31, 1974*

A squat, broad-shouldered tycoon with a boxer's face, Sam Goldwyn was the prototype movie mogul, renowned for the consistently high quality of his productions and his uncanny ability to spot potential stars – Ronald Colman, Gary Cooper and David Niven among them. His association with director William Wyler proved one of the most fruitful producer/director relationships in Hollywood history, giving us such classics as *Wuthering Heights* (1939) and *The Best Years of Our Lives* (1946), whilst his "Goldwynisms" – "Include me out"; "A verbal contract isn't worth the paper it's written on" – became the stuff of Hollywood legend. Goldwyn arrived in the US, penniless, at the age of 13 and became a successful glove salesman before forming the Jesse L. Lasky Feature Play Company in 1914 with his father-in-law and Cecil B. DeMille. Their first film, *The Squaw Man* (1913), was a huge success, and Goldwyn formed The Goldwyn Picture Corporation in 1916, then, in 1922, his own independent company, Samuel Goldwyn Incorporated, and, finally, in 1924 Metro-Goldwyn-Mayer. Thereafter he spared no expense in producing a series of classic family movies: *Ben Hur* (1925); *Dodsworth* (1936); *The Bishop's Wife* (1947); *Guys And Dolls* (1955). A legend in his own lifetime, he received the Irving Thalberg award in 1946 in recognition of the unique quality of his work as a producer.

Elliott Gould

Actor
Born: ELLIOTT GOLDSTEIN, *Brooklyn, NY, August 29, 1938*

Crumpled and mournful-looking, Gould is an unforgettable face in a career collection of often forgettable movies, but his cynical wit summed up a generation's disillusionment, most spectacularly in *M*A*S*H* (1970). A native New Yorker, his city-boy's guile in impersonating an agent promoting his own praises earned him his first job in theatre, where he met Barbra Streisand, marrying her on her way to superstardom in 1963. *Quick, Let's Get Married* (1964), his film debut, was not released until 1971, by which time he had been Oscar-nominated as the wife-swapping lawyer in *Bob & Carol & Ted & Alice* (1969), and played a leading role in Robert Altman's phenomenally successful Korean War farce, *M*A*S*H*, which shocked studio executives with its popularity and led to the long-running TV spin-off series. Despite being the first American star to be directed by Ingmar Bergman, in *The Touch* (1971), he is most closely associated with

Altman, who rescued Gould from rumours of a drug problem after he pulled out of *A Glimpse of Tiger*. Altman argued successfully for Gould to play private investigator

Elliott Gould: *Crumpled star of the 70s*

Philip Marlowe in *The Long Goodbye* (1972), but not before the studio had insisted Gould provide a medical certificate to prove his sanity. They were reunited for *Nashville* (1974) and *California Split* (1974), but Gould was reduced to *The Muppets Take Manhattan* (1984) before returning older and heavier in *Bugsy* (1991).

Betty Grable

Actress, singer, dancer
Born: ELIZABETH RUTH GRABLE, *St Louis, Mo., December 18, 1916*
Died: *July 2, 1973*

The vivacious, eager-to-please blonde star of 1940s Fox musicals seemed ready for anything and gave her modest all in a collection of fondly remembered pictures, despite being best known as the most popular GI pin-up of World War Two, whose legs were insured with Lloyd's for £250,000. If not outstanding as a singer, dancer or actress, she was extremely popular with the public and was among the top box-office draws for 10 straight years. Grable started dancing at 12 and two years later was signed as a chorus girl by Fox, debuting in *Let's Go Places* (1930). Invariably cast in backstage musicals or as the charming but scheming pursuer of

rich men, she appeared in well over 20 films before reaching stardom. The advent of colour boosted her appeal and she sparkled in three consecutive films with Victor Mature (beginning with *Song of the Islands* in 1942). Poor reviews for films such as *Four Jills in a Jeep* (1944) and *The Dolly Sisters* (1945) did little to hurt her popularity. She took over as queen of the Fox lot from Alice Faye in 1943, but was eventually herself supplanted by Marilyn Monroe, her co-star in *How to Marry a Millionaire* (1953). Grable's final film *How to Be Very, Very Popular* (1955) was very, very ordinary, and she returned to the stage, appearing in several musicals before succumbing to cancer aged 56.

Stewart Granger

Actor
Born: JAMES LABLANCHE STEWART, *London, England, May 6, 1913*
Died: *August 16, 1993*

This debonair, good-looking and self-confessedly arrogant English actor served his apprenticeship in the British repertory theatres, where he changed his name to avoid confusion with the Hollywood James Stewart. After being invalided out of the army, he took over the romantic role in *The Man In Grey* (1943) from James Mason, who had been promoted to play the villain, and the film made them both Britain's top leading men throughout the 1940s. In 1949 Granger and his second wife, Jean Simmons, went to Hollywood, where Granger was cast in *King Solomon's Mines* (1950), after which he swashbuckled his way through a host of costume dramas and other he-man roles, which were by no means art but usually good entertainment for their time. They include A remake of *The Prisoner of Zenda* (1952), *Salome* (1953), *Young Bess* (1953) and the wonderfully dreadful *Beau Brummell* (1954)

with Robert Morley as mad King George, making it the most tactless choice ever for a British Royal Command Film Performance! *Footsteps in the Fog* (1955) and *Bhowani Junction* (1956) fared better critically. In the 1960s Granger found work in Europe; *Sodom and Gomorrah* (1962), and a trio of westerns, shot in Yugoslavia and based on German writer Karl May's novels. His last major film appearance was *The Wild Geese* (1978), after which he worked in television movies and mini-series.

Cary Grant

Actor
Born: ARCHIBALD ALEXANDER LEACH, *Bristol, England, January 18, 1904,*
Died: *November 29, 1986*

"A personality at work" was Katharine Hepburn's verdict on Cary Grant. This sounds like a putdown, but in a way it's what all the great stars have in common. Who wanted Newman, Monroe or even Hepburn to be anything but themselves? Grant's reputation rests firmly on his unsurpassed flair for sophisticated comedy, especially screwball comedy such as *Bringing Up Baby* (1938), *His Girl Friday* (1940) or *Arsenic and Old Lace* (1944). Hepburn went on to say, "He can't play a serious part, the public isn't interested in him in that way," but Hitchcock exploited him cannily in *Suspicion* (1941), *Notorious* (1946) and *North by Northwest* (1959), in which you really do believe Grant is capable of betrayal and even murder before his charisma wins you over. In real life there were revelations about supernatural dabblings, wife-beating, LSD-taking and being bisexual, but the public didn't want to know. In real life too, his charisma won us over. As the master of the double and treble take, Grant was admired for a great sense of timing that never deserted him. He retired in his prime at 62, still looking famously

Cromwell (1970) and made a hardy hero in both the *Jaws* exploiter *Orca* (1977) and the pulpy 1978 actioner *The Wild Geese*. Rather less successful was his noisy show-boating turn opposite an unclad Bo Derek in the plotless *Tarzan the Ape Man* (1981). But Harris has matured well, in recent years regaining his high reputation. A powerful role in the rural saga *The Field* (1990) earned another Oscar nomination; he contributed an eye-catching cameo to Clint Eastwood's mighty *Unforgiven* (1992) and notably held his own against arch scene-stealer Robert Duvall in the likeable buddy heartwarmer *Wrestling Ernest Hemingway* (1994).

Sir Rex Harrison

Actor
Born: REGINALD CAREY, *Huyton, England, March 5, 1908*
Died: *June 2, 1990*

Harrison had enough debonair charm and sophisticated style to keep him popular for six decades and to sweep innumerable women off their feet, including six wives, making him a gossip column regular as Sexy Rexy. He thought of himself primarily as a theatre actor, but had an equally successful run in films from 1930. Harrison made his first screen impact as a jaunty journalist in *Storm in a Teacup* (1937), followed by Carol Reed's thriller *Night Train to Munich* (1940) and Shaw's *Major Barbara* (1940). Then Noel Coward's *Blithe Spirit* (1945) and *The Rake's Progress* (1946) made him an international star. Hollywood didn't know what to do with him, though *Anna and the King of Siam* (1946), *The Ghost and Mrs Muir* (1947) and *Unfaithfully Yours* (1948) were all worthwhile. The theatre kept him in work till, pushing 50 in 1956, the role of Professor Higgins in Alan Jay Lerner's musical *My Fair Lady* turned him into a superstar and his movie career ignited. Harrison was Oscar-nominated as Caesar in

Cleopatra (1962), then won Best Actor Oscar for the film of *My Fair Lady* (1964) in the role he'll always be remembered for. He worked in a series of international movies of variable and increasingly feeble quality, but a lot of them gave considerable pleasure and he always achieved his ambition – "to communicate enjoyment".

William S. Hart

Actor, writer, director
Born: *Newburgh, NY, December 6, 1870*
Died: *June 23, 1946*

A tall, laconic, stone-faced loner, Hart was the model for many of Hollywood's greatest cowboys. Clint Eastwood, John Wayne and Gary Cooper all adopted a measure of the tough, solitary good-guy persona that Hart had created. Born in New York, he actually grew up in the Wild West, working as a ranch-hand, then for 20 years was an actor on Broadway before moving to California, determined to develop the western film and move it away from the comic-book world of Bronco Billy Anderson and other early film stars. His first movie, *The Bargain* (1914), which he both scripted and starred in, brought to the genre an unimagined realism and visual poetry, and created for the first time a complex, multi-layered western hero. He thereafter carried his gaunt stone face through a succession of minor masterpieces, most of which he also wrote and directed: *The Darkening Trail* (1915), *The Return of Draw Egan* (1916), *Hell's Hinges* (1916), *The Aryan* (1917) and *The Toll Gate* (1920). The austerity and realism of his work were, however, ahead of their time, and when Hart refused to supply more glamour and thrills audiences turned to more showy cowboy stars such as Tom Mix. His final film was the mournful *Tumbleweeds* (1925), after which he retired, returning only for the odd cameo appearance.

Rutger Hauer

Actor
Born: *Breukelen, Netherlands, January 23, 1944*

Strikingly handsome, Rutger Hauer brings an intriguing air of danger to his screen persona, which doesn't fit the Hollywood star hero mould. Hauer became a popular star in the Netherlands during the 1970s, where he played the promiscuous sculptor in Paul Verhoeven's *Turkish Delight* (1973) and a resistance fighter role in *Soldier of Orange* (1979). The latter won them both international recognition and a ticket to Hollywood, where Hauer was cast as a terrorist who fought Sylvester Stallone (off screen as well as on) in *Nighthawks* (1981). Subsequent Hollywood roles were of varying quality with the accent on villains, of which the blond android in *Blade Runner* (1982) was one of the

Rutger Hauer: Pure genius

best. He was in Nicolas Roeg's underrated *Eureka* (1983), persuaded Sam Peckinpah to cast him as the hero not the villain in *The Osterman Weekend* (1983), helped out Verhoeven with the lead in the medieval epic *Flesh and Blood* (1985) (known to some as Flash and Bleed!), then played a psychopath in a flashy chiller, *The Hitcher* (1986). After turning down the lead in *Robocop*, he returned to

the cultural springs of Europe for the poetic fable *The Legend of the Holy Drinker* (1988), based on Arthur Roth's novella. Philip Noyce's thriller *Blind Fury* (1990) and *Buffy the Vampire Slayer* (1992) saw him back in Hollywood, but Hauer is best known in Britain for his television commercials for Guinness.

Jack Hawkins

Actor
Born: *London, England, September 1, 1910*
Died: *July 18, 1973*

An actor at 13 and on screen at 20, Jack Hawkins slowly emerged as one of Britain's most dominant acting presences, with a cool, commanding air and a powerful, distinctive husky voice. Very much a figure of his post-war time, he achieved stardom in his middle years, playing macho heroes, often in one of the services. As the vogue for war films ended and he grew older, Hawkins managed a seamless transition to character actor parts in the 1960s. But in 1966 he cruelly forfeited his voice after being operated on for throat cancer, though he continued to make minor, dubbed appearances in films like *Waterloo* (1970) and *Young Winston* (1972). During Hawkins's heyday in the 1950s he made a handful of films upon which his reputation rests: his obstinate pilot in *Angels One Five* (1952), his touching portrayal of the father of a deaf girl in *Mandy* (1952), his quintessential performance as ship's captain in the war story *The Cruel Sea* (1953) and his seedy officer planning the perfect crime in *The League of Gentlemen* (1959). Somehow epics weren't right without him: Lean hired him twice, first for *The Bridge on the River Kwai* (1957) and then *Lawrence of Arabia* (1962), and he appeared in *Ben-Hur* (1959) and *Zulu* (1963) too. His entertaining autobiography was published posthumously: *Anything for a Quiet Life*.

Howard Hawks

Director, writer, producer

Born: *Goshen, Ind., May 30, 1896*
Died: *December 26, 1977*

Howard Hawks was the supreme film craftsman, the unobtrusive hand behind many of Hollywood's best-loved productions. His exclusion from many all-time great lists is solely down to his chameleon-like ability to work in a variety of genres. Hawks's breakthrough movie was 1932's controversial gangster saga *Scarface*, a springboard from which he would diversify into westerns with *Rio Bravo* (1959) and *Red River* (1948), musicals with *Gentlemen Prefer Blondes* (1953) and science-fiction with 1951's *The Thing from Another World* – a picture nominally directed by Christian Nyby, though producer Hawks is rumoured to have had a hand in the shooting. But given their immense range, Hawks's pictures display a remarkably organic quality, typified by their spare, well-oiled dialogue. It says much for the director's skill that he was also able to coax the best from a trio of very different Hollywood players. He had John Wayne in tough cowboy mode in the westerns, Humphrey Bogart at his hard-boiled peak in the *noir* thrillers *The Big Sleep* (1946) and *To Have and Have Not* (1944), and sent Cary Grant through his expert comic paces with *Bringing Up Baby* (1938), *I Was a Male War Bride* (1949) and *Monkey Business* (1952). Towards the close of his career, Hawks worked with a cast of youthful unknowns that included a pre-stardom James Caan in the motor-racing yarn *Red Line 7000* (1965).

Goldie Hawn

Actress, producer

Born: *Washington, DC, November 21, 1945*

The irresistibly kooky Hawn came to movies a fully fledged star with a fully defined persona through TV's *Laugh-In*, but unlike her equally popular series co-stars she has stayed the course, hardly changing her image or suffering any career dips over a quarter of a century. Like a latterday Lucille Ball, Goldie may play the dizzy blonde but she's got the brains and power to be a major Hollywood player, producing her own movies and controlling the final form of her films. In only her second film, the comedy *Cactus Flower* (1968), cast in her first main role, she won a Best Support Oscar, upstaging co-stars Walter Matthau and Ingrid Bergman. In 1980 she was nominated as Best Actress for the deliciously funny take on women soldiers, *Private Benjamin* (1980), one of her major hits. Although she's tended to play safe and stick to tried and tested, lightweight comedy vehicles, she has successfully bitten on something more serious like Richard Brooks's thriller *Dollars* (1972) or Spielberg's *The Sugarland Express* (1973). She's often been at her best when bouncing opposite a particularly sparky, sympathetic co-star like Peter Sellers in *There's a Girl in My Soup* (1970), Chevy Chase in *Foul Play* (1978) or Mel Gibson in *Bird on a Wire* (1990). Disappointingly, she's made only a couple of films with her long-time companion, Kurt Russell, *Swing Shift* (1984) and *Overboard* (1987).

Will Hay

Actor

Born: *Aberdeen, Scotland, 1888*
Died: *April 19, 1949*

Although he never gained widespread popularity abroad, Hay, with his creased oblong face, little round glasses and bumbling professorial personality, was one of the great delights of British comedy. Born in Aberdeen, he worked extensively in music hall, gradually perfecting a sketch entitled "The Fourth Form of St Michael's" which was to be the prototype for all his future film work. He played a pompous, bumbling, incompetent teacher who refused to admit that his students were brighter than him, a formula he later applied to a succession of masterful British comedies: as a schoolmaster in *Boys Will Be Boys* (1935), a private eye in *Where There's a Will* (1936) and a ship's skipper in *Windbag the Sailor* (1936). The last of these was his first teaming with two characters who were thereafter perfectly to complement his pompous authoritarianism: Graham Moffat, the fat, lazy, insolent smart-alec, and Moore Marriott, the crafty, gaptoothed old codger. Together they made some of the funniest British films ever: *Oh Mr Porter* (1937), *Convict 99* (1938), *Ask a Policeman* (1939) and *Where's That Fire?* (1939). Hay then went it alone for the *The Black Sheep of Whitehall* (1941) and the blackly humorous *My Learned Friend* (1943), but overall they lacked the sparkle of his earlier work. He retired due to ill health in 1943.

Susan Hayward

Actress

Born: *EDYTHE MARRENER, Brooklyn, NY, June 30, 1918*
Died: *March 14, 1975*

The flame-haired, tough-acting former model Hayward came to Hollywood in 1937 to test as Scarlett O'Hara, but won a film contract instead, finally reaching star status a decade later with her archetypal role as a singer battling alcoholism in the first of her five Oscar nominations, for *Smash-Up: the Story of a Woman* (1947). It set the pattern for her career of noble stricken heroine fighting for survival which she alternated with as-tough-as-any-man roles in adventure movies. Oscar nominations followed for J. D. Salinger's wartime romancer *My Foolish Heart* (1950), and three roles based on real lives – crippled singer Jane Froman in *With a Song in My Heart* (1952), alcoholic star Lillian Roth in *I'll Cry Tomorrow* (1956) and hooker criminal Barbara Graham wrongly sent to the gas chamber in *I Want to Live!* (1958). She finally won Best Actress Oscar for her rousing acting in the latter. Hayward was a top star throughout the 1950s, but succumbed to a series of feebly made weepies in the 1960s and semi-retired after Harold Robbins's *Where Love Has Gone* in 1964. The movies – and the world – had changed and she'd gone out of fashion but she retired far too early and a trio of late movies showed she still had the stuff: *The Honey Pot* (1967), *Valley of the Dolls* (1967) and *The Revengers* (1972).

Rita Hayworth

Actress

Born: *MARGARITA CARMEN CANSINO, Brooklyn, NY, October 17, 1918*
Died: *May 14, 1987*

Her wide smile, flashing eyes and sensuous figure made her a leading love goddess and favourite forces pin-up of the 1940s. She followed her parents into a dancing career at the age of 12, played some bit parts in movies in the late 1930s, usually as a dancer, and in 1937 married businessman Edward Judson, who moved out of car sales into promoting his wife's career. Her first good role was in Howard Hawks's *Only Angels*

Rita Hayworth: *Sensuous love goddess*

101

Have Wings (1939). She was Fred Astaire's dancing partner in *You'll Never Get Rich* (1941) and *You Were Never Lovelier* (1942), and Gene Kelly's in *Cover Girl* (1944), after which she turned virtually full-time screen siren, as in *Gilda* (1946), *The Lady from Shanghai* (1948), *Salome* (1953) and *Miss Sadie Thompson* (1953), an inferior rehash of Somerset Maugham's short story. Her screen image was reflected in her turbulent private life and short-lived marriages, her husbands including Orson Welles and Prince Aly Khan. In the 1950s time turned her to ageing beauty roles, most notably the rich woman pursuing *Pal Joey* (1957) and a good dramatic performance as Burt Lancaster's ex-wife in *Separate Tables* (1958). She became victim at an early age to Alzheimer's Disease in 1977 and spent the last six years of her life in the care of her daughter, Princess Yasmin Aly Khan.

Audrey Hepburn

Actress
Born: *Brussels, Belgium, May 4, 1929*
Died: *January 20, 1993*

Few actresses have inspired such genuine affection as Belgian-born Audrey Hepburn. In a movie world full of canny screen sirens, there was a dignified fragility about her that appealed across traditional age and gender boundaries. Beautiful without ever quite being sexy, Hepburn was a child-woman with soul. Her popularity rests on a glittering string of 1950s romantic comedies. An Oscar-winning Hollywood debut as the princess heroine of William Wyler's *Roman Holiday* (1953) was the perfect calling-card, showcasing an airy charm which a clutch of big-league directors – Billy Wilder, Stanley Donen, Fred Zinnemann – instantly queued up to use. Her enchanting mix of catwalk class and quirky humour lent polish to a number of fairly

feathery comedies but Hepburn's broad-based allure sometimes prompted over-zealous producers to overlook the specialized, particular nature of her persona. She struck an odd note as the street-smart, all-American Holly Golightly in Blake Edwards's *Breakfast at Tiffany's* (1961) or struggling with Eliza Doolittle's cockney accent in *My Fair Lady* (1964). In the 1970s and 1980s, acting took a back seat to charity

Audrey Hepburn: *Angelic queen of the catwalk*

work, with Hepburn serving as the UN ambassador for UNICEF, but in her rare screen forays she continued to dazzle. She was poignant and affecting in Richard Lester's *Robin and Marian* (1976) and her cameo as a serene, white-clad angel lit up Spielberg's *Always* (1989) and proved a fitting swansong to a magical career.

Katharine Hepburn

Actress
Born: *Hartford, Conn., November 9, 1907*

If Elizabeth Taylor is the queen of Hollywood, Hepburn is the queen mother. The Americans affectionately call her the Great Kate, though not to her face. In a society where everyone is on first-name terms, she is held in due reverence as Miss Hepburn. In her eighties, the actress with the famous strong jaw, high cheekbones, flaring nostrils, outbreak of freckles and

inevitable baggy trousers is a beloved national monument. Hepburn's place in movie history is secure. She is a long-distance performer who notched up over a period of 60 years a record that looks unbeatable. She's the only actress to win four Oscars and has starred in several of Hollywood's best movies, including *Bringing Up Baby* (1938) and *The Philadelphia Story* (1940) with Cary Grant, and 1951's *The African Queen* with Humphrey Bogart. She was an immediate sensation from her debut in 1932 in *A Bill of Divorcement*, followed by a run of hits like *Morning Glory* (1933), *Little Women* (1933) and *Stage Door* (1937) until she was for a time declared "box-office poison". Her clutch of nine films with her friend Spencer Tracy is rightly admired, particularly *Woman of the Year* (1942),

The great Kate: *Hollywood's queen mother*

Adam's Rib (1949), *Pat and Mike* (1952) and their last together, *Guess Who's Coming to Dinner* (1967). In old age she managed to find a few golden roles, usually opposite other great veterans: *Love among the Ruins* (1974) with Laurence Olivier, *Rooster Cogburn* (1975) with John Wayne and *On Golden Pond* (1981) with Henry Fonda.

Werner Herzog

Director
Born: WERNER STIPETIC, *Sachrang, Germany, September 5, 1942*

Film-maker Werner Herzog has drawn on ancient myth and the conventions of early expression-

ism to fashion a film *oeuvre* of startling impact and originality. The picture that established him, 1972's *Aguirre: The Wrath of God*, still stands as his masterpiece, a meaty Conrad-style fable of Spanish conquistadors sliding toward savagery in 16th-century South America. In fact the film's breathtaking opening shot can now be seen to spotlight the essence of Herzog's artistic concerns, with its exotic landscape and ant-like protagonists – slaves to some all-consuming collective impulse that negates individual action. Other 1970s outings took Herzog to the wilds of Wisconsin for the cultural satire *Stroszek* (1977) and back to his native Germany for the alluring but unloved modern-day fairytale *Heart of Glass* (1976). But it is in tandem with Klaus Kinski, the bug-eyed, strung-out star of *Aguirre*, that this erratic, fiercely talented director has produced his best work. Conjuring up art-house tales of compelling verve and vigour, Herzog cast Kinski as the ghoulish anti-hero of *Nosferatu the Vampyre* (1979), a soldier in crack-up in the disturbing *Woyzeck* (1978) and as a barbaric bandit in *Cobra Verde* (1988). Most memorably he gave Kinski the lead role in the epic *Fitzcarraldo* (1982), an absurdist, beguiling, Peru-set saga that won its creator the Best Director Award at the Cannes Film Festival.

Charlton Heston

Actor, director
Born: JOHN CHARLES CARTER, *St Helen, Mich., October 4, 1924*

Most moviegoers' strongest image of Heston is Moses talking to the Almighty amid much thunder and lightning in DeMille's *The Ten Commandments* (1956), or putting up a granite-jawed struggle with a team of unruly chariot horses in *Ben-Hur* (1959) for which he won the Best Actor Oscar. Though he did very occasionally play less noble parts, these set the tone for a career filled with characters of towering, tooth-grinding integrity. Two of his subtler and more interesting performances were the Mexican detective tracking police corruption in Orson Welles's classic *Touch of Evil (1958)* and the accidental time traveller in *Planet of the Apes* (1968), one of his few sci-fi appearances, but he is better known for epics like *El Cid* (1961), *55 Days at Peking* (1962) and *Antony and Cleopatra* (1970), which he also directed, and jeopardy movies like *Earthquake* (1974) and *Airport 1975* (1975). He also appeared in a television ver-

Charlton Heston: *Taking the tablets*

sion of of *A Man for All Seasons* (1988). Six times president of the Screen Actors' Guild and a regular performer in 1980s soap opera (*The Colbys*), he was, more recently, paid something of a tribute by being cast as "Good Actor" in the teen comedy *Wayne's World 2* (1993), though one might observe that, having started off with Moses and risen via John the Baptist, in George Stevens' unwieldy *The Greatest Story Ever Told* (1965), he gained the ultimate casting promotion in Paul Hogan's *Almost an Angel* (1990) where he played God. Where can an actor go from there?

Sir Alfred Hitchcock

Director, writer, producer, cameoist

Born: ALFRED JOSEPH HITCHCOCK, *Leytonstone, England, August 13, 1899*

Died: *April 28, 1980*

Universally recognized, Hitchcock is the undisputed king of the thriller and first director superstar thanks to his signature cameo appearances and droll introductions to his popular TV series. His own unique mix of suspense, humour, sex and violence spawned a host of imitators. He joined the business as title designer in 1919, directed his first silent in 1925 (*The Pleasure Garden*) and made his first "Hitchcockian" thriller with *The Lodger* (1926). 1928's *Blackmail* was Britain's first talkie, and throughout the 1930s Hitch honed his talent in a series of dazzling pictures: *The Man who Knew Too Much* (1934), *The Thirty-Nine Steps* (1935) and *The Lady Vanishes* (1938). Hitchcock went to Hollywood for bigger budgets, stars and markets, working with David Selznick on the untypical Best Picture romancer *Rebecca* (1940). More typical was the paranoia-fest *Suspicion* (1941), with his favourite actor Cary Grant, and *Shadow of a Doubt* (1943), his own favourite picture. He wrapped psychological studies inside thriller formats with *Spellbound* (1945), *Notorious* (1946) and *Under Capricorn* (1949), all with his

Sir Alfred Hitchcock: *"Actors are cattle"*

beloved Ingrid Bergman. He set himself technical puzzles: a single set for *Lifeboat* (1944), the 10-minute take in *Rope* (1948), 3D in *Dial M for Murder* (1954). The 1950s were a decade of prodigious achievement: *Strangers on a Train* (1951), *Rear Window* (1954), *Vertigo* (1958), *North by Northwest* (1959). None of these prepared the world for the stark horror of *Psycho* (1960) which set the cinema on an unending wave of violent chillers.

Dustin Hoffman

Actor

Born: *Los Angeles, Calif., August 8, 1937*

"I lived below the official American poverty line until I was 31," Dustin Hoffman once remarked and even today, reclining in respectable, moneyed middle age, there is something engagingly crumpled and worn about this most respected of movie actors. Amid the traditional square-jawed leading men, Hoffman's breakthrough role as *The Graduate* (1968) heralded a new breed of film hero: a more cerebral, introverted view of American youth that was perfectly in keeping with the uncertainty and disillusion of late 1960s culture. But with typical lack of compromise Tinseltown's new star refused to trade on his assigned image, following the film with two acting *tours de force* as nervy, tragic street-punk Ratso Rizzo in *Midnight Cowboy* (1969) and transforming from gauche youth to 121-year-old crone in the Red Indian fable *Little Big Man* (1970). These three roles effectively put Hoffman's place among history's "great actors" beyond dispute and by the mid-1970s he was already conducting himself as one of film's elder statesmen, winning an inevitable Oscar for his grandstand turn in the soapy but affecting *Kramer vs Kramer* (1979). It says much for Hoffman's continued hunger, though, that he continues

to hunt for roles that stretch his acting talents. Huge success greeted his quirky cross-dressing comedy *Tootsie* (1982), he gave a searing portrait of the anguished

Dustin Hoffman: *New breed of movie hero*

Willy Loman in 1985's *Death of a Salesman*, while his turn as Tom Cruise's autistic elder brother in *Rain Man* (1988) brought a deserved second Oscar.

William Holden

Actor

Born: WILLIAM FRANKLIN BEEDLE JR, *O'Fallon, Ill., April 17, 1918*

Died: *November 16, 1981*

Dependable, handsome star Holden did some of his best work playing half-hero, half-heel characters for director Billy Wilder, who described him as "the ideal motion picture actor", perhaps because Holden, on his own admission, did not enjoy acting, so was never tempted to "ham it up". Spotted by a talent scout at the age of 19 playing an 80-year-old man in a radio play, his first major role was as Clifford Odet's *Golden Boy*, about a would-be violinist boxer, but he first won critical acclaim as Gloria Swanson's toy boy in Wilder's *Sunset Blvd* (1950), as Judy Holliday's tutor in *Born Yesterday* (1950) and in an Oscar-winning performance as the cynical POW capitalist of *Stalag 17* (1953). A top box-office star throughout the 1950s, he became one of Hollywood's highest-paid actors after *The Bridge on the River Kwai* (1957) but his box-office success rate was sinking until Sam Peckinpah's *The Wild Bunch* (1969) put him back on top. He gave one of the best performances of his career as the television executive struggling to keep his moral integrity in *Network* (1976), and stayed with that profession, on celluloid at least, for *Fedora* (1978) with Wilder once more and a telling support role in *S.O.B.* (1981). He died alone of suspected alcohol poisoning aged 63.

Judy Holliday

Actress, comedienne
Born: JUDITH TUVIM, *New York, NY, June 21, 1922*
Died: *June 7, 1965*

From a short but memorable career – she only made 11 films – the scene in *Born Yesterday* (1950) where she's playing cards with Broderick Crawford is a classic example of the acuteness of Holliday's comedic genius. Playing the dumb blonde gangster's moll to a T, she drives hood Crawford crazy by singing to herself while whipping him at gin rummy, and a scene which could have been just amusingly silly in the hands of a lesser talent is turned into a hilarious cat-and-mouse game of sexual politics with Crawford as the mouse. She first appeared in the role on stage, a part she got when Jean Arthur whom she was understudying dropped out. Cukor's film version brought her the Best Actress Oscar nomination in a year (1950) when the competition was formidable and included Bette Davis in *All About Eve* and Gloria Swanson in *Sunset Blvd*, but the Oscar went to Holliday, type-casting her for the rest of a career during which she played variations on the same character. She gave other memorable performances in *The Marrying Kind* (1952), the sparkling *It Should Happen to You* (1954) with Jack Lemmon, and her last film

Bells Are Ringing (1960) with Dean Martin. A brilliantly measured actress and comedienne and a criminally underused talent, she never got to make half the number of films she should have.

Bob Hope

Actor, wisecracker, golfer
Born: LESLIE TOWNES HOPE, *Eltham, England, May 29, 1903*

London-born wisecracker Bob Hope is an American institution, as rich and famous as the Rockefellers, and rather funnier. He's golfed, dined and joked with every president since Franklin Roosevelt. They've named hospitals and schools after him, and he's even been decorated by the Queen. He emigrated to the States aged five and at 19 started in vaudeville with Fatty Arbuckle's travelling show, establishing his persona of smart-aleck, fast-talking coward who rarely gets the girl. While cutting his teeth on Broadway and as a radio star, he made his short film debut in 1934, and *The Big Broadcast of 1938* (1938) launched him into features. He became a superstar with *Road to Singapore* (1940), the first of seven *Road* pictures with Bing Crosby and Dorothy Lamour. Although he made movies regularly up until *How to Commit Marriage* in 1969, his years at Paramount were his film heyday. The *Road* films were major hits, as were 10 other of his pictures for the studio, *My Favorite*

Laugh with Hope: Rich and famous

Blonde (1942), *Monsieur Beaucaire* (1946), *The Paleface* (1948) and *Fancy Pants* (1950) among them. Despite his worldwide success, his appeal is specially to WASP Americans, and he's been accused of being politically reactionary and professionally dependent on teams of gag-writers etching on cue cards. But the old trouper's timing is wonderful and his place is secure as the century's most popular comedian since Chaplin. He's still working in his nineties.

Sir Anthony Hopkins

Actor, director
Born: *Port Talbot, Wales, December 31, 1937*

A broad-built performer with haunted eyes, Anthony Hopkins has emerged, after a career blighted by alcoholism, as the elder statesman of his profession, an actor's actor whose every role

Anthony Hopkins: *The actor's actor*

commands attention. After an acclaimed period on the London stage, he took time adapting to the film medium, languishing in supporting roles before impressing in a set of high-class projects during the 1980s. He was assured in David Lynch's *The Elephant Man* (1980), heartwarming as a crusty bookseller in *84 Charing Cross Road* (1986), while his searing turn as Captain Bligh in 1984's mutiny remake *The Bounty* trumped even Charles Laughton's original interpretation. But it was a horror role, playing urbane, gracious serial

killer Hannibal Lecter in Jonathan Demme's psycho-thriller *The Silence of the Lambs* (1991) that sealed his reputation. His memorable turn won a well-deserved Oscar but Hopkins suddenly seemed to back-pedal from the role, apparently concerned by the public's favourable response to the character. On safer ground he turned in two finely judged portraits of British repression in the Merchant-Ivory period pieces *Howards End* (1992) and *The Remains of the Day* (1993). With his South Wales background and mesmeric voice, Hopkins has long been looked on as a pretender to Richard Burton, and while he may not possess Burton's superstar aura he could now arguably rank as the better actor.

Dennis Hopper

Actor, director, writer
Born: *Dodge City, Kan., May 17, 1936*

Movie maverick Dennis Hopper's giddying slump-and-comeback career is partly due to fickle ever-changing fashions, partly due to his own once-legendary chemical indulgences. He started on a high, with a debut alongside pal James Dean in *Rebel without a Cause* (1955), but clashes with director Henry Hathaway during the making of *Manhunt* (1958) stymied his ascent, relegating him to the B-movie treadmill. Increasingly aligned to the counter-culture in the 1960s, he triumphed in directing the landmark hippie call-to-arms *Easy Rider* (1969). The picture made Hopper Hollywood's hottest ticket, a position he quickly squandered – moseying off to Mexico and blowing a fortune in filming the haemorrhaging, near-incoherent *The Last Movie* (1971). With his name poison at home, he spent much of the 1970s drifting through European art movies, but his drug intake was reaching epic proportions and a babbling, boiling-eyed cameo in Coppola's

Apocalypse Now (1979) revealed a man on accelerated self-destruct. Amazingly, Hopper cleaned up, channelling his acting and film-making skills with a new-found maturity. Rehabilitation came with his terrifying turn as the helium-snorting Frank in David Lynch's *Blue Velvet* (1986), while his directing career was revitalized in 1988 with the vivid and impactful streetgang drama *Colors*. Now an elder statesman of the Hollywood elite, Hopper looked to be slipping towards genuine legitimacy with his role in the 1994 summer blockbuster *Speed*.

John Houseman

Producer, actor, writer, author, insurance salesman
Born: JACQUES HAUSSMANN, *Bucharest, Romania, September 22, 1902*
Died: *October 31, 1988*

"When people buy insurance from me," said Houseman, "they buy it from Professor Kingsfield, they don't buy it from John Houseman the crooked producer." Most familiar to audiences from his much-loved Oscar-winning role as the cantankerous old law professor in *The Paper Chase* (1973), the subsequent TV series and a good many TV adverts, Houseman had by then already had a very successful career as a film producer and before that had co-founded the Mercury Theatre with Orson Welles, with whom he had produced and written the notorious radio version of *War of the Worlds* (1938). They also collaborated on the classic *Citizen Kane* (1941), but litigation over the authorship of the script led to the end of their partnership. His career in film production included such popular successes as *The Blue Dahlia* (1946), *Julius Caesar* (1953) and *Lust for Life* (1956), and he was a scriptwriter on *Jane Eyre* (1944), but it was his film and TV appearances that brought him to public attention.

The very picture of an archetypal spiky elder statesman, he was natural casting for *Paper Chase*, which made him a star and led to a succession of similar roles, most notably the chilling executive Bartholomew in the bleak sci-fi parable *Rollerball* (1975), a typically well-judged performance of velvety menace.

Leslie Howard

Actor, director
Born: LESLIE HOWARD STAINER, *London, England, April 3, 1893*
Died: *June 1, 1943*

During his 1930s peak Hollywood bosses regarded Leslie Howard as the archetypal English romantic – polished, quick-thinking, coolly charismatic. His two key roles were subtle variations on this carefully honed screen image. Nominally transplanted to France in 1935's The *Scarlet Pimpernel* and juggling disarming wit with prefect-style dominance as the scheming Higgins in *Pygmalion* (1938), which he also co-directed with Anthony Asquith, Howard's majestically easy unobtrusive manner led him naturally from stage success to film stardom, maintaining a balance with the more macho, inarticulate heroism of James Cagney and Paul Muni. But while he memorably romanced a youthful Ingrid Bergman in 1939's *Intermezzo*, Howard's intellectual stance did not fit well with Hollywood's concept of the great screen lover. The same year's *Gone with the Wind* (1939) saw his honourable but anaemic Ashley Wilkes significantly lose out to the more rugged, go-getting Clark Gable. Howard's last feature outing was a typically dashing turn in the heated World War Two call to arms *49th Parallel* (1941), directed by Michael Powell, who admired his acting panache but had little regard for him personally. "His charm ... was entirely artificial," Powell concluded. Howard was killed in

1943, when his plane was shot down by the Nazis who mistakenly believed Winston Churchill was his airplane.

Trevor Howard

Actor
Born: *Kent, England, September 29, 1916*
Died: *January 7, 1988*

Trevor Howard, in his heyday, was the quintessential Britisher. While never quite the Hollywood stereotype of an Englishman – a roguish, urbane gent like David Niven or Rex Harrison – Howard seemed to represent the average, unsung Brit; solid, middle-class, quietly heroic. Howard's moment of screen immortality came for his role as the reserved doctor impassioned by housewife Celia Johnson in *Brief Encounter* (1945), David Lean's evergreen ode to the romantic English spirit. Other key turns amid a mountainous film list include his performance as a corrupted clerk in *An Outcast of the Islands* (1951) and his Oscar-nominated turn as an embittered miner in Jack Cardiff's *Sons and Lovers* (1960). Even in sketchy support roles Howard's range and quality were never hard to spot. Amid the flashy direction and flamboyant acting of Carol Reed's *The Third Man* (1949), Howard's performance as the officious Major

Calloway steadily grows in significance, searing as the irascible angel battling Orson Welles's devil for the soul of hero Joseph Cotten. Fashions changed in the 1960s when Howard's brand of decency was judged outmoded against the gritty kitchen-sink realism typified by younger players like Albert Finney or Tom Courtenay. But when rewarding roles were unearthed, Howard seized them with his usual alacrity. He lit up Lean's overstuffed *Ryan's Daughter* (1970) and gave a resonant interpretation of the doomed Dr Rank in Losey's adaptation of Ibsen's *A Doll's House* (1973).

Rock Hudson

Actor
Born: ROY HAROLD SCHERER JR, *Winnetka, Ill., September 17, 1925*
Died: *October 2, 1985*

After high school and war service in the army, clean-cut handsome Hudson, seemingly hewn from the solid rock, did a variety of jobs until he was discovered by Raoul Walsh, who directed him in his film debut *Fighter Squadron* (1948). A year later he landed a contract with Universal and after five more years of small roles mostly in westerns –*Winchester '73* (1950), *Tomahawk* (1951), *Horizons West* (1952), *Taza, Son of Cochise* (1954) –

Rock Hudson: *In genial mood with co-star Doris Day*

Douglas Sirk's cult melodrama *Magnificent Obsession* (1954) turned him into a star. Then he joined Dean and Taylor for the legendary *Giant* (1956) where he matched his co-stars' sparkle. Also adding to the Hudson legend, he did three more for Sirk, *All That Heaven Allows* (1955), *Written on the Wind* (1956) and *The Tarnished Angels* (1958). In 1959 he began his hugely popular series of comedies with Doris Day in *Pillow Talk*, and throughout the 1960s was a major star, alternating comedies with dramas and action pictures. One of his best displays of acting was in John Frankenheimer's cult film *Seconds* (1966). When his career dipped, he switched successfully to TV with the long-running series *McMillan and Wife* (1971–77), but trying to revive his film career in the 1980s he found good work scarce. Though married, Hudson was gay, and he finally came out shortly before he succumbed to AIDS in October 1985, but now we can see the underrated talent behind the lurid headlines.

Holly Hunter

Actress
Born: *Conyers, Ga., February 2, 1958*

An independent-minded dynamo with a drawling Georgia accent, Holly Hunter appears to slide in and out of major-league stardom with an ease perfectly in keeping with her earthy, determinedly non-starlet nature. A film debut as a menaced teen in the stalk'n'slash pic *The Burning* (1981) could hardly have been less auspicious and it was not until 1987 that she seized the public's attention with a trio of cracking character turns in three films suddenly worthy of her talents. She was the head-strong girl confronting racism in *A Gathering of Old Men*, a broody ex-cop in the Coen Brothers' wildly inventive *Raising Arizona* and took the lead role in yuppie comedy *Broadcast News* as a principled TV

producer torn between clownish Albert Brooks and bland William Hurt. At the decade's end a typically vigorous turn as a bereaved airwoman injected a little heart into Spielberg's slick *Always* (1989). Her Oscar-winning turn in Jane Campion's *The Piano* (1993), though, revealed astounding new depths and nuances to Hunter's talent. Her portrayal of a mute, musically minded bride in semi-civilized New Zealand – all emoting eyes in a chalk-white face – was a performance of true majesty

Holly Hunter: Making sweet movie music

and should ensure that, however recklessly she flirts with the movie limelight, Hunter's status as one of America's leading actresses remains rock-solid.

William Hurt

Actor
Born: *Washington, DC, March 20, 1950*

"I am a character actor in a leading man's body", Hurt was a 1980s hit, with a series of both popular and critical successes beginning with his very first film, Ken Russell's psychedelic *Altered States* (1980), in which his cerebral performance set the pattern for what followed. Next came *Body Heat* (1981), a reworking of *Double*

Indemnity with Hurt in the Fred MacMurray role and Kathleen Turner in the Stanwyck part, which was the beginning of his collaboration with director Lawrence Kasdan, with whom he also made *The Big Chill* (1983) and *The Accidental Tourist* (1988). A risky gay role in *Kiss of the Spider Woman* (1985) won him a Best Actor Oscar and Best Actor at Cannes, which he followed with another success in *Children of a Lesser God* (1986). Here his warm performance as a teacher in a deaf school gained him an Oscar nomination and helped his co-star and friend Marlee Matlin win an Oscar. He went on to win another nomination for *Broadcast News* (1987), a satire of TV news reworked from *The Front Page*. Suddenly his daring wish to take risks turned against him when his poor performance in *A Time of Destiny* (1988) started a run of flops. Despite appearing in *The Doctor* (1991), an attempt to recapture a popular audience, he has not yet succeeded in recovering his previous form.

Anjelica Huston

Actress
Born: *Los Angeles, Calif., July 8, 1951*

Daughter of John, grand-daughter of Walter, Anjelica Huston is a grand performer in her own right, with a film roster that fairly bristles with distinctive and challenging roles. Angular, striking, faintly forbidding, she made an inauspicious debut as a teenager in her dad's 1969 picture *A Walk with Love and Death*, before setting off for a lucrative career as a catwalk model. Major-league movie success arrived with two supporting performances alongside then-partner Jack Nicholson in 1981's *The Postman Always Rings Twice* and John Huston's black-comedy thriller *Prizzi's Honor* (1985), which won her an Oscar. Rewarding character work followed, with

starring roles in her father's James Joyce-inspired swan song *The Dead* (1987), the overlooked human drama *Enemies: A Love Story* (1989) and a brilliantly twitchy, dangerous turn as the wronged mistress of Woody Allen's masterful *Crimes and Misdemeanors* (1989). More impressive still was her immaculately complex and sustained turn as an icy, hustling mum in the stylish *noir* homage *The Grifters* (1990). In the 1990s she enjoyed big box-office success as star ghoul Morticia in the genial comedy-chiller *The Addams Family* (1991) and *Addams Family Values* (1993), and turned in another smart support turn as a go-getting novelist in Allen's *Manhattan Murder Mystery* (1993). Despite a determinedly non-star persona, Huston is Hollywood royalty, and always worth a look.

John Huston

Director, writer, actor, producer
Born: *Nevada, Mo., August 5, 1906*
Died: *August 28, 1987*

John Huston is a legend of American cinema – the consummate film-maker and master of the hard-boiled contemporary yarn in a male-oriented universe. The son of actor Walter, he worked as a painter and screenwriter before rising to fame with an intense directing debut in the *film noir* blueprint *The Maltese Falcon* (1941). It was the first of several classic collaborations with Humphrey Bogart, an actor he used as the epitome of the cynical, world-weary modern-day hero, teaming with him again for *Key Largo* (1948) and *The African Queen* (1952) and casting him against type as a paranoiac gold-digger in *The Treasure of the Sierra Madre* (1948). Huston's works are distinguished by their clean, hard narratives, luminous deep-focus photography and willingness to tackle tricky moral topics, though his elegant Civil War essay *The Red Badge* of *Courage* (1951) was notoriously hacked by an uncomprehending studio. While the 1960s saw a slump in Huston's fortunes, he was still able to produce the odd gem, most notably *The Night of the*

John Huston: *Grizzled father of* film noir

Iguana (1964) and the camp *Reflections in a Golden Eye* (1967), oddly the director's own favourite picture. The 1970s and 1980s saw him back on searing form with 1975's *The Man Who Would Be King*, the oddball religious masterwork *Wise Blood* (1979) and the stylish black comedy *Prizzi's Honor* (1985). After a career loaded with thunderous movie classics, he went out on a beautifully intimate note, directing the low-key, poignant *The Dead* in 1987.

Walter Huston

Actor
Born: *Toronto, Canada, April 6, 1884*
Died: *April 7, 1950*

The Huston family has made two inestimable contributions to the art of film, one behind the camera and one in front of it. It is fitting that Walter Huston's greatest performance, and the one which finally gained him an Oscar (Best Supporting Actor), was in a film directed and scripted by his son John – *The Treasure of the Sierra Madre* (1948). It was the culmination of an extraordinary film

acting career, one which didn't actually start until he was well into his forties. He had trained as an engineer, performed to great critical acclaim on Broadway and made his screen debut as a journalist in *Gentlemen of the Press* (1928). He was superb, and rarely let the standard slip, even if the films weren't always as good as his performances in them. He was a villain in the western *The Virginian* (1930); a magnetic *Abraham Lincoln* in D. W. Griffith's movie of the same name (1930); a prison governor in Hawks's *The Criminal Code* (1931); and an overzealous policeman in *The Beast of The City* (1932). He scored huge successes in *Dodsworth* (1936) and *All That Money Can Buy* (1941), was by far the best thing in *Duel in The Sun* (1946), and capped a brilliant career with *The Treasure of the Sierra Madre.* José Ferrer called him "One of the greatest actors who ever lived," and there are few people who would disagree.

Betty Hutton

Actress, singer
Born: BETTY JUNE THORNBURG, *Battle Creek, Mich., February 26, 1921*

Blond, blue-eyed and uninhibited actress and singer, who could grab audiences with the sheer power of her high spirits. After her father's death, Hutton sang on the streets to feed her family and at 13 began singing in bands. "The Blond Bombshell", as she was now known, caught Hollywood's attention, and after her first film *The Fleet's In* (1942) she played largely sassy comedy roles laced with the odd dramatic one. Despite the moral film climate, she played a girl who gets drunk and then pregnant in Preston Sturges's *The Miracle of Morgan's Creek* (1944) and was in two successful biopics: *Incendiary Blonde* (1945), as nightclub queen Texas Guinan, and *The Perils of Pauline* (1947), playing

silent screen star Pearl White. She is best remembered as the tough yet vulnerable heroine of *Annie Get Your Gun* (1950) – a role she took over from the ailing Judy Garland. She then partnered Fred Astaire in *Let's Dance* (1950), led a starry cast in De Mille's circus epic *The Greatest Show on Earth* (1952), and played vaudeville star Blossom Seeley in *Somebody Loves Me* (1952). Shortly afterwards she walked out on her contract when the studio refused to let her then husband direct, and apart from *Spring Reunion* (1957) never made another film. In the mid-1970s she was discovered working as a maid in a Catholic rectory.

Jeremy Irons

Actor
Born: *Cowes, England, September 19, 1948*

Jeremy Irons, with his gaunt frame, soft voice and sallow, haunted face, is one of the most technically proficient British actors of his generation. A master of mood and understatement, he brings an extraordinary intellectual intensity to his work, imbuing roles with the sort of exact, humourless precision that tends to arouse admiration rather than affection. Classically trained, he started his career in theatre before coming to widespread attention as the laconic, introverted intellectual Charles Ryder in the TV series *Brideshead Revisited* (1981). He was one of the few good things about *The French Lieutenant's Woman* (1981); was excellent as a literary agent in *Betrayal* (1983), a French aristocrat in *Swann in Love* (1984) and a Jesuit priest in *The Mission* (1986); and stunning as identical twins in the chilling *Dead Ringers* (1988). His masterpiece, however, was as the stone-faced murder suspect Claus von Bulow in *Reversal of Fortune* (1990), a beautifully controlled, bravura performance that deservedly won him a Best Actor Oscar. He was almost

as good playing an obsessive lover in *Damage* (1992), and as the title role in Steven Soderbergh's *Kafka* (1991), and looks set to remain a considerable force in the world of cinema acting for some time to come.

Glenda Jackson

Actress, politician
Born: *Birkenhead, England, May 9, 1936*

Jackson was the liberated woman's actress. Intelligent, independent, witty and sexually freewheeling, she perfectly captured the swinging mood of the early 1970s. Attractive in an unconventional way, with a deep gritty voice, she studied at RADA, worked with The Royal Shakespeare Company, and first appeared on screen in a couple of largely forgettable experimental shorts. She burst out of her corset and into the international limelight in Ken Russell's *Women in Love* (1969). Her powerful portrayal of a self-aware, sexually liberated schoolteacher won her an Oscar, and marked out the territory she was to make her own over the next few years. She was exceptional as a woman in love with a bisexual man in *Sunday, Bloody Sunday* (1971) and netted another Oscar for *A Touch of Class* (1972), as married George Segal's shrewish lover. *A Bequest to the Nation* (1973), *The Maids* (1975) and Losey's *The Romantic Englishwoman* (1975) were also good, if little noticed. The buzz that surrounded her early work tailed off through the 1970s, however and, with the exception of the amusing *House Calls* (1978) with Walther Matthau, she gradually slipped from public favour. The 1980s saw her returning to TV and theatre work, and she has now moved into politics, a perfectly natural progression from the forceful, dominant and opinionated screen characters she so loved to play.

Emil Jannings

Actor

Born: THEODOR FRIEDRICH EMIL JANENZ, *Rorschach, Switzerland, July 23, 1884*

Died: *January 2, 1950*

Jannings, with his huge pudding face and permanent scowl, was once regarded as the greatest actor in the world. He certainly starred in some of the masterpieces of the early German cinema, and his screen presence was never less than commanding. However, he was essentially a stage actor, and, for all his blustering power, much of his work now seems mannered and outdated. He started as a touring repertory actor, made his film debut in 1914 and went on to work with some of the finest German directors of the age – Murnau, Dupont, Pabst and Lubitsch. This was a German golden age, and Jannings's screen creations were central to it – *Othello* (1922); a camp Haroun Al Raschid in *Waxworks* (1924); Nero in *Quo Vadis* (1924); and, most memorably, a proud hotel doorman reduced to a lavatory attendant in Murnau's masterful *The Last Laugh* (1924). He went to Hollywood and won the first-ever Best Actor Academy Award for his performances in *The Way of All Flesh* (1927) and *The Last Command* (1928,) and then returned to Germany to give one of his greatest performances, opposite Marlene Dietrich in *The Blue Angel* (1930). He happily turned out Nazi propaganda films, and was blacklisted. At the end of the war, his career was finished, and he died five years later in Austria.

Derek Jarman

Director, writer, painter, saint

Born: *Northwood, England, January 31, 1942*

Died: *February 19, 1994*

Of all modern British film-makers, Jarman most embodies the spirit of quietly determined criticism of the establishment's heart of darkness. His directorial debut, *Sebastiane* (1976), a gay take on the life of St Sebastian, created the world's only film in Latin, causing a stir on account of its sexual frankness. The films that followed mixed an expression of his poetic vision with an affirmation and celebration of gay sensibility and cultural heritage – like his camp, delightful version of *The Tempest* (1979), the darkly poetic *The Angelic Conversation* (1985) and *Caravaggio* (1986), reclaiming the painter as a gay icon. He made a direct, vocal challenge to the complacent, brutish extremes of the 1970s' and 1980s' right-wing government – as in *The Last of England* (1987), his broadside against Thatcherite Britain, his poetic anti-war film *War Requiem* (1989), built

Jarman: St. Derek of Dungeness

around Benjamin Britten's music, and *Jubilee* (1978), his punk antidote to the royalist hysteria of the Queen's silver jubilee. Learning that he was HIV-positive, he bought a desolate coastline shack where he created a stone and driftwood garden, celebrated in *The Garden* (1990), followed by his overtly gay, updated version of *Edward II* (1991) and *Wittgenstein* (1993) a homo-aware view of the philosopher. Succumbing to AIDS and blind, he responded positively as ever to his limited resources with *Blue* (1993), his extraordinary, moving final film with just a blue screen and voices. A gay champion, vociferous humanist and icon of the alternative, Jarman always spoke in a language accessible to anyone with the guts to listen and the intelligence to understand, and was an important voice in a time when few others were raised.

Jim Jarmusch

Director, writer

Born: *Akron, Oh., January 22, 1953*

Jim Jarmusch feels that his movies – high on concept, light on plot – are made up of the bits other filmmakers would instantly cut from their pictures. His fascination is the minutiae of existence, the "time between" events when characters are inadvertently thrown together, unsheltered and exposed. Jarmusch's movies offer a lazily hip trip through an everyday world turned suddenly unfamiliar. His principal players are often outsiders, foreigners to whom the American experience is a glorious but indecipherable puzzle. The work also proves a lovely alliance of contemporary concerns with antiquated forms. Jarmusch's two most recent releases, *Mystery Train* (1989) and *Night on Earth* (1991), are portmanteau pieces, the first recounting a Canterbury Tales-style pilgrimage to Memphis, the second transforming five taxi cabs into confession boxes on wheels, sacred, self-contained spots where strangers meet in moments of unguarded self-revelation. Similarly, the director's much-loved *Down by Law* (1986) takes a picaresque form, following the jumbled misadventures of a bunch of ex-cons as they strike out through Louisiana's bayou country. While at times too meandering and self-consciously eccentric to rank as all-time cinema classics, Jarmusch's work possesses wit and charm in abundance. In an increasingly grey and conformist industry, he's an artist of rare originality, conjuring up a sublimely strange yet oddly benevolent world, peopled by protagonists who continually confound audience expectations. Folk-tales from the fringe.

Dame Celia Johnson

Actress

Born: *Surrey, England, December 18, 1908*

Died: *April 25, 1982*

Marvellously English in her ability to suffer stoically, Johnson will forever be remembered as the nearly adulterous, nearly suicidal, nearly-woman of David Lean's *Brief Encounter* (1945). Born in Richmond, Surrey, she attended RADA. Her screen debut was *Dirty Work* (1934) but Carol Reed's propaganda film, *A Letter From Home* (1941) brought her more attention. Three highly successful collaborations with David Lean and Noel Coward began as the latter's wife in *In Which We Serve* (1942). She struggled to overcome her distinctively clipped, well-bred accent to be working class for *This Happy Breed* (1944), but *Brief Encounter* found her on more familiar territory. Her despairing, self-restrained housewife was the central performance, ahead of Trevor Howard's romantic commuter, and won her an Oscar nomination, rare for a player in a British film at the time. Her marriage took precedence over her career, though, and she was so selective over scripts that she made less than a dozen features in all, but she expanded her range to include comedy in *The Captain's Paradise* (1953), and as the embittered Scottish headmistress in *The Prime of Miss Jean Brodie* (1969),

Johnson: Suffering stoically in Brief Encounter

despite opposition from 20th Century-Fox. She was reunited with Howard in television's *Staying On* (1980) before being honoured as a Dame in 1981. A fine actress with whom many of her audience identified closely, she died of a stroke two days before opening a play in London's West End.

Al Jolson

Singer, actor

Born: ASA YOELSON, *Srednike, Lithuania, May 26, 1886*
Died: *October 25, 1950*

The first person ever to speak in a feature-length film, his "you ain't heard nothing yet" proved prophetic, the blacked-up singer of "Mammy" going on to become the first genuine pop star. Russian-born to Jewish parents, he moved to Washington, DC aged

Al Jolson: "You ain't heard nothin' yet"

four, where he learnt to sing in the synagogue, but ran away to join a circus. He graduated to vaudeville and, following the 19th-century minstrel tradition, first wore blackface in 1906, later appearing on stage with Mae West. D. W. Griffith's attempt to make a silent film with Jolson ended in lawsuits and acrimony, but *The Jazz Singer* (1927) truly revolutionized the movies. Jolson sang a few songs, spoke a few lines, and massive money was made, surpassed only by his second talkie, *The Singing Fool* (1928), which set and held a box office record until *Gone With The Wind*, 11 years later.

Hollywood clung to the stereotypical depiction of blacks, even attempting to pass Jolson for the genuine article until the very end of *Big Boy* (1930). His popularity waned until the wartime troops he entertained took to him. This prompted *The Jolson Story* (1946) in which he sang, dubbing Larry Parks, but was peeved at not being allowed to play himself. *Jolson Sings Again* (1949) was the successful sequel, and he was still planning an on-screen comeback when he died of a heart attack.

Jennifer Jones

Actress

Born: PHYLLIS ISLEY, *Tulsa, Okla., March 2, 1919*

An actress of fragile beauty, more suited to the gentle image of the saintly Bernadette than the tempestuous roles with which she later tried to broaden her range. Jones arrived in Hollywood in 1939, played leads in a B western and a *Dick Tracy* serial, and was taken up by producer David O. Selznick, who after careful grooming launched her in *The Song of Bernadette* (1943), which won her an Oscar. The "women at home" theme of *Since You Went Away* (1944) struck a wartime nerve and she did well in Lubitsch's *Cluny Brown* (1946). She played the tempestuous female love interest in Selznick's big-budget western *Duel in the Sun* (1947), and two years later they were married. She was an unlikely Emma in Minnelli's *Madame Bovary* (1949), tried her hand at steamy melodrama as *Ruby Gentry* (1953) and was a big hit as the Eurasian doctor opposite William Holden in *Love Is a Many Splendored Thing* (1955). Well cast as Elizabeth in *The Barretts of Wimpole Street* (1957), she held her ground against John Gielgud's powerful performance, but was brutally dismissed by novelist Ernest Hemingway as "too old for the part" in Selznick's last film, the

overinflated flop *A Farewell to Arms* (1957). Selznick died in 1965 and in 1971 Jones married industrialist Norton Simon, since when, apart from *The Towering Inferno* (1974), she has not made another film.

Tommy Lee Jones

Actor

Born: *Suba, Tex., September 15, 1946*

The 1990s have seen the dark-haired, raw-boned Tommy Lee Jones make a belated ascent to the front rank of Hollywood stardom. It's a deserved reward for 20 years on the B-movie treadmill, a respected but largely untapped talent. He made an unlikely debut in 1970 with a bit part in the high-gloss weepie *Love Story* and later acted alongside Laurence Olivier in 1978's trashy *The Betsy*. Three better projects followed, though each relegated Jones to second-fiddle roles – playing support to Faye Dunaway in *The Eyes of Laura Mars* (1978), Sissy Spacek in *Coal Miner's Daughter* (1980) and Sally Field in *Back Roads* (1981). But when Jones happened on a prize role he always attacked it with passion, winning an Emmy award for his searing central portrait in the 1982 TV dramatization of Norman Mailer's *The Executioner's Song*. A sea-change in Jones's fortunes occurred in the early 1990s. His turn as a shady New Orleans homosexual was one of the high spots of Oliver Stone's *JFK* (1991) and paved the way for his Oscar-winning breakthrough role as Harrison Ford's dogged pursuer in the 1993 summer sensation *The Fugitive*. Jones promptly consolidated his position with a majestic performance as the traumatized Vietnam soldier of Stone's *Heaven and Earth* (1993), engaged in a spot of superstar showboating in the same director's ferocious *Natural Born Killers* (1994) and turned in a meaty lead turn in *Cobb* (1994). Long may he reign.

Louis Jouvet

Actor

Born: JULES EUGÈNE LOUIS JOUVET, *Crozon, France, December 24, 1887*
Died: *August 16, 1951*

Theatre was his love and a man of the theatre was how he always saw himself. Yet despite regarding films as a means of earning money to sponsor additional stage productions, Jouvet's forceful screen personality resulted in a number of outstanding performances. Ironically in view of his later celebrity, Jouvet was rejected three times by the Paris Conservatoire but, determined to be an actor, he crept into the theatre by the back door of administration and once he got on stage there was no stopping him. He made his silent film debut in *Shylock* (1913), and the same year became director of the Théâtre du Vieux-Colombier, then the Théâtre des Champs Élysées and one of Paris's leading actors. His first major film role in *Topaze* (1933), as a wily schoolteacher-turned-businessman, gives an early example of the Hollywood remake syndrome. A version starring John Barrymore was released the following year, and later remakes featured Fernandel and Peter Sellers, but the character is still identified with Jouvet. Other major roles include the crafty Spanish chaplain of *La Kermesse Heroïque* (1935); the gambler count in Renoir's film of Gorki's *The Lower Depths* (1936); the sanctimonious bishop in *Drôle de Drame* (1937); and the sleazy pimp of *Hôtel du Nord* (1938), both for Carné; and the ageing actor in the old people's home in *La Fin du Jour* (1939). He toured South America during the war but re-established himself in French theatre in 1945. His first film role after the war was the police inspector with a perpetual cold in Clouzot's murder mystery *Quai des Orfèvres* (1947), and he was the inspector again in his final film, *A Story of Love* (1951).

Boris Karloff

Actor
Born: WILLIAM HENRY PRATT,
London, England, November 23, 1883
Died: *February 2, 1969*

Universal had planned *Frankenstein* (1931) as a vehicle for Bela Lugosi to follow his success in *Dracula (1931)*, but he refused the role due to other commitments and it was offered to Karloff, then in another film at the same studio. Thus creating the single best-known image of the genre, Karloff lumbered and growled his way into a career spanning five decades, redolent with murderers, mad scientists and devil worshippers, that made him a household name in films like *The Raven* (1935), *The Man They Could Not Hang* (1939) and *The Body Snatcher* (1945). In real life a mild-mannered gentleman with a love of lit-

Boris Karloff: G-r-r-r-r-r-r-r-r-r-r-r-r-r-r-r-r-r-r

erature and cricket, the screen Karloff, with his gaunt features, heavy-lidded gaze and that characteristic lisping delivery, became one of the most abiding figures in horror movies. Made as cheap entertainments, these films were approached in earnest by the people involved, and this serious-minded, conscientious actor was capable of much more than simply shocking an audience. By a single cavernous stare Karloff could fill the screen with the expectation of terror, an ability rarely seen in modern horror performers.

Regarded with great affection and with over 100 movies to his credit, he is still best remembered for *Frankenstein*, *The Mummy* (both 1932) and *Bride of Frankenstein* (1935), three films that made him an icon of Western cinema culture.

Aki Kaurismaki

Director, writer, producer
Born: *Helsinki, Finland,*
April 4, 1957

Kaurismaki's inventive films are marked by a dour and sardonic humour, a gritty black realism and the imaginative use of music. He is one of the few Finnish directors to make a mark on the international scene in the 1980s. He worked as a film critic, co-founded the film co-operative Filmtotal with elder brother Mika and Anssi Mänttäri and was co-writer and assistant director for Mika in the early 1980s, with whom he co-directed the "rockumentary" *The Saimaa Gesture* (1981). His first solo film was *Crime and Punishment* (1983). His prolific output throughout the 1980s of features, shorts, documentaries and rock videos includes *Shadows in Paradise* (1986), the first of a trilogy completed with *Ariel* (1988) – the misadventures of a redundant miner and Kaurismaki's first British release – and *The Match Factory Girl* (1990). One of his best-known films is *Leningrad Cowboys Go America* (1989), a rock n' roll road movie, shot in the United States. The Cowboys also featured (with the ex-Red Army Choir) in the concert documentary *Total Balalaika Show* (1993) – Woodstock meets Vladivostok. In 1990 he came to Britain to make his tribute to the Ealing comedies in *I Hired a Contract Killer* with French icon Jean-Pierre Léaud. It was deliciously odd and funny. *Take Care of Your Scarf, Tatiana* (1994) is another road movie about what Kaurismaki describes as "the amazing frame of mind of Finnish man".

Danny Kaye

Actor
Born: DAVID DANILE KOMINSKI,
Brooklyn, NY, January 18, 1913
Died: *March 3, 1987*

Highly talented comic actor Kaye was skilled in mime, impersonation and the vocal agility needed for the tongue-twister songs which became his trademark. He boasted a personality which was invariably sunny, in public if not always in private that made him a darling with audiences worldwide; the clean-living boy scout with the hyperactive wit. Kaye, a tailor's son, started in vaudeville and nightclubs, broke into Broadway revue in 1939, and made a big impact in *Lady in the Dark* (1941), where he stopped the show with "Tchaikovsky", a song in which he named 54 Russian composers in 38 seconds. Samuel Goldwyn put him into *Up in Arms* (1944), the first of a series of lavish, Technicolor comedies, which included Thurber's compulsive daydreamer in *The Secret Life of Walter Mitty* (1947). Later Kaye helped Goldwyn fulfil his long-cherished dream to make *Hans Christian Andersen* (1957). Other hits include the spy comedy *Knock on Wood* (1953); the feel-good Yuletide caper *White Christmas* (1956) with Bing Crosby; *The Court Jester* (1956), a delightful costume comedy – and the biopic of bandleader Red Nichols, *The Five Pennies* (1959). From the 1950s Kaye's work for the charity UNICEF took up more of his time. He returned to films in *The Madwoman of Chaillot* (1969) for Bryan Forbes in Britain, where he was more popular than in his native America, and played Hook to Mia Farrow's television *Peter Pan* (1976). He received a special Oscar in 1954 for his unique talents, and was married from 1940 to composer/lyricist Sylvia Fine, who wrote much of his material.

Elia Kazan

Director
Born: *Istanbul, Turkey,*
September 7, 1909

One of the legendary figures of American screen, Elia Kazan infused post-war cinema with the pioneering acting styles and political edge of New York's famed Group Theater. By introducing the method school of acting to American picture-houses, Kazan brought a new sense of realism to the film medium, showcasing the generation's two most compulsive male actors. He plucked James Dean from obscurity for the lead role in 1955's *East of Eden* and immortalized the young Marlon Brando in Tennessee Williams's heated *A Streetcar Named Desire* (1952) and the majestic *On the Waterfront* (1954). The driving force behind many of the era's most urgent and provocative pictures, Kazan spotlighted antisemitism in *Gentleman's Agreement* (1947), child sexuality in *Baby Doll* (1956) and the corrosive influence of celebrity with the dazzling *A Face in the Crowd* (1957). He sprang from a socially conscious age that truly believed that it could change the world. But despite his revered position Kazan is not without his detractors. Contemporary critics dismiss his lesser work as faded and heavy-handed and argue that his films' liberal zeal is undermined by Kazan's own forced complicity with the House Un-American Activities Committee in 1952, which blacklisted many left-leaning Hollywood artists. Nevertheless, there's little doubting the rigour and purpose of Kazan's *oeuvre*, nor his immense influence on the American filmmakers who followed. His last film teamed him with Jack Nicholson and Robert De Niro, two actors he'd surely influenced, for a faithful adaptation of Scott Fitzgerald's Hollywood tragedy *The Last Tycoon* (1976).

Buster Keaton

Actor, director, writer, producer

Born: JOSEPH KEATON, *Piqua, Kan., October 4, 1895*
Died: *February 1, 1966*

The cinema of Buster Keaton looks to have aged better than that of his great silent-screen rival Charlie Chaplin. Whereas Chaplin's combination of pratfalls and sentimentality can now appear tinged with mawkishness, Keaton – with his sphinx-like impassivity, uncanny athleticism and subtle genius at gag creation – is now viewed as the more sophisticated artist. Raised in a vaudeville family, Keaton took instinctively to the medium of cinema and two of his films, 1924's *Sherlock Jnr* and 1928's *The Cameraman*, were even set in the world of movie-making. Though he generally credited an assistant as "director" during his

Buster Keaton: *Comic genius well on-track*

peak 1920s period, he enjoyed absolute control: scripting, starring and directing. Keaton was the lugubrious, soulful clown, trapped in an aggressive world that his passive elusiveness helps him triumph over; whether caught between feuding southern broods in *Our Hospitality* (1923), stuck aboard an abandoned liner in *The Navigator* (1924), buffeted by a cyclone in *Steamboat Bill Jnr* (1928) or tackling runaway saboteurs in 1927's *The General*. But Keaton's fine-tuned artistry was eventually savaged by the onset of sound cinema. He rashly decided to surrender creative control to MGM studios who misused his talents as Keaton – always something of a Hollywood hellraiser – slid into a sad alcoholic decline. The 1950s saw a partial renaissance, with luminous cameos in *Sunset Boulevard* (1950) and as Chaplin's stage partner in the elegiac 1952 tragicomedy *Limelight*.

Diane Keaton

Actress, director, photographer

Born: DIANE HALL, *Los Angeles, Calif., January 5, 1946*

Keaton's combination of Californian hippyism with Manhattan sophistication and underlying insecurity epitomized much of the spirit of 1970s America, particularly in her Oscar-winning performance as *Annie Hall* (1977). She studied drama in New York aged 19 and played a lead role on Broadway in *Hair* in 1968 – even though she refused to strip off. She began her long-running personal and professional partnership with Woody Allen in *Play It Again Sam*, first on stage (1969), then reprised on film (1972). Apart from *Annie Hall*, other notable work together includes *Manhattan* (1979) and the Bergmanesque *Interiors* (1978). As a dramatic actress she showed her muscle as the teacher with a dangerous night life in *Looking for Mr Goodbar* (1977), with subsequent partner Warren Beatty in *Reds* (1981), in Gillian Armstrong's Hollywood debut picture *Mrs Soffel* (1984), and as a single parent in the underrated *The Good Mother* (1988) with Liam Neeson. She made the most of her limited opportunities playing Al Pacino's wife in the three *Godfather* films (1972, 1974 and 1990). She was recently reunited with Allen for the delightful *Manhattan Murder Mystery* (1993), which combined Nick and Nora Charles-style comedy thriller with Allen's urban angst trademark. Her directing credits include a documentary, *Heaven* (1987) and a teleplay, *The Girl with a Crazy Brother* (about schizophrenia). She has also published two volumes of photography.

Michael Keaton

Actor

Born: MICHAEL DOUGLAS, *Pittsburgh, Pa., September 9, 1951*

Talented comic and engaging dramatic player, Keaton has had his fair share of flops on the way to his rather unlikely stardom. Though a natural comedian and not built in the heroic mould, he plays heroes and prefers dramas of significance to the comedy fluff he's so funny in. After unsuccessful TV series and movies, Keaton's film career got off to a bright start in 1982 with Ron Howard's *Night Shift* and the hit *Mr Mom* (1983). His career was in minor key until he triumphed as "the ghost with the most" in Tim Burton's *Beetlejuice*, one of the big smashes of 1988, leading to his landmark lead role in Burton's megahit *Batman* (1989), in which he was impressively grave and haunted as the Caped Crusader. He's used his star power to vary the roles so much he's a difficult actor to pigeonhole: an alcoholic in *Clean and Sober* (1988), a mental patient in *The Dream Team* (1989), a loopy tenant in *Pacific Heights* (1990), a dad dying of cancer in *My Life*, ace reporter in *The Paper*. Perhaps the actor he most closely resembles is Jack Lemmon; like him he combines the natural comedian's perfect timing with an urge to be serious and intelligent. He takes risks, boldly goes and, though a lack of clear-cut star image blunts his broad public appeal, every Keaton appearance is one to look forward to.

Howard Keel

Actor, singer

Born: HAROLD CLIFFORD LEEK, *Gillespie, Ill., April 13, 1917*

A big star of 1950s Hollywood musicals, Keel boasted a strong and lusty untrained baritone voice, warm grin and good looks, exactly right for the heyday of the screen musical. Son of a coal-miner, Keel broke into musical theatre via a spell entertaining workers in aircraft plants. While playing the lead in the London production of *Oklahoma* he was cast in a minor British film, *The Small Voice* (1958). He found instant stardom in *Annie Get Your Gun* (1950), where his likeable personality made the swaggering male lead palatable, and went on to become one of the cornerstones of the MGM musicals, many of them co-starring Kathryn Grayson: *Show Boat* (1951), *Lovely to Look At* (1952) and *Kiss Me Kate* (1953), where he redeemed another male chauvinist character with his warmth. Other musicals include *Calamity Jane* (1953) with Doris Day, *Rose Marie* (1954) with Ann Blyth, and *Seven Brides for Seven Brothers* (1954), one of the last of the original screen musicals. When musicals declined, Keel moved into dramatic roles in often minor films, including the British sci-fi movie *The Day of the Triffids* (1962), loosely based on John Wyndham's novel. He continued to draw huge audiences on stage, television and the nightclub circuit, sometimes with former co-stars Grayson and Jane Powell. In 1981 he was a big hit in the cast of the television soap *Dallas*.

Ruby Keeler

Actress, dancer, singer

Born: ETHEL KEELER, *Halifax, Canada, August 25, 1909*
Died: *February 28, 1993*

Good-natured actress, energetic performer and pretty dancer, Keeler specialized in playing the chorus girl who took over the lead from the temperamental leading lady and became a star. Keeler's family moved to New York when she was three. Her father scraped a living delivering ice, but somehow found the money for his daughter's tap-dancing lessons. She became a chorus girl at 14, graduated to feature roles and turned down a Broadway lead in 1929 to join her new husband Al Jolson in Hollywood. Initially taken up by Warners because her tap-dancing sounded so good in talkies, she starred in a string of their naively plotted, now classic backstage musicals, many of them characterized by Busby Berkeley's surreal choreography, in which her romantic interest was usually Dick Powell – an on-screen partnership which prospered through such films as *42nd Street* (1933), *Gold Diggers of 1933* (1933) and *Footlight Parade* (1934) – but also with James Cagney: *Dames* (1934) and *Colleen* (1936). She made only one film with Jolson, *Go Into Your Dance* (1935), and shortly afterwards she left Warners at Jolson's insistance. Two years later they were divorced. After one more film, *Sweetheart of the Campus* (1941), she married a real estate broker and retired. After her husband died in 1969, she made a guest appearance in *The Phynx* (1970) and starred in the very successful Broadway revival of *No No Nanette* (1971).

Harvey Keitel

Actor
Born: *New York, NY, May 13, 1941*

Brooding, tenacious former US marine Harvey Keitel ranks as one of cinema's most driven and committed performers, shooting to fame in his first four movies along-side director Martin Scorsese. Most significant of these collaborations was his role as the troubled hero of *Mean Streets* (1973), the film that ironically saw him eclipsed by second-billed Robert De Niro, thereafter

Scorsese's preferred film player. By the time of the next key Scorsese outing, 1976's *Taxi Driver*, Keitel's involvement was reduced to a scant support turn as a lank-haired pimp and he was not to work with the director again until 1988's controversial *The Last Temptation of Christ*. Fortunately Keitel's impact as a performer guaranteed rewarding roles away from the Scorsese stable, most notably in Ridley Scott's *The Duellists* (1977) and Tony Richardson's *The Border* (1982). In the 1990s his uncompromising hunt for testing work belatedly lifted him from respected middle-ranker to cutting-edge film icon. His turn as the likeable cop-in-pursuit in *Thelma and Louise* (1991) laid the ground for his portrayal of a very different breed of law-enforcer in Abel Ferrara's nightmarish *Bad Lieutenant* (1992). Keitel's support of little-known directors also paid a double dividend, with career-topping turns in Jane Campion's *The Piano* (1993) and as a suited-up hoodlum in Quentin Tarantino's feverish *Reservoir Dogs* (1992), a picture his championing presence had largely helped to finance.

Gene Kelly

Actor, dancer, director, choreographer
Born: EUGENE CURRAN KELLY, *Pittsburgh, Pa., August 23, 1912*

In any history of the screen musical, Gene Kelly merits a starring role. Though a capable actor and director, his genius is as dancer and choreographer. His imaginative, story-based approach and spontaneous and virile personal style advanced the art of cinematic dance by several giant leaps. After Broadway chorus work, Kelly played stage lead in *Pal Joey* (1940) and made his first film *For Me and My Gal* (1942) with Judy Garland. He later co-choreographed *Cover Girl* (1944) with fellow Broadway hoofer Stanley

Gene Kelly: The musical's raining king

Donen. Other landmarks of the 1940s include his ground-breaking dance with the cartoon mouse of *Tom and Jerry* in *Anchors Aweigh* (1945) and his *Slaughter on 10th Avenue* ballet in *Words and Music* (1948). *On the Town* (1949) was the first of three co-directed with Donen, the others being the thrilling *Singin' in the Rain* (1952) and the less successful *It's Always Fair Weather* (1955). Minnelli's *An American in Paris* (1951,) with its climactic Gershwin ballet, introduced Kelly's discovery Leslie Caron. *Invitation to the Dance* (1956), an all-ballet musical, won the West Berlin Film Festival Grand Prize and was a commercial flop. Later work includes straight roles such as the reporter in *Inherit the Wind* (1960), directing Barbra Streisand in *Hello Dolly* (1969) and major contributions to the three *That's Entertainment!* compilations (1974, 1976 and 1994). He was awarded a special Oscar in 1951 for his choreographic achievements.

Grace Kelly

Actress
Born: *Philadelphia, Pa., November 12, 1929*
Died: *1982*

When Grace Kelly married Prince Rainier of Monaco it was seen as the dream conclusion to a fairytale career. While her period as a jobbing actress may have been brief, her serene, translucent beauty marked her, along with Marilyn Monroe, as a key female star of 1950s cinema. Poised and pol-

ished, she was used by directors as the embodiment of sophisticated but unthreatening womanhood, playing Gary Cooper's pacifist fiancée in Fred Zinnemann's *High Noon* (1952) and a marrying debutante in the plush 1956 musical *High Society*. But Kelly was anxious to prove herself more than an elegant ornament, winning a Best Actress Oscar for her star turn as Bing Crosby's frumpy wife in 1954's *The Country Girl*. The most significant collaboration in Kelly's career was with Alfred Hitchcock, who appeared to take an unhealthy delight in burrowing beneath her ice-cool exterior. The

Kelly: Grace under fire

director had her baffled by Cary Grant in *To Catch a Thief* (1955), throttled by an assassin in *Dial M for Murder* (1954) and menaced by Raymond Burr in *Rear Window* (1954) – the film which paradoxically provided her with her most rounded and empowered role as James Stewart's dress designer girlfriend. Retiring in 1956 at the peak of her silver screen fame, Kelly lived her princess's existence until a tragic car crash death 26 years later.

Deborah Kerr

Actress
Born: DEBORAH JANE KERR-TRIMMER, *Helensburgh, Scotland, September 30, 1921*

Trained as a dancer and marked out by her snobbish air for lady-like roles, Kerr still suggested untapped depths of resourcefulness and passion beneath the gentle exterior. She made her mark in British films such as *Major Barbara* (1941), *Love on the Dole* (1941), *The Life and Death of Colonel Blimp* (1943) and *Black Narcissus* (1947), after which she went to Hollywood to play opposite Clark Gable in *The Hucksters* (1947). Along with costume dramas such as *Quo Vadis?* (1951), *The Prisoner of Zenda* (1952) and *Young Bess* (1953), she enjoyed stronger dramatic roles. These included her six Oscar-nominated performances: *Edward My Son* (1949) as Spencer Tracy's hard-pressed wife; *From Here to Eternity* (1953) where she showed that hidden passion in the famous beach love scene with Burt Lancaster; the governess in *The King and I* (1956); Huston's *Heaven Knows, Mr Allison* (1957) as the nun to Robert Mitchum's rough diamond; the crushed spinster daughter of *Separate Tables* (1958); and with Mitchum again as Australian homesteaders in *The Sundowners* (1960). Other notable roles include the protective governess in Jack Clayton's *The Innocents* (1961) and the gentle but spirited spinster artist of Tennessee Williams's *The Night of the Iguana*. After stage work in the 1970s, she did the television mini-series *A Woman of Substance* (1984) and *Hold the Dream* (1986), and impressed as an ex-Raj widow befriending an Indian family in *The Assam Garden* (1985).

Ben Kingsley

Actor
Born: KRISHNA BANJI, *Scarborough, England, December 31, 1943*

Kingsley's sudden emergence as a star when he won the Oscar and a British Film Academy award for 1982's *Gandhi* startled cinemagoers unaware of his distinguished stage career. Though he'd enjoyed high times at the Royal Shakespeare Company, his movie career didn't begin until 1972 with a support role in *Fear Is the Key* and there it might have stopped if Richard Attenborough hadn't cast him as the loinclothed leader. Since then, he's overcome difficulties in casting and energetically pursued a high-profile transatlantic film career. Two of his best films so far are from Harold Pinter scripts: *Betrayal* (1982) with Jeremy Irons and *Turtle Diary* (1985) with Glenda Jackson. His search for differing roles has taken him from his kidnapping Arab prince in *Harem* (1984) to the period thriller with *Pascali's Island* (1988), and from futuristic fantasy with *Slipstream* (1989) to comedy as Dr Watson opposite Michael Caine's Sherlock Holmes in *Without a Clue* (1988). And he made a success of all of them. In the 1990s, working much in America, he's come up with an Oscar-nominated role in the grand gangster movie *Bugsy* (1991), the baddie in the caper thriller *Sneakers* (1992), the kindly chess teacher in *Innocent Moves* (1993), and a searing performance for Spielberg in *Schindler's List* (1993). Nothing has yet topped his *Gandhi*, but you know he'll keep trying, and coming up with polished performances.

Klaus Kinski

Actor
Born: NIKOLAUS GUNTHER NAKSZYNSKI, *Zoppot, Poland, 1926*
Died: *November 23, 1991*

Father of the ravishing Nastassja, gaunt, wild-eyed German character actor Klaus Kinski had a long and varied career, making an extraordinary number of films though few of any real consequence. He is now chiefly known through his work with director Werner Herzog, a partnership which brought out the best of both of them and propelled him into an international career of variable fortune. His films spanned every genre, including Billy Wilder's comedy *Buddy Buddy* (1981) as a stereotypical mad scientist, the horror film *Venom* (1982), the sci-fi hit *Android* (1982), playing a slightly less mad scientist, the war film *Code Name: Wild Geese* (1986) and the John Le Carré thriller *The Little Drummer Girl* (1984). Kinski made his first film, *Morituri*, in 1948 and followed it with memorable appearances in films like *For a Few Dollars More* (1965) and *Doctor Zhivago* (1965). His ability to project enormous screen intensity made him perfect for creepy villains and characters on the edge. Though he was prone to gilding the lily when anyone would let him, he could be electrifying when handled properly by the right director. Now a cult figure, Kinski is best remembered for his magisterial films with Herzog: *Aguirre Wrath of God* (1972), *Woyzeck* (1978), *Nosferatu* (1979), *Burden of Dreams* (1982), *Fitzcarraldo* (1982) and *Cobra Verde* (1988).

Nastassja Kinski

Actress
Born: *Berlin, Germany, January 24, 1960*

Nastassja Kinski made her bid for stardom early. At 16 she bagged a supporting role in Wim Wenders's *Wrong Movement* (1975) and by 20 was already a bona fide sex symbol, the anguished heroine of lover Roman Polanski's lush Thomas Hardy adaptation *Tess* (1979). The daughter of actor Klaus, this strong-featured, hauntingly beautiful performer brought an elusive extra dimension to some of the most unusual and intriguing films of the early 1980s. She played the demonically possessed heroine of Paul Schrader's *Cat People* (1982), upstaged Gérard Depardieu in the wobbly *The Moon in the Gutter* (1983) and her turn as a fragile showgirl lit up Francis Coppola's glorious folly *One from the Heart* (1982). But it was her role in Wenders's American odyssey *Paris, Texas* (1984) that truly burnt her into film iconography. As the object of Harry Dean Stanton's desperate quest, Kinski doesn't even appear until the last quarter of the film and even then, hidden behind glass in a down-at-heel peep-

Nastassja Kinski: *Peroxide vision of* Paris, Texas

show, there is a mirage-like quality about her, something undefined and unobtainable. Since a co-starring turn in the disastrous *Revolution* (1985), Kinski has ceased to be such a potent force within cinema, although she impressed in a supporting role as an angel in Wenders's low-powered fable *Faraway, So Close* (1993). As to future plans, her approach seems a typical blend of steely ambition and philosophic detachment. "I want absolutely everything," she says. "I'm not saying I want it right away. But I do want it."

Kris Kristofferson

Actor, musician
Born: *Brownsville, Tex., June 22, 1936*

Kris Kristofferson is one of the few male rock stars to have made any significant impression as a film actor. With his handsome grizzled face and hell-raising reputation, he was tailor-made for those free-wheeling renegade roles that became so fashionable in the late 1960s and 1970s; and although his persona was limited, he proved on more than one occasion that with the right script and director he could produce a perfectly ade-

113

quate performance. He was already established as a popular recording artist when he was given his first major role, as a washed-up pop star in Cisco Pike (1972). It remains his finest screen performance, and introduced the cool, haggard, edge that was to inform his best work. He impressed as the outlaw hero of Peckinpah's *Pat Garrett and Billy The Kid* (1973), and had one of his most sympathetic roles as Ellen Burstyn's lover in *Alice Doesn't Live Here Anymore* (1975). He was typecast as a fading rock star in *A Star Is Born* (1976), and as a wacky rebel truck-driver in *Convoy* (1978); and proved surprisingly effective as a US marshal in Cimino's underrated *Heaven's Gate* (1980) which was his last film of any note, though he gave a fine restrained turn in Alan Rudolph's *Trouble in Mind* (1985).

Stanley Kubrick

Director, writer
Born: *New York, NY, July 26, 1928*

Kubrick is one of cinema's most imaginative, daring and controversial film-makers. An obsessive perfectionist, he has turned out relatively few movies in a 40-year career, yet each in its way has been a minor masterpiece. He has consistently demanded, and enjoyed, absolute artistic control over his creations – usually scripting, producing and editing them, as well as directing – and his body of work thus displays an extraordinary consistency of vision. A world teetering on the brink, peopled by humans struggling to come to terms with their own failings, is the theme that dominates his films, and even his more overtly comic offerings such as *Dr Strangelove* (1963) are underscored by this dark sense of fatality. Born in New York, he worked as a photographer before coming to prominence with *The Killing* (1956), and his searing anti-war movie *Paths of Glory* (1957). He enjoyed a huge

hit with *Spartacus* (1960), which he later disowned, and produced a satirical masterpiece in *Dr Strangelove*, the story of a renegade

Stanley Kubrick: *Uncompromsing movie genius*

American general's decision to blow up the world. *2001: A Space Odyssey* (1968) and *A Clockwork Orange* (1971) proved extraordinary, complex, diverse visions of a future world, but he has since made only three movies – *Barry Lyndon* (1975); *The Shining* (1980); and *Full Metal Jacket* (1987). Frustration at his sporadic output, however, must always be tempered by its extraordinary quality.

Akira Kurosawa

Director, writer
Born: *Tokyo, Japan, March 23, 1910*

Most internationally famous of his film-directing countrymen, Kurosawa made his breakthrough with the Oscar-winning *Rashomon* (1950), the story of a bandit attack and rape from four different viewpoints. It was the first Japanese film to be widely shown in the west, winning Best Film award at Venice in 1951, and became the first of three of his films to be remade as westerns (*The Outrage*). It was followed by *The Seven Samurai* (1954) – perhaps still his best-loved film – reworked in 1960 as *The Magnificent Seven* and *Yojimbo* (1961), turned into *A Fistful of Dollars* in 1964 by Sergio Leone. Apart from *Ikiru* (*Living*) (1952), a rare and bleak look at modern Japanese society, and *The*

Lower Depths (1957), his version of the Gorky play, Kurosawa is best known in the west for his Samurai epics, most notably the magnificent *Throne of Blood* (1956) – the Macbeth story translated to medieval Japan – and his late-period masterpiece *Ran*, an epic version of King Lear made in 1985 when he was 75. Just when the world thought he'd retired, he came back with *Kurosawa's Dreams* (1990), a mixed bag of short stories which found room for Martin Scorsese as the painter Van Gogh, and *Rhapsody in August* (1991) which starred Richard Gere – neither of whom seems, at least to western eyes, to be natural casting for such exotic material, but when a genius like Kurosawa says "come", you go.

Alan Ladd

Actor
Born: *Hot Springs, Ark., September 3, 1913*
Died: *January 29, 1964*

Small but perfectly formed star Ladd was born to play opposite the equally vertically challenged Veronica Lake, and they joined together as one of the cinema's most luminous teams for *This Gun for Hire* (1942), an Americanized thriller version of Graham Greene's story *A Gun for Sale*. His role defined his persona, that of soft-talking hard man propelled by inner rage and zeal for justice, a portrayal author Raymond Chandler dismissed as a kid's idea of a gangster. Ladd and Lake went on to more success in *The Glass Key* (1942), *The Blue Dahlia* (1946) and *Saigon* (1948), helping him to stay at the very top for a decade. He was surprisingly able as Scott Fitzgerald's *The Great Gatsby* (1949) and in 1953 gave his subtlest performance in one of cinema's most famous westerns, *Shane*, as the archetypal loner hero who helps a family of homesteaders, but he was bitter that he wasn't even nominated for an Oscar.

Oddly this high spot was virtually the end of Ladd's run of success, and he immediately fell into a trough of routine action films from which his career never really recovered. By the 1960s he was outmoded and depressed, but ironically he'd just staged a triumphant popular comeback as the cowboy Nevada Smith in Harold Robbins's *The Carpetbaggers* (1964) when he died of a mix of sedatives and alcohol.

Veronica Lake

Actress
Born: CONSTANCE FRANCES MARIE OCKELMAN (*aka* CONSTANCE KEANE), *Brooklyn, NY, November 14, 1919,*
Died: *July 7, 1973*

Raymond Chandler always insisted on referring to her as "Moronica", but if the Lake was shallow the image scored deep and thousands of girls all over America and Britain sported the famous peekaboo hair-do, which obscured one side of her face. So many in fact that the US government officially asked Paramount to change her look, because an alarming number of (female) munitions workers were getting their hair caught up in the machinery. Though her range was limited, Lake was an enormous star in her day, outstanding in Preston Sturges's freewheeling satire *Sullivan's Travels* (1941) but at her best as the shadowy "broads" she played in thrillers like *The Glass Key* (1942) and *The Blue Dahlia* (1946), opposite Alan Ladd. In her most successful screen partnership, Lake was to Ladd what Bacall was to Bogey. It was not her talent or her films that were of importance to screen culture, however, it was her image. Lake was one of the first *film noir* shady ladies, virtually inventing the role and influencing most of the actresses that played it since. Even Bacall's tough cookies – though much more skilfully acted – owe a debt to this original image. Her success only lasted a decade and 20 years after the height of her fame *The New York Post* magazine found her working as a cocktail waitress in a Manhattan bar. But that's showbiz.

Burt Lancaster

Actor
Born: BURTON STEPHEN LANCASTER, *New York, NY, November 2, 1913*
Died: *October 21, 1994*

Harlem postman's son Burton abandoned college to establish a circus acrobatic duo with tiny Nick Cravat who was later to appear in many of his films. After war service in North Africa, he landed a Broadway role, was spotted by Hollywood agents and made a star-making debut in Ernest Hemingway's *The Killers* (1946). He moved gracefully from athletic roles in escapist fun like *The Flame and the Arrow* (1950) and *Crimson Pirate* (1952) to thoughtful portray-

Burt Lancaster: "Match me, Sidney"

als in prestige dramas like *All My Sons* (1948) and *Come Back, Little Sheba* (1953). Lancaster spearheaded the trend for actors to become producers with agent Harold Hecht and producer James Hill, who included *Sweet Smell of Success* (1957) and *Separate Tables*

(1958) among their notable product. He made a series of top westerns like *Apache*, *Vera Cruz* (both 1954) and *Gunfight at the OK Corral* (1957), but in the 1960s increasingly turned to posh movies like his Oscar-winning *Elmer Gantry* (1960), *Birdman of Alcatraz* (1962), *Seven Days in May* (1964) and *The Swimmer* (1967), though he always kept the popular touch with *The Professionals* (1966) and *Airport* (1969). He gained the fourth of his Oscar nominations for his overpowering performance as the old gangster in Louis Malle's *Atlantic City* (1980) and two of his other best roles were for European maestros – Visconti's magnificent epic *The Leopard* (1963) and Bertolucci's *1900* (1977). This fine star actor grew old gracefully and worked regularly throughout his seventies.

Fritz Lang

Director, writer, producer
Born: *Vienna, Austria, December 5, 1890*
Died: *August 2, 1976*

The great German-based filmmaker, Lang made his name with several enduring silent classics, including the revered sci-fi masterpiece *Metropolis* (1926). At the onset of sound he made *M* (1931), based on the case of a Düsseldorf child murderer. His next, *The Testament of Dr Mabuse* (1933), was banned by the Nazis and Lang fled to Paris. In 1935 he went to America with an MGM deal, and made the acclaimed mob violence film *Fury* (1936). During the 1940s he divided his time between westerns like *The Return of Frank James* (1940) and *Western Union* (1941); thrillers with a theme of obsessive love like *The Woman in the Window* (1944) and *Scarlet Street* (1945); and spy dramas like *Ministry of Fear* (1944) and *Cloak and Dagger* (1946). He was on a winning streak in the early 1950s with his best western *Rancho Notorious* (1952), the sinister crime melodrama *The Big Heat* (1953), and another essay on desire

and destiny, *Human Desire* (1954). But after two more tense crime dramas, *While the City Sleeps* (1956) and *Beyond a Reasonable Doubt* (1956), Lang felt he'd had enough of rows with interfering studio bosses. After a none too profitable period of wandering, he returned to America to retire in Beverly Hills. Lang mixed commerce with art to produce a unique body of work for which he's deservedly adored among cineastes, while his American films crop up regularly on TV to provide the most civilized entertainment.

Jessica Lange

Actress
Born: *Cloquet, Minn., April 20, 1949*

This special actress has battled to overcome the Hollywood second-string stereotype her golden good looks force her into. She has it all: looks, talent, love and success – and she deserves it. With a too short filmography, she has racked up two Oscars and four nominations. Lange started her career at the top in 1976 in *King Kong*'s paw, but then was unemployed for over two years until her friend Bob Fosse cast her as an angel of death in *All That Jazz* (1979), leading to a memorable turn as Nicholson's adulteress/murderess co-star in *The Postman Always Rings Twice* (1981). But 1982 was her year, with an Oscar for Best Supporting Actress as a soap opera star in *Tootsie* and an Oscar nomination for playing tortured actress Frances Farmer in *Frances*. When she decided to devote more time to her family, her career inevitably suffered. She had a child with dancer Mikhail Baryshnikov and now has two more with actor/playwright Sam Shepard. In the next six years there were only three films, but they included *Country* (1984) and *Sweet Dreams* (1985) as country singer Patsy Cline, both of which won her Oscar nominations, while a fourth followed with her poignant performance as a lawyer defending her

father for war crimes in Costa-Gavras's *Music Box* (1989). The 1990s found her busy, scoring well in two roles with Robert De Niro, *Cape Fear* (1991) and *Night and the City* (1992), before winning a Best Actress Oscar for *Blue Sky* (1992).

Mario Lanza

Singer, actor
Born: ALFREDO COCOZZA, *Philadelphia, Pa., January 31, 1921*
Died: *1959*

The fiery Italian American, as famous for his temper as his stentorian tenor, got his first film contract after his operatic debut in *Madame Butterfly* in 1948, when MGM scouts heard him at the Hollywood Bowl. Because he was an operatic singer/actor Hollywood had to find, or construct, vehicles that fitted his talents, which they did with varying success, *The Toast of New Orleans* (1950) and *Because You're Mine* (1952) being two of their better attempts. Still, Lanza's relationships with his studio, and anyone else he worked with, were always uneasy, and partly because of this his films were variable. Drug and alcohol abuse together with a chronic weight problem and his notorious temperament ended his short film career and he spent some time touring and making guest appearances at night spots like the London Palladium, until his untimely death at 38 from a heart attack. He retains a loyal fan following, his records are still popular sellers and his movies are often seen on TV internationally. His (best) film *The Great Caruso* (1951), in which he played the celebrated tenor, has probably done more to popularize opera over the years than all the televised efforts of more modern exponents put together, with the possible exception of Luciano Pavarotti, himself a great admirer of Lanza's, and his rendition of football's 1990 World Cup theme of Puccini's *Nessum Dorma*.

Lassie

Actor, dog
Whelped: PAL *(date unknown)*

Not many people know that Lassie was in fact a laddie, real name Pal, whom some wag called "the only star who could play a bitch better than Bette Davis". MGM animal handler Rudd Weatherwax had been asked to provide a good female dog for the part, but when shooting began the expensive and highly trained female shed heavily and became unco-operative. Luckily Rudd had Pal – a dog he had bought for $10 – with him and swapped animals,

Lassie: Paws for thought

turning Pal into an instant star and creating perhaps the world's only canine female impersonator. The first film was MGM's *Lassie Come Home* (1942) with Roddy – "I think she wants us to follow her" – McDowall, overshadowed by his two hairier co-stars, Lassie and Elizabeth Taylor. Its huge success produced the inevitable sequels: *Son of Lassie* (1945), with the same cast, *Courage of Lassie* (1946) again with Taylor, *Hills of Home* (1948), *Challenge to Lassie* (1949), *The Sun Comes Up* (1949) – featuring a different animal – and *The Painted Hills* (1951), the last at MGM. Lassie was hugely successful on TV with one of the longest-running series ever, from 1954 (when it won Best Children's Program Emmy) to 1973. It was followed by a cartoon series (1973–74), then started all over again with *Lassie: The New Beginning* (after which

one critic growled "If I were a Collie I'd sue") and *The Magic of Lassie* (1978). But you can't keep a good dog down and our heroine sprang back to the big screen in 1995 with the long-awaited new *Lassie* motion picture. "Woof!"

Charles Laughton

Actor
Born: *Scarborough, England, July 1, 1899*
Died: *December 15, 1962*

Laughton was the outsized scene-stealing character actor par-excellence. During a 30-year career he proved himself a player of terrific depth and versatility, rarely giving a performance that was anything less than absorbing. The son of a family of Scarborough hoteliers, he studied at London's Royal Academy of Dramatic Arts, worked on the stage in London and New York, and took the cinema-going public by storm with his lusty, Holbeinesque portrayal of Henry VIII in Alexander Korda's *The Private Life of Henry VIII* (1933). This won him an Oscar (the first-ever Englishman to lay hands on the coveted statuette), and there followed an extraordinary succession of dramatic creations: Javert in *Les Misérables* (1935); Captain Bligh in *Mutiny on the Bounty* (1935); *Rembrandt* (1936); and Quasimodo in *The Hunchback of Notre Dame* (1939). After a bad spell when he played second fiddle to Abbott and Costello, he was as forceful at at the end of his career in *Hobson's Choice* (1954), *Witness for the Prosecution* (1957), *Spartacus* (1960) and *Advise and Consent* (1962) as he had been at its start. He directed only one picture, the chillingly malevolent *Night of the Hunter* (1955), which leaves posterity begging for more. His glory was to bring not merely a power and physical magnitude to his performances, but also a pathos and vulnerability arising, most likely, from a lifetime of hiding his

homosexuality, though married to actress Elsa Lanchester. He died of cancer in 1962.

Laurel and Hardy

Comics
Born: ARTHUR STANLEY JEFFERSON (LAUREL), *Ulverston, England, June 16, 1890*
Died: *February 23, 1965*
Born: OLIVER NORVELL HARDY, *Harlem, Ga., January 18, 1892*
Died: *August 7, 1957*

The cinema's finest comedy team first paired up accidentally in *Lucky Dog* (1917) but both Stan and Ollie's talents were largely wasted until producer Hal Roach brought them together in 1926, first for a series of silent shorts (*Slipping Wives*), then from 1930 (*The Rogue Song*) for a run of classic features. They complemented each other perfectly. Laurel was the skinny, creative, serious one; joke-writer and sometimes director. Hardy was the tubby, funny one who just came in and did it, like Ginger Rogers in the Astaire-Rogers partnership. 1929 was a golden year for them with a dozen or so vintage shorts, among which *Big Business*, *Double Whoopee*, *Berth Marks*, *Men O' War* and *The Perfect Day* see them at near their best, topped only by their Oscar-win-

ning two-reeler *The Music Box* (1932). Until 1935 they alternated shorts with features, perhaps the best of which are *Fra Diavolo*, *Sons of the Desert* (both 1933), *Babes in Toyland* (1934), *Our Relations*, *Way Out West* (both 1936), *Blockheads* (1938) *The Flying Deuces* (1939) and *A Chump at Oxford* (1940). After this concentrated spell of 1930s comic masterpieces, their work tailed off dramatically on splitting with Roach in 1940. They made their final film together in 1952 (*Atoll K*) before taking off for the theatre where they were warmly received. "The Boys" were the greatest of friends: when Ollie died, Stan was devastated and never recovered.

Sir David Lean

Director, editor, writer
Born: *Croydon, England, March 25, 1908*
Died: *April 16, 1991*

The ultimate cinema craftsman, Lean directed only 16 films in nearly 50 years, but almost all of them are remarkable. He started in films in 1928, pursuing a distinguished career as an editor, a credit he liked to keep on his movies, until he teamed up with Noel Coward for *In Which We Serve* (1942), *This Happy Breed* (1944),

Laurel and Hardy: Another fine mess

Blithe Spirit (1945) and *Brief Encounter* (1945). Two superb Dickens adaptations followed – *Great Expectations* (1946) and *Oliver Twist* (1948) – then three rather disappointing films with his wife Ann Todd. Suddenly in the late 1950s he launched into the then fashionable international epics with controversial results. *The Bridge on the River Kwai* (1957), *Lawrence of Arabia* (1962) and *Doctor Zhivago* (1965) were truly spectacular, enormous successes with difficult, complex subjects, garnering Oscar glory (he won Best Director for the first two). But the critics worried, saying they detected empty canvasses, sentimentality and populist pandering. *Ryan's Daughter* (1970), a slight, romantic tale at the mercy of an enormous budget, nearly sank Lean, who wanted to retire after the lacerating reviews and public indifference. There followed a long period of despair and abandoned projects, but he lived long enough to turn around his fortunes and reputation. His triumphant version of Forster's *A Passage to India* (1984) was, after 14 years, the cinema's most remarkable comeback, though ill-health prevented his final film of Conrad's *Nostromo*.

Bruce Lee

Actor

Born: LEE YUEN KAM (Protector of San Francisco), (*aka* LI SIU-LUNG [Little Dragon]), *San Francisco, Calif., November 27, 1940*
Died: *July 20, 1973*

Single-handedly popularizing kung-fu with his all-action, martial-art massacres, Lee was a major international star for only the last two years of his life before his mysterious death cemented cult figure status. His father was a stand-up comedian who moved Lee to Hong Kong aged three, where he appeared in several films beginning with *The Birth Of Mankind* (1946). Returning to the US at 18, he studied philosophy in Washington, DC, teaching kung-

Bruce Lee: *Martial artist of the silver screen*

fu to supplement his studies, and after a spell on television made his adult film debut in *Marlowe* (1969) alongside James Garner, a former pupil who won him the role. When he returned to Hong Kong to star in the low-budget *Fists of Fury* (1972) he really arrived, though. Suddenly he was a household name the world over, famous for doing his own stunts, and displaying incredibly athletic fighting skills. He had a hand in scripting and directing *Return of the Dragon* (1973), which was also made in Hong Kong, before returning to Hollywood for *Enter the Dragon* (1973), for which he had his underarm sweat glands removed so he would look better on screen. His sudden death at the age of 32 prompted wild speculation of drugs, triads, and even that he was still alive. His imitators have failed to match him, including his own son Brandon; mysteriously killed on a film-set in 1993.

Christopher Lee

Actor

Born: *London, England, May 27, 1922*

Tall, imposing and aristocratic, Lee was perfect casting for Count Dracula in Hammer's 1959 classic *The Horror of Dracula*, a performance for which he will always be remembered. An intelligent actor of subtlety and depth, one of the mainstays of Hammer horror and a key figure in the modern develop-

ment of the genre, his career has been closely linked with that other icon of British horror, Peter Cushing. Starting off with *The Curse of Frankenstein* (1956), in which Lee was the monster and Cushing the misguided Baron, they made more than 20 films together between 1957 and 1973. These included their wonderful remake of *The Hound of the Baskervilles* (1959), with Lee as a surly Sir Henry Baskerville opposite Cushing's sparkling Sherlock Holmes, *The Mummy* (1959) with Lee in the bandages, and of course their resurrection of the evil Count Dracula himself, nobly fought by Cushing's equally memorable Van Helsing. Among the other highlights of this long and prolific career, of well over 200 films, have been *The Face of Fu Manchu* (1965), the first of a series of five in which he starred as the devilish oriental villain, the fascinating *The Devil Rides Out* (1967), based on Denis Wheatley's black magic novel, *The Man with the Golden Gun* (1974), with Lee as James Bond's chilling nemesis, and his exquisitely lampooned mad scientist in *Gremlins 2* (1990).

Spike Lee

Director, writer, producer, actor

Born: *Atlanta, Ga., March 20, 1956*

"The biggest lie is that if you're American it doesn't matter what race, creed, nationality you are," says Spike Lee. "The colour of your skin doesn't matter, it's the person that you are ... Bullshit! Race has everything to do with everything." Lee is America's foremost black film-maker – provocative, uncompromising, prodigiously talented. His feature debut was a bolt from the blue: 1986's *She's Gotta Have It*, a witty look at female sexuality, shot in two weeks on a shoestring budget. He followed this up with a raucous comedy in *School Daze* (1988) and took time out to direct campaign ads for presidential hopeful Jesse

Jackson before rustling up a genuine classic in *Do the Right Thing* (1989), a brilliantly choreographed examination of a race riot in sun-soaked Brooklyn. While there's little doubting the wizardry of his crisp, vibrant film-making style, Lee has attracted criticism for his anti-semitic portrayal of Jewish characters in *Mo' Better Blues* (1990) and the harsh depiction of a mixed-race relationship in *Jungle Fever* (1991). But Lee is committed to documenting the Afro-American experience, complete with all its undiluted grievances and hints of inverse racism, and this made him the obvious choice to film 1992's sprawling, colourful biopic of *Malcolm X*. A raw, erratic talent, Lee faltered with the semi-autobiographical family drama *Crooklyn* (1994), but has opened the floodgates for a wealth of new black directors.

Mike Leigh

Director, writer

Born: *Salford, England, February 20, 1943*

Mike Leigh is a film-maker in direct descent from the kitchen-sink "free cinema" movement of 1960s Britain, rejecting sweeping saga for the overlooked life-and-death struggles of everyday folk. Coping, Leigh argues, is both the most honourable and the most consistent state of being. He made his debut in 1971 with the gruelling, aptly titled family drama *Bleak Moments* and grabbed the limelight in the late 1970s with two first-rate TV films. The Dorset-based *Nuts in May* (1976) was followed by the acclaimed *Abigail's Party* (1977), a nightmarish satire on the galloping pretensions of middle-class suburbia – both starring Leigh's wife and regular interpreter Alison Steadman. 1988's *High Hopes* proved a poignant tale of life in Thatcher's Britain while the hilarious tragicomedy *Life Is Sweet* (1990) brought him to a wider audience and was a surprise Stateside hit.

Although a unique artist of British cinema, Leigh is not without his detractors, with critics complaining that his protagonists verge on the caricature and dismissing him as a dour gloom-monger: "There's a lot of shit written about me and pessimism," Leigh retorts. But, employing a loose, improvisatory approach, Leigh has built up a film canon of startling worth and originality. 1993's *Naked* was his finest yet, a savage study of youthful alienation on the streets of inner-city London that ranks among the decade's most significant pictures.

Vivien Leigh

Actress
Born: VIVIAN MARY HARTLEY, *Darjeeling, India, November 5, 1913*
Died: *July 1967*

A vibrant, brittle, unpredictable, sporadically brilliant actress of stage and screen, Leigh was famed for her exquisite beauty, exotic lifestyle and glamorous marriage to Laurence Olivier. Ironically, though, it was this cut-crystal-voiced Englishwoman's snatching of the most famous American role of the 1930s, Scarlett O'Hara, that

Vivien Leigh: "Tomorrow is another day"

has secured her place for posterity. Born in India to English parents, she made her screen debut in *Things Are Looking Up* (1934) after a brief spell at RADA. Success in the stage play *The Mask of Virtue* (1935) led to her signing a five-year contract with producer

Alexander Korda during which she played opposite Olivier in *Fire Over England* (1937) and in *21 Days* (1937). While visiting Olivier in Hollywood in 1938, she tested for the coveted role of Scarlett O'Hara in *Gone with the Wind* (1939) and impressed producer David Selznick enough to win over the likes of Bette Davis. The result was an enormous personal and Oscar-winning triumph. Though her career was repeatedly interrupted by ill-health, she toured widely with the Old Vic and Stratford theatre companies. Having recovered from TB, she played Blanche Dubois in Tennessee Williams's *A Streetcar Named Desire*, scooping a second Oscar for the 1951 film version. After suffering a nervous breakdown in 1953 while shooting *Elephant Walk*, Leigh filmed only twice more till her final movie, *Ship of Fools* in 1965. She died at 53 after a recurrence of TB.

Jack Lemmon

Actor, director
Born: JOHN UHLER LEMMON III, *Boston, Mass., February 8, 1925*

While middle-aged men may fantasize about being Humphrey Bogart, they know they are really Jack Lemmon: the insecure Mr Everyman, well-meaning, naive, muddling through. But while he's the kind of guy you wouldn't actually choose to be, he's the kind you love to see in the movies. Funny and likeable, he's cannily elevated his dithering anti-hero act, normally the sidekick role, into a star turn. Few performers give us more sheer pleasure. Lemmon is one of the rare star actors who never gives a bad performance. His films with director Billy Wilder and his buddy Walter Matthau are great fun entertainments, the best of them – *Some Like It Hot* (1959), *The Apartment* (1960) and *The Front Page* (1974) – now cherished Hollywood classics. It's a measure of his enduring magic with light comedy that he's easily

Bitter Lemmon: Jack in The Apartment

adapted the persona he established back in the mid-1950s to suit his age and changing fashions. Perhaps Matthau can be more spontaneous and hilarious, but Lemmon is more thoughtful and possesses the greater range and depth. More recently he's at his best in serious films like *The China Syndrome* (1979), *Missing* (1982), *Glengarry Glen Ross* (1992), and *Short Cuts* (1993). This universally admired star won Oscars for *Mister Roberts* (1955) and *Save the Tiger* (1973), both good performances but not his best, and half a dozen nominations include *Days of Wine and Roses* (1962) and *Tribute* (1980). Married to actress Felicia Farr, he's directed once – Matthau in *Kotch* (1971).

Sergio Leone

Director, writer, producer
Born: *Rome, Italy, January 23, 1921*
Died: *April 30, 1989*

Sergio Leone couldn't have arranged a better start in movies – while still a teenager he had a minor role in Vittorio De Sica's neo-realist masterwork *Bicycle Thieves* (1948). Working in the US, Leone became the most influential director of westerns after John Ford, revitalizing the genre with a weird, wonderful, utterly distinctive film-making style. The *Dollars*

trilogy – *A Fistful of Dollars* (1964), *For a Few Dollars More* (1966), *The Good, the Bad and the Ugly* (1966) – established both Leone and rookie star Clint Eastwood and coined the "spaghetti western" sub-genre. Leone's westerns are played out in a near-surrealistic American west, a godless world fired by greed and random violence. Its inhabitants are invariably loners, skittering about on the crust of a hostile landscape. Plot is skeletal, but the films mesmerize thanks to Leone's rich visual sense – extreme close-ups, languid panning shots, an ever-present undertone of tension. The spaghetti western reached its apogee with *Once Upon a Time in the West* (1968), an operatic, lavishly staged saga of how the west was really won. As the spaghetti western slid into self-parody, Leone withdrew from directing, only to make a dramatic comeback the year before his death with *Once Upon a Time in America* (1984), an elegiac gangster epic starring James Woods and Robert De Niro.

Barry Levinson

Director, writer, producer, actor
Born: *Baltimore, Md., April 6, 1942*

One of the more highly valued directors within the studio system, Barry Levinson cut his teeth as a comic-writer, co-scripting and grabbing bit-parts in two of Mel Brooks's funniest 1970s pictures, *Silent Movie* (1976) and *High Anxiety* (1977). Shifting towards dramatic writing, he was Oscar-nominated for his contribution to the screenplay of *... And Justice for All* (1979) and made a belated but acclaimed writer-director debut with the popular 1950s-set, coming-of-age drama *Diner* (1982). Levinson followed the film's success with two alluring minor hits in *The Natural* (1984) and *Tin Men* (1987), before hitting the jackpot with the uproarious Robin Williams vehicle *Good Morning*

Vietnam (1987) and 1988's tearjerking *Rain Man* (1988), which won him a Best Director Oscar. While hardly regarded as a film *auteur*, Levinson's easy, unobtrusive style and sumptuous, softly lit visuals make for some eye-catching pictures. His most personal work remains 1990's *Avalon*, set in his home town of Baltimore a sensitive, generation-hopping saga of a family of Russian immigrants. Undeterred by its relative lack of success, he forged on with the lavish gangster epic *Bugsy* (1991) and reunited with Williams for the ambitious but uneven *Toys* (1992). Levinson now occupies a spot near the top of the Hollywood tree.

Jerry Lewis

Comic, actor, director, producer, writer
Born: JOSEPH LEVITCH, *Newark, NJ, March 16, 1926*

To the French he's a second Charlie Chaplin. He has been honoured at Cannes and festivals of his work have been arranged in places as dissimilar as Spain and Norway. In America he is revered for his series of 17 films with his nightclub partner Dean Martin from their debut in *My Friend Irma* in 1949 to *Hollywood or Bust* in 1956, a partnership that split acrimoniously. Yet in Britain his rubber body, constantly flailing arms and outrageous mugging just hardened the hearts of critics and public alike. But if you can get past the sentimentality and gargantuan gurning, there is a clever acrobat and mime at work. His classic "silent" set pieces, for example the music lesson in *The Patsy* (1964) or the movie mogul in *The Errand Boy* (1961), equal anything Chaplin or Keaton put on celluloid. And the subtlety with which he plots his routines is every bit as painstaking as that supreme perfectionist Jacques Tati, whom perversely the French admire less than the British. In

1983 Lewis more or less played himself opposite Robert De Niro in Scorsese's acid showbiz black comedy *The King of Comedy*. It was a fascinating chance to see some of the clockwork tick, but showing so starkly Lewis's outsize ego put off many would-be admirers. Being funny is a tough business and Lewis drove himself to two major heart attacks just trying to please his voracious public.

Val Lewton

Producer, writer, novelist
Born: VLADIMIR IVAN LEVENTON (*aka* CARLOS KEITH *and* COSMO FORBES), *Yalta, Russia, May 7, 1904*
Died: *1951*

Lewton emigrated to the United States with his mother when he was seven and was educated at Columbia. By the time his potential was spotted by producer David Selznick, who took him on as his editorial assistant in the early 1930s, Lewton had already published 10 novels, six works of non-fiction, a book of poetry and a book of pornography, *Yasmine*. He sometimes used pseudonyms for his books and later his screenplays. Lewton is remembered as the producer of a series of successful, cheaply-made 1940s chillers at the RKO studios. They were strongly stamped with his love of detail and concentrated on horrors imagined rather than seen as in today's gory fashion. He was very influential on the work of later film-makers in this genre. Among his best-known works are *Cat People* (1942), remade in 1982 by Paul Schrader; its psychological sequel *Curse of the Cat People* (1944); *I Walked with a Zombie* (1943), inspired by the first Mrs Rochester from *Jane Eyre* and predating Jean Rhys's 1966 novel *The Wide Sargasso Sea* by more than 20 years; *The Body Snatcher* (1945), starring Boris Karloff and Bela Lugosi in a version of Robert Louis Stevenson's Burke and Hare story; and Karloff again in *Bedlam*

(1946), set in an 18th-century Hogarthian asylum. He worked on the scripts of the last two as Carlos Keith. In mid-career Lewton died of a heart attack at 46.

Max Linder

Actor
Born: GABRIEL LEVIELLE, *Saint-Loubes, France, December 16, 1883*
Died: *1925*

A dapper, moustachioed dandy in top hat and tails, Max Linder was not only the first truly great screen comedian, but also proved one of the first generally acknowledged international film stars. Most of the great silent comics in one way or another incorporated and adapted his ideas as their own, while the persona he developed – the sartorially elegant, unflappable cad Max – was for a while as popular a creation as Charlie Chaplin's little tramp. Linder started his career in theatre, but moved to films in 1905, drawn by the lure of big money. He worked extensively with the Pathé studio in Paris, starring in over 400 shorts between 1905 and 1915, and becoming a comic superstar in the process. "Max" – with his top hat, tails and cloak – first appeared around 1910, while from 1913 onwards Linder wrote and directed his movies as well as starring in them. Much of his output was disposable crowd-pleasing escapism, but *Max's Duel* (1913) was a minor masterpiece. His relocation to Hollywood in 1916 resulted in some extraordinarily witty and inventive film-making – *Max in a Taxi* (1917), *Seven Years' Bad Luck* (1921), *Be My Wife* (1921); and *The Three Must-Get-Theres* (1922). Linder simply could not accept that his career was on the wane in the early 1920s, and, when his last film, *The King of The Circus* (1925) flopped, he and his wife killed themselves in a tragic joint suicide pact.

Harold Lloyd

Actor
Born: *Burchard, Nebr., April 20, 1893*
Died: *1971*

Behind Harold Lloyd's trademark spectacles lurked a brawny, ruggedly handsome athlete, a figure of startling physical difference to his popular silent-screen persona. Just as Chaplin devised the image of the shuffling tramp and Keaton the glum, soulful adventurer, so Lloyd evolved the character of a gawky wimp, the gauche would-be playboy whose hot pursuit of damsels lands him in all manner of trouble. Shunning the pathos and plot nuances of his rivals, Lloyd's pictures served up shameless, carefree escapism, a frantic series of comic misadventures stitched together around a tried and tested premise of the

Harold Lloyd: *Gawky wimp in hot water*

little guy succeeding against the odds. But Lloyd went at these films with an almost mechanical precision, choreographing the action and editing the finished film footage. The *Freshman* (1925), with its grand football finale, was the era's most successful comedy picture, while his dazzling sky-scraper foray in *Safety Last* (1923) occupies a unique place in movie folklore and was a device Lloyd fell back on again with the talkies *Feet First* (1930) and the misfired Preston Sturges outing *Mad Wednesday* (1947). Arguably a more savvy businessman than either Keaton or Chaplin, Lloyd made a partially successful transition to sound cinema, most spectacularly with the Hollywood satire *Movie Crazy* (1932). But, aware that his fine-tuned skills would never truly mesh with the new medium, he withdrew into millionaired middle age, one of film's finest pioneers reclining in revered, comfortable retirement.

Ken Loach

Director

Born: KENNETH LOACH, *Nuneaton, England, June 17, 1936*

A maverick and often controversial left-wing director, Ken Loach's films are characterized by a strong social conscience and a preference for unknown or non-professional actors. The son of an electrician, Loach was the first in his family to go to university. In the 1960s he made socially realistic television plays about working-class life, such as *Up the Junction* (1965) and *Cathy Come Home* (1966), a drama about homelessness which hit the headlines. His first feature film *Poor Cow* (1967) followed a similar vein, but in *Kes* (1970), the story of a boy and a kestrel, the social message was implicit rather than overt, and therefore the more powerful. During the 1970s Loach worked mainly in television. His controversial documentary series about trade unions, *A Question of Leadership* (1981) was never screened. He returned to the big screen with the children's adventure *Black Jack* (1979); *Looks and Smiles* (1981); *Fatherland* (1986) about an East Berliner's disillusionment with the West; and the controversial Irish political thriller *Hidden Agenda* (1990). In *Riff Raff* (1991) and *Raining Stones* (1993) he returned to social politics laced with affectionate humour, followed by the harrowing *Ladybird Ladybird* (1994), about a woman who loses her children to the social services. He then achieved a long-time ambition together with writer Jim Allen to make *Land and Freedom* (1994), whose subject was the left-wing conflicts in 1930s Civil-War Spain.

Margaret Lockwood

Actress

Born: MARGARET DAY, *Karachi, India, September 15, 1916*
Died: *July 15, 1990*

Lockwood was a good actress and a great star, one of Britain's most celebrated and popular film actresses, beautiful, vivacious and indomitable. On stage at 12, she became an appealing twinset and pearls spunky starlet of the 1930s, making her debut in 1935 with *Lorna Doone*. Hitchcock used her to resounding effect in *The Lady Vanishes* (1938) as a carefree play-girl baffled by Dame May Whitty's disappearance on a transcontinental train, and Carol Reed followed it up with the similar *Night Train to Munich* (1940). She was also effective in others for Reed: *Bank Holiday* (1938) as a sinning week-ender, *The Stars Look Down* (1940) as the baddie, and *The Girl in the News* (1940) as a murder suspect. In the 1940s she played a wide range of roles but delighted most as a scheming, wicked lady, and her quintessential films of this period were *The Man in Grey* (1943), *The Wicked Lady* (1945), as a tempting tomboy who teams up with high-wayman James Mason, and *Jassy* (1947), as a gypsy accused of her husband's death. When she told her studio, Rank, she was weary of being wicked, they tried to put her in other roles, but her appeal faded in the late 1940s. Her film career was effectively over by 1957, though she turned into a much-loved, busy star on the British stage and television.

Carole Lombard

Actress

Born: JANE ALICE PETERS, *Fort Wayne, Ind., October 6, 1908*
Died: *January 16, 1942*

Versatile and glamorous blond actress whose career was tragically cut short by her death in a plane crash when only 33. Lombard made her film debut while a 12-year-old schoolgirl in *A Perfect Crime* (1921) and began her film career proper three years later, playing standard ingenues, interspersed with a series of Mack Sennett slapstick comedies, after which the roles became more sophisticated and she achieved minor star status. Her comedy talent was given full rein in Howard Hawks's *Twentieth Century* (1934), the first of several screwball comedies which established her position as one of Hollywood's top stars. They included: *My Man Godfrey* (1936) in which she was ironically pursuing William Powell, by now her ex-husband (they divorced in 1933 after a two-year marriage); and *Nothing Sacred* (1937) for William Wellman, who became a staunch admirer. She turned for a while to more serious roles: *Made for Each Other* (1939), combining comedy with tragedy; *Vigil in the Sun* (1940) as the dedicated nurse; and *They Knew What They Wanted* (1940) as immigrant Charles Laughton's mail-order bride. But she returned to laughter for her last two films: *Mr and Mrs Smith* (1941), Hitchcock's only screwball comedy, and Ernst Lubitsch's *To Be or Not To Be* (1941). Her sudden death stunned her fans and devastated her second husband, Clark Gable, whom she had married in 1939.

Sophia Loren

Actress

Born: SOFIA SCICOLONE, *Rome, Italy, September 20, 1934*

Earthy and voluptuous Loren was spurred by her poverty-stricken upbringing in wartime Naples into the iron ambition to succeed – and nature gave her the beauty and sympathetic personality to make it happen. As a struggling 14-year old model and bit-part player, Loren was noticed by Carlo Ponti, who some years later married her in the teeth of public scandal. Under Ponti's guidance she was in the international spotlight by 1954 as a big Italian star. In America she was glamorized and sometimes miscast. However she did well in *Black Orchid* (1959) and sparkled in *Houseboat* (1958), *It Started in Naples* (1960) and the British comedy *The Millionairess* (1960) with Peter Sellers. *Two Women* (1960), made in Italy for her friend, Vittorio De Sica, showed her genuine dramatic power and she won an Oscar for her performance as a mother in war-ravaged Italy. Subsequent films in Britain and America ranged from accomplished to mediocre – *El Cid* (1960), *The Fall of the Roman Empire* (1964), *A Countess from Hong Kong* (1967) and *Man of La Mancha* (1972). Back home De Sica teamed her to great acclaim with Marcello Mastroianni for *Yesterday, Today and Tomorrow* (1963) but *Marriage Italian Style* (1964) failed to ring the international bell when repeated in the 1970s. Loren lost her way in anonymous international pictures in the 1970s and TV movies in the 1980s, yet she is still perceived in the public mind as a star.

Peter Lorre

Actor

Born: LASZLO LOWENSTEIN, *Rosenberg, Hungary, June 26, 1904*
Died: *March 24, 1964*

For over 30 years Lorre was a unique star character actor, usually a memorable villain, with bulging, infinitely sad eyes and an indefinable European accent. Seven years after his stage debut in Zurich and still an unknown, director Fritz Lang picked him as the child murderer in the German classic *M* (1931), perhaps the quintessential Lorre performance. Established in Germany, when the Nazis gained control he took off for Britain where Hitchcock employed him effectively in *The Man Who Knew Too Much* (1934) and *Secret Agent* (1936), and America, where, oddly cast, Lorre was a hit as John P.

Peter Lorre: *Creepy but versatile*

Marquand's oriental sleuth in Fox's short series of fondly remembered *Mr Moto* films (1937–39), curtailed by the war. But his high spots were in the 1940s Warner melodramas, often opposite Bogart or Greenstreet. These included several cinema classics like *The Maltese Falcon* (1941), *Casablanca* (1942) and *The Mask of Dimitrios* (1944). In light-hearted mood, Lorre scored more successes in *My Favorite Brunette* (1947), *Beat the Devil* (1953) with Bogart again, and in Disney's *20,000 Leagues under the Sea* (1954). He later showed a gift for comedy, often broad, in horror spoofs like *Tales of Terror* (1962) and *The Raven* (1963), and he even cheered up Jerry Lewis's *The Patsy* (1964). But then there was always a suggestion of a twinkle somewhere in Lorre's eye, even in his darkest roles.

Joseph Losey

Director, producer, critic
Born: JOSEPH WALTON LOSEY III (*aka* ANDREA FORZANO, VICTOR HANBURY, *and* JOSEPH WALTON), *La Crosse, Wis., January 14, 1909*
Died: *June 22, 1984*

Born into a family whose American roots predate the revolution, this "most European of American directors" was driven from his homeland by the iniquitous McCarthy witch-hunts and from 1951 lived and worked in Europe. After college, Losey had worked in New York theatre and studied under Eisenstein in Moscow, where he met Bertolt Brecht, whose *Galileo Galilei* he directed for the stage in 1947 with Charles Laughton, and later filmed (1974). He made a distinguished debut with *The Boy with Green Hair* (1948), an allegorical plea for tolerance, then shot thrillers like *The Prowler* (1950) and *M* (1951). Exiled to England, he cast his pessimistic outsider's eye over the British class system in *King and Country* (1964) – officer Dirk Bogarde defending private Tom Courtenay in a World War One court martial – and in three brilliant collaborations with Harold Pinter: *The Servant* (1963) – master and servant; *Accident* (1967) – academic power play; and *The Go-Between* (1971) – the destructiveness of the class system. Less successful was his collaboration with Tom Stoppard on *The Romantic Englishwoman* (1975), but the intriguing *Secret Ceremony* (1968) is memorable for Elizabeth Taylor's performance and the art deco interiors of its London location. In the mid-1970s he moved to France, where his work includes an enlightening version of Mozart's *Don Giovanni* (1979). He died while completing his last English-language film, *Steaming* (1985), based on Nell Dunn's all-female stage play.

Myrna Loy

Actress
Born: MYRNA WILLIAMS, *Raidersburg, Mont., August 2, 1905*
Died: *December 14, 1993*

Loy was the Queen of Hollywood, reigning supreme through the 1930s and early 1940s with Gable as her king. Witty, sophisticated and beautiful, she was a consummate actress, as effective trading one-liners with long-time co-star William Powell in the *Thin Man* series as she was in tougher, more dramatic roles such as the soldier's wife in *The Best Years of Our Lives* (1946). She fought her way to the top through a succession of minor roles in minor films, starting in silents and playing just about every part imaginable, including orientals, vamps, negroes and natives. She gained a certain notoriety when gangster John Dillinger was shot after watching her in *Manhattan Melodrama* (1934) and hit the big time in *The Thin Man* (1935), co-starring with William Powell as a husband and wife detective team. The combination of witty repartee and tongue-in-cheek adventure was a huge suc-

Myrna Loy: *Queen of Beverly Hills*

cess, spawning six sequels and establishing Loy as "The Perfect Screen Wife". There followed a succession of massive hits – *Libeled Lady* (1936), *Double Wedding* (1937), *Too Hot to Handle* (1938), *Love Crazy* (1941) – culminating in her transcendent performance opposite Fredric March in *The Best Years of Our Lives*. Thereafter she tended to concentrate on her work with the UN, but will always be remembered as one of cinema's truly great performers, fully deserving her regal epithet.

Ernst Lubitsch

Director
Born: *Berlin, Germany, January 28, 1892*
Died: *1947*

The lightness of the famous Lubitsch touch with its stylish, subtle sexiness made him a master of cinema, admired by fellow filmmakers such as Hitchcock, Truffaut and Orson Welles. As a young member of Max Reinhardt's *Deutsches Theater*, Lubitsch developed the character of *Meyer*, a slapstick Jewish archetype, later featured in a series of comedy shorts loved by audiences. Typecast by his own creation, Lubitsch turned to directing, and soon his reputation reached America, where Mary Pickford invited him to direct her in *Rosita* (1923). He quickly established himself as a maker of sophisticated comedies packed with visual detail. The coming of sound revealed his ear for witty dialogue and his subtle and impishly satirical comedies of sex and money, such as the elegant soufflé *Trouble in Paradise* (1932), and his "naughty but nice" musicals teaming Jeanette MacDonald and Maurice Chevalier – *The Love Parade* (1929), *One Hour With You* (1932) and *The Merry Widow* (1934) – were equally popular with audiences. He created screen history when Garbo laughed in *Ninotchka* (1939), and other comedy successes include *To Be or Not To Be* (1942), with Jack Benny and Carole Lombard as Shakespearean thespians taking on the Nazis; and playboy Don Ameche confessing his sins to the Devil in *Heaven Can Wait* (1943). Lubitsch died of his sixth heart attack while making *That Lady in Ermine* (1948), which was completed by Otto Preminger.

George Lucas

Producer, director, writer
Born: *Modesto, Calif., May 14, 1944*

West-coast whizz-kid George Lucas was a key member of the new generation of American filmmakers who rose to prominence in the early 1970s. His assistance on Francis Coppola's *Finian's Rainbow* (1968) led the director to help him raise funding for Lucas's first feature, 1971's *THX-1138*, an Orwellian thriller set in a futuristic hell where human emotions are fiercely suppressed. Slow-burning and cerebral, it was to prove a misleading start for this most

Broadway acting debut in a David Mamet play. But cinema success has eluded her. "I've always wanted to be a movie star," she says. "Even when I was a child I behaved like one." This is all the more frustrating because back in 1985 she surprised and delighted audiences as the kookie temptress in her second film *Desperately Seeking Susan*. But follow-ups – the thriller *Shanghai Surprise* (1986), with her then husband Sean Penn, and *Who's That Girl?* (1987) – led critics to say said she couldn't act. After her Sondheim-singing floozie in Warren Beatty's *Dick Tracy* (1990) and self-promo documentary *Truth or Dare* (1991), her engaging character part as a baseball player in *A League of Their Own* (1992) put her back on the acting map, but a star role in the over-sexed thriller *Body of Evidence* (1993) sent her back down. Beatty said: "She's got energy and generosity of spirit and works harder than anybody I know. And she's gifted." She may yet achieve her film star ambition.

Anna Magnani

Actress
Born: *Alexandria, Egypt, March 7, 1909*
Died: *September 26, 1973*

Magnani, with her unglamorous mop of black hair, fierce eyes and pale, lived-in face, is one of the few Italian actresses to gain wide credence outside her native cinema. She was the earth-mother of Italian films, a tragic comedienne who perfectly captured both the bitterness and humour of post-war Italy. An illegitimate child, she began her career as a variety performer and stage actress before making her film debut in *The Blind Woman of Sorrento* (1934). She first made a mark as a music-hall star in *Teresa Venerdí* (1941), and then burst onto the international scene with her compelling performance as a pregnant widow shot down by the Germans in Rossellini's *Rome, Open City* (1945). She was

equally powerful in *The Honourable Angelina* (1947) as the leader of a group of tenement-dwellers complaining about their conditions, and showed off her comedic talents in *Molti Sogni per la Strada* (1948) and *Bellissima* (1951). The high point of her career came as an Italian widow who falls for Burt Lancaster in *The Rose Tattoo* (1955), for which she deservedly won an Oscar. She was affecting in *Wild is the Wind* (1957) with Anthony Quinn and *The Fugitive Kind* (1960) opposite Marlon Brando, but thereafter made few films of any note.

John Malkovich

Actor
Born: *Benton, Ill., December 9, 1953*

Malkovich is arguably the finest actor working in America today. This is not to say he's incapable of a bad performance – he was colourless in Bertolucci's *The Sheltering Sky* (1990), deeply embarrassing in *Of Mice and Men* (1992) – but on form, with the right script and a director able to contain and channel his energies no one can top him. An intense blend of menace and vulnerability, Malkovich graduated to films after touring with his own theatre company, providing an achingly authentic portrait of

John Malkovich: *Dangerous when roused*

blindness in the neglected *Places in the Heart* (1984). In more villainous mood, he brought a gleeful panache to the Machiavellian Valmont in *Dangerous Liaisons* (1988), a box-office hit that sealed his reputation. Equally memorable

was his psychotic turn opposite Clint Eastwood in the escapist thriller, *In the Line of Fire* (1993), evading capture through a dizzying set of disguises, none of which incidentally are quite able to dilute the wearer's weird, instantly recognizable features. One critic wrote that Malkovich and Eastwood's warring was a one-sided contest between the great actor and the great movie star. At times Eastwood looks quite dazed by Malkovich's acting pyrotechnics. More recently Malkovich, long hailed as the natural successor to Marlon Brando, reprised the master's *Apocalypse Now* (1979) role as Kurtz, the prospector "gone native", in Nic Roeg's brooding adaptation of Conrad's *Heart of Darkness (1994)*.

Louis Malle

Director, writer
Born: *Thumeries, France, October 30, 1932*

A leading light of the French New Wave, Louis Malle moved into direction on the back of an apprenticeship assisting such film-makers as Jacques Cousteau, Jacques Tati and Robert Bresson. His classic directing style may have displayed little of the rough-hewn subversiveness of compatriot Jean-Luc Godard but Malle has never shied from controversy, most notably with *Lacombe Lucien* (1974) and the incest-tinged *Souffle au Coeur* (1971). Where Godard turned his camera lovingly on Anna Karina, so Malle enjoyed a sparkling collaboration with actress Jeanne Moreau, casting her as a dissatisfied housewife in the erotic *Les Amants* (1958) and teaming her with Brigitte Bardot in the vibrant *Viva Maria* (1965). Controversy followed Malle's move to the US. *Pretty Baby* (1978), featuring a coquettish, pubescent Brooke Shields, raised hackles but was neither as focused or potent as the elegiac *Atlantic City* (1980), powered by Burt Lancaster's outstanding performance as a skid-

row crook. *Au Revoir, les Enfants* (1987), a piercing, heart-tugging semi-autobiographical tale of growing up in Nazi-occupied France, was lavished with praise but another English-language excursion, adapting the glitz novel *Damage* (1992) proved less auspicious. Malle's formal film-making prowess, usually so graceful, now looked merely flashy while the would-be controversial content, once daring and provocative, suddenly seemed just an excuse to be wilfully risqué.

Rouben Mamoulian

Director
Born: *Tiflis, Georgia, Russia, October 8, 1898*
Died: *December 4, 1987*

A man of the theatre who was over 30 before going near a film camera, Mamoulian proved to be a great orchestrator of visual and aural cinematic techniques, unfettered by any suggestion of the restrictions of the stage. He trained at the Moscow Art Theatre and directed theatre, opera and operetta in England and New York in the early 1920s, staged the play *Porgy* on Broadway and later the premiere of Gershwin's *Porgy and Bess* (1935). He turned his imagination to cinema with *Applause* (1929), where his free-ranging shots of New York and orchestration of city sounds were an innovation. *Dr Jekyll and Mr Hyde* (1932) is renowned for its light and shade camera work and Fredric March's on-screen transformation, while in the Rodgers and Hart musical *Love Me Tonight* (1932) he integrated music, dialogue and action, and introduced the then revolutionary technique of cutting from scene to scene inside a musical number. *Queen Christina* (1933) boasts the memorable "objects recalling a love affair" scene and the final enigmatic shot of Garbo's impassive face, while with *Becky Sharp* (1935) he rose to the challenge of directing the first feature in three-colour Technicolor. His last two films were *Summer Holiday* (1948) and *Silk Stockings* (1957), the under-rated musical remake of *Ninotchka*, though in 1961 he was fired as director of *Cleopatra*. His other theatre work includes the first Broadway stagings of *Oklahoma* (1943) and *Carousel* (1945).

Joseph Mankiewicz

Director, producer, writer
Born: JOSEPH LEO MANKIEWICZ, *Wilkes-Barre, Pa., February 11, 1909*
Died: *February 5, 1993*

A multiple Oscar-winner, Joseph Mankiewicz often betrayed his writer's instinct in subordinating cinematographic showiness to an intelligent script. His finest film was *All About Eve* (1950) which brilliantly revived Bette Davis's flagging career. The son of a German-Jewish newspaperman, Mankiewicz began work as a journalist in Berlin, then translated film titles into English. He followed his screenwriter brother Herman to Hollywood, where he wrote titles for talkies in silent cinemas, beginning with *The Dummy* (1929). He appeared in *The Woman Trap* (1929), wrote dialogue for *Fast Company* (1929) and was Oscar-nominated for his first credited screenplay, *Skippy*, in 1931. After a second nomination for *Manhattan Melodrama* (1934), he asked to direct but was forced to produce instead, most notably *The Philadelphia Story* (1940). His directorial debut came when Ernst Lubitsch was too ill for *Dragonwyck* (1946). *A Letter to Three Wives* (1949) with its flashbacks and comic dialogue won him Oscars for Director and Screenwriter, followed a year later by the sparkling *All About Eve* (Best Film, Director and Screenplay). A fine *Julius Caesar* (1953) and a sparkling *Guys and Dolls* (1955) preceded his rescue job on the overblown *Cleopatra* (1963), for which he said, "It was,

on my part, knowingly an act of whoredom". He was much criticized for his films' talkiness, and *Sleuth* (1972) certainly lived up to that charge, but it remains a delight. The Director's Guild and Venice Festival honoured him in 1986, but the wit of his work is best savoured on the tongue.

Anthony Mann

Director
Born: EMIL ANTON BUNDSMANN, *San Diego, Calif., June 30, 1906*
Died: *April 29, 1967*

Anthony Mann's eye for the loner lost in a big country helped develop the western genre he is best known for, before he applied the same approach to historical epics with less success. The son of philosophy teachers, he moved to New York as a child, leaving school when his father died to look for acting work. He eventually formed his own theatre company where he first met James Stewart, later his favourite star, before moving into film in 1938 as a talent scout and casting director, supervising the screen-tests for *Gone With The Wind* (1939). His directorial debut was *Dr Broadway* (1942), but *Winchester 73* (1950) proved his first major production. Stewart had recommended him for the job, and of Mann's next 17 films, 10 were westerns, and seven in succession were with Stewart, including his most violent and successful, *The Man from Laramie* (1955), and the considerably gentler *The Glenn Miller Story* (1954). After teaming up with an ageing Gary Cooper for the pessimistic *Man of the West* (1958), he risked a change of genre but was sacked for clashing with the producer and star of *Spartacus* (1960), Kirk Douglas, after just a few weeks. *El Cid* (1961) was a success and *The Fall of the Roman Empire* (1964) highly regarded, but Mann died having been largely denied critical acclaim by all but the

French New Wave. Only posthumously has his talent for understatement, western mythology and fluid camera movement been properly recognized.

Jean Marais

Actor
Born: JEAN ALFRED VILLAIN-MARAIS, *Cherbourg, France, December 11, 1913*

Lover and muse of the great artist, poet and film-maker Jean Cocteau, the beautiful Marais inspired the older man to make some of his best work on film, particularly the enchanting fantasy *La Belle et la Bête*/Beauty and the Beast (1945), his film masterpiece *Orphée* (1950), an allegorical update of the

Jean Marais: *A striking and beautiful actor*

Orpheus myth, and its sequel *Le Testament d'Orphée* (1959). Though little-known outside France apart from these three performances, he has had a long and prolific career spanning five decades, with over 100 films. Through period romances like *Le Secret de Mayerling* (1949) and swashbucklers like *Nez de Cuir* (1952) and *Le Comte de Monte Cristo* (1954), he became the French Errol Flynn. He has also worked with several of the big names of world cinema, appearing in two of Sacha Guitry's historical epics, Renoir's *Eléna et les Hommes* (1957) with Ingrid Bergman and Visconti's *Le Notti Bianche* (1958) with Marcello Mastroianni. He started in pic-

tures as the discovery of the director Marcel L'Herbier, in whose 1933 film *L'Epervier* he made his debut and starred in five more of his pictures, until Cocteau wrote *La Belle et la Bête* for him and instantly established him as an international star – a position he held for the rest of his career and even to the present day, though he is now retired.

Fredric March

Actor
Born: FREDERICK MCINTYRE BICKEL, *Racine, Wis., August 31, 1897*
Died: *April 14, 1975*

Fredric March was one of the most reliable actors of American cinema, making his presence felt in a number of key films from the 1930s to the 1960s. His initial casting as a romantic lead merely scratched the surface of his abilities and it was not until 1932's *Dr Jekyll and Mr Hyde* that he came into his own, scooping an Oscar with a searing dual interpretation that has probably yet to be equalled. He cemented his reputation by playing a declining actor in *A Star Is Born* (1937) and in 1946 earned a second Oscar as a war hero adapting to civvie life in the homecoming fable *The Best Years of Our Lives*. With these roles March honed the knack of portraying a peculiarly American brand of tragedy – the cheated dreamer, too rigid to drop his false, destructive ideals – that made him perfect for the role of the doomed, desperate Willy Loman in the 1951 adaptation of Arthur Miller's *Death of a Salesman*. While the dark-haired, sober-looking March once dismissed himself as "just an old ham", others regard him as a supreme product of the American school of acting – serious, diligent and always value for money. The highlight of his later years was a towering turn as the inflexible opponent of liberal lawyer Spencer Tracy in *Inherit the Wind*

(1960), a grand-scale slice of US history that fitted March's talents like a glove.

Dean Martin

Actor, singer

Born: DINO PAUL CROCETTI, *Steubenville, Oh., July 7, 1917*

Having been a boxer, petrol pump attendant and croupier, the dark-haired, laconic, amiable rascal, most often seen on screen as laid-back cowboys, playboy spies and drunken lounge lizards, started his performing career as a club

Dean Martin: *Likeable lounge lizard*

singer, later teaming up with Jerry Lewis as the suave straight man in their popular comedy act. Their film partnership ran from 1949 to 1956, when it ended in acrimony, and was one of America's most successful comedy duos. Like Lewis he went on to have a big solo career and was phenomenally successful as a recording artist and in TV specials which slightly overshadowed his prolific film career. He churned out films regularly until 1974 and, though most of them were routine but popular, they included several highly regarded films like Minnelli's *Some Came Running* (1958), Howard Hawks's *Rio Bravo* (1959) and Billy Wilder's *Kiss Me, Stupid* (1964), playing a character who is a parody of himself. Though he specialized in light comedy, when he was persuaded to play in a tough western or a dark comedy

he could show his mettle as a serious actor of some depth. He will always be remembered, though, for the froth: the Matt Helm spy pictures, and the so-called Rat Pack movies with his friend Frank Sinatra (such as *Ocean's Eleven* [1960]), while the films he made with Lewis crystallized his screen persona.

Steve Martin

Actor, comedian, director

Born: *Waco, Tex., 18 August, 1945*

Steve Martin is a performer whose air of solemn respectability – impassive features, prematurely grey hair – masks a comedian of tremendous mental and physical agility. He's taken the rocky route to movie glory, with early success as *The Jerk* (1979) followed by a series of worthwhile but costly bombs like the misguided Americanized rejig of Dennis Potter's *Pennies from Heaven* (1981). Martin faced a common comedian's dilemma – finding a script that both contained and showcased his manic comic energies. Modest success with 1984's *All of Me* paved the way for a leap to the heights with the delicious *Roxanne* (1987), with Martin co-scripting and donning a vast latex snout as a small-town Cyrano de Bergerac. Quite suddenly the stand-up sensation had gone from cult item to megastar and a stream of hit turns followed, playing a prickly traveller in *Planes Trains and Automobiles* (1987), a bogus preacher in *Leap of Faith* (1992) and a luckless con-man opposite Michael Caine in 1988's *Dirty Rotten Scoundrels*. Martin's true strength, though, stems from a deceptive versatility. Time and again he has shown himself to be surprisingly deft in roles that combine comedy and drama, none better than his beautifully restrained turn in Ron Howard's *Parenthood* (1989). Martin's comic style, while often savagely anarchic, never appears cruel. "Making

yourself look stupid seems much more human," he says. "Making other people look stupid just seems cheap."

Lee Marvin

Actor

Born: *New York, NY, February 19, 1924*
Died: *August 29, 1987*

There is something inherently cruel and violent about Marvin's thick, pale lips, huge bony face and gruff voice. He had the appearance of a brutal man, and violence was never far from the surface of the characters he portrayed. He served a long apprenticeship as a Hollywood heavy, throwing scalding coffee over Gloria Grahame in *The Big Heat* (1953), tormenting one-armed Spencer Tracy in *Bad Day at Black Rock* (1954), and fighting it out with heroic John Wayne

Lee Marvin: *A violent man?*

in *The Man Who Shot Liberty Valance* (1962). He graduated, against the odds, from bad guy to hero, eventually winning an Oscar for his superb double portrayal of the cruellest gunfighter in the west and his drunken twin in *Cat Ballou* (1965). Even as a good guy, however, there was always a sense he might flip and do something really nasty. His finest performances – as a shipwrecked marine on a desert island in *Hell in the Pacific* (1968); the leader of a World War Two suicide mission in *The Dirty Dozen* (1967); and an ageing gunslinger in *Monte Walsh* (1970) – were extraor-

dinary essays in nihilistic anti-heroism. Always powerful, Marvin never failed to dominate the screen although he was never an actor to attract real warmth or empathy from an audience. He didn't care what people thought either, which was part of his appeal.

The Marx Brothers

Comedy team

GROUCHO
Born: JULIUS HENRY, *October 2, 1890*
Died: *August 19, 1977*
HARPO
Born: ADOLPH, (*aka* ARTHUR), *November 21, 1888*
Died: *September 28, 1964*
CHICO
Born: LEONARD, *March 26, 1886*
Died: *October 11, 1961*
ZEPPO
Born: HERBERT, *February 25, 1901*
Died: *December 13, 1979*
All born in New York, NY

The craziest comedy team in Hollywood history. Groucho with glasses, moustache and fat cigar was the wisecracker, Harpo never uttered a word but grinned insanely, tooting a bicycle horn, while Chico interpreted, hamming an Italian accent. The Brothers started out as a musical team but by 1924 they were in comedy on Broadway, and by 1929 debuted in the movie *The Cocoanuts* (with the straight-laced Zeppo in their first five films). *Animal Crackers* (1930) was more cinematic, and followed by the stowaway farce *Monkey Business* (1931), college romp *Horse Feathers* (1932), and their best film, *Duck Soup* (1933), with Groucho as the inept politician, Rufus T. Firefly, and a truly magnificent mirror sequence. Mussolini banned it, and a waning box-office performance saw them leave Paramount for MGM where their popularity was revived at the expense of their characters being made more sympathetic. Fortunately plot still fell by the wayside of their anarchic slapstick and nonsense logic. In *A Night at the Opera* (1935) they sold popcorn, yelled boogie and punctured pomposity with a series of inappropriate backdrops, a success repeated in *A Day at the Races* (1937), but rarely again. *Love Happy* (1950) was their last appearance as a team, though they all featured separately in *The Story of Mankind* (1957). Groucho

The Brothers Marx: Zeppo, meet Groucho, Chico and Harpo

finally collected an honorary Oscar for the Brothers in 1974, and a special award at Cannes. He became a TV star and returned to the stage aged 82 with a one-man show.

Giulietta Masina

Actress
Born: GIULIA ANNA MASINA, *Giorgio di Pano, Italy, February 22, 1920*
Died: *March 23, 1994*

Elfin-faced Masina, often compared to Chaplin for her ability to combine pathos and comedy, is best known for the films she made with her director husband, Federico Fellini. Masina first acted at university in Rome. In 1942 she appeared in a radio play written by Fellini, and they married the following year. She made her film debut in Rossellini's *Paisan* (1946) and her first film for her husband was *Variety Lights* (1951), about a

third-rate theatre troupe. She became an international name with the simple-minded, sensitive gamine of *La Strada* (1954), followed by the naive prostitute of *Le Notti di Cabiria* (1954), both for Fellini, who describes her as not just the actress of the roles, but their inspiration. *Cabiria* was also the inspiration for the 1960s musical *Sweet Charity*. She fell out of critical favour in subsequent films without Fellini, such as de Filippo's *Fortunella* (1958) and Duvivier's *La Grande Vie* (1960), where her much-praised, clown-like pathos was now dismissed as "mugging", and she virtually disappeared from the screen, apart from Fellini's *Juliet of the Spirits* (1965) and a brief role in *The Madwoman of Chaillot* (1969). She made one more film for her husband, *Ginger and Fred* (1984), a nostalgic tale with an ironic real-life subtext for her, where she and Mastroianni play two ageing dancers reuniting for a television show.

James Mason

Actor
Born: *Huddersfield, England, May 15, 1909*
Died: *July 27, 1984*

One of cinema's most enduring actors, the velvet-voiced James

Mason honed his screen persona of sophisticated, quietly menacing charm to a practised art. After cutting his teeth in high-class British productions – playing a dashing highwayman in *The Wicked Lady* (1945), an IRA gunman in Carol Reed's *Odd Man Out* (1946) – he embarked on a lengthy Hollywood career but was only rarely given the room to flex his acting muscles properly. He contributed a performance of exquisite villainy to Alfred Hitchcock's *North by Northwest* (1959) and lit up Disney's live-action fantasy *20,000 Leagues Under the Sea* (1954) as the demagogic Captain Nemo. Even in later years Mason radiated intensity, playing the "Prince of Darkness" in Sidney Lumet's courtroom drama *The Verdict* (1982) and sign-

James Mason: Velvet-voiced 'Prince of Darkness'

ing off with an assured, beautifully fashioned turn as a doomed aristocrat in his film swan song *The Shooting Party* (1985). But in a career roll-call topping 100 movies, two Mason performances bear the unmistakable stamp of greatness. As the paedophile protagonist of Stanley Kubrick's *Lolita* (1962), Mason nimbly navigates an acting minefield, audaciously juggling pathos, melodrama and wry comedy, while his Oscar-nominated role as a self-destructive actor in George Cukor's *A Star Is Born* (1954) is equally majestic, catching this supreme film performer at the peak of his considerable powers.

Marcello Mastroianni

Actor
Born: *Fontana Livi, Italy, September 28, 1924*

While Italian actor Marcello Mastroianni is most closely identified with Federico Fellini, in the course of a 150-film career he has also worked with the likes of Visconti, De Sica, Robert Altman, Louis Malle, "and eight films directed by women," he adds. "I believe I have a world record. Not another actor in the world can say this." Square-built and dusky, Mastroianni came to embody the man-of-the-world Latin lover. After a long list of support turns he impressed as a lovelorn clerk in Visconti's *White Nights* (1957), before leaping to worldwide fame in Fellini's *La Dolce Vita* (1960). It is the role he remains most associated with, the jaded journalist through whose trademark spectacles Fellini views the decadence of modern Rome. It was the first of five collaborations with the director, who was memorably to cast him as the moviemaker in meltdown in his autobiographical Oscar-winning drama *8 1/2* (1963). Another significant collaboration, teaming Mastroianni with sultry Sophia Loren, reached its peak with *A Special Day* (1977) driven by his high-octane turn as a homosexual broadcaster in Fascist Italy. Now in old age, Mastroianni refuses to rest on his laurels, alternating high-profile outings like 1992's *Used People* with small-scale labours of love, such as his role as an elderly playboy in *We Don't Want to Talk About It* (1994).

Walter Matthau

Actor, director, producer
Born: WALTER MATUSCHANASKAVASKY, *New York, NY, October 1, 1920*

Jowly, crumpled, and with an elastically expressive face, Hollywood's leading grouch Walter Matthau has turned such apparent drawbacks to comic advantage, his timing and double-takes ensuring lasting success. The son of poor Jewish-Russian immigrants, he worked in theatre from the age of 11, selling soft drinks initially but was soon on stage. He trained to be a journalist, but worked as a boxing instructor and basketball coach before enlisting as a radioman-gunner on World War Two bombers. Back in civvies, his Hollywood debut was

Walter Matthau: Hollywood's leading grouch

The Kentuckian (1955), bull-whipping Burt Lancaster and establishing himself as a villain in movies such as *A Face in the Crowd* (1957), *King Creole* (1958) and *Gangster Story* (1958), which he also directed. *The Fortune Cookie* changed all that, winning him an Oscar alongside Jack Lemmon, and the two were reunited as "husband and wife" in *The Odd Couple* (1968), the hit role specially written for him by Neil Simon. He was by now a major star – *Hello Dolly!* (1969) and *Plaza Suite* (1971) were followed by Oscar nominations for *Kotch* (1971) and *The Sunshine Boys* (1975). He displayed his versatility – from action adven-

ture in *The Taking Of Pelham 123* (1974), to romance in *House Calls* (1978), to executive production of *Little Miss Marker* (1980). His cynical style brings a touch of class to the least promising of material – see 1993's *Dennis* – and he has since traded insults with Lemmon again in the most aptly titled *Grumpy Old Men* (1994).

Louis B. Mayer

Producer, studio boss
Born: ELIEZER MAYER, *Minsk, Russia, July 4, 1885*
Died: *October 29, 1957*

Known as "the Czar of all the rushes", archetypal movie tycoon Mayer emigrated to America via Canada and leased a chain of New England cinemas before graduating to distribution and major success with D. W. Griffith's *The Birth of a Nation* (1915). He then went into production and in 1917 formed his own company but in 1924 merged with Metro and Samuel Goldwyn, forming the enormously powerful studio Metro-Goldwyn-Mayer, which in 1994 celebrated its 70th birthday, its roaring lion symbol still the most famous of all movie trademarks. When Goldwyn bought himself out of the studio, leaving him king of the lot, the wily Mayer appointed Irving Thalberg as his head of production, while he himself held tight on to the purse strings and promoted or stifled stars' careers at whim. He fostered the careers of Garbo, DeMille, Gable and (his favourite actor) Lionel Barrymore, encouraging the idea of an extended family of movie stars – "more stars than there are in the heavens", as MGM boasted. But Mayer could be as despotic as he was supportive: even a star as big as Joan Crawford was dispensable if L. B. decided she had had her day. Mayer won a special Academy Award in 1959 for distinguished service to the motion picture industry, but even the mightiest

have to fall and his one-time assistant Dore Schary kicked him out of MGM in 1951, a piece of poetic justice which must have been greeted with a wry smile on at least one well-lipsticked mouth.

Leo McCarey

Director, producer, writer
Born: *Los Angeles, Calif., October 3, 1898*
Died: *July 5, 1969*

McCarey's films were typified by his warm and irreverent humour and likeable characterizations which capitalized on the personalities of his star actors, while his tear-jerkers are regarded either as honest or sentimental, depending on taste. McCarey abandoned his law career and joined the Hal Roach studio in 1923, where as vice-president from 1926 to 1929 he supervised the Laurel and Hardy comedies, directing four of them. Turning to features, he worked with some of the leading comedy talent of the day: Eddie Cantor, in *The Kid from Spain* (1932), plus films with Mae West, W. C. Fields and one of the best of the Marx Brothers' movies, *Duck Soup* (1933). His big successes included *Ruggles of Red Gap* (1935) with Charles Laughton as the perfect English butler; *The Awful Truth* (1937), an Oscar-winning comedy with Cary Grant and Irene Dunne; *Make Way for Tomorrow* (1937), an unusual tear-jerker about deserted old people; *Love Affair* (1939), a Charles Boyer/Dunne weepie which he remade less memorably as *An Affair to Remember* (1957) with Grant and Deborah Kerr; and the wartime spy comedy *Once Upon a Honeymoon* (1942), with Grant and Ginger Rogers. He also scored with the Bing Crosby "priestly parables" – the double Oscar-winner *Going My Way* (1944) and *The Bells of St Mary's* (1945). From 1937 he produced practically all his films, writing the stories and screenplays for most.

Joel McCrea

Actor
Born: *Los Angeles, Calif., November 5, 1905*
Died: *October 20, 1990*

Tall, handsome, workmanlike Joel McCrea had neither the charisma nor the inclination to become a major star. He worked with some of Hollywood's greatest directors – Hawks, De Mille, Hitchcock, Sturges – and turned in a number of sturdy performances in a popular career spanning 30 years. But by his own admission he was no great actor, and rarely commanded a film in the way some of his more illustrious contemporaries did. Having worked as an extra, he got his first notable screen role in *The Jazz Age* (1929). Throughout the 1930s he turned in a string of reliable performances as a flyer in *The Lost Squadron* (1932), a hunted man in *The Most Dangerous Game* (1932), a gold prospector in *Barbary Coast* (1935) and a heroic railman in De Mille's *Union Pacific* (1938). In the early 1940s, however, his career blossomed with a series of fine performances in successful films. He was great as the journalist hero of Hitchcock's *Foreign Correspondent* (1940) and exceptional in two Sturges comedies – *Sullivan's Travels* (1942) and *The Palm Beach Story* (1942). He was equally endearing in *The More the Merrier* (1943) and *Buffalo Bill* (1944). Thereafter his career tailed off into a series of crowd-pleasing westerns, riding into the sunset on a high note as an ageing cowboy in Peckinpah's *Ride The High Country* (1962).

Hattie McDaniel

Actress
Born: *Wichita, Kan., June 10, 1895*
Died: *October 2, 1952*

The first black actor to win an Oscar, McDaniel was frequently cast as subservient maid or mammy, but was able to project her sassy personality on to the screen to great scene-stealing effect. The daughter of a Baptist minister, she progressed from church choir to showband, becoming the first black woman to sing on American radio. Her film debut was as Marlene Dietrich's protective maid in *Blond Venus* (1932), but she was soon raising comical eyebrows at her screen employers' follies (*Judge Priest*, 1934; *Alice Adams*, 1935). She was sharply witty as Queenie alongside Paul Robeson in *Show Boat* (1936), and in *The Mad Miss Manton* (1938) yells, "I ain't deaf. Sometimes I wish I was", at a guest's persistent knocking. She gave such spice to limited roles that there were complaints from some moviegoers that she was too "uppity", but as Scarlett's mammy and occasional adviser in *Gone With The Wind* (1939) she was rewarded with the Oscar for Best Supporting Actress. Black critical opinion was divided, the film condemned, but public acclaim for McDaniel complicated matters. McDaniel's problem was where to go from here. She had the talent, but Hollywood didn't offer blacks the roles. Nevertheless, McDaniel was responsible for a relative thaw in racial depictions in Hollywood. Her last film was *The Big Wheel* (1949), before she hosted her own television show, finally retiring because of ill-health.

Steve McQueen

Actor

Born: TERRENCE STEVEN McQUEEN, *Slater, Mo., March 24, 1930*
Died: *November 7, 1980*

The coolest of all film stars, with rugged good looks and ice-blue eyes, Steve McQueen made every character – however flawed – an irresistible hero, becoming one of the biggest names and icons of the 1960s and 1970s. Abandoned by his father aged only three, he was sent to reform school, escaped, was jailed, became a sailor, lumberjack, bookie's runner, poker player and marine, before drifting into acting in New York. His film debut was a bit part in *Somebody Up There Likes Me* (1956), and his first lead came in *The Blob* (1958). After television's *Wanted Dead or Alive* (1958), he became one of the first small-screen names to make the leap to major movie fame. If *The Magnificent Seven* (1960) sug-

Steve McQueen: *Electric blue*

gested big-time stardom, *The Great Escape* (1963) confirmed it. He was supercool on and off his motorbike, doing his own stunts throughout the legendary two-wheel chase. He returned to poker for *The Cincinnati Kid* (1965), was Oscar-nominated for *The Sand Pebbles* (1966), and was perfect as the casual, lone cop *Bullitt* (1968). He appeared with his second wife, Ali MacGraw, in *The Getaway* (1972), then *Papillon* (1973) which was another escape story, but while he fought flames in *The Towering Inferno* (1974) he was unable to overcome cancer, which killed him aged 50. His last film was *The Hunter* (1980). McQueen is best remembered for his terrific restlessness and for creating an atmosphere of electric expectancy, where something – anything – was certain to happen soon.

Jean-Pierre Melville

Director, writer

Born: JEAN-PIERRE GRUMBACH, *Paris, France, October 20, 1917*
Died: *August 2, 1973*

The poised, poetic visionary behind many of Europe's most challenging post-war pictures, film-maker Jean-Pierre Melville is looked on as the forefather of the French New Wave. His feature debut, the literary, low-budget *Le Silence de la Mer* (1948) set the stage for the Cocteau-inspired *Les Enfants Terribles* (1949), a simmering, unsettling tale of childhood games in 1940s France. Most influential was Melville's 1955 underworld outing *Bob le Flambeur*. A self-styled "love letter to Paris", vigorously filmed on the sodium-lit streets of Pigalle and Montmartre, it charts the misadventures of cardsharp criminal Roger Duchesne and proved the prototype for such Paris-set outings as Truffaut's *The 400 Blows* (1958) and Godard's *Breathless* (1959). Melville splendidly kept pace with the younger generation of French film-makers throughout the 1960s, even plucking their great star, Jean-Paul Belmondo, for the lead role of his intense metaphysical essay *Léon Morin, Priest* (1961). But it was a trio of gangster pictures that sealed his reputation, with *Le Doulos* (1963) and *Le Deuxième Souffle* (1966) building to 1967's *Le Samourai*, a bewitchingly minimalistic celebration of the *film noir* thrillers of 1940s Hollywood. In his last years, Melville's delicate style became a shade too clogged and self-referential. His final films, *The Red Circle* (1972) and *Dirty Money* (1972), were worthy but downbeat swansongs for one of French cinema's brightest talents.

Bette Midler

Actress, comedienne, singer

Born: *Honolulu, Hawaii, December 1, 1945*

"I wouldn't say I invented tack, but I definitely brought it to its present high popularity"; rude, raucous and raunchy, La Midler made her first screen impression in *The Rose* (1979) playing – and singing – a character reminiscent of the tragic Janis Joplin, and proving beyond doubt that, apart from being extremely funny when she wanted, the gal could act. She started off with a singing/comedy spot in a gay bath-house that formed the basis of her Tony award-winning Broadway review *Clams on a Half Shell*, which she followed with an Emmy for her TV special *Ol' Red Hair Is Back*, but it was her terrific performance in *The Rose* that started the movie career she'd always wanted, made her internationally popular and won her an Oscar nomination. The hysterical *Divine Madness* followed in 1980 with a taste of her stage show, a dazzling bolt of energy, trash and below-the-belt humour – who could forget the wheelchair-bound mermaid "Dolores del Lago, the toast of Chicago": "the problem before us, is where's her ...'"? But though this, and its aptly named successor *Jinxed* (1982) both flopped at the box office, her career was back on course with *Down and Out in Beverly Hills* (1986), since when she's gone from strength to strength with movies like *Ruthless People* (1986) and *Beaches* (1988). In recent years she has been trying to tone down her outrageous image – "underneath all this drag I'm a librarian". Yeah, right Bette!

Toshiro Mifune

Actor, producer, director

Born: *Tsingtao, China, April 1, 1920*

A strong, intelligent and subtle actor, and probably the most internationally famous of his countrymen, Mifune is best known to western audiences in the work of the great Japanese director Akira Kurosawa, a collaboration that established his career. The first actor ever to have received the Best Actor award at the Venice Film Festival twice – for Kurosawa's *Rashomon* (1950) and *Yojimbo* (1961) – he combines toughness, sensitivity and acute observation to make intelligent and believable portrayals of real

129

people caught in human situations. Kurosawa said of him: "His reactions are extraordinarily swift. If I say one thing he understands ten. He reacts very quickly to the director's intentions." It is with the ideal samurai figures that he has

Toshiro Mifune: *The ideal samurai*

played in films like the classic *The Seven Samurai* (1954), which established his popularity outside Japan, and *Throne of Blood* (1957), a samurai version of the Macbeth story, that audiences most associate him. Some of his better-known appearances have been *Hell in the Pacific* (1969) with Lee Marvin, as two stranded soldiers from opposite sides of World War Two, pursuing a stolen sword across the wide open spaces of Wild West America in *Red Sun* (1971), playing a Japanese ambassador whose son is kidnapped in *Paper Tiger* (1975), a star cameo in Spielberg's *1941* (1979) as the bewildered Japanese submarine commander, and the American mini-series *Shogun* with Richard Chamberlain in 1980.

Lewis Milestone

Director
Born: LEVIS MILSTEIN, *Chisinau, Russia, September 30, 1895*
Died: *September 25, 1980*

Milestone emigrated to America aged 18, and worked on army training films in World War One. He started his Hollywood career as an assistant cutter and in 1927 won the only Oscar ever awarded for Best Comedy Director with

Two Arabian Knights (1927). His real place in history, though, comes with the deeply felt anti-war film *All Quiet on the Western Front* (1930), for which he won his second Oscar. He returned to this theme in *A Walk in the Sun* (1945), set in World War Two, and *Pork Chop Hill* (1959), in the Korean War. His strong grasp of technique made him able to handle many different genres: the frantic pace of Hecht/McArthur's farce about journalism *The Front Page* (1931) – the first of many film versions; the innovative depression musical *Hallelujah I'm a Bum* (1933); and *Of Mice and Men* (1939) from Steinbeck's novel, which opened audiences' eyes to another side of Lon Chaney Jr as Lenny. From the 1950s Milestone worked mainly in television, and many critics claim his later film material was not worthy of his talent. But *Ocean's Eleven* (1960), starring Frank Sinatra and his pals, was not without entertainment value, nor was the maligned remake of *Mutiny on the Bounty* (1962), with a strong Bligh from Trevor Howard and an intriguingly bizarre "English" accent from Marlon Brando.

John Milius

Writer, director
Born: *St Louis, Mo., April 11, 1944*

John Milius is the chief of America's macho cinema – a screenwriter who strives for a tough, Hemingwayesque vision, a director who boasts that he runs his film crew like a crack military unit. Rejected from real military service because of his asthma, Milius turned to movies, scripting the 1969 actioner *The Devil's Eight*, biking biopic *Evel Knievel* (1971) and contributing uncredited to the script for Clint Eastwood's *Dirty Harry* (1971). At the end of the 1970s he collaborated memorably with buddy Francis Coppola on the screenplay for the Vietnam fable *Apocalypse Now* (1979), where

the gung-ho romanticism of his initial script was eventually tempered by his more measured and sensitive co-writer. By that time Milius had established his own directing pedigree with a trio of distinguished pictures, kicking off with a fine debut in the dime-store gangster fantasy *Dillinger* (1973), moving through the adventurous sprawl of *The Wind and the Lion* (1975) and climaxing with a mini-masterwork in the elegiac surf movie *Big Wednesday* (1978). But Milius's undisputed storytelling skills are often hamstrung by a slide into crude jingoism – witness his 1984 commie-bashing caper *Red Dawn* or the comic-strip knockabout of the wildly popular *Conan the Barbarian* (1982). In the 1990s Milius looked back on form, contributing to the script of the Harrison Ford blockbuster *Clear and Present Danger* (1994) and co-authoring the undervalued revisionist western *Geronimo* (1994).

Ray Milland

Actor, director
Born: REGINALD ALFRED TRUSCOTT-JONES, *Neath, Wales, January 3, 1905*
Died: *March 10, 1986*

Milland joined films in 1929 in *The Flying Scotsman* credited as Spike Milland. A few movies later, he went Hollywood in 1930 where he quickly made his mark in striking support roles, then as polished, resolutely cheerful romantic star in a wide range of different kinds of films. His best films of this period were *The Jungle Princess* (1936), *Beau Geste* (1939) and *French without Tears* (1939). By the time of *Arise My Love* (1941), *The Major and the Minor* (1942), and *The Uninvited* (1944), he'd developed into a proficient, sometimes outstanding actor and won an Oscar for perhaps his best performance, the drunken writer in Billy Wilder's *The Lost Weekend* (1945). Only occasionally cast as the

baddie, he excelled as the devil in *Alias Nick Beal* (1949) and the wife-killer in Hitchcock's *Dial M for Murder* (1954), but he was also ideal in Fritz Lang's Hitchcock-style thriller *Ministry of Fear* (1944) and in John Farrow's *film noir The Big Clock* (1948). In the 1950s and 1960s Milland had several intriguing stabs at direction, including *A Man Alone* (1955), *The Safecracker* (1958), *Panic in Year Zero* (1962) and *Hostile Witness* (1968). Later he did a couple of fine Roger Corman creepers, *The Premature Burial* (1962) and *The Man with X-Ray Eyes* (1963), but he didn't stay with the burgeoning genre, and experienced a late-1960s career slump, rescued by his role as dad in *Love Story* (1970). Thereafter Milland acted tirelessly in horror films and TV movies.

Sir John Mills

Actor
Born: LEWIS ERNEST WATTS MILLS, *North Elmham, England, February 22, 1908*

In a film career of over 60 years, Sir John Mills has passed from being one of the most popular, reliable English actors of his generation to becoming a beloved British showbiz legend. He won his star status thanks to Noel Coward, who had seen him in repertory theatre in Singapore and back in London recommended him for the lead in *Charley's Aunt* (1930). The following year Mills made his film debut in *The Midshipmaid* as a sailor with an eye for Jessie Matthews. He was soon a busy worker in double-bill movies, among them *The Green Cockatoo* (1937), in which he played his former real-life role as a chorus boy. He often specialized in cheeky Cockneys and overcame his short stature with high-energy, high-charm performances. He excelled for Coward in *In Which We Serve* (1942) and *This Happy Breed* (1944), and two of his best films were literary adaptations, *Great Expectations* (1946) and *The*

History of Mr Polly (1949). In the 1950s he turned to another character he made his own, the terribly British star of popular war films such as *Ice Cold in Alex* (1959), *Tunes of Glory* (1960) and *King Rat* (1965). In 1970 he won an Oscar for *Ryan's Daughter* and he was still working in his eighties, most recently with Madonna in *Who's That Girl?* (1987) and the 1994 horror spoof *Deadly Advice*.

Liza Minnelli

Actress, singer

Born: *Los Angeles, Calif.,*
March 10, 1946

It is impossible to forget that Liza Minnelli is Judy Garland's daughter. She has inherited her mother's looks and extraordinary singing voice; and, like her mother, comes to the fore in musical extravagan-

Liza Minnelli: *Life is a cabaret*

zas. But Liza is far more than just a Garland clone, and has brought to her screen roles a fast-talking contemporary toughness and street-wisdom that is entirely her own. She made her screen debut as a secretary in Albert Finney's *Charlie Bubbles* (1967), and took the world by storm in her first musical role, as Sally Bowles in Kander and Ebb's *Cabaret* (1972). It was one of the immortal musical per-

formances, mixing vulnerability with toughness, guts with absolute self-assurance. It was an Oscar-winning turn she has rarely come close to topping, although her skill was evident in Scorsese's big band musical, *New York New York* (1977), and she scored a massive hit as the sassy love interest in the comedy *Arthur* (1981). Since then she has concentrated mainly on stage and concert work, and her sporadic film outings have been mostly forgettable, despite valiant performances as a mother with a disabled son in *A Time To Live* (1985), and a tap-dance teacher in *Stepping Out* (1991). Inevitably overshadowed by the legend of her mother, she remains an exceptionally gifted performer in her own right, one of modern cinema's great contemporary entertainers.

Vincente Minnelli

Director

Born: *Chicago, Ill.,*
February 28, 1910
Died: *July 25, 1986*

Director of some of the best pure entertainment films of the 1940s and 1950s, Minnelli's show-business blood (he was a dancer and tumbler in his parents' act from age three) expresses itself in a love of flamboyance, colourful costumes and decor, movement and imagination. After working as a set and costume designer, he graduated to art director at New York's Radio City Music Hall and thence to the direction of Broadway musicals. He went to Hollywood in 1940 as a director of musical sequences, taking the director's chair for the all-black musical *Cabin in the Sky* (1943). Musicals were among the most memorable of his films: *Meet Me in St Louis* (1944), with his first wife Judy Garland; *An American in Paris* (1951), an Oscar-winner in which Minnelli's visual imagination combined with Gene Kelly's choreographic one; the delightful *The*

Band Wagon (1953); *Gigi* (1958), another Oscar-winner; and the reincarnation fantasy *On a Clear Day You Can See Forever* (1970), with Barbra Streisand. However, much of Minnelli's considerable output was non-musical, including comedy hits like *Father of the Bride* (1950) and the Lucille Ball vehicle *The Long, Long Trailer* (1954), as well as dramas like *The Bad and the Beautiful* (1952), a "behind-the-screen" tale of ruthless Hollywood people. The Van Gogh biopic *Lust for Life* (1956) allowed him openly to indulge his love of painting.

Carmen Miranda

Actress

Born: MARIA DO CARMO MIRANDA DA CUNHA, *Marco de Canavezes, Portugal,*
February 9, 1909
Died: *August 5, 1955*

Miranda, with her ludicrous fruit-bowl head-dresses, boundless vitality and hip-wiggling Brazilian charm, was one of the most extraordinary forces ever to burst on to the silver screen. She was no great actress, never played a lead role, and only appeared in some 14 films, yet for the early part of the 1940s enjoyed an unparalleled popularity in Hollywood musicals. The Brazilian Bombshell, as she was known, was actually born in Portugal, moving to South America as a child and embarking on a successful career as a night-club singer and recording artist. She was already a household name south of the border when she landed a part in a Betty Grable musical, *Down Argentine Way* (1940), singing "South American Way" and becoming an instant hit. There followed a succession of lightweight musicals – *That Night in Rio* (1941), *Weekend in Havana* (1941), *The Gang's All Here* (1943), *Greenwich Village* (1944) – in which she did little except dance and sing and deliver as few lines as possible. She was always fun,

though, and her searing energy, together with her undoubted skill as a musical entertainer, made even the most risible projects palatable. However, as the decade progressed audiences tired of her tropical flamboyance. She returned to night-club singing, making a final appearance in a Jerry Lewis comedy, *Scared Stiff* (1953).

Robert Mitchum

Actor

Born: *Bridgeport, Conn.,*
August 6, 1917

There's a danger in underestimating the man Charles Laughton (who directed him in one of his finest films 1955's *Night of the Hunter*) called "one of the best actors in the world". Like Michael Caine, Mitchum has always given the erroneous impression that he doesn't take acting seriously – "movies are a turn-off, especially mine". His most famous feature, the heavy-lidded snake-eyes – from an old boxing injury – accounted for a lot of his sex appeal in the early days of his career in the 1940s, but they also help foster the myth that he has sleepwalked through much of his career. While Mitchum is never seen to be acting, he's one of the screen's most powerful and respected players, who always rises to the occasion. Though he has probably appeared in more

Robert Mitchum: *"Movies are a turn-off"*

131

poor movies than any other great star (he started out in a Hopalong Cassidy pic), his once-despised RKO films *Out of the Past* (1947) and *Angel Face* (1953) are now deemed minor classics. When the films were good, Mitchum was invariably excellent, as in *The Sundowners* (1960), *Cape Fear* (1962), *Ryan's Daughter* (1970) or *The Yakuza* (1975). He came to the role he was born to play, Philip Marlowe, too late (he was 58) but *Farewell My Lovely* (1975) is still a high spot. In the 1980s TV lured him, and his 18-hour mini-series *The Winds of War* (1983) gave him one of his biggest hits.

Tom Mix

Actor
Born: *Mix Run, Pa., January 6, 1880*
Died: *October 12, 1940*

Mix was *the* cowboy star of the 1920s, a glamorous, gung-ho showman who packed his films with stunts, daredevil action routines and fancy costumes. By his own admission most of his movies had much the same plot – "getting into trouble when doing the right thing for somebody else" – but audiences in the Roaring Twenties wanted thrills and spills and glamour, and Mix happily provided them, setting a trend for westerns that continued well into the 1950s. Born in 1880, he worked as a rodeo performer before making his first western in 1910. He enjoyed no real success until *The Daredevil* (1919), which he also directed, and thereafter his crisp, check shirts, enormous sombreros and trusty black steed, Tony, galloped their way through over 60 movies, all of them distinguished by groundbreaking stuntwork, gleaming photography and Mix's faintly ridiculous get-ups. There was nothing particularly subtle about his work, the complete opposite of the brooding, realistic westerns of William S. Hart, but action romps such as *Just Tony* (1922), *The Lone Star Ranger* (1923)

and *The Great K & A Train Robbery* (1926) were extremely good fun, and much of the stuntwork has never been bettered. However, his career faded with the coming of talkies. His last great film was *Destry Rides Again* (1932) and he died in a car crash in 1940.

Kenji Mizoguchi

Director, actor
Born: *Tokyo, Japan, May 16, 1898*
Died: *August 24, 1956*

It's hard to get a true grasp on Mizoguchi's career and importance since, although he made over 85 films in a 30-year career from 1923 onwards, more than 50 of them have been lost because of fire or war and of the remainder few have been screened outside Japan. His work in the 1950s finally brought him an international audience with his three Venice prize-winning films *The Life of Oharu* (1952), *Ugetsu Monogatari* (1953) and *Sansho the Bailiff* (1954) – his masterpieces. He is known for his painstaking direction and his meticulous attention to visual quality, prompted no doubt by his training as a painter, though his early career as an actor gave him a sympathetic attitude to performers. He favoured long takes, non-symmetrical composition and a theatrical approach to the cinema also seen in the work of Ozu and Bergman. Mizoguchi made extraordinary demands of his collaborators, both technical and performing, who responded with a fierce loyalty establishing a valuable continuity within the *oeuvre* that's again common to some of the cinema's greats. He suffered a series of failures before *Oharu* and staked all his finances on his adaptation of a classic novel about a samurai's daughter who falls for lower-caste Toshiro Mifune, but this was the film that established his reputation outside Japan and spurred the masterpieces of his final years. He died with his next script by his bedside.

Marilyn Monroe

Actress
Born: NORMA JEAN MORTENSON, *Los Angeles, Calif., June 1, 1926*
Died: *August 5, 1962*

Marilyn Monroe remains the most exhaustively documented yet somehow elusive of all Hollywood icons. Her legendary status stems from a potent combination of glowing blond locks, poetic curves, low, breathy vocals, vulnerable bearing and premature demise – dead at 36 from a drug overdose. In her early days Monroe was just another jobbing actress on the movieland circuit, providing vivid bit parts in *All About Eve* (1950), *Monkey Business* (1952) and *The Asphalt Jungle* (1950) before landing a star role with her 18th film as a devious bride in the 1953 potboiler *Niagara*. Her range was narrow but within it her fooling was exquisite, sugaring her all-accommodating sexual-

Marilyn Monroe: Ballyhoo and sensation

ity with a wide-eyed comic gloss. She held audiences spellbound as a myopic gold-digger in *How to Marry a Millionaire* (1953), the wayward ukulele-strummer of *Some Like It Hot* (1959) and an uncomprehending engine of lust, skirt billowing about an hourglass waist, in 1955's *The Seven Year Itch*. Branching out, she impressed in more dramatic roles, in *Bus Stop*

(1956) and her last completed picture *The Misfits* (1961), scripted by then-husband Arthur Miller. Described by one-time co-star Laurence Olivier as "the victim of ballyhoo and sensation – exploited beyond anyone's means", she could be awkward and unreliable on set, while her private life has been linked to both presidents and mobsters. But on film, damaged, insecure Norma Jean was always Monroe – incandescent immortal of the silver screen.

Yves Montand

Actor, singer
Born: IVO LIVI, *Monsummano Alto, Italy, October 13, 1921*
Died: *November 9, 1991*

The archetypal popular image of the sophisticated, world-weary Frenchman, Montand was brought up in Marseilles after his Jewish peasant family fled Mussolini's persecution. He left school at 11 and after various menial jobs, became a nightclub singer. He was discovered at the Moulin Rouge by Edith Piaf, who made him her lover and guided him to singing stardom. His first film role was with her in *Etoile sans Lumière* (1946), but he stayed primarily a singer until Clouzot cast him in *The Wages of Fear* (1953). After leads in many European films, some with his wife Simone Signoret, he starred opposite Marilyn Monroe in *Let's Make Love* (1960), but failed to sparkle in that and subsequent Hollywood films. The unknown Costa-Gavras tapped into his dramatic talent with the whodunnit *Compartiment Tueurs/The Sleeping Car Murder* (1965); then *Z* (1969), a powerhouse of a film about political assassination; and *L'Aveu* (1970), a harsh indictment of anti-democracy in Communist Czechoslovakia. Most of his films of the 1970s and early 1980s were seen only in France, so it was a shock for the rest of the world to see him in fine form but grown old as the scheming, acquisitive peasant in Claude Berri's two-parter *Jean de Florette* (1986) and

Yves Montand: World-weary Gaul

Manon des Sources (1986). He died while making Jean-Jacques Beineix's mystical road movie *IP5* (1992), a role which required him to swim naked in a lake and possibly contributed to the heart attack which killed him.

Dudley Moore

Actor, comedian, composer, pianist
Born: *London, England, April 19, 1935*

By the mid-1960s, Oxford graduate Moore had formed a duo with fellow B*eyond the Fringe* revue alumnus Peter Cook, appearing first on TV, making their movie debut in *The Wrong Box* (1966) and thereafter moving easily between TV, theatre and movies. In 1978 Moore was cast solo in a key cameo in Goldie Hawn's comedy thriller *Foul Play* and the Americans loved his broadly funny turn. It landed him the star role in Blake Edwards's '*10*' the following year and the extraordinary success of this spicy comedy conferred a wholly unexpected international fame on the diminutive Dud. But what to do with it? Certainly not the wholly awful *Wholly Moses* (1980) or *Romantic Comedy* (1983), but definitely *Arthur* (1981), even if his star-

drunk turn was upstaged by the great Gielgud's Oscar-winning acid butler. Little Dud was by now big enough to survive a series of indifferent comedies from which he always emerged unscathed, thanks to his personal warmth, a rare enough commodity in Hollywood leading men. There hasn't been a Dudley Moore film since *Arthur* that you could put your hand on your heart and say was hilarious, though quite a few have been funny enough. *Like Father Like Son* (1987), *Crazy People* (1990) and *Blame It on the Bell Boy* (1991) were all made strictly to formula perhaps, but were passably entertaining as vehicles for this likeable little man.

Roger Moore

Actor
Born: *London, England, October 14, 1927*

Roger Moore squeezed into the movie pantheon when he took over from Sean Connery in *Live and Let Die* (1973) as a lightweight but definitely not wooden James Bond for seven 007 pictures before calling it a day in 1985 with *A View to a Kill*. It's easy to underestimate the debonair Moore and overlook the skill beneath his cool, polished, ironic-toned performances. There may be little variety, but that was what was often expected of stars in his heyday of the 1950s, and there's no doubt he plays Roger Moore better than anyone – to perfection in fact. Moore's appeal is that he is suave in an age when no one is suave any more and his self-mockery is disarming – on his narrow range: "left eyebrow raised, right eyebrow raised". Though critics often sneer, the public has long enjoyed his laid-back elegance and laconic humour, first in a collection of unmemorable British and Hollywood pictures, then on TV in the *Saint* series, then as Bond, and finally in some decent star

vehicles which his 007 status commanded. RADA-trained, he had a surprisingly long struggle to establish himself, starting right back in 1946 with *Caesar and Cleopatra*. Hollywood groomed him for stardom with *The Last Time I Saw Paris* (1954), but it wasn't till the TV series *Ivanhoe* (1957–58) and *Maverick* (1960–61) that his star persona clicked smoothly into place, leading to *The Saint* and *The Persuaders*.

Agnes Moorehead

Actress
Born: *Clinton, Mass., December 6, 1906*
Died: *April 30, 1974*

Graduating from college in the mid-1920s and appearing in provincial theatre, Agnes Moorehead started appearing on Broadway in 1928, then worked on radio and toured vaudeville halls with her partner Phil Baker. Her career took off when she joined Orson Welles's and John Houseman's Mercury Theatre players in 1940. This striking and incisive star character actress started at the top and never strayed far away, with *Citizen Kane* (1941), playing Kane's mother, and as the hysterical, frustrated spinster in *The Magnificent Ambersons* the following year. Her hawkishly handsome features and powerful screen presence destined her for highly strung or nasty characters and it's an ironic postscript on such a distinguished career that she's now most famous as the witch mother-in-law Endora in the TV series *Bewitched* (1964–72), although her appearances as this character were expertly timed and exquisitely arch. From Welles to the witches there were four Academy nominations, for *The Magnificent Ambersons* (1942), *Mrs Parkington* (1944), *Johnny Belinda* (1948), and *Hush Hush Sweet Charlotte* (1964), while among her other memorable movies were *The Lost Moment* (1947), *The Woman in*

White (1948), *Show Boat* (1951), *Magnificent Obsession* (1954) and *The Bat* (1959). In 1954 she toured with a solo show, *The Fabulous Red Head*, which she eventually played in over 200 towns across the globe.

Jeanne Moreau

Actress, director
Born: *Paris, France, January 23, 1928*

The incisive French stage and screen actress Moreau, classically trained at the Paris Conservatoire, was an icon of the French New Wave cinema of the early 1960s. Her tough demeanour and aloof allure earned her the respect of fans and fellow artists. She lit up a host of key New Wave films, particularly Malle's *Lift to the Scaffold* (1957), *The Lovers* (1958) and *Viva Maria* (1965), Truffaut's *Jules and Jim* (1961) and *The Bride Wore Black* (1968), and Jacques Demy's *Bay of Angels* (1963). These successes brought calls from all the top arthouse directors. Buñuel cast her in *Diary of a Chambermaid* (1963), Welles in *The Trial* (1962), *Chimes at Midnight* (1966) and *The Immortal Story* (1968), Fassbinder in *Querelle* (1982), and Losey in

Jeanne Moreau: Aloof muse of the nouvelle vague

Eva (1962) and *The Trout* (1982). Having established her worldwide reputation, she appeared to less acclaim in international productions like *The Train* (1964), *Great Catherine* (1968), *Monte Walsh* (1970) and *The Last Tycoon* (1976). In the 1970s she worked with up-

and-coming directors like Bertrand Blier (*Les Valseuses*, 1973), André Techiné (*Souvenirs d'en France*, 1975) and Guy Gilles (*Le Jardin Qui Bascule*, 1975), helping to promote their careers. Moreau became a praised director herself in 1976 with *Lumière*. She remains adored and – better still – busy. Though few of her films are now seen outside France, she graced *Nikita* (1990) and 1991's *The Old Woman who Walked in the Sea*.

Paul Muni

Actor

Born: MUNI WEISENFREUND, *Lemberg, Austria, September 22, 1895*
Died: *August 25, 1967*

Paul Muni's painstaking and committed approach to his craft made him one of the 1930s' greatest actors, with full-blooded performances in some of the Depression era's most hard-hitting and socially conscious productions. Already a respected stage performer, he shot to stardom in Howard Hawks's S*carface* (1932), a gritty and urgent dissection of underworld America that laid the ground for the gangster movie genre. A jittery establishment, unnerved by Muni's white-hot performance and troubled by the film's glorification of crime, were only pacified when the studio added the disclaiming sub-tag "the shame of the nation" below the title. The actor followed *Scarface*'s success with another controversial, acclaimed role as a wrongly convicted prisoner in the fact-based *I Am a Fugitive from a Chain Gang* (1932), while his forceful turn as an impoverished coalminer put fire in the belly of the banned *Black Fury* (1935). By the mid-1930s Muni had moved on to the historical epic, bagging an Oscar for his central performance in *The Story of Louis Pasteur* (1935) and proving histrionic but compelling in the title role of William Dieterle's *Juarez* (1939). In the

1940s and 1950s Muni's film forays were fewer and farther between, though he signed off with a flourish, Oscar-nominated for his role as a good-hearted doctor in 1959's *The Last Angry Man*, his final film appearance.

F. W. Murnau

Director

Born: FRIEDRICH WILHELM PLUMPE, *Bielefeld, Germany, December 28, 1888*
Died: *March 11, 1931*

In his brief but prolific career, F.W. Murnau left an indelible impression on the early history of cinema through his powerful ability to tell a story with action, light, camera movement and editing. After working with Max Reinhardt in Berlin, Murnau served in World War One as a combat pilot. The mood of his early film work was in tune with the expressionists' pessimistic postwar view of human frailty and despair in a tragic world, yet was atypically filmed against naturalistic backgrounds, as in the mesmerising *Nosferatu* (1922), based on the Dracula story, where the horror of the supernatural is intensified by being set against the everyday. *The Last Laugh* (1924) tells the story of a proud man's descent into humiliation without any of the customary titles of the silent film. *Faust* (1926) makes great use of pictorial backcloths echoing Bosch, Breughel and Rembrandt. Hollywood seized on Murnau's talent for *Sunrise* (1927), a film since praised for its lyrical pessimism, about a young farming couple in the big city who find a (Hollywood-imposed) happy ending after many trials. It failed, however, to find an audience with cinema-goers of the day. *Four Devils* (1928) and *City Girl* (1930) were equally unsuccessful, and he was sacked by the money men. His next film, *Tabu* (1931), a documentary about Polynesian customs, became a great success, but a week before the premiere Murnau was killed in a car crash.

Audie Murphy

Actor, war hero

Born: *Kingston, Tex., June 20, 1924*
Died: *May 31, 1971*

The baby-faced kid from a poor Texan cotton-cropping family entered films because of his World War Two fame as the most honoured serviceman in American history with 24 citations of bravery, including the Congressional Medal of Honor. His fame, laddish good looks (he seemed born to play the title role in *Billy the Kid* in 1950) and a modicum of acting talent ensured him a good 20-year career from 1948, mainly in war or cowboy pictures. Like Randolph Scott, he was one of the few bankable stars of B-westerns in the 1950s, starring in films like *Sierra* (1950), *Destry* (1954), *Kansas Raiders* (1950) and *Ride Clear of Diablo* (1954). But the talent he showed when he got the chance – in John Huston's version of Stephen Crane's *The Red Badge of Courage* (1951), in his filmed autobiography *To Hell and Back* (1955), or in Joseph Mankiewicz's adaptation of Graham Greene's *The Quiet American* (1958) – was increasingly demoted to low-cost, low-interest movies. In the 1960s his kind of movies were not attracting the interesting cult directors like Don Siegel and Kurt Neumann who had switched to TV, and indeed the B-movie itself was terminally sick. His last years were sad – made bankrupt in 1968, accused of attempted murder in a bar-room fight in 1970 and killed in a plane crash the following year. Murphy is an unfashionable figure with a fervent cult following whose work is ripe for re-evaluation.

Eddie Murphy

Actor, comedian, producer, director, writer

Born: *Hempstead, NY, April 3, 1961*

Sassy, talented, confident and good-looking young black actor/comedian, Eddie Murphy hosted a

talent show at 15, performed in nightclubs at 16 and had made his mark before he was 20 in the popular satirical *Saturday Night Live* TV show. His film debut *48 HRS* (1982), as the fast-talking, street-smart, con sprung from jail by cop Nick Nolte to track down killers, was a huge hit, and made Murphy an instant box-office draw. He was winning in John Landis's enjoyable comedy *Trading Places* (1982) as the clever beggar who changes places with smug yuppie Dan Aykroyd, while the high-action comedy *Beverly Hills Cop* (1984) was a laugh-a-minute surprise. Then came the downside, created by unwise choices and

Eddie Murphy: Comedy's golden child

poor advice: *The Golden Child* (1986), followed by the limp sequel *Beverly Hills Cop II* (1987); *Coming to America* (1988) as an African prince looking for an American bride; and *Harlem Nights* (1989), a one-man disaster area. Little better were two predictable sequels, *Another 48 HRS* (1990) and *Beverly Hills Cop III* (1994), plus the unpleasantly chauvinistic comedy *Boomerang* (1992). But it is far too early to write him off as a burned-out victim of too much, too soon. *The Distinguished Gentleman* (1992) displays some of the old Murphy charisma as the cool senator elected by default, showing there is still room for him at the top.

Dame Anna Neagle
Actress
Born: MARJORIE ROBERTSON, *London, England, October 20, 1904*
Died: *June 3, 1986*

A genteel, demure English rose, Neagle was a major star in England in the years around World War Two. Invariably directed by her husband Herbert Wilcox, she made few films of great worth, and was never popular outside Britain, yet the refined, faintly glamorous Englishness that she brought to all her movies struck a chord with the British public, and fulfilled a need for home-grown heroines at a time of national crisis. She worked as a dancer and on the stage before Wilcox starred her in the film musical *Goodnight Vienna* (1932). She first caught the public eye in the title role of *Nell Gwyn* (1934), then produced three of her finest, most flag-waving performances, as Queen Victoria in *Victoria the Great* (1937) and *Sixty Glorious Years* (1938), and as *Nurse Edith Cavell* (1939). She enlivened the austere post-war years with a number of faintly ludicrous, escapist romances – *Piccadilly Incident* (1946), *Springtime in Park Lane* (1948) – but was surprisingly forceful as a wartime heroine in *Odette* (1950) and as Florence Nightingale in *The Lady with a Lamp* (1951). Filmgoers tired of her persona in the 1950s but she returned to hit stage work, becoming a Dame of the British Empire in 1969.

Pola Negri
Actress
Born: BARBARA APPOLONIA CHALUPEC, *Janowa, Poland, December 31, 1894*
Died: *August 1, 1987*

A capricious, magnetic, larger-than-life performer, Negri was the first in a long line of European actresses imported into Hollywood as much for their exotic novelty value as for their dramatic skills. Like Dietrich and Garbo, she became a legend in her own lifetime, but unlike her illustrious successors never made a happy transition from German to American cinema. Born in Poland, she worked in theatre and made her screen debut in *Love and Passion* (1914), which she both wrote and financed. She was soon the leading film star in Poland, and then moved to Germany, where she started making movies with Ernst Lubitsch, the only director fully to exploit her rawness, vitality and passion. Together they made a series of milestone movies, including *Carmen/Gypsy Blood* (1918), *Madame Dubarry/Passion* (1919), *One Arabian Night* (1921) and *Montmartre* (1923). *Madame Dubarry* was her finest creation, a tempestuous, roller-coaster performance which brought her international acclaim. She was snapped up by Hollywood, but the studios failed to capitalize on the animal magnetism that had so enlivened her German movies. She was superb in Lubitsch's *Forbidden Paradise* (1924) and scored big successes with *Hotel Imperial* (1927) and *Barbed Wire* (1927), but these were exceptions. Her career on both sides of the Atlantic petered out, and, despite the odd cameo appearance, she never again displayed the irresistible, driving energy of her early roles.

Paul Newman
Actor, director
Born: *Cleveland, Oh., January 26, 1925*

Not only does Newman have the most devastating, sapphire-blue eyes, but he is also one of the finest screen actors of the modern cinema age. Others are more showy, but Newman outdoes them because, at his best, he is so laid back you would never actually think that he was acting at all. He studied at the Actor's Studio, made his screen debut in *The Silver Chalice* (1954) and entered the big league as boxer Rocky Graziano in *Somebody Up There Likes Me* (1956). *Cat on a Hot Tin Roof* (1958) confirmed his excellence, and her-

Paul Newman: Does he ever miss?

alded three decades of extraordinary performances in great films: *The Hustler* (1961); *Sweet Bird of Youth* (1962); *Hud* (1963); *Cool Hand Luke* (1967); *Butch Cassidy and the Sundance Kid* (1969); and *The Sting* (1973). The 1980s and 1990s have seen the hair whitening, but he has made the transition from virile heart-throb to grizzly elder statesman with little apparent effort, and continues to produce work of outstanding quality: *Absence of Malice* (1981); *Fort Apache, the Bronx* (1981); *The Verdict* (1982); and *The Color of Money* (1986), for which he finally won a criminally overdue Oscar for Best Actor. In 1994, he turned in a show-stealing performance as the bad guy – one of the few he has ever played – in the Coen Brothers' *The Hudsucker Proxy* and in 1995 he impressed again in *Nobody's Fool*..

Jack Nicholson
Actor, director, writer
Born: *Neptune, NJ, April 22, 1937*

The perpetual rebel outsider is now very much part of the Hollywood establishment but, with his ironic grin and receding don't-care hair, Nicholson continues to be one of the most charismatic stars of the screen. Deserted by an alcoholic father, he was brought up in a household of women. A trip to California landed him a job in MGM's cartoon department, and from there he joined an actors' group, soon making his way into stage productions and television soaps. His first film experience came amid Hollywood's fringe film industry. His debut was the lead in Roger Corman's *Cry Baby Killer* (1958), and in such low-budget quickies he gained vast experience as writer, director and producer as well as actor. His big break came when Rip Torn dropped out of the surprise bikers-on-dope hit, *Easy Rider* (1969), earning Jack his first Oscar nomination, followed by others for *Five Easy Pieces* (1970) which made him a star, *The Last Detail* (1973) and *Chinatown* (1974), before finally winning with *One Flew Over the Cuckoo's Nest* (1975) and *Terms of Endearment* (1983). There were more nominations for *Reds* (1981), *Prizzi's Honor* (1985) and *Ironweed* (1987). Free-spirited individuals are his speciality but inevitably his great talent has attracted the big money. His outrageous performance as the villainous Joker in *Batman* (1989)

Nicholson: *Jack's back*

may have earned him $60 million. His later, seemingly effortless performances in the hits *The Witches of Eastwick* (1987), *A Few Good Men* (1992) and *Wolf* (1994) made up for the occasional flop like *Man Trouble* and *Hoffa* (both 1992).

Leslie Nielsen

Actor
Born: *Regina, Canada, February 11, 1925*

A genial stalwart of many, mostly forgotten, 1950s and 1960s adventure films, Leslie Nielsen rocketed to stardom in his silver-haired sixties in the most unexpected way, displaying a precision-tooled talent for po-faced alternative comedy in *Airplane!* (1980) and especially *The Naked Gun* (1988). He was a huge international success in a film that, according to Hollywood physics, should never have been made, based as it was on the flop TV series *Police Squad* (1982), cut off in its prime because of poor ratings. The ABC TV network admired the Zucker brothers' spoof disaster movie *Airplane!* and had commissioned a cop show in the same vein. The series' reputation grew during the 1980s and Paramount took a chance on the big-screen version, and its enormous success was topped by the sequel *The Naked Gun 2 1/2* (1991) – "the only sequel with a fraction in the title to take more money than the original" – and a second sequel *The Naked Gun 33 1/3* (1994). With all due respect

to funny scripts and the genial co-stars, the film's success is entirely down to Nielsen's expert performances, a far cry from his first incarnation as matinee idol leading man in vintage movies like *Forbidden Planet* (1956) and *Beau Geste* (1966) or when he captained *The Poseidon Adventure* in 1972.

David Niven

Actor, author, gentleman
Born: JAMES DAVID GRAHAM NIVEN, *Kirriemuir, Scotland, March 1, 1910*
Died: *July 29, 1983*

Niven was Hollywood's cherished idea of the quintessential English gentleman with his dulcet voice, laconic smile, pencil moustache and stiff upper lip. Actually he was Scottish-born and a lovable rogue, at odds with authority. Expelled from prep school, he drifted to America after a spell in the Highland Light Infantry, working first in New York as a bootlegger, then in Hollywood as an extra. His rise was swift. Compensating for his lack of acting experience with his enormous charm, he landed a seven-year contract with producer Sam Goldwyn and was soon starring alongside his close friend Errol Flynn in *Dawn Patrol* (1938). After *Wuthering Heights* (1939), he returned to wartime Britain to serve as a commando officer. Goldwyn welcomed him back to Hollywood in 1946 and, through notable performances in *The Moon Is Blue* (1953) and *Around the World in 80 Days* (1956), he re-established himself as a reliable star actor specializing in light comedy. His portrayal of a bogus war hero in *Separate Tables* (1958), for which he won an Oscar, revealed him as a dramatic actor of unexpected depth. A brilliant raconteur, his romanticized memoirs *The Moon's a Balloon* (1971) and *Bring on the Empty Horses* (1975) were international bestsellers. Niven remained a star for five decades, regarded the world over

as a member of the family, and, despite a neuromuscular disorder, performed until the year of his death.

Philippe Noiret

Actor
Born: *Lille, France, October 1, 1930*

One of cinema's most thoughtful performers, Noiret is up there with Raimu, Louis Jouvet and Michel Simon in the pantheon of great French character actors. His droopy, bloodhound face and large nose have adorned a host of classic French and European movies; but, unlike his illustrious predecessors, he has also enjoyed considerable success in English-speaking films. He worked in theatre before making his film debut in an experimental feature, *La Pointe Courte* (1955) and his first notable role came with Louis Malle's *Zazie dans le Métro* (1960), as a flamboyant, avuncular female impersonator, the first in a series of perfectly crafted character performances. He was a wonderfully slobbish farmer in *Alexandre le Bienheureux* (1967); a man who eats himself to death in *La Grande Bouffe* (1973); a vengeful army surgeon in the poignant *Le Vieux Fusil/The Old Gun* (1975); a romantic professor in *Tendre Poulet* (1977); an indolent police chief in *Clean Slate* (1981) and an exuberantly bent cop in *Le Cop* (1984). Noiret has enlivened a number of English-language films – notably *Justine* (1969) and *Murphy's War* (1971) – and, like a good wine, has improved with age, giving one of his finest, most popular performances as the wistful, nostalgic cinema projectionist in *Cinéma Paradiso* (1988).

Nick Nolte

Actor
Born: *Omaha, Nebr., December 8, 1940*

Blond, bear-like Nick Nolte is a Hollywood player in the Bogart mould, adept at portraying brood-

ing, beat-up rough diamonds. As with Bogart, movie stardom arrived relatively late, with Nolte moving from TV roles (especially 1975's *Rich Man, Poor Man*) to give a powerhouse turn as a drug-smuggling Vietnam vet in Karel Reisz's high-fuelled *Who'll Stop the Rain?* (1978). Even then, mainstream box-office success had to wait until 1981 when he was fortuitously teamed with rising star Eddie Murphy for the fast and furious comedy-thriller *48 HRS* Rumoured to be awkward and inflexible, Nolte has seen his career hampered by dud outings, including uncertain turns in Barbra Streisand's *The Prince of Tides* (1991) and 1994's hamfisted screwball attempt *I Love Trouble*. But with the right handling he can be one of the business's most compelling actors in both dramatic and comedy roles – witness his performance as a wily, dog-food-eating destitute in *Down and Out in Beverly Hills* (1986). Predictably, perhaps, it has been the most skilled directors who have wrestled the best from this unruly, undervalued actor. Sidney Lumet's otherwise formulaic *Q & A* (1989) was splendidly beefed up by the star's role as a corrupt police chief while Martin Scorsese coaxed out two classic Nolte performances, as a boorish painter in the director's *New York Stories* (1989) segment and the lawyer-under-threat in the ambiguous psycho-chiller *Cape Fear* (1991).

Mabel Normand

Actress
Born: MURIEL FORTESCUE, *Boston, Mass., November 16, 1894*
Died: *February 23, 1930*

Mabel Normand, with her huge brown eyes and delicate 5'3" frame, could conceivably have made it as one of the silent screen's early sex sirens. It is to the inestimable enrichment of film culture that she opted instead to pursue her talents as a comedienne, becoming one of cinema's first, and greatest, female comics. She was a model before starting her film career at Biograph under D. W. Griffith and making her name with Mack Sennett's Keystone Film Company. Here, alongside the likes of Fatty Arbuckle and later Chaplin, she brought her irresistible vitality and inventiveness to dozens of one- and two-reel comedies, most of them totally forgettable, but including enough minor slapstick masterpieces to ensure her reputation: *Mabel's Lovers* (1912); *Tillie's Strange Predicament* (1914); *Tillie's Punctured Romance* (1914); *Mabel's Simple Life* (1915); *Fatty and Mabel Adrift* (1916); *Mabel and Fatty's Wash Day* (1916). Her first solo feature, *Mickey* (1917), was a triumph, amply demonstrating her natural magnetism and ability to carry a film. She continued producing fine work into the twenties – *Molly O* (1921); *The Extra Girl* (1923); and Hal Roach's *The Nickel Hopper* (1926) – but her wild living (including suspected drug addiction) was starting to catch up with her. She was implicated in two notorious murder scandals and, like her close friend Fatty Arbuckle, never really recovered from the bad press. She died in 1930.

Kim Novak

Actress
Born: MARILYN PAULINE NOVAK, *Chicago, Ill., February 13, 1933*

An icy blonde beauty launched as a sex symbol in a major studio publicity drive. While much maligned as an actress, Novak produced a number of well-judged performances in several of the 1950s' most crucial films. She proved a convincing *femme fatale* in Richard Quine's stock thriller *Pushover* (1954) and gave a rounded, sympathetic turn as the concerned girlfriend of junkie Frank Sinatra in the provocative *The Man with the Golden Arm*

(1955). Most notable is her dual role as Madeleine and Judy, James Stewart's double obsession in Hitchcock's *Vertigo* (1958). Hitch was unimpressed with Novak, finding her wooden and unresponsive, but in fact she's precisely in tune with the movie's mood, her blank carnality bringing an almost otherworldly sleaze to what remains the director's most masterly elusive and oblique thriller. After revealing surprisingly effective comic skills in Quine's *Bell Book and Candle* (1958) and Billy Wilder's *Kiss Me, Stupid* (1964), rewarding work began to dry up. But Novak deserves credit for possessing the talent and determination to break out of her allocated starlet mould. "The head of publicity of the Hollywood studio told me, 'You're a piece of meat, that's all'," Novak recollected. "When I made my first screen test the director explained to everyone: 'Don't listen to her, just look'."

Ryan O'Neal

Actor
Born: PATRICK RYAN O'NEAL, *Los Angeles, Calif., April 20, 1941*

Handsome, clean-cut all-American boy Ryan O'Neal was just what the 1970s moviegoing public needed. TV had turned him into a pin-up and a star in *Peyton Place*, (1964–69) and a contract with Warners launched him in his movie debut *The Big Bounce* (1969), opposite wife and *Peyton Place* co-star Leigh Taylor-Young. Romancing Ali MacGraw in Erich Segal's soppy tearjerker *Love Story* (1970) (motto: "Love means never having to say you're sorry") turned him into a red-hot, Oscar-nominated attraction. During his 1970s superstar period, he admirably tried to widen his range, enjoying hits with Barbra Streisand in the screwball farce *What's Up Doc?* (1972), in the hard-hitting chase thriller *The Driver* (1978), and alongside daughter Tatum in the comedy drama *Paper

Moon* (1973). It's upon these three fine films that his reputation rests and they indicate a depth of talent that hasn't been exploited since. He pocketed $3 million for *Oliver's Story* (1978), the feeble sequel to *Love Story*, and worked again with Streisand in *The Main Event* (1979). But though he was pulling in the dollars, he wasn't pulling in the crowds and a comedy with Shelley Long, *Irreconcilable Differences* (1984), was his only hit in the 1980s. In recent years, his turbulent private life has attracted more attention than any of his movies and he's virtually retired from the screen, an extraordinary eclipse of a former superstar.

Peter O'Toole

Actor
Born: *Connemara, Ireland, August 2, 1932*

O'Toole had already enjoyed a blossoming stage career and a couple of movie roles when David Lean picked the golden-haired, blue-eyed, dashing young actor for the title role in his *Lawrence of Arabia* in 1962. One of the best epics of the 1960s, its success brought O'Toole immediate world stardom. He stayed at the top throughout the 1960s, though

Peter O'Toole: *The perfect Lawrence*

some of the vehicles were shaky. Curiously his other best two roles were the same: Henry II – with Burton in *Becket* (1963) and with Katharine Hepburn in *The Lion in

Winter* (1968). He has always been at his best in historical roles, but he showed a happy lightness of touch with comedy in *What's New Pussycat?* (1965) and *How to Steal a Million* (1966). He was convincing in the underrated musical version of *Goodbye, Mr Chips* (1969) and brilliant as a loopy aristocrat in *The Ruling Class* (1972). There were several flops in prestige productions like *Lord Jim* (1964), *Great Catherine* (1968), even *Man of La Mancha* (1972), while his 1970s career is a list of disappointments. But O'Toole is a survivor. Battling with alcoholism, then a jeering public for his London stage *Macbeth* (1980), he came back with *The Stunt Man* (1980) and the TV satire *My Favorite Year* (1982). In 1987 he scored as Pu Yi's tutor in Bertolucci's *The Last Emperor*, was funny in *High Spirits* (1988) and hilarious as a drunken Elizabeth I in *Rebecca's Daughters* (1991).

Sir Laurence Olivier

Actor, director, producer
Born: LAURENCE KERR OLIVIER, *Dorking, England, May 22, 1907*
Died: *July 11, 1989*

Lord Olivier, the British theatre's first peer, was often described as the century's greatest actor, though some critics allege he was just a dazzling bag of tricks, while others argue he was a chameleon who got deep under the skin of every role he tackled. At any rate there were many great performances in a long filmography and he was Oscar-nominated 10 times, winning for *Hamlet* (1948). After a slow start in films from 1930, his career got going under his Alexander Korda contract, but it was a trio of American films – *Wuthering Heights* (1939), *Rebecca* (1940) and *Pride and Prejudice* (1940) – that established him as a dashing box-office success. His three Shakespeare entries, *Henry V* (1944) for which he won a special Oscar, *Hamlet* and *Richard III*

(1956) are British film classics. He displayed the showman side of his character when he directed Marilyn Monroe in the soufflé *The Prince and the Showgirl (1957)*, but showman and intellectual merged for his thrilling portrayal of a broken-down comic in *The Entertainer (1958)*. In the 1960s he mixed running Britain's National

Sir Laurence Olivier: A call to acting arms

Theatre with high-profile performances in character parts like the Mahdi in *Khartoum* (1966), the mystery writer in *Sleuth* (1972), the Nazi dentist in *Marathon Man* (1976) and the Nazi-hunter in *The Boys from Brazil* (1978). In old age with failing health no part seemed too shallow, including Harold Robbins's *The Betsy* (1978) and the Neil Diamond *Jazz Singer* (1980), but all was redeemed with his majestic TV *King Lear* (1984).

Max Ophüls

Director
Born: MAX OPPENHEIMER *(aka* MAX OPULS*)*, *Saarbrücken, Germany, May 6, 1902*
Died: *March 26, 1957*

Ophüls is best known for his elegant romantic melodramas featuring women misused in love by men, often in lush *fin de siècle* settings. He had a penchant for circular stories leading to an inevitable conclusion, whose structure is

reflected in the fluid mobility of his camerawork. His own story is one of determination triumphing over adversity, though his early life promised much. Born into a prosperous Jewish family, he became a successful stage director while still a young man, before turning his attention to films. The rise of Nazism necessitated flight to France, where he resumed filmmaking, until the occupation uprooted him again, sending him to Hollywood in 1941 and several years of unemployment. Ophüls was eventually invited by Preston Sturges to direct *Vendetta* (1950) but was dismissed after a few days' work, then made *The Exile* (1947) with Douglas Fairbanks Jr. He followed this with one of his greatest successes, *Letter from an Unknown Woman* (1948) – Joan Fontaine in a story of unrequited love – and two *films noirs, Caught* (1949) and *The Reckless Moment* (1949), both starring James Mason. Ophüls then returned to France for the internationally renowned *La Ronde* (1950) with its witty chain of love affairs; *Le Plaisir* (1951), based on stories by de Maupassant; *Madame de ...* (1953), another circular tale; and his first venture into colour, the masterwork *Lola Montes* (1953).

Yasujiro Ozu

Director, writer
Born: *Tokyo, Japan, December 15, 1903*
Died: *December 4, 1963*

One of Japan's most distinguished directors, Ozu created minutely planned and observed studies of lower-middle-class Japanese life, largely shot from the still, low-angle viewpoint of an observer sitting on the floor in traditional Japanese position. His films are also characterized by the stylized composition of shots, the absence of virtually any form of camera movement, their unusual transitions and their use of 360°C space, as opposed to the conventional

180°C, which preserves the viewer's sense of reality. Ozu went into films as an assistant director in 1923, and was directing by 1927. His early films were comedies with an undertone of sadness, such as *Life of an Office Worker* (1929), where an expected sum of money never arrives, and *Tokyo Chorus* (1931), about a man who loses his job and becomes a sandwich worker. During the war he was sent to Singapore to make propaganda films and spent much of his time viewing captured prints of American films. He was however uninfluenced by them in his own work, which he continued after the war in the style he had already established, merely refining it in such films as *The Flavour of Green Tea over Rice* (1952), and *Good Morning* (1958), looking at the world of a child. In the 1950s the merits of his masterworks like *Late Spring* (1949), *Early Summer* (1951), *Tokyo Story* (1953) and *Early Spring* (1956) became recognized outside Japan and they are now world cinema classics.

G. W. Pabst

Director
Born: GEORG WILHELM PABST, *Raudnitz, Bohemia, August 27, 1885*
Died: *May 29, 1967*

Brought up in Vienna, as a young man Pabst worked as an actor and director in America. Returning home in 1914 he was trapped in France for the duration of the war. He entered films in 1921, soon rejecting the overriding expressionist style for his own pessimistic realism, evident in the film which established him, *Joyless Street* (1925), a gloomy story about the effects on one street of post-war corruption and inflation. In the cast was the young Greta Garbo while Marlene Dietrich was among the extras. *Secrets of a Soul* (1926), with its famous dream sequences achieved through multiple exposure, dramatized Freudian

theory, and the blatantly sexual *Pandora's Box* (1929) and *Diary of a Lost Girl* (1929) both featured erotic performances from Louise Brooks. Pabst upset Brecht by making changes to *The Threepenny Opera* (1930) when filming it and, more dangerously, put his head on the Nazi block with two pacifist films showing comradely feeling between French and Germans: *Westfront 1918* (1929), his first talkie, and *Kameradschaft* (1930). He wisely removed himself to France, but unwisely allowed himself to become trapped by war for a second time on a trip home in 1939. He was later accused of collaboration because of the films he made in Germany during World War Two, despite the anti-Nazi and pro-Semitic tone of some of his later work.

Al Pacino

Actor
Born: ALFREDO PACINO, *Harlem, New York, NY, April 25, 1940*

Pacino is an actor of extraordinary power, depth and sensitivity who has never quite claimed his rightful place in the pantheon of screen greats. His pale, haggard face and huge brown eyes have scowled their way through half a dozen classic movies, yet he has failed to put together the sort of consistently excellent body of work that might be expected of someone of

Al Pacino: Mobbed by the fans

his talent. After extensive work in theatre he burst into the public conscious with his extraordinary performance as Mafia man Michael Corleone in *The Godfather* (1972). There followed a four-year period of extraordinary creativity – *Scarecrow* (1973); *Serpico* (1973); *The Godfather, Part II* (1974); *Dog Day Afternoon* (1975). The failure of Hugh Hudson's costly civil war epic *Revolution* (1986) devastated him and he stopped filming for three years. The superb thriller *Sea of Love* (1989) brought him back to public attention, and he has remained there firmly ever since with a series of highly popular and critically acclaimed vehicles: *Dick Tracy* (1990); *The Godfather, Part III* (1990); *Glengarry Glen Ross* (1992), and *Scent of a Woman* (1992), for which he won an Oscar as a blind army officer having one last fling before committing suicide. He was spellbinding as a reformed mobster in *Carlito's Way* (1993), and if he continues in this form should achieve the wide popular adoration that has so far eluded him.

Sergei Paradjanov

Director, writer
Born: SARKIS PARADZHANOV, *Tbilisi, Georgia, January 1, 1924*
Died: *July 21, 1990*

Graduating from the Institute of Cinematography in 1951, Paradjanov co-directed his first feature *Andriesh* (1954) and shot some noteworthy realist dramas until 1964 when he made *Shadows of Our Forgotten Ancestors*, memorable for its original lyrical approach to narrative and unnaturalistic use of the cinematic vocabulary to convey emotions, a style common to his best-known work. He became a focus for dissidents and joined the human rights campaign, to the fury of the authorities, who quashed his film projects. His next film was made in Armenia in 1969, *The Colour of Pomegranates*, the biopic of an

18th-century monk and Armenian national icon, martyred by invaders for his Christianity, but this thinly veiled political allegory wasn't seen in the west until 1977, when it was a huge success. In 1974 he was jailed for four years for homosexuality and on invented charges of dealing in currency, pornography and art works. Sick, dispirited and banned from working, he wrote scripts about his prison hard-labour but Brezhnev's assumption of power allowed him to return to filmmaking and he produced two masterworks; *The Legend of the Suram Fortress* (1984) and *Ashik Kerib* (1988), extraordinarily being allowed to visit America for the New York premiere of what turned out to be his last film. He died of lung cancer shortly afterwards. A man of conscience and a complete original, Paradjanov leaves behind a body of work with a strong resonance as well as a strange alien beauty.

Alan Parker

Director, writer, cartoonist, lyricist
Born: *London, England, February 14, 1944*

Parker is a man of contradictions. This most British of film directors has worked mostly in America where he looks happiest with American subjects and large-scale projects aimed at the widest audiences. He was one of Britain's brightest directors in commercials (Hovis bread) and television (*The Evacuees*) yet Parker remains a cinema careerist through and through. Three of his first five films were youth-oriented musicals – *Bugsy Malone* (1976), *Fame* (1980), *Pink Floyd – The Wall* (1982) – yet he seems most at home with the raw emotions of adults: M*idnight Express* (1978) and *Shoot the Moon* (1982). The man who despises the press ("turnip heads") and intellectual film-makers like Peter Greenaway says he wants to

make films for a popular audience, yet he seems forever to be straining to make a masterpiece. Even a thriller like *Angel Heart* (1987) is heavy with meaning, not to mention a touch of artistry. His best film to date, *Birdy* (1984), is an arthouse movie, but made with so much of the skill of a born entertainer that it reaches out to everybody. He says the Oscars are worthless, yet in 1978 (*Midnight Express*) and 1988 (with the searing race thriller *Mississippi Burning*) he might well have been pleased to have won one of his Best Director nominations. One day he'll probably get one, though he didn't for the inert 1940s romance *Come See the Paradise* (1990), for the populist soul musical *The Commitments* (1991), nor for the coarse farce *The Road to Wellville* (1995).

Pier Paolo Pasolini

Director, writer, novelist, poet, essayist, critic
Born: *Bologna, Italy, March 5, 1922*
Died: *November 2, 1975*

Pasolini's rebellion against the views of his Fascist father expressed itself in more than his Communist beliefs. A brilliant multi-faceted gay artist, he was unafraid of controversy through the often uncompromising nature of his work, while showing a passionate concern for the underprivileged and a personal spirituality, as he juggled his conflicting allegiances to Marx, Freud and Jesus Christ. A published poet at 19, Pasolini had established himself as a novelist and essayist by the time he collaborated on the screenplay of Fellini's *Le Notte di Cabiria* (1956). His clear-eyed humanist debut *Accatone* (1961), about a pimp in the Roman slums, brought him international acclaim, followed by *Mamma Roma* (1961), with Anna Magnani as a prostitute. He fell foul of the Church with his parody of biblical epics in *Rogopag* (1961), countering it with his own uncompromising and realistic

telling of *The Gospel According to Matthew* (1964). He vividly reinterpreted the classical *Oedipus Rex* (1967) and *Medea* (1970) with Callas, made a teasing sexual exploration in *Theorem* (1968), then put all his imagination into a bawdy, liberating trilogy based on classical literature, reworking *The Decameron* (1971), *The Canterbury Tales* (1972) and *The Arabian Nights* (1974). His final film *Salò – The 120 Days of Sodom* (1975), an allegory of Fascist Italy packed with sexual depravities, was declared obscene by the Church and banned in Britain. That same year Pasolini mysteriously met a violent death at the hands of a 17-year-old youth.

Gregory Peck

Actor
Born: ELDRED GREGORY PECK, *La Jolla, Calif., April 5, 1916*

Peck radiates integrity in a world where that's a rare virtue. He is probably the sincerest actor ever to have come out of Hollywood, playing a long line of decent, dignified heroes. He has taken lead

Gregory Peck: *Hollywood's bastion of integrity*

roles since his debut in *Days of Glory* (1944), and at his best can be a spellbinding performer. As the general in charge of a potentially suicidal bombing mission in *Twelve o'Clock High* (1949) and as the world-weary gunslinger Jimmy Ringo, desperately trying to go straight, in *The Gunfighter*

(1950) he brilliantly, and movingly, explores the darker side of moral correctness. His career reached its peak as liberal lawyer Atticus Finch in *To Kill a Mockingbird* (1962), for which he deservedly won a Best Actor Oscar for the quintessential Peck performance. He has starred in plenty of enjoyable films – *Roman Holiday* (1953), *The Big Country* (1958), *The Guns of Navarone* (1961), *The Omen* (1976) – but always comes unstuck when playing characters who aren't essentially good. He struggled as a lecher in *Duel in the Sun* (1946); and looked and sounded ridiculous as Captain Ahab in *Moby Dick* (1956). He continues to lend his weighty presence to the odd television series, and will always remain a force for decency in the world of film.

Sam Peckinpah

Director

Born: *Fresno, Calif., February 21, 1925*
Died: *December 28, 1984*

Sam Peckinpah was one of the visionaries of 1960s and 1970s cinema, the man who overhauled the western genre and dragged American film into its gritty, gory new era. Peckinpah's West is Wild in every sense of the word; a harsh, unstable world built around a series of suppressed contradictions, symbolized by the surrealistic wedding ceremony at the mining camp in 1961's *Ride the High Country*. *Major Dundee* (1965) debunked the myth of the Wild West hero, subverting Charlton Heston's square-jawed image by casting him as a racist, borderline-crazy Federal officer, while *The Wild Bunch* (1969), a bloody tale of outmoded gunslingers in a changing territory, probably stands as the summation of Peckinpah's themes and style. But many viewers were upset both by Peckinpah's ritual, stylized violence – all reeling bodies in slow-

motion – and by the complete absence of the genre's traditional notions of right and wrong, of good men winning through over bad. In Peckinpah's work, life was messy and violence random. His obsession with violence reached its apogee with the uncomfortable *Straw Dogs* (1971). But the 1970s saw the director's westerns mellowing, with the low-key *The Ballad of Cable Hogue* (1971) paving the way for the lovely, nostalgia-tinged *Junior Bonner* (1972). While making his last film, espionage thriller *The Osterman Weekend* (1983), Peckinpah humorously reflected on his more benevolent stance. "I'm getting so fond of these characters," he said. "I'm tempted to keep them alive."

Arthur Penn

Director

Born: *Philadelphia, Pa., September 27, 1922*

Penn is a director of variety and quality, whose films reflect his interest in the destructive relationship of society to the outsider, combined with the arbitrary nature of violence. After studying acting, Penn turned to directing television plays in the early 1950s. In 1958 he directed his first Broadway play, *Two for the Seesaw* and his first film, *The Left Handed Gun*, an offbeat psychological approach to the story of Billy the Kid, played by Paul Newman. He sensitively filmed *The Miracle Worker* (1962) with Anne Bancroft and Patty Duke, whom he had already directed on Broadway. *The Chase* (1966), about the conflict between honest sheriff Marlon Brando and a corrupt town, was both praised and slated, as was *Mickey One* (1965), with Warren Beatty as a nightclub comic on the run. But Beatty had a winner with *Bonnie and Clyde* (1967), Penn's violent and compassionate film about young bankrobbers in the Depression. *Little Big Man* (1970) was a quirky epic about the pio-

neer/Indian conflict, built round Dustin Hoffman as a tall-tale-telling turncoat in the Old West, *Night Moves* (1975) a gripping thriller with Gene Hackman as a Los Angeles private eye, while *The Missouri Breaks* (1976), another western, brought Brando into conflict with Jack Nicholson. Penn has rarely worked for the cinema since then, his most powerful piece of recent years being an intelligent thriller, *Target* (1985), with Hackman again as a former CIA agent whose past is destroying his family.

Michelle Pfeiffer

Actress

Born: *Santa Ana, Calif., April 29, 1957*

Of course it's Pfeiffer's drop-dead gorgeous looks you notice first, but while America isn't short of blondes who won beauty pageants, it hasn't got many box-office queens. For Pfeiffer's captivating smile conceals two qualities in even greater demand than honeyed skin and high cheekbones – mystery and excitement. She started out in the late 1970s with only the Miss Orange County

Michelle Pfeiffer: *Drop-dead gorgeous*

beauty contest prize, a few months of acting lessons and a hefty chunk of ambition. After her 1980 debut in *Falling in Love Again*, she made an impression in her first starring roles in the teen pic *Grease*

2 (1982) and the mobster movie *Scarface* (1983) opposite Al Pacino. But it was John Landis's 1984 mystery *Into the Night* that showed what she could really do, shaping up as a Marilyn Monroe for the 1980s with a talent for comedy underpinned by a haunting vulnerability. *The Witches of Eastwick* (1987) opposite Jack Nicholson really made her career hot and it's been a non-stop rollercoaster since, Oscar-nominated for *Dangerous Liaisons* (1988), *The Fabulous Baker Boys* (1989) and *Love Field* (1992). Her Catwoman in *Batman Returns* (1992) outclassed her co-stars, and she showed her versatility in Scorsese's period romance *Age of Innocence* (1993). Reunited with Pacino, she was miscast as a frumpy waitress in *Frankie and Johnny* (1991), but she had plenty of bite in her reteaming with Nicholson in 1994's *Wolf*.

Gérard Philipe

Actor

Born: GÉRARD PHILIP, *Cannes, France, December 4, 1922*
Died: *November 25, 1959*

One of the great figures of modern French cinema and the most lauded actor of his generation, Gérard Philipe was a uniquely talented performer who, in his brief career, came to personify both the frivolity and the turbulence of post-war French society. A sensitive, impish figure with a childlike grin and huge, glistening eyes, he started in theatre, made his screen debut in *La Boîte aux Rêves* (1943) and gained widespread acclaim as a gentle, well-meaning idealist in *The Idiot* (1946). His breakthrough movie was *Le Diable au Corps* (1947), playing a schoolboy who has an affair with a soldier's wife. It was a blisteringly poignant portrayal, combining playfulness with acute inner turmoil, and was the first in a series of complex, spellbinding performances: as a romantic officer in *La Ronde* (1950); a happy-go-lucky swashbuckler in

Fanfan-la-Tulipe (1951); a lovelorn teacher in *Le Rouge et Le Noir* (1954); and a soldier again in *Les Grandes Manoeuvres* (1955). His directorial debut – *Les Aventures de Till l'Espiègle* (1957) – was a critical failure, but his portrayal of the painter Modigliani in *Montparnasse 19* (1958) was one of the finest performances of his career. He died of a heart attack in 1959, aged 36, a tragically premature yet somehow appropriate end for one so closely identified with the mood and aspirations of post-war French youth.

River Phoenix

Actor

Born: *Madras, Oreg., August 23, 1970*
Died: *October 31, 1993*

The world was devastated when "Hollywood's Mr Clean" died aged 23 of a drug overdose at Hollywood's starry Viper Club, accompanied by Johnny Depp and his girlfriend Samantha Mathis, star of his last complete film *The Thing Called Love* (1993). Happily the films live on and this cute kid with the intense look and cornfed charisma had already shown his stylish and sensitive acting in a dozen or so top movies. Phoenix started a busy TV career when he was just 10. Then at 15 came his movie break – playing a science whiz-kid who magics up a spaceship in Joe Dante's enchanting sci-fi film *Explorers* (1985). This won him a role in Rob Reiner's surprise hit *Stand by Me* (1986) as the leader of a gang of 1950s pals. He made a strong impression playing Harrison Ford's son in Peter Weir's *The Mosquito Coast* (1986), leading to his first starring role as a high school Romeo falling from grace in *Jimmy Reardon* (1988) and scooping an Oscar nomination for Lumet's *Running on Empty* (1988). Playing the young Indie in the prologue to *Indiana Jones and the Last Crusade* (1989) and one of the break-in merchants in Robert

Redford's *Sneakers* (1992) helped him reached a wider mainstream audience. But it was his performance of astonishing maturity and power as the narcoleptic hustler in *My Own Private Idaho* (1991) that has clinched his place in movie legend.

Mary Pickford

Actress

Born: GLADYS SMITH, *Toronto, Canada, April 8, 1893*
Died: *May 28, 1979*

Mary Pickford's fluffy golden curls and vulnerable but plucky little-girl image made her "America's Sweetheart" and the most famous star of the silent screen. But inside cute "Little Mary" lived an astute business-woman – an attitude formed in childhood, as breadwinner to her widowed mother and siblings, touring in theatre as "Baby Gladys". At 14 she charmed Broadway producer David Belasco into giving her a leading role and two years later persuaded D. W. Griffith at Biograph to take her on, completing her debut film *Pippa Passes* (1909) on her initial day, and negotiating her first salary increase, from $5 to $10. She quickly became a star as "Little Mary" in *The Little Teacher* (1910), and by moving cleverly from company to company built her career in terms of ever-increasing salary and creative control. In 1919 she formed United Artists with Griffith, Charlie Chaplin and Douglas Fairbanks Sr, who shortly afterwards became her second husband. Despite efforts to break away from "Little Mary" she was forced by public demand to continue to play little-girl roles into her twenties and thirties: *The Little Princess* (1917); *Rebecca of Sunnybrook Farm* (1917); *Pollyanna* (1920) – her first UA film; *Little Lord Fauntleroy* (1921) and *Little Annie Rooney* (1925). She finally grew up on screen playing a flapper in her first talkie, *Coquette*

(1929), for which she won an Oscar but lost audiences. Shortly after she and Fairbanks flopped in *The Taming of the Shrew* (1929), she retired from the screen, though she and Chaplin retained control

Mary Pickford: 'America's Sweetheart'

of UA until 1953. In 1935 the famous "Hollywood Royalty" marriage to Fairbanks fell apart and she married Charles "Buddy" Rogers, her co-star from *My Best Girl* (1927). Pickford was awarded a Special Oscar in 1975.

Walter Pidgeon

Actor

Born: *New Brunswick, Canada, September 23, 1897*
Died: *September 25, 1984*

The tall, handsome Canadian gentleman actor started in silent pictures with *The Mannequin* (1925) and became a busy star right up to the mid-1950s, though he continued working steadily in urbane character roles till he was 80, bowing out after Mae West's *Sextette* (1976). Pidgeon was a much-needed trusty actor of the kind who give films their texture and depth. He was the reliable movie consort for a number of Hollywood's strong-willed women, but is especially linked with the ladylike Greer Garson, with whom he formed a popular team in such "women's pictures" as the orphanage tearjerker *Blossoms in the Dust* (1941), the

wartime weepie *Mrs Miniver* (1942), *Madame Curie* (1943), Galsworthy's *That Forsyte Woman* as Young Jolyon (1949) and *The Miniver Story* (1950). Pidgeon flew highest in the 1940s, as the loose cannon in Fritz Lang's spy thriller *Man Hunt* (1941) and courting Maureen O'Hara in the John Ford heartwarmer *How Green Was My Valley* (1942). When he wasn't in weepies and biopics, his polished exterior made him ideal in mysteries, whether as crime solver Nick Carter in MGM's 1939–40 series or as Sapper sleuth in *Calling Bulldog Drummond* (1951). He scored a hit as the Prospero figure in *Forbidden Planet* (1956), the sci-fi reworking of Shakespeare's *Tempest*, was senate leader in Preminger's political thriller *Advise and Consent* (1962), and played Florenz Ziegfeld in Streisand's *Funny Girl* (1968).

Christopher Plummer

Actor

Born: ARTHUR CHRISTOPHER ORME PLUMMER, *Montreal, Canada, December 13, 1927*

Hailed as "the finest classical actor of the Americas" by the *Washington Post*, Plummer's career has spanned stage and screen, classic and contemporary roles, heroes and villains. He started in radio and theatre in his native Canada in the late 1940s and made his Broadway debut in 1954. He became a major stage star of Broadway and London's West End in such plays as Anouilh's *The Lark*, Brecht's *Arturo Ui* and Peter Shaffer's *The Royal Hunt of the Sun* as the Inca Emperor Atahualpa, a role he later re-created in the film (1969). He also scaled the heights of the great Shakespearean and other classical roles with the National Theatre and Royal Shakespeare Company in Britain, and the Stratford Festival, Ontario. Plummer made his film debut in Sidney Lumet's *Stage Struck* (1958), and achieved popular recognition as Captain von Trapp in *The Sound of Music* (1965) and Rommel in *The Night of the Generals* (1966). He was storyteller Rudyard Kipling in *The Man Who Would Be King* (1975); solved the mystery of Jack the Ripper as Sherlock Holmes in *Murder by Decree* (1979) with James Mason as Watson; and added an effective chill to the offbeat thriller *Eyewitness* – aka *The Janitor* (1980). His performance in *Souvenir* (1987), as the ageing expatriate pork butcher returning to Europe to confront his Nazi past, was a piece of memorable character work. Plummer played Jack Nicholson's ruthless publisher boss in *Wolf* (1994). He is married to English actress Elaine Taylor, and is the father of actress Amanda Plummer by his first wife, Tammy Grimes.

Sidney Poitier

Actor, director
Born: *Miami, Fla., February 20, 1924*

Sidney Poitier was Hollywood's first black superstar, challenging Afro-American stereotypes with roles in a series of high-profile liberal movies throughout the 1950s and 1960s. An impactful movie debut, cast as a principled doctor in the cogent race-riot thriller *No Way Out* (1950), set the trend. He was the fugitive chained to racist runaway Tony Curtis in *The*

Sidney Poitier: America's first black superstar

Defiant Ones (1958), an unnerving house-guest in 1967's *Guess Who's Coming to Dinner*, a northern cop in the Deep South classic *In the Heat of the Night* (1967) and became the first black man to win an Oscar for his role in 1963's *Lilies of the Field*. America's number-one box-office draw in 1968, Poitier was increasingly dismissed by more radical black activists. But despite his clean-cut screen image, Poitier's achievements were considerable, preaching across the racial spectrum and subtly but significantly altering the perception of a people previously consigned to bit parts as shifty criminals or doltish servants. In the 1970s he turned more towards directing, helming 1974's *Uptown Saturday Night*, the first of three comedy vehicles in which he starred opposite Bill Cosby, and directing the 1980 hit *Stir Crazy*. Acting outings have become less frequent, though Poitier enjoyed himself with a neat turn in the star-driven comedy-thriller *Sneakers* (1992).

Roman Polanski

Director, writer, producer, actor
Born: *Paris, France, August 18, 1933*

Rootless *auteur* Roman Polanski is the inspiration behind many of modern cinema's finest productions. Paris-born and Poland-raised, he moved to Hollywood as one of the 1960s' sharpest talents, only to flee the country in 1977 to avoid a jail term for the alleged rape of a 13-year-old girl. Since then he has worked solely in Europe. With his mother dead in the Nazi holocaust and his wife (Sharon Tate) killed by the disciples of Charles Manson, Polanski's best work probes at the nature and causes of human evil. His debut feature *Knife in the Water* (1962) enraged the Polish Communist authorities with its subversive worldview, *Repulsion* (1965) painted a vivid portrait of mental

breakdown in Swinging-60s London, while 1971's *Macbeth* proved a provocatively blood-soaked and naturalistic Shakespeare adaptation. These concerns reached their apogee with Polanski's two greatest films, *Rosemary's Baby* (1968) and *Chinatown* (1974), but even his bleakest work is shot through with a wry black humour, a delicate wit and observation. In Europe Polanski turned in a taut French chiller in *The Tenant* (1976) and a successful British period saga in *Tess* (1979) before floundering in 1986 with the rollicking folly *Pirates*. Though he bounded back with the underrated thriller *Frantic* (1988), 1992's *Bitter Moon* proved indulgent and overheated, notably missing the crazed conjury of his earlier, incandescent pictures.

Sydney Pollack

Director, producer, writer, actor
Born: *South Bend, Ind., July 1, 1934*

One of the hallmarks of Pollack's work is the fine performances he draws from Hollywood stars, probably because he started out as an actor himself. Another is his strong sense of accessible narrative when dealing with complex subjects. After training at New York's Neighborhood Playhouse, Pollack worked as an actor and acting coach. An introduction to Burt Lancaster led to a five-year career directing for television, including the popular *Ben Casey* series. He also worked with Lancaster as supervisor of the American dub of Visconti's *The Leopard* (1963) and directed a sequence of Frank Perry's *The Swimmer* (1968). His first film as director was *The Slender Thread* (1965). His long association with Robert Redford began as fellow actors in *War Hunt* (1962), leading to Redford's casting in *This Property Is Condemned* (1966); *Jeremiah Johnson* (1972); *The Way We Were* (1975), an audience- if not

a critic- pleaser; *Three Days of the Condor* (1975), an ingenious thriller; *The Electric Horseman* (1979), a much-praised romantic comedy with Jane Fonda; *Out of Africa* (1985), for which Pollack won Best Director and Film Oscars; and the disappointing *Havana* (1991). Other notable films are the powerful Depression dance marathon drama *They Shoot Horses Don't They?* (1969) and *Tootsie* (1982), in which Pollack also played a small but effective role as Dustin Hoffman's agent. He also made screen appearances in *Death Becomes Her* (1992) and *Short Cuts* (1993) and was first-class in a leading role in Woody Allen's *Husbands and Wives* (1992). Pollack brought John Grisham's bestseller, *The Firm,* (1993) to the screen, and has also supported upcoming directors as producer, for example Steve Kloves's *The Fabulous Baker Boys* (1989) and Luis Mandoki's *White Palace* (1990).

Michael Powell

Director, writer, producer, editor
Born: *Bekesbourne, England, September 30, 1905*
Died: *February 19, 1990*

One of Britain's most imaginative, original and cinematic film-makers, Powell is famed for his 1938–57 collaboration with Emeric Pressburger, which represents a high spot of world cinema. Together as The Archers, they filmed half a dozen undisputed masterpieces in *The Life and Death of Colonel Blimp* (1943), *A Canterbury Tale* (1944), *I Know Where I'm Going* (1945), *A Matter of Life and Death* (1946), *Black Narcissus* (1946) and the all-time great ballet film *The Red Shoes* (1948). In these subversive, often mystifying films, they confronted the complacency and parochialism of the British cinema, sometimes angering the powers-that-be, like Premier Churchill who tried to ban *Colonel Blimp* which dared show a good German in wartime. Almost alone among British directors of the period, their work had international appeal, gaining more fans as the years went by, and influencing directors like Roeg, Russell, Scorsese and Coppola, for whom Powell went to work in the 1970s as creative adviser. Now they are considered second only to Hitchcock as the great British filmmakers. After The Archers broke up, Powell made the notorious chiller *Peeping Tom* (1960), whose outraged reception effectively killed his career, though he lived long enough to see his reputation re-evaluated and to produce two enthralling autobiographical volumes. Powell also directed an intriguing series of British 1930s B-movies, and co-directed the gorgeous fantastic adventure *The Thief of Bagdad* (1940).

William Powell

Actor
Born: *Pittsburgh, Pa., June 29, 1892*
Died: *March 5, 1984*

An angular actor with a distinctive pencil moustache, William Powell's combination of easy wit and impeccable appearance ensured a smooth transition from silent-screen villainy to well-bred charmer in a stream of 1930s and 1940s talkies. His six *Thin Man* outings, playing Dashiell Hammett's unflappable detective Nick Charles were the epitome of 1930s sophistication – tightly scripted cocktails of mysterious murders, firecracker dialogue and tinkling dry martinis. The *Thin Man* series also threw up one of the eras great screwball partnerships, Powell and worldly-wise Myrna Loy, who were eventually to appear in 13 movies together. Nobody would ever have taken Powell for a hobo. His forte was characters from the professional classes or the upper echelons of society. He was an aristocrat turned butler in the delicious *My Man Godfrey* (1936), an ambitious

politician in *The Senator Was Indiscreet* (1947), while his turn as an ageing playboy brought extra sheen to Negulesco's *How to Marry a Millionaire* (1953). Although he lived into the 1980s, his last performance was an acclaimed supporting turn as the suave doctor in Ford and Le Roy's star-studded World War Two drama *Mr Roberts* (1955). No squalid fall from the pinnacle for Powell. He left with the minimum fuss, just as he had come in – immaculate, urbane, resolutely uncrumpled.

Tyrone Power

Actor
Born: *Cincinnati, Oh., May 5, 1913*
Died: *November 15, 1958*

This easy-going, good-natured star with his dashing good looks and Irish charisma was exactly what the 1940s needed. The son of actor Tyrone Sr, with radio and stage experience, he landed a Fox contract in 1936, starting off a lightweight but high-profile career. Early high spots include a run of Fox musicals with Alice Faye, including *Alexander's Ragtime Band* (1938), *In Old Chicago* (1938) and *Rose of Washington Square* (1939). In tougher mode he played the title outlaw in Henry King's *Jesse James* (1939) and starred ideally in two Rouben Mamoulian films, as the bandit in *The Mark of Zorro* (1941) and the bullfighter in *Blood and Sand* (1941). After the war he made a notable comeback in one of his best roles as the lost soul in Somerset Maugham's *The Razor's Edge* (1946). During the 1950s his looks hardened and the films became more routine, but he remained a top star in adventure films like *Diplomatic Courier* (1952) and *King of the Khyber Rifles* (1953). He bowed out on a couple of high notes as an impotent reporter in the Hemingway yarn *The Sun Also Rises* (1957) and as the murder case defendant in Billy Wilder's film of the Agatha Christie mys-

tery *Witness for the Prosecution* (1957). He suffered a fatal heart attack after acting a fight with George Sanders on *Solomon and Sheba* (1958).

Otto Preminger

Director, actor, writer
Born: *Vienna, Austria, December 5, 1905*
Died: *April 23, 1986*

Otto Preminger was one of Hollywood's most forceful and driven directors, a film-maker who unflinchingly pushed the mainstream picture into previously unexplored territories. Born and raised in Austria, he emigrated to the US in 1935, working first in theatre and distinguishing the first phase of his career with a string of fiendishly fashioned *film noir* thrillers. 1944's *Laura* proved an engrossing exploration of the genre conventions while the Freudian-tinged *Angel Face* (1952) benefited from the saintly looking Jean Simmons's impish turn as a deranged murderess. Working increasingly outside the confines of the studio system, Preminger cultivated the image of film maverick, perfecting an ice-cool approach to tricky social topics. *Anatomy of a Murder* (1959), starring James Stewart, stands as perhaps his most fine-tuned and fully realized work, a clinical, utterly unsentimental dissection of the

American legal network. But the director's compulsive risk-taking unsurprisingly threw up the occasional film failure. His two efforts with teenaged beauty Jean Seberg – *Saint Joan* (1957) and *Bonjour Tristesse* (1957) – were intriguing but misconceived, as was the daring all-black musical *Carmen Jones* (1954). Perhaps 1955's controversial drug exposé *The Man with the Golden Arm* best captures the essence of Preminger – reaching for greatness, tackling tough issues head on and surviving thanks to the crisp, pure economy of his film-making vision.

Elvis Presley

Singer, actor, hip-swiveller
Born: ELVIS AARON PRESLEY, *Tupelo, Miss., January 8, 1935*
Died: *August 16, 1977*

The King holds a unique place as the only pop star (Sinatra apart) to enjoy prolonged success in the movies – 33 in all between 1956 and 1972. They were carefully constructed showcases for his sexy but shy personality, often directed

Elvis Presley: *Unshackled energy in* Jailhouse Rock

by old-timers from Hollywood's golden years (Norman Taurog directed nine of his films) but he was rarely supported by stars of equal magnitude. His homespun films, custom-built for the fans, have never been well regarded by critics or general audiences, though some – *Jailhouse Rock*

(1957), *GI Blues* (1960), *Flaming Star* (1960), *Viva Las Vegas* (1964) – are rousingly done and are now fascinating period pieces. Nor were the songs, with exceptions like Lieber and Stoller's score for *Jailhouse Rock*, always that exciting, particularly in the later films. Nevertheless the films performed powerfully in cash terms, taking nearly $200 million in pre-inflationary currency. In the late 1960s as his star faded, the movies themselves were noticeably much poorer, and his last drama film, *Change of Habit* (1969), became the first American film to have its British premiere on TV. He was to re-emerge as a cabaret performer in the 1970s, and his last two films are valuable records of those now legendary shows. Presley died of a heart attack aged 42, after weight and drink problems. The King was dead, but the legend lives on and the films are a regular TV favourite.

Vincent Price

Actor
Born: *St Louis, Mo., May 27, 1911*
Died: *October 25, 1993*

Price was a tall, handsome, cultured character star in films for 50 years, with inimitably honey-toned speech and a camp manner which held him back as a leading man in the 1940s, but served him well in the 1950s as a backstabbing baddie and in the 1960s and 1970s as the king of the chillers. He made his theatre debut in London, then became a Broadway star before Universal offered him a film contract, making his debut in 1938 with *Service de Luxe* and *Elizabeth and Essex* (1939). He was sporadically effective in the 1940s with films like *The Song of Bernadette* (1943), *Laura* (1944), *Dragonwyck* (1946) and *The Three Musketeers* (1948). He started making horror films with the 3D *House of Wax* (1953) and its sequel *The Mad Magician* (1954), and he's especially admired for *The Fly*

(1958), *House on Haunted Hill* (1958) and *The Abominable Dr Phibes* (1971). He's fondly remembered for his series of films with Roger Corman, including *The Fall of the House of Usher* (1960), *The Pit*

Vincent: *The Price is right*

and the Pendulum (1961), *Tales of Terror* (1962), *The Raven* (1963) and 1964's *The Comedy of Terrors*. An extraordinarily civilized man, Price was an art and cookery expert, and in 1974 married actress Coral Browne whom he met while filming *Theatre of Blood* (1973). Among his admired last performances were Lindsay Anderson's *The Whales of August* (1987) and 1990's *Edward Scissorhands*.

Richard Pryor

Actor, comedian, writer, producer, director
Born: *Peoria, Ill., December 1, 1940*

The trenchant American stand-up comedian, labelled the black Lenny Bruce, developed his act in nightclubs, and from 1966 became a star on TV, on records and at Las Vegas. Several of his live shows are recorded as feature films, including *Richard Pryor Here and Now* (1983) with which he made his debut as director. He toned down his abrasive style and raunchy material to find success in conservative Hollywood, showing himself a gifted actor as well as a hilarious comic. His films, starting with *The Busy Body* in 1967, have been very variable, but he's part-

nered Gene Wilder several times to great box-office, though less critical, acclaim. Their first together, *Silver Streak* (1976), was by far the best, though *Stir Crazy* (1980) was a huge hit and they were paired again in *See No Evil, Hear No Evil* in 1989 and in *Another You* in 1991. He starred in several important films of the 1970s – *Lady Sings the Blues* (1972), *Car Wash* (1976) and *Blue Collar* (1978). But in the 1980s strong opportunities eluded him, though his high spirits enlivened even weak films like *Superman III* (1983), *Brewster's Millions* (1985) and Eddie Murphy's *Harlem Nights* (1989). Like Wilder, he has also directed (*Jo Jo Dancer, Your Life Is Calling* in 1985) and co-wrote the majestic *Blazing Saddles* (1974) with Mel Brooks. He was badly burned in an accident, and in *Another You* his failing health was evident.

David Puttnam

Producer
Born: DAVID TERENCE PUTTNAM, *London, England, February 25, 1941*

Britain's best-known producer, Puttnam has always kept a close "hands on" control of his films. He started in advertising and produced his first film, *Melody* (1970), from a screenplay by fellow advertising man Alan Parker, with whom he later made the off-beat musical *Bugsy Malone* (1976) and *Midnight Express* (1978), an Oscar-winner which left him regretting its exploitative effect – probably the reason for the sense of film-maker's moral responsibility governing his later choice of subjects. Other early films include Ken Russell's *Mahler* (1973) and *Lisztomania* (1975) and the rock musicals *That'll Be the Day* (1974) and *Stardust* (1975). He produced the big-screen directorial debuts of Ridley Scott (*The Duellists*, 1977) and Hugh Hudson (*Chariots of Fire*, 1981) – the outsider which won him a Best Picture Oscar and

made Hollywood take serious notice. However, his next films were the modestly budgeted Bill Forsyth comedy *Local Hero* (1982) and the Northern Ireland drama *Cal* (1984). Puttnam returned to a larger scale with Roland Joffé's debut film *The Killing Fields* (1984), set in Cambodia at the fall of Phnom Penh, followed by Joffé's second film *The Mission* (1986). That same year Puttnam was recruited as production head of Columbia Studios, where his lean approach to budgeting, contempt for Hollywood values and egos and his European tastes made him many enemies. After 18 months, he returned to his own country for *Memphis Belle* (1990), *Meeting Venus* (1991), *Being Human* (1993) and *The War of the Buttons* (1994), an Irish-based remake of Yves Robert's 1962 film.

Anthony Quinn

Actor
Born: ANTHONY RUDOLPH OAXACA QUINN, *Chihuahua, Mexico, April 21, 1915*

Always strong, often vulnerable, and invariably sounding like he's got a mouthful of something sour on board, the bear-like Quinn has been the quintessential growling foreigner, both friend and foe, in over 300 films. Half-Mexican, half-Irish, as a child he moved to the US, where his father was a cameraman. Determined to make it in

The Mighty Quinn: *Refusing to go quietly*

acting, Quinn paid for an operation on his tongue to eradicate a speech defect, but was fated to mumble incomprehensibly as a series of bad guys until winning his second Oscar in *Lust for Life* (1956). After signing up as a Cheyenne warrior in Cecil B. De Mille's *The Plainsman* (1936), he married the director's daughter but with little effect on his career. An Oscar for Best Supporting Actor alongside Marlon Brando, in *Viva Zapata!* (1952), signalled a brighter future, while Federico Fellini's *La Strada* (1954) earned him international acclaim. His portrayal of Paul Gauguin in *Lust for Life* was followed by a memorable *Hunchback of Notre Dame* (1957), a single attempt at directing, *The Buccaneer* (1958), and Oscar nominations for *Wild is the Wind* (1957) and *Zorba the Greek* (1964), with which he will always be associated. Now a highly regarded painter and sculptor, his vigour remains undimmed. In 1993 he was dubbed "The Mighty Quinn" when, at the age of 78, after undergoing quadruple heart bypass surgery, he fathered his 11th child. Truly the stuff of legend.

George Raft

Actor
Born: GEORGE RANFT, *New York, NY, September 26, 1895*
Died: *November 24, 1980*

The classic screen gangster complete with zoot suit and spats, Raft had first-hand experience of the underworld to draw on, having been a boxer, gigolo, club dancer and a close friend of Owney Maddon, a hoodlum liquor smuggler, who supported him until he achieved movie stardom. His screen debut was a walk-on in The *Queen of the Night Clubs* (1929) and he continued in bit parts as heavies until his role in the vintage *Scarface* (1932) as the coin-flipping Guido Rinaldo, brought stardom, a Paramount contract and *Night*

After Night (1932) which crystallized his movie persona. He played detectives as in *Midnight Club* (1933), danced in *Bolero* (1934), was unconvincingly Chinese in *Limehouse Blues* (1934) and made the musical *Every Night at Eight* (1935) with Alice Faye, but the quintessential Raft was that gangster with the smooth oily surface, masking the animal within, and he scored big in films like *Each Dawn I Die* (1939) with Cagney, *Invisible Stripes* (1939) with Bogart and *They Drive by Night* (1940) with Edward G. Robinson. But Raft did not always make the shrewdest film choices, turning down *Casablanca* (1942), *The Maltese Falcon* (1941) and *High Sierra* (1941), all of which went to Bogey. After a lull in his career, he resurfaced with guest appearances in Billy Wilder's *Some Like It Hot* (1959), the Jerry Lewis movies *The Ladies' Man* (1961) and *The Patsy* (1964), and the Bond spoof *Casino Royale* (1967).

Claude Rains

Actor
Born: *London, England, November 10, 1889*
Died: *May 30, 1967*

British theatre actor Rains, with his cultivated manner and beautiful, distinctive voice, became a film star in the oddest way, by playing (transparently except for the final seconds) The *Invisible Man* (1936) in a role Boris Karloff rejected as insignificant. Rains made it the springboard for an exciting career. He was under contract from 1936 to Warners, where he gave a series of memorable and diverse performances as a silkily menacing Prince John in *The Adventures of Robin Hood* (1938), as Napoleon III in *Juarez* (1939) and as a midwest doctor in *King's Row* (1941). Memorably he was the devil's messenger in *Here Comes Mr Jordan* (1941) and the phantom in *Phantom of the Opera* (1943). He worked particularly well with

Bette Davis, giving three of his finest performances opposite her – in *Now Voyager* (1942), *Mr Skeffington* (1945) and *Deception* (1946) – with his self-effacing style working effectively in tandem with her histrionics. *Skeffington* won him one of four Oscar nominations, the others being for his corrupt senator in *Mr Smith Goes to Washington* (1939), his cynical police chief in *Casablanca* (1942) and as Ingrid Bergman's doting Nazi husband in Hitchcock's *Notorious* (1946). The movies thinned out in the 1950s but he was always a welcome presence, still busy in old age in films like *The Lost World* (1960), *Lawrence of Arabia* (1962) and *The Greatest Story Ever Told* (1965).

Basil Rathbone

Actor
Born: PHILIP ST JOHN BASIL RATHBONE, *Johannesburg, South Africa, June 13, 1892*
Died: *July 21, 1967*

Silky smooth, elegant and aristocratic, Rathbone was quite simply the finest arch-villain the cinema has ever seen. A dazzling swords-

Basil Rathbone: *Diamond sharp and dashing*

man who used his tongue like his blade, delivering his lines like rapier thrusts, he was at his serpentine best as the evil Sir Guy of Gisborne in the 1938 *Robin Hood* with Errol Flynn. An actor of some range, who appeared on both sides of the screen battle between good

and evil, he was equally at home with the intellectual purities of his definitive Sherlock Holmes in *The Hound of the Baskervilles* (1939), a performance touched by lightning. He had been doing small parts in films for some time and became a stage star on both sides of the Atlantic before starting his film career in earnest with *The Last of Mrs Cheyney* (1929), which brought him an MGM contract. Throughout the early 1930s he appeared in minor films playing assorted cads and ne'er-do-wells until his role as Mr Murdstone in *David Copperfield* (1935), creating a truly loathsome image of the wicked stepfather and establishing himself as the villain of choice for the next three decades in roles like Richard III in *Tower of London* (1939) and Tyrone Power's oily opponent in *The Mark of Zorro* (1940), parts that complemented his immortally heroic Holmes, a role he played 14 times on film.

Nicholas Ray

Director, writer
Born: RAYMOND NICHOLAS KIENZLE, *Lu Crosse, Wis., August 7, 1911*
Died: *June 16, 1979*

American *auteur* Nicholas Ray is best known for a series of moody films about disaffected misfits, the most celebrated of which, *Rebel Without a Cause* (1955), won both star and director cult-favourite status. His builder father died when he was 15. By 16 a radio script won him a scholarship in Chicago, before he switched to studying architecture, a discipline evident in his films where environment bears a strong effect on his characters' relationships. In New York he worked with Elia Kazan, wrote for a Communist newspaper (but was never subsequently blacklisted) and directed radio propaganda programmes before his feature debut about fugitives from justice, *They Live By Night* (1948). *Knock On Any Door*

(1949) was a dry run for *Rebel Without a Cause*, which followed 1950's *In a Lonely Place* (starring his wife Gloria Grahame) and psychological western *Johnny Guitar* (1954). *Rebel* won an Oscar for Best Story, but James Dean's death four days before its release made it a sensation. Thereafter Ray had few hits but became a hero of the French New Wave critics. Although *The Savage Innocents* (1959) and *King of Kings* (1961) supported their judgement, he couldn't raise the money to turn independent, and by 1974 was reduced to shooting pornography in Holland. A line from *Johnny Guitar*, "I'm a stranger here myself," was his motto. Ray's career and life ended collaborating with Wim Wenders on *Nick's Film/ Lightning Over Water* (1980), documenting his death by cancer.

Satyajit Ray

Director, writer
Born: *Calcutta, India, May 2, 1921*
Died: *April 23, 1992*

One of the greatest film-makers of the century, India's own Renaissance man wrote his own scripts and music, illustrated children's books, edited magazines and transformed the world's perception of a continent. Born into a family of writers, Ray was first inspired by the poet Rabindranath Tagore, and later by the filmmaker Jean Renoir whom he met in 1950. After seeing world cinema classics while in London as a commercial artist, he returned to India where he struggled to complete his first film on a negligible budget, but was eventually rescued by a Government grant. *Pather Panchali* (*Father Panchali* – 1955), a dusty rites of passage tale, won a prize at Cannes, enabling Ray to fund a sequel. International recognition kept him working in India where he was hindered by the bulk of his work being in the minority language, Bengali, and his dramatic realism, a rarity

among the glossy escapism of Indian cinema, often under threat of censorship. Ray won two Silver Bears, for *Mahanagar* (*The Big City* – 1963) and *Charulata* (*The Lonely Wife* – 1964), a Special Award of Honour (1966) at the Berlin Film Festival, the Légion d'Honneur at Cannes (1987) and an honorary Oscar for a Lifetime Achievement in Cinema (1992) – his proudest moment – while on his deathbed in Calcutta. *Agantuk* (*The Stranger* – 1991) was his 39th and last film in an extraordinarily prolific career that brackets him up alongside the all-time cinema greats.

Robert Redford

Actor, director, producer
Born: *Santa Monica, Calif., August 18, 1937*

Robert Redford's unshiftable "golden boy" label stems from his two contrasting favourites of 1960s cinema – *Barefoot in the Park* (1967) and 1969's *Butch Cassidy and the Sundance Kid*. In the first his turn as a newlywed in a leaky Manhattan loft captured the era's unbridled youthful optimism, while the latter audaciously re-

Robert Redford: *Ageless Hollywood golden boy*

drew the hoary western genre as an irreverent buddy caper. The film's successful partnership with Paul Newman was dutifully repeated in 1973's conman romp *The Sting*. In the 1970s Redford moved into more serious drama,

spotlighting political corruption with *The Candidate* (1972) and *All the President's Men* (1977), which he also co-produced. But those corn-fed good looks – coupled with an avoidance of truly testing roles – have always counted against him, despite playing a Bogart-style anti-hero in *Havana* (1990) and having director Sydney Pollack emphasize his pock-marked skin in *Comes a Horseman* (1979). "They see me as having the temperament of the Sundance Kid, the charm of *The Candidate*, the wit of *The Sting* and the wardrobe of *The Great Gatsby*," he once ruefully commented. Behind the camera Redford is treated with more deference. His four directorial efforts, including the Oscar-winning *Ordinary People* (1980), *A River Runs Through It* (1992) and *Quiz Show* (1995) were well received, while his annual Sundance Film Festival admirably serves to champion the work of lesser-known moviemakers.

Sir Carol Reed

Director
Born: *London, England, December 30, 1906*
Died: *April 25, 1976*

To many, Carol Reed stands as the archetypal British film director. Although his early films were in keeping with the bulk of home-grown 1930s output – stagy, static and studio-bound – with 1939's socially conscious *The Stars Look Down*, Reed appeared to hit on a more fluid, naturalistic style, honing this approach with his Oscar-winning wartime documentary *The True Glory* (1945) and injecting a new realism and energy into his late 1940s work. *Odd Man Out* (1946), driven by a committed turn from the young James Mason, is a tense, terrifically paced tale of a hounded IRA gunman, while his three collaborations with novelist Graham Greene show the director at the peak of his ability. *The Fallen Idol* (1948) turns a piercing gaze on

the alliance that grows between an upper-class child and the family's below-stairs servant (Ralph Richardson), while *Our Man in Havana* (1960) proves an engagingly played satire on espionage shenanigans in Cuba. Best of Reed's three forays into Greeneland is that all-time gem *The Third Man* (1949), with the director providing a safe pair of hands to marshal the diverse talents in cast and crew. During the latter half of his career Reed, knighted in 1952, was increasingly dismissed by *auteur* theorists in favour of more distinctive, stylistic practitioners, with compatriot Michael Powell describing him as "a watchmaker, passionless". His last film hit was the populist romp *Oliver!* (1968), an enjoyable musical that lacked the poise and depth of his finest work.

Oliver Reed

Actor
Born: *Wimbledon, England, February 13, 1937*

The barrel-chested, sullenly handsome Oliver Reed has spent so long squandering his ability that one forgets what a fine performer he once was. A public-school drop-out, he spent the 1960s toiling away in the acting second division, notably spicing up the schlock Hammer creeper *The Curse of the Werewolf* (1961) and making a splendidly malevolent Bill Sykes in his uncle Carol Reed's hit Dickens-based musical *Oliver!* (1968). But it was to be a fellow maverick, director Ken Russell, who provided Reed with his two finest film opportunities. His turn as a wealthy cad in *Women in Love* (1969), notorious for its nude wrestling scene between Reed and co-star Alan Bates, exposed (no pun intended) an unexpected depth to his ability, gifts Russell was quick to exploit further with his controversial satanism saga *The Devils* (1971). But Reed has always had to juggle conflicting callings as a serious actor and a pub-crawling, home-counties roustabout and, poised on the edge of movie greatness, he seemed suddenly to choose the easier route. This is not to say that his work since has been without merit. His swaggering turn in 1973's *The Three Musketeers* demonstrated an Errol Flynn-like gift for swashbuckling while his portrait of a boorish writer in Nic Roeg's *Castaway* (1986) was amiably rounded and restrained, evidence of a residual but very real talent.

Christopher Reeve

Actor, Superman

Born: *New York, NY, September 25, 1952*

Tall, elegant and handsome, Reeve became an overnight sensation playing the hunky, be-stockinged comic-strip hero *Superman*. Like Sean Connery with James Bond, he has struggled ever since to throw off the cumbersome mantle of this enormously popular screen character; but, unlike Connery, has so far not quite managed to do so. Reeve enjoyed early success on the stage before a low-key screen debut as an officer in the submarine drama *Gray Lady Down* (1978). With *Superman* (1978) he became an international star, filling the role with a wholesome, all-American mixture of courage, strength, romance and integrity, and attaining popular icon status into the bargain. He reprised the part in three sequels of decreasing merit, and applied those decent, upright *Superman* qualities to a series of more earthly roles: as a writer in *Somewhere in Time* (1980); a lawyer in *The Bostonians* (1984); a pilot in *The Aviator* (1985); Kathleen Turner's fiancé in *Switching Channels* (1988) and, less predictably, a corrupt, scheming priest in 1982's *Monsignor*. More recently he turned in an excellent screen performance as a pragmatic US politician in *The Remains Of The Day* (1993), and it seems that he is

at last in the process of shedding the *Superman* image, if not the decency, uprightness and integrity that went with it.

Keanu Reeves

Actor

Born: *Beirut, Lebanon, September 2, 1964*

Reeves's Hawaiian-Chinese father gave him a name that means "Cool breeze over the mountains", and cool is mostly what this handsome dude has built his career on, especially in his *Bill and Ted* breakthrough movies – *Excellent Adventure* (1989) and *Bogus Journey* (1991) – as gormless high-school time-traveller Theodore Logan, prone to frequent grinning and ejaculations of "E-x-c-e-l-l-e-n-t!". They made Keanu a name to remember, though their brow was

Keanu Reeves: *The cool dude who's hot stuff*

so low as to be virtually invisible, unlike the classy *Dangerous Liaisons* (1988) which preceded them. But it was his next big success, *Point Break* (1991), playing a surfing cop, which confirmed his status as Hollywood hot property. *My Own Private Idaho* (1991) broke the mould of what a hot young star is allowed to do, teaming up with the late River Phoenix as gay hustlers in Gus Van Sant's visionary road movie. A pair of ill-advised period pieces saw him working in posh company, as Jonathan Harker in

Bram Stoker's Dracula (1992) and in Kenneth Branagh's *Much Ado About Nothing* (1993), struggling in both with an improbable English accent. Even more improbable was his role and make-up as Prince Siddhartha in Bertolucci's well meaning Buddhist biopic *Little Buddha* (1994), though he brought just enough dignity to it to get away with it. Then came the real surprise – a Bruce Willis-style, action-man role in the relentless thriller *Speed* (1994). Reeves said he was nervous, but with his new cool crewcut and even trimmer body he was E-x-c-e-l-l-e-n-t!

Lee Remick

Actress

Born: *Boston, Mass., December 14, 1935*
Died: *July 2, 1991*

Among the brightest of young stars in the late 1950s and early 1960s, Remick mixed a demure ladylike demeanour with a sizzling sexuality and considerable acting talent to produce a unique screen presence. Remick made her film debut in *A Face in the Crowd* (1957) and followed it up with *The Long Hot Summer* (1958), but it was as Ben Gazzara's flirtatious wife in *Anatomy of a Murder* (1959) that she really signalled her arrival in the cinema. The thriller *Experiment in Terror* (1962) and particularly her Oscar-nominated performance, as Jack Lemmon's wife, in the study of alcoholism *Days of Wine and Roses* (1963) confirmed her star status. Throughout the next decade she ploughed a busy furrow through films of all kinds, romancing Steve McQueen in *Baby the Rain Must Fall* (1965), hitting the western trail in *The Hallelujah Trail* (1965) and supporting Paul Newman in *Sometimes a Great Notion* (1972). She lived and worked in Britain for many years where she was cast in smart films with literary sources – Iris Murdoch's *A Severed Head* (1970), Joe Orton's *Loot* (1970) and

Edward Albee's *A Delicate Balance* (1972). She also hit the thriller trail with *Hennessy* (1975) and *Telefon* (1977), and the horror trail with *The Omen* (1976) and *The Medusa Touch* (1977). Though in middle age she retained her beauty and allure, the cinema had no idea what to do with her, no doubt provoking her comment "I'd really like to make movies for adults again", and her last decade and a half was spent on the TV movie treadmill, apart from *The Europeans* (1979), *Tribute* (1980) and *Emma's War* (1986). It was a good career but she deserved a great one.

Jean Renoir

Director, writer, producer, actor

Born: *Paris, France, September 15, 1894*
Died: *February 12, 1979*

Jean Renoir is arguably European cinema's most influential filmmaker. The son of impressionist painter Auguste Renoir, he brought a new artistry to a fledgling medium; first in his native France, later in the heady climes of 1940s Hollywood. The Gallic period caught Renoir at his peak, filming with a fluid beauty and fashioning pictures with playful, multi-layered wit underpinned by a basic understanding and compassion. Many of these pictures remain undisputed masterworks: the subversive comedy of manners *Boudou Saved from Drowning* (1932), the melodramatic *La Bête Humaine* (1938), the uplifting parable *Le Crime de Monsieur Lange* (1935), the banned social satire *La Règle du Jeu* (1939) and his seminal anti-war, anti-class essay *La Grande Illusion* (1937). Fleeing to the US during World War Two, Renoir laboured to match the organic magic of the 1930s output with subsequent films. His first Hollywood outing, *Swamp Water* (1941), was an uneven Deep South potboiler but Renoir gradually settled into his new environment with more graceful work in *The Southerner* (1945) and *Diary of a Chambermaid* (1952). In the 1950s he returned to Europe for a string of pictures, beginning with the joyous *The Golden Coach* (1952) and closing in 1970 with his last movie, *Le Petit Théâtre de Jean Renoir*. The following year Hollywood awarded Renoir an honorary Oscar, celebrating a career few directors have come close to rivalling.

Alain Resnais

Director, writer, editor
Born: *Vannes, France, July 3, 1922*

Half a century a film-maker and still experimenting, Alain Resnais is hailed as one of the most important directors to emerge from the French New Wave, but unlike others associated with that movement he worked as a technician within the traditional film industry before his complex narrative structures of multiple temporality hit the screen. Renais made his first film at 14, and after dropping out of teaching in Paris flirted with theatre before becoming a professional film-maker in his mid-twenties. His first commission was for the short *Van Gogh* (1948), but his Auschwitz exploration *Night and Fog* (1956) was his best before he moved into features with *Hiroshima Mon Amour* (1959). With its complex flashback structure attempting to reconcile memory with reality, it is judged by some as the first masterpiece of the New Wave. *Last Year at Marienbad* (1961), a surreal, plotless stream of consciousness, won prizes, and *Muriel* (1963) introduced the now-standard technique of allowing sound to overlap scenes. Unfortunately 1968's *Je t'Aime, Je t'Aime* lost money, and he was unable to complete another until the conventional *Stavisky* (1974), and the beguiling *Providence* (1977), his first English-language film. The 1980s trilogy of

Mon Oncle d'Amérique (1980), *La Vie est un Roman* (1983) and *L'Amour à Mort* (1984) were commercial successes, and in his two-part epic *Smoking/No Smoking* (1994) – with nine characters, two actors, and multiple endings – he continues to test and please audiences. It won the César (French Oscar) for best film.

Burt Reynolds

Actor, director
Born: BURTON LEON REYNOLDS JR., *Waycross, Ga., February 11, 1936*

Hollywood's leading 1970s macho man, Burt Reynolds was a TV star with the hit 1950s series *Riverboat*, *Gunsmoke* (1962–65), *Hawk* (1966–67) and *Dan August*

Burt Reynolds (right)*: Action hero with a rare sense of self-parody*

(1970) long before he made it in movies. He edged into films with TV-style actioners like *Sam Whiskey* (1969), *100 Rifles* (1969) and *Fuzz* (1972), but film stardom came with his turn as a menaced city-slicker in John Boorman's *Deliverance* (1972). Basically an adventure film with serious undertones, its success gave him star clout to work with top directors like Robert Aldrich – *The Longest Yard* (1974) *and Hustle*

(1975) – and with Peter Bogdanovich in *At Long Last Love* (1975) and *Nickelodeon* (1976). He shrewdly alternated broad comic adventures like *Smokey and the Bandit* (1977) and *The Cannonball Run* (1980) with thoughtful dramas like *Semi-Tough* (1977), *The End* (1978) and *Starting Over* (1979). In common with Clint Eastwood, Reynolds began a career as actor/director with *Gator* (1976) and *Sharkey's Machine* (1981). But the 1980s were a fallow period and attempts to repeat the *Cannonball Run/Smokey and the Bandit* formula didn't reproduce the original success. He made a welcome comeback with *Switching Channels* (1988) and a first successful character

role as an elderly safe-cracker in Bill Forsyth's *Breaking in* (1989). TV maintained his popularity with the private eye series *B L Stryker* and the sitcom *Evening Shade*, and in 1992 Reynolds scored his biggest cinema hit for years in *Cop and a Half*. He is well known for his self-deprecating humour, and sums up his career: "Nowadays they only screen my pictures in jails and jets – no one can escape!"

Sir Ralph Richardson

Actor, director
Born: *Cheltenham, England, December 19, 1902*
Died: *October 11, 1983*

Ralph Richardson stands alongside John Gielgud and Laurence Olivier as one of British cinema's most respected performers. The theatrically trained star's screen career

Sir Ralph Richardson: *Stage ham or acting deity?*

was managed in the early years by producer Alexander Korda. An inauspicious debut as a bogus priest in the 1933 creeper *The Ghoul* led to better roles in two Korda-produced HG Wells adaptations, *Things To Come* and *The Man who Could Work Miracles* (both 1936), and an impressive starring role in the involving Yorkshire-set potboiler *South Riding* (1937). His careful turn in the underpowered *Anna Karenina* (1948) laid the ground for a belated Hollywood debut: magnificently icy and imperious as Olivia de Havilland's manipulative father in William Wyler's *The Heiress* (1949). For such a dignified, restrained-looking figure, Sir Ralph's film roster proved dismayingly erratic. Key pictures include David Lean's *Doctor Zhivago* (1965) and Lindsay Anderson's *O Lucky Man!* (1973), while the stagy but satisfying thriller *Home at Seven* (1953) marked his sole directing foray. Richardson's most compelling performance, though, came as the tortured patriarch in Sidney

Lumet's 1961 version of Eugene O'Neill's *Long Day's Journey into Night*. Knighted in 1947, Richardson continued to work until his death, memorably portraying God as an irascible, well-meaning country gent in Terry Gilliam's super-imaginative fantasy *Time Bandits* (1982). It was a role this elder statesman of British screen appeared born to play.

Tony Richardson

Director
Born: CECIL ANTONIO RICHARDSON, *Shipley, England, June 5, 1928*
Died: *November 14, 1991*

The Oxford-educated, BBC-trained Tony Richardson was at the forefront of the "Free Cinema" movement that flooded stuffy British cinema with a cornucopia of dingy backstreets, malcontent protagonists and the obligatory kitchen sinks. The movement's ideals were crystallized in Richardson's feature-film debut, adapting John Osborne's toxic play *Look Back in Anger* (1959). He followed up that success by giving old-school luminary Laurence Olivier one of his finest roles as *The Entertainer* (1960), directed the faded but affecting *A Taste of Honey* (1961) and created perhaps the most rounded and detailed kitchen-sink fable, *The Loneliness of the Long Distance Runner* (1962). 1963's *Tom Jones*, his Oscar-winning hit that cut a roguish dash through 18th-century England, topped off one of the most white-hot spells of productivity of any British filmmaker. Unfortunately it was a period Richardson was never again to match, with his subsequent British efforts, *The Charge of the Light Brigade* (1968), *Laughter in the Dark* (1969) and *Joseph Andrews* (1977), looking mediocre by comparison. His increasing number of Hollywood forays also lacked the flair and focus of his early work, despite impressing with the indiscriminately inventive *The Loved*

One (1965), the corruption saga *The Border* (1982) and his witty but undervalued version of John Irving's *The Hotel New Hampshire* (1984). Richardson died of AIDS in 1991.

Martin Ritt

Director, actor
Born: *New York, NY, March 2, 1914*
Died: *December 8, 1990*

A stage and screen actor who made his Broadway debut in *Golden Boy* in 1937, Ritt turned to television directing after service in World War Two, until he was blacklisted in the 1950s. He taught at the Actors' Studio of "Method" fame, until one of his stage productions caught the eye of Hollywood and he was asked to direct *Edge of the City* (1957), a powerful waterfront drama featuring Sidney Poitier and John Cassavetes. Ritt's early experience gave him great skill in handling actors and an appreciation of literate drama, resulting in some of the best-acted and most intelligent films of his era. They include *The Long Hot Summer* (1958) featuring former Actors' Studio students Paul Newman, Joanne Woodward and Lee Remick; *Hud* (1963) with Newman as an early example of the anti-hero; and the stark world of Le Carré's *The Spy Who Came in from the Cold* (1965). In *The Front* (1976) Ritt drew on his own experience of television blacklisting, with Woody Allen in the title role and a moving performance from Zero Mostel as one of its victims. Much of Ritt's work demonstrates his interest in ordinary working people: Pennsylvania coal miners in *The Molly Maguires* (1969); *Pete 'n' Tillie* (1972), a character-led comedy romance between Walter Matthau and Carol Burnett; trade union organizer *Norma Rae* (1979); and the slow-burning mature love affairs of *Murphy's Romance* (1985) and *Stanley & Iris* (1990), a drama about illiteracy.

Jason Robards

Actor
Born: JASON NELSON ROBARDS JR, *Chicago, Ill., July 22, 1922*

One of America's best-known, most-admired star character actors, Robards, son of character actor Jason Robards Sr, had his screen debut in *The Journey* (1959). He worked primarily on stage at this time, winning the New York Drama Critics' Award for *Toys in the Attic* and taking bit parts in movies until landing the role of the drunken older brother in *Long Day's Journey into Night* (1962). His biggest acclaim came in three roles as real-life American icons when he won Oscars in successive years for *All The President's Men* (1976) as *Washington Post* editor Ben Bradlee and as Dashiell Hammett in *Julia* (1977), then was Oscar-nominated for his part as Howard Hughes in *Melvin and Howard* (1980). In 1977 he also got to play the bad guy in the Watergate scandal as the President Nixon character in the milestone TV drama *Washington Behind Closed Doors*. A prolific and much-in-demand character actor who has occasionally broken out of the rut of eye-catching cameos to produce virtuoso star performances in *Something Wicked this Way Comes* (1983), *Black Rainbow* (1989) and as the Russian dissident in *Sakharov* (1984), this actor with an affinity for the dark side has hardly ever been cast in comedy but displayed a real talent for it in *The Night They Raided Minsky's* (1968) and *The Adventures of Huck Finn* (1994).

Tim Robbins

Actor, director, writer, songwriter
Born: *New York, NY, October 16, 1958*

Playing *The Player* helped Tim Robbins develop a reputation as one of the most important stars of the 1990s, and the smirking giant

with the Mensa forehead has since displayed the independence and versatility to back that up. He grew up in Greenwich Village where his father was a folk singer with The Highwaymen, and by the age of 12 he had joined an experimental agitprop theatre. After moving to college in Los Angeles he co-founded The Actors' Gang, later becoming artistic director and playwright. A television appearance in *St Elsewhere* was followed by the movie *Toy Soldiers* (1984), though Rob Reiner's more substantial *The Sure Thing* (1985) is often cited as his film debut. He escaped his minor role in the flop comedy *Howard The Duck* (1986) and co-wrote the songs for *Tapeheads* (1988) before his eccentric baseball pitcher for *Bull Durham* (1988) attracted attention, not least from co-star Susan Sarandon who has since stayed his partner. But it was Robbins's nightmare-suffering Vietnam vet in *Jacob's Ladder* (1990) that really signalled his arrival, and Robert Altman's Hollywood exposé *The Player* (1992) confirmed it. But instead of cashing in, he chose to script, direct and star in *Bob Roberts* (1992), a satirical mockumentary about the rise of a folk-singing politician. Robbins possesses that extra edge that lights up a role, and his ability in comedy or drama seems limitless, ably demonstrated in *Short Cuts* (1993) and *The Hudsucker Proxy* (1994).

Julia Roberts

Actress, pretty woman
Born: *Smyrna, Ga., October 28, 1967*

A rangy, red-headed, rubber-lipped beauty, Julia Roberts proved the first sex symbol of the 1990s. After amassing favourable reviews in supporting roles in *Mystic Pizza* (1988) and the star-laden *Steel Magnolias* (1989), she hit the big time as the tart-with-a-heart heroine of 1990's *Pretty Woman*, a role that had Hollywood studios rushing to concoct projects that capitalized on her sex appeal and brand of coltish vulnerability. Roberts sealed her superstar status by single handedly powering the slick thriller *Sleeping with the Enemy* (1991) and, to a lesser extent, the wobbly, leadenly paced weepie *Dying Young* (1991). But although Hollywood's number-one female star, Roberts looked an increasingly harassed presence, with an abandoned wedding behind her and rumours of difficult behaviour on the set of Spielberg's *Hook* (1991), where she made an oddly spacy, frayed-at-the-edges Tinkerbell. After a risky

Julia Roberts: Pretty woman drawn to trouble

recuperative break from the movie maelstrom, Roberts made a grand comeback as a law student under threat in Alan Pakula's *The Pelican Brief* (1993). There's no doubt she still has the box-office Midas touch, despite the sometimes wayward judgement that led her to look uncomfortable and miscast opposite Nick Nolte in the lame-brained paper caper *I Love Trouble* (1994).

Edward G. Robinson

Actor
Born: EMMANUEL GOLDENBERG, *Bucharest, Romania, December 12, 1893*
Died: *January 26, 1973*

Short, frog-like, spitting words from his mouth like bullets from the machine-gun he often wielded, Edward G. had a charismatic

screen presence, a versatile talent, a humanitarian nature and a passion for art. From the age of 10 he grew up in New York. He abandoned plans for a career as a rabbi to study acting. After 17 years on stage, he turned to films with the talkies, making his mark as gang boss Rico in *Little Caesar* (1930),

Edward G.: Here's to you Mr Robinson

which both set an archetype and largely typecast Robinson in dramatic and sometimes comic variations on underworld types through Warner's 1930s crime cycle. He widened his range in the 1940s as the German-Jewish discoverer of a cure for syphilis in *Dr Ehrlich's Magic Bullet* (1940) and the news agency founder of *A Dispatch from Reuters* (1940). Other highlights include the determined insurance agent of *Double Indemnity* (1944); tracking down Nazi Orson Welles in New England in *The Stranger* (1946); the paranoiac gangster of Huston's *Key Largo* (1948); and the father in the film of *All My Sons* (1948). In the 1950s he fell foul of McCarthyism and, though he was cleared, his career suffered. In the 1960s he played supporting roles, including a scene-stealing performance as a world-weary poker king opposite Steve McQueen in *The Cincinnati Kid* (1965). His last film, the well thought-out science fiction tale *Soylent Green* (1973), came out a few days before his death from cancer and he was awarded a posthumous Special Oscar two months later.

Nicolas Roeg

Director, cinematographer
Born: *London, England, August 15, 1928*

Roeg is one of the few film-makers to graduate from technician to director. He began as tea boy at Marylebone Studios in London in 1947, became clapper boy on *The Miniver Story* for MGM in 1950, then was second unit photographer on Lean's *Lawrence of Arabia* (1962). He soon rose to noted cinematographer, working on several famous 1960s British films, beginning with the real-life chiller *Dr Crippen* (1962). His colour work on Roger Corman's *Masque of the Red Death* (1964), Truffaut's *Fahrenheit 451* (1967) and Schlesinger's *Far from the Madding Crowd* (1967) was outstanding. Roeg broke into direction as co-director of the extraordinary gender-bending gangster picture *Performance* (1970), then made the imaginative, exquisitely shot adventure film *Walkabout* (1971) in Australia. The occult chiller *Don't*

Look Now followed (1973), his first commercial hit, but he's remained strictly offbeat and adventurous, a dangerous combination for the box office. He sent David Bowie into space in *The Man who Fell to Earth* (1976), but alienated audiences with the weirdness of both *Bad Timing* (1980) and *Eureka* (1983). *Insignificance* (1985), *Castaway* (1987) and *The Witches* (1990) restored some of his box-office allure, while he's never lost his critical reputation as an artist true to his own individual vision at the cost of career advantage. His wife, Theresa Russell, has given eye-catching performances in many of his films.

Ginger Rogers

Actress, dancer, singer
Born: VIRGINIA KATHERINE McMATH, *Independence, Mo., July 16, 1911*
Died: *April 25, 1995*

Rogers's status as a Hollywood legend is based firmly on her 10 musicals (1933–49) with Fred

Ginger Rogers: Gotta sing, gotta dance

Astaire. Like it or not, they were each just half of one of the screen's most magical partnerships. They will always be Fred and Ginger, and it's a measure of her stylish quality as a hoofer that Astaire was never as successful with any other partner. He worried and planned meticulously; she just came in and did it with ease and grace. But this obscures Ginger's second claim to enduring fame: her success in dramatic roles. During the 1940s she starred in a series of RKO films in which she showed her versatile range as a straight actress and light comedienne. Though she won an Oscar for a serious part in *Kitty Foyle* (1940), she was at her best in comedy, masquerading as a child in Billy Wilder's *The Major and the Minor* (1942), playing a cabaret singer in *Vivacious Lady* (1938) or a phone operator in *Tom, Dick and Harry* (1941). Ginger carried on moving successfully between funny and serious roles until she started looking mature and the supply of movie work dried up – too early – in the mid-1950s. Her last part was mom in *Harlow* (1965), but the vivacious lady turned to the stage in the 1960s and was a hit all over again in *Hello Dolly* (Broadway) and *Mame* (London).

Will Rogers

Actor
Born: WILLIAM PENN ADAIR ROGERS, *Oologah, Okla., November 4, 1879*
Died: *August 15, 1935*

The folk hero whose rustic philosophy could elect presidents, Rogers had 20 hit movies after the introduction of talkies, before his death in a plane crash. Of Irish and Cherokee ancestry, he began his showbusiness career in Wild West shows in Johannesburg, South Africa, after delivering mules during the Boer War. He was initially a silent rope twirler and trick rider until a chance ad-lib got him a laugh. Thereafter he

gradually wove an inoffensive brand of humour into his act. Working his way into vaudeville, by 1917 he was starring with the Ziegfield Follies. His movie debut was as *Laughing Bill Hyde* (1918), but silent film robbed him of his act, and after a spell of producing and directing he went broke. A successful newspaper column and books including *The Cowboy Philosopher* kept Rogers's name alive until the advent of sound pictures. After *They Had To See Paris* (1929) his career never faltered, and by 1934 he was the number one cinema draw. His best work was his three films with director John Ford, *Doctor Bull* (1933), *Judge Priest* (1934) and *Steamboat Round the Bend* (1935). His support of Franklin Roosevelt helped the Democrat to the presidency, but he declined the offered reward of governorship of Oklahoma, and instead became honorary mayor of Beverly Hills. One of the great American showbusiness personalities, his last film, *In Old Kentucky* (1935), was released posthumously after his untimely death.

Mickey Rooney

Actor, singer, dancer
Born: JOE YULE JR, *Brooklyn, NY, September 23, 1920*

A popular child star with a rare spunkiness and edge, Rooney was the son of old-style vaudevillians and debuted on stage aged two. He started his film career aged six in comic shorts and made his debut proper in *My Pal the King* (1932). His cheeky energy made him an instant hit with the public, playing a plucky Puck in *A Midsummer Night's Dream* (1934). He had a string of successes at MGM like *Captains Courageous* (1937) before starting the long-running Hardy Family series as Andy Hardy with *A Family Affair* in 1937. In 1938 he was matched with Judy Garland in *Love Finds Andy Hardy* and MGM put the pair in a string

of hit musicals together including *Babes in Arms* (1939), *Strike Up the Band* (1940) and *Girl Crazy* (1943). He won a special Oscar for *Boys' Town* (1938) and his youthful success continued until the end of the Andy Hardy series proper in 1946 ("I didn't get out of short pants till I was 50") but he suffered the usual career hiccup experienced by most child stars trying to re-establish themselves as adult performers. He has kept working in a busy career of varied quality. He was remarkable in Siegel's gangster pic *Baby Face Nelson* (1957) and enlivened films as diverse as the thriller *Pulp* (1973) and the children's classic *The Black Stallion* (1959). In 1983 he got an Oscar for 50 years in movies.

Francesco Rosi

Director
Born: *Naples, Italy, November 15, 1922*

In the 1960s Francesco Rosi became known as the cinematic social conscience of Italy and "the journalist with a camera" for his neo-realist stories of the politically corrupt south and the exploitation of the poor. It is an interest which could be attributed to his youthful law studies and early days as a radio reporter, before he broke into films in the 1940s as assistant to Visconti. After working with other eminent directors, he turned to solo directing in the 1950s, proving himself a major talent with *Salvatore Giuliano* (1961), the story of a Sicilian bandit and folk hero, which pointed out, as did several of Rosi's later films, the links between the Mafia and the state. *Hands over the City* (1963), about a ruthless developer, and *Lucky Luciano* (1973), a gangster thriller, both starring Rod Steiger, along with *Illustrious Corpses* (1976) used strong storylines to continue Rosi's examination of corruption in high places. Rosi changed to a more lyrical and literary style with *Christ Stopped at*

Eboli (1979), the story of writer Carlo Levi's Fascist-induced exile in a southern village and *Chronicle of a Death Foretold* (1987), based on Gabriel García Márquez's novel. He also brought Bizet's opera *Carmen* (1983) to the screen in a sumptuous and accessible piece of film storytelling shot on location, with Julia Migenes-Johnson in the title role and Plácido Domingo as Don José.

Isabella Rossellini

Actress, model
Born: *Rome, Italy, June 18, 1952*

How could Isabella Rossellini fail? The daughter of Ingrid Bergman and the Italian director Roberto Rossellini, she inherited all her mother's looks and speaking voice, giving her an uncanny resemblance to the great star, and she has used those looks to advan-

Isabella Rossellini: Breathtakingly Bergmanesque

tage in a high-profile modelling career. She made her film debut with her mother in Vincente Minnelli's *A Matter of Time* (1976) and, after some Italian films, made the cold war thriller *White Nights* (1985), but it was David Lynch's dark masterpiece *Blue Velvet* (1986) that thrust her to the forefront of world attention as the abused singer in this art-house cult shocker. Since then she's pursued the oddest of careers, moving from cult item to art-house movie, to mainstream comedy with the gayest of abandon. Maybe it's a career plan, but it looks as though she's at the mercy of having to take the best offer at the time. There have been one or two good offers, romancing Ted Danson in the literate comedy *Cousins* (1989), a guest spot in Lynch's *Wild at Heart* (1990) and a mysterious purveyor of potions in *Death Becomes Her* (1992). John Schlesinger used her to evoke memories of her mother in his cold war thriller *The Innocent* (1992), but her part as Katie Elder was cut to a couple of lines in Kevin Costner's *Wyatt Earp* (1994). She landed a much better opportunity as Jeff Bridges's distraught wife in *Fearless* (1993). It's a tenuous hold on stardom but in her forties she has the talent, looks and staying power to survive.

Roberto Rossellini

Director, writer, producer
Born: *Rome, Italy, May 8, 1906*
Died: *June 4, 1977*

The inspiring Italian neo-realist film-maker Rossellini is a major though neglected figure in international cinema who spearheaded the renaissance of Italian movies after World War Two. Recruited by the Fascists in 1938 to work on propaganda films, he electrified the world's screens in 1945 as the creator of a new kind of humanist documentary-style cinema with *Rome, Open City*, the first of a trilogy completed by the equally renowned *Paisan* (1946) and *Germany Year Zero* (1948). In the 1950s he achieved even wider fame – or notoriety – as the man Ingrid Bergman left Hollywood for. Although both married, they had an affair and a baby before they divorced and remarried. One of their daughters is cinema darling Isabella Rossellini (born 1952), star of *Blue Velvet* (1986) and *Fearless* (1993). The films Roberto and Ingrid made together, including *Stromboli* (1949) and *Voyage to Italy* (1953),

were banned and reviled at the time, but they have since been revalued and are now held in high esteem. In 1957 the marriage broke up when Rossellini shocked popular opinion again, this time through a relationship with Indian writer Somali Das Gupta. Rossellini's career suffered until, in the 1960s, he embarked on a series of landmark films for television, most notably *The Rise of Louis XIV* (1966). His work influenced the 1960s generation of European film-makers like Godard, Bergman and Bertolucci.

Mickey Rourke

Actor
Born: *Schenectady, NY, February 4, 1950*

A defiant maverick by reputation, Rourke has a soft voice, a strong screen presence, can be effectively

Mickey Rourke: Heart of an angel

sexy, sleazy and menacing, but his choice of roles and quality of performance vary from good to horrid. Of Scots-Irish descent, Rourke was brought up with five stepbrothers, whom he claims made him a tough street fighter. An amateur boxer, he then trained at the Actors' Studio and went to Hollywood, where after 78 auditions he got a couple of small film roles and some television leads. He was first noticed as the arson-

ist in Lawrence Kasdan's *Body Heat* (1981) and the lothario hairdresser in Barry Levinson's *Diner* (1982). Francis Coppola cast him in *Rumble Fish* (1983), then Michael Cimino gave him his first grown-up lead as the drug-busting cop in *Year of the Dragon* (1985). He co-starred with Kim Basinger in *Nine and a Half Weeks* (1986), a film whose valid observations on female masochism were swamped by accusations of porn – a charge again levelled at a later Rourke film, *Wild Orchid* (1990). Meanwhile he was ideally cast as a scruffy private eye in 1950s' New Orleans wrestling with Robert De Niro's Satan in Alan Parker's intriguing *Angel Heart* (1987); played another scruff in *Barfly* (1987); came to England to star as an IRA gunman in *A Prayer for the Dying* (1987); and caused a sensation at the Cannes Film Festival two years later, when he was associated with support for the IRA cause. He also played a boxer in his own script for *Homeboy* (1988), indulged his personal passions again in *Harley Davidson and the Marlboro Man* (1991), and mumbled through the Bogart role in Cimino's indifferent remake of *Desperate Hours* (1990).

Jane Russell

Actress, singer
Born: ERNESTINE JANE GERALDINE RUSSELL, *Bemidji, Minn., June 21, 1921*

"Mean, Moody and Magnificent!" went the poster publicity for *The Outlaw* (1943), or rather Russell's low-cut cleavage, which attracted the censor's attentions, establishing her as the first of the bosomy sex symbols that dominated the 1950s and beyond. The daughter of a former actress, she was a chiropodist's assistant and a model before Howard Hughes sought her out to debut in *The Outlaw*. Briefly opening in 1943, it was not properly released until 1950, although Russell was only in bed with her co-star once, and that to

keep a sick man warm! The movie made her name, but also hampered her career. While she should have been capitalizing, Hughes kept her under wraps through most of the 1940s lest she flop and damage the film's eventual release. Yet disregarding the suggestive *Double Dynamite* (1951), Russell showed she had more on offer than the obvious. Always sharp, she was canny at comedy – 1948's *The Paleface* – and musicals, most notably with Marilyn Monroe in *Gentlemen Prefer Blondes* (1953), but gradually drifted away from the screen in favour of Broadway and her nightclub act. Still handsome and vibrant in her 50s, Russell was the ideal 1970s spokeswoman for Playtex bra, and she was last seen in *The Jackass Trail* (1981). Her enduring status in screen history is evidence of the triumph of image over content, as while she is unforgettable, her films often were.

Ken Russell

Director, writer, producer
Born: HENRY KENNETH ALFRED RUSSELL, *Southampton, England, July 3, 1927*

The flamboyant, unpredictable and hugely creative director Russell still rejoices at unsuitably advancing years in his title of *"wunderkind* of British films"! After a varied career in the merchant navy, the RAF, as a ballet dancer and then a photographer, Russell joined BBC Television, where he created a series of brilliantly original and inventive fictionalized documentaries, whose imaginative frankness gave him his first taste of the controversy which became a corollary of much of his later work. After two feature films – the comedy *French Dressing* (1963) and Michael Caine's third outing as Harry Palmer in *Billion Dollar Brain* (1967) – his lush, erotic and groundbreaking film version of D.H. Lawrence's *Women in Love* (1969) hit the international scene. He continued his exploration of art and sensuality with a sensational biopic of Tchaikovsky, *The Music Lovers* (1971), which he described as "a love story between a homosexual and a nymphomaniac" and, big-budget bit between his teeth, galloped into further excesses with *The Devils* (1971) and the birthday cake vulgarity of *The Boy Friend* (1971). *Savage Messiah* (1972) was a restrained and sensitive biopic of sculptor Gaudier-Brzeska, followed by three more overblown but original and visually exciting biopics: *Mahler* (1973), *Lisztomania* (1975) and *Valentino* (1977); the rock musical *Tommy* (1975); and the intriguing, psychedelically mystic sci-fi of *Altered States* (1979). He returned to shock tactics with the startling black satire on sexual fantasies *Crimes of Passion* (1984); comical excess with *Gothic* (1986) and *The Lair of the White Worm* (1988); high camp in *Salome's Last Dance* (1988) and an almost sentimental sensuality in *The Rainbow* (1989). *Whore* (1991) was for him low-key but, knowing Russell, this state of play should not last for long.

Kurt Russell

Actor

Born: *Springfield, Mass., March 17, 1951*

Brawny, some say handsome, with heavily dimpled chin, Kurt Russell was a Disney kid before a memorable film impersonation of Elvis Presley propelled him to stardom, often in tandem with long-term lover Goldie Hawn. The son of *Bonanza's* deputy sheriff, Bing, Russell established himself as a blue-eyed, cute blond by the time he was 10, making his debut in *The Absent-Minded Professor* (1960). By a quirk of fate he was required to kick the real Elvis Presley on the shin in *It Happened at the World's Fair* (1963), and first briefly met Hawn in *The Family Band* (1968). His main interest was baseball

until a promising career was ended by a shoulder injury. Fortunately, John Carpenter cast him in black leather as a convincing *Elvis! The Movie* (1979), winning him an Emmy nomination, and his transition from Disney innocent was completed with his macho eye-patched hero in Carpenter's *Escape From New York* (1981). *Silkwood* (1983) was followed by *Swing Shift* (1984) and *Overboard* (1987), his first adult appearances with Hawn, but there are some bum movies on his resumé *Big Trouble in Little China* (1986) was white kung-fu nonsense, while his pairing with Sylvester Stallone in *Tango & Cash* (1990), proved little better. *Backdraft* (1991) beats *Unlawful Entry* (1992) hands down, and *Tombstone* (1993), the western he helped re-write, was a notable improvement. But Russell has never quite broken through into the stellar super-league.

Rosalind Russell

Actress

Born: *Waterbury, Conn., June 4, 1908*
Died: *November 28, 1976*

A stylish exponent of sophisticated comedy, Russell was the daughter of a lawyer and a fashion editor. She started her career on stage in the late 1920s, turning to film in 1934 in mainly dramatic parts, though in the comedy *Four's a Crowd* (1938) she first played the snazzy female reporter-type character she was to make her own, most memorably in *His Girl Friday* (1940), for which director Howard Hawks had the bright idea of turning Ben Hecht's Hildy Johnson into a female role. Russell had now found her niche for most of the 1940s: the well-dressed, in-control business gal trading wisecracks with the men in her life. At her own estimate she played 23 of them, dressed in smart suits for most of the film and confessing towards the end that what they really wanted was to be "a dear little housewife". She received

three Oscar nominations in this period, for *My Sister Eileen* (1942), which she later took to Broadway as the stage musical *Wonderful Town* (1953); *Sister Kenny* (1946); and a dramatic role in *Mourning Becomes Electra* (1947). Her film career then took a downturn and she returned to the stage. She took her first character role as the spinster in *Picnic* (1956) and returned triumphantly to screen big-time as *Auntie Mame* (1958) – another Oscar nomination – in the film version of her Broadway triumph. She is also well remembered as the monstrous but sympathetic stage mother of *Gypsy* (1962). Russell was awarded a Special Oscar in 1972 for her charity work.

Dame Margaret Rutherford

Actress

Born: *London, England, May 11, 1892*
Died: *May 22, 1972*

Dame Margaret led with her copious chins in deliciously dotty

Dame Margaret Rutherford: *Deliciously dotty*

performances in a host of British film comedies. She was spinsterish and jolly-hockey-sticks, had a lovely ripe voice and, like fellow eccentric Alastair Sim, started out teaching elocution and playing the piano. She studied at London's prestigious Old Vic School, but it was a long wait for her first movie, *Dusty Ermine* (1938) as the

wily agent of a gang of forgers. She became a star on stage in the late 1930s playing Madame Arcati, Miss Prism and Mrs Danvers, and the films enshrining the first two of these, *Blithe Spirit* (1945) and *The Importance of Being Earnest* (1952) are enduring records of her brilliance. *Passport to Pimlico* (1949) cast her in a memorable cameo as a medieval charter expert and in 1950 she re-created her stage success in *The Happiest Days of Your Life* as a headstrong headmistress. She worked in diligent support of many of the greats of 1950s British comedy, usually upstaging and outclassing them – including Norman Wisdom, Frankie Howerd and Ian Carmichael. She even supported Danny Kaye when he came to Britain for 1961's *On the Double*. Her greatest international fame came in the 1960s when she impersonated Miss Marple in four Agatha Christie films for MGM to general delight, not ideally cast but making the part her own. Rutherford won an Oscar as a Heathrow passenger in the Burton-Taylor soaper *The V.I.P.s* (1963). She was married to actor Stringer Davis who appeared in many of her pictures.

Winona Ryder

Actress

Born: WINONA HOROWITZ, *Winona, Mont., October 29, 1971*

Elfin, doe-eyed Winona Ryder is the hottest of Hollywood's rising stars, with a short but sure-footed career that has taken her from kooky teen icon to mainstream sex symbol. She first grabbed attention as the sensitive-souled, misfit heroine of Tim Burton's *Beetlejuice* (1987), a role she was to reprise – with subtle variations – in *Welcome Home, Roxy Carmichael* (1990) and the big-budget hit *Mermaids* (1990). But the most significant role of this first phase of her career came with her turn as a rebelling high-school insider in the sly black comedy *Heathers* (1988), a part described by Ryder as "the role of my life". But Winona was growing up, yearning to spread her wings. A part as a chain-smoking cab driver in Jim Jarmusch's *Night on Earth* (1991) heralded a change of pace, quickly followed by a trio of elaborate costume dramas. Though these were intended to reveal the slender, attractive star as an actress of real weight, Ryder ended up looking a touch over-stretched: ill-at-ease in *Bram Stoker's Dracula* (1992), sporadically impressive as a devious debutante in Martin Scorsese's *The Age of Innocence* (1993), awkward and unconvincing as a feisty rebel in the overblown *The House of the Spirits* (1994). Back on safer ground, she proved far more appealing in the Generation-X caper *Reality Bites* (1994) and clearly has a glittering future ahead of her.

Marianne Sägebrecht

Actress, producer
Born: *Starnberg, Germany, August 10, 1945*

A trio of 80s films by German director Percy Adlon tuned his compatriot Sägebrecht into an internationally renowned character actress. Adlon discovered her work as a leading producer and performer of Germany's fringe and experimental theatre and cast her as a star of *Herr Kischott* (1980), his made-for-TV version of *Don Quixote*, then gave her her cinema debut in *Die Schaukel* (1983), the tale of an 1880s Munich family. But it was in *Sugarbaby* (1985) that she caught the public imagination with her performance as a lovelorn undertaker, and consolidated her success as the lost German tourist who turns up at the isolated California diner and is adopted by the wacky inhabitants in the delightfully quirky, atmospheric and funny *Bagdad Café* (1983). This hit in America made her hot and spawned the inevitable TV spin-off series but she turned down an

offer to play in it. The success of these films earned her Hollywood's respect, leading Paul Mazursky to cast her in his banana republic comedy *Moon Over Parador* (1988) and Danny De Vito to use her in his *The War of the Roses* (1989). She then starred in Adlon's *Rosalie Goes Shopping* (1989) in which she has settled in Arkansas adopting the local consumer values. But she turned down a part in Penny Marshall's *Awakenings* (1990), and preferred to return to Europe to work in such films as *Martha and I* (1991) and *The Milky Way* (1992).

John Sayles

Director, actor, writer
Born: *Schenectady, NY, September 28, 1950*

John Sayles appears a throwback to such old-style American film-makers as Huston, Welles and John Ford. A fiercely intelligent, socially committed director, screenwriter, actor and novelist, he's the driving force behind some of the most challenging low-budget works of recent years. His inventive script for 1980's *Alligator* turned what should have been a toothless *Jaws* rip-off into an audaciously tongue-in-cheek monster pic pastiche and an instant classic of junk cinema. In more serious mode, *The Return of the Secaucus 7* (1980) provided the $60,000 blueprint for both Lawrence Kasdan's *The Big Chill* (1983) as well as Kenneth Branagh's syrupy ensemble-piece *Peter's Friends* (1992). But it's with the political picture that Sayles really demonstrates his film-making prowess. *Matewan* (1987), an engrossing miners' strike study, is political drama at its most cogent and affecting and, with Sayles scripting, directing, starring as the local preacher and co-writing the songs, there's only one man to thank. The agreeable *Passion Fish* (1993) paved a neat route into the movie mainstream but Sayles's career

peak remains the majestic *City of Hope* (1991), a vigorous, visionary dissection of a fictional East Coast city tottering under racial tensions and a crumbling infrastructure. Seamlessly fusing a fistful of parallel plotlines, Sayles rustled up a state-of-the-nation address that confirmed his place at the cutting-edge of American cinema.

John Schlesinger

Director, actor
Born: *London, England, February 19, 1926*

One of Britain's most gifted, intelligent and exciting directors, Schlesinger won an Oscar for *Midnight Cowboy* (1969). A paediatrician's son, he entertained troops in World War Two as a conjurer, attended Oxford University (1945–50) and joined Colchester repertory theatre. He played small roles in British plays, films and TV series (*Robin Hood*), and, after making amateur movies, from 1956 directed 26 documentaries for the BBC's *Monitor* arts programme and *Tonight* news magazine. In 1961 he scooped the top award at Venice for his *Terminus* documentary on London's Waterloo station, and his subsequent debut feature, the realist *A Kind of Loving* (1962), based on Stan Barstow's novel, won first prize at the Berlin Film Festival. Two decades of almost non-stop success followed, with British landmarks like *Billy Liar* (1963), *Darling* (1965), *Far from the Madding Crowd* (1967), *Sunday Bloody Sunday* (1971) and *Yanks* (1979), and American masterworks *The Day of the Locust* (1975) and *Marathon Man* (1976). But it ended with the costly flop of *Honky Tonk Freeway* (1981) and film work has been scarce for Schlesinger since. Television provided two of his best opportunities, the Alan Bennett spy pieces *An Englishman Abroad* (1983) and *A Question of Attribution* (1991). In the 1990s Schlesinger turned to commercial thrillers for cinema survival, with mixed suc-

cess – *Pacific Heights* (1990) delivering him a hit and *The Innocent* (1993) a flop.

Volker Schlöndorff

Director
Born: *Wiesbaden, Germany, March 31, 1939*

The stylish, professional German director Volker Schlöndorff appears to steer an even course while his more erratic compatriot Wim Wenders veers regularly between the sublime and the ridiculous. Although his output tends towards the socially critical, it bears less unity of vision than Wenders's and Schlöndorff is probably best known as a master-craftsman who has brought poise, polish and atmosphere to a variety of upmarket film projects. After flirting with television work and opera productions, Schlöndorff moved into the feature film industry, first as an assistant director, before grabbing world attention with his Oscar-winning adaptation of Günter Grass's *The Tin Drum* (1979). He appears particularly drawn to the literary adaptation and has proved adept at translating the elusive mood and intent of a novel to the big screen. He has turned in fine movies from the work of Proust, with *Swann in Love* (1984), and of Max Frisch with 1991's *Voyager*, as well as a less successful attempt at Margaret Attwood's *The Handmaid's Tale* (1990) which was marred by tonal uncertainty and the miscasting of Natasha Richardson as a rebelling *femme*. High points in a career of enviable quality include his 1985 TV treatment of Arthur Miller's *Death of a Salesman*, staged in a stylized, oppressive set and driven by two Emmy-award-winning turns from Dustin Hoffman and John Malkovich. *Voyager*, too, proved a gleaming showcase for the director's skills, serving up a slow-burning, bewitching study of forbidden love in 1950s Europe.

Romy Schneider

Actress

Born: ROSEMARIE ALBACH-RETTY, *Vienna, Austria, September 23, 1938*
Died: *May 29, 1982*

The daughter of a well-known actor and actress (she later took the name of her mother, film star Magda Schneider), Romy Schneider became a major juvenile star in Germany and was particularly popular as the young Empress Elisabeth in three films, later cut together for US release as *Forever My Love* (1962). She rebelled against her sugary roles for *Mädchen in Uniform* (1958) and went to France for a remake of Ophuls's *Liebelei* as *Christine* (1959). Visconti cast her in *Boccaccio '70* (1962) and Welles in *The Trial* (1962) at a time when Hollywood was becoming interested in European talent, leading to roles in Foreman's *The Victors* (1963) and other American films. In England she joined a bevy of 1960s beauties surrounding Peter O'Toole in *What's New Pussycat?* (1965) and featured in the spoof spy thriller *Otley* (1969) opposite Tom Courtenay. Having turned down *Accident* when she was pregnant, she worked with Losey on *The Assassination of Trotsky* (1972) and played Empress Elisabeth as an adult for Visconti in *Ludwig* (1973). When both films flopped, the international scene lost interest in Schneider's enigmatic – or, as some saw it, wooden

Romy Schneider: Enigmatic or wooden?

– style of playing, and she concentrated on French cinema thereafter, such as Chabrol's *Les Innocents aux Mains Sales* (1975), Costa-Gavras's *Clair de Femme* (1979) and Tavernier's *Deathwatch* (1979), set in Glasgow. She died unexpectedly of a heart attack shortly after completing *La Passante du Sans Souci* (1982).

Paul Schrader

Writer, director

Born: *Grand Rapids, Mich., July 22, 1946*

Sleaze and violence are what fascinate and disgust Schrader, the writer most associated with Martin Scorsese, and now a powerful director in his own right. From strict Calvinist parents of Dutch-German descent, he was protected from the depravity of cinema until he was 17, when a guilty visit led to him abandoning theology to attend film school. He began as a critic in Los Angeles, before turning down a job offer from Pauline Kael, thus kicking off a famous feud. His first script sale was *The Yakuza* (1975), whose commercial failure upset him, but he was glad to be uncredited for an early version of *Close Encounters of the Third Kind* (1977). The real break came with *Taxi Driver* (1976), a tale of violence and disillusion written in two frenzied weeks in hospital while recuperating from divorce, drink and depression. His directorial debut was of his own script, *Blue Collar* (1978), but he had to wait for *American Gigolo* (1979) for commercial success. An Oscar nominee for co-writing *Raging Bull* (1980), his other screenwriting credits include *The Mosquito Coast* (1986) and *The Last Temptation of Christ* (1988). Among his director's credits are *Mishima: A Life In Four Chapters* (1985), *Patty Hearst* (1988), *The Comfort of Strangers* (1990) and, in a return to the insomniac underworld of *Taxi Driver*, 1992's *Light Sleeper*. In recent times no one has better dealt with his con-

sistent theme of redemption through confession or cathartic violence. Except old pal Scorsese, of course.

Arnold Schwarzenegger

Actor, bodybuilder, director

Born: *Graz, Austria, July 30, 1947*

Schwarzenegger's progress from incredible hulk to box-office number one is as unexpected and delightful as any celluloid dream.

Arnie Schwarzenegger: Speak seldom and carry a big gun

How did a muscleman with a strong Austrian accent ever make it in American movies? After a false start as Arnold Strong, the seven-time Mr Olympia kicked off his film career with a Golden Globe-winning part in *Stay Hungry* (1976) and *Pumping Iron* (1977), a documentary about an Olympia contest. John Milius's shrewd casting in *Conan the Barbarian* (1982) grossed $100 million and made Schwarzenegger an overnight star. A sequel, *Conan the Destroyer* (1984), was just as successful and *Terminator* (1984) proved he wasn't a one-part star, sparking a long run of 1980s hit action movies – *Commando* (1985), *Predator* (1987), *Raw Deal* (1986), *Red Heat* (1988) – with a high violence factor. The films and the star had style, and Arnie seemed to have taken acting

lessons. He always suggested he has a sense of humour, and wisely turned to comedy. *Twins* (1988), as Danny De Vito's slightly improbable brother, is a revelation: Big Arnie is gentle, charming and very funny. Back in violent mode, he had his biggest successes with the costly and imaginative sci-fi actioners *Total Recall* (1990) and *Terminator 2* (1991) until the public mood seemed to turn against him. Arnie's post-modernist attempt to comment on screen violence in *The Last Action Hero* (1993) was an unnerving box-office disaster, but he bounced back with *True Lies* (1994).

Martin Scorsese

Director, writer, actor

Born: *New York, NY, November 17, 1942*

One of the world's most innovative and exciting directors, Scorsese has audaciously used a series of complex, flawed anti-heroes – Travis Bickle in *Taxi Driver* (1976), Jake La Motta in *Raging Bull* (1980), Rupert Pupkin in *The King of Comedy* (1982) – to illuminate the wider failings of American culture. He made award-winning shorts before releasing his first feature – *Who's*

That Knocking at My Door? – in 1969. *Mean Streets* (1973), his raw, witty study of small-time Italian-American hoodlums, won him international recognition, displaying the earthy realism and imagination that was to be his hallmark and signalling the start of his collaboration with Robert De Niro,

Martin Scorsese: *No misdirection here*

which has produced such masterworks as *Taxi Driver*, *Raging Bull*, *The King of Comedy* and *Goodfellas* (1990). *Raging Bull* is Scorsese's masterpiece, a brutal, groundbreaking biopic, at once the poignant story of one man's fall and a radical critique of society and its values. *The Color of Money* (1986) and *Cape Fear* (1991) showed that he could make popular mainstream movies, while *The Age of Innocence* (1993) saw him launching, not altogether successfully, into eyecatching costume drama. He is at his most effective when not only entertaining an audience, but also challenging and provoking them.

George C. Scott

Actor, director
Born: GEORGE CAMPBELL SCOTT, *Wise, Va., October 18, 1927*

A forceful, outspoken, always professional and sometimes inspired actor of the old school, Scott grew up in Detroit, served in the marines, studied journalism, then acted while working as labourer and clerk. His theatre breakthrough came as *Richard II* in New York (1958) and his film debut came straight after, in a Gary Cooper western *The Hanging Tree*

(1958), followed by *Anatomy of a Murder* (1959), *The Hustler* (1961) – he was Oscar-nominated for both – and *Dr Strangelove* (1964). These, along with his TV series *East Side West Side* (1963–64), turned him into a star. For two decades the cinema showed him equally powerful in a wide variety of moods from comic (*The Flim Flam Man*, 1967) via tender (*Petulia*, 1968) and angry (*The New Centurions*, 1972) to romantic (*Jane Eyre*, 1971). He won an Oscar for his dazzling impersonation of the renegade US World War Two general in Coppola's *Patton* (1970), and after-

George C. Scott: *Might be a giant*

wards played some intriguing offbeat movies like *They Might Be Giants* and *The Hospital* (both 1971) that harmed his box-office reputation but have worn well. He then plumped for international crowd-pleasers like *Beauty and the Beast* (1977), *The Prince and the Pauper* (1978), *Oliver Twist* (1982), *A Christmas Carol* (1984) and *Exorcist III* (1990) to prop up his sagging appeal. Film work has been scarce in the 1990s though TV helped him out. He directed twice: *Rage* (1972) and *The Savage Is Loose* (1974).

Randolph Scott

Actor, cowboy
Born: RANDOLPH CRANE, *Orange County, Calif., January 23, 1898*
Died: *March 2, 1987*

Like the title of one of his movies, Scott was high, wide and handsome, the very model of a major

western hero. As a struggling stage actor in the late 1920s, he encountered producer Howard Hughes during a round of golf, his passport to Hollywood Boulevard. He debuted in walk-on parts in 1929 and blossomed in the mid-1930s as a somewhat soppy romantic hero in musicals like *Roberta* (1935) and *Follow the Fleet* (1936). But adventure roles were more his thing as he showed in *She* (1935) and *The Last of the Mohicans* (1936). Soon he'd established himself as a cowboy star in top films like *Jesse James* (1939), *Frontier Marshal* (as Wyatt Earp) (1939) and *Western Union* (1941). But it was in the 1950s that he carved his main niche with a run of now classic B-westerns made for his own company Ranown and directed by Budd Boetticher. The films, including *The Tall T* (1957), *Buchanan Rides Alone* (1958) and *Ride Lonesome* (1958), were gilt-edged financial successes and helped turn Scott into a very rich man (he invested in oil wells). He rode into the sunset at the best possible moment when, at over 60, he played an old gunfighter in Sam Peckinpah's magnificent elegy to the western, *Ride the High Country* (1962). And then he lived long enough to enjoy his retirement.

Ridley Scott

Director
Born: *South Shields, England, November 30, 1939*

Ridley Scott is one of the most visually daring and innovative directors currently working. Films such as *Alien* (1979) and *Blade Runner* (1982) have established him not only as a master of mood and atmosphere, but as one of the great imaginative forces of modern cinema, melding exciting, intelligent storylines with stunning visual effects to create some of the most satisfying action movies of the last 15 years. He worked as a freelance director –

mainly on commercials – before winning a Special Jury Prize at Cannes with his debut feature *The Duellists* (1977), becoming a household name with the cult sci-fi horror flick *Alien*. The latter's blend of strong characters, complex, faintly esoteric script and extraordinary set design proved a massive winner, establishing a formula that he has applied to all his subsequent projects. The futuristic *film noir Blade Runner* (1982) – with its unique combination of gripping plot and unparalleled visual flair – is his masterpiece, although the thrillers *Someone to Watch Over Me* (1987) and *Black Rain* (1989) are almost as memorable. *Thelma and Louise* (1991), his free-wheeling feminist road movie, underlined once again his extraordinary skill as both a screen artist and creator of complex, engaging characters. And although his Columbus epic *1492* (1992) was uncharacteristically stodgy, he remains one of cinema's most intelligent, thought-provoking and stylish filmmakers.

Peter Sellers

Comedian, actor
Born: RICHARD HENRY SELLERS, *Southsea, England, September 8, 1925*
Died: *July 24, 1980*

Sellers first came to prominence in the 1949 BBC radio *Goon Show* whose anarchic, surreal brand of humour was the precursor of Monty Python and in fact most modern alternative comedy. Starting his film career in shorts like *Let's Go Crazy* (1950), *Down Among the Z-Men* (1952) and on TV, he didn't hit his stride until *The Ladykillers* (1955) with Alec Guinness. By the late 1950s, already established as a British comedy stalwart, Sellers appeared regularly in films like *Carlton-Browne of the F.O.* (1959), the successful *The Mouse That Roared* (1959), in which he played multiple parts including a grand duchess, and *I'm All Right Jack* (1959), which brought him a British Film Academy Award for Best Actor. But it was Blake Edwards's *The Pink Panther* (1964)

Peter Sellers: *One of his many faces*

that really established him as an international star and created the character of bumbling French police inspector Clouseau, a part he would return to for several popular sequels. Next came Kubrick's apocalyptic masterpiece *Dr Strangelove* (1964), Sellers again playing multiple roles, this time a *tour de force* as the American President, the mad scientist and an R.A.F. officer. After a lull in his career, during which the material he chose was less than popular, *The Return of the Pink Panther* (1975) restored his prestige and he was Oscar-nominated for his subtlest, most endearing characterization in *Being There* (1979).

David O. Selznick

Producer

Born: DAVID OLIVER SELZNICK, *Pittsburgh, Pa., May 10, 1902*
Died: *June 22, 1965*

A huge, chain-smoking bear of a man, David Selznick will always occupy a unique place in cinema history as the producer of *Gone with the Wind* (1939). A tireless worker and legendarily hard taskmaster, he was the prototype of the creative independent pro-

ducer, a maverick perfectionist operating outside the Hollywood studio system and involving himself in every aspect of film production. The son of film magnate Lewis J. Selznick, and brother of agent Myron, he worked for his father until the latter went bust in the mid-1920s. After short spells at MGM, Paramount and RKO, he formed his own company Selznick International Pictures (S.I.P.) in 1936, thereafter producing a steady trickle of high-quality, prestige films, notable for their stringent production values and strong story-lines: *The Prisoner of Zenda* (1937), *A Star Is Born* (1937), *Gone with the Wind* (1939) and *Rebecca* (1940). Despite winning Best Film Oscars for the latter two productions, S.I.P. folded in 1940, and although he continued to produce films for the next two decades – *Duel in the Sun* (1946), *The Paradine Case* (1948), *The Third Man* (1949) – he never again displayed his earlier creative vigour. One of Hollywood's greatest and most engaging of producers, Selznick once avowed he wanted to stand out from the crowd. His independence, creativity, and unerringly high standards ensured that he did.

Mack Sennett

Director, producer

Born: MIKALL SINNOTT, *Danville, Quebec, Canada, January 17, 1880*
Died: *November 5, 1960*

Sennett almost single-handedly invented the American silent comedy. An irreverent, larger-than-life figure, he directed and produced an extraordinary number of films, honing chaos to a fine art and launching the careers of some of the screen's great comedians – Chaplin, Normand, Arbuckle, Lloyd. There was nothing subtle about his humour, which was brash, childish and vulgar, but he had the unique vision to understand how film could be used to develop the

comic art. He performed in burlesque before joining the pioneering Biograph Film Company in 1908, where he worked as an actor, writer and, after 1910, director. In 1912 he moved to Hollywood and founded the Keystone Film Company, directing their movies until 1914, and thereafter producing. He assembled a talented repertory company of comic performers and churned out a dizzying array of comic shorts, some of the more notable being *In the Clutches of the Gang* (1913), *The Alarm* (1914), *The Knockout* (1914), *Kid Auto Races at Venice* (1914) and *His Prehistoric Past* (1914). *Tillie's Punctured Romance* (1914), which he directed as well as produced, was the first ever comedy feature, but Keystone folded in the late 1910s, and although he continued working well into the 1930s, Sennett's real importance rests with those frantic, innovative Keystone years. He retired in 1935, and in 1937 received a special Academy Award for his contribution to screen comedy.

Norma Shearer

Actress

Born: EDITH NORMA SHEARER, *Montreal, Canada, August 10, 1900*
Died: *June 12, 1983*

One of Hollywood's top stars in the 1930s, Shearer owed her success to her air of well-bred elegance, determination, total professionalism and to her marriage, rather than to sheer acting talent. She moved with her family to New York in her teens, worked as a bit-part player in films, and was spotted by Irving Thalberg in *The Stealers* (1920). It took him three years to track her down and put her under contract. They married in 1927. As a partner in MGM and Hollywood's top producer, Thalberg made her the studio's leading lady. The public loved her in comedies and dramas, including *Their Own Desire* (1929), *The*

Divorcee (1930), for which she won an Oscar, and *A Free Spirit* (1931). She also played some of the top theatre hits of the day on film: the title role in *The Last of Mrs Cheyney* (1929); Amanda in Noel Coward's *Private Lives* (1931); and Elizabeth in *The Barretts of Wimpole Street* (1934). Although she had been unimpressive with John Gilbert performing the balcony scene in *The Hollywood Revue of 1929*, she still had a yen to play Juliet, and eventually her husband indulged her by setting up the film of *Romeo and Juliet* (1936). Though a touch old for the part, she acquitted herself admirably. She played the title role in *Marie Antoinette* (1938), planned for her by Thalberg before his death in 1936. Thereafter the loss of his advice on her career showed with some poor choices, including the turning-down of *Gone with the Wind* (1939) and *Mrs Miniver* (1942). In 1942 she married a ski instructor 20 years her junior and retired.

Charlie Sheen

Actor

Born: CARLOS ESTEVEZ, *Los Angeles, Calif., September 3, 1965*

Son of Martin Sheen and brother of Emilio Estevez, Sheen Jr started acting professionally as a child. One of his jobs was as an extra on *Apocalypse Now* (1979) starring his father. He was one of the youngsters who save America in John Milius's paranoiac right-wing *Red Dawn* (1984) and likeable as a football hero in the above-average teen sex comedy *Lucas* (1986). Oliver Stone made Sheen a leading man in *Platoon* (1986) as the green Vietnam recruit who narrates the story, and as the ambitious young trader in *Wall Street* (1987), in which Sheen Sr played his blue-collar, union-leader father. Sheen was one of the western "Brat Pack" group led by brother Emilio in *Young Guns* (1988) and showed a good sense of comedy in *Major League* (1989) as the slobby star of a deadbeat baseball team, which was virtually re-run with most of the original cast but none of the sparkle in *Major League II* (1994). He was also adept at handling the pastiche-and-puns style of humour in *Hot Shots!* (1991), and was sympathetic as the wrongly accused runaway hero of *The Chase* (1994), which made some perceptively tart observations on media morality. A hellraiser in his youth, Sheen now seems to have calmed down personally, but could do with a bit more fire, excitement and power in his future film roles.

Martin Sheen

Actor

Born: RAMON ESTEVEZ, *Dayton, Oh., August 3, 1940*

There is an oddly defined symmetry to the career of American actor Martin Sheen, with the year 1980 serving as a dividing benchmark. During the 1970s Sheen

Martin Sheen: *Painted and primal in* Apocalypse Now

proved one of the keenest interpreters of youthful alienation and disillusion; the doomed anti-hero of *Badlands* (1973) and *Apocalypse Now* (1979) or the intrusive town creep of *The Little Girl Who Lives Down the Lane* (1976). Post-1980 he appeared transformed, seemingly overnight, into a mature, well-adjusted elder statesman, turning in a memorable impersonation of JFK in the 1983 TV mini-series *Kennedy* and playing the principled father to real-life son Charlie in *Wall Street* (1988). After early roles in TV, Sheen commanded attention as the runaway killer Kit Caruthers in Terrence Malick's mesmerizing *Badlands*. His complex performance – polite, deferential and utterly insane – created a memorable screen psycho, though his major role to date remains that of Captain Willard, the army assassin protagonist of Francis Coppola's *Apocalypse Now*. During the film's gruelling shoot, Sheen suffered a heart attack that

almost killed him – a Catholic priest was summoned to administer the last rites. Amid the grandstand turns of Robert Duvall and Marlon Brando, his playing is arguably the most resonant, serving as a horrified witness, a burnt-out mediator between the audience and the surreal wartime experiences the movie depicts. It's a mighty achievement, marking Sheen out as a fine film actor who rarely finds work that fully stretches his considerable talents.

Don Siegel

Director

Born: DONALD SIEGEL, *Chicago, Ill., October 26, 1912*
Died: *April 20, 1991*

In view of Siegel's tough and uncompromising movies, often based round loners or psychopaths and where nice guys usually get a raw deal, his background comes as a surprise. His father was a mandolin virtuoso, who brought his son up in England, where he studied at Jesus College, Cambridge, and RADA. He returned to America and joined Warner's film library in 1933, where he became their top montage compiler, particularly of newsreel action sequences in war films. He eventually got his directing opportunity, firstly with two shorts, *Star in the Night* (1945) and *Hitler Lives?* (1945), both Oscar-winners, and then his first feature *The Verdict* (1946). Films like *Riot in Cell Block 11* (1954), *Baby Face Nelson* (1957) and *The Killers* (1964) caused the French New Wave critics to hail Siegel as an important American *auteur*. *Invasion of the Body Snatchers* (1956) is a grippingly handled B-movie sci-fier, which became a cult classic. Siegel was directorial mentor to Clint Eastwood, whom he directed in *Coogan's Bluff* (1968); *Two Mules for Sister Sara* (1970) with Shirley MacLaine, an unusual story for Siegel whose movie world normally has little space for women;

The Beguiled (1971); *Dirty Harry* (1971), which made Eastwood a megastar and spawned a series; and the relentlessly tense *Escape from Alcatraz* (1979). Siegel also directed John Wayne's last film *The Shootist* (1976) where the star poignantly played a gunfighter dying of cancer.

Simone Signoret

Actress

Born: SIMONE HENRIETTE CHARLOTTE KAMINKER, *Wiesbaden, Germany, March 21, 1921*
Died: *September 30, 1985*

Signoret remains one of the most compelling of all French screen actresses. With her rich mouth and sensual features, she was once considered the most attractive women in cinema – a byword for magnetism and charisma. Her greatest roles came as prostitutes or obsessive lovers, making her an archetype of post-war French womanhood – passionate, sexual, determined yet vulnerable. She worked as a film extra and walk-on before gaining widespread acclaim as a whore in *Dédée d'Anvers* (1948). She was superb as a slut in *Manèges* (1949), a prostitute in *La Ronde* (1950), a courtesan in *Casque d'Or* (1951); and a murderer in *Les Diaboliques* (1954); before giving the finest performance of her career as a married woman in love with Lawrence Harvey in *Room at the Top* (1958). An extraordinarily powerful portrayal of passion and rejection, it won her a Best Actress Oscar and led to a number of Hollywood movies before fading looks pushed her into older character parts, notably as a bitter housewife in *Le Chat* (1971) and an aged prostitute in *La Vie Devant Soi* (1977). An actress of spellbinding power and authority, her later performances were just as notable as her early work, although it is as the sex symbol of the 1950s that she remains best remembered.

Alastair Sim

Actor
Born: *Edinburgh, Scotland,*
October 9, 1900
Died: *August 19, 1976*

With his weary, hangdog face, shifty eyes and rich Scottish accent, Sim is one of the eccentric glories of British film. His shady,

Alastair Sim: Eccentric glory of British cinema

manic, oddball personality exuded a likeable hint of corruption, and was equally effective in both comic and straight roles, although he is now best known for the string of hilarious British comedies he made through the 1940s and 1950s. Born in Edinburgh, he worked extensively on the London stage before making his film debut in *Riverside Murder* (1935). There followed a string of supporting character roles – *The Big Noise* (1936), *The Mysterious Mr Davis* (1936), *The Squeaker* (1937), *Hornleigh on Holiday* (1938) – but despite rave reviews it wasn't until Launder and Gilliat's *Green for Danger* (1946), as a detective, that he really hit the big time. Thereafter he starred in some of the all-time great British comedies, including Ealing's *Hue and Cry* (1947) as a befuddled scriptwriter, *The*

Happiest Days of Your Life (1950) as a put-upon headmaster, *Scrooge* (1951), *The Belles of St Trinians* (1954) as both the headmistress and her dodgy brother, and *School for Scoundrels* (1960). He also shone in serious roles in films like *Innocents in Paris* (1953) and *An Inspector Calls* (1954), but it is as the scowling, sly and avuncular comic genius that he will always be best remembered.

Jean Simmons

Actress
Born: *London, England,*
January 31, 1929

With her clipped, girlish voice, porcelain features and huge liquid eyes, Simmons is one of the most beautiful women to have graced the screen. More significantly, she is also a consummate actress, a mistress of timing and nuance who has never quite achieved the stardom or legend that her appearance and talent deserve. She became a teenage star as the wilfully gorgeous Estella in David Lean's *Great Expectations* (1946), was stirring as an Indian girl in *Black Narcissus* (1946) and stunning as Ophelia in Olivier's screen version of *Hamlet* (1948). This confirmed her as one of the leading players of her generation and catapulted her into the Hollywood spotlight, where she remained a major star for over 20 years. However, her talent was almost invariably wasted on a succession of dire projects, with producers more anxious to show off her looks than use her acting skill. *The Actress* (1953), *Guys and Dolls* (1955), *The Big Country* (1958), *Elmer Gantry* (1960), *Spartacus* (1960) and *Life at the Top* (1965) count among the few really good films in which she starred, although even in the turkeys she shone out as something special. She has continued to work sporadically in film and television, but has never quite managed to fulfil her early promise.

Michel Simon

Actor
Born: FRANÇOIS SIMON, *Geneva, Switzerland, April 9, 1895*
Died: *May 30, 1975*

Simon's corpulent frame and jowled face graced some of the masterpieces of French cinema, and disturbed audiences around the world for over 50 years. A complex, obsessive, anarchic spirit, he was at once repugnant and magnetic, a grotesque outsider who attracted horror and fascination in equal measure. Born in Switzerland, he worked as an acrobat and comedian before entering films in the 1920s. His first big role was as a valet in Renoir's *Tire-au-Flanc* (1928), and there followed a string of offbeat, anti-social and

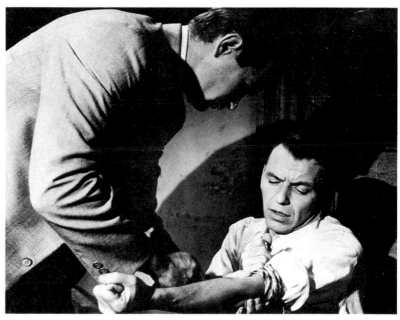

Frank Sinatra: Old Blue Eyes shoots to stardom

upsetting performances, starting with the ugly, middle-aged bank clerk who murders a prostitute and gets away with it in Renoir's *La Chienne* (1931). He was both hilarious and shocking as a truculent tramp in *Boudu Saved from Drowning* (1932); and was memorably villainous as the possessive guardian of a beautiful orphan in Carné's *Quai des Brumes* (1938). In between he gave one of the most ingratiatingly odd-ball of all

cinema performances, as the eccentric but lovable mate of a Seine river barge in *L'Atalante* (1934). He continued to turn in top-notch performances right up to the end of his career, and his last great role, as a sexually obsessed medieval baron in *Blanche* (1971), was a performance as dark, disturbing and powerful as any of those he had given 40 years previously.

Frank Sinatra

Singer, actor, director, producer
Born: *Hoboken, NJ, December 12, 1915*

Sinatra has always been a fighter and took pride in being the man who did it his way: if he hadn't fought, he'd never have had a screen career at all. His work as a crooner with the Harry James and Tommy Dorsey orchestras led to his huge "bobbysoxer" pop success in the early 1940s, bringing him a career in musicals like *Anchors Aweigh* (1945) and *On the Town* (1949). He was amiable and eager to please, but seemed a minor, transient talent. By 1952 he looked like yesterday's news, suffering from haemorrhaged vocal chords and let go by Universal

159

and Columbia Records. He had to beg for a supporting role in *From Here to Eternity* (1953), but it won him an Oscar and sudden recognition as an actor, and his comeback was sealed by his role as a drug addict in *The Man with the Golden Arm* (1955). He continued to score in musicals like *Guys and Dolls* (1955), *High Society* (1956) and *Pal Joey* (1957), but also indulged in popular froth like *The Tender Trap* (1955) and *Ocean's Eleven* (1960). In the 1960s he made a successful switch to action hero in *The Manchurian Candidate* (1962), *Von Ryan's Express* (1965) and *Tony Rome* (1967). It was a film career of great variety in a life of variety. And when it was time to quit the movies in 1970, Sinatra bowed out suddenly and gracefully, returning to the stage where he'd started.

Robert Siodmak

Director
Born: *Memphis, Tenn.,*
August 8, 1900
Died: *March 10, 1973*

Robert Siodmak's American birth was an accident of geography and he was brought up in Germany from early infancy. Failure of his business ventures in the 1920s forced him into the film industry as a title writer. He liked it so much he became an editor, and co-directed the feature documentary *People on Sunday* (1929), also a career launchpad for Billy Wilder as scriptwriter and Fred Zinnemann, assistant cinematographer. As a Jew, Siodmak was forced into exile by the rise of the Nazis, first to Paris and then to America, where he first directed B-pictures until he found his ground with a series of darkly menacing, suspenseful psychological thrillers. This eight-year period was the creative high point of Siodmak's career and proved him a true master of *film noir*. His first big success was *Phantom Lady* (1944). Other masterworks include *The Suspect* (1944) with Charles

Laughton as a sympathetic wife-killer; *Christmas Holiday* (1944) where he cast Deanna Durbin and Gene Kelly against type; *The Strange Affair of Uncle Harry* (1945), another anti-type casting – of George Sanders as the repressed central character; *The Spiral Staircase* (1945), a superb chiller about a serial killer whose victims are maimed women; *The Dark Mirror* (1946), a dual role for Olivia de Havilland as good and evil twins; and *The Killers* (1946), coaxing suppressed menace from Burt Lancaster and Ava Gardner as the *femme fatale*. Siodmak changed tack for *The Crimson Pirate* (1952), a wonderfully entertaining spoofy piece with Lancaster at his swashbuckling best. It promised to launch Siodmak into a new phase, but shortly afterwards he returned to Europe, where his work never again reached the heights of his American period.

Douglas Sirk

Director
Born: HANS DETLEF SIERCK, *Hamburg, Germany, April 26, 1900*
Died: *January 14, 1987*

Mr Melodrama directed some of the most popular pictures of the 1950s and made a star of Rock Hudson. Derided by critics of the time as a maker of "women's weepies", he has latterly been re-evaluated as an ironic expressionist, important for parodying the American dream from within mainstream Hollywood. He grew up in Denmark but returned to Germany to pursue a career in theatre. Successful as a stage director, he was subject to Nazi harassment and escaped into the film business. His debut, *It Was In April* (1935), was a great success but, fearing for his Jewish wife, he fled Germany for the US. He spent five years re-establishing himself before directing *Hitler's Madman* (1943), having changed his name to avoid anti-German prejudice.

His career only really took off with a move to Universal studios, where he fashioned a series of melodramas that includes *Magnificent Obsession* (1954), *All That Heaven Allows* and *Written on the Wind* (both 1956). His last film, *Imitation of Life* (1959), dealing with the consequences of a black girl trying to pass as white for social acceptance, is a classic of its genre, and was a huge hit for Universal. Sick of health and sick of Hollywood, Sirk retired to Europe and lived to witness reappraisal of his over-the-top movies whose artificiality some consider to be a sophisticated Brechtian distancing technique. Revisionist film criticism at its best.

Alf Sjöberg

Director
Born: *Stockholm, Sweden,*
June 21, 1903
Died: *April 17, 1980*

Little-known Alf Sjöberg rates his place in the world cinema pantheon as Sweden's most important director before the advent of Ingmar Bergman, who started his own career as one of Sjöberg's scriptwriters. Sjöberg trained as an actor, graduating to directing in 1927. Seeing one of Eisenstein's films turned his attention to cinema, and he wrote and directed *The Strongest* (1929), a powerful silent documentary-style drama about seal hunters. The advent of sound disillusioned him with the cinema and he returned to the theatre for the next ten years, as head of the Royal Dramatic Theatre and one of Sweden's leading directors. Meanwhile Swedish cinema remained dormant until Sjöberg started making films again, such as the pacifist story *They Staked Their Lives* (1940) and his internationally successful drama *Torment* (1944), Bergman's first screenplay, which starred Mai Zetterling, herself a future director. Much of Sjöberg's film work was adapted from theatre and literary works.

His version of Strindberg's *Miss Julie* (1951) was joint winner of the Grand Prize at that year's Cannes Film Festival and he later adapted *The Father* (1969), another famous play by the same writer, for the cinema. Other noteworthy films include *The Road to Heaven* (1942) and *Only a Mother* (1949) .

Victor Sjöström

Director, actor
Born: *Silbodal, Sweden,*
September 20, 1879, (aka VICTOR SEASTROM)
Died: *January 3, 1960*

Although Victor Sjöström was one of the founding fathers of Swedish cinema and an undoubted master of silent film-making, it is doubtful if his films would now be known outside his native land had it not been for the seven years he spent in Hollywood. As a child Sjöström moved to America with his family. Hating his tyrannical father, he returned to Sweden after his mother's death and became an actor and director. He started directing films in 1913, soon establishing a reputation with European intellectuals, who regarded *Thy Soul Shall Bear Witness* (1920) as a masterpiece. A slump in Swedish film production sent him to America to study production methods there. He quickly adapted to the new milieu of sets and studios, as opposed to location shooting of the Swedish landscape which had been an important element of his films back home, and made *He Who Gets Slapped* (1924), a showcase for Lon Chaney's talents with a good role for MGM's new discovery, Norma Shearer. He teamed them again in a Swedish story, *The Tower of Lies* (1925), then made two films with Lillian Gish: *The Scarlet Letter* (1926) and his American masterwork *The Wind* (1928), a tale of mental disintegration and one of Gish's best performances. He also directed Garbo as *The Divine Woman* (1928). Sjöström lost interest in Hollywood with the advent of sound. He returned home to share his updated technical knowledge and started acting again. His last performance was the poignant leading role of the old scholar in Bergman's *Wild Strawberries* (1957).

Christian Slater

Actor

Born: *New York, NY, April 18, 1969*

The hip, laidback, vulpine young star, clearly under the influence of Jack Nicholson, whom he seems to have used as a role model since his performance in the 1989 hit *Heathers*, has been in movies since the age of 14. Slater made his debut in the Richard Thomas TV movie *Living Proof: The Hank Williams Jr Story* (1983), but he made his breakthrough oddly cast as a medieval monk in *The Name of the Rose* (1986). He gained his first cinema lead in the teenage skateboarding thriller *Gleaming the Cube* (1989), in which he gleamed but the film fizzled. Then it was the cult black comedy *Heathers* cast opposite Winona Ryder that established his cool image and his box-office potential. He turned his role as an underground high school DJ in *Pump Up the Volume* (1990) into a personal *tour de force* and hit the Hollywood mainstream as a gunslinger in *Young Guns II* (1990). He was miscast as a Brooklyn-accented Will Scarlett in *Robin Hood: Prince of Thieves* (1991), he also floundered in *Mobsters* (1991), a misguided attempt at a gangster film for teenyboppers, while *Kuffs* (1992) was an equally misjudged teen cop film. He took two big chances in 1993 trying to redefine his image: on the one hand with the sickly love story *Untamed Heart* and on the other the ultra-violent *True Romance*. He emerged with credit from both and managed not to be swamped by his scene-stealing co-stars. No longer

a teen heart-throb, Slater is still in search of a vehicle that will give him adult box-office appeal.

Dame Maggie Smith

Actress

Born: *Ilford, England, December 28, 1934*

With her pinched face, scatty personality and clipped accent, Maggie Smith is one of the more distinguished of British screen comediennes. She's also one of the most successful, having won Academy Awards both as Best Actress (1969's *The Prime of Miss Jean Brodie*) and Best Supporting Actress (1978's *California Suite*), and might have reached even greater heights had she not preferred to concentrate on stage work. Having performed in comic revue, she first made her mark as a screen actress playing Richard Burton's mousy, scene-stealing secretary in *The V.I.P.s* (1963). There followed a number of notable characterizations – as a lodger in *The Pumpkin Eater* (1964); Desdemona in *Othello* (1965); and a secretary again in *The Honey Pot* (1967) – before she gained international acclaim as an oddball Scottish schoolteacher in *The Prime of Miss Jean Brodie*. She was uproariously funny as a bitchy, hard-drinking actress in *California Suite*, and has continued to turn in memorable performances ever since, particularly as a priggish

Maggie Smith: *Scatty, scene-stealing comedienne*

provincial snob in *A Private Function* (1985), a shy Irish spinster in *The Lonely Passion of Judith Hearne* (1987), and a mother superior in *Sister Act* (1992). Peter Ustinov once said of Smith: "I'd really have to search my memory to find any actress to equal her; and after a long time I'd probably have to give up."

Sissy Spacek

Actress

Born: MARY ELIZABETH SPACEK, *Quitman, Tex., December 25, 1949*

Texas small-town girl Sissy Spacek moved to New York after the death of her beloved brother to stay with her cousin, actor Rip

Sissy Spacek: *Wide-eyed All-American*

Torn, and his wife Geraldine Page, who got her a walk-on in Warhol's *Trash* (1970). After a role in *Prime Cut* (1972) Spacek made real impact in *Badlands* (1973), where her childlike looks enabled her at 23 to play the disturbed 15-year-old heroine. Brian De Palma cast her in another disturbed teen role, *Carrie* (1976), as the telekinetic victim wreaking lethal revenge on her tormentors. She was a kooky housewife in *Welcome to L.A.* (1976), one of Robert Altman's *Three Women* (1977) and the female pivot of the triangular relationship between beat writer Jack Kerouac and Carolyn and Neal Cassidy in

Heart Beat (1979). In *Coal Miner's Daughter* (1980) she illuminated the working-class cultural roots of country music as Loretta Lynn, proving she could sing and also winning an Oscar. She gave a strong performance in the Costa-Gavras political thriller *Missing* (1982) as Jack Lemmon's daughter-in-law, then co-starred with Mel Gibson in *The River* (1984), one of a trio of films at the time extolling the virtues and hardships of farming life. She played one of three Mississippi sisters with broken dreams in Bruce Beresford's *Crimes of the Heart* (1986) but many of her subsequent films, including those made with her husband, production designer-turned-director Jack Fisk, had little impact. Not true though of Oliver Stone's *JFK* (1991), in which she shone out as investigator Kevin Costner's wife.

Steven Spielberg

Director, producer

Born: *Cincinnati, Oh., December 18, 1947*

Spielberg is not only cinema's greatest storyteller but also its most commercially successful director. His dinosaur romp *Jurassic Park* (1993) became the biggest-grossing film of all time, seizing the top slot from another Spielberg work, *E.T. The Extra-Terrestrial* (1982). More than any other director, he has the ability to connect with his audience, instinctively understanding their need not merely for thrilling storylines, but for something magical and mysterious. He experimented with film from an early age, and first came to note with his TV movie *Duel* (1971), and hit the big time with the shark horror flick *Jaws* (1975). Already the key elements of the Spielberg *oeuvre* were in place – a simple story masterfully told; giant measures of suspense, sentiment, and excitement; and, above all, a fascination with the unknown. He thereafter used

Steven Spielberg (middle): *Storytelling magic*

them to fashion some of the most enjoyable and popular movies of all time: *Close Encounters of the Third Kind* (1977), *Raiders of the Lost Ark* (1981) and *Indiana Jones and the Last Crusade* (1989). His three-and-a-half hour Holocaust epic *Schindler's List* (1993) saw him displaying a new maturity. A cinematic masterpiece, it won him a long-overdue Oscar for Best Director and marked him out as one of the movie greats.

Sylvester Stallone

Actor, director, writer
Born: *New York, NY, July 6, 1946*

Sly Stallone is something of a throwback to the movie stars of Hollywood's Golden Age. He's a larger than life figure, a self-styled Renaissance man – scriptwriter, director, restaurateur (with the much-hyped *Planet Hollywood*), abstract artist and, occasionally, actor. Stallone's superstar status rests on the brawny back of two immortal action heroes, Rocky Balboa and Vietnam vet John Rambo. His five *Rocky* films, which started as a labour-of-love, follow the fortunes of a lion-hearted heavyweight boxer and, in their better moments (1976's Oscar-winning *Rocky* in particular), the movies offer honest, involving escapism in the classic Hollywood fashion. More dubious were the three *Rambo* pictures (1982, 1985 and 1988) – crass, jingoistic comic-book outings that

many felt epitomized the worst aspects of Reagan's America. Concerned with being stuck with Rambo's wild-eyed, shaggy-mopped image, Stallone celebrated the new decade by donning spectacles and Armani for 1990 cop-caper *Tango & Cash*. But the change was only cosmetic –

Sylvester Stallone: Abstract artist with an Uzi

Stallone still blew the baddies away with the same ferocity of old. A brave foray into comedy began nicely with John Landis's *Oscar* (1991) before floundering with the execrable *Stop! or My Mom Will Shoot* (1992), sending Sly hurrying back to more familiar action movie territory. But in the mid-1990s, Stallone seems at a career crossroads, unsure whether he's an actor or a personality, touring the celebrity chat-show circuit to plug his Hollywood hamburgers.

Terence Stamp

Actor, author
Born: *London, England, July 23, 1940*

While still at drama school, East End cockney Terence Stamp was chosen by Peter Ustinov to play the angelic cabin boy *Billy Budd* (1962). He scored a great success as the loner who kidnaps the girl with whom he is obsessed in William Wyler's *The Collector* (1965) and his startling good looks and pale blue eyes brought him

parts as juvenile leads and juvenile delinquents: the heroine's cockney sidekick in Losey's comic caper *Modesty Blaise* (1966); Julie Christie's dashing soldier lover in Schlesinger's lush *Far From the Madding Crowd* (1967); and a petty crook in *Poor Cow* (1967). He was very much part of the "swinging London" scene, sharing a flat for a while with Michael Caine, and was the long-time boyfriend of top model Jean Shrimpton. He also worked for top continental directors such as Pasolini (1968's *Theorem*) and Fellini (1968's *Extraordinary Stories*). In the 1970s he took time out to travel in the East, returning to appear in Peter Brook's film about an Eastern mystic, *Meetings with Remarkable Men* (1979), and in contrast played the arch-villain from Krypton in *Superman II* (1980). He seized the opportunities of his leading role as the target for *The Hit* (1984) in Stephen Frears's offbeat British thriller and has since played a selection of English villains and other untrustworthy types in American films, including *Wall Street* (1987), *Young Guns* (1988) and *The Real McCoy* (1993), and startled audiences by playing a transsexual in the delightfully funny/sad Australian road movie *The Adventures of Priscilla, Queen of the Desert* (1994). Stamp has published three volumes of autobiography and a novel.

Harry Dean Stanton

Actor
Born: *West Irvine, Ky., July 14, 1926*

Stanton is particularly powerful when playing bad guys and crazies, but equally impressive at the other end of the spectrum in kindly, sympathetic or fatherly characters. This hard-working support actor was propelled into the ranks of cult stardom through a string of extraordinary movies, starting in the 1970s with *Alien* (1979) and continuing to the pre-

sent day. Stanton was already making films back in the late 1950s with such westerns as *Dragoon Wells Massacre* and *Tomahawk Trail* (both 1957). Over the years the parts got bigger and the films got better and he graced such pictures as *How the West Was Won* (1962), *Cool Hand Luke* (1967), *Dillinger* (1973), *Farewell My Lovely* (1975) and *The Missouri Breaks* (1976). But it was in John Huston's religious drama *Wise Blood* and Ridley Scott's sci-fi classic *Alien*, both made in 1979, that cinemagoers first really noticed his name. Thereafter it was a name to conjure with and he was in the Joseph Wambaugh thriller *The Black Marble* (1980), Goldie Hawn's comedy *Private Benjamin* (1980) and Francis Coppola's musical *One from the Heart* (1982). Truly vintage Stanton followed with his role as Emilio Estevez's mentor in Alex Cox's cult item *Repo Man* (1984), and his superb performance as the abandoned husband in Wim Wenders's poignant quest for lost love *Paris, Texas* (1984), films that etched him indelibly into filmgoers' memories.

Barbara Stanwyck

Actress
Born: RUBY STEVENS, *Brooklyn, NY, July 16, 1907*
Died: *January 20, 1990*

Perhaps Stanwyck was never a brilliant actress like Hepburn, a dazzling beauty like Dietrich, or a great box-office hit like Monroe, but she was the most thorough professional, greatly admired by the film industry, critics and public alike. Though she shared with Davis and Crawford the ability to appear strong, cynical and down-to-earth, for sheer likeability she beat them hands down. For 60 years Stanwyck was always good value and never gave a poor performance. A protégée of directors Frank Capra and William Wellman, she established herself in the early 1930s in a wide variety of parts, but she became classified as the spirited, spunky dame who was more than the equal of any guy. She hit it rich in the 1940s, both professionally with a great run of hits like *The Lady Eve* (1941), *Ball of Fire* (1941) and *Double*

Barbara Stanwyck: *Barbed-witted beauty*

Indemnity (1944), and materially (she was America's top-salaried woman in 1944). She moved successfully between thrillers, comedies and westerns like *Annie Oakley* (1935), but one of her best-loved films is the classic woman's weepie *Stella Dallas* (1937). When she quit the movies in 1965, her greatest fame was ironically yet to come. The TV series *The Barbara Stanwyck Show* (1960–61) and her western show *The Big Valley* (1965–68) were both huge hits and Emmy-winners for her, and she was a sensation again in the 1980s in her Emmy-winning *The Thorn Birds* (1983) and *The Colbys* (1985–86).

Rod Steiger

Actor
Born: RODNEY STEPHEN STEIGER, *Westhampton, NY, April 14, 1925*

Stocky, sad-eyed Rod Steiger was one of the 1950s' foremost method actors. While often accused of overacting, he simmers brilliantly, usually as a villain about to explode off the deep end. Steiger's parents were a song-and-dance partnership who split up shortly

after he was born, and he grew up in Newark, New Jersey. After quitting school for the Navy, he was a civil service clerk before studying theatre at the Actors' Studio in New York. From Broadway he moved into television, but apart from his film debut, a small part in *Teresa* (1951), audiences had to wait until *On the Waterfront* (1954), where he was Oscar-nominated for supporting Brando, holding his own in the famous "I coulda been a contender," exchange. He sang for his supper in *Oklahoma!* (1955) but, apart from *Al Capone* (1959), *The Longest Day* (1962) and *Dr Zhivago* (1965), worked mainly in Europe until, outstanding as a concentration camp survivor in *The Pawnbroker* (1965), he won another Oscar nomination. Academy success finally came for his redneck sheriff tormenting Sidney Poitier *In The Heat of the Night* (1967). He impersonated Napoleon (*Waterloo*, 1971), Mussolini (*The Last Four Days*, 1974), and W. C. Fields (*W. C. Fields And Me*, 1976), but has since been underused. Seemingly out of place in Hollywood's glitz, he continues to love the work and enjoyed a cameo role in *The Player* (1992).

George Stevens

Director, writer
Born: *Oakland, Calif., December 18, 1904*
Died: *March 8, 1975*

An obsessive perfectionist and one of the all-time great director-producers, Stevens was a unique creative force in cinema for over 40 years, winning two Best Director Oscars (for *A Place in the Sun*, 1951, and *Giant*, 1956) and an Irving Thalberg Award for services to film production. Having worked as an actor and cameraman, he made his directorial debut with the comedy *The Cohens and Kellys in Trouble* (1933), and scored his first success with the Katharine

Hepburn vehicle *Alice Adams* (1935). There followed a series of well-made, lightweight hits, *Annie Oakley* (1935); *Swing Time* (1936); *Vivacious Lady* (1938 – also his first film as a producer); *The More The Merrier* (1943) – before he spent three years as a cameraman during World War Two. His post-war work was less populist but more dramatic than the earlier features, with films such as *I Remember Mama* (1948), *A Place in the Sun* (1951), *Shane* (1953) and *Giant* (1956) bringing a new darkness and intensity to his directorial style. Despite the quality of these films, his extravagant perfectionism became increasingly unfashionable. *The Diary of Anne Frank* (1959) was a minor masterpiece, but his biblical epic *The Greatest Story Ever Told* (1965) was a sprawling, outdated dinosaur of a movie, and thereafter he only made one more film (1970's underrated *The Only Game in Town*) before his death in 1975.

James Stewart

Actor, author, cowboy
Born: *Indiana, Pa., May 20, 1908*

The profoundly loved American institution Stewart is admired the world over for his slow-on-the-drawl delivery, upright demeanour and sheer good nature. Now that he's a national monument, he's underrated as an actor, able to move suddenly from upstanding hero to reveal reserves of toughness or even nastiness. In 1935 gossip columnist Hedda Hopper recommended Stewart for a screen test, landing him an MGM contract, but they stuck the non-singer in musicals like *Born to Dance* (1936) and cast him as the killer in *After the Thin Man* (1936). His best early successes were all for other studios – Capra's *You Can't Take It with You* (1938), *Mr Smith Goes to Washington* (1939) and *Destry Rides Again* (1939). Back at MGM, he had hits with Lubitsch's *The Shop around the*

Corner (1940) and Borzage's *The Mortal Storm* (1940), then won an Oscar for *The Philadelphia Story* (1940). After war service he returned for Capra's *It's a Wonderful Life* (1946), a national institution itself. He took to the saddle in middle age to revive a flagging career with a series of classic westerns, like *Winchester '73* (1950), *Broken Arrow* (1950) and *The Man from Laramie* (1955), revealing a new tough Stewart. His quartet of flawed heroes for Hitchcock are other high spots, especially *Rear Window* (1954) and *Vertigo* (1958), and he'll be remem-

James Stewart: *Slow-on-the-drawl*

bered too for his warmhearted *The Glenn Miller Story* (1954) and as the rabbitman in *Harvey* (1950), which he re-created on the London stage in the 1970s.

Dean Stockwell

Actor
Born: *Hollywood, Calif., March 5, 1936*

Stockwell is the exception that proved the rule – the child star who grew up to have an adult career of great longevity, consistently in demand over half a century. He started out as a child actor with an MGM contract at the age of nine, making his first film, *Anchors Aweigh* in 1945, dancing with Gene Kelly, but his most memorable early appearances were in *The Green Years* (1946),

163

Gentleman's Agreement (1948) and particularly Joseph Losey's prejudice parable *The Boy with Green Hair* (1948) where he was singled out and rejected because he looked different. *Kim* (1950) and *Cattle Drive* (1951) signalled the end of his childhood career. But after five years he returned as a mature, handsome, though still sensitive young man in such films as Richard Fleischer's *Compulsion* (1959), the story of the Leopold-Loeb "killing for kicks" murders, as a British miner's son in a version of D. H. Lawrence's *Sons and Lovers* (1960) and in *Long Day's Journey into Night* (1962) with Hepburn and Ralph Richardson. In the late 1960s he hit the exploiter trail with films such as *Psych-Out* (1968) and *The Dunwich Horror* (1970), and in the 1970s he appeared in cult films like Dennis Hopper's *The Last Movie* (1971) and *Werewolf of Washington* (1973). Appearances in key films like *Paris, Texas* (1984), *Dune* (1984), *Blue Velvet* (1986), Coppola's *Gardens of Stone* (1987) and particularly his Oscar-nominated performance in Demme's *Married to the Mob* (1988) secured him a niche as a key star character actor. His TV series *Quantum Leap*. which began in 1989, ensures that he remains a familiar and welcome screen presence throughout the world.

Oliver Stone

Director, writer, producer
Born: *New York, NY, September 15, 1946*

In less than 10 years Oliver Stone turned himself into one of Hollywood's most important directors for his uncompromising and often controversial treatment of social and political themes in films which he writes or co-writes himself. He first made his name as the Oscar-winning writer of *Midnight Express* (1978), followed by *Conan the Barbarian* (1982), *Scarface* (1983) and *Year of the*

Dragon (1985). His first major film as director was the coruscating *Salvador* (1986), but the film that made his name was the multi-Oscared *Platoon* (1986), a stark treatment of the Vietnam War, based on his own experience there. It became the first of a Vietnam trilogy. He won another Oscar for *Born on the Fourth of July* (1989), in which Tom Cruise gives one of his best performances as paraplegic Vietnam veteran Ron Kovac. But he had a flop with his soft-focus treatment of Le Ly Hayslip's autobiography, *Heaven and Earth* (1993). He examined the moral corruption of insider traders in *Wall Street* (1987); turned Eric Bogosian's one-man play *Talk Radio* (1988) into a hard-hitting film but was psychedelically soft on the Jim Morrison story in *The Doors* (1991). Not an accusation you could level against *JFK* (1991), a disturbing documentary-style drama about the conspiracy theory surrounding Kennedy's assassination, nor at 1994's *Natural Born Killers*. This black satire on media promotion of violent crime caused massive controversy because of its own graphic violence. Stone also produced *Reversal of Fortune* (1990), *South Central* (1992) and television's *Wild Palms* (1993).

Sharon Stone

Actress
Born: *Meadsville, Pa., March 10, 1957*

The first-ever actress to undress for *Playboy* as a career move went largely unnoticed in 18 duff movies before becoming an "overnight sensation" for her psycho-sexual role in *Basic Instinct* (1992). Like Marilyn Monroe, the green-eyed blonde with drop-dead sex appeal began as a small-town beauty queen, but after giving up a Fine Arts degree, Stone moved out to become a successful model. Woody Allen picked her from a queue of extras to play his fantasy girl in *Stardust Memories* (1980), but she went on to worse

things, with *Irreconcilable Differences* (1984), *King Solomon's Mines* (1985) and *Police Academy 4* (1987). She finally caught the eye as Arnold Schwarzenegger's robo-wife in *Total Recall* (1990), raising cheers when she was spectacularly blown into marital oblivion. *Basic Instinct* (1992) shot Stone into the Hollywood Hall of Infamy with the most famous uncrossing of the legs ever. Stone's knickerless minute was the 1990s' equivalent of Monroe's air-ventilated dress, and generated fevered publicity. Increasing her fee tenfold for *Sliver* (1993), she pronounced, "If you have a vagina and a point of view in Hollywood, that's a dangerous combination" but, despite a look-no-hands solo love scene, the expected success of the film never materialized. *Intersection* (1994) was another disappointment. Stone has yet to prove whether she's one of a new powerful breed of actress, or just a great talker with a gift for self-publicity.

Meryl Streep

Actress
Born: MARY LOUISE STREEP, *Summit, NJ, June 22, 1949*

As *Silkwood* co-star Cher once famously remarked, "Meryl Streep is an acting machine in the same way that a shark is a killing machine." Poised and striking, she has been hailed as America's greatest actress, though detractors argue that there is something too mannered and clinical about her style. Streep first came to public notice with the marathon TV mini-series *Holocaust,* moving on to impress in an underwritten role in Michael Cimino's Vietnam odyssey *The Deer Hunter* (1978). She won an Oscar for her portrayal of Dustin Hoffman's icy ex-wife in *Kramer vs Kramer* (1979) and another as the fey, windswept, enigmatic *French Lieutenant's Woman* (1981). Throughout the early to mid-1980s she was regarded as her country's

principal dramatic lead, the heartfelt heroine of Alan Pakula's old-style epic *Sophie's Choice* (1982) and the African adventuress romanced by Robert Redford in *Out of Africa* (1986). "For a while there it was either me or the Ayatollah on the covers of national magazines," she wryly observed. "Major hype." Streep's continuing high standing is thanks both to talent and an exquisite career surefootedness. She affected a broad Aussie twang for the fact-based *A Cry in the Dark* (1988), contributed a bravura bag-lady impersonation to 1987's *Ironweed* and in the 1990s edged more towards comedy with *Postcards From the Edge* (1990) and Robert Zemeckis's flashy *Death Becomes Her* (1992).

Barbra Streisand

Actress, singer, producer, director, writer
Born: BARBARA JOAN STREISAND, *Brooklyn, NY., April 24, 1942*

It is said that Streisand's accomplishment as a singer, comedienne and dramatic actress is offset by a reliance on technique rather than feeling. Her looks have always been ridiculed and her professional conduct attacked, perhaps because her tireless quest for perfection has led her to interfere in the making of movies, upsetting several of her co-stars. The real

Barbra Streisand: *Spells 'Star'*

complaint against Streisand should be that she has neglected the cinema. There have been only 15 films in a quarter century, and just four since 1980. Sadly her forte, musicals, are out of fashion. Her first movie *Funny Girl* (1968), for which she won an Oscar re-creating her Broadway and London stage success, and *A Star Is Born* (1976) were huge hits, but a cherished personal project like *Yentl* (1983) was touch and go and so was the seemingly safe, all-time great *Hello Dolly* (1969), which she made too young. She's also a natural comedienne and comedies are always in vogue: *What's Up Doc?* (1972), *For Pete's Sake* (1974) and *The Owl and the Pussycat* (1970) were all funny and popular. But she has a hankering to be a serious actress with a penchant for big dramatic parts. *The Way We Were* (1973), *Nuts* (1987) and *The Prince of Tides* (1991) all bit off important themes and gave her room to emote. They're just the kind of pictures this old-style great star should be making.

Preston Sturges

Director, writer
Born: EDMUND PRESTON BIDEN, *Chicago, Ill., August 29, 1898*
Died: *August 6, 1959*

For a short time in the early 1940s the urbane, witty Sturges reigned supreme as Hollywood's favourite son, the brains behind eight of filmdom's greatest, boldest satirical comedies, all made between 1940 and 1945. Aged 16 he took charge of his parents' cosmetics company, beginning a long series of inventions with kiss-proof lipstick. In 1927, recovering from an appendix operation, he adapted a comic book for the stage. Broadway success followed and Paramount hired him as a writer. His first hit, *The Power and the Glory* (1933), was a precursor to *Citizen Kane* (1941), but his other scripts were in the light-hearted screwball style he was to

make his own. His longed-for breakthrough as a director came in 1940, adapting his own script *The Great McGinty* for a $10 fee. Sturges won an Oscar for it, setting off a giddying run of great critical and popular successes, including *The Lady Eve* (1941), *Sullivan's Travels* (1951), *The Palm Beach Story* (1942), *The Miracle of Morgan's Creek* (1944) and *Hail the Conquering Hero* (1944). These remain among comedy classics of the cinema. But the fall of this master film-maker was as sudden as his rise. After he parted company with Paramount in the mid-1940s, he fatefully hitched his wagon to producer Howard Hughes, which proved a disastrous career decision. Sturges's subsequent works were weary, leaden box-office failures and by 1950 he was finished. He went into exile in France and died in relative poverty in 1959.

Margaret Sullavan

Actress
Born: *Norfolk, Va., May 16, 1911*
Died: *January 1, 1960*

Sullavan boasted a magnetic screen presence, with huge eyes and light husky voice, but she only made a handful of films in a career spanning some 17 years. Her performances, however, were always of the highest quality and, had she not preferred theatre to film acting, she might well have become one of the great Hollywood stars. Such was the impact of her screen debut in the sentimental *Only Yesterday* (1933) that Universal signed her to an immediate contract, leading to a string of powerhouse performances through the 1930s. She was notable in a variety of roles – as a pregnant wife in *Little Man What Now?* (1934), a simple philanthropist in *The Good Fairy* (1935), a truculent film star in *The Moon's Our Home* (1936), a tubercular wife in Frank Borzage's *Three Comrades* (1938) and espe-

cially as a lovelorn shop assistant wrangling with James Stewart in Ernst Lubitsch's charming comedy *The Shop Around the Corner* (1940). In the 1940s she suffered increasing emotional problems and her career faltered, but she was still impressive in the vintage weepie *Back Street* (1941) and the nurses' war saga *Cry Havoc* (1943). Thereafter she made only one more film – *No Sad Songs for Me* (1950) – and died from a barbiturate overdose 10 years later.

Donald Sutherland

Actor
Born: *St John, Canada, July 17, 1934*

Tall and gaunt, with large lips and bulging eyes, Donald Sutherland has always looked vaguely unhinged, imbuing his roles with an unpredictable, odd-ball quality that made him one of the most eye-catching performers of his generation. He worked in radio before making his screen debut in *Castle of the Living Dead* (1964). He thereafter had a number of smallish supporting roles – notably as a psychopath in *The Dirty Dozen* (1967) – before gaining widespread acclaim as army surgeon Hawkeye in Altman's zany black comedy *M*A*S*H* (1970). His intelligent, wacky portrayal was both amusing and disturbing, and he has played variations on it ever since, notably as a detective in *Klute* (1971), a tormented father in *Don't Look Now* (1973), a gauche misfit in *The Day of the Locust* (1975), and the head of a dysfunctional family in *Ordinary People* (1980). He has concentrated increasingly on character roles in high-quality films – *Max Dugan Returns* (1983); *JFK* (1991); *Backdraft* (1991) – although he was mesmerizing as the lead in the anti-apartheid feature *A Dry White Season* (1989). Sutherland has produced a host of unusual performances over the last two

decades and, however small the role, never fails to lend an intriguing edge of uncertainty to all his movie projects.

Gloria Swanson

Actress, producer
Born: GLORIA JOSEPHINE MAE SWENSON (*aka* GLORIA MAE), *Chicago, Ill., March 27, 1897*
Died: *April 4, 1983*

One of the great legendary silent film stars, Swanson began filming in 1913 in her Chicago home town, marrying her co-player Wallace Beery in 1916. They went to Hollywood and starred in a run of Mack Sennett romantic comedies, but when Swanson switched to Paramount she became a star in Cecil B. DeMille's adult screwball comedies. Around the middle 1920s she was a mega-star and in 1927 her banker (as well as her lover) Joseph Kennedy backed her as a producer, leading to her

Gloria Swanson: Ready for her close-up

Oscar-nominated films *Sadie Thompson* (1928) and *The Trespasser* (1929). But Erich von Stroheim's outrageously expensive folly *Queen Kelly* (1928) sent her company on the rocks, though she regained control of the movie and it was released in a heavily truncated form. She made only a partially successful adaptation to sound and retired in 1934, but staged a number of comebacks, including most spectacularly her legendary Oscar-nominated performance as a dotty silent screen star uncannily mirroring her own persona in Billy Wilder's ghoulish melodrama *Sunset Blvd* (1950), a great popular hit and now a classic, with a showy role for her one-time nemesis von Stroheim and a cameo by her old director DeMille. "I'm ready for my close-up now, Mr DeMille," says the wild-eyed star and descends the staircase towards the camera. Fittingly, in her last film, *Airport 75* (1974), she played her finest role of all – herself.

Patrick Swayze

Actor, dancer
Born: *Houston, Tex., August 18, 1954*

Ex-ballet dancer Swayze starred in the Broadway production of *Grease*, made his film debut in *Skatetown U.S.A.* (1979) and hit the big-time in Coppola's *The Outsiders* (1983), as a (senior) member of the "Brat Pack". A splashy start, but Swayze, like the others, had to struggle to maintain career momentum, making movies like *Uncommon Valor* (1983), *Red Dawn* (1984) and *Youngblood* (1986). One film turned him into a major attraction: the 1987 box-office surprise, semi-musical *Dirty Dancing*, where his butt-wiggling performance set many a heart fluttering. Even though he was barely established as a romantic lead, he then did a couple of ill-advised actioners, *Next of Kin* and *Road House* (both 1989), but *Ghost* (1990) came along and recaptured his faltering audience with its mix of comedy, drama and supernatural romance. Swayze was ideal as a recent ghost trying to help his lover Demi Moore out of the clutches of the villains, and the movie grossed over $200 million in America alone. Swayze was hot but still determined to have an action hit and he struck lucky playing against type as the bad guy opposite Keanu Reeves in the hit *Point Break* (1991). The ambitious *City of Joy* (1992) and the low-aiming

Fatherhood (1993) showed how quickly a career could get back into trouble, but as Swayze enters his 40s he retains his box-office potential – provided he continues to find the right vehicles.

Quentin Tarantino

Director, writer, actor
Born: *Knoxville, Tenn., March 27, 1963*

Taking junk culture into the art-house, Tarantino burst into the big time with his stylishly violent directorial debut, *Reservoir Dogs* (1992), and profited from being tagged "a Scorsese for the 90s". Born to a 16-year-old mother, he never met his father and claims an education on comic books, movies, television – and proud of it. He tried to make it first as an actor and then a screenwriter, playing

Quentin Tarantino: *Junk culture's wonderkid guru*

an Elvis impersonator in TV's *The Golden Girls*, and alongside Woody Allen in Jean-Luc Godard's *King Lear* (1987). Writing while working in a video rental store, he was preparing to shoot his sixth script, *Reservoir Dogs*, on a $10,000 guerrilla-movie budget, when actor Harvey Keitel stepped in to executive produce it, elevating it to a $1.5m debut. Critical opinion was divided between masterwork, or violent trash. Either interpretation brought the punters in and suddenly Tarantino was hot property. He declined to direct his earlier

rejected scripts, instead selling the pistol-packing Romeo and Juliet road movie, *True Romance* (1993), to Tony Scott, and *Natural Born Killers* (1993) to Oliver Stone. His second attempt at directing, the contemporary *film noir*, *Pulp Fiction* (1994), won him the Palme d'Or at Cannes, and the future looks bright for Tarantino, if his designer violence tag doesn't become too much of a hindrance.

Andrei Tarkovsky

Director, writer
Born: *Laovrazhe, USSR, April 4, 1932*
Died: *December 29, 1986*

Along with Eisenstein and Paradjanov the most important Russian film-maker so far, Tarkovsky made his debut in 1962 with *Ivan's Childhood*, the story of a Russian boy avenging the death of his parents at the hands of the Nazis, proclaimed the Venice Film Festival's Best Film. *Andrei Rublev*, the spiritual biopic of the 15th-century icon painter, followed in 1966, but it brought problems with the Soviet authorities for its barely veiled comment on the situation of Soviet artists. Officially suppressed until 1971, it was hailed as a masterwork when it was finally screened outside Russia. He didn't work again until *Solaris* (1972), proclaimed as Russia's answer to *2001*, and there was another long gap before the film widely regarded as his political and social masterpiece, *Mirror* (1974); the story of a Russian poet at odds with himself, his family and his country. Tarkovsky had to move outside Russia to work in the 1980s, filming the wistful and Bergmanesque *Nostalgia* (1983) in Italy. In 1985 he went to Sweden to make his final and greatest work *The Sacrifice* (1986) with some of Ingmar Bergman's famous collaborators, including star Erland Josephson and world-famous director of photography Sven Nykvist. This story of an artist

saving the world whose values he has rejected is a striking distillation of his personal and artistic vision. He died of lung cancer in Paris aged 54 in the year *The Sacrifice* won the Cannes Special Jury prize. A film-maker who has stretched the limits of the medium, a deeply poetic visionary and a vocally spiritual humanist, Tarkovsky is one of the important voices of the cinema's first century.

Jacques Tati

Director, actor, writer
Born: JΛCQUES TATISCHEFF, *Le Pecq, France, October 9, 1908*
Died: *November 5, 1982*

Tall, gangling and stork-like, Tati is one of cinema's all-time great comedians. The direct heir to Chaplin and Keaton, he worked exclusively in the silent tradition, eschewing dialogue in favour of virtuoso slapstick clowning; and although he made only five features in a 35-year career, each was, in its own way, an unparalleled comic treasure. He worked as a mime artist before moving into films in the 1930s with a series of highly imaginative comic shorts. *L'École de Facteurs* (1947) – the story of a bewildered postman – was his first real hit, and he re-employed the same character for his first feature, *Jour de Fête* (1948). 1953's *Monsieur Hulot's Holiday* brought worldwide recognition. Hulot – an attenuate, blank-faced, pipe-smoking bungler – was one of cinema's great creations: a confused, well-meaning alter ego who never spoke (although he occasionally mumbled), created anarchy wherever he went, and was perpetually and hilariously at odds with the mechanics of the modern world. It was a classic comic archetype, used to wonderful effect in all Tati's future films: *Mon Oncle* (1958); *Playtime* (1967); and *Traffic* (1971). His unyielding perfectionism, however, eventually bankrupted him, and with the exception of *Parade* (1974) – a video of his early mime routines – the greatest comic genius of modern cinema spent his last ten years in enforced retirement.

Bertrand Tavernier

Director, critic
Born: *Lyons, France, April 25, 1941*

As a student Tavernier abandoned his law studies in favour of his attraction to the cinema, becoming a film critic and feature writer for *Cahiers du Cinéma*. He collaborated on a number of books, including one on American cinema, his particular passion, then entered the film industry as a publicist. He started directing shorts in 1963 and finally his first feature *L'Horloger de St Paul* (1973). Based on a Simenon novel and with Philippe Noiret in the title role, it immediately established Tavernier as a major talent. Tavernier's work appeals to international audiences and he often works with stories or actors from outside France. *Deathwatch* (1980), an unusual sci-fi story shot in English, starred Harvey Keitel as a television reporter with a camera concealed in his head, with Romy Schneider as his unwitting subject; *Clean Slate* (1981) was a Jim Thompson thriller relocated from the American Deep South to French North Africa. Noiret starred again as the eccentrically vengeful central character. *Sunday in the Country* (1984) was a totally French tale of family relationships and the relationship of art to life, while *Round Midnight* (1986) captured the authentic atmosphere of the "American in Paris" jazz scene of the 1950s. In *These Foolish Things* (1990), Tavernier returned to a family subject in a moving story of a father and daughter exploring their relationship in the shadow of his impending death, beautifully played by Dirk Bogarde and Jane Birkin. *L627* (1993) is an atypically brutal thriller about Parisian drugs cops which caused controversy over what was perceived as racism in its depiction of the drug dealers. Tavernier continues to fire the imagination.

Elizabeth Taylor

Actress
Born: *London, England, February 27, 1932*

The queen of Hollywood became a star at the age of 11 with *Lassie Come Home* (1943) and *National Velvet* (1944). Her personal life is a glitzy soap opera, with extraordinary love affairs and epic battles against her yo-yoing weight overshadowing real acting talent. Still a teenager, she was playing grown-ups in *Father of the Bride* (1950) and *A Place in the Sun* (1951), though it was *Giant* (1956) that fixed her acting reputation.

Elizabeth Taylor: *Winning by a Nile*

Three Oscar-nominated roles in *Raintree County* (1957), *Cat on a Hot Tin Roof* (1958) and *Suddenly Last Summer* (1959) led to her first Oscar as a classy hooker in *Butterfield 8* (1960). Her association with Richard Burton began on *Cleopatra* (1963). They married twice and made a series of hit films, the best of which, *Who's Afraid of Virginia Woolf?* (1966), won her a second Oscar. After they split, her films deteriorated, with such fiascos as *X Y and Zee* (1972), *Ash Wednesday* (1973), *Night Watch* (1973) and *A Little Night Music* (1977). When big-screen roles dried up after the failure of *The Mirror Crack'd* (1980), she dipped her toe cautiously in TV to considerable acclaim. *The Flintstones* (1994) tempted her back to the movies, hilarious as Fred's mother-in-law from hell. After five decades of stardom, 60 films, two Oscars, four children, eight marriages and countless illnesses, she's more famous than ever with her perfume, her diet book and her groundbreaking AIDS campaigning.

Shirley Temple

Actress, singer
Born: *Santa Monica, Calif., April 23, 1928*

The world's most famous child star, at least until Macaulay Culkin, was the epitome of cuteness for 1930s audiences. Her films were as sugary as the grenadine in the non-alcoholic cocktail named after her, but in a world coming out of the Great Depression, they struck a vital chord. By the age of eight she was the biggest box-office draw in the world. After a series of short spoofs called Baby Burlesks, she came to prominence with her rendition of *Baby Take a Bow* in 1934's *Stand Up and Cheer*. An astonishing four more films followed that same year, including *Bright Eyes* (1934), which gave her the immortal hit *On the Good Ship Lollipop*, establishing her as an international star, and Hollywood's biggest attraction for three consecutive years. By 11 she had amassed a fortune of over $3 million, wisely invested for her by her band-manager father, but her popularity fell away rapidly and she all but disappeared from the screen during her teenage years. An attempted comeback as a young woman was not a success and after her second marriage in 1950 she quietly announced a premature movie retirement. In 1957 she narrated a popular TV series, *Shirley Temple's Story Book,* and later became involved in politics.

She was appointed US ambassador to Ghana (1974–76) and is now ambassador to the Czech Republic.

Terry-Thomas

Actor, comic
Born: THOMAS TERRY HOAR-STEVENS, *London, England, July 14, 1911*
Died: *January 8, 1990*

Terry-Thomas specialized in playing British upper-class twits, bombastic rogues and comic cads, his catchphrases – "How do you do", "You absolute shower" or just "crikey" – choked out through moustache, gap-teeth and cigarette holder. But as fellow character comedian Lionel Jeffries says, "He was much more than a good comedian, he was a very good actor as well. He often played himself, but that is one of the most difficult things." Three films in quick succession established him as a star in Britain: *Private's Progress* (1956) as a disdainful CO; *Brothers in Law* (1957) as a posh spiv; and *Lucky Jim* (1957) as a fatuous painter. He consolidated his reputation as the diplomatic clot in 1959's *Carlton-Browne of the FO*, the personnel manager in *I'm All Right, Jack* (1959) and the rotter in *School for Scoundrels* (1960). Then in 1961 he got the call from Hollywood, playing the trouserless English professor in *Bachelor Flat* (1961). There followed the international hits *It's a Mad Mad Mad Mad World* (1963), *Those Magnificent Men in Their Flying Machines* (1965) and his own favourite, as Jack Lemmon's butler in *How to Murder Your Wife* (1965). He was a big star as the typical Englishman for non-British audiences, though the top echelons of stardom enjoyed by people such as Peter Sellers eluded him, perhaps because his range was narrow. In the 1970s good roles became hard to find, though this British comic institution kept working until Parkinson's disease forced an early retirement after he had completed the 1977 spoof *The Hound of the Baskervilles*.

Emma Thompson

Actress

Born: *London, England, April 15, 1959*

With her unconventional good looks and forceful nature, Thompson has excelled in the sort of eccentric, strong-willed female roles Glenda Jackson once made her own. A formidable actress, she is equally at home in both character and lead parts and, with husband Kenneth Branagh, is the closest thing Britain now has to screen royalty. She first came to note in the British TV serials *Tutti Frutti* and *Fortunes of War* before making an unforgettable screen debut as Nurse Lemon, the no-nonsense love interest in the comedy *The Tall Guy* (1989). She excelled in the pivotal role of Princess Katherine in Branagh's *Henry V* (1989); and shone as an intelligent, freewheeling Edwardian eccentric in *Howards End* (1992). It won her an Oscar, bringing her a series of equally memorable roles: an acid-tongued Beatrice in Branagh's *Much Ado About Nothing* (1993); a lovelorn housekeeper in *The Remains of the Day* (1993); and a strong-willed lawyer in Jim Sheridan's controversial *In the Name of the Father* (1993). An actress of great sensitivity and insight, Thompson has brought a unique strength to her roles, creating in the process some of the most vivid female screen characters of the last decade.

Gene Tierney

Actress

Born: *Brooklyn, New York, NY, November 20, 1920*
Died: *November 6, 1991*

She might not have revolutionized the actor's craft, but with her pouting lips, high cheekbones and watery eyes, Tierney was one of the most attractive women ever to have graced the silver screen. She worked as a model before being cast opposite Henry Fonda in Fritz Lang's *The Return of Frank James* (1940). Her role wasn't much to speak of, and after a similarly inauspicious turn in Ford's *Tobacco Road* (1941) one magazine dubbed her "The Worst Discovery of the Year". Despite critical sniping, however, she was good in Lubitsch's comedy *Heaven Can Wait* (1943); and excellent as the enigmatic heroine of the mystery thriller *Laura* (1944). The success of the latter gave her the clout to demand better parts and, although there were plenty of turkeys, there were enough good films to ensure her continued popularity: *Leave Her to Heaven* (1945); *Dragonwyck* (1947); *The Ghost and Mrs Muir* (1948); and *Whirlpool* (1949). However, her career came off the rails in 1955 when she had a breakdown and was in a mental home for three years. Thereafter she had a minor role in *Advise and Consent* (1962), and featured parts in *Toys in the Attic* (1963) and *The Pleasure Seekers* (1964), but her career was effectively over. Critics derided her acting abilities, but in the right vehicle she could be extremely effective. Such was her beauty that you could always forgive the woodenness.

Spencer Tracy

Actor

Born: *Milwaukee,Wis., April 5, 1900*
Died: *June 10, 1967*

Like Robert Mitchum, Spencer Tracy appeared never to be acting. Though players like this are very easy to underrate, the measure of Tracy's greatness as a screen actor is how well his performances have worn. He spent the 1920s as a stage actor but from his film debut in John Ford's *Up the River* (1930) worked solely in the movies. Often cast as priests, lawmen and other characters of craggy integrity who were

at ease with themselves, this wasn't the real Tracy at all. In reality a turbulent, insecure man and lifelong heavy drinker, he pretended to have no regard for himself as an actor or for the profession but privately took it very

Spencer Tracy: *The image of dogged decency*

seriously and worked hard to improve his acting skills. He had a long personal and professional relationship with Katharine Hepburn, beginning with *Woman of the Year* (1942) and including many fine films like *State of the Union* (1948) and *Adam's Rib* (1949). Their contrasting natures and acting styles proved beautifully complementary. He won Oscars for *Captains Courageous* (1937) and *Boys' Town* (1938) but among his best films are *Fury* (1936), *Father of the Bride* (1950), *Bad Day at Black Rock* (1955) and a clutch of films he made at the end of his life with director Stanley Kramer – *Inherit the Wind* (1960), *Judgment at Nuremberg* (1961) and *Guess Who's Coming to Dinner* (1967).

John Travolta

Actor

Born: *Englewood, NJ, February 18, 1954*

The sexy Latino-looking 1970s star was a hit on TV as a numbskull schoolkid in *Welcome Back, Kotter*

(1975–78) before making *Saturday Night Fever* (1977) and *Grease* (1978), two of the most popular films of all time which nearly brought musicals back into fashion. He was the darling of the discos with a slew of hit records and he danced so nimbly he was dubbed the new Fred Astaire by none other than the old Fred Astaire. It was downhill all the way from these dizzy heights in a series of flop movies. Some – *Moment by Moment* (1978) and *Two of a Kind* (1983), an ill-starred rematch with his *Grease* co-star Olivia Newton-John – were undeniably awful. Others were intriguing like Brian De Palma's thriller *Blow Out* (1981) and the aerobics comedy *Perfect* (1985) with Jamie Lee Curtis. Sylvester Stallone thought he could make Travolta a hit with a sequel to *Saturday Night Fever, Staying Alive* (1983), but nobody came to that either. Not working and hooked on junk food, Travolta got fat until, teamed with Kirstie Alley for the baby comedy *Look Who's Talking* (1989), he suddenly scored a number one at the box office. But the 1990s brought only one poor youth comedy *Shout* (1991) and two feeble *Look Who's Talking* sequels, until Quentin Tarantino cast him triumphantly against type as a goofy killer in his ultra-violent *Pulp Fiction* (1994).

François Truffaut

Director, writer, critic, actor, producer

Born: *Paris, France, February 6, 1932*
Died: *October 21, 1984*

Truffaut's first feature film *The 400 Blows* (1959) is largely a reflection of his own unhappy childhood. After a spell in a reformatory and deserting from the army, he was rescued by André Bazin, who employed him to write for *Cahiers du Cinéma*. Truffaut quickly became one of the most caustic of the young "New Wave" film critics, many of whom later became film-makers themselves. Truffaut made several shorts before touching an international nerve with *The 400 Blows*, whose main character, always played by Jean-Pierre Léaud, he followed into adolescence and adulthood in *Love at Twenty* (1962), *Stolen Kisses* (1968), *Bed and Board* (1970) and *Love on the Run* (1979). The romantic triangle story *Jules et Jim* (1961) featured Jeanne Moreau as the first example of the obsessive women characters who fascinated him. Truffaut employed a wide choice of storylines and styles. *Fahrenheit 451* (1966) used sci-fi to discuss the importance of literature to political freedom. *The Bride Wore Black* (1968) was a thriller homage to Hitchcock. In *Day for Night* (1973), a celebration of the process of film-making and one of his most popular films, winning him two Oscars, he also played the director of the film within the film. He took the lead in his own *The Wild Child* (1969) as the sympathetic doctor; appeared in as well as directed *The Story of Adèle H* (1975); and played the stoic scientist in Spielberg's *Close Encounters of the Third Kind* (1977). His last films were love stories: *The Last Metro* (1980), set in Nazi-occupied Paris, *The Woman Next Door* (1981), Fanny Ardant's film debut, and *Confidentially Yours* (1983), a mystery romance also starring Ardant. Truffaut died aged 52 of a brain tumour.

Kathleen Turner

Actress
Born: *Springfield, Mo.,*
June 19, 1954

Daughter of a diplomat, Kathleen Turner travelled the world as a child. After university she went to New York, got work in television soap operas and quickly set the big screen alight as the smouldering, double-dealing heroine of Lawrence Kasdan's first film *Body Heat* (1981). She played a dowdy spinster with a night life as a

hooker in Ken Russell's eyebrow-raiser *Crimes of Passion* (1984), and has since shown her strong talent for comedy, often with a touch of self-mockery, as in the tongue-in-cheek romantic adventure *Romancing the Stone* (1984) and its inferior sequel *The Jewel of the Nile* (1985), both co-starring Michael Douglas. She was elegantly funny in Huston's mafia comedy *Prizzi's*

Kathleen Turner: *The temperature is rising*

Honor (1985) and managed the difficult trick of playing both a mature woman and her teenage self in Coppola's time-travel fantasy *Peggy Sue Got Married* (1986). As William Hurt's ex wife, Turner drew a lot of attention and sympathy away from leading lady Geena Davis in *The Accidental Tourist* (1988), but failed to rise above memories of Rosalind Russell in *Switching Channels* (1988), an ill-judged remake of *His Girl Friday* (1940). After giving sexy voice to "bunny wife" Jessica in *Who Framed Roger Rabbit* (1988), she was teamed again with Douglas for the explosive marital battle-ground of *The War of the Roses* (1989). Private eye *V. I. Warshawski* (1991) and *Undercover Blues* (1993) flopped, but she was back on form sending up her former sexy image as a predatory soap queen in Dan Algrant's debut film *Naked in New York* (1993) and scored a great hit as the suburban housewife killer in John Waters's hilariously black *Serial Mom* (1994).

Lana Turner

Actress
Born: JULIA JEAN MILDRED FRANCES TURNER, *Wallace, Idaho, February 8, 1920*

Most famous for the manner of her discovery, working as a waitress in a soda fountain, Turner was a girl from the wrong side of the tracks who became, if not Hollywood's greatest actress, the epitome of glamour stardom. Her screen debut in the *They Won't Forget* (1937) – sipping soda in a drug store – impressed director Mervyn LeRoy enough to land Turner a contract with MGM, who sold her as the new Jean Harlow under the sex symbol label "the Sweater Girl", turning her into a popular pin-up. Films like *Ziegfeld Girl* (1941) and the Spencer Tracy *Dr Jekyll and Mr Hyde* (1941) caught the public imagination, and she sizzled as the *femme fatale* in James M. Cain's thriller *The Postman Always Rings Twice* (1946) at the height of her popularity. Her star waned in the 1950s but her Oscar-nominated performance as the neurotic mother in the small-town melodrama *Peyton Place* (1957) brought her back. This and Douglas Sirk's *Imitation of Life* (1959) are her acting high spots. Though her last film *Witches' Brew* was in 1978, throughout the 1980s she was still appearing in the theatre and starring in the US soap *Falcon Crest*. Turner's reputation was unfairly tarnished by the sensational headlines of seven marriages and her daughter's murder trial, but she will ever be remembered as the quintessence of Hollywood glamour.

Liv Ullmann

Actress, director, writer
Born: *Tokyo, Japan, December 16, 1939*

Ingmar Bergman's favourite actress is blonde, beautiful, subtly splendid and endlessly tormented on screen – and now a director in

her own right. Born in Japan to Norwegian parents, she moved with her family to Canada and later to New York during World War Two, then back to Norway after her father's death. She briefly studied acting in London when she was 17, made her film debut in *Fools in the Mountains* (1957), and had already established her stage career (which she frequently returned to) when Bergman picked her for the emotionally mixed-up lead in *Persona* (1966), thereby making her internationally famous in the process. Though most of her best work was with Bergman (*Shame*, 1968; *Cries and Whispers*, 1972; *Scenes from a Marriage*, 1973), she became more widely known and earned her first Oscar nomination for Jan Troell's *The Emigrants* (1971). Another nomination came for Bergman's *Face to Face* (1976), but she subsequently told him she didn't wish to work with him again; not for personal reasons, but because the emotional hoops he forced her through were too agonizing. Excursions to Hollywood turned out to be unhappy affairs too. *Lost Horizon* (1973) was a musical, *40 Carats* (1973) a comedy, and *A Bridge Too Far* (1977) really was one too many. Ullmann now serves as a Goodwill Ambassador for UNICEF, and won further critical approval as a writer/ director for *Sofie* (1993), the tale of a young Jew's journey through anti-semitic Denmark at the turn of the century.

Sir Peter Ustinov

Actor, writer, director
Born: *London, England, April 16, 1921*

Ustinov is the portly polymath of world cinema. He has won two Best Supporting Actor Oscars – for his performances as a sly slave-dealer in *Spartacus* (1960), and a deliciously clumsy thief in *Topkapi* (1964) – and is equally at home acting, directing or writing. His interests, however, are so varied, that he has never quite assumed the central position in the development of film that his ability would seem to warrant. Born in London of Russian parents, he made his screen debut in a short, *Hullo Fame* (1940), and came to international attention as a superbly neurotic Nero in *Quo Vadis?* (1951). He was chubby and amusing as a prisoner on the run in *We're No Angels* (1955), and exceptional in Max Ophuls's *Lola Montez* (1955). The early 1960s saw him at his peak, winning his two Oscars, and in between directing and acting in probably the finest film of his career – his own adaptation of Melville's *Billy Budd* (1962). He has since concentrated on eccentric character roles, most notably his definitive portrayal of Belgian detective Hercule Poirot in *Death on the Nile* (1978). He is guaranteed – literally – to bring extra weight to any project in which he is involved, but is now more of a charming oddity than key player in the world of cinema.

Rudolph Valentino

Actor
Born: RODOLFO ALFONZO RAFFAELE PIERRE PHILIBERT GUGLIELMI, *Castellaneta, Italy, May 6, 1895*
Died: *August 23, 1926*

The archetypal Latin lover, the great romantic idol of the 1920s and the man who put the flapper generation into a flap, Valentino is one of the most lustrous names of the silent cinema. He first arrived in New York in 1913 and quickly graduated from waiter and dancer to bit parts in the movies. His first starring role was in *My Official Wife* (1914), but it was Rex Ingram's *The Four Horsemen of the Apocalypse* (1921) that turned him into one of the first worldwide mega-stars. His spectacular reign included seminal romantic performances in *The Sheik* (1921), *Blood*

and Sand (1922), *Monsieur Beaucaire* (1924), *The Eagle* (1925) and *Son of the Sheik* (1926). But at the height of his fame, aged only 31, he died suddenly from a perforated ulcer, causing unprecedented scenes of mass public hysteria which allegedly caused women to commit suicide. The funeral was an occasion of international significance and it sparked off a Valentino cult. His movies are rare among silent films in being among the few still admired by a general audience apart from silent comedies, and

***Rudolph Valentino:** The first great sex symbol*

are still re-released at intervals to the renewed acclaim of successive generations. The films may have faded but Valentino's sexual magnetism continues to fascinate. He was played by another Rudolf, the famous ballet dancer Nureyev, in the intriguing Ken Russell biopic *Valentino* (1976).

Conrad Veidt

Actor
Born: *Potsdam, Germany, January 22, 1893*
Died: *April 3, 1943*

Although an actor of enormous range, Conrad Veidt's tall, gaunt frame, huge mouth and pale, sinister face were especially suited to

playing villains and horror characters. It's within these fantasy genres that he's best known – as the macabre Cesare in *The Cabinet of Dr Caligari* (1919), the dreadfully scarred hero of *The Man Who Laughs* (1928) and the wicked grand vizier in Michael Powell's rip-roaring *The Thief of Bagdad* (1940). Born in Germany, he worked extensively in theatre before starring in some of the masterpieces of German expressionist film: *The Cabinet of Dr Caligari*, *Waxworks* (1924), *The Hands of Orlac* (1924) and *The Student of Prague* (1926). The last brought him international fame, and he went to Hollywood, making a number of significant films – notably *The Man Who Laughs* – before the coming of sound forced his return to Germany. He fled to England to escape the Nazis, achieving great success with a number of villainous roles – as a crook in *Rome Express* (1932), a German officer in *I Was a Spy* (1933) and a German sailor in Powell's *The Spy in Black* (1939). At the peak of his fame, he made two of the most popular movies of all time – *The Thief of Bagdad* and *Casablanca* (1943). He died soon after completing the latter.

King Vidor

Director, writer
Born: *Galveston, Tex., February 8, 1894*
Died: *November 1, 1982*

One of the pioneers of American film, Texas-born King Vidor struggled through his first years in Hollywood as a screenwriter, poverty-row director and head of his own mini-studio, before breaking it big as a contract director with MGM. Vidor's most typical output as a writer/director tends toward the large-scale and serious, essays on mankind's futile tussles with nature. His two finest silent-screen pieces, *The Big Parade* (1925) and *The Crowd* (1928), are set in

harsh urban environments. The latter employed concealed cameras to capture real life on New York's streets as it traced an office clerk's timid progress through the big bad city. Vidor was remarkably unfazed by the advent of talkies, with *The Fountainhead* (1949) perhaps his most pointed and successful sound picture, an expressionistic fable focusing on the trials of an architect loosely based on Frank Lloyd Wright. But Vidor also proved adept at human drama and the immaculate *Stella Dallas* (1937), starring Barbara Stanwyck as a struggling mom, remains his most perennially popular work. In the last third of his career, though, Vidor's grand style came to blunt his intentions as a film-maker. *Duel in the Sun* (1946) and *War and Peace* (1956) became lumbering, lurid melodramas while his final effort, the messy *Solomon and Sheba* (1959), gave evidence of a once-mighty talent slipping into bloated self-parody.

Luchino Visconti

Director, writer
Born: COUNT DON LUCHINO VISCONTI DI MODRONE, *Milan, Italy, November 2, 1906*
Died: *March 17, 1976*

Born into one of Italy's leading aristocratic families, Visconti spent his youth cultivating his tastes for music, art and breeding horses. Aged 30, he worked as Jean Renoir's costume designer in Paris and became that most interesting of paradoxes, an aristocratic Marxist. Returning to Italy, Visconti managed to get his script based on James M. Cain's novel *The Postman Always Rings Twice* (1946) past the Fascist censors, but when *Ossessione* (1942) was completed the realism of its political/social subtext caused its mutilation by the authorities. After a period directing opera and theatre, he moved in *Senso* (1954) towards the elaborately decorative, operatic style of much of his later work. The destruction of the family by social forces is a recurrent theme. In *The Leopard* (1963) it is an aristocratic one, with Burt Lancaster as the *paterfamilias* learning to accept social change; in *Rocco and his Brothers* (1960), a proletarian one, broken by the migratory search for work; while *The Damned* (1969) is a Wagnerian study of decadence in a German industrial dynasty during Hitler's rise to power. One of Visconti's most popular films internationally was his personal interpretation of Thomas Mann's *Death in Venice* (1971), with a heart-wrenching central performance by Dirk Bogarde, underscored by Mahler's 5th Symphony. His last two films are lower-key: *Conversation Piece* (1975) with Lancaster as an elderly intellectual confused by contemporary materialism and sexual conflict, and *The Innocent* (1976) an elegant and touching period tale of adultery.

Jon Voight

Actor
Born: *Yonkers, NY,*
December 29, 1938

Jon Voight: *Home on the range*

One of the most challenging and least appreciated actors of his generation, Voight has consistently explored the down-side of the American dream. A handsome, broad-featured all-American intellectual, he has deliberately chosen parts in which his looks and intelligence are inverted and negated –

dumb boxers, crippled war veterans, brainless hustlers. In Schlesinger's *Midnight Cowboy* (1969), probably his finest role, he plays a straw-haired hunk who comes to New York to make his fortune and ends up as a sordid gay hustler turning tricks in the back seats of seedy cinemas. It was an extrordinary portrayal of wasted perfection and crushed ideals, and its inherent cynicism was thereafter to inform all of his best work. After performing extensively in theatre, he made his film debut in 1967, and gained international recognition with *Midnight Cowboy*. *The Revolutionary* (1970), *Deliverance* (1972), and *Conrack* (1974) all explored the theme of failed ideals; while his Oscar-winning portrayal of a crippled Vietnam veteran in *Coming Home* (1978) was a searing, indictment of American culture and aspirations. He was punchy as a struggling boxer in *The Champ* (1979) but with the exception of *Runaway Train* (1985) has done little of note since. It is somehow a perverse extension of his on-screen persona that such a talented actor should have produced so few good films.

Josef von Sternberg

Director
Born: JONAS STERNBERG,
Vienna, Austria, May 29, 1894
Died: *December 22, 1969*

An obsessive, extravagant, truculent maverick, von Sternberg proved a true visionary of early sound cinema. Best known as the man who discovered Marlene Dietrich, he was the consummate visual artist, a master of atmosphere, lighting and set design, who produced, in the late 1920s and early 1930s, a succession of memorable, moody, dazzlingly innovative movies. Born in Vienna but educated in the US, von Sternberg worked his way up through the ranks of the film industry, gaining widespread

recognition as the director of a series of memorable silents, notably *The Last Command* (1928) and *The Docks of New York* (1928). But it was *The Blue Angel* (1930), shot in Germany and starring an unknown Marlene Dietrich, that saw his reputation rocket. He had a unique relationship with Dietrich, instinctively knowing how best to light and direct her, and the seven films they made together – especially *The Scarlet Empress* (1934) and *The Devil Is a Woman* (1935) – stand as the greatest examples of his unique visual artistry. After the partnership split in 1935 he continued to work – *Crime and Punishment* (1935) was terrific – but his career gradually tailed off. Over the next 30 years he made few films of any note – the epic Japanese *Saga of Anatahan* (1953) excepted – as this bravura artist of early Hollywood slid into a sad, slow decline.

Erich von Stroheim

Actor, director, writer
Born: ERICH OSWALD STROHEIM,
Vienna, Austria, September 22, 1888
Died: *May 12, 1957*

Stroheim enjoyed an illustrious dual career in films. With his close-cropped bullet head and arrogant, pugnacious face, he was one of Hollywood's most menacing character actors – billed as "The Man You Love To Hate". During the silent era he was also a highly innovative director, and might well have gone on to become one of the greatest film-makers had creative differences with studio heads not truncated his directorial career. Born in Vienna, he emigrated to the US in 1906 and ended up as an adviser on D. W. Griffith's groundbreaking *Birth of a Nation* (1915). He made his directorial debut in 1918 with *Blind Husbands*, in which he also starred, a trend he continued with both *Foolish Wives* (1921)

and *The Wedding March* (1928). *Greed* (1923), the tale of a drunk who murders his wife, was his masterpiece, but thereafter he only directed five more movies, and quit the director's chair at the end of the 1920s. There followed a succession of marvellously nasty Teutonic performances: as a ventriloquist taken over by his dummy in *The Great Gabbo* (1929); a German aristocrat in *La Grande Illusion* (1937); and Rommel in *Five Graves to Cairo* (1943). He was, however, always a frustrated director, and it is fitting that his finest screen performance, in *Sunset Boulevard* (1950), was as fading film star Gloria Swanson's one-time director and husband, now humiliatingly reduced to the role of butler.

Max von Sydow

Actor, director
Born: CARL ADOLF VON SYDOW,
Lund, Sweden, April 10, 1929

Sydow became internationally famous as a key member of Ingmar Bergman's stock company, an association which took him

Max von Sydow: *Quiet strength and dignity*

from *The Seventh Seal* (1956), via *The Face* (1959), *The Virgin Spring* (1960), *Through a Glass Darkly* (1961) and *Winter Light* (1962) to *The Best Intentions* (1992). He made his debut film, Alf Sjöberg's *Only a Mother*, in 1949 and his first international mark in Sjöberg's Cannes award-winning *Miss Julie* (1951), but it was his haunting performance as the knight who confronts death at chess in *The Seventh Seal* that set the seal on his worldwide reputation. In 1965 Hollywood beckoned him to play Jesus in *The Greatest Story Ever Told* and, though many wondered whether the title was entirely accurate, the quality of his performance was unquestionable. After *Hawaii* (1966) and *The Quiller Memorandum* (1966), he returned to Bergman for *Hour of the Wolf* (1967), *The Shame* (1968) and *The Touch* (1971). He started to appear more frequently in American movies including *The Kremlin Letter* (1969) and *The Exorcist* (1973), but many films were unworthy of his talent. Andrei Konchalovsky cast him in *Duet for One* (1986), the fictionalized story of the cellist Jacqueline du Pré, and Bergman fan Woody Allen gave him his best opportunity for years in *Hannah and Her Sisters* (1986). In 1987 he won his only Oscar nomination for his role as the widowed farmer in the Cannes award-winner *Pelle the Conqueror*, directed by Bille August, and he scored again in the same director's second Cannes triumph *The Best Intentions* (1992), Bergman's family story.

Andrzej Wajda

Director, writer
Born: *Suwalki, Poland, March 6, 1927*

Andrzej Wajda became a resistance fighter at 16 after the death of his cavalry officer father in World War Two. He studied painting, then at the Lodz Film School, and with his first feature film *A Generation* (1954) established his importance in the new Polish cinema. This story of young people under Nazi occupation became the first of a masterly trilogy questioning the supposed glory of war. *Kanal* (1956) was about the Warsaw uprising of

1944; *Ashes and Diamonds* (1958) the victory of corruption over idealism in post-war Poland. Wajda returned to the subject of war and its futility in *Lotna* (1959), *Ashes* (1965) and *Landscape after a Battle* (1970). Another of his themes is entrapment, either physical, as with the resistance fighters in the sewers in *Kanal*, or political, as in *Man of Marble* (1977) and his other films of the late 1970s, when he became an indicator of his country's social and political unrest. *Man of Marble* deals with a student's attempt to uncover the truth about a propaganda-hero bricklayer who fell from party grace. *Without Anaesthesia* (1979) deals with a journalist whose career collapses when he makes a politically incorrect choice in a literary discussion; and *Man of Iron* (1980) charts the beginnings of the Solidarity movement and foretells its subsequent suppression. When that suppression came, Wajda went to France and made *Danton* (1982), a grim meditation on revolution, returning with the unexpected liberalization of Eastern Europe in 1989 to be elected to the Polish parliament as a Solidarity candidate.

Anton Walbrook

Actor
Born: ADOLF WOHLBRUCK, *Vienna, Austria, November 19, 1896*
Died: *August 9, 1967*

Angular and aquiline, Viennese-born Anton Walbrook rose to fame during the dark days of World War Two, a vital reminder to British audiences of the dignity and strength of the average Continental. Though he made a memorable Prince Albert in two biopics of Queen Victoria and was effective as a piano-playing Polish airman in *Dangerous Moonlight* (1941), it was his collaborations with Michael Powell and Emeric Pressburger that truly forged his reputation. After playing the voice of reason in the propaganda piece

49th Parallel (1941), he gave a splendidly realized and heartfelt turn as Roger Livesey's German officer friend in *The Life and Death of Colonel Blimp* (1943). It was Powell and Pressburger, too, who provided Walbrook with his most famous role, casting him as the icy, driven impresario Lermontov in the bright-hued classic *The Red Shoes* (1948). Walbrook followed this triumph with another bravura turn as an impoverished soldier in Thorold Dickinson's baroque extravaganza *The Queen of Spades* (1948) and took the lead role in *La Ronde* (1950), Max Ophüls's circular tale of romance in 19th-century Vienna. His last film appearance, before comfortable retirement as a British citizen in London, was a co-starring role opposite actor/director José Ferrer in the intriguing, fact-based courtroom drama *I Accuse* (1957).

Christopher Walken

Actor
Born: *New York City, NY, March 31, 1943*

No one looks quite like Walken. His triangular face, which mixes a poised, mantis-like menace with a strained and alien beauty, is at its most disturbing when he smiles, a small action with all the screen intensity of a punch from most other actors. A serious, talented and controlled performer, he started on stage, making his film debut with a walk-on, but his first big part was a criminal electronics whizzkid in *The Anderson Tapes* (1971), followed by appearances in films as varied as *Annie Hall* (1977), as Diane Keaton's psychotic brother (1977), *The Deer Hunter* (1978), for which he won Best Supporting Actor Oscar, and David Cronenberg's *The Dead Zone* (1983) as a clairvoyant coma victim. He was inspired casting for the comic psycho-sergeant in *Biloxi Blues* (1988) and enjoyed high-profile roles in mainstream movies like *A View to a Kill* (1985)

and *Batman Returns* (1992). He's equally at home in violent cult thrillers like *King of New York* (1990), playing an out-of-control mobster, and *The Comfort of Strangers* (1991), as a dangerous

Christopher Walken: *Strained and alien beauty*

Italian aristocrat. Now at the cutting edge of modern movie-making, he has reached cult status himself as shown by his iconic cameos in two Tarantino films *True Romance* (1993) and *Pulp Fiction* (1994). A literally fascinating performer, Walken can steal a scene just by standing still.

Andy Warhol

Painter, film-maker, pop-culture icon
Born: ANDREW WARHOLA, *Cleveland, Ohio, August 8, 1927*
Died: *February 22, 1987*

Most famous now for his multiple soup can and Marilyn paintings, Warhol was a prolific film-maker with over 70 movies between 1963 and 1976. His concerns with the surface of popular culture translated themselves to celluloid in films like *Kiss* (1963) – his first film; *Sleep* (1963) – an eight-hour film of a sleeping man; *Empire* (1964) – entirely consisting of a single take of the Empire State Building; *Harlot* (1964) – his first sound movie; *Vinyl* (1965) – based on the Burgess novel *A Clockwork Orange*; and *The Chelsea Girls* (1966) – made for two screens, each showing different situations. In 1968 Warhol survived attempted murder and thereafter his assistant Paul Morrissey took over the direction of Warhol-brand movies, making successive films more coherent and reaching a wider audience with *Flesh* (1968), *Heat* (1972), *Flesh for Frankenstein* (1973) and *Blood for Dracula* (1974), the last two entirely shot by Morrissey. Warhol had nothing to say. His films, like his paintings, pass no comment, make no reaction to their – often loosely defined – subject, except an impersonal and dissociated irony. Falling between fantasy and documentary, they mix a self-consciously arty approach with liberal doses of sexual voyeurism, gutter-life chic and straightforward camp. For the most part, this controversial artist didn't make art films, he made film art. Whether you see his product as an avant garde exploration of cinematic possibilities, or a skilful and cynical exploitation of the mass media, or simply as poorly made, camp and often boring personal indulgences, their impact on the popular culture of their time is undeniable.

Denzel Washington

Actor

Born: *New York, NY, December 28, 1954*

One of 1990s Hollywood's biggest stars, the striking, highly talented Denzel Washington is America's principal black actor. His ascent has been slow but steady, making his small screen debut in the 1977 telefilm *Wilma* and first feature appearance as George Segal's unlikely teenage son in the patronizing race comedy *Carbon Copy* (1981). A lengthy stint on television in the hospital comedy-drama *St Elsewhere* made him a household name and increased his box-office standing, leading to a handful of minor movie roles. Washington's Oscar-nominated breakthrough came when Richard

Attenborough cast him as murdered South African activist Steve Biko in the acclaimed *Cry Freedom!* (1987) and his position was sealed with an Oscar win for his support turn in the Civil War drama *Glory* (1989). Washington's star peformance as a troubled band leader brought some heart to Spike Lee's jazz soaper *Mo' Better Blues* (1990) and he was affecting as a southerner romancing an Asian girl in 1991's *Mississippi Masala*. A far more profitable collaboration with Lee came in 1992 with his muscular interpretation in the title role of the director's exhaustive biopic of *Malcolm X*. It remains Washington's most significant role to date, though he followed it with a well-calculated change of pace, enjoying himself in support in Kenneth Branagh's Shakespearean romp *Much Ado about Nothing* (1993).

John Wayne

Actor, director

Born: MARION MICHAEL MORRISON, *Winterset, Ia., May 26, 1907*
Died: *June 11, 1979*

More American than apple pie, the giant, drawling Duke is the ultimate action hero, an inseparable weave of man and legend. Raised in California, he was a football player before working behind the cameras, developing a relationship with director John Ford who encouraged him to act. His debut was *Brown of Harvard* (1926), but he made 80 low-budget pictures, even playing a singing cowboy, before Ford cast him for the lead in *Stagecoach* (1939), propelling him to stardom. *Fort Apache* (1948) and *She Wore a Yellow Ribbon* (1949) cemented his bankability, and even his right-wing politics and McCarthyite connections could be turned to advantage. Howard Hawks's *Red River* (1948), and especially Ford's *The Searchers* (1956) played the contradictions of stubborn racism against his more

admirable qualities of skill and tenacity to excellent effect. Wayne always played himself, tough and proud, but with variations of self-assurance and cussedness, summing himself up best by claiming, "I just sell sincerity". He directed

An American legend: Big John Wayne

himself in *The Alamo* (1959) and *The Green Berets* (1968), his jingoistic salute to the Vietnam War, and finally won an Oscar for *True Grit* (1969), by which time he had to be lifted into the saddle by crane. Wayne's elegiac portrayal of a dying gunman, *The Shootist* (1976), was made while he was withering from cancer, the last performance from the most consistently popular of post-war Hollywood stars.

Sigourney Weaver

Actress

Born: SUSAN ALEXANDRA WEAVER, *New York, NY, October 8, 1945*

Hollywood has never known what to do with powerful women and they don't come much stronger

than tall, chiselled, strikingly beautiful Weaver. Daughter of NBC president Sylvester Weaver and actress Elizabeth Inglis, Sigourney – a name she adopted from *The Great Gatsby* – debuted with a walk-on in Woody Allen's *Annie Hall* (1977). She seized the public's imagination as tough first-officer Ripley in Ridley Scott's classic sci-fi horror *Alien* (1979), turning male/female action stereotypes on their head and creating a powerful feminist icon, who, fortunately for her fans – and Weaver's career – survived to make two sequels. Following *The Year of Living Dangerously* (1982) and the enormously successful *Ghostbusters* (1984), the second of the trilogy, *Aliens* (1986), brought her first Oscar nomination which she capped with two more, for a refreshingly funny turn in *Working Girl* (1988) and for the popular *Gorillas in the Mist* (1988). Next came *Ghostbusters II* (1989), a profitable but frustrating outing as a piece of window-dressing in a boys' picture. But *Alien 3* (1992) brought her back to centre-stage, dramatically shaven-headed and more powerful than ever. She

Sigourney Weaver: *Bald, brave and beautiful*

remains a criminally underused talent, making far too few movies – either by choice or because she isn't offered good roles. "I think I get sent the roles Meryl's not doing," she says. Whatever the truth, it's the cinema's loss.

Clifton Webb

Actor
Born: WEBB PARMELEE HOLLENBECK, *Indianapolis, Ind., November 19, 1891*
Died: *October 13, 1966*

With his haughty, aristocratic face, thin moustache and superior, tight-lipped expression, Webb was always destined for a career as an offbeat character actor. His finest creation was Mr Belvedere, an idiosyncratic, pompous intellectual who first appeared in the comedy *Sitting Pretty* (1948) and thereafter became something of an American institution. It was a wonderfully prim, charismatic performance, and perfectly summed up a man who was always a little disdainful of Hollywood and the success he enjoyed there. After early careers as a dance teacher and musical comedian, Webb entered movies in the 1920s, but it wasn't until

Laura (1944), playing Gene Tierney's suave, possessive admirer, that he came to general notice. He impressed as a jealous gallery owner in *The Dark Corner* (1946) and was even better as an insufferable snob in *The Razor's Edge* (1946). But it was with *Sitting Pretty* (1948) that he really hit the big time and there were two hugely popular sequels – *Mr Belvedere Goes to College* (1949) and *Mr Belvedere Rings the Bell* (1951). These were followed by probably the finest performance of his career, as a ham actor in *Dreamboat* (1952), and he stood out in *Three Coins in the Fountain* (1954). In his final movie, *Satan Never Sleeps* (1962), Webb displayed a hitherto unexplored poignancy and depth.

Peter Weir

Director
Born: *Sydney, Australia, August 21, 1944*

Peter Weir is at the forefront of the new wave of Australian directors, and one of the few filmmakers from his native country to have gained widespread international recognition. He is not only a superb storyteller, but one of cinema's great stylists, filling the screen with rich colours, memorable panoramas and powerful, thought-provoking imagery. He learnt his craft with the Commonwealth Film Unit, directing a number of notable shorts before making his feature debut with *The Cars that Ate Paris* (1974). He attracted universal attention with *Picnic at Hanging Rock* (1975), an eerie, atmospheric slow-burner about three girls who disappear on a jaunt into the outback; and followed it up with the mysterious, beautifully shot thriller *The Last Wave* (1977). The success of *Gallipoli* (1981) and *The Year of Living Dangerously* (1982) brought him to America, where he struck gold with his first film, 1985's *Witness*. More than any other movie, this latter demonstrates

Weir's ability to combine a dramatic storyline, sumptuous visual artistry and elements which have dominated all his future work: *The Mosquito Coast* (1986); *Dead Poets Society* (1989); and *Green Card* (1990). One of the era's most interesting directors, Weir might lack the radicalism of a Scorsese or Coppola, but his uniquely poetic visual style is constantly alluring.

Johnny Weissmuller

Actor
Born: JANOS WEISSMULLER, (*aka* PETER JOHN WEISSMULLER), *Freidorf, Hungary, June 2, 1904*
Died: *January 20, 1984*

Tall, lean and muscular, Weissmuller's wholesome good looks and champion swimming prowess made him the most famous and memorable of 18 Tarzans so far. Having moved to Winbear, Pennsylvania, Weissmuller's parents registered him as Peter John, enabling him to claim American nationality. He grew up in Chicago and won Olympic gold for the US in 1924, repeating the feat in 1928. His easy popularity encouraged MGM to

Johnny Weissmuller: *Young, free and swinging*

make him the star of *Tarzan the Ape Man* (1932), and an institution was born. In Edgar Rice Burroughs's *Tarzan* novels, the hero was an educated English

lord, but Weissmuller's appeal was much more primitive. Scantily clad, alongside Maureen O'Sullivan as Jane, he used to joke that the secret of his success was his ability to grunt well. After 12 Tarzan movies he hung up his loin-cloth, aged 44, instead covering up in a white suit to become the similar *Jungle Jim* (1948). He continued to play the character in 16 adventure films for children, although by *Devil Goddess* (1955) he was credited as simply playing himself. He had just one attempt at a different role, *Swamp Fire* (1946), until *Won Ton Ton, the Dog Who Saved Hollywood* (1976). On retirement to Acapulco, Mexico, he prospered by lending his name to a pool company as his fellow swimmer/actor, Esther Williams had done. He was less successful in love, though, with six marriage certificates to display alongside his Olympic medals.

Orson Welles

Director, actor, writer
Born: *Kenola, Wis., May 6, 1915*
Died: *October 10, 1985*

Even in jaundiced, corpulent middle age there was something of the mischievous child about Orson Welles. This, after all, is the man who at 16 blagged his way into Dublin's Gate Theatre, at 23 terrorized the nation with his *War of the Worlds* broadcast and by 26 had effortlessly conjured up the cinematic milestone *Citizen Kane* (1941), generally held to be the greatest film ever made. Regrettably it was to prove the most creative control he would ever enjoy. His follow-up, *The Magnificent Ambersons* (1942), was vandalized by crass editing ("cut in my absence by the studio janitor," Welles said) while his low-budget adaptation of *Othello* (1952) was ignored by distributors. For the rest of his life Welles's childlike genius was constantly reined in by wary studio heads. Despite this, he was always liable to spring the occasional film treasure. *The Lady from Shanghai* (1948), starring then-wife Rita Hayworth, proved a labyrinthine *film noir* puzzle, and 1962's *The Trial* vividly evoked Kafka's nightmare world. The tangy *Touch of Evil* (1958) led the viewer on a dastardly jaunt through a corrupt, crumbling Mexico, while his menacing support role memorably lit up Carol Reed's *The Third Man* (1949). In later years Welles increasingly fell back on lucrative cameo turns and voice-over work and appeared frustrated by his lack of support and recognition. Critic Kenneth Tynan recalled Welles introducing himself at a sparsely attended lecture in the American Midwest: "I will tell you the highlights of my life," he began. "I am a director and producer of plays. I am a writer of motion pictures. I am a motion picture actor. I write, direct and act on the radio. I am a magician. I also paint and sketch and I am a book publisher. I am a violinist and a pianist. Isn't it strange that there are so many of me – and so few of you?"

Wim Wenders

Director, writer, producer
Born: WILHELM ERNST WENDERS, *Düsseldorf, Germany, August 14, 1945*

Wim Wenders grew up in a West Germany dominated by American culture, which provided a diversion for Germans eager to forget the recent past, and he has said that all his films have as their underlying current the Americanization of Germany. He studied at Munich Film School, where he completed his first feature *Summer in the City* (1970). His first professional film, *The Goal Keeper's Anxiety at the Penalty Kick* (1971), was well received, *The Scarlet Letter* (1972) less so, but his trilogy of road movies, particularly *Kings of the Road* (1976), struck a chord with audiences. *The*

American Friend (1977), based on Patricia Highsmith's novel *Ripley's Game*, developed Wenders's theme of Germany's Americanization in its story of a picture restorer (Bruno Ganz) seduced by a psychotic underworld figure (Dennis Hopper) into committing murder. It also seduced Francis Coppola, who invited Wenders to direct *Hammett* (1983); interesting for Frederic Forrest's performance but muddied by Wenders's artistic disagreements with Coppola. However *Paris, Texas* (1984), with a Sam Shepard script and Harry Dean Stanton as the drifter seeking reunion with his family, was a Cannes Palme d'Or winner and an international success. Wenders returned to Berlin to make the intriguing mystic fantasy *Wings of Desire* (1987) with Ganz as an angel yearning to be human. *Until the End of the World* (1991) was a worldroving road movie with a bizarre sci-fi second half. *Faraway So Close* (1993), the eagerly anticipated sequel to *Wings of Desire*, with Ganz, Otto Sander and Peter Falk recreating their characters, received less than its due respect.

Lina Wertmüller

Director, writer, actress, playwright
Born: ARCANGELA FELICE ASSUNTA WERTMÜLLER VON ELGG, *Rome, Italy, August 14, 1928*

The rebellious daughter of an aristocratic Swiss lawyer, Lina Wertmüller became an actress, director and writer in touring theatre, where she first met Giancarlo Giannini, later the star of her films. Through her friendship with Marcello Mastroianni, Wertmüller became assistant to Fellini on *8 1/2* (1963), and later, with Fellini's support, directed her first film, *The Lizard* (1963). She won Best Director prize at Cannes with *The Seduction of Mimi* (1972), in which Giannini as a puny David is pitted against a Goliath of social, sexual and political figures drawn with

broad caricature strokes in a Fellini-influenced style. *Love and Anarchy* (1973) won Giannini a Cannes Best Actor prize and earned Wertmüller a cult following in America, which grew with her subsequent films *All Screwed Up* (1973); *Swept Away* (1974), a battle-of-the-sexes story in which both participants behave monstrously; and particularly *Seven Beauties* (1976), which combined Wertmüller's grotesque humour with the horrors of the Nazi concentration camp. The high praise heaped on this by American critics led to a Warner contract to direct in the United States. The resulting film, *The End of the World in Our Usual Bed in a Night Full of Rain* (1978), teamed Giannini with Candice Bergen and was so critically slated that the contract was cancelled. Wertmüller returned to Italy, where she has continued to make films, though her international cult following seems to have largely been swept away.

Mae West

Actress
Born: *Brooklyn, NY, August 17, 1892*
Died: *November 23, 1990*

Mae West once declared: "There'll never be another star like me" – and she was right. One of the most ebullient, flamboyant and outrageous of screen comediennes, she was not just a cinematic icon, but an integral part of American culture. Her epigrams – "I used to be Snow White but I drifted"; "Whenever I'm caught between two evils I take the one I haven't tried before" – became part of popular 1930s parlance, and her name a byword for gaudy sexual satire. A charismatic, buxom blonde, she achieved widespread notoriety as the author and star of a series of risqué stage plays before making her Hollywood debut, aged 40, in *Night after Night* (1932), for which she also wrote her own lines. According to co-

star George Raft, "she wasn't averse to stealing the best lines", and continued to do so for the next 10 years, notably in *She Done Him Wrong* (1933) when she invited Cary Grant to "come up some time and see me"; *I'm No Angel* (1933); *Belle of the Nineties* (1934); *Goin' to Town* (1935); and *Go West, Young Man* (1936). Her star was so incandescent it was inevitable it would burn itself out,

Mae West: *Icon of the outrageous*

and, after her famed pairing with W. C. Fields in *My Little Chickadee* (1940), she returned to theatre. A transcendent comedienne, she will always occupy a special place in the Hollywood Hall of Fame, and was still a legend in her eighties, parodying her old self in *Myra Breckinridge* (1970) and *Sextette* (1978).

James Whale

Director
Born: *Dudley, England, July 22, 1896*
Died: *May 30, 1957*

The director of some of the finest horror films of the 1930s, James Whale injected his own brand of black humour into his expressionist vision of *Frankenstein* (1931) et al., smartening the genre up, before his premature retirement and mysterious death. His parents were an ironworker and a nurse, though Whale took much care later to eradicate any evidence of his working-class background. Captured in the trenches, he was sent to a POW camp where he acted to entertain the troops, continuing his stage career after the war, and directing by 1928. His Hollywood debut came with *Journey's End* (1930), but he made his reputation with the classic *Frankenstein*, a ground-breaking Gothic extravaganza that remains one of cinema's most influential horror films. *The Old Dark House* (1932) starred his friend Charles Laughton with Boris Karloff, who refused 1933's *The Invisible Man*, Claude Rains appearing – or rather not appearing – instead. Karloff returned for the seminal *The Bride of Frankenstein* (1935) which broke box-office records. Whale was even successful with Paul Robeson's musical, *Showboat* (1936), but abandoned cinema for painting after *The Man in the Iron Mask* (1939) and *They Dare Not Love* (1941), possibly an apt title since some suggest he was driven out of Hollywood for his homosexuality. Whale died in suspicious circumstances, drowning in his swimming pool. The verdict was accidental death, but suicide is widely favoured as an explanation.

Pearl White

Actress
Born: *Green Ridge, Mo., March 4, 1889*
Died: *August 4, 1938*

Pre-talkie heroine Pearl White was the unchallenged megastar of the serials; caught at the end of each episode in some inextricable predicament, from which she would be rescued in the next chapter only to find herself yet again faced with an equally hair-raising danger by the end of that episode. A farmer's daughter, she made her stage debut aged six as Little Eva in *Uncle Tom's Cabin*, followed by other child roles, which earned her enough to buy her own horse. White joined a circus as an equestrienne, until she suffered a spinal injury from a fall. She also did some stunt work, but it was

her job as a secretary for a film company, which brought her to the attention of director Joseph A. Golden, who cast her in *The Life of Buffalo Bill* (1910), after which she starred in around a hundred one- and two-reelers. White's big break came when Pathé gave her the title role in what became the best-known serial ever, *The Perils of Pauline* (1914). This and others, such as *The Exploits of Elaine* (1915), made her for several years even more popular than Mary Pickford. From 1920 to 1923 she moved into feature films for Fox including *Know Your Men* (1921) and *A Virgin Paradise* (1921), which were less successful, so she returned to Pathé and serials, the last of which, *Perils of Paris* (1924) was made in France, which she liked so much she retired and settled there.

Richard Widmark

Actor, producer
Born: *Sunrise, Minn., December 26, 1914*

After radio and Broadway roles, golden-haired, steely-looking Widmark was Oscar nominated for his first film as a laughing killer in *Kiss of Death* (1947) and was subsequently shoehorned into a slew of such parts before fighting to play straight up good guys and hard-nosed but decent misfits, though he was always more entertaining as the baddie. Throughout the 1950s and 1960s he proved himself a fine actor and one of America's more enduring, dependable stars, though success in comedy and romance eluded him. He took to westerns like a duck to water, becoming a staple of the genre, with *Yellow Sky* (1949), *Red Skies of Montana* (1952), *The Last Wagon* (1956), *The Alamo* (1960), *Two Rode Together* (1961), *How the West Was Won* (1963), *The Way West* (1967) and *When the Legends Die* (1972). He also scored in two Sam Fuller thrillers, *Pickup on South Street* (1953) and *Hell and High Water* (1954), while his char-

acter work impressed in *Judgement atNuremberg* (1961) and *The Bedford Incident* (1965). In the 1970s he re-established himself as an important supporting actor in films like *Murder on the Orient Express* (1974), *Rollercoaster* (1977), *Coma* (1978), *Who Dares Wins* (1982) and *Against all Odds* (1983), and made several TV movies plus a hit television series, *Madigan*, based on his acclaimed 1968 Manhattan cop thriller. Widmark occasionally produced, including *The Secret Ways* (1961), written by his ex-actress wife Jean Hazelwood.

Billy Wilder

Writer, director, producer
Born: SAMUEL WILDER, *Vienna, Austria, June 22, 1906*

Wilder is a king of comedy without a kingdom, banished to those distant shores where writer/directors are only allowed to scribble and appear at Oscar ceremonies and not make films any more. Admittedly his latest, *Buddy Buddy* (1981) was patchy but it did have the peerless Matthau/Lemmon team and some good fun. Wilder's problem is that in late middle age he made a number of fine movies the public just didn't want to see, including *The Private Life of Sherlock Holmes* (1970), *Avanti* (1972) and *Fedora* (1978). No wonder that in 1990s interviews he seems bitter. But then he was always bitter. His classics *Double Indemnity* (1944), *Sunset Blvd* (1950), *Ace in the Hole* (1951) and *Kiss Me Stupid* (1964) are dangerous films that explore life's dark corners. But his acid has always been leavened by a gleefully malevolent sense of humour. *Some Like It Hot* (1959), the cinema's greatest drag comedy, has a layer of darkness, but like *The Seven-Year Itch* (1955) it's a film of truth, warmth and good nature, mostly thanks to the vibrant presence of Marilyn Monroe. Jack Lemmon provides the warmth in *The*

Apartment (1960), *The Fortune Cookie* (1966) and *The Front Page* (1974), all great fun films to balance the darkness of the classic alcohol-addiction film *The Lost Weekend* (1945) or POW saga *Stalag 17* (1953).

Gene Wilder

Actor, writer, director, producer
Born: JEROME SILBERMAN, *Milwaukee, Wis., June 11, 1935*

The frizzy-haired American comedian with a talent for frenzied but warm-hearted comedy attended New York's Actors' School and came to films from the stage. He made his debut in a notable bit part as a comic undertaker in *Bonnie and Clyde* (1967), and he won an Oscar nomination for Mel Brooks's *The Producers* (1968), only his second picture. Two more hilarious satires for Brooks, *Blazing Saddles* and *Young Frankenstein* (both 1974), turned him into a star. Since then he's split from Brooks to write and direct several movies of his own, with variable results, starting with *The Adventure of Sherlock Holmes' Smarter Brother* (1975), and he's partnered Richard Pryor several times to great box-office, though less critical, acclaim. Their first together, *Silver Streak* (1976), was by far the best, though *Stir Crazy* (1980) was a huge hit, much revived on TV, and they were paired again in 1991 in *Another You*. He co-starred in *Hanky Panky* (1982), *The Woman in Red* (1984) and *Haunted Honeymoon* (1986) with comedienne Gilda Radner to whom he was married from 1984 until her untimely death four years later. Through moderately amusing films like these, Wilder held on as a star through the tough times of the 1980s, but in 1990 an admirable attempt to change gear with a drama-driven, non-slapstick comedy about fertility, *Funny About Love*, found very little favour.

Robin Williams

Actor, comedian
Born: *Chicago, Ill., June 21, 1952*

Stocky, bright-eyed and quicksil-
ver-witted, Robin Williams graduated to the big screen on the back
of his success as the manic alien
hero of the TV series *Mork and
Mindy* (1978–81). His movie debut,
buried under latex in the title role
of Robert Altman's *Popeye* (1980),
boded well but the film floundered, consigning him to
Hollywood's second division,
turning in decent performances in

Robin Williams: Comedy to shout about

little-seen works like *Seize the Day*
(1986) and *The World According to
Garp* (1982). Williams's star rocketed when Barry Levinson cast
him as DJ Adrian Cronauer in his
1987 smash *Good Morning Vietnam*
and let him improvise much of his
own dialogue, fleshing out a near-
skeletal plot with off-the-cuff
comic fireworks that left audiences
reeling. A string of sleekly packaged comedy-dramas followed,
culminating in 1994's gender-
bending blockbuster *Mrs
Doubtfire*. If there is any problem
with Williams it is not so much a
lack of talent as a surfeit. His
indiscriminate zeal as a film performer leads him to tread a per-
ilously fine line, occasionally
blunting a gag's impact through
overwork. Similarly, Williams can
sometimes overdo his dramatic
turns – while he was heartfelt and

affecting in *Dead Poets Society*
(1989) and *Awakenings* (1990), his
role as the grown-up Peter Pan in
Spielberg's *Hook* (1991) bordered
on the mawkish. But among a
growing number of bland, pro-
grammed stars, Williams is a true
original, possessed of a giddying
skill that should ensure he stays at
the top of the Hollywood tree.

Bruce Willis

Actor
Born: *Germany, March 19, 1955*

Bruce Willis proved one of the
1980s' quintessential action stars,
battling through hell, high water
and hails of bullets with ruddy
good looks and cocky grin always
intact. Small-screen success as a
wisecracking gumshoe in the
Moonlighting (1985–89) series had
studio chiefs grooming him for
stardom, capitalizing on his sex
appeal and gift for light comedy in
the enjoyable romance-gone-awry
caper *Blind Date* (1987). Willis's
Hollywood status is mainly
thanks to his two *Die Hard* outings
(1988 and 1990), playing a New
York cop whose estranged wife
(Bonnie Bedelia) is forever
embroiling him with international
terrorists. Structurally the two
films are almost identical – flashy
siege thrillers set, respectively, in a
skyscraper and an airport – but
there's no denying their white-
knuckle worth. However his
career fluctuates, Willis – married
to film star Demi Moore – seems
guaranteed a hit with an actioner,

Bruce Willis: Hard as nails

and impressed with a wry support
turn in *Pulp Fiction* (1994). Only
when he ventures off familiar territory does the muscular Willis
appear suddenly enfeebled. An
obligatory trip into serious drama,
lank-haired and bearded as a
Vietnam vet, in Norman Jewison's
In Country (1989) looked strained
and underpowered while his overstuffed labour-of-love *Hudson
Hawk* (1991) bombed at the box
office. Most damaging of all, perhaps, was Willis's mugging, miscast turn in Brian De Palma's
Manhattan odyssey *The Bonfire of
the Vanities* (1990), a notorious
fiasco that singed the careers of all
concerned.

Debra Winger

Actress
Born: *Cleveland, Oh, May 17, 1955*

Earthy, dark-eyed and intense,
Debra Winger is one of the industry's most undervalued performers. She made a mark in her first
significant role, as John Travolta's
no-nonsense bride in the coarse-
grained *Urban Cowboy* (1980). "I
loved that movie," Winger recalls.
"It was a slice of life." She proved
a vibrant love-interest in the 1982
blockbuster *An Officer and a
Gentleman*, was Oscar-nominated
for her role as Shirley MacLaine's
warring daughter in the high-
gloss *Terms of Endearment* (1983)
and used her famous husky tones
to provide the voice of Steven
Spielberg's *ET* (1982). Winger's
lack of true superstardom is partly
due to her determinedly vocal,
uncompromising nature. She
clashed memorably with
MacLaine and has dismissed co-
stars Richard Gere and Robert
Redford as "a brick wall" and
"white meat" respectively, though
her rise has also been hampered
by a lack of truly great movies.
Key roles in a chequered but
always ambitious career include
her performance as the frumpy
heroine of the alluring *Black
Widow* (1987), as an FBI agent con-

fronting racism in the engrossing
Betrayed (1988) and as writer Jane
Bowles in Bertolucci's mesmeric
but overstretched *The Sheltering
Sky* (1990). In the mid-1990s
Winger looked to be steering a
steadier course. She was effec-

Debra Winger: Soft eyes, acid tongue

tively cast opposite Anthony
Hopkins in *Shadowlands* (1993) and
impressed in one of her most
demanding roles, playing a
gauche, unworldly misfit in the
1994 psycho-drama *A Dangerous
Woman*.

Robert Wise

Director, producer
Born: *Winchester, Ind.,
September 10, 1914*

Wise started his career as a cut-
ting-room trainee, progressing to
being Orson Welles's editor on
Citizen Kane (1941) and *The
Magnificent Ambersons* (1942). His
chance to direct came when producer Val Lewton's director for
Curse of the Cat People (1944)
couldn't cope with the tight schedule and Wise was asked to take
over. His first big critical success
was *The Set-Up* (1949), a gritty
boxing film with Robert Ryan, and
a genre he returned to with equal
success with *Somebody Up There
Likes Me* (1956), the Rocky
Graziano biopic starring Paul
Newman. *The Day the Earth Stood
Still* (1951) became a sci-fi classic;
another hit was the melodramatic

I Want to Live (1958) in which Susan Hayward played the real-life defendant in a sensational murder trial. Wise won a Best Director Oscar with Jerome Robbins for the thrilling *West Side Story* (1961), returning to the musical genre with the phenomenally successful *The Sound of Music* (1965), another Oscar-winner, and with *Star!* (1968), another Julie Andrews picture. Despite top production values and a good score, this underrated musical biopic of Gertrude Lawrence was a flop. Also underrated was *Two for the Seesaw* (1962), featuring Shirley MacLaine and Robert Mitchum as a couple tentatively building a relationship. Wise was the first to bring Captain Kirk and crew to the big screen with *Star Trek – The Motion Picture* (1979), and returned to the musical with *Rooftops* (1989), a likeable but minor story of teenage outsiders.

Natalie Wood

Actress

Born: NATASHA VIRAPAEFF, (*aka* NATASHA GURDIN), *San Francisco, Calif., July 20, 1938*
Died: *November 29, 1981*

Most memorable for her anguished teen tears, the youthful brunette with the hair in her eyes successfully negotiated the transition from child actress to adult star, but a waning career ended with her dramatic death by

Natalie Wood: Three Oscar nominations

drowning in 1981. Born to Russian and French parents, Wood was aged five when picked out of her local neighbourhood for a part in *Happy Land* (1943). There followed a succession of roles as daughter to the famous, including Orson Welles, Bing Crosby, James Stewart and Bette Davis. She earned the first of three Oscar nominations flirting with dangerous James Dean in *Rebel without a Cause* (1955), and was the object of John Wayne's mixed-up feelings, as the white girl kidnapped by Indians in *The Searchers* (1956). She was then suspended by Warner Bros for refusing a role but returned as wishful peacemaker Maria in the phenomenally successful *West Side Story* (1961), her singing voice dubbed by Marnie Dixon. *Splendor in the Grass* (1961) and *Love with the Proper Stranger* (1963) brought her further nominations. Wood married actor Robert Wagner for the second time in 1972, but starring roles petered out. Her tragic drowning off Santa Catalina Island, California, during the filming of *Brainstorm* (1983) generated fevered speculation. Wagner and co-star Christopher Walken were reputedly quarrelling on board their yacht when Wood went missing. Afraid of water all her life, she was found hours later, drowned with a high blood-alcohol level.

Joanne Woodward

Actress

Born: *Thomasville, Ga., February 27, 1930*

Blonde and talented, but less glamorous than her contemporaries Marilyn Monroe and Grace Kelly, Woodward's undoubted ability has been overshadowed by her husband Paul Newman's star status, and she has appeared with him in almost half of her screen outings. She began playing sexy slatterns from the deep south, and had picked up an Oscar before her

association with Newman, though, later maturing into playing ordinary women under pressure. Born into a well-to-do southern family, she met Newman while understudying on Broadway. Her cinema debut was *Count Three and Pray* (1955) and she lasted just 20 minutes in *A Kiss Before Dying* (1956), before an electric perfor-

Joanne Woodward: An Oscar at 27

mance as a schizophrenic in *The Three Faces of Eve* (1957) won her the Oscar for Best Actress. She first co-starred with Newman in *The Long Hot Summer* (1958), but her rigorous script selections bought her a reputation as "box office poison", until Newman directed her as the middle-aged schoolmarm out for a final fling in *Rachel, Rachel* (1968), for which she was again an Oscar nominee. *The Effect of Gamma Rays on Man-in-the-Moon Marigolds* (1972) won her the Cannes Best Actress accolade, but she chose to work less and involve herself more in liberal political campaigns, until her role as Newman's wife in *Mr & Mrs Bridge* (1990) confirmed them as everybody's favourite celebrity couple.

William Wyler

Director

Born: *Mulhausen, Germany, July 1, 1902*
Died: *July 27, 1981*

Insiders used to call him William "Ninety-Take" Wyler because of his insistence on filming the same

shot over and over again. Such perfectionism evidently worked, because he won three Best Director Academy Awards – for *Mrs Miniver* (1942), *The Best Years of Our Lives* (1946) and *Ben-Hur* (1959) – and created some of Hollywood's most memorable pictures. A master of visual composition, his movies were meticulously crafted, notable for their taut scripts, heartfelt performances and ground-breaking camerawork. He had come to America as a teenager and, after working as an assistant director, made his own debut with the two-reeler *Crook Buster* (1925). Features such as *Hell's Heroes* (1930) and *A House Divided* (1932) were hugely popular, but it wasn't until *Dodsworth* (1936) and *These Three* (1936) that he came to be recognized as a major creative force. Over the next decade he made a string of classic movies – *Jezebel* (1938); *Wuthering Heights* (1939); *Mrs Miniver*; *The Best Years of Our Lives* – before turning to more grandiose productions in the 1950s and 1960s, notably *The Big Country* (1958) and the Roman epic *Ben-Hur*. Although generally very popular, these big-budget spectacles lacked the subtlety of his early work, and it is on his more intimate films of the period 1936–46 that his reputation as one of the directing greats must truly rest.

Jane Wyman

Actress

Born: SARAH JANE FULKS, *St Joseph, Mo., January 4, 1914*

After a failed attempt by her mother to make her a child star, Wyman broke into show business in her late teens as Jane Durrell, radio singer, then moved into films as a chorus girl and bit player. She graduated to supporting roles, often as the heroine's dizzy blonde best friend. During her marriage to Ronald Reagan (1940–48), when playing Betty Grable's sidekick in *Footlight Serenade* (1942), Wyman had the retrospectively ironic line: "You have as much chance of doing that routine as I have of being the First Lady". The turning point for her came when Billy Wilder gave her the small but important role of Ray Milland's fiancée in *The Lost Weekend* (1945). Her dramatic abilities now recognized (and her hair restored to its natural brunette), Wyman played Gregory Peck's embittered, wife in *The Yearling* (1946) and her Oscar-winning role as the deaf-mute rape victim in *Johnny Belinda* (1948). Then followed a series of lush "Wyman weepies", including Tennessee Williams's *The Glass Menagerie* (1950) as Gertrude Lawrence's shy, crippled daughter; *The Blue Veil* (1951) as a self-sacrificing children's nanny; and the object of Rock Hudson's *Magnificent Obsession* (1954). After the sudsy wartime romance *Miracle in the Rain* (1956) Wyman decided she had had enough of screen suffering. She hosted a television drama show in the 1950s, starred in several TV movies and in her sixties played America's favourite matriarch in the soap *Falcon Crest* (1981–90).

Loretta Young

Actress
Born: GRETCHEN MICHAELA YOUNG, *Salt Lake City, Ut., January 6, 1913*

Young will always be remembered as Hollywood's favourite fashion model. A glamorous beauty with delicate features and ebony-black hair, she became known for the richness and style of her on-screen outfits, enlivening almost 100 films with her stunning looks and sartorial elegance. Most of her movies weren't outstanding, but she won an Oscar for *The Farmer's Daughter* (1947) and was more than capable of turning in a powerhouse performance. One of four actress sisters, she appeared on screen as a child, and first made a

mark with Lon Chaney's *Laugh Clown Laugh* (1928), as a high-wire performer. She was good opposite Jean Harlow in *Platinum Blonde* (1931), outstanding with James Cagney in *Taxi!* (1932), and gave memorable performances in *The Hatchet Man* (1932), *Zoo in Budapest* (1933), *Man's Castle* (1933), *Love Is News* (1937) and *Four Men and a Prayer* (1938). Her career hit the doldrums in the late 1930s and early 1940s, partly due to run-ins with studio heads, but she bounced back with *The Stranger* (1946), followed by *The Farmer's Daughter* and the taut psychological thriller *The Accused* (1949). Her last film was the enjoyable comedy *It Happens Every Thursday* (1953), after which she went into television, enjoying huge success with her *Loretta Young Show* (1953–61), scooping her three Emmies.

Darryl F. Zanuck

Producer, scriptwriter
Born: *Wahoo, Nevada, September 5, 1902*
Died: *December 22, 1979*

The winner of three Academy Awards for Best Film – for *How Green Was My Valley* (1941); *Gentleman's Agreement* (1947); and *All About Eve* (1950) – and an unprecedented three Irving Thalberg Awards for achievements in production, Zanuck was one of the most successful and enduring producers in movie history. A tough, dynamic businessman, he had an instinctive understanding of what the moviegoing public wanted to see, and rarely failed to deliver. He began as a scriptwriter for Warners in the mid-1920s, rising to chief of production and supervising a series of popular hits – notably *Little Caesar* (1930) and *The Public Enemy* (1931) – before forming 20th Century Pictures in 1933. In 1934 this merged with Fox to form 20th Century Fox with Zanuck as head of production, and over the next 20 years he released a formidable

string of classic films: *Les Miserables* (1935), *The Grapes of Wrath* (1940), *How Green Was My Valley*, *Gentleman's Agreement*, *All About Eve* and *Viva Zapata* (1952). He went independent in 1956, but, after the hugely successful *The Longest Day* (1962), returned as head of 20th Century Fox and remained there until his resignation in 1971. One of the most influential figures in cinema history, Zanuck was Hollywood's arch-populist, with a Midas touch which, it seems, has now been inherited by his mogul son Richard (*Jaws, Cocoon*).

Franco Zeffirelli

Director, writer, producer
Born: GIANFRANCO CORSI, *Florence, Italy, February 12, 1923*

Franco Zeffirelli is a true Renaissance man. An unashamedly extravagant, theatrical film-maker, he imbues his work with the sort of dramatic, colourful romanticism one normally associates with big-budget stage productions. It is, indeed, with opera and theatre that his heart truly lies, and in a movie career spanning 30 years he has made only ten feature films, most of them adaptations of classic stage works. After working briefly as an actor, he moved into set design and direction in the mid-1940s. He eventually made his feature debut in 1966 with an opulent, boisterous version of Shakespeare's *The Taming of The Shrew*, starring Elizabeth Taylor and Richard Burton, and followed it up with the equally invigorating *Romeo and Juliet* (1968), portraying the doomed lovers as flower-children. *Brother Sun, Sister Moon* (1972), about St Francis, wasn't so good, but his epic tele-movie *Jesus of Nazareth* (1977) was stunning. *The Champ* (1979) and *Endless Love* (1981) were horribly over-sentimental and over-directed, but he bounced back with *La Traviata* (1982), *Otello* (1986), and an excel-

lent rendition of *Hamlet* (1990) with Mel Gibson as the Dane. With his bombastic, over-the-top pictures, Zeffirelli has described himself as "a flag-bearer of the crusade against boredom", though the flag was fluttering limply with 1994's tame costume-romance *Sparrow*.

Fred Zinnemann

Director, producer, writer
Born: *Vienna, Austria, April 29, 1907*

The distinguished Vienna-born, Paris-trained director who says he's in pictures for the joy of it has given audiences plenty of joy. He's moved easily between genres and is known as a craftsman par excellence. He arrived in Hollywood in 1929, immediately became an extra in *All Quiet on the Western Front* (1930), then an editor and in 1937 director of shorts for MGM, one of them (1938's *That Others Might Live*) winning an Oscar. He directed his first feature, B-movie thriller *Eyes in the Night*, in 1942, but it was the classic western *High Noon* (1952) and the army life saga *From Here to Eternity* (1953) that put him on the map, the latter winning him his second Oscar. Then he opened out Rodgers and Hammerstein's musical *Oklahoma!* (1955) into a widescreen hit. Intelligent, often inspiring dramas followed, such as *The Nun's Story* (1958) with Audrey Hepburn and Peter Finch and *The Sundowners* (1960), for both of which he was Oscar-nominated. He won his third Oscar for his version of Robert Bolt's *A Man for All Seasons* (1966). Since then there have been only three more films, but they've included two satisfying real-life dramas, *The Day of the Jackal* (1973) with Edward Fox as President De Gaulle's would-be assassin, and *Julia* (1977), teaming Jane Fonda and Oscar-winning Vanessa Redgrave in the stirring story of author Lillian Hellman.

Landmark Movies

Whittling the total of 280,000 or so films made worldwide in the cinema's first century down to just 250 Landmark Movies has proved a Herculean task. The following selection is bound to infuriate as well as delight our readers, and it's certain to contain films you detest or, perhaps even worse, films that had no effect on you at all. Equally it's bound to omit some of your all-time favourites. What this selection hopes to achieve is to cover those works that have had an undeniable influence on the development of world cinema. Normally that impact is beneficial, though in some instances such as *Triumph of the Will* (1935) or *Wayne's World* (1992) the influence is more open to debate. This section is arranged on an annual basis, and some years have produced a richer harvest than others. It's a job for cultural historians to figure out why this may be. The rest of us can just simply enjoy and read on.

1903

The Great Train Robbery

12 min.
Director: *Edwin Porter*
Origin: *USA*
Distributor: *Edison*
Cast: *Broncho Billy Anderson, George Barnes, Marie Murray*

For many years *The Great Train Robbery* was regarded by film historians as the first narrative film, which is strange as, apart from other contenders, Porter's own version of *Uncle Tom's Cabin* earlier the same year was narrative in content. However, *The Great Train Robbery* is undoubtedly one of the most important milestones in screen history. It was the longest film of its time – records of its length vary from eight to 12 minutes – but in the context of the period it was an epic action picture, with all the elements of its modern descendants, such as careful and briskly paced editing and a sense of cinema showmanship. The story was based on a 1903 British cops-and-robbers film, *A Daring Daylight Burglary*, but was far more sophisticated, with a cast of 40 and a logical, semi-scripted narrative. It used existing cinema techniques to maximum effect, ending with the famous close-up of a bandit shooting a pistol at the audience. The story of the robbery is shown in 14 scenes, with the bandits tying up the telegraph operator and robbing the train, their escape, subsequent pursuit and capture. Though Porter made the film in New Jersey, the costume of the pursuers suggests that they are cowboys, and it is possible that *The Great Train Robbery* started the fashion for westerns, and could indeed be described as the first of this genre. The film caused a sensation at the time and remained the most famous and profitable film until D. W. Griffith's *The Birth of a Nation* in 1915.
ACTION ADVENTURE

1915

The Birth of a Nation

187 min.
Director: *D. W. Griffith*
Origin: *USA*
Distributor: *Epoch*
Cast: *Miriam Cooper, Lillian Gish, Mae Marsh, Robert Harron, Wallace Reid, George Siegman, Henry B. Walthall*

D. W. Griffith's sweeping silent masterpiece, based around the American Civil War, is not only the most popular silent movie of all time – by 1946 over 200 million people had seen it – but also the first true feature film, introducing narrative and visual techniques still in use today. Its contemporary impact was immense and, although its overt racism is repugnant to modern audiences, it is impossible not to be swept away by its panoramic battle scenes and beautifully crafted, intimate family exchanges. Adapted from Thomas Dixon Jr's novel *The Clansman*, it follows the fortunes of two friendly families, the Camerons of the South and the Stonemans of the North. Deftly weaving historical fact with narrative fiction, Griffith provides us with three separate sequences – a pre-war visit by the Stonemans to the Camerons; scenes from the Civil War itself; and a post-war drama in which the defeated South is overrun by rapacious black soldiers. A dazzling array of memorable characters – notably Henry B. Walthall's "Little Colonel"; Mae Marsh's "Little Sister"; and George

touching performance by Claude Rains, which made the revelation of his scarred face, less terrifying than Chaney's, both piteous and horrific. The low-key Hammer version in 1962 relocated the story to London, while Brian De Palma's inventively satirical *Phantom of the Paradise* (1974) was set in a contemporary pop palace.
HORROR

1926

Ben-Hur

145 min.
Director: *Fred Niblo*
Origin: *USA*
Distributor: *MGM*
Cast: *Betty Bronson, Francis X. Bushman, May McAvoy, Carmel Myers, Ramon Novarro*

Several silent versions were made of Lew Wallace's semi-biblical adventure novel, but Fred Niblo's film, the silent screen's biggest epic, remains the best-known. His telling of the story of the trials and tribulations of a Jewish noble in conflict with the Romans when Jesus was alive was huge in the scale of its conception, boasting a cast not merely of thousands but of 125,000, according to the publicity. It also included some early sequences filmed in colour. The film's most memorable moments were the clash at sea and, of course, the chariot race. The novel was filmed again in 1959 by William Wyler, with Charlton Heston as the hero and Stephen Boyd as his Roman rival, with Heston selected after stars like Tony Curtis and Marlon Brando had rejected the role. Like its 1926 predecessor, the film was able to boggle its audience's minds with statistics. The chariot race sequence, directed by action expert Andrew Marton, required for its arena 18 acres, 8,000 extras to fill the stands and 40,000 tons of sand for the track. The film garnered mixed reviews and huge audiences. Its huge budget for a time nearly bankrupted MGM but they came up smiling eventually with a $40 million gross take.
HISTORICAL EPIC

Metropolis

120 min.
Director: *Fritz Lang*
Origin: *Germany*
Distributor: *UFA*
Cast: *Alfred Abel, Gustav Fröhlich, Brigitte Helm, Rudolf Klein-Rogge, Fritz Rasp*

Metropolis is the cinema's first great futuristic fantasy. Fritz Lang's costly silent sci-fi classic, with its political allegory about oppressed workers in a mechanized society who are stirred to revolt, has worn extremely well thanks partly to a still-timely message and partly to the extraordinary images thrown up by the set designs (Otto Hunte, Erich Kettelhut, Karl Vollbrecht) and camerawork (Karl Freund, Günther Rittau). A complex, intelligent and thought-provoking story, *Metropolis* is set in the then distant future of the year 2000, when the son of the wealthy ruling capitalist rebels against his comfortable life. Below them in the underground city of Metropolis (a future projection of New York), where the workers are slaves to industry, a mad scientist (Rudolf Klein-Rogge) creates an evil robot who's a replica of the people's heroine Maria (Brigitte Helm). Sweet Maria has calmed the rumblings of the workers by preaching goodwill, but they're stirred up by the robot. Extraordinarily, after 70 years the special effects still have the power to amaze thanks to the vision of master cinematographer Eugen Shuftan who, years later, won an Oscar for *The Hustler*. But the mastermind of it all is the visionary Lang. The film's 1984 revamp and restoration by rock musician Giorgio Moroder may not please purists but it's a real pleasure for those who like his jolly electronic score, the colour-tinted visuals and the driving pace he's brought by removing the inter-titles, which accounted for a quarter of its length.
SCI-FI

Son of the Sheik

74 min.
Director: *George Fitzmaurice*
Origin: *USA*
Distributor: *United Artists*
Cast: *Agnes Ayres, Vilma Banky, Rudolph Valentino*

Hailed by columnist Louella Parsons as "the very picture for which the world's wife, mother and daughter have been waiting", *Son of the Sheik* was Valentino's last movie before his untimely death at 31, and a belated sequel to his kitsch 1921 smash-hit *The Sheik*. In the latter – unimaginatively directed by George Melford – he had played a smouldering desert prince who abducts and romances a swooning English Lady (Agnes Ayres). Now five years later, under the more assured direction of George Fitzmaurice, he reprised the role, playing both the Sheik and his son Ahmed, upon whom the new story focuses. Plotwise it wasn't much sharper than the original, with Ahmed falling for dusky nomadic dancer Yasmin (Vilma Banky), doubting her faithfulness

Ben-Hur: *Chariots of fire and a cast of tens of thousands*

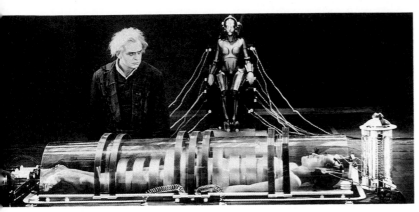

Metropolis: *A mad scientist creates an evil robot*

after he's captured by bandits, but then discovering she's true after all and fighting his way back into her arms and a happy sunset ending. What distinguishes it from its predecessor is Valentino's charismatic, tongue-in-cheek performance (by far the finest of his career) and the thrilling succession of fights, rescues and stunts with which director Fitzmaurice relentlessly drives the action onwards. George Barnes's stirring photography was among the finest of the silent era, while the psychological analysis of how violence and passion are passed down from father to son proved way ahead of its time. A luscious, rip-roaring romantic adventure, it was both a fascinating insight into the social tastes of 1920s Hollywood and a fitting epitaph to a screen legend.
ADVENTURE/ROMANCE

1927

Napoléon

378 min.
Director: *Abel Gance*
Origin: *France*
Distributor: *WESTI*
Cast: *Anabella, Antonin Artaud, Pierre Batcheff, Albert Dieudonné, Abel Gance, Nicolas Koline, Alexandre Koubitsky Gina Manés, Wladimir Roudenko, Edmond van Dale*

Although *Napoléon* has been criticized by some for its crude

psychological view of its subject as a man of destiny and the Fascist thinking behind the climactic invasion of Italy, few will dispute Abel Gance's achievement in terms of the visual splendour of this work and his innovative use of cinema techniques. He pushed the language of cinema further than anyone else had done with his daring use of montage and rapid and split-time editing, as in the intercutting between Napoléon facing a storm at sea and the political storm at home. He introduced advances in lighting effects, masking, tinting and innovative camera movement, particularly for action sequences, placing his camera on anything that moved – trucks, horses, pendulums and in the human hand – and experimented with 3D and colour, though these sequences were cut from the final version. His most spectacular innovation was the triptych or triple-screen process, which showed different aspects of the invasion simultaneously, then combining into one giant picture – predating 50s wraparound screens. *Napoléon* was shown in its entirety in only eight European cities. In America MGM cut it drastically, junked the triptych technique as too confusing for an audience already bewildered by the arrival of sound, and the film's reception was disastrous. Gance himself revised the film in 1934, adding another of his innovations, stereophonic sound. But it was not until 1981 that he received the recognition due to him, when

British documentary director Kevin Brownlow carefully restored the film from extensive research, including some of the colour sequences, and presented it with live orchestral accompaniment. Unveiled after 54 years, *Napoléon* shocked modern audiences with its force and vigour.
HISTORICAL EPIC

The General

74 min.
Director: *Buster Keaton*
Origin: *USA*
Distributor: *United Artists*
Cast: *Glen Cavender, Jim Farley, Buster Keaton, Joseph Keaton, Marion Mack*

"*The General* was my pet," remarked Buster Keaton. "It was a page out of history." A jewel of silent cinema, the film was loosely inspired by an actual event during the American Civil War when a bunch of Northern soldiers hijacked a locomotive, the "General", in order to sabotage a Confederate supply line sustaining Southern troops. In the hands of Keaton (the picture's writer, director, editor and star), this bitter struggle is condensed into one dazzlingly sustained chase sequence with "Old Stone Face" nominally cast as hero Johnny Gray, the dogged Southern engineer in pursuit. "You can't make villains out of the Confederate army," Keaton insisted. "They lost the war anyway, so a motion picture audience resents it. And the same goes if I was in Michigan, Maine, Massachusetts." In *The General* little Johnny Gray isn't truly battling for either side anyway. He's just trying to get his engine back. While set in the wooded hills of Georgia, the picture was actually filmed in the Pacific Northwest state of Oregon, where the scenery was better and the country was honeycombed with the narrow-gauge lumber railroads that fitted Keaton's period engines. Luminous and

consistently thrilling, *The General* has arguably worn better than all other silent comedies. Rather than using the camera as a simple gag-recording device, Keaton was determined to explore its full potential – filming on location, constructing elaborate stunts and shooting long tracking shots from a customized vehicle that ran alongside the speeding train. Perhaps the movie marked the moment when comic cinema slipped the chains of its stage-bound vaudeville origins, turning airy, fluid and poetic. "Railroads are a great prop," concluded Keaton. "You can do some awful wild things with railroads."
COMEDY

The Jazz Singer

89 min.
Director: *Alan Crosland*
Origin: *USA*
Distributor: *Warner*
Cast: *Eugenie Besserer, William Demarest, Al Jolson, Otto Lederer, May McAvoy, Warner Oland*

The Jazz Singer owes its place in history not to its merits as a film, but for being the very first "talkie". Perhaps "singie" would be more accurate, as the sound consisted mainly of music and songs, with a few lines of dialogue, one of which is Jolson's prophetic line: "You ain't heard nothin' yet". The songs were in pairs and originally on disc synchronized to the action, and it is not surprising that, because of the limited nature of the early sound techniques, few realized that this film would mean the end of the silent cinema. The story is a well worn and sentimental one about a cantor's son who refuses to follow in his father's Jewish footsteps but becomes a vaudeville entertainer, finding showbiz success as a blackface singer. It made a star of Al Jolson but, as is so often the case with these things, he was not the first choice. *The Jazz Singer* was based on a play by Samson Raphaelson, and the

movie role was offered to George Jessel, who had played the part on Broadway, but he wanted a much increased fee to sing and talk in a film. Eddie Cantor turned it down on the grounds that he could not follow Jessel in the role, so Jolson got lucky. There was a sentimental rejig in 1953 by director Michael Curtiz, and in 1980 another version, starring Neil Diamond and Laurence Olivier, in which the mother character became a patient wife and "jazz", as still misleadingly used in the title, became Diamond's particular brand of ballad singing. It made for a good record album, a night out for Neil Diamond fans and otherwise a pretty pointless movie exercise.
MUSICAL

Wings

137 min.
Director: *William Wellman*
Origin: *USA*
Distributor: *Paramount*
Cast: *Richard Arlen, Clara Bow, El Brendel, Gary Cooper, Jobyna Ralston, Charles "Buddy" Rogers*

Wings was the first film to win an Oscar for Best Picture, and the only silent movie ever to receive the award in that category. Directed by William Wellman to the tune of $2 million, it remains, despite a wafer-thin plot, one of the most visually stunning

of all silent movies, thrilling for its protracted aerial combat sequences and Harry Perry's extraordinary airborne photography. It is the story of two small-town boys (Charles "Buddy" Rogers and Richard Arlen) – both in love with the same girl (Clara Bow) – who enlist as flyers in the Army Air Corps during World War One, an enterprise that ends in tragedy when one accidentally shoots down the other. The storyline alone is insufficient to maintain interest over the 137 minutes, but the project is sustained by the graphic flying scenes, with up to 18 planes at a time battling it out in a succession of dramatic dogfights, crashes and explosions (the film won another Oscar in the now defunct category of Best Engineering Effects). Tinting of the black and white background enhanced these sequences by highlighting the sky, clouds and spouts of flame, while a re-released version in 1929 was accompanied by sound effects and a musical score. The performances are outstanding,

Wings: High-flying aerial stuntwork and in-your-face battle scenes

especially from the two white-faced protagonists (Wellman wouldn't let them use make-up). Screen legend Gary Cooper has one of his earliest film roles, winning a studio contract on the basis of his single brief, blink-and-you'll-miss-it appearance.
ADVENTURE EPIC

1928

Un Chien Andalou

AN ANDALUSIAN DOG   17 min.
Director: *Luis Buñuel*
Origin: *France*
Distributor: *Luis Buñuel*
Cast: *Pierre Batcheff, Luis Buñuel, Salvador Dali, Simone Mareuil, Jaime Miravilles*

Seventeen infamous, intoxicating minutes of Surrealist dreamlike delight from Luis Buñuel and Salvador Dali. Sensational in its time, this short is still eye-popping, opening with a woman's open eye (though supposedly human, in close-up it's actually a bull's eye) apparently dissected by a cut-throat razor. The film's

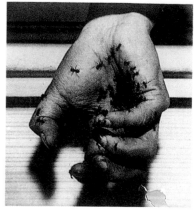

Un Chien Andalou: Getting a big hand

nightmarish images follow in a random, unconnected, illogical succession that nevertheless satisfies as a whole entity as if in an altered state. Audiences are forced to engage their brains, to use their imagination, to provide their own meaning. As if to reassure viewers fumbling for a narrative, the makers helpfully added: "Nothing means anything." Buñuel's first film, made at the age of 28, burns with the tongue-in-cheek, fresh humour of youth, and was a calling card for the masterpieces to come. We see the anti-clerical stance of his later works in the moment where the priests are pulled along the ground. Other renowned images include the hand leaking with crawling ants ("I've always found insects exciting," Buñuel said teasingly), a woman's breasts turning into buttocks and dead donkeys lying on pianos (bewilderingly, later referred to in the 1929 Laurel and Hardy short, *Wrong Again*, which features a horse balanced on a grand piano). Buñuel co-wrote the script with Dali, and directed and edited the film. The two men served as joint producers, while photographer Albert Dubergen captured their fantastical images. Buñuel obtained the funding from his mother, the Vicomte de Noailles (who also financed his second film *L'Age d'Or* and Cocteau's *The Blood of a Poet)* and from a friend's fortuitous lottery win.
SURREALISM

1929

Applause

80 min.
Director: *Rouben Mamoulian*
Origin: *USA*
Distributor: *Paramount*
Cast: *Fuller Mellish Jr, Helen Morgan, Joan Peers, Henry Wadsworth*

Rouben Mamoulian's debut feature, and probably the finest film he ever made, *Applause* is an epoch-making, multi-hankie classic, revolutionary both for its combination of complex soundtrack with moving camera, and for its intense psychological study of a troubled mother-daughter relationship. It appeared in the very earliest days of talkie films, when the new sound cameras, enclosed in special booths, were largely immobile. Mamoulian insisted that such limitations were unnecessary, combining long tracking shots with a multi-layered soundtrack to create the first truly satisfying sound movie. Based on Beth Brown's tear-jerking novel, it showcases a towering central performance from Helen Morgan as Kitty Darling, a fading burlesque star with a two-timing lover (Fuller Mellish Jr) who is gradually eclipsed and rejected by her convent-educated daughter April (Joan Peers), eventually committing suicide so as not to shame the

Applause: Epoch-making, multi-hankie classic

latter. A melodramatic plot is elevated by the strength of characterization and by Mamoulian's ground-breaking direction, perfectly capturing, in his Expressionist use of lighting and camera-angle, the seedy backstage atmosphere of a small-time vaudeville hall and the lonely, windswept streets of night-time New York. Unforgettable cinematic and emotional touches – an erotic chorus-line dance silhouetted against a backcloth, Morgan singing her daughter to sleep as the latter mumbles a prayer – create a uniquely moving tragedy. Also the debut of Morgan, who succumbed to alcoholism and died of liver failure at 41.
MELODRAMA

Pandora's Box

DIE BÜCHSE DER PANDORA
140 min.
Director: *G. W. Pabst*
Origin: *Germany*
Distributor: *Nero Film*
Cast: *Louise Brooks, Gustav Diessl, Fritz Kortner, Franz Lederer*

G. W. Pabst's silent masterpiece, restored to its original glory in 1983 after 50 years of circulation in a heavily cut format, is notable chiefly for the transcendentally erotic performance of its 23-year-old star, Louise Brooks. Despite the skilful editing and Expressionist photography, it is Brooks who carries the piece with her sexual magnetism and unique mastery of movement and expression. In a slimline plot drawn from two Franz Wedekind plays – *Erdgeist* (1893) and *Die Büchse der Pandora* (1904) – she plays Lulu, a provocative circus performer who marries a rich doctor (Fritz Kortner), murders him, becomes a prostitute and ends up as a victim of Jack the Ripper. Essentially a series of dislocated vignettes charting Lulu's social rise and fall, the storyline is given coherence by Brooks's mesmerizing performance and Pabst's imaginative direction.

His technique of cutting while his actors were in motion provided the film with a poetic fluidity, trapping the characters in an onward rush of events. Likewise his clever use of soft-focus lighting and claustrophobic interiors suggested a heroine irrevocably trapped within her own destiny. There is a host of memorable set-pieces – a gambling sequence on board a giant floating casino, the intrusion by Lulu's low-life friends into her newly respectable surroundings – but all is dominated by the exquisite Brooks. Her work here, combined with that in her other film for Pabst, *Diary of a Lost Girl* (1929), established her reputation as one of the key icons of the silent cinema.
MELODRAMA

1930

All Quiet on the Western Front

105 min.
Director: *Lewis Milestone*
Origin: *USA*
Distributor: *Universal*
Cast: *Ben Alexander, Lew Ayres, Russell Gleason, Raymond Griffith, Slim Summerville, Louis Wolheim, John Wray, Fred Zinnemann*

Still the benchmark anti-war movie, *All Quiet on the Western Front* was the first film of its kind to acknowledge the enemy as human, scared victims. It depicts the horror and futility of war as seen by seven German schoolboy volunteers for World War One. The central character, Paul (Lew Ayres) briefly escapes the horror, travelling home on leave, but is so disillusioned by the misplaced patriotism there that he returns to die at the front. The last-but-one scene is the film's most famous motif, Paul carelessly reaching out to grasp a butterfly, his hand (in fact a close-up of the director's)

smothering the creature as a sniper's bullet finishes him off. Adapted from Erich Maria Remarque's landmark novel, the film abandons the book's flashback structure in favour of a chronological account, but remains an emotionally draining experience. Pacifists criticized it for failing to suggest how to make a stand against war, though in Poland it was banned as pro-German, and in Germany the Nazis organized riots at screenings, enabling them to ban it as detrimental to the country's image. Ironically, peaceful Southern California was turned into a war zone for the making of the film, with 1,000 acres dug up for trenches and 2,000 ex-servicemen recruited as extras. Milestone's tracking through the trenches and use of crane-shots were both startlingly innovative, as was his camera-as-machine-gun technique, mowing down troops as they appear on screen. James Whale made a sequel, *The Road Back* (1937), and the original was remade for TV in 1980.
WAR

The Blue Angel

103 min.
Director: *Josef von Sternberg*
Origin: *Germany*
Distributor: *UFA*
Cast: *Hans Albers, Marlene Dietrich, Kurt Gerron, Emil Jannings*

Marlene Dietrich first hit the world's headlines as Lola, the promiscuous cabaret singer who casts her spell over a fussy professor of English (Emil Jannings). The infatuated academic persuades her to marry him, but soon the worthless good-time girl grows bored and despises him. It's filmed in dazzling high style by director Josef von Sternberg, Dietrich's Svengali-figure who took her to America for a series of exotic triumphs, including *Morocco*, *Dishonoured*, *Shanghai Express*, *Blonde Venus*, *The Scarlet Empress* and *The Devil Is a Woman*. Sternberg brings out the potency of the sleazy German cabaret settings and the smouldering glances of Dietrich who sings a clutch of Frederick Hollander's haunting songs, notably "Falling in Love Again" and "They Call Me Naughty Lola". Jannings's silent-cinema-style acting, which so impressed in its day, has dated a little but it still touches the heart, while Dietrich's turn (a parody favourite from Madeline Kahn in *Blazing Saddles* to Helmut Berger in *The Damned*) is as fresh and lustrous as ever, giving a diamond-sharp cutting edge to her sex appeal. She reveals the mesmerizing Lola as a woman without kindness or pity, whom (in the words of the song) men cluster round like moths around the flame, and if they burn then they know she's not to blame. Made back to back in German and in English, it's best seen in the subtler Teutonic version. Robert Liebmann's script is based on Heinrich Mann's novel *Professor Unrath*, but this film is the director's and actors' triumph. ROMANTIC DRAMA

1931

City Lights

87 min.
Director: *Charles Chaplin*
Origin: *USA*
Distributor: *United Artists*
Cast: *Charles Chaplin, Virginia Cherrill, Florence Lee, Harry Myers*

An unforgettable mixture of pantomime humour and tear-jerking pathos, this poetic tale of the Little Tramp and the blind flower girl catches Charlie Chaplin at the very height of his powers. He produced, directed, starred, scripted, scored and edited; and, at a time when every other film-maker had gone over to sound, stubbornly and triumphantly continued in

City Lights: Chaplin lights up hearts around the world

the silent tradition, adding sound effects and music, but no dialogue. A project 18 months in the making, and one into which Chaplin sank most of his fortune, *City Lights* stars Chaplin as the shabby, bowler-hatted vagrant who falls for blind flower-seller Virginia Cherrill, embarking on a series of hilarious money-making schemes to pay for an operation to restore her sight. He finally takes the money from an eccentric millionaire (Harry Myers), placing it in the girl's hands before being imprisoned for robbery. In one of the most moving of all Chaplin finales, the tramp emerges from jail to find the girl, sight restored, working in a flower shop. Pitying him, she gives him some money from the cash register and discovers, by the feel of his hands, that he is her mysterious benefactor. Such heart-rending poignancy is offset by wonderful comic touches and, despite its outmoded silent format, the film was a massive hit: "*City Lights* has no dialogue," said critic Rose Pelwick after the first-night preview. "And it's just as well, because if the picture had words the laughs and applause of last night's audience would have drowned them out." SENTIMENTAL COMEDY

Frankenstein

71 min.
Director: *James Whale*
Origin: *USA*
Distributor: *Universal*
Cast: *John Boles, Mae Clarke, Colin Clive, Dwight Frye, Boris Karloff, Frederick Kerr, Edward van Sloan*

The most famous and seminal horror film ever, *Frankenstein* is also one of the cinema's finest fairytale works of the imagination. Universal decided to remake the Frankenstein story (after three silent versions) as a follow-up vehicle for Bela Lugosi after his hit *Dracula*, but cast him as the monster opposite Leslie Howard's doctor. Bela objected to having a mute role and Universal wouldn't agree to his self-devised make-up so he left for another project. British director James Whale inherited the film, cast his fellow countrymen Colin Clive as the Doc and Boris Karloff as the Creature, then brought in Jack Pierce as make-up man. The film's dark, Germanic style is clearly influenced by Paul Wegener's *The Golem* (1920) and there are many great moments, not least the thrilling and much-copied creation sequence. But Karloff's mesmerizing performance as a sympathetic monster – clearly and subversively the film's hero – turns

the ghoulish story to poetry, capturing his chilling transformation from naive innocent to playful learner to vengeful killer. The Creature that Mary Shelley invented in her 1818 novel was a handsome, articulate and sophisticated self-teacher, unlike Universal's mute, rampaging movie monster with his stitched forehead and neck bolts. Though the discrepancy between Shelley's Gothic romance and the crowd-pleasing horror film is significant, it is entirely due to the film's success that the word Frankenstein entered almost every language on earth. Who but the academic few would now know the name Mary Shelley were it not for the lumbering and growling Boris Karloff? HORROR

M

99 min.
Director: *Fritz Lang*
Origin: *Germany*
Distributor: *Nero Film*
Cast: *Inge Landgut, Peter Lorre, Gustav Gründgens, Ellen Widmann*

Fritz Lang's favourite picture *M* allowed him the freedom to make overt social criticism in an unsettling tale of the disturbed, overweight psychotic Franz Becker (memorably played by Peter Lorre) who cannot help his impulse to murder children. In detailing so sympathetically the case of a sick individual reviled as a criminal, Lang speaks up for the mentally ill in a startlingly modern fashion. Both the Berlin police and the underworld of criminals, outraged at being associated with his crimes and trying to prevent the cops probing their activities, organize to track Becker down, but it's the latter group who find him. Then Lang goes in for another kind of social criticism – that of the sickness in society at large – as he shows the criminals giving the terrified Becker a citizens' trial. Of course he's found guilty, and is killed in revenge for the children's

deaths, a theme later reflected in Lang's American film *Fury* (1936). Lang shot *M* as a thriller, weaving a series of imaginatively staged set-pieces in the German Expressionist style of the period and somehow transcending the difficulties of early sound shooting with its cumbersome cameras and equipment. For the sake of authenticity, Lang – who had mixed with the underworld – employed real criminals on the film, leading to a large fallout of extras as more than 20 of them were arrested.
THRILLER

1933

42nd Street

89 min.
Director: *Lloyd Bacon*
Origin: *USA*
Distributor: *Warner*
Cast: *Warner Baxter, George Brent, Bebe Daniels, Ruby Keeler, Guy Kibbee, Una Merkel, Dick Powell, Ginger Rogers, Ned Sparks*

This quintessential backstage musical that invented all the clichés, *42nd Street* still stands up as perhaps the best of the genre thanks to the brightest of showbiz performances and dazzling choreography by Busby Berkeley. Star Warner Baxter sweats nervously as the obsessive impresario with failing health who's determined to make his swan-song show into a Broadway hit. But trouble looms. His star Bebe Daniels takes the advice you're supposed to give actors on opening night – break a leg – and Baxter promotes young Sawyer (Ruby Keeler) from the chorus. But Ruby isn't quite good enough yet, so the two go through hell and high water to get her ready. Baxter's pre-show pep talk has become legendary: "Sawyer, you're going out a youngster but you've gotta come back a star". Of course she does thanks to the love of co-star Dick Powell, a clutch of great showtunes by Al Dubin and Harry Warren, and of course Berkeley's kaleidoscopic stagings, filmed in groundbreaking overhead camera shots. All the show numbers ("42nd Street", "Shuffle off to Buffalo", "Young and Healthy", "You're Getting to be a Habit with Me") arrive back to back at the film's finale – a risky strategy that should rock its structure, but it's so strong and pacy through the drama scenes you forget it's a musical at all. Talking of plucking someone from the chorus to be a star, that's Ginger Rogers hovering in the background as Anytime Annie, and we all know what happened to her! Lloyd Bacon is the director whose handling is Hollywood professional, but it's Berkeley and the stars who well and truly bring home the bacon.
MUSICAL

Duck Soup

70 min.
Director: *Leo McCarey*
Origin: *USA*
Distributor: *Paramount*
Cast: *Louis Calhern, Margaret Dumont, Edgar Kennedy, Groucho, Harpo, Chico and Zeppo Marx, Raquel Torres*

A critical and commercial failure on release, *Duck Soup* is now generally recognized as the Marx Brothers' finest hour. The last release in a five-picture deal with Paramount, it marked the last outing for Zeppo, the group's clean-cut straight man, and proved one of the few pictures where the team were marshalled by a seasoned director, comic master Leo McCarey. Set in the fairytale Ruritanian principality of Freedonia, the film spins a freewheeling, absurdist yarn, bristling with espionage, military skulduggery and deconstructed diplomatic backchat. Amid a wealth of beautifully complementary comic performances Groucho Marx provides a turbo-charged turn as President Rufus T. Firefly, who declares instant war on a neighbouring principality when he's dubbed an upstart and then refuses to re-think the declaration. "I've paid a month's rent on the battlefield," he explains. While *Duck Soup* has been lauded as a savage satire on the dead language and double-dealing of international diplomacy, it is unlikely that the film's intentions were so pointed. The Marx Brothers' assaults always seemed more anarchic and indiscriminate than that, an audacious juggling of wordplay and exquisite physical comedy, best evidenced in the hilarious mute artistry of the mirror sequence. In hindsight *Duck Soup* can be seen to mark the apogee of this exuberant comic style, as later pictures found the team equally funny but less blatantly disruptive, sucked gently into the formula movie mainstream. In *Duck Soup* the Brothers still had teeth.
COMEDY

King Kong

100 min.
Director: *Merian C. Cooper*
Origin: *USA*
Distributor: *RKO*
Cast: *Robert Armstrong, Bruce Cabot, Frank Reicher, Fay Wray*

The beloved monster movie *King Kong*, which set the standard by which all fantasy films are now judged, is a triumph of storytelling and special effects in developing a myth about the impossibility of love. It turned the 50ft giant gorilla Kong into one of the cinema's most famous images, while Fay Wray became the movies' greatest screamer as the object of his desire, forever associated with just this one role. The picture shows its age only in the slow start before the adventure-party reach the island jungle inhabited by Kong, but the island sequences are thrilling. When Kong is captured, he's brought to America to appear as a theatre attraction but, untamed, the beast escapes into the streets of Manhattan to search for his beloved Wray. The finale atop the Empire State Building is justly celebrated, and when Kong is shot down by evidently toy planes, with Wray snatched from his hand, he dies a tragic, sympathetic figure. Willis O'Brien's pioneering stop-motion animation trick-work, though jerky, is still impressive and persuasive after all the 20th century's technical innovations. While the story clearly owes something to Conan Doyle's *The Lost*

42nd Street: Come and meet those dancing feet

King Kong: *Manhattan monkey business*

World, it creates a unique world of its own. *King Kong* was proclaimed a masterpiece by the Surrealists who saw Kong as an expression of the darker side of human sexuality. Underpinning the picture are unforgettable moments of true psychological darkness, for example Kong's first appearance from the forest, a symbol of the emergence of this uncontrollable bestiality from the shadowy depths of the subconscious.
FANTASY

The Private Life of Henry VIII

97 min.
Director: *Alexander Korda*
Origin: *GB*
Distributor: *London Films*
Cast: *Binnie Barnes, Wendy Barrie, Robert Donat, Franklin Dyall, Charles Laughton, Elsa Lanchester, Miles Mander, Merle Oberon*

Alexander Korda's rip-roaring, bawdy biopic of Britain's corpulent Tudor monarch bore little

relation to historical fact, but is still hugely enjoyable and was roundly praised by contemporary critics as the finest picture to have come out of England. Although British films had long been shown abroad, this was the first to have a major international impact, largely due to Charles Laughton's monumental, Oscar-winning performance in the title role (the first English actor ever to receive the prized statuette). Shot in five weeks and costing only £60,000, it is a light-hearted, Holbeinesque romp through five out of Henry's six marriages. Historical and psychological analysis are pushed aside in favour of lavish scenery (designed by the director's brother Vincent Korda), opulent costumes and some wonderful, tongue-in-cheek comedy, especially in its gluttonous banqueting scenes, and Laughton's sequences with fourth wife Anne of Cleves (real-life spouse Elsa Lanchester), who takes him for half his kingdom at cards and, when her portly husband lumbers into the marital bedchamber, utters the immortal line: "The things I've done for England!" Georges Périnal's photography is elegant if unexceptional, while the supporting cast – many of whom made their names in this movie – reads like a who's who of classic British screen talent: Robert Donat, Merle Oberon, Binnie Barnes. A minor classic, it established Laughton as one of the all-time great character actors, and thrilled audiences worldwide with its witty dialogue and quaint, traditional Englishness – something of a paradox considering that director Korda was actually Hungarian.
HISTORICAL

1934

It Happened One Night

105 min.
Director: *Frank Capra*
Origin: *USA*
Distributor: *Columbia*
Cast: *Ward Bond, Claudette Colbert, Walter Connolly, Clark Gable, Alan Hale, Roscoe Karns, Jameson Thomas*

The only film to scoop all the five main Oscars (Best Picture, Actor, Actress, Screenplay, Director) until *One Flew Over the Cuckoo's Nest* in 1975 has worn extremely well, thanks mainly to Clark Gable and Claudette Colbert's captivating performances as a news reporter and the runaway heiress he meets on the road. The story's a model of its kind but it's best remembered for two classic scenes – both considered sexy and risqué in their day. In the first, Colbert hitches up her dress to show her stocking when she wants to hitch a lift after Gable has failed to attract a driver – Colbert has instant success, of course.

In the second, when they're forced to share a room for the night, Gable displays a manly chest, but hangs up a blanket between them ("the walls of Jericho!") in a display of mutual modesty, though we're given the impression the embarrassment's more his than hers. In the sexual equality stakes, Colbert clearly has the upper hand, making this seem a truly modern picture, putting the actress in a long line of 1930s strong women like Davis, Hepburn, Crawford and Stanwyck who portrayed a new image of femininity, mostly to appeal to other women in the audience. It is 1930s screwball comedy at its most typical, endearing and enduring, with a witty script by Robert Riskin from a *Cosmopolitan* story. Perfectly paced by director Frank Capra, whose sophisticated handling doesn't betray a single hint of the populist Capracorn that softened his later outings.
ROMANTIC COMEDY

It Happened One Night: *Two thumbs up from Gable and Colbert*

L'Atalante

89 min.
Director: *Jean Vigo*
Origin: *France*
Distributor: *J. L. Nounez-Gaumont*
Cast: *Jean Dasté, Gilles Margaritis, Dita Parlo, Michel Simon*

L'Atalante is a deceptively simple story, shot in gleaming black and white, about a barge captain sailing down the Seine with his new wife to Paris, which she longs to see but never does. Not a lot happens in terms of plot – the couple fall out, lose each other, find each other and realize how much they love each other. Jean Vigo tells his story through detail, small incident and atmosphere, blending the dingy surface reality of life on the cramped barge with a romantic surrealism of landscape and the way he reveals his characters. The overall effect manages to be charming, touching, poetic and sometimes comic, while avoiding cloying sentimentality. In terms of performances, Michel Simon steals every scene he is in, as the wise but eccentric old boat-hand whose tales enchant the young bride. L'Atalante was one of only four films by Vigo, who is now regarded as one of the major talents and influences of French cinema of this period. He was taken ill with leukaemia during the production of this film and died shortly afterwards at the early age of 29. The film was severely cut by its producers, who feared that its attack on the attitudes of the French bourgeoisie would upset and alienate the public. It was largely vilified by the critics, as were Vigo's other films, and it was not until the 1940s that his work was rediscovered by the post-war cinema movement and his talent and contribution to the development of French film-making were acknowledged. L'Atalante was restored and reissued to a new public in 1990.
POETIC REALISM

1935

The 39 Steps

87 min.
Director: *Alfred Hitchcock*
Origin: *GB*
Distributor: *Gaumont British*
Cast: *Peggy Ashcroft, Madeleine Carroll, Robert Donat, Helen Haye, John Laurie, Lucie Mannheim, Godfrey Tearle, Wylie Watson*

Hitchcock's freewheeling version of the John Buchan adventure classic sees the master at his most intoxicating, conjuring up a spirited spy thriller, crammed with enough wit, plot, scares and thrills for half a dozen movies. Robert Donat plays the typical Hitch innocent hero Richard Hannay accidentally embroiled with villains, like so many Hitchcock protagonists after him – he's almost a prototype for Cary Grant's Roger Thornhill in North by Northwest. It is exciting to watch a cheeky, almost abrasive Donat before he was overtaken by taking himself too seriously. Madeleine Carroll is the obligatory ice-cold blonde, and very alluring she is too as the perfect bantering opponent for Donat, even though she's never given quite enough to do. How Hitchcock enjoyed making the two actors play a large section of the movie in handcuffs! – daring in its day, and much copied since, either as homage or just borrowed. "I used one idea after another," said Hitchcock, "eliminating anything that interfered with the swift pace." Two remakes weren't at all in the same class, though they were OK in their own right. The 1959 version with Kenneth More is a virtual frame-by-frame copy, while the 1978 Robert Powell version stays close to the plot of the original novel. But what these two films

The Bride of Frankenstein: *A hair-raising experience for Elsa Lanchester*

lack is any of Hitchcock's unerring flair, imagination, energy and taste for the bizarre. The 39 Steps is, with The Lady Vanishes, the high spot of Hitchcock's British work, his calling card to America where he carried on ploughing the same profitable furrow, except with bigger stars and bigger budgets – and to bigger acclaim.
SPY THRILLER

The Bride of Frankenstein

75 min.
Director: *James Whale*
Origin: *USA*
Distributor: *Universal*
Cast: *Colin Clive, E. E. Clive, Dwight Frye, Gavin Gordon, O. P. Heggie, Valerie Hobson, Boris Karloff, Elsa Lanchester, Una O'Connor, Ernest Thesiger, Douglas Walton*

This sequel to the 1931 Frankenstein is sometimes claimed to be "perhaps the greatest horror film ever". At any rate The Bride of Frankenstein is one of the rare cases where the sequel keeps up the standard of a classic original. Exploring a strain of Mary Shelley's original story not included in the 1931 Frankenstein, director James Whale reprised his earlier success with the tale of the making of a monstrous consort for the original creature, casting Boris Karloff again as the Creature with Elsa Lanchester as the Bride with what must be the most unforgettable hair-do in film history. Universal get round their Creature's inability to speak articulately by using the camp and creepy character of the overwrought mad scientist Dr Pretorius (played by elderly Ernest Thesiger) as the Creature's mouthpiece. Meeting the monster accidentally in a crypt while grave robbing, Pretorius promises him a wife and forces the reluctant, regretful Baron Frankenstein (Colin Clive again) to construct him a mate, appealingly played by Lanchester, who is also cast as the demure author Mary Shelley in a literary preamble. It is Lanchester who sets off the final terror, rejecting her partner with a startled hiss. By any yardstick it's a great horror film, constructed with a chilling script laced with dashes of dark-toned humour. It's graced by memorable performances, with Karloff again outstanding and Thesiger triumphant, terrific Franz Waxman music and stylish Expressionist photography. This was the film that set the seal on Hollywood's burgeoning horror genre first clearly defined by Dracula and Frankenstein.
HORROR

Top Hat

99 min.
Director: *Mark Sandrich*
Origin: *USA*
Distributor: *RKO*
Cast: *Fred Astaire, Lucille Ball, Eric Blore, Helen Broderick, Edward Everett Horton, Erik Rhodes, Ginger Rogers*

The one and only Fred Astaire is at his most entrancing in this archetypal Astaire-Rogers musical, dancing and sparring memorably with Ginger Rogers as he pursues her through vast hotel suites and a breathtaking studio-conjured Venice. The two stars, who eventually notched up ten films together, are supported in the finest possible way by RKO's stock comedy support team (Edward Everett Horton, Helen Broderick, Eric Blore and Erik Rhodes). With an almost identical cast, it's all very much the mixture of the previous year's *The Gay Divorcee*, but even better, as everybody gets caught up in a silly, highly theatrical musical plot of muddled identities. But no matter the story. Irving Berlin's 11 songs (including "Cheek to Cheek", "Isn't This a Lovely Day?", "Top Hat, White Tie and Tails", "No Strings") are nothing short of perfection. Also terrific are Van Nest Polglase's art deco sets, which create wonderfully imaginative fantasy versions of London and Venice you would only dare go for in a musical film, and the choreography of Astaire's regular collaborator Hermes Pan, who keeps the Piccolino dance tune going with endless inventiveness. Pan and Fred rehearsed exhaustively, with Pan dancing Ginger's steps. Then when they were finally ready, Rogers would just arrive on set and perform. This is the artificial, sophisticated 1930s musical at its peak, the equivalent of Broadway on the silver screen, taking the high ground at the opposite end to the realism of Warner musicals like *42nd Street*.
MUSICAL

Fury: Sylvia Sidney and Spencer Tracy are locked up in love

1936

Fury

94 min.
Director: *Fritz Lang*
Origin: *USA*
Distributor: *MGM*
Cast: *Walter Abel, Frank Albertson, Walter Brennan, Bruce Cabot, Edward Ellis, Sylvia Sidney, Spencer Tracy*

Fritz Lang's blistering Hollywood debut, made more than a year after his exile from Nazi Germany and arrival in America, was an intense and classic analysis of bigoted small-town violence, later described by Graham Greene as "The only film I know to which I have wanted to attach the epithet 'Great'." Based on the novel *Mob Rule* by Norman Krasna, it is a film in two halves. In the first upright citizen Joe Wilson (Spencer Tracy) is on his way to meet his fiancée Katherine (Sylvia Sidney) when he is mistakenly arrested for kidnap and incarcerated in the town jail, which is then burnt down by a furious lynching mob. Unbeknown to the masses, Tracy survives the conflagration, watching from the safety of his brother's home as the 22 mob members – including the woman who actually torched the jail – are brought to trial, setting the stage for the second section of the movie. At once taut thriller and biting social commentary, *Fury* boasts a formidable central performance from Tracy – one of the finest of his career – and a wonderful character turn from Walter Abel, whose gruff district attorney dominates the courtroom scenes. With its punchy script (by Lang and Bartlett Cormack), tense, moody atmosphere and ground-breaking use of newsreel footage, it is widely considered Lang's finest American film. Despite its unnaturally upbeat ending – with a conscience-stricken Tracy appearing in court and halting the trial – it remains one of cinema's most powerful indictments of bigotry and mob rule.
THRILLER

La Grande Illusion

GRAND ILLUSION   117 min.
Director: *Jean Renoir*
Origin: *France*
Distributor: *Réalisations d'Art Cinématographique*
Cast: *Julien Carette, Marcel Dalio, Jean Dasté, Pierre Fresnay, Jean Gabin, Gaston Modot, Dita Parlo, Erich von Stroheim*

Jean Renoir's immortal study of World War One prisoners of war, based on his own experiences, is an absorbing masterpiece of characterization and social analysis – the most revered of all his films. Although it begins in the headquarters of the German and French armies, and concludes with an extended epilogue following the fortunes of two escaped prisoners, the main body of the film takes place in a prison camp, focusing on the interaction of four central characters – aristocratic German commandant von Rauffenstein (Erich von Stroheim); French officer de Boeildieu (Pierre Fresnay); working-class French soldier Maréchal (Jean Gabin); and *nouveau-riche* Jewish soldier Rosenthal (Marcel Dalio). "My preoccupation," Renoir once said, "is with the meeting: how to belong, how to meet", and it is this theme of loyalty and belonging that he develops here, using intricate plotting, subtle dialogue and unexpected humour to probe the issues of nationality, class and creed that unite and divide his four protagonists. Replete with pregnant images – a recurring shot of a camp window, signifying the sense of inside (belonging) and outside (rejection); von Rauffenstein's neck brace, which leaves him as much a prisoner as those he is guarding – the film is both a moving humanist indictment of war, and an unparalleled critique of the faultlines that divide our society. The script (by Renoir and Charles Spaak) is perfect, as are the performances and Christian Matras's claustrophobic interior photgraphy. A poignant, thought-provoking masterpiece, it was banned in Germany and Italy for its forceful anti-war sentiment.
ANTI-WAR

Modern Times

85 min.
Director: *Charles Chaplin*
Origin: *USA*
Distributor: *United Artists*
Cast: *Henry Bergman, Charles Chaplin, Chester Conklin, Paulette Goddard, Tiny Sandford*

Almost a decade after the coming of talkies, Chaplin remained steadfastly silent with this hilariously imaginative critique of industry, mechanization and the modern urban world. Two years in the making, and Chaplin's most overt social comment, *Modern Times* was inspired by René Clair's 1931 film

A Nous La Liberté, and provides a series of witty, nightmarish scenarios in which Chaplin's tramp character enters into disastrous conflict with different aspects of the industrialized landscape. In its most renowned sequence Chaplin lands a job as a bolt-tightener on a factory production line, getting caught up in the cogs of a giant machine and eventually becoming so dehumanized by his work that he goes around tightening people's noses and buttons. *Modern Times*'s surreal, pantomimic humour is balanced by the tramp's relationship with an exquisite waif (Paulette Goddard) with whom he eventually runs off to seek a new life in a less mechanical environment. Despite containing some of Chaplin's finest visual clowning – frantically operating one machine as another feeds him his lunch; playing football with a duck while working as a waiter; diving gracefully into two feet of water outside Goddard's run-down lakeside shack – it met a cool critical reception, and was banned in Germany and Italy for supposedly containing Communist propaganda. For all its biting social commentary, however, it is first and foremost a sublime piece of entertainment, a sentimental backward glance at the great days of silent humour and, in its unforgettable blend of comedy and pathos, quintessential Charlie Chaplin.

COMEDY

Mr Deeds Goes to Town

118 min.
Director: *Frank Capra*
Origin: *USA*
Distributor: *Columbia*
Cast: *Jean Arthur, George Bancroft, Walter Catlett, Gary Cooper, Douglas Dumbrille, Lionel Stander, Raymond Walburn, H. B. Warner*

Graham Greene called Frank Capra's warmly whimsical tale of an eccentric country hick who inherits $20 million "A comedy quite unmatched on the screen". It

is vintage Capra, jammed full of humour, sentiment, deft social observation and an unfailing belief that the good guys will always win through in the end. Based on a Clarence Budlington Kelland short story – *Opera Hat* – it has Gary Cooper as Longfellow Deeds, a simple, kind-hearted bumpkin from Vermont who ups sticks to New York after unexpectedly coming into a $20 million inheritance. His generosity and eccentricity – sliding down the bannisters of his palatial mansion, playing his tuba to help him think – cause more than a few raised eyebrows, and hard-boiled ace reporter Jean Arthur is dispatched to dig a bit of dirt and cut him down to size. Cooper, of course, falls for her but, when he discovers what she's really up to, decides to give all his money to the poor, sparking a hilarious courtroom climax in which his greedy relatives contest his sanity. All ends happily, however, with Cooper winning the trial, Arthur and Cooper getting it together, and the baddies suffering a humiliating and richly deserved comeuppance. It's heart-warming, fairytale stuff, handled with Capra's usual flair, insight and lightness of touch, and enhanced by spot-on performances from all concerned. The critics and public adored it. Capra won his second Best Director Academy Award and the word "pixilated" – used by two doddery old ladies to describe Deeds's eccentricity – entered common American parlance.

COMEDY

Triumph of the Will

TRIUMPH DES WILLENS   110 min.
Director: *Leni Riefenstahl*
Origin: *Germany*
Distributor: *UFA/Nazi Party*
Cast: *Adolf Hitler*

A hymn to the master-race, Leni Riefenstahl's Hitler-assisted propagandist documentary of the Nazis' 1934 Nuremberg rally is a

frightening paean to Fascism's all-consuming love affair with strength and discipline. Riefenstahl had 30 cameras and 120 staff at her disposal to shoot the rally which was stage-managed for maximum cinematic effect, helping to produce a film that's technically brilliant. *Triumph of the Will* opens with Hitler's descent from the skies, a messiah in a light aircraft, then there is a parade, some wreath-laying, and on to speeches intercut with grand symbolism: eagles, swastikas, flags, banners and, of course, a rapt crowd. Often only Hitler has a discernible face, with a disturbing use of people as architectural backdrop. The result was a great success with Hitler and Goebbels, who both recognized early on the power of film to communicate their ideas, but the German public never took to it. Goebbels awarded it the National Film Prize in 1935, it won the Venice Biennale Gold Medal in 1936 and another award in Paris, but Riefenstahl's appearance there to collect it was disrupted by protesting workers. Riefenstahl considered it an "heroic film of fact", but after the war argued for it to be judged solely as a work of art rather than propaganda. The Allies never

blacklisted her but she was never able fully to resume her career, turning to photo-journalism instead. The film is a landmark for its manipulative techniques of style and editing, but it is one the world could have done without.

PROPAGANDIST DOCUMENTARY

1937

Oh, Mr Porter!

83 min.
Director: *Marcel Varnel*
Origin: *GB*
Distributor: *Gainsborough*
Cast: *Will Hay, Agnes Lauchlan, Moore Marriott, Graham Moffat, Sebastian Smith, Dennis Wyndham*

Oh, Mr Porter! remains one of British cinema's most consistently entertaining comedies and was the peak picture of comic Will Hay, in collaboration with regular foils Graham Moffat and Moore Marriott. Filched from the Arnold Ridley stage farce *The Ghost Train*, the plot is a wry parody of the vintage *Boys' Own* adventure yarn. Crumpled, officious Hay is put out to pasture by his exasperated family, posted to manage a semi-derelict railway station in the wilds

Oh, Mr Porter!: (left to right) *Graham Moffat, Will Hay, and Moore Marriott get all steamed up*

195

of Southern Ireland. Once there, he discovers the place shunned by passing trains and encounters an unlikely pair of helpmates in a corpulent, helium-voiced porter (Moffat) and a scrawny, gap-toothed clerk (Marriott). Hay's subsequent dogged efforts at revitalizing the station and solving a ghoulish local mystery are met with fatalistic discouragement ("yer wastin' yer time"), but by the end our hero has redeemed himself – snaring a bunch of gun-runners after a madcap skirmish aboard the rotating blades of a neighbouring windmill. A plot that in other hands might seem throwaway is buoyed by the eye-pleasing surrounds, Marcel Varnel's capable direction and the sparkling three-way chemistry between Hay, Moffat and Marriott – raising the playing of their music-hall archetypes to a kind of art form. *Oh, Mr Porter!* won't shake you to the core, or change the way you view the world, but there aren't many more uplifting, truly pleasurable ways to while away a damp Sunday afternoon. What's the cinema there for, anyway?
FARCE

Snow White and the Seven Dwarfs

82 min.
Director: *David Hand*
Origin: *USA*
Distributor: *Walt Disney*
Cast: Voices of *Roy Atwell, Stuart Buchanan, Adriana Caselotti, Pinto Colvig, Billy Gilbert, Otis Harlan, Lucille La Verne, Scotty Mattraw, Moroni Olsen, Harry Stockwell*

A milestone in cinema history and the fulfilment of Walt Disney's long-held dream of extending the scope of animation into full-length feature-film making. *Snow White* was known as "Disney's folly" among his film contemporaries, who thought it was bound to fail. How wrong they were for, both then and now, the film has stood the test of time in absolute terms.

Admittedly it softens the Grimms' fairy tale of the princess whose stepmother, jealous of her beauty, orders her death, only to be thwarted by the girl's finding a safe haven with seven short fellows who shelter her until her handsome prince comes. Admittedly the romantic leads are wishy-washy and the forest animals cute beyond belief. But it scores with its comic creations, particularly the precisely differentiated characters of Bashful, Grumpy, Sleepy, Sneezy, Happy, Dopey and Doc, and its magnificently villainous Wicked Queen, who can still make toddlers' toes curl. The brilliance of the animation, particularly the scary bits, still stands up well against the standards of contemporary animation, and even in today's climate this politically incorrect tale of a heroine washing and cleaning for her seven vertically challenged male flatmates while waiting for her prince to come is a popular crowd-pleaser. *Snow White* also boasts a collection of tuneful songs and was the first film to generate a soundtrack album: "Whistle While You Work", "Some Day My Prince Will Come" and "Heigh Ho, Heigh Ho" (its "off to work we go" lyrics an ironic rallying call to the jobless).
CARTOON

1938

Bringing up Baby

102 min.
Director: *Howard Hawks*
Origin: *USA*
Distributor: *RKO*
Cast: *Walter Catlett, Cary Grant, Barry Fitzgerald, Fritz Feld, Jonathan Hale, Katharine Hepburn, May Robson, Charles Ruggles*

In the memorable opinion of critic Pauline Kael, the narrative of *Bringing Up Baby* gives the impression of having been "spun from

gossamer". Brilliantly showcasing the comic playing of stars Cary Grant and Katharine Hepburn, it's the most enduringly popular film of the super-sophisticate screwball genre. *The Philadelphia Story* may have been more sure-footed, *His Girl Friday* might have boasted more gags per minute; neither could quite match the giddying soda-stream rush of this most joyful, free-spirited, engagingly scatterbrained of cinema treasures. Although it unravels a fraction in its hectic final reel, director Howard Hawks maintains exquisite control of a quick-stepping plot that has buttoned-up palaeontologist David Huxley (Grant) whirled into a double-taking, cross-dressing wreck by nutty socialite Susan Vance (Hepburn). The armoury that Susan employs against her hap-

less target includes a speeding convertible, the bright-eyed Scots terrier who pinches Huxley's cherished dinosaur bone and Baby, a wayward leopard who needs to be constantly serenaded with the lyrics from a contemporary pop song. *Bringing Up Baby* is a *tour de force* of sexual sparring, driven by witty interplay and outrageous mishaps and anchored by the effortless ease of its principal players, with Grant at his most charismatically bemused and Hepburn all brittle energy and breathless irresponsibility. To this pair the farcical script adds a frazzled fiancée, a wealthy dowager, a doltish town cop and an extended climactic jail sequence. The result is the headiest of cocktails; a genuine classic of comic cinema.
SCREWBALL COMEDY

Baby love: *Jailbirds Cary Grant and Katharine Hepburn*

1939

Gone with the Wind

220 min.
Directors: *Victor Fleming, George Cukor and Sam Wood*
Origin: *USA*
Distributor: *MGM*
Cast: *Ward Bond, Laura Hope Crews, Jane Darwell, Harry Davenport, Olivia de Havilland, Clark Gable, Leslie Howard, Victor Jory, Evelyn Keyes, Vivien Leigh, Hattie McDaniel, Butterfly McQueen, Thomas Mitchell, Ona Munson, Barbara O'Neil, Ann Rutherford*

Probably the greatest single misjudgement in cinema history was made by Irving Thalberg, who infamously cautioned fellow producer Louis B. Mayer against any involvement in *Gone with the Wind*, saying that the American public wouldn't pay to see a Civil War film. In fact, as produced by David O. Selznick, it went on to become the most popular film of all time, winning nine Academy Awards, recouping its $4.5 million cost many times over, and remaining one of the small handful of movies always guaranteed to draw an audience. An epic, awe-inspiring Technicolor treasure, it explores the fortunes of a group of wealthy Confederate landowners against a dramatic backdrop of society balls, battles and the eventual collapse of the South. At its heart is the romance between hot-headed Southern belle Scarlett O'Hara (the then little known Vivien Leigh in an Oscar-winning performance) and dashing beau Rhett Butler (Clark Gable), a uniquely charismatic pairing that has tended to overshadow the excellence of supporting cast members Olivia de Havilland, Leslie Howard and Hattie McDaniel (the first Afro-American to win an Oscar, as Best Supporting Actress). The complexity of the film's production was legendary –

a two-year search for the right Scarlett, thousands of extras, a small army of writers and three directors (Victor Fleming, George Cukor and Sam Wood) – but the end product is seamless, an ever-green combination of drama, romance and spectacle that has wowed audiences ever since.
CIVIL WAR EPIC

La Règle du Jeu

THE RULES OF THE GAME   113 min.
Director: *Jean Renoir*
Origin: *France*
Distributor: *La Nouvelle Edition Française*
Cast: *Julien Carette, Marcel Dalio, Nora Gregor, Gaston Modot, Mila Parély, Jean Renoir, Roland Toutain*

The great pre-war French satirical comedy of manners, *La Règle du Jeu* is widely regarded as Renoir's masterpiece, marking his move away from naturalism towards a more classical and poetic style. It boasts a deceptively simple story about a count organizing a shooting party for his friends, which becomes the setting for a complex of romantic intrigues. Renoir took this by no means original set-up, added a Beaumarchais-style subplot, in which the servants aped the behaviour of so-called betters, and created a bleakly pessimistic but often hilarious comedy of social mores, which dissects the games people play in their relationships, set against a society riven by class distinctions. As the unblinking eye of his camera records the intrigues, social rivalries and foibles of the characters, the mood switches daringly from comedy to tragedy, realism to fantasy, melodrama to farce. Renoir himself also acted in the film, turning in a beautiful performance as the well-meaning muddler Octave. Ironically the film proved one of Renoir's greatest commercial failures, was cut drastically and not seen again in its entirety until 1956, after careful restoration.
SATIRICAL COMEDY

Ninotchka

110 min.
Director: *Ernst Lubitsch*
Origin: *USA*
Distributor: *MGM*
Cast: *Felix Bressart, Richard Carle, Ina Claire, Melvyn Douglas, Greta Garbo, Alexander Granach, Bela Lugosi, Sig Ruman*

This sparkling Ernst Lubitsch comedy, sold on the advertising slogan "Garbo laughs", owes much of its appeal to the successful on-screen chemistry between Greta Garbo and co-star Melvyn Douglas. The story is about a Communist iceberg, sent to Paris to reclaim errant comrades and the people's jewels from a Grand Duchess, who is wooed, warmed and won under the spell of Paris and the romancing of a sophisticated playboy. The style is a subtle mixture of farce, romance and satire, with the Lubitsch touch evident in terms of lightness and nuances of shading, relying on telling gestures and meaningful sidelong looks. It also benefits from a witty script by Charles Brackett, Billy Wilder and Walter Reisch, writing in the first year of World War Two, who seize the opportunity for impish political jokes, such as Garbo's line, "It would have been very embarrassing for people of my sort to wear low-cut gowns in the old Russia. The lashes of the Cossacks across our backs were not very becoming, and you know how vain women are." Much of the joy, though, comes from watching Garbo, in her fourth Oscar-nominated performance, move from icy intensity to playfulness under the warmth of Douglas's assured performance. The film was remade as the musical *Silk Stockings* (1957) which featured brilliant dancing from Fred Astaire and Cyd Charisse but otherwise suffered in comparison with the original.
ROMANTIC COMEDY

Stagecoach

96 min.
Director: *John Ford*
Origin: *USA*
Distributor: *United Artists*
Cast: *John Carradine, Berton Churchill, Andy Devine, Donald Meek, Thomas Mitchell, Louise Platt, Claire Trevor, John Wayne*

This prototype for the modern western transformed the genre from simplistic action movie into something to be taken seriously – and propelled John Wayne to stardom. Director John Ford's first talking western involved more complex and in-depth characterization than anything preceding it, although the premise has since been copied so often it can look like a hackneyed group-in-peril carriage across Utah when viewed today. The story is simple but compelling. An outlaw (John Wayne), ex-prostitute (Claire Trevor), drunk doctor (Thomas Mitchell), mysterious gambler (John Carradine), crooked banker (Berton Churchill), pregnant "lady" (Louise Platt) and timid salesman (Donald Meek) journey through Apache country towards the town of Lordsburg. After struggling among themselves, they fight off Indians before the brave and true (Wayne and Trevor) head off together, with the Doc announcing the theme, "Well, they're saved from the blessings of civilisation!", for anyone still in doubt. *Stagecoach* was Ford's first film of nine made in Monument Valley, causing the area to be dubbed "Ford Country" by industry insiders, and included chase sequences much studied by Orson Welles, who ran the film over 40 times to learn about camera angles and cutting before making *Citizen Kane* (1941). Ford held out to cast his drinking partner Wayne as the Ringo Kid, and eventually won, although the studio initially wanted Gary Cooper and Marlene Dietrich in the wagon. There were numerous Oscar nominations but

it was up against *Gone with the Wind* (1939) and lost out, winning only for best score and Thomas Mitchell's rousing acting. But now it is regarded as perhaps cinema's most influential western.
WESTERN

The Wizard of Oz

103 min.
Director: *Victor Fleming*
Origin: *USA*
Distributor: *MGM*
Cast: *Clara Blandick, Ray Bolger, Billie Burke, Judy Garland, Charley Grapewin, Jack Haley, Margaret Hamilton, Bert Lahr, Frank Morgan*

Hollywood's best-loved retelling of a fairytale survived initially grudging reviews and shaky business to go on to claim a special place in the hearts of adults trying to recapture their lost childhood. L. Frank Baum's book had been filmed before in silent days (1925) with Oliver Hardy and was reworked in an all-black version in 1978's *The Wiz*, but this is the only version that matters. Its chief pleasures are the gorgeous Technicolor for the dream sequences, MGM's spectacular artwork, the attractive score by Harold Arlen and Yip Harburg and the legendary cast. It includes most memorably Jack Haley as Tin Man, Bert Lahr as Cowardly Lion, and Ray Bolger as Scarecrow – called the "three dirty hams" by the director Victor Fleming. Plus, of course, a teenage Judy Garland, innocent and appealing as Dorothy, the little girl who seeks salvation over the rainbow, following the Yellow Brick Road to find the Wizard (Frank Morgan). Shooting was a nightmare. Whenever they could, the three hams tried to upstage Garland, whose plumpness and maturity were becoming increasingly difficult to hide. Buddy Ebsen, originally cast as Tin Man, ended up in hospital for six months when the metallic dust they powdered on his head and face got into his lungs. Margaret

Hamilton, the wonderfully Wicked Witch of the West, was seriously burnt on her right hand and face when her broomstick caught fire.The midget actors playing the Munchkins ran amok on the set, though three of the original 124 survived into the 1990s to tell the tale.
FANTASY MUSICAL

1940

The Bank Dick

73 min.
Director: *Eddie Cline*
Origin: *USA*
Distributor: *Universal*
Cast: *W. C. Fields, Shemp Howard, Una Merkel, Franklin Pangborn, Grady Sutton, Cora Witherspoon*

A comedy gem about a grouchy small-town ne'er-do-well who becomes a hero after foiling a bank robbery, *The Bank Dick* is W. C. Fields's penultimate starring feature and the funniest film of his

career. Naturally it's Fields's show all the way. He wrote the script (under the pseudonym Mahatma Kane Jeeves) and dominated the action, giving director Eddie Cline little more to do than keep the whole thing moving and balance Fields's decidedly eccentric working methods. Made on a modest budget and essentially a series of interconnected sketches and vaudeville routines – many drawn from Fields's previous movies – it features W. C. as grumpy town lush Egbert Souse (pronounced Soo-zay) who, after cornering a couple of robbers, is rewarded with a job as dick (detective) at the local bank. There follows a series of madcap scenarios, with Fields persuading gullible clerk Og Oggilby (Grady Sutton) to embezzle money from the bank to fund a dubious mining enterprise; Fields outwitting bank examiner J. Pinkerton Snoopington (Franklin Pangborn); Fields foiling another bank robbery; and Fields becoming a millionaire movie-maker. It's all wildly improbable and deliciously funny, held together

The Bank Dick: *W.C. Fields* (right) *rules the roost*

by its star's supremely cantankerous clowning and a series of unforgettable gags, most notably Fields's disastrous attempts at helping an old lady mend her car and the wacky high-speed car chase down a mountainside. A subversive, idiosyncratic comic winner, the film's name was changed in Britain to *The Bank Detective* for fear British audiences might misconstrue the word "dick".
COMEDY

A *Wizard* **musical:** *Judy Garland with the friends of Dorothy – (left to right) Jack Haley, Ray Bolger and Bert Lahr*

The Grapes of Wrath

128 min.
Director: *John Ford*
Origin: *USA*
Distributor: *20th Century Fox*
Cast: *Dorris Bowdon, John Carradine, Jane Darwell, Henry Fonda, Charley Grapewin, Grant Mitchell, John Qualen, Eddie Quillan, Russell Simpson, Zeffie Tilbury, O. Z. Whitehead*

Ford's masterwork, *The Grapes of Wrath* is based on John Steinbeck's great Depression-era tragedy about Oklahoma farmers – victims of the dust bowl and capitalist greed – trekking west to California for a better life. Their story is told through the experiences of one family, the Joads. The stark conclusion of Steinbeck's novel has been softened to one of hope for the future and belief in the American people – understandable in the political and film-making context of the time. But the film's magnificently tragic picture of people clinging to their human dignity and self-respect in the face of an indifferent and inhumane society teaches a universal lesson for all time and is a beautiful and moving piece of storytelling. Nunnally Johnson's dialogue is emotionally and dramatically engaging, and visually the film is set against the stark landscape and the real-life migrant camps, vividly captured by Gregg Toland's black and white photography. Fonda is outstanding as Tom Joad, the eldest son, as is Carradine as the preacher turned union activist, while Jane Darwell more than earned her Oscar for her portrayal of the indomitable, undefeated Ma Joad, struggling to hold her family together. The film also won a well-deserved Oscar for Ford's direction and five other nominations. Ford is to be saluted for both his artistic achievement and his courage in making the film at a time when government and studios were in no mood to encourage unions and criticism of capitalism.
REALIST DRAMA

The Great Dictator

127 min.
Director: *Charles Chaplin*
Origin: *USA*
Distributor: *United Artists*
Cast: *Charles Chaplin, Henry Daniell, Reginald Gardiner, Billy Gilbert, Paulette Goddard, Maurice Moscovich, Jack Oakie*

Chaplin's first proper talkie, the first film he scripted in advance, and his biggest box-office success – with five Oscar nominations, including three for Chaplin – *The Great Dictator* is a blistering comic satire on Hitler and the rise of Nazi Germany. Although its message was overtly political, it remains one of Chaplin's most amusing and innovative features, brilliantly employing burlesque and pantomime buffoonery to parody not just Hitler, but the entire concept of dictatorship itself. It centres on two characters: the psychotic Adenoid Hynkel, Dictator of Tomania, and his compatriot, a meek Jewish barber – both played by Chaplin. Their contrasting stories unfold side by side until, in the film's final reels, the barber is mistaken for the dictator and stands in for him at a rally, delivering a six-minute polemical speech on the importance of freedom and democracy. Actually, the film's impassioned climax works less well than its earlier comic routines, in which Chaplin masterfully lampoons Hitler's mannerisms and rhetoric, talking in nonsensical gibberish, delivering a speech so fiery that the microphones melt and performing a ludicrously balletic dance with an inflatable globe. There are memorable supporting turns, notably from Jack Oakie as the Mussolini-like Benzino Napaloni, Dictator of Bacteria; while the scene in which the barber shaves a customer in time to Liszt's Hungarian Rhapsody is one of the most dazzling of all Chaplin routines. It's triumphantly daring and supremely witty, though Chaplin later claimed he wouldn't have made the film had he understood the full horror of Hitler's regime.
POLITICAL SATIRE

The Thief of Bagdad

106 min.
Directors: *Ludwig Berger, Michael Powell and Tim Whelan*
Origin: *GB*
Distributor: *London Films*
Cast: *June Duprez, Rex Ingram, John Justin, Miles Malleson, Mary Morris, Sabu, Conrad Veidt, Tim Whelan*

Producer Alexander Korda employed an army of top directors to help him make his beguiling and exhilarating Arabian Nights fantasy epic, assembling a legendary cast of eccentric performers for a tale in which a thief attempts to thwart the wicked Grand Vizier who has thrown the good Prince Ahmad of Bagdad into prison. Charismatic young Sabu as the thieving Abu and Conrad Veidt as the usurping Jaffar sweep along an established British classic, lavishly filmed in glorious Technicolor, and brimming with still dazzling special effects, including a spectacular magic carpet and a stunning flying horse. It's all topped off by Rex Ingram's larger-than-life performance as the gigantic genie. This labour of love, a work of art and great popular entertainment, took 20 months to make, starting with all the interior shots in Britain's Denham Studios, and finishing with the exterior filming in Grand Canyon and the Arizona desert after the outbreak of World War Two. The huge task was supervised by three credited directors – Michael Powell, Ludwig Berger and Tim Whelan – plus Geoffrey Boothby, Zoltan Korda, William Cameron Menzies and Alexander Korda himself. But the script was

The Great Dictator: *Chaplin takes a global view*

199

mostly by one hand – that of beloved British character actor Miles Malleson (who also has a cameo role in the film as the Sultan), though Lajos Biro was also credited. It went on to win four Oscars, and appropriately perhaps, since this is such an achievement of cinema wizardry, they were all technical Oscars – for Photography, Special Effects, Art Direction and Sound Effects. If the luscious Technicolor has now faded, the pleasure the movie brings never does.
FANTASY EPIC

1941

Citizen Kane

119 min.
Director: *Orson Welles*
Origin: *USA*
Distributor: *RKO*
Cast: *Ray Collins, Dorothy Comingore, Joseph Cotten, George Coulouris, Alan Ladd, Agnes Moorehead, Everett Sloane, Paul Stewart, Ruth Warwick, Orson Welles*

The revered motion-picture landmark from Orson Welles, *Citizen Kane*, conjures up an exhilarating fable on the corrupting nature of power. Boy wonder Welles, just 26, rocked the RKO studios with the costly, unexpected failure of his baroque-filmed, poison-penned portrait of a William Randolph Hearst-style newspaper tycoon, who suffers a doomed marriage with a pretty nobody (Dorothy Comingore). Welles gives a towering performance as the thrusting media baron, eaten away by the emptiness of his success, while Joseph Cotten is equally impressive as his reporter friend who tells the tale in a series of flashbacks. Made with an obvious joy in exploring the possibilities of cinema and a cast of fresh, bright names from Welles's Mercury Theatre, it is one of those few films where every viewing yields further pleasures and

Casablanca: *Claude Rains (one from left)* rounds up the usual suspects

nuances. *Kane* is a milestone technically as well as artistically since it is renowned for its pioneering use of low-angle shots, Expressionist images, deep-focus photography, and the use of looming ceilings in shot. Probably the greatest movie in the world, certainly the most famous, usually the one voted by critics as best ever and – almost incredibly for a revered art work – it's darned entertaining too. The Oscar-winning script is credited to Herman J. Mankiewicz and Welles, though Cotten and John Houseman had a hand in it too, and who actually did what is the subject of an on-going controversy, greatly fuelled in 1971 by Pauline Kael's pro-Mankiewicz viewpoint in her *The Citizen Kane Book*. The picture enraged Hearst who campaigned to stop it, by banning mentions or reviews of it in his newspaper empire, and this was a key factor in its box-office failure and in sabotaging Welles's career.
NEWSPAPER TYCOON DRAMA

The Maltese Falcon

100 min.
Director: *John Huston*
Origin: *USA*
Distributor: *Warner*
Cast: *Mary Astor, Humphrey Bogart, Ward Bond, Elisha Cook Jr, Jerome Cowan, Gladys George, Sidney Greenstreet, Peter Lorre, Barton MacLane, Lee Patrick*

John Huston made an unforgettable directorial debut (he also penned the script) with this taut, atmospheric *film noir* masterpiece. A triumph of suspenseful plotting, magnetic performances and ingenious camera-work, *The Maltese Falcon* is at once a gripping thriller and a razor-sharp analysis of greed, deceit and paranoia. Based on crime-writer Dashiell Hammett's novel of the same name, already filmed in 1931 and 1936 (as *Satan Met a Lady*), it features Humphrey Bogart at his sardonic best, playing tough, wise-cracking gumshoe Sam Spade.

Employed by mysterious *femme fatale* Brigid O'Shaughnessy (Mary Astor) to find her lover's murderer, Spade becomes hopelessly tangled in a web of intrigue and double-dealing centred upon the search for a priceless, bejewelled statue, the Maltese Falcon. The investigation brings him into contact with a host of memorably nasty characters – Peter Lorre as sycophantic, toad-like Joel Cairo; Sidney Greenstreet, in his film debut, as the treacherously urbane fat man, Kasper Gutman – and provides Bogart with some of the snappiest dialogue of his career. Huston's moody lighting, enclosed, claustrophobic sets (contrary to usual Hollywood practice he constructed many of his interiors with ceilings), and unusual style of framing his shots – characters in the foreground, their faces covering half the screen; close-ups of characters who are listening as opposed to talking – made for a uniquely dark, intense atmo-

sphere, enlivened with flashes of cynical humour. Superb performances, the heavyweight script and a marvellous sting in the tail make this the last word in screen thriller-making; the stuff that dreams are made on.
THRILLER

1942

Casablanca

102 min.
Director: *Michael Curtiz*
Origin: *USA*
Distributor: *Warner*
Cast: *Ingrid Bergman, Humphrey Bogart, Marcel Dalio, Sidney Greenstreet, Paul Henreid, Peter Lorre, Claude Rains, S. Z. Sakall, Conrad Veidt, Dooley Wilson*

Ah, you must remember this. The wartime Humphrey Bogart-Ingrid Bergman romantic adventure just gets better and better as time goes by, acquiring a greater and greater aura of myth and magic. Everything's just right. At the top there's the archetypal Bogart performance, tough and wisecracking on the outside, vulnerable, even sentimental within, while Bergman is at her most glowingly luminous with beauty and allure. Then there's a superb line-up of the cinema's greatest character actors of the day: Sidney Greenstreet, S. Z. Sakall, Conrad Veidt, Peter Lorre and Claude Rains, all being eccentric or villainous or both. At heart, it's a classic love story with waspishly witty dialogue from the Epstein twins, Julius and Philip, and Howard Koch, fashioning something brilliant from an unproduced play called *Everybody Comes to Rick's* by Murray Burnett and Joan Alison, writing the pages of the script nightly so no one knew the outcome. Would Bergman go off with Bogey, or stay true to her dull but noble resistance fighter husband Paul Henreid? Who

would have thought in an ironic ending Bogart would walk off together with Claude Rains who has conspired to let the married couple fly free ("Round up the usual suspects!"). As Bogey says, "This could be the start of a beautiful friendship." The portrait of wartime Casablanca is artfully painted in the Warner studio: a watering hole for criminals, refugees, resistance fighters and Nazis. The cynical, expatriate American bar-owner of Rick's Cafe sticks his neck out for no one until the arrival of beautiful Bergman whom he'd romanced to the tune "As Time Goes By" in Paris. Bogart tells his piano-player Dooley Wilson, "If you can play it for her, you can play it for me. Play it, Sam!" Audiences preferred to believe he said: "Play it again Sam" and thus it's fixed forever.
WARTIME ROMANTIC MELODRAMA

The Palm Beach Story

90 min.
Director: *Preston Sturges*
Origin: *USA*
Distributor: *Paramount*
Cast: *Sig Arno, Mary Astor, Roscoe Ates, Claudette Colbert, Jimmy Conlin, William Demarest, Robert Dudley, Joel McCrea, Jack Norton, Franklin Pangborn, Rudy Vallee*

Writer-director Preston Sturges burned too brightly, too quickly. Between 1940 and 1945 he conjured up a seemingly effortless series of comic masterworks – an output he was never subsequently to match. *The Palm Beach Story* is one of these masterworks, a typical Sturges combination of screwball, genial farce and rapier-like satire. The plot is a dazzling bit of narrative trickery, playing gleeful games within a self-consciously conventional framework. Bright-eyed Claudette Colbert marries idealistic architect Joel McCrea but, dissatisfied with her lot, takes off to gold-dig herself a Florida millionaire. En route she falls in with the boorish Ale and Quail Club and is romanced by the hugely wealthy,

impossibly fussy J. D. Hackensacker III (Rudy Vallee). Enter McCrea, to be instantly preyed on by Hackensacker's sister (Mary Astor), who is herself lumbered with a buffoonish hangdog gigolo (Sig Arno). But just as the tale looks to be getting too tangled and unresolvable, Sturges comes up with a breathtakingly outrageous exercise in storytelling sleight-of-hand and – hey presto – everyone is magically set free to live happily ever after. This marvellously managed picture has the look of a contained laboratory experiment, with Sturges providing a clinical examination of the lives of America's idle rich within the confines of a light comedy escapade. While *The Palm Beach Story* may lack the extra bite and intent of *Sullivan's Travels*, *The Miracle of Morgan's Creek* or *Hail, The Conquering Hero*, it stands as Sturges's most representative comedy. Terrific fun.
COMEDY

To Be or Not to Be

99 min.
Director: *Ernst Lubitsch*
Origin: *USA*
Distributor: *Korda/United Artists*
Cast: *Jack Benny, Carole Lombard, Robert Stack, Stanley Ridges, Felix Bressart, Lionel Atwill, Sig Ruman, Tom Dugan*

German film-maker Ernst Lubitsch, concocter of some Hollywood's most elegant soufflés in the 1930s, shocked the wartime public by taking the Nazi occupation of Poland as a subject for comedy. Critics and audiences alike accused *To Be or Not to Be* of being heartless and insensitive, though it's now hailed as one of cinema's greatest satires. This bold effort had a role model in Chaplin's *The Great Dictator* in 1940, poking fun at the Nazis with a similar mix of slapstick and satire. Like Chaplin, Lubitsch views the Nazis as ineffec-

The Palm Beach Story: *Joel McCrea and Claudette Colbert wrap it up*

tual idiots and, although this comforting view was far from the truth, Edwin Justus Mayer's screenplay hit the target as wartime propaganda more tellingly than most dramatic films, and has passed the test of time – still hilarious now its original purpose has long vanished. Jack Benny finds the perfect comic showcase, cast as a conceited Polish ham actor, married to Lombard. Together they lead a troupe of Shakespearian thespians through war-ravaged Warsaw. Amidst the devastation, Erhardt (Ruman) archly equates the troupe's treatment of Shakespeare with the Nazi destruction of Poland. *To Be or Not to Be* is a film imbued with deep-rooted bitterness and anger as well as endowed with big laughs, and it's the deft balance of these two elements that makes it so palatable. The director with the famed "Lubitsch touch" knew precisely how far to go.
BLACK COMEDY

The Life and Death of Colonel Blimp: *Roger Livesey gives a pointed performance as Colonel Clive Candy*

162 min.
Director: *Michael Powell and Emeric Pressburger*
Origin: *GB*
Distributor: *Archers/Gaumont*
Cast: *Roland Culver, David Hutcheson, Ursula Jeans, Deborah Kerr, Albert Lieven, Roger Livesey, James McKechnie, Anton Walbrook, Arthur Wontner*

Colonel Blimp is one of the most celebrated films by the matchless creative partnership of Michael Powell and Emeric Pressburger. Their story follows the fortunes of one British soldier, from his days as a dashing young officer in the Boer War through World War Two to his twilight days as a crusty old codger in the London Blitz, remembering his lost youth. The title, taken from

cartoonist David Low's pompous and blustering creation, is a misnomer for Roger Livesey's stuffy but likeable Clive Candy. He is a beautifully realized revelation of a long life and a character changed by time and experience, who is finally faced with a modern world and war where the fair play and chivalry of his youth have become as outdated as the horse and cart. The film is also a quirky romance, revealing the romantic feelings smouldering underneath the English stiff upper lip. Deborah Kerr is delightful as the three loves of Candy's life. Though the film was made in war-time, Powell and Pressburger included a sympathetic German character – Anton Walbrook as the sensitive Prussian officer with whom Candy fights a duel in his youth, loses his first love to and befriends for life. For two years British Prime Minister Winston Churchill prohibited export of the film, saying it was "detrimental to the morale of the army". Its British success forced him to lift the ban, but the version

shown in America was a butchered 93-minute one. The film was restored in 1986 by the British National Film Archive.
DRAMA/WAR

1944

Double Indemnity

106 min.
Director: *Billy Wilder*
Origin: *USA*
Distributor: *Paramount*
Cast: *Porter Hall, Jean Heather, Fred MacMurray, Tom Powers, Edward G. Robinson, Barbara Stanwyck*

A dying man records his murder confession but time is running out... *Double Indemnity* is the king of the 1940s crime melodramas, told in the flashback style typical of the genre and period, in which Fred MacMurray (cast plausibly against type) plays an insurance salesman lured by sexy *femme fatale* Barbara Stanwyck to murder her

oilman husband for the life insurance. But they've reckoned without Edward G. Robinson as MacMurray's canny and dogged boss, who's suspicious about the man's death after he notices there has been a recent change in the insurance policy. Then MacMurray gets scared at the idea of faking an accidental death from a moving train to claim their fraudulent double indemnity insurance jackpot. Superb acting from the three stars at their peak illuminates this compelling, classic *film noir* thriller, atmospherically directed by the right man in cynical Billy Wilder. But then it should be good: it's got at its disposal a razor-sharp script by none other than Philip Marlowe's creator Raymond Chandler, adapting the novel *Three of a Kind* by James M. Cain, the author of *The Postman Always Rings Twice*. *Double Indemnity* was greeted with great critical and public acclaim, and scooped seven Oscar nominations, including Wilder as Best Director and Stanwyck as Best Actress, though it scandalously won none.

The story has parallels in a real 1927 New York murder case when Ruth Snyder and her lover Judd Gray killed her husband Albert for his insurance.
THRILLER

Meet Me in St Louis

113 min.
Director: *Vincente Minnelli*
Origin: *USA*
Distributor: *MGM*
Cast: *Leon Ames, Mary Astor, Lucille Bremer, Joan Carroll, Hank Daniels, Harry Davenport, Tom Drake, Judy Garland, June Lockhart, Marjorie Main, Margaret O'Brien*

A witty, warm and thoroughly entertaining musical, which follows the ups and downs of an affectionate middle-class family at the turn of the century, particularly the romantic problems of the two elder daughters. Judy Garland, at her best under the direction of her future husband Vincente Minnelli and looking wonderful thanks to the skills of Carole Lombard's former make-up artist Dottie Pondell, plays Esther, who falls for the boy next door, while Lucille Bremer is Rose of the rival beaux. The film has been compared to a period valentine and its nostalgic charm was certainly well timed to meet a need in wartime. The story is told within a formal four-act structure, each act introduced by a photograph from the family album which then springs to life and colour. It is a prime example of Minnelli's strengths as a director of musicals: his love of rich, flamboyant colour, movement and swirling patterns of light, as in the dreamlike Hallowe'en sequence, and his eye for detail in the beautifully recreated World's Fair in St Louis of 1904, which gives the film its title. Above all there is his skill at integrating into the narration the musical numbers which include standards forever associated with Garland: "Meet Me in St Louis", "The Trolley Song", "The Boy Next Door" and "Have Yourself a Merry Little Christmas". Although MGM did not originally set great store by *Meet Me in St Louis*, it became the most popular film produced by the company at this time.
MUSICAL

1945

Brief Encounter

85 min.
Director: *David Lean*
Origin: *GB*
Distributor: *Eagle Lion/Cineguild*
Cast: *Joyce Carey, Valentine Dyall, Stanley Holloway, Trevor Howard, Celia Johnson, Cyril Raymond*

This quintessentially English tale of buffet love, taken from Noel Coward's one-act play *Still Life*, combines stiff upper lip and quivering lower labial, with not a kiss to be seen between them, yet remains a Desert Island Movie favourite. Mostly set in the fictional Milford Junction railway station, *Brief Encounter* tells how a housewife (Celia Johnson) and doctor (Trevor Howard), both married with children, accidentally meet and fall in love. They continue to see each other once a week until, realizing they are in the grip of a passion they cannot control, he does the decent thing and moves abroad, leaving her to contemplate suicide before returning to her safe, secure but stodgy husband (Cyril Raymond). Coward, Lean and Johnson had worked together twice previously but never to such glorious effect. The central pair are perfectly restrained, Stanley Holloway's and Joyce Carey's flirty banter is their ideal foil, and Rachmaninov's Piano Concerto No 2 swells to marvellous melodramatic effect. The effect of war-enforced separations on couples gave the film a topical poignancy and, although set in Kent, it was filmed on location in the Lake District because of blackout restrictions and bombing raids on the south coast. Despite its commercial failure in the US, it earned three Oscar nominations for Lean, Johnson and the screenplay, and much prestige for British cinema. A 1974 remake bizarrely cast Richard Burton and Sophia Loren as the unlikely couple, but more interestingly, *Flames of Passion* (1990) was a gay tribute to the original.
ROMANCE

Les Enfants du Paradis

CHILDREN OF PARADISE   195 min.
Director: *Marcel Carné*
Origin: *France*
Distributor: *Pathé*
Cast: *Arletty, Jean Louis-Barrault, Pierre Brasseur, Maria Casares, Marcel Herrand, Jane Marken, Gaston Modot, Pierre Renoir, Louis Salou*

Widely considered to be the greatest French film ever made, and likened to *Gone with the Wind* with its epic scope and themes, *Les Enfants du Paradis* is a delightful concoction of thwarted desire in the theatre underworld of 19th-century Paris. Filmed in studios during German occupation, it boasts a cast that includes many Resistance fighters and is often seen as an allegory of the enduring vitality of the French spirit, particularly in the character of the beautiful Garance (Arletty) – the independent woman who refuses to be owned by any man. Originally shot in two parts, the film has a story that is rich, complicated and based on real characters of 1840s Paris. It is set in the Boulevard of Crime (theatre-land), and the "Paradis" of the title refers to the cheap balcony seats ("the gods") where the common people watched the actors try to win their favour. A mime (Jean-Louis Barrault), a daring criminal (Marcel Herrand), a romantic actor (Pierre Brasseur) and a powerful count (Louis Salou) vie for Garance's love. Their struggle for her ends in tragedy, and she sets off alone, pursued by the mime who seems to call after her (we have never heard him speak) when the curtain falls. The earlier "poetic realism" of Marcel Carné and Marxist screenwriter Jacques Prévert was banned under the Nazis, but they outwitted them with this film, hiding incriminating reels of film and stalling the premiere until Paris was liberated. During the war Arletty, France's Dietrich, refused to work for Nazi film companies, but when she married a German she was accused of being a collaborator and her career never really recovered.
HISTORICAL EPIC

Henry V

136 min.
Director: *Laurence Olivier*
Origin: *GB*
Distributor: *Rank*
Cast: *Renee Asherson, Felix Aylmer, Leslie Banks, Leo Genn, Esmond Knight, Robert Newton, Laurence Olivier, George Robey, Ernest Thesiger*

With World War Two still raging, Laurence Olivier celebrated Britain's glorious past and drew out the theme of victory over the enemy against the odds. Made as a wartime morale booster for beleaguered British audiences, *Henry V* was one of the few UK colour films of the period due to a shortage of film stock, and it is extraordinarily effective as propaganda as well as a great version of the play. Olivier gives a dashingly heroic performance as the warrior King Henry V, who wins the support of the Archbishop of Canterbury (Felix Aylmer) for his claim to the French throne and prepares an army of invasion. Throughout, the verse is beautifully spoken by an outstanding cast which includes Robert Newton as Pistol, Leslie Banks as Chorus and the English comedian George Robey as Sir John Falstaff. In his first film as director, Olivier's bold experiment of beginning in a mock-up of Shakespeare's original Globe Theatre in 1603 then switching to realistic settings is a spectacular success. Olivier, who in an extraordinary, sentimental gesture was awarded a special Oscar "for outstanding achievement as actor, producer and director in bringing *Henry V* to the screen", puts all he's got into the emotional pre-battle speech, whose relevance to a nation at war was inescapable. When the Battle of Agincourt comes, it's as spectacularly staged as any sequence in British cinema. Henry V is arguably the best of Olivier's Shakespeare trilogy, though he won Best Actor and Picture for *Hamlet* (1948), and his *Richard III* (1955) was much admired.

SHAKESPEARIAN EPIC

Rome, Open City

ROMA, CITTÀ APERTA   100 min.
Director: *Roberto Rossellini*
Origin: *Italy*
Distributor: *Minerva*
Cast: *Aldo Fabrizi, Anna Magnani, Maria Michi, Marcello Pagliero*

A glorious boost for the Italian movie industry after the deprivations of the war years, Roberto Rossellini's melodramatic tale of Italian resistance fighters was central to the development of the neo-realist style – a pioneering style very much dictated by the shortages of the post-war era. Filming just two months after the Allied liberation of Rome, Rossellini could only obtain a documentary permit, was forced to use silent film stock because of the prohibitive black-market cost of sound film and – with the exception of music-hall performer Anna Magnani – had to pack the film entirely with non-professionals. The result is a compellingly authentic, black-and-white, documentary-style narrative in which a group of Italian resistance workers, aided by pregnant Magnani and priest Aldo Fabrizi, oppose the Nazis during the final days of the

occupation of Rome. Although the script – co-written by a young Federico Fellini – was functional and simplistic, with characters clearly defined as either good or bad, Rossellini was able to coax heartfelt performances from his cast, further enhancing the film's immediacy by shooting many of its key incidents in locations where similar events had actually taken place in real life. Gritty, realistic and replete with powerful images – notably the use of babies and children to signify the birth of a new, post-Fascist Italy – *Rome, Open City* was hailed as an instant classic, winning the Best Film award at Cannes and profoundly influencing a generation of European film-makers.

WAR REALISM

1946

A Matter of Life and Death

STAIRWAY TO HEAVEN   104 min.
Directors: *Michael Powell and Emeric Pressburger*
Origin: *GB*
Distributor: *Archers/Gaumont*
Cast: *Richard Attenborough, Robert Coote, Marius Goring, Kim Hunter, Roger Livesey, Raymond Massey, David Niven, Abraham Sofaer*

Powell and Pressburger's lavishly imaginative tale of an airman reprieved from death because of a heavenly mix-up remains one of their finest collaborations. A profound, multi-layered romantic fantasy, originally commissioned by the British Ministry of Information as a piece of Anglo-American propaganda, *A Matter of Life and Death* stars David Niven as Squadron-Leader Peter Carter who, after a final radio conversation with American wireless operator Kim Hunter, is forced to bail out over the Channel without a parachute. Miraculously surviving, he meets

and falls in love with Hunter before a heavenly emissary (Marius Goring), visible only to Niven, arrives to spirit him to the afterlife. The subsequent development of Carter's case in Heaven is parallelled by his deteriorating physical condition on earth, resulting in a dual climax in which he undergoes an earthly operation for a brain tumor and a heavenly trial for a renewed lease of life. Extraordinary imaginative flair – the contrasting of a monochrome heaven with a Technicolor earth; a vast escalator leading upwards from this world to the next; a heavenly court attended by the legions of the dead – combines with vintage performances, notably from Niven, Roger Livesey as his doctor and Raymond Massey as Heaven's prosecutor, to make for a uniquely enchanting visual, intellectual and emotional feast, at once light-hearted fairytale and, according to one film historian "one of the most metaphysically complex films ever made".

WAR FANTASY DRAMA

It's a Wonderful Life

129 min.
Director: *Frank Capra*
Origin: *USA*
Distributor: *RKO*
Cast: *Lionel Barrymore, Ward Bond, Beulah Bondi, Frank Faylen, Gloria Grahame, Thomas Mitchell, Donna Reed, James Stewart, Henry Travers*

Home from the war as one of the top-ranked officers in the American Auxiliary Air Force, James Stewart turned his back on his 1930s studio MGM and joined producer Frank Capra instead. The result was his best-loved performance as the doubting 30-year-old hero planning suicide when everything seems to go wrong, and saved by an elderly, bungling guardian angel (sprightly Henry Travers) who takes him through all the small, positive aspects of his wonderful life. Capra's shamelessly sentimental and inherently conservative toast to homespun

American values was surprisingly a turnoff for postwar audiences, but *It's a Wonderful Life* has long gripped television viewers with its resounding cinema artistry, good-hearted feeling and appealing acting displays. These include charismatic turns from Lionel Barrymore as the miserly banker, Thomas Mitchell as Stewart's hard-drinking uncle and Donna Reed as his love. It's a Christmas TV favourite every year in America, and only Scrooge himself would object to the treacly family-Christmas finale of the flashback-told tale, based on a short story called *The Greatest Gift*, which author Philip Doren Stern apparently first penned on a Christmas card. It's for everyone who believes in love, angels, Christmas – and black-and-white movies. But the post-war mood had turned against Capra and it was to be the director's last great film, with nearly all his big successes comings in the extraordinary five years between *It Happened One Night* (1934) and *Mr Smith Goes to Washington* (1939).

COMEDY/DRAMA

Mildred Pierce

113 min.
Director: *Michael Curtiz*
Origin: *USA*
Distributor: *Warner*
Cast: *Eve Arden, Bruce Bennett, Ann Blyth, Jack Carson, Joan Crawford, Butterfly McQueen, Lee Patrick, Zachary Scott, George Tobias*

Mildred Pierce is Hollywood melodrama *par excellence*. Joan Crawford won an Oscar for the part of a lifetime as the eponymous heroine which fell to her only after her deadly rivals Bette Davis and Barbara Stanwyck turned it down. She relishes the quintessential Crawford role of young thrusting woman who rises from humble waitress to restaurant boss, but her business success is hardly reflected in her private life. Cool on the outside, this dis-

Darling *performances: Henry Fonda, Ward Bond, Victor Mature and Alan Mowbray at the OK Corral*

turbed heroine is in turmoil within. Her unnaturally doting fondness on her daughter Ann Blyth isn't returned since Blyth is a selfish piece of work. Rejected, Crawford succumbs to the slimy charms of Zachary Scott as the cad from Pasadena, but old Zach attracts the attentions of jealous Ann. And with both mother and daughter after the same fella, the stage is set for some explosive consequences. The obvious parallels with Crawford's own emotionally stunted personal life are uncanny, adding a new dimension to an already highly emotionally charged story, neatly adapted by Ranald MacDougall from James M. Cain's novel. There's a terrific ensemble of actors (Eve Arden, Jack Carson, Bruce Bennett, Lee Patrick, Butterfly McQueen, all on their best form), while ideally cast Blyth and Scott are especially creepy. But the real star is Joan Crawford, utterly believable, touching and vulnerable – the latter two adjectives not normally associated with her – in a complex part people might once have dismissed as just soap opera. This is the very kind of film they don't make any more, and should. Frank, risqué material for its day, with a tough, cynical edge and gritty dialogue have helped it to age well and stay fresh.
THRILLER/MELODRAMA

My Darling Clementine

97 min.
Director: *John Ford*
Origin: *USA*
Distributor: *20th Century-Fox*
Cast: *Ward Bond, Walter Brennan, Linda Darnell, Cathy Downs, Henry Fonda, Tim Holt, John Ireland, Victor Mature, Alan Mowbray, Roy Roberts*

The classic Ford western, *My Darling Clementine* tells the oft-repeated story of how Wyatt Earp cleaned up Tombstone and, with the help of his friend Doc Holliday, wiped out the Clanton gang at the OK Corral. Joseph MacDonald's black-and-white photography creates a world of brooding shadows by night, and never-ending blinding skyline by day. Ford is more concerned with the myth of the west than historical accuracy, and with character and atmosphere more than action for action's sake. Fonda is the lanky, socially awkward but honourably manly Earp; Mature, while somewhat robust for the tubercular Doc Holliday, is convincing in his uneasy friendship with Fonda; and Alan Mowbray is a joy as a drunken itinerant thespian. Linda Darnell plays a Hispanic-looking Native American firecracker, whose treatment by Earp is distinctly politically incorrect by modern standards, and Cathy

Downs as Clementine is the personification of the east coast civilization that the emergent west aspires to. The most memorable scenes are those which illuminate the community and its attitudes: Earp's civilizing visit to the barber's and the dance held in the unfinished church. Compared to later versions of the Earp legend, such as *Gunfight at the OK Corral* (1957) and more recently *Tombstone* (1993) and *Wyatt Earp* (1994), *My Darling Clementine* has an old-fashioned innocence, directness and simple morality which is nostalgically appealing, lacking the lingering detail in its killings, or indeed in Doc's operation on Darnell, which would be *de rigueur* today. The later Earp films, which lay claim to greater historical accuracy, also raise the question of whatever happened to darling Clementine, who is ousted in the 1990s by much more worldly ladies.
WESTERN

Notorious

101 min.
Director: *Alfred Hitchcock*
Origin: *USA*
Distributor: *RKO*
Cast: *Ingrid Bergman, Louis Calhern, Cary Grant, Leopoldine Konstantin, Moroni Olsen, Claude Rains, Reinhold Schünzel*

Notorious is the most cleanly plotted yet morally murky of Alfred Hitchcock's espionage thrillers. The picture's prophetic use of a secret stash of uranium ore landed Hitchcock in trouble with America's nuclear-obsessed secret service. But ironically the uranium is the best example of what the director termed "the MacGuffin", a nominal plot device to spur the story forward and set the film's more significant elements into motion. At its heart *Notorious* is a steely-eyed study of male-female relations hamstrung by outside demands, wounded pride, petty point-scoring and a near-fatal lack of communication. The plot sees federal agent Devlin (Cary Grant) dispatch damaged, dissolute Alicia Huberman (Ingrid Bergman) into the jaws of danger, infiltrating a group of Brazil-based Nazis by marrying one of their number – mother's boy Alex Sebastian (Claude Rains). Devlin and Alicia are in love, but their love is complex, compromised, scarcely articulated until the picture's close when Alicia, poisoned and perhaps dying, is finally sprung from Sebastian's lair. *Notorious* catches its principal players on career-best form, with Bergman all aching, vulnerable beauty and Rains masterfully turning bad-guy Sebastian into an oddly dignified and sympathetic figure.

Notorious: Cary Grant and Ingrid Bergman bottle up their emotions

Easter Parade: *Fred Astaire and Judy Garland are a couple of swells*

Most impressive is Grant, cast against type as a hard-bitten misogynist, his moral ambiguity signified in the opening scene where Hitchcock films him faceless – a brooding, shadowy guest at the party. It's merely the first of a veritable treasure chest of directorial flourishes from the master, garnishing this thrilling, multi-layered, super-tense outing with the visual wizardry it deserves.
SPY THRILLER

The Big Sleep

114 min.
Director: *Howard Hawks*
Origin: *USA*
Distributor: *Warner*
Cast: *Lauren Bacall, Humphrey Bogart, Elisha Cook Jr, Louis Jean Heydt, Dorothy Malone, John Ridgely, Regis Toomey, Martha Vickers*

Humphrey Bogart is at his hard-boiled best as Raymond Chandler's private eye Philip Marlowe, shooting quips and bullets as he encounters myriad corpses, wayward women and a heated blackmail case. Some audiences have complained they can't follow *The Big Sleep's* story, and director Howard Hawks admitted he, Chandler and screenwriter William Faulkner couldn't either. But that isn't the point. For the plot, though characteristic, isn't anything out of the ordinary. Marlowe is hired to protect general's daughter Martha Vickers but gets embroiled in murder and love with the girl's sister, played by Lauren Bacall in her second charismatic teaming with Bogey. Instead, it's the acting, atmosphere, characters, motives, dialogue, suspense, the pace and sheer verve of the whole thing that count. And if it even looked as though it was going to get dull, they just brought on another corpse. Great! Britain's Michael Winner remade it in 1978 with Robert Mitchum, who seemed born to play Marlowe, and he'd played to great effect, aged 58, in *Farewell, My Lovely* in 1975. But

Winner made the cardinal error of switching the film to the 1970s and moving the mean streets to London, so it was just another thriller. Marlowe has thrown up a number of distinguished interpreters: Dick Powell in the original *Farewell, My Lovely* (1944), Robert Montgomery in *The Lady in the Lake* (1946), George Montgomery in *The Brasher Dubloon* (1947), James Garner in *Marlowe* (1969) and Elliott Gould in *The Long Goodbye* (1972).
DETECTIVE THRILLER

1948

Bicycle Thieves

THE BICYCLE THIEF/LADRI DI BICICLETTE   90 min.
Director: *Vittorio De Sica*
Origin: *Italy*
Distributor: *Mayer/PDS*
Cast: *Vittorio Antonucci, Elena Altieri, Lianella Carell, Lamberto Maggiorani, Enzo Staiola*

A deceptively simple story about Antonio, a long-unemployed man struggling to keep his family alive, whose happiness at finding a job gives way to despair when his precious bicycle, on which the job depends, is stolen. He and his young son Bruno tramp the streets of Rome looking for the thief. De Sica's neo-realistic treatment combined with Cesare Zavattini's script give the story the true resonance of tragedy. *Bicycle Thieves'* richness lies in the telling detail it gives of the lives of its characters and of post-war Rome itself: the hungry crowd of men competing for work outside the employment office; the pawn shop where the wife pawns her sheets to raise money for her husband to redeem his bicycle; the streets, the flea markets and the poverty-stricken, overcrowded tenements where Antonio and the child desperately search for the stolen bicycle; and the restaurant, where a wealthy family stuff them-

selves while father and son share a simple meal at a nearby table. All the while we see in their faces the looming spectre of no work, no money, no food, if the bicycle is not found. All the performers, including Maggiorani as Antonio and Staiola, heartrending as the little boy, are non-professional and the whole film is seared through with a sense of honesty, supported by the documentary-style truth of the black and white camerawork, which induces pity and anger for the characters' plight. The film won a special Oscar in 1949 for Best Foreign Film.
REALIST DRAMA

Easter Parade

103 min.
Director: *Charles Walters*
Origin: *USA*
Distributor: *MGM*
Cast: *Fred Astaire, Judy Garland, Peter Lawford, Ann Miller, Jules Munshin, Clinton Sundberg*

The ever-ingratiating Irving Berlin backstage musical *Easter Parade* boasts perfect performances and great tunes, lifting a merely functional story about Fred Astaire's bid to erase the memory of his old partner Ann Miller who's left him in the lurch to join a Ziegfeld show. In pained revenge, Astaire swears he can make a star out of anybody, and plucks Judy Garland from the chorus line to try to boost the at-first clumsy youngster up on the stairway to success, falling in love by the final reel. But it's not the story so much as the music that makes this MGM show special. The multi-faceted musical numbers – there are 17 in all – are vintage Berlin, and the musical directors, Roger Edens and Johnny

Green, won Oscars for their lovely work. There's a continual unravelling of essential sequences for all musical fans here, including Astaire's "Steppin' out with My Baby" and his inventive "Drum Crazy", Miller's "Shakin' the Blues Away" and "The Girl on the Magazine Cover", Astaire-Garland's duet "A Couple of Swells", and of course the "Easter Parade" song itself, included in the Fifth Avenue finale. An on-form Garland has one beautifully soulful number, "Better Luck Next Time", to balance all her glorious upbeat tunes, and she's especially sparky in a series of old-time tunes – "When the Midnight Choo-Choo Leaves for Alabam", "Snooky Ookums", "Ragtime Violin" and "I Love a Piano" – which perfectly suit this great showbiz trouper's exuberant style.
MUSICAL

The Red Shoes

133 min.
Director: *Michael Powell*
Origin: *GB*
Distributor: *Archers/Gaumont*
Cast: *Frederick Ashton, Albert Basserman, Marius Goring, Robert Helpmann, Esmond Knight, Leonide Massine, Moira Shearer, Ludmilla Tcherina, Anton Walbrook*

The unique film-making partnership of Michael Powell and Emeric Pressburger hit its creative heights with *The Red Shoes*, a "ballet film" only in the sense that *Raging Bull* is a film about boxing, or *Citizen Kane* a movie about newspapers. A feast of colour-soaked imagery, the film charts the development of a ballet production, *The Red Shoes*, in which a girl's magical footwear impels her to keep dancing, long after her head has decided to stop. In the course of the film, life duly comes to imitate art as lead dancer Victoria Page (Moira Shearer) finds herself torn between the human love offered by composer Julian Craster (Marius Goring) and the strict demands of her craft, embodied by the driven, piercing-eyed impresario Boris Lermontov (a never-better Anton Walbrook). *The Red Shoes* is a potentially deadly hotch-potch of styles that somehow blend perfectly – part gritty naturalism, part flamboyant melodramatics, part bewitching fairy-tale fantasy. But the end of this spellbinding, celebratory confection sees director Powell dropping us abruptly back into the real world with the controversial image of his heroine stretched bloody and torn on the railway tracks – a shocking yet somehow appropriate finale to a film always on the outer edge of self-control. "I think the real reason why *The Red Shoes* was such a success," mused Powell, "was that for ten years we had all been told to go out and die for freedom and democracy, for this and for that, and now that the war was over, *The Red Shoes* told us to go and die for our art." DANCE/FANTASY/MELODRAMA

1949

Gun Crazy

86 min.
Director: *Joseph H. Lewis*
Origin: *USA*
Distributor: *Universal/King Brothers*
Cast: *Morris Carnovsky, Peggy Cummins, John Dall, Barry Kroeger, Harry Lewis, Mickey Little, Annabel Shaw, Rusty Tamblyn, Nedrick Young*

The low-budget cult classic *Gun Crazy* is the prototype for *Bonnie and Clyde*. Told in flashback, principally from the point of view of the anti-hero

Bart (John Dall), it begins with his childhood obsession with firearms, leading to his shooting a chicken, after which he vows never to kill again. But returning from the war he gets into a shooting contest with carnival queen Annie (Cummins), who gets him a gun and persuades him to hold up banks with her. "We go together like guns and ammunition," he tells her as they flee to the mountains, hunted by a posse of Bart's former school-friends. Refusing to surrender, Bart is finally driven to kill again when Annie is about to shoot his chums. He guns her down before dying in a barrage of bullets himself. Despite, or perhaps because of, being made so quickly, the film boasts some daring direction, most notably the single-shot robbery scene filmed from inside the car. The camera begins in the back seat with Bart and Annie talking nervously in front. When he goes into the bank the camera moves up to see her diverting a nosy policeman's attention, climbing onto the back seat again when they make their getaway. Lewis's refusal to cut away is significantly claustrophobic, suggesting they are cornered and doomed, and was later borrowed by Godard in *Bande à Part* (1964). Dalton Trumbo wrote the script from a MacKinlay Kantor newspaper article, but Trumbo was blacklisted and had to use the pen-name Millard Kaufman. The movie's original title was *Deadly Is the Female*. GANGSTER THRILLER/CULT

Kind Hearts and Coronets

106 min.
Director: *Robert Hamer*
Origin: *GB*
Distributor: *Ealing*
Cast: *Joan Greenwood, Hugh Griffith, Alec Guinness, Valerie Hobson, Arthur Lowe, Miles Malleson, Dennis Price, Jeremy Spenser*

Alec Guinness gives a remarkable display of his versatility and

comic touch in eight different parts (one of them a woman) as almost the entire aristocratic D'Ascoyne family in this marvellous, elegantly cynical, multiply murderous black comedy. Co-star Price plays Louis Mazzini, a lowly and broke member of the D'Ascoyne clan who starts murdering each member of the family who stands between him and the dukedom and its riches. Guinness plays, quite hilariously as well as ingen-iously, the Duke, the Banker, the Canon, the General, the Admiral, Young Ascoyne D'Ascoyne, Young Henry and even Lady Agatha. The part he doesn't go for is Edith D'Ascoyne, taken by Valerie Hobson, while breathy Joan Greenwood is headstrong Sibella. The director, Robert Hamer, and John Dighton base their witty and polished script, full of Wildean epigrams (the Canon says: "I always say that my west window has all the exuberance of Chaucer without, happily, any of the concomitant crudities of his period"), on Roy Horniman's novel *Israel Rank*. The story unfolds in flashback, narrated by our murderous hero as he rushes to finish his memoirs while the public hangman (Miles Malleson) arrives at the prison for the great day. The portrait of Edwardian English society is sharp, shot

Kind Hearts: *"She fell to earth in Berkeley Square"*

through with pointed satirical barbs, but it's for the film's malicious fun as well as its literate intelligence and the cut-crystal acting that this delightful British gem is to be so prized. One of the sparkling jewels in the crown of Ealing studios. BLACK COMEDY

The Third Man

100 min.
Director: *Carol Reed*
Origin: *GB*
Distributor: *British Lion*
Cast: *Joseph Cotten, Ernst Deutsch, Trevor Howard, Wilfrid Hyde-White, Bernard Lee, Alida Valli, Orson Welles*

The Third Man is one of those rare instances when a clutch of fiercely independent talents mesh to create an organic whole. Graham Greene scripted, Carol Reed directed, Robert Krasker won an Oscar for his camerawork, Joseph Cotten played the lead and Orson Welles, improvising his own dialogue, created an immortal screen villain in Harry Lime. But the result is seamless, a film masterpiece. Indeed, if a movie's worth is measured by its number of classic set-pieces, *The Third Man* goes down as one of the finest ever made: Cotten's hounding through Vienna by an angelic, moon-faced infant; Welles's gleeful grin in a darkened doorway; the dazzling exchange aboard the empty ferris wheel; fingers poking through a sewer grate; and the last lingering shot as Cotten waits on the cemetery path, an ending that turned the cosy expectations of the 1940s viewer upside down. All these moments burn into the mind's eye with an intensity that's startling. The city of Vienna is an inspired choice of location and the perfect symbol for an uncertain post-war world – rationed and rubble-strewn, split between the occupying Allied powers, none of whom has a clue what the others are up to. Amid this shaky terrain, Cotten proves an ideal modern hero in the Greene mould – a

faintly ludicrous dime-store writer who discovers his basic dignity when confronted by Lime's demonic malevolence.
THRILLER

White Heat

114 min.
Director: *Raoul Walsh*
Origin: *USA*
Distributor: *Warner*
Cast: *John Archer, James Cagney, Steve Cochran, Virginia Mayo, Edmond O'Brien, Margaret Wycherly*

James Cagney's reputation may rest on his gangster outings of the 1930s but it was this tough-toned 1949 classic, made after a decade away from the genre, that proved his movie peak. Directed by Raoul Walsh, *White Heat* is an exhilarating amalgam of styles. The basic premise, with crime boss Cody Jarrett (Cagney) shadowed by an undercover police agent (Edmond O'Brien) is pure 1930s: hard, fast and uncomplicated. But just below the surface matters are less straightforward, sullied by the darker elements of the 1940s *film noir*. Far from Cagney's typical no-nonsense mobster, Cody is borderline insane and unnaturally devoted to his "Ma" (Margaret Wycherly), climbing into her lap to be nursed through one of his crippling migraines. When Cody, banged up in jail, hears of Ma's death, his tentative hold on sanity is permanently severed. *White Heat* boasts a raw, contemporary urgency, with Cagney seemingly representative of a world "liable to crack up any minute". In this uncertain post-war climate there is no longer any honour among thieves. The old rules no longer apply; treachery is endemic. This vision of a volatile new era is made explicit in a devastating final scene which finds the cornered Cody emptying his pistol into the tanks of an oil refinery and crying out hysterically to his dead mother ("Made it Ma! Top of the world!"). The ensuing apocalypse – mushroom clouds in a night sky –

makes for a chillingly significant denouement; the point where the American thriller first met the nuclear age.
GANGSTER THRILLER

1950

All About Eve

138 min.
Director: *Joseph L. Mankiewicz*
Origin: *USA*
Distributor: *20th Century-Fox*
Cast: *Anne Baxter, Bette Davis, Celeste Holm, Hugh Marlowe, Gary Merrill, Marilyn Monroe, Gregory Ratoff, Thelma Ritter, George Sanders*

"Fasten your seat belts, it's going to be a bumpy night!" The great Bette Davis shows why she was nicknamed Mother Goddam in a quintessential performance in one of Hollywood's most incisive backstage looks at the world of the theatre and the neuroses of thespians. Oscar-nominated Davis makes the most of Joseph L. Mankiewicz's terrific script, playing the aging Broadway actress Margo Channing, laid low by star-struck youngster Anne Baxter (as Eve) who turns up in her dressing room as a fan one day. The unsuspecting Davis employs the innocent-seeming young woman as her secretary, but the new assistant begins ruthlessly to undermine Davis's career. Writer/director Mankiewicz's piercing gaze at the showbiz bear-pit is a cornucopia of bitchy wit and greasepaint atmosphere, while the stars in the top-drawer cast cover themselves with glory. George Sanders is particularly impressive as the waspish, Machiavellian theatre critic Addison De Witt, and so is Thelma Ritter as Birdie. Marilyn Monroe sparkles briefly as a dumb but ambitious starlet, and Davis, by turns bitchy, vulnerable and compassionate, gives one of her most successful performances without a

hint of archness or self-parody. A triumph for Mankiewicz, it was nominated for an all-time record 14 Oscars and won six, including Best Picture, Direction, Screenplay, and Best Supporting Actor for Sanders, but nothing for Davis who should certainly have won. It was the second year running Mankiewicz won both Director and Writer Oscars. The film, taken from Mary Orr's short story *The Wisdom of Eve*, was the basis for the 1970s Broadway hit musical *Applause!* with Lauren Bacall.
BACKSTAGE DRAMA

Orphée

ORPHEUS   95 min.
Director: *Jean Cocteau*
Origin: *France*
Distributor: *André Paulvé*
Cast: *Maria Casarès, Marie Déa, Edouard Dermithe, Juliette Greco, Jean Marais, François Périer*

The Parisian poet and artist Jean Cocteau creates cinema magic in the French *avant-garde* masterpiece *Orphée*, pursuing the Surrealist and Freudian idea of ancient myth as a doorway to the modern subconscious and encapsulating his main concerns: death and the situation of the artist, torn between the real world of everyday life and the "underworld" of the human mind's imagining depths. In this modern retelling of the Orpheus myth, Death (Maria Casarès) appears to the poet Orphée (Jean Marais) as a muse sending coded messages over the radio. Fascinated, Orphée follows her through a mirror (in one of cinema's most evocative special effects) into the underworld on a mystical search for inspiration. He neglects his wife Eurydice (Marie Déa) who turns to female friends, the Bacchantes, at an all-women dancing club, for comfort. Death falls for Orphée and has her leather-clad motorcyclists run down Eurydice, but Orphée persuades Death's sidekick Heurtebise (François Périer) to lead him back into the underworld to recover

her. There a Supreme Tribunal orders that he can take Eurydice back on condition that he never looks at her again. Cocteau's provocative subtext is that, for the artist, a love affair with death is ultimately preferable to the meat-and-two-veg bourgeois ideal offered by Eurydice. *Orphée* is the purest expression of poetry in the cinema, with striking imagery and a darkly enigmatic story, which is both universal and highly personal. Cocteau revisited this fertile material nine years later in the elegiac *Le Testament d'Orphée*, mixing his friends and obsessions to produce a unique statement of his life and art.
SURREALIST FANTASY

Sunset Blvd

110 min.
Director: *Billy Wilder*
Origin: *USA*
Distributor: *Paramount*
Cast: *Fred Clark, Cecil B. DeMille, Lloyd Gough, William Holden, Hedda Hopper, Buster Keaton, Nancy Olson, Gloria Swanson, Erich von Stroheim, H. B. Warner, Jack Webb*

One of Hollywood's most mordant and bitter takes on its own legacy, *Sunset Blvd* is recounted by a dead man floating in a Beverly Hills pool. Billy Wilder's dark and humorous Hollywood classic, fusing black comedy with *film noir* melodrama, showcases one-time silent-screen icon Gloria Swanson in her most famous role as unbalanced former star Norma Desmond and William Holden as down-on-his-luck scriptwriter Joe Gillis. Out of work, he stumbles upon the neglected mansion of the doomed Desmond who lives in dotty seclusion with her manservant (Erich von Stroheim) but is planning a triumphant comeback. Spookily, the aging Norma takes on young Joe as her script helper and gigolo. This was adult, risky and challenging stuff for 1950 moviegoers, of the kind that Hollywood wouldn't consider in the smoothed-out

1990s. The only similar-veined movie it calls to mind is 1962's *What Ever Happened to Baby Jane? Sunset Blvd* is one of those rare treasures where everything's just right: a clever, Oscar-winning script from Wilder, Charles Brackett and D. M. Marshman Jr; delightfully eccentric, eerie performances reflecting their own histories from Swanson and Erich von Stroheim; and priceless cameos from cinema legends Buster Keaton and Cecil B. DeMille. In 1993 Andrew Lloyd Webber fashioned a British stage musical version of the movie, with the first American version starring Glenn Close as Desmond. Wilder gave his blessing to the show: "This man Sir Andrew is on a roll," he said. "You should put your chips where he does."

BLACK COMEDY/MELODRAMA

1951

Rashomon

90 min.
Director: *Akira Kurosawa*
Origin: *Japan*
Distributor: *Daiei*
Cast: *Minoru Chiaki, Fumiko Homma, Daisuke Kato, Toshiro Machiko Kyo, Mifune, Masayuki Mori, Takashi Shimura, Kichijiro Ueda*

Set in eleventh-century Japan, *Rashomon* is the story of the rape of a nobleman's wife by a bandit in the forest, the death of her husband, and the woodcutter who witnessed the incident. It is told from the different viewpoints of the four participants, one them now a ghost, each of whom has a different version of what happened. Framing the telling is a priest sheltering from the rain under the ruined Rashomon gate and describing the bandit's trial. This study in ambiguity, rich in symbolism and psychological

understanding, has become a benchmark in cinema for its experimental style. Though by no means typical of Kurosawa's work, it is a monument to both his artistry and his humanity. It also contains a group of remarkable performances, particularly from Toshiro Mifune as the bandit. There are two contradictory interpretations of the story: that it illustrates the philosopher's contention that there are many truths versus the widely accepted crude logic that there is only one set of true facts, therefore three out of the four testifying characters are lying; and that the film is about human fallibility and dishonesty and that humanity, like the Rashomon gate, is crumbling. *Rashomon* reintroduced Japanese film to the world market, winning the top prize at the 1951 Venice Film Festival and a Best Foreign Film Oscar. This and subsequent films made Kurosawa a cinema figure of world stature, although *Rashomon* is probably still his most widely seen film.

PUZZLE DRAMA

Strangers on a Train

101 min.
Director: *Alfred Hitchcock*
Origin: *USA*
Distributor: *Warner*
Cast: *Leo G. Carroll, Farley Granger, Patricia Hitchcock, Marion Lorne, Ruth Roman, Robert Walker*

Stiletto-sharp and fiendishly fun, *Strangers on a Train* marked a huge return to critical and popular acclaim for Alfred Hitchcock after the intriguing waywardness of *The Paradine Case* and *Under Capricorn*. Patricia Highsmith may have written the source-novel, Raymond Chandler may have penned the script, but the end result is quintessential Hitch: a bag of irresistibly devilish entertainment. The premise is absurdly simple. Tennis star Guy (Farley Granger) meets playboy Bruno (Robert Walker) in an anonymous train dining-car. Guy wants to be rid of

his wife, Bruno can't abide his bullying father, so Bruno hatches a plan. The ideal solution is to "criss-cross" – swap murders, so removing the incriminating taint of motive. Believing his companion to be joking, Guy agrees that it's a fine idea, unconsciously giving Bruno the nod to stalk Guy's grasping, estranged missus around the village fair where, after a trip through the Tunnel of Love, he lovingly throttles her. With his monogrammed necktie and silky patter, Walker's creation is one of Hitchcock's finest screen monsters. By contrasting Bruno's unholy charisma with Guy's flat, po-faced heroism, the director playfully splits the audience's loyalties, forcing us into an identification with both hero and villain. This reaches its peak in the film's accelerating, cross-cutting finale with Guy's sun-drenched tennis tussle mirrored by Bruno's shadowly fumbling in a streetside drain. Jam-packed with vibrant incidents and wrapped up by an immortal merry-go-round climax, *Strangers on a Train* finds Hitchcock on peak form, rustling up a crowd-pleasing classic of 1950s cinema and one of his crispest, canniest, most purely pleasurable pictures.

THRILLER

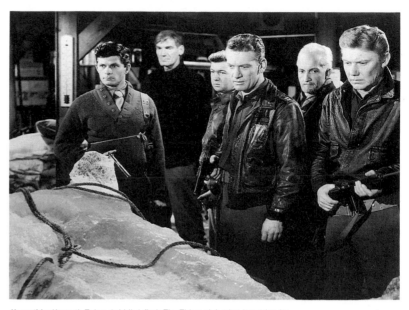

Unearthly: *Kenneth Tobey* (middle) *finds* The Thing *ain't what it used to be*

The Thing from Another World

THE THING   87 min.
Director: *Christian Nyby*
Origin: *USA*
Distributor: *RKO*
Cast: *James Arness, Robert Cornthwaite, Dewey Martin, William Self, Margaret Sheridan, Douglas Spencer, Kenneth Tobey*

A vintage slice of 1950s sci-fi chiller, *The Thing from Another World* lives up to its cult status as a work of grand imagination and suspense, notably giving life to the cinema's first space monster. Though directed by Christian Nyby, the film betrays the hand of its esteemed producer, Howard Hawks, bearing his hallmarks of an intense study of a group in crisis, the quick-fire, naturalistic dialogue, the simple, direct acting and the brisk, unfussy film-making. Charles Lederer's script makes a tasty soup out of the bones of J. W. Campbell Jr's source story *Who Goes There?* about a party of American scientists, working in an isolated Arctic base, who unearth and accidentally defrost an unfriendly eight-foot alien. Kenneth Tobey plays an air force captain who leads a crew to Polar Expedition Six to investigate reports that a spaceship has

crashed into the ice. Tobey heads a cast of B-movie stalwarts all working above their usual form, while James Arness, who became a star in TV's *Gunsmoke*, plays the Thing – an unrewarding part since he's kept off screen for most of the time and then seen only in shadow. The final speech is a classic: "I bring you warning... keep looking – watch the skies!" John Carpenter's 1982 big-budget remake is a horror film with an emphasis on bodily gore but, intriguingly, it follows the original story, with its *Alien*-style premise where the shape-changing Thing hides in every character one by one. No doubt this was too strong a subject for the 1950s – or maybe they just didn't have the special effects.
HORROR/SCI-FI

1952

High Noon

84 min.
Director: *Fred Zinnemann*
Origin: *USA*
Distributor: *United Artists*
Cast: *Lloyd Bridges, Lon Chaney Jr, Gary Cooper, Katy Jurado, Grace Kelly, Otto Kruger, Ian Macdonald, Thomas Mitchell, Henry Morgan, Lee Van Cleef*

Dubbed the first adult western, *High Noon* is Gary Cooper's finest hour, reviving his flagging career, and a key moment on the road towards the more psychologically complex westerns of the 1950s. There is little action but plenty of suspense as Sheriff Will Kane (Cooper) has his wedding day to Quaker pacifist Amy (Grace Kelly) ruined by his inability to raise a posse to help him fight the killers coming for him on the midday train. With the action unfolding in real time, Kane refuses to desert the ungrateful town and survives the inevitable shoot-out with the aid of Amy. *High Noon* is a western

with a difference, Will being a reluctant loner, afraid of death and willing to ask for help (John Wayne was so disgusted that he made 1959's *Rio Bravo* as a belated riposte). Marlon Brando, Charlton Heston and Kirk Douglas were all offered the part before Cooper took it at a cut-price. His lonely agony was for real since he was suffering from a bleeding ulcer and injured hip, and finished filming with the comment, "I'm all acted out". Fortunately he was rewarded with his second Oscar, one of four for the film, including an award for Dmitri Tiomkin's persistent ballad, "High Noon (Do Not Forsake Me)", sung by Tex Ritter. Screenwriter Carl Foreman was subsequently blacklisted for refusing to co-operate with the House Un-American Activities Committee and *High Noon* was written to express his outrage at Hollywood's cowardice in failing to back artists like himself.
WESTERN

Singin' in the Rain

102 min.
Directors: *Gene Kelly and Stanley Donen*
Origin: *USA*
Distributor: *MGM*
Cast: *Madge Blake, Cyd Charisse, King Donovan, Douglas Fowley, Jean Hagen, Gene Kelly, Millard Mitchell, Rita Moreno, Donald O'Connor, Debbie Reynolds*

An all-time favourite comic musical, arguably the best MGM ever made, and also one of the funniest films to deal with the evolution from silent movies to talkies, *Singin' in the Rain* is directed at a dazzling pace by Gene Kelly and Stanley Donen, appropriate to the era of its story – the Roaring 20s. The story was created by screenwriters Adolph Green and Betty Comden to showcase the best numbers from MGM musicals. The discovery that many of them came from this period of movie history gave them their framework. Kelly

always maintained that every dance should tell a tale, which it certainly does in this, most demonstrably with the title song, first heard in *Hollywood Revue of 1929*. Kelly's show-stopping version of the number, as he saunters and splashes through the puddles with the joy of his new-found love for bouncy flapper heroine Reynolds, was described by one critic as "the most enchanting dance in history" and must be one of the most often seen film clips. Other musical highlights include Donald O'Connor's spoof on the voice coaches much in demand at this time, "Moses Supposes"; and his energetic vaudeville-style dance "Make 'Em Laugh"; plus one of Kelly's inventive climactic ballets with Cyd Charisse and her crazy 25-foot veil, a sequence which took a month to rehearse, two weeks to shoot and cost about a fifth of the overall budget – and was money well spent. All this plus Jean Hagen's high comedy performance as Kelly's silent screen co-star, whose squeaky voice spells curtains for her career.
BACKSTAGE MUSICAL

1953

From Here to Eternity

118 min.
Director: *Fred Zinnemann*
Origin: *USA*
Distributor: *Columbia*
Cast: *Claude Akins, Ernest Borgnine, Montgomery Clift, Deborah Kerr, Burt Lancaster, Philip Ober, Donna Reed, George Reeves, Mickey Shaughnessy, Frank Sinatra, Jack Warden*

Burt Lancaster as Sgt Milton Warden and Deborah Kerr as Karen Holmes romp around on the beach famously – and in its day shockingly – in Fred Zinnemann's potent adaptation of James Jones's bestseller. Superb acting from the host of stars and Zinnemann's res-

onant handling of the theme of sexual frustration helped turn it into an eight-Oscar winner. Along with the sex on the sand scene, its vulgarity, barracks language and depiction of women of easy virtue (all transferred intact from the novel) were milestones of frankness in their day. Set in the summer of 1941 on the eve of Pearl Harbor, the drama focuses on the relationships within an army unit stationed in Hawaii. The story sparks off when Montgomery Clift, as the independently-minded Prewitt, is posted to the barracks and refuses to join the boxing team. Frank Sinatra's comeback film was a particular triumph for him in a crowd-pleasing, career-moulding performance as the tough but appealing Italian-American soldier Angelo Maggio, and he won an Academy Award for it. He replaced Eli Wallach while the normally demure Kerr, cast against type as the commanding officer's nymphomaniac wife, was a replacement too – for Joan Crawford, after a row about her wardrobe. Among the other famous faces are Ernest Borgnine as the brutal Sgt Fatso Judson, Donna Reed as hostess Alma Lorene, Jack Warden as Cpl Buckley and Philip Ober as the weak CO. The Oscars included Best Picture, Director, Supporting Actor, Supporting Actress, Screenplay, Black and White Cinematography, Sound Recording, and Editing.
ACTION ADVENTURE/WAR DRAMA

Mr Hulot's Holiday

LES VACANCES DE MONSIEUR HULOT 93 min.
Director: *Jacques Tati*
Origin: *France*
Distributor: *Cady/Discina*
Cast: *Valentine Camax, Nathalie Pascaud, Michèle Rolla, Jacques Tati*

Jacques Tati's silent comic masterpiece, based around the holiday misadventures of his gangling alter ego, Monsieur Hulot, is both

Mr Hulot's Holiday: *Jacques Tati finds that life's a beach*

a high point of 1950s film and an enduring cinematic paradox – at once revolutionary in its rejection of conventional narrative structures, yet traditional in its revival of the silent format and backward references to the golden age of burlesque comedy. Although each scene is painstakingly crafted, there is no plot to speak of, just a loosely interconnected selection of gags and scenarios as the sublimely unawareHulot wreaks chaos during a trip to the sea. The film delights in breaking almost every established rule of conventional cinema. Gags are set up and dropped without climax or punchline; Hulot himself is often marginalized, proving irrelevant to much of the humour; and there is no obvious attempt to direct or influence the viewer's opinions. Camerawork and editing are totally objective, with the director preferring to observe scenes in lingering long-shot and to leave it to the audience to decide what is important or unimportant. The whole is given coherence, however, by Tati's uniquely absurdist sense of humour and acute observation of the vagaries of human behaviour. Exquisite parodies, such as a holidaying businessman continually called away to the phone, combine with hilarious set-pieces – Hulot lighting a match in a room full of fireworks; the solemnity of a funeral destroyed by the flatulent sounds of a deflating inner tube – to create one of the most innovative

feasts of humour ever to grace the world's cinemas.

SILENT SLAPSTICK COMEDY

Tokyo Story

TOKYO MONOGATARI 136 min.
Director: *Yasujiro Ozu*
Origin: *Japan*
Distributor: *Shochiku*
Cast: *Setsuko Hara, Chieko Higashiyama, Chishu Ryu, Haruko Sugimura, Eijiro Tono, So Yamamura*

There are many who consider *Tokyo Story* one of the finest films ever made. It was certainly the best of Yasujiro Ozu's 54 movies: a virtuoso display of craft, insight and sensitivity that captured the essence of post-war Japan and cemented Ozu's reputation as one of the world's leading directors. An elegiac tale of disillusionment and changing values, it follows an elderly couple (Chishu Ryu and Chieko Higashiyama) who leave their home in southern Japan to visit their offspring in the country's capital. Their doctor son (So Yamamura) and beautician daughter (Haruko Sugimura), however, resent the old couple's presence, and it is only with their widowed daughter-in-law (Setsuko Hara) that they find any kindness or understanding. Bitter and broken they return home, where greater tragedy awaits with the unexpected death of the old woman. Clear-eyed ensemble playing is complemented by Ozu's unique visual style, with each scene care-

fully structured to mirror the rigid formality of Japanese society and family. The result provides an uncanny documentary realism, with characters laid bare and the audience drawn into the very thick of the emotional action. Tokyo itself represents not merely a modern, urbanized society, but a new value system, a sprawling concrete family that has replaced the traditional kinship structure upon which the elderly couple depend. It is a bleak analysis, but an unflinchingly honest one, and remains one of cinema's most poignant studies of family, society, and the generational divide.

FAMILY DRAMA

The Wages of Fear

LE SALAIRE DE LA PEUR 140 min.
Director: *Henri-Georges Clouzot*
Origin: *France/Italy*
Distributor: *Filmsonor/CICC/Vera*
Cast: *Vera Clouzot, Folco Lulli, Yves Montand, William Tubbs, Peter Van Eyck, Charles Vanel*

One of the all-time great exercises in suspense, Henri-Georges Clouzot's nihilistic fable of four men transporting an explosive cargo of nitroglycerine across South America works as both a heart-stopping adventure story and a gripping existential commentary. A huge contemporary success, *The Wages of Fear* established Clouzot as one of the leading directors of his day, made international stars of Yves Montand and Charles Vanel and has, with its dour imagery and deft weaving of action and philosophy, exercised a profound influence on film-makers ever since. Based on a novel by Georges Arnaud, the picture divides into two halves, with the first hour spent introducing us to a cast of international misfits stranded in a dead-end Venezuelan town. Clouzot then focuses on four of the characters – Mario (Montand), Jo (Vanel), Luigi (Folco Lulli) and Bimba (Peter Van Eyck) – who, in a desperate effort to improve their lot, undertake a sui-

cide mission steering two lorryloads of nitro-glycerine to the site of an oil-well fire. Their gruelling trip through inhospitable terrain is at once a masterpiece of suspense and a pointed metaphor for the human condition, the hopelessness of which is underlined when Mario, the only man to survive the mission, is killed in a road accident on his way home. Unflinchingly pessimistic, and replete with dramatic images, it presents a near-perfect blend of taut script, insightful direction and eloquent performances. A precursor of the French New Wave, it was remade in 1977 as *Sorcerer*, although to considerably less effect.

ROAD MOVIE/THRILLER

1954

A Star Is Born

181 min.
Director: *George Cukor*
Origin: *USA*
Distributor: *Warner*
Cast: *Charles Bickford, Amanda Blake, Jack Carson, Judy Garland, Lucy Marlow, James Mason, Tom Noonan*

George Cukor's part-musical drama of a loving but doomed Hollywood couple is a terrific reworking of William Wellman's 1937 version, with Judy Garland and James Mason giving magnificent performances in their archetypal parts as the rising actress and fading star. In Moss Hart's story, celebrated screen star Norman Maine (Mason) is saved from drunkenly making a fool of himself in public by struggling young singer Esther Blodgett (Garland). Impressed by her talent, Maine encourages her to try the movies, little knowing that Esther's spectacular rise to stardom will mirror his own spectacular fall. It's perhaps Garland's best film thanks to her energy, vulnerability, sure comic touch and her vocal power

in marvellous numbers by Harold Arlen and Ira Gershwin like the Oscar-nominated "The Man That Got Away". Leonard Gershe and Roger Edens's extended (18-minute) "Born in a Trunk" sequence is Garland's other real show-stopper. The Warner studio, fearful of its investment inflated by $5 million from production delays, recut it after poor initial reactions, but in 1983 it was restored to its full, nearly complete, glory (though stills replace some missing footage), which reinstated 16 minutes of material cut from the original print. It's a tale for all seasons: Cukor filmed the first version of this story as *What Price Hollywood?* in 1932 with Constance Bennett and Lowell Sherman, which was remade in 1937 as the Janet Gaynor-Fredric March version, and filmed yet again in 1976 with Barbra Streisand and Kris Kristofferson, with the story transferred to the pop world. But this 1954 version is the definitive Hollywood backstage drama.
MUSICAL/BACKSTAGE DRAMA

Bad Day rising: *Spencer Tracy on the track of baddies at Black Rock*

Bad Day at Black Rock

81 min.
Director: *John Sturges*
Origin: *USA*
Distributor: *MGM*
Cast: *Walter Brennan, Ernest Borgnine, Russell Collins, John Ericson, Anne Francis, Dean Jagger, Lee Marvin, Robert Ryan, Spencer Tracy*

Director John Sturges's finest film, *Bad Day at Black Rock* is a brooding drama of greed and intolerance in the badlands of America's midwest. While not technically a western, the picture spills over with the stylistic properties of the genre, anticipating the rise of the 60s spaghetti-western with its pungent, slow-burning atmosphere and harsh re-examination of the myths of the American frontier. The story casts Spencer Tracy in vintage loner mould, an aging one-armed war veteran who arrives at the deadbeat township of Black

Rock in search of an Asian farmer, the father of a member of his platoon. His quiet, dogged investigation antagonizes the thuggish local heavies (Robert Ryan, Lee Marvin, Ernest Borgnine) but Tracy keeps going until the closet door is open and the skeleton revealed. The farmer is dead – killed four years before by Black Rock's inhabitants, who were enraged by his racial origins and success at finding water in an otherwise barren land. With its spare CinemaScope vistas and ever-present undertow of tension, *Bad Day at Black Rock* makes for a mesmerising morality play. The first Hollywood picture to recognize the nation's oppressive treatment of Asian-Americans during World War Two, it goes deeper still in its implications, questioning the entire basis on which the west was won. If Black Rock counts as the nation in microcosm, Sturges's film paints a particularly bleak picture, evoking a society founded on violent acquisition and maintained through intimidation and force. Thank goodness Spencer Tracy was on hand to put everything right.
SUSPENSE THRILLER/WESTERN

La Strada

THE ROAD   115 min.
Director: *Federico Fellini*
Origin: *Italy*
Distributor: *Trans Lux (Italy)*
Cast: *Richard Basehart, Giulietta Masina, Anthony Quinn, Marcella Rovere, Aldo Silvani, Livia Venturini*

One of the most moving and memorable films of world cinema, *La Strada* is Federico Fellini's first unquestioned masterpiece, which both established his international fame and marked his break from neo-realism to a more fanciful and symbolic style. It is also his first starring his wife, Giulietta Masina, who did her best work with her husband in this and subsequent films. It won an Oscar for Best Foreign Film. The story is simple, focusing on a naive peasant girl who is sold for a plate of pasta by her family into virtual slavery with a wandering muscleman and their adventures in the grey, desolate towns they visit. The film is dominated by Masina's performance as the waif. Her gamine clown, always laughing through her tears whatever life throws at her, has a Chaplinesque laughter-and-pathos quality, which is ultimately uplifting, particularly in its conclusion as to where the real strength and need lies in the master/slave relationship. Anthony Quinn is both repellent and touching as the bewildered bully who buys her body but never owns her spirit, while Richard Basehart is sympathetic as the tightrope-walking clown who befriends her and is killed by Quinn. This tragi-comic road movie of pain, cruelty and solitude was both hailed by the Catholic Church as "a parable of charity, love, grace and salvation" and attacked by leftist critics, who objected to Fellini's abandonment of neo-realistic principles and saw the film as justifying political repression through the tolerant nature of its heroine.
TRAGI-COMIC DRAMA

On the Waterfront

108 min.
Director: *Elia Kazan*
Origin: *USA*
Distributor: *Columbia*
Cast: *Marlon Brando, Lee J. Cobb, Leif Erickson, John Hamilton, Pat Henning, Karl Malden, Nehemiah Persoff, Eva Marie Saint, Rod Steiger*

Based on a series of late 1940s news-paper articles about corruption on the New York docks, *On the Waterfornt* is a milestone movie in every sense of the word. Directed by Elia Kazan from a Budd Schulberg script, its uncompromising dialogue, blistering performances and controversial subject matter redefined the boundaries of screen drama and set new standards of cinema realism. The major studios refused to back it, convinced that such gritty social analysis would never do business (it was eventually financed by independent producer Sam Spiegel). Yet it transfixed audiences, swept the board at the 1954 Oscars (eight awards in all, including Best Picture, Director, Actor and Screenplay) and established Brando as the most compelling performer of his generation. He plays Terry Malloy, an ex-boxer and dockyard stevedore who, prompted by the murder of his brother (Rod Steiger), takes on corrupt waterfront racketeer Johnny Friendly (Lee J. Cobb). It was a part originally intended for Frank Sinatra, but elicits from Brando his finest screen performance, supported all the way by Cobb, Steiger, Eva Marie Saint, and Karl Malden as a tough-talking local priest. Kazan's use of genuine dockyard locations lent the film a sense of dour, unrelenting immediacy, while close similarities between Malloy's betrayal of Friendly and Kazan's own willingness to shop friends to Senator McCarthy's House Un-American Activities Committee gave the project a gripping political undertone. At once poignant morality

tale and raw social commentary, *On the Waterfront* changed the face of screen drama and is rightly considered one of the transcendent classics of American film.
SOCIAL DRAMA

Seven Samurai

SHICHININ NO SAMURAI   208 min.
Director: *Akira Kurosawa*
Origin: *Japan*
Distributor: *Toho*
Cast: *Minoru Chiaki, Yoshio Inaba, Ko Kimura, Kuninori Kodo, Toshiro Mifune, Seiji Miyagachi, Takashi Shimura*

Akira Kurosawa's enthralling medieval drama of samurai honour is an action-packed masterpiece with depth, drawing on Hollywood models such as John Ford's westerns, and in turn inspiring John Sturges's classic American western *The Magnificent Seven*. The story is vintage stuff. A 16th-century Japanese village is annually attacked by marauding bandits who steal their food, prompting the farmers to hire samurai to defend them. But, through lack of funds, the villagers can only hire seven ill-assorted samurai who, despite the huge odds of the numbers stacked against them, marshal their forces and await the arrival of the bandits. The film's climax sees the samurai and villagers wipe out the bandits in a breathtaking battle sequence played out in the mud and driving rain. These exciting scenes are in stark contrast to the film's long, slow but equally engrossing build-up when each of the warriors is introduced to the viewer in turn, establishing their individual characters with crispness and economy. The later sequences of the villagers' training are made equally riveting through Kurosawa's insistent focus on the detail and facts, building up empathy with how the villagers think and feel. The film is visually breathtaking, particularly in its restored 35mm print and, oddly, works equally well in its cut 155-

minute and restored 208-minute versions. The shorter version is taut and terrific but even in the longer version there looks to be no fat at all.
ACTION ADVENTURE

1955

Pather Panchali

SONG OF THE LITTLE ROAD
112 min.
Director: *Satyajit Ray*
Origin: *India*
Distributor: *Government of West Bengal*
Cast: *Karuna Bannerjee, Kanu Bannerjee, Subir Bannerjee, Uma Das Gupta, Chunibala Devi*

Ray's first film signalled the emergence of a major new director, and was effectively Indian cinema's Western breakthrough. Set in the 1920s, it is the first of the Apu trilogy, with *Aparajito* (1956) and *Apur Sansur* (1959) following, and is based on a popular novel that Ray had acquired the rights to after illustrating the book. Apu (Subir Bannerjee) is a small boy from a Bengali village whose father has to move to the city for work, leaving the family to struggle together. There is no clear storyline, just a series of ordinary events recounted with overwhelming emotional force. Ray had been encouraged by Jean Renoir whom he met while the French director was making *The River* (1951), but working with an inexperienced weekend crew and no budget, he almost gave up after two years of struggle. He was saved when John Huston and the New York Museum of Modern Art intervened, pressurizing the government into financing the project to completion. They took the title literally, expecting it to be an account of road building, and were so embarrassed by its criticism of village poverty that they

gave it minimal publicity. Fortunately for Ray, word of mouth made it a popular success and international prizes at Cannes and Berlin earned enough prestige to enable him to complete the trilogy. Ray's influence on Indian cinema eventually filtered through to the principal production centre, Bombay, establishing humanist realism as a form able to exist alongside the operatic tradition of that country.
REALIST DRAMA

Rebel without a Cause

111 min.
Director: *Nicholas Ray*
Origin: *USA*
Distributor: *Warner*
Cast: *Corey Allen, Nick Adams, Jim Backus, James Dean, Ann Doran, Dennis Hopper, Sal Mineo, Natalie Wood*

Legendary screen idol James Dean starred in just three films, and this powerful work gave him his most famous role – a delinquent teen misunderstood by both his parents and society. Warner Brothers cashed in on the huge success of 1955's *East of Eden*, which turned Dean into an overnight sensation, by quickly casting their new star in another prestige drama with similar Freudian alienated-youth themes, but this time they shrewdly transferred the setting to contemporary California, making it seem even more relevant to the burgeoning American teenage audience. The film's poetic title is perfectly tailored to Dean's image, and triggered off audience identification in a big way not just in America but across the world, and as it turned out not just for the 1950s but for all time. Again Dean gives an electric and moving performance as Jim, an archetypal American teenager alienated from his dull and uncomprehending folks (Jim Backus, Ann Doran) and a community which doesn't understand him, but reaching out for love with Judy (Natalie Wood) and

friendship with Plato (Sal Mineo). Jim's the prototype new kid in town, with a lot of psychological baggage to sort out and a lot to prove. Stewart Stern's feverish script and Nicholas Ray's direction with its restless visual style still possess all their original power to move and thrill, complemented by the exotic Warnercolor and CinemaScope photography. Wood and Mineo were Oscar-nominated for their impressive acting, as was Ray for his original story. There's also a key early performance from Dennis Hopper as Goon.
TEENAGE MELODRAMA

The Ladykillers

97 min.
Director: *Alexander Mackendrick*
Origin: *GB*
Distributor: *Ealing*
Cast: *Kenneth Connor, Danny Green, Alec Guinness, Frankie Howerd, Katie Johnson, Herbert Lom, Cecil Parker, Peter Sellers, Jack Warner*

Lovable British character actress Katie Johnson suddenly became a star at age 77, playing the elderly landlady who comes up against sly, creepy lodger Alec Guinness and his comic cut-throats in this incisively written vintage black comedy from writer William Rose and director Alexander Mackendrick. When the crazy gang of robbers fear they've been rumbled by their dotty old landlady, they decide she must be silenced, but none of these softies can bear to murder her, and they're in much more danger than she is. The casual, frivolous approach to sudden death blows like a breath of fresh air through the stuffy corridors of British post-war cinema, packed to the gunwales with stiff upper lips and outmoded attitudes. Surprisingly perhaps for a reticent race, black comedy is a vein of humour the British do well, and it's the other side of the Ealing Studios coin from the cosy conservative comedies, dramas and war films they were expert at. The acting is

The Ladykillers: *Houseguests from hell (from left) Guinness, Sellers and Green intimidate Katie Johnson*

impeccable. Guinness, doing his canny Alastair Sim impersonation resplendent with ill-fitting dentures, leads an accomplished cast of comic actors – a tubby Peter Sellers, Cecil Parker, Herbert Lom and Danny Green are the other gang members – who play it all to the hilt. Apparently the complete script came to the writer in a dream, so it's ironic (and hilarious) that some po-faced critics have treated the story seriously and seen it as a parable of British post-war stagnation, with the gang as the first post-war Labour Government. But there's no need to ponder its implications; just enjoy and treasure it.
BLACK COMEDY

The Night of the Hunter

93 min.
Director: *Charles Laughton*
Origin: *USA*
Distributor: *United Artists*
Cast: *Don Beddoe, Sally Jane Bruce, Billy Chapin, Lillian Gish, Peter Graves, James Gleason, Robert Mitchum, Evelyn Varden, Shelley Winters*

If a director's worth was judged on just one picture Charles Laughton would rank among the all-time great film-makers. The actor's only directorial effort is a genuine one-off; a uniquely creepy stroll through a storybook American South described by its creator as "a nightmarish sort of Mother Goose

tale". At its centre lies the monstrous, demagogic performance of Robert Mitchum as Harry Powell, a hellfire-and-brimstone preacher with the words LOVE and HATE tattooed across his knuckles. In his obsessive hunt for their dead father's loot, Powell comes to terrorize two young children, plucky John (Billy Chapin) and his feckless sister Pearl (Sally Jane Bruce). Their mother murdered, the children go on the run, escaping to the sanctuary of saintly spinster Rachel (Lillian Gish), their only guardian in an adult world the snakelike Powell has clearly bewitched. *The Night of the Hunter* is a haunting fable of lost innocence, rendered more chilling by its non-naturalistic, child's-eye view of Depression-era USA. Laughton's deep-shadowed interiors and fairytale landscapes, primarily magicked up in the studio, lend the picture a dreamlike quality, best seen in the children's otherworldly flight downstream, watched over by looming riverside wildlife. With its weird hybrid of genre thrills, light humour and religious ponderings, *The Night of the Hunter* did not kick off any new artistic trend and cannot truly be said to fit anywhere. But this mesmerizing curio of 1950s cinema is that rarest of beasts – a wholly unclassifiable exercise in film-making originality.
THRILLER

1956

A Man Escaped

UN CONDAMNÉ À MORT S'EST ECHAPPÉ   102 min.
Director: *Robert Bresson*
Origin: *France*
Distributor: *Gaumont/SNE*
Cast: *Maurice Beerblock, Jacques Erland, Charles Le Clainche, François Leterrier, Roland Monot, Jacques Oerlemans*

Based on a true story, Robert Bresson's masterpiece is obsessively concerned with the details of a POW's escape from a Gestapo prison. Opening with the words, "This is a true story. I show it as it happened, without any embellishment", the film is indeed documentary-like, with Bresson going to great lengths in his search for authenticity. He used non-professional actors (François Leterrier was a philosophy graduate and army lieutenant), and appointed André Devigny (on whom Leterrier's character, Fontaine, is based) as technical adviser. Devigny's actual cell in Lyon's Montluc fortress was used for filming, with the actors kept in neighbouring cells between scenes. Concentrating on how the escape was executed rather than why Fontaine was so driven, Bresson spurns traditional dramatic methods. There is no obvious race against time, although he *is* condemned to be executed, and the chiselling of the door with a spoon, and the building of rope from bedding are painfully but lovingly observed. The film's alternative title, *The Spirit Breathes Where It Will*, is a biblical quote handed to Fontaine by another prisoner when his faith is foundering. The use of camera angles also hints at fate or divinity as a force (little is seen from Fontaine's point of view), and he is aided by unseen characters who smuggle letters out and provide lock-pick-

ing pins for his escape. Even the title, in giving the ending away, suggests predestination. Bresson struggled for five years to get backing for *A Man Escaped*, but was rewarded with the Best Director Award at Cannes.
PRISON DRAMA

Forbidden Planet

98 min.
Director: *Fred McLeod Wilcox*
Origin: *USA*
Distributor: *MGM*
Cast: *Richard Anderson, Anne Francis, Earl Holliman, Jack Kelly, Leslie Nielsen, Walter Pidgeon, Warren Stevens, George Wallace*

Prized among the most imaginative and entrancing 50s science-fiction film, *Forbidden Planet* loosely reworks ideas and characters from Shakespeare's *The Tempest* as Leslie Nielsen (long before he joined *Police Squad*) journeys into space to land on Walter Pidgeon's planet. MGM coughed up $1 million for the first big-studio, big-budget SF film, and their artists are clearly having a great time in designs that influenced many later sci-fi movies. Its trailblazing style and specific sequences (particularly the crane shot when the cast cross a bridge over a huge chasm filled with strange machinery) have been much copied in subsequent films and TV episodes. In the year 2200 a space cruiser visits the remote planet of Altair-4 to investigate the disappearance 20 years before of the spaceship *Bellerophon*. Despite an order not to land, Commander Adams (Nielsen) and the crew touch down to be welcomed by Robby, a robot that can speak in 88 languages. They discover that there are two survivors – the mysterious Dr Morbius (Pidgeon) and his daughter Altaira (Anne Francis) – and are warned of an invisible monster (the Id) roaming the planet. In Shakespearian terms

Forbidden Planet: *Walter Pidgeon in full flight*

Morbius equals the magician Prospero, Altaira is Miranda, Robby corresponds to the spirit Ariel, and the Id is the monster Caliban. Robby (a design classic himself) was a major hit in his day, and starred in *The Invisible Boy* (1957) and many TV segments, but it's the authoritative acting of MGM stalwart Pidgeon that gives the film its weight and dignity.
SCI-FI

Invasion of the Body Snatchers

80 min.
Director: *Don Siegel*
Origin: *USA*
Distributor: *United Artists*
Cast: *Whit Bissell, Virginia Christine, King Donovan, Larry Gates, Carolyn Jones, Kevin McCarthy, Dana Wynter*

This uniquely chilling 1950s sci-fi film develops a serious metaphorical subtext that works successfully on both scare and intellectual levels – and it's all the more notable for that when viewed in the 1990s era when chillers are reduced to being merely stalk-and-slashers or gorefests. Don Siegel, king of the 1950s B-movie, turns in the original and best film version of Jack Finney's novel *The Body Snatcher*, in which California townsfolk are taken over by parasitic Pod People. Kevin McCarthy stars as a doctor who struggles to save the US when hostile aliens land in his small-town community and the pods hatch into living-dead doubles of the local population. The atmosphere of mounting paranoia, reflecting 1950s unease over Commie-bashing and Senator Joseph McCarthy's investigations in America (its final eerie message is "You're next"), is uniquely gripping and creepy in this low-budget, black-and-white version. Don't expect costly special effects because there aren't any – only intelligence and imagination. The Allied Artists studio imposed a prologue and epilogue in an attempt to make the story's message less pessimistically gloomy, though these were duly removed in the director's 1978 cut. Siegel and Kevin McCarthy had cameos in Philip Kaufman's big-budget 1978 remake, located in a dark and threatening San Francisco for a parable on the paranoia of 1970s big-city life. Then in 1993 Abel Ferrara made it again as *Body Snatchers*, filming in widescreen and pop-video style visuals for a younger generation, and serving up a vision of nihilistic chaos.
HORROR/SCI-FI

The Searchers

119 min.
Director: *John Ford*
Origin: *USA*
Distributor: *Warner*
Cast: *Ward Bond, Jeffrey Hunter, Vera Miles, John Wayne, Natalie Wood*

The Searchers is one of the all-time classic westerns and probably John Ford's most fully realised film. Accurately described by Ford as a "psychological epic", it portrays its western hero as a savage racist, a breakthrough in maturity for the genre at a time of heightened racial tension in America. John Wayne gives a malevolent *tour-de-force* performance as Ethan Edwards, searching for the Indians who have slaughtered his family and captured his niece (who might just be his daughter, although this is barely touched upon). He is accompanied by Martin (Jeffrey Hunter), who is one-eighth Cherokee, but it is Ethan who has adopted such brutal customs as scalping, and Martin who proves the civilizing influence. They search for five years, Ethan planning to kill Debbie (Natalie Wood) rather than save her, until a dramatic change of heart in the picture's thunderous finale. The film's final shot is one of the most famous ever: Wayne framed in a doorway, the eternal outsider. It is a homage to early Ford star Harry Carey Sr, whose hand-on-elbow pose Wayne imitates as he walks away from the homemaker, Mrs Jorgensen, played by Carey's widow, Olive. *The Searchers* has great comedy to relieve its grim theme, and inspired countless tributes, including Martin Scorsese's *Taxi Driver* (1976) and Buddy Holly's songwriting (when Martin spits "I hope you die", Wayne drawls back, "That'll be the day"). It was also Ford's best use of Monument Valley out of the nine films in which he featured the bleak American landscape he had made his own.
PSYCHOLOGICAL WESTERN

1957

The Bridge on the River Kwai

161 min.
Director: *David Lean*
Origin: *GB*
Distributor: *Columbia*
Cast: *James Donald, Alec Guinness, Jack Hawkins, Sessue Hayakawa, William Holden, Geoffrey Horne, André Morell*

David Lean's masterful, Technicolor World War Two epic, recipient of seven Academy

Awards – including Best Film, Director and Actor – boasts an extraordinary central performance from Alec Guinness, and a theme tune that set people whistling worldwide. Based on a Pierre Boulle novel and shot largely on location in Sri Lanka, it follows a group of British prisoners forced by their Japanese captors to build a bridge in occupied Burma. Guinness deservedly won an Oscar as the truculent, stiff-upper-lip English colonel who becomes obsessed with the project, seeing it as a means to both improve morale and demonstrate the innate superiority of British spirit. In a style reminiscent of Renoir's classic prisoner-of-war drama *La Grande Illusion* (1936), Lean uses the interplay of his three main characters – Guinness, Sessue Hayakawa's authoritarian Japanese commandant and William Holden's renegade American sailor – to present a gripping study of the psychology of conflict and duty, deftly analysing the way in which loyalty to the rule-book often overshadows the interests of humanity, nationality or commonsense. Exquisitely shot (by Oscar-winning Jack Hildyard) and constructed with as much care and precision as the bridge itself, this is at once a thrill- ing action adventure, a matchless study of obsession and misplaced duty and, above all, a crushing indictment of the futility of war. It won Lean the first of his two Best Director Oscars and was the year's top British moneymaker.
ANTI-WAR EPIC

Paths of Glory

86 min.
Director: *Stanley Kubrick*
Origin: *USA*
Distributor: *United Artists*
Cast: *Timothy Carey, Kirk Douglas, George Macready, Ralph Meeker, Adolphe Menjou, Wayne Morris*

One of the best war films of all time met a chilly reception from the critics and the public of the

Paths of Glory: *Kirk Douglas in turmoil*

day, no doubt due to its unrelenting bleakness and a feeling that it was old-fashioned material for 1957. Now it seems simply a realistic, timeless masterpiece. Stanley Kubrick forged his name worldwide with this searing World War One anti-war film about a French army mutiny after a regiment is ordered by the General Staff to take an impregnable hill long held by the Germans. Based on a factual novel by Humphrey Cobb, the story centres on the court martial of three innocent soldiers (Ralph Meeker, Timothy Carey, Joseph Turkel), unjustly charged with cowardice after the attack fails. With an unstinting attention to the situation's harsh reality, Kubrick painfully conveys the general absurdities of war and the particular evils of fighting in the trenches, and brings off an incisive examination of the French leaders' shocking callousness. On the acting front, Kirk Douglas turns the main role into one of his finest opportunities as the regiment's idealistic, stoical commander, Colonel Dax, who has to carry out the order to make the attack. Hollywood veteran Adolphe Menjou is equally remarkable as the uncomprehending General Groulard, while George Macready gives a memorable portrait of the stern old-style General Mireau whose obstinacy and outmoded ideas precipitate

the tragedy. It's a great indictment of the Oscars and suchlike that there were no awards anywhere for this important picture. It was made by Douglas's Bryna company; star and director reunited for *Spartacus* (1960).
ANTI-WAR

The Seventh Seal

DET SJUNDE INSEGLET   96 min.
Director: *Ingmar Bergman*
Origin: *Sweden*
Distributor: *Svensk Filmindustri*
Cast: *Bibi Andersson, Gunnar Björnstrand, Bengt Ekerot, Gunnel Lindblom, Nils Poppe, Max von Sydow*

One of Ingmar Bergman's greatest and most accessible films, with a towering performance by great Bergman interpreter Max von Sydow as the disillusioned knight Antonio Block who returns from the Crusades to find his homeland wasted by the plague. He challenges Death (Bengt Ekerot) to a game of chess on the beach, but must play the game of his life, because if he loses he dies. It's a beautiful-looking film full of famous haunting images, lovingly photographed by Gunnar Fischer, and the director's own script offers a quintessential Bergman discussion on religion, life and death. Among the other renowned players from the regular Bergman repertory company are Gunnar

Björnstrand as the knight's squire and Bibi Andersson as Mia. Nothing about its perfect form suggests the speed with which it was filmed – in a mere 35 days. *The Seventh Seal* encapsulates the essence of Bergman: as a portrait of medieval life it's typically austere and rigorous; as a morality play it has enormous dignity and gravity; as an expression of his spiritual outlook it cuts deep into the psyche. It deals as no other film with the ultimate, as man faces the inevitability of death, the hopelessness of his situation, the complete mystery of life, the uncontrollability of his fate and, ultimately, the uselessness of any effort to resist it. This film, which won the Special Jury Prize at Cannes in 1957, was the one which set the seal on Bergman's international reputation after 16 previous pictures, few of which have been widely seen.
MORALITY PLAY

Wild Strawberries

SMULTRONSTÄLLET   92 min.
Director: *Ingmar Bergman*
Origin: *Sweden*
Distributor: *Svensk Filmindustri*
Cast: *Bibi Andersson, Gunnar Björnstrand, Victor Sjöström, Ingrid Thulin*

1957 was Ingmar Bergman's breakthrough year, soaring to

Wild Strawberries: *Victor Sjöström and Bibi Andersson hit the road, Bergman-style*

global significance on the back of two milestones of world cinema. But where *The Seventh Seal* was grandiose and allegorical, *Wild Strawberries* proved a more intimate, self-contained affair. Initially overshadowed by its much-mimicked companion piece, it has grown in stature down the years. *Wild Strawberries* is a physical and spiritual journey, a prototype road-movie charting the voyage of elderly medical professor Isak Borg (Victor Sjöström) to receive an honorary degree from the University at Lund. En route Borg clashes with his estranged daughter (Ingrid Thulin) and falls in with a trio of young hitchhikers led by a vivacious teen (Bibi Andersson). A beautifully observed study in character, the film uncovers its protagonists' past in gentle, probing layers. In Borg's defining consciousness, age-old memories and contemporary reality run concurrently, with the narrative dipping back into his youth to revisit a lost, painful love affair with the bewitching Sara (Andersson again). As a bond develops between Borg and Andersson's present-day incarnation, the film sees the old man making peace with his past, laying the ghosts that have haunted his adult years and imperceptibly preparing himself for death. *Wild Strawberries* is a *tour de force* of acting and directorial talent. An acclaimed filmmaker himself, Sjöström's detailed playing as the crusty, cantankerous Borg conjures the script into glowing, heartfelt life, though in the final analysis it's undeniably Bergman's picture. Borg's eerie dream sequence that opens the tale was, in fact, taken from the director's own memory and brings a further personal touch to this evergreen cinema artwork; a film brimming with droll humour, gleaming with compassion and a devastating moral truth.
SPIRITUAL DRAMA / ROAD MOVIE

1958

Carry On Sergeant

88 min.
Director: *Gerald Thomas*
Origin: *GB*
Distributor: *Anglo Amalgamated*
Cast: *Eric Barker, Dora Bryan, Kenneth Connor, Shirley Eaton, William Hartnell, Charles Hawtrey, Hattie Jacques, Bob Monkhouse, Kenneth Williams*

This gleeful British comedy turned out to be the first *Carry On* film, though back in 1958 it was just another army farce about life in the British National Service, based on a comic play, *The Bull Boys*, about conscripts by R. F. Delderfield. The series regulars assembled only over the course of several sequels, though lovely comic performers Kenneth Williams, Kenneth Connor, Hattie Jacques and Charles Hawtrey are already in place, while the relishable or ghastly (depending on taste) silly word-plays and smutty gags are all present and correct. The notoriously cheaply made series, produced by Peter Rogers and directed by Gerald Thomas, was hugely popular – at least in Britain – assuming the status of a national institution and elevating its main regular players (who later included Sid James, Barbara Windsor, Joan Sims, Bernard Bresslaw, Terry Scott, Peter Butterworth and Jack Douglas) to comedy icons. It carried on for an astonishing 29 movies till changing tastes forced it out of business after the 1978 sex spoof *Carry On Emmanuelle*. But the continuing popularity of the series on TV brought a one-off revival in 1992, with a diabolically awful *1492* parody in *Carry On Columbus*, scuppered by the absence of most of the original stars. Like the best wine, the series didn't travel well, though one or two, like *Carry On Nurse* (1959), were hits in America,

prompting an attempt to widen the appeal by importing American star Phil Silvers, and even to drop the *Carry On* name for *Follow that Camel* (1967) and *Don't Lose Your Head* (1966). But it remained essentially and quite properly a great British phenomenon and institution.
COMEDY

The Four Hundred Blows

LES QUATRE CENTS COUPS
99 min.
Director: *François Truffaut*
Origin: *France*
Distributor: *Films du Carrosse*
Cast: *Patrick Auffay, Jean-Claude Brialy, Jacques Demi, Jean-Pierre Léaud, Claire Maurier, Jeanne Moreau, Albert Rémy, François Truffaut*

Key French New Wave director François Truffaut's debut picture is a marvellous dip into childhood autobiography, with young Jean-Pierre Léaud heartrending as the 12-year-old tearaway hero who runs away from home because he's neglected by his unfeeling parents. He turns to a life of petty crime (including, significantly, stealing a movie still) and is eventually sent to a reform school. This incisive study of the pains of growing up in Paris is one of the central films of the Nouvelle Vague of the late 1950s and early 1960s, spun off on the back of the film criticism of the writers of the *Cahiers du Cinéma* (among them Truffaut, Godard and Chabrol). The film is brought to life by Henri Decaë's black-and-white photography in the streets of Paris, one of the central devices of these film-makers who rejected the studio-based work of their predecessors. Truffaut conjures up a movie that's warmhearted and nostalgic, while still being razor-sharp and intellectually penetrating in its judgments, particularly on the shortcomings of adults and the sadness of childhood. It's one of the best films about childhood in the whole of the cinema and

after all these years it still seems as fresh as the day it was made. Truffaut returned to his autobiographical story about Antoine Doinel periodically through his film career, and the part was always played by Truffaut's protégé and friend Léaud.
DRAMA / AUTOBIOGRAPHY

Touch of Evil

108 min.
Director: *Orson Welles*
Origin: *USA*
Distributor: *Universal*
Cast: *Ray Collins, Joseph Calleia, Joseph Cotten, Marlene Dietrich, Zsa Zsa Gabor, Charlton Heston, Janet Leigh, Joanna Moore, Akim Tamiroff, Dennis Weaver, Orson Welles*

The Orson Welles touch of genius conjured an otherwise standard B-movie script into a lavish feast of baroque imagery, a roguish essay on law and disorder and the last great picture Hollywood's aging boy-wonder was ever able to make. Originally only contracted to act, Welles arrived determined to direct and won what proved to be decisive support from the film's influential star Charlton Heston. There were to be no regrets. "He was the most

Touch of Evil: *Orson Welles as Hank Quinlan; 'a good man, but a bad cop'*

talented man I ever worked with," Heston later commented – "Indeed, ever seen." Few pictures begin as memorably as *Touch of Evil*, with its urgent, endless opening shot – loitering with intent around the border into Mexico until an exploding car breaks the spell, kicking off the main body of action. It's a film fixated on the notion of borders, boundaries, definitions; with the US representative of clean-cut order and Mexico a teeming, volatile cesspit; Hispanic narcotics agent Vargas (Heston), a rigid, righteous do-gooder, and American cop Hank Quinlan (Welles), sullied and corrupted by his years in the game. Around these moral markers Welles spins a wealth of complementary elements, making room on the cast list for old pal Joseph Cotten, Janet Leigh (as Vargas's milk-pure girlfriend) and fading Teutonic beauty Marlene Dietrich, eccentrically cast as a Mexican gypsy. Amidst a rogues' gallery of harshly lit grotesques, Welles hogs centre-stage as the sweaty, bug-eyed Quinlan, audaciously making a bonus of his 300lb bulk and the moral implications of a golden-boy gone to seed. "You're a mess honey," quips Dietrich's floozie, appraising him through smoky, hooded eyes. "You've been eating too much candy."
THRILLER

Vertigo

128 min.
Director: *Alfred Hitchcock*
Origin: *USA*
Distributor: *Paramount*
Cast: *Raymond Bailey, Barbara Bel Geddes, Ellen Corby, Tom Helmore, Henry Jones, Kim Novak, Lee Patrick, James Stewart*

Alfred Hitchcock's marvellously elusive and oblique thriller *Vertigo* is a key work in the director's *oeuvre*, regarded by many as his most fully realized picture. A 1990s survey of French critics placed it second, behind *Citizen Kane*, as the greatest movie ever made. A cre-

ation of perfect symmetry and strangeness, it is the closest the master of suspense ever came to an out-and-out art movie. Set in a steeply graded dreamscape San Francisco, *Vertigo*'s vision is subjective to the point of distortion, rooted in the consciousness of "Scottie" Ferguson (James Stewart), haunted by the suicide of a beautiful blonde housewife and obsessively trying to mould a brunette lookalike into the dead woman's image. There's a hypnotic, otherworldly pull to *Vertigo* that's communicated through a weird blend of ingredients – Bernard Herrmann's moody score, Hitchcock's pioneering use of the disorientating "pull-back zoom-in" camera shot and Kim Novak's distant, passively sexual turn as the dual object of Scottie's unhealthy desire. The picture also sees the culmination of Hitchcock's reinvention of Stewart – formerly American cinema's perennial good guy. It's a process that began with *Rope* (1948) where the director cast him as a clinical Nietzschean professor and continued with the splendid *Rear Window* (1954), which found him playing an impotent, compulsive voyeur. With *Vertigo* the process is complete, rendering homespun Jimmy unrecognizable as the unstable, unreliable hero-figure; sexually obsessed and a would-be necrophiliac. It's just another indispensable piece to

this beguiling abstract puzzle, a hall-of-mirrors movie that demands multiple viewings.
THRILLER

1959

Anatomy of a Murder

160 min.
Director: *Otto Preminger*
Origin: *USA*
Distributor: *Columbia*
Cast: *Eve Arden, Orson Bean, Ben Gazzara, Kathryn Grant, Arthur O'Connell, Lee Remick, George C. Scott, James Stewart*

"Crazy Otto" Preminger had a long and distinguished career that included *Laura* (1944), *Carmen Jones* (1954) and *Advise and Consent* (1961), but his movie of the 1950s Robert Traver courtroom bestseller was two-and-a-half of his finest hours. Indeed it's perhaps his most highly regarded work, with Preminger at the height of his powers as he explores the mainsprings of mankind's motives and encourages his talented cast – all seen at their best. He keeps a vice-like control as he tells a long, complex and thought-provoking yarn in which James Stewart's effortlessly canny, deliciously laid-back defence lawyer tries to help army lieutenant Ben Gazzara beat the rap for the murder

of a bar owner he believes tried to rape his sexy young wife (Lee Remick). Terrific though Wendell Mayes's script is, it's the performances you remember. As well as Stewart and the young couple, there's Arthur O'Connell as Stewart's drunken Irish attorney ally, George C. Scott as the silkily threatening prosecutor, and real judge Joseph Welch sitting in judgment. The film's racy language, which shocked in its day, proved a milestone in the liberalization of what was permitted on the screen, though now it sounds as tame as Eliza Doolittle's use of the word "bloody" in Pygmalion. Incidentally the author of the source novel is a pseudonym for another real-life judge, John D. Voelker. And, in an extraordinary feat of organization, Preminger screened his film only three weeks after concluding shooting in the small Michigan town where the film is set. Seven Oscar nominations but no wins. Though Duke Ellington's score is a major asset, it wasn't even nominated.
COURTROOM DRAMA

Shadows

81 min.
Director: *John Cassavetes*
Origin: *USA*
Distributor: *Lion*
Cast: *Ben Carruthers, Rupert Crosse, Lelia Goldoni, Hugh Hurd, Anthony Ray*

When Cassavetes mentioned on a radio show in the late 1950s his desire to make an improvisational film, to his surprise $20,000 of public donations flowed in unbidden. Scraping together the rest, largely from his earnings as TV detective *Johnny Staccato*, he made *Shadows*, based on improvisations with actors from the Variety Arts Studio, of which Cassavetes was director, and shot with a 16mm camera. The story, in which the characters are known by the names of the actors playing them, is about

Shadows: *Improvising* ciné verité *from Cassavetes*

two black brothers and their sister, struggling for survival on the streets of Manhattan. The eldest, a jazz musician, is embittered by the restrictions his colour places on his life; his brother and sister both pass for white. The editing is jumpy, the camerawork free-focus and the improvised dialogue often difficult to hear but, in its story, performances and edgy atmosphere, moody music by Charlie Mingus and steely black-and-white photography, the film captures a particular aspect of its era. American distributors were uninterested, but Cassavetes took the film to the Venice Film Festival, where it was greeted as a sign that the US now had a *cinéma verité* new wave movement, rejecting Hollywood stereotypes. An important difference, though, was that Cassavetes approached film-making from an actor's rather than a critic's perspective. The film was picked up for British distribution and eventually found a showing in the States, where it created a minor sensation with Cassavetes hailed as a genius. While flawed by its technical limitations, *Shadows* is immensely important to the development of the American independent movement, introducing a powerful new force in US cinema.
IMPROVISED DRAMA

Some Like It Hot

119 min.
Director: *Billy Wilder*
Origin: *USA*
Distributor: *United Artists*
Cast: *Joe E. Brown, Tony Curtis, Jack Lemmon, Marilyn Monroe, Pat O'Brien, Nehemiah Persoff, George Raft, Edward G. Robinson, Joan Shawlee*

Some Like It Hot remains Hollywood's best-loved drag comedy – arguably better than its nearest rivals *I Was a Male War Bride*, *Tootsie* and *Mrs Doubtfire*. Arch-cynic Billy Wilder creates a spiral of jokes through an inspired story of two musicians who dress in flappers' frocks to flee from gangsters after they witness the St Valentine's Day Massacre in the Prohibition-era Chicago of 1929. Their only escape is to join a jazz band heading on the train for Florida – but it's an all-girl orchestra. Wise-cracking Jack Lemmon and Tony Curtis supply oodles of extravagant, unrestrained comedy. Lemmon is effortlessly hilarious, not looking for a moment like anything except a man in drag, while it's one of Curtis's best performances, switching from fussy female to a brilliantly sustained impersonation of *War Bride*'s Cary Grant. Vulnerably gorgeous Marilyn Monroe proves the perfect foil, giving the film warmth, sympathy and heart as the simpleminded siren Sugar Cane. Despite the on-screen chemistry between Curtis and Monroe, Curtis uncharitably compared kissing her to smooching with Hitler. But the main laurels must go to Wilder, who directs and writes (with partner I. A. L. Diamond) with even more than his accustomed brio and astringency. If the film has any flaw, it's only that it's perhaps just a fraction overlong, but then as the daft millionaire Joe E. Brown says at the fade-out to "fiancée" Lemmon, "Nobody's perfect." Fitting that the movie should win an Oscar for Best Costumes, but it was a lone win for one of cinema's greatest comedies.
DRAG COMEDY

1960

A Bout de Souffle

BREATHLESS   90 min.
Director: *Jean-Luc Godard*
Origin: *France*
Distributor: *SNC/Imperia*
Cast: *Jean-Paul Belmondo, Daniel Boulanger, Jean-Luc Godard, Jean-Pierre Melville, Jean Seberg*

Jean-Luc Godard's dazzling debut *A Bout de Souffle* heralded the arrival of one of the 60s' most important film-makers and was the clearest signal yet that the Nouvelle Vague's time had come. Petty crook Michel (Jean-Paul Belmondo) kills a cop and goes on the run, stopping only to try to persuade his American girlfriend (Jean Seberg) to go with him. After a philosophy-in-bed session she phones the police, and he is gunned down in the street. Shooting on a tiny budget within a month, Godard was not the first radical French critic to switch to film-making but his was the most spectacular debut. François Truffaut and Claude Chabrol had already made the transition, Truffaut writing the story and providing the funds here, with Chabrol serving as technical adviser. Godard, though, set about inventing his own cinema language, fragmenting the narrative with jump-cuts, extending scenes beyond their natural narrative function, and making full use of the new hand-held cameras in what is still his most conventional and profitable film. Its enduring appeal owes a lot to Belmondo, a study of Bogart-ian cool and Brando-esque prize fighter's sex-appeal, leading to his being branded "the male Bardot". Godard himself appears briefly as a police informer. The title, originally mistranslated as "at the end of his tether", signals Godard's intention to leave the viewer breathless while he breathes new life into cinema. He was rewarded with Best Director's prize in Berlin and an unchallenged place among the movie greats.
NEW WAVE CRIME THRILLER

La Dolce Vita

THE SWEET LIFE   180 min.
Director: *Federico Fellini*
Origin: *Italy/France*
Distributor: *Riama*
Cast: *Anouk Aimée, Alain Cuny, Anita Ekberg, Yvonne Furneaux, Marcello Mastroianni, Magali Noel*

Federico Fellini's famous film won him the Best Film award at Cannes

Mastroianni and Ekberg: *Finding life is sweet*

in 1960 and fans across the world, bringing a new phrase into the English language, for somehow its unresonant English title, *The Sweet Life*, just doesn't work. "Sweet" won't cut it for the life Fellini shows us. His alter ego and regular interpreter Marcello Mastroianni is on his best form as a newspaper gossip writer with serious ambitions (just like the young Fellini) who wanders through Rome, simultaneously shocked and tolerant, or at least intriguingly ambiguous, about the lack of morals and purpose of the city's middle classes. This is entertaining, almost tabloid cake-and-eat-it exposé stuff: Fellini delights in displaying the decadence of Rome while he quietly, cynically tuts-tuts in the background. The set-pieces are among the cinema's most famous and eye-catching: not very profound as an intellectual image to show a statue of Christ flying from a helicopter over St Peter's, but visually and emotionally it amazes and excites. As a study in boredom, loss of purpose, of a stagnant society, the film has been accused of seeming prosaic, but Fellini's playful cynicism reveals a clever Wildean loftiness, mirroring the characters and situations while commenting on them. Fellini's obviously in love with all the things and people he affects to despise. Viewers worldwide were beguiled by Fellini's *Dolce Vita*, lapping up all of Rome's beautiful

people and the voluptuous Anita Ekberg as a visiting film star. For three hours you can just sit back and enjoy the society of extravagant decadents, and wish you were there on the beach or in the street cafes. It's an astounding postcard from a Rome of long ago.
AUTOBIOGRAPHICAL MELODRAMA

Peeping Tom

109 min.
Director: *Michael Powell*
Origin: *GB*
Distributor: *Anglo Amalgamated*
Cast: *Maxine Audley, Carl Boehm, Brenda Bruce, Shirley Anne Field, Michael Goodliffe, Pamela Green, Esmond Knight, Anna Massey, Martin Miller, Moira Shearer, Jack Watson*

A brilliant psychological chiller, *Peeping Tom* focuses on an abused child who becomes an adult serial killer of women. The elements of the story are sensational for any time: the psychopath recording his victims' fear as they face death; the method of murder, with a dagger hidden in the camera tripod; the killer's part-time job as a pornographic photographer; and the psychological abuse inflicted on him as a child by his father's

Peeping Tom: *Carl Boehm shoots to kill*

experiments with fear. But Michael Powell's treatment of his material is comparatively restrained by modern standards. The background chosen for the story – the murderer is a focus puller in a film studio – emphasizes the central

issue, which is even more relevant today, of the audience's own voyeurism in watching these events as entertainment and therefore its share in the central character's sickness. The film is also marked by Powell's modern touches of black humour and features a sympathetic performance from Carl Boehm as the killer, with Anna Massey as the girl who befriends him and Maxine Audley strong as her astute, blind mother. The film was vilified by the British press, who found it repugnant, butchered by the studio and, because of the controversy, never gained the mass audience it merited. Shown briefly in the United States in second-run houses, it then disappeared until a restored version was released in 1979 due to the efforts of Martin Scorsese, a great admirer of Powell's work. *Peeping Tom* virtually finished Powell's career although, with Scorsese's help, his place as one of Britain's most important filmmakers was restored before his death in 1990.
HORROR/THRILLER

Psycho

109 min.
Director: *Alfred Hitchcock*
Origin: *USA*
Distributor: *Shamley/Paramount*
Cast: *Martin Balsam, John Gavin, Patricia Hitchcock, Ted Knight, Janet Leigh, John McIntire, Vera Miles, Simon Oakland, Anthony Perkins*

Psycho is Alfred Hitchcock's most nakedly subversive picture, shot cheaply in oppressive black-and-white after a decade on high-profile Technicolor projects. Part bag of sly storytelling tricks, part voyeuristic dissection of a world in collapse, it's the logical culmination of the director's own psychological obsessions. A disorientating, super-tense thriller that whips the rug out from under the feet of even the most attentive viewer, *Psycho* leads us to the edge and points out the abyss. The film's

Psycho: *Perkins prepares to mop up mummy's mess*

heroine is Marion Crane (Janet Leigh) who in a moment of weakness steals some money and flees west, finally fetching up at the backwater Bates Motel. But our natural identification with Marion is wrecked when she is shockingly murdered, hacked to death in the legendary shower-scene montage (45 seconds, a frenzied 70 camera set-ups). Cast adrift, we switch our sympathies to Norman Bates (Anthony Perkins); nervy, pathetic Bates, the prisoner of a grotesque Oedipal scenario. But by nudging the viewer down that route, Hitchcock sets us up for the most devastating twist of all. "The public likes to be one step ahead of the story," he once explained. "So you deliberately play on that fact to turn the viewer in one direction and then another; you keep them as far as possible from what's actually going to happen." Only in the final moments is the horrible truth revealed, as the director tugs us right inside Bates's twisted psyche as he sits straitjacketed in the police-cell, the "mother side" of his personality now in full control. Horror movies would never be the same again, and neither would the magnificent Perkins – typecast ever after as the all-American crazy, and returning to the role for three sequels in the 80s.
HORROR/THRILLER

Saturday Night and Sunday Morning

90 min.
Director: *Karel Reisz*
Origin: *GB*
Distributor: *Woodfall*
Cast: *Hylda Baker, Shirley Anne Field, Albert Finney, Bryan Pringle, Rachel Roberts, Norman Rossington*

Saturday Night and Sunday Morning proved one of the best of the British New Wave efforts of the late 1950s and 1960s launched Albert Finney's career as a filmstar, was briefly banned, and earned "beer-and-sex-in-the-Midlands" headlines. Produced by Tony Richardson and written by Alan Sillitoe from his own novel, the social realism story follows a bullish young lathe operator surviving a life of dull work with the weekend promise of pale ale and wild women. Finney's character of Arthur Seaton begins an affair with a workmate's wife (Rachel Roberts, after Diana Dors turned the part down), while pursuing a determinedly virginal Shirley Anne Field. Roberts gets pregnant, an abortion arranged by Finney fails, and her husband's brother beats him up. Finney gets engaged to Field and ends up hurling stones at the prim housing estate she expects them to live in, threatening "it won't be the last I'll throw". The Nottingham regional dialect had to be dubbed for American audiences, and in retrospect some of the lines seem infelicitous ("I'm a fighting pit-prop who likes a pint of beer") but they do have an energetic poetry of their own, and it was a breakthrough for stories about ordinary people's lives to be told so convincingly. Director Karel Reisz's first feature caught the mood of changing British attitudes to work and leisure, and the film, Finney, and Roberts all won British Academy Awards, though in parts of Warwickshire, near where it is set, councils banned it, demanding cuts which were wisely refused.
REALIST DRAMA

1961

Accatone
120 min.
Director: *Pier Paolo Pasolini*
Origin: *Italy*
Distributor: *Cino del Duca/Arco*
Cast: *Adriana Asti, Franco Citti, Silvana Corsini, Paolo Guidi, Franca Pasut, Roberto Scaringella*

Pier Paolo Pasolini's acclaimed first feature *Accatone* is loosely based on his own novel *Una Vita Violenta*, published in the late 1950s and drawing on his own experiences of life in the squalid, poverty-stricken section of Rome where he had lived in 1949. The title character is a small-time pimp, played by previously non-professional actor Franco Citti. When his lover and meal ticket Maddalena (Silvana Corsini) is jailed, he attempts to turn his naive new love, Franca Pasut, to prostitution. Failing in that, his struggle to survive in the face of starvation forces him into petty thievery and ultimately death. Unlaudable though the main character is, the viewer is made to feel pity for his stunted life and the trap in which he finds himself, created by social conditions and his response to them, while the female characters, such as Accatone's deserted wife, struggling to raise her children in poverty, and Adriana Asti's perky, pimp-free prostitute, demonstrate an admirable courage. The film is a fascinating marriage of documentary realism with creative originality. Accatone's pimp friends have an almost Greek-chorus quality in their sarcastic observations on his life, but have their roots in the "ragazzi", the streetwise young men Pasolini encountered when he first came to the city in the 1940s. While the graphic depiction of poverty and the grim environment might appear to classify the film as a study in neo-realism, its shooting and editing style and elegant Bach score are pointers towards the studied stylization of Pasolini's later work.
SOCIAL REALIST DRAMA

Jules et Jim
JULES AND JIM   104 min.
Director: *François Truffaut*
Origin: *France*
Distributor: *Films du Carrosse*
Cast: *Marie Dubois, Jeanne Moreau, Henri Serre, Vanna Urbino, Oskar Werner*

Amid the feverishly creative burst of films to emerge from the French New Wave, *Jules et Jim* stands today as the most whole and self-assured. It was François Truffaut's third feature, adapted from a novel by Henri-Pierre Roché and played out against the bohemian backdrop of Paris in the years surrounding World War One. But despite this period setting, the picture's mood and sensibility are pure 1960s, with its modish study of the shifting *ménage-à-trois* between restrained German Jules (Oskar Werner), urbane Parisian Jim (Henri Serre) and the woman they both grow to love: wilful, enigmatic Catherine (Jeanne Moreau). *Jules et Jim* catches Truffaut at his most stylistically inspired, shooting with abandon and using all the tricks in the directing textbook – swirling camera movements, jump-cuts, freeze-frames, crane-shots and spliced-in archive footage. It's evidence of a man in love, intoxicated both with muse Moreau and by the infinite possibilities of his chosen medium, like a kid with a new train set. But *Jules et Jim* is not simply art for art's sake. These visual flourishes have a featherlight touch, meshing harmoniously with a tale somehow in tune with the elusive ebb and flow of life, love and lasting friendship. Each of the three characters is highly distinctive, precisely drawn and yet somehow unknowable, moved by desires beyond their control. Truffaut observes their wavering progress with an eye that might seem detached were it not for the compassionate warmth that glows just beneath the surface. Exquisite.
NEW WAVE ROMANCE

Last Year at Marienbad
L'ANNÉE DERNIÈRE À MARIENBAD
94 min.
Director: *Alain Resnais*
Origin: *France/Italy*
Distributor: *Terra/Cormoran/Precitel/Como/Tamara/Silver-Cineriz*
Cast: *Giorgio Albertazzi, Françoise Bertin, Sacha Pitöeff, Delphine Seyrig*

Variously perceived by audiences of the time as intriguing, baffling, enigmatic, irritating, impenetrable, masterly, boring or endlessly inventive, *Last Year at Marienbad* is a true

Marienbad: *Lovers in a dream-like landscape*

cinema landmark for the way it expanded screen language to the limits of the subjunctive. The main characters are the elegant Delphine Seyrig, Sacha Pitöeff (who may or may not be her husband) and Giorgio Albertazzi, a handsome stranger, who attempts to convince Seyrig that they may or may not have met last year, perhaps in Marienbad, perhaps somewhere else, where she may or may not have promised to run away with him this year. The viewer never learns whether the meeting took place, will take place in the future, or is a total fantasy. Or indeed could all the possibilities be true and is this a philosophical treatise on the nature of time and the split universe? This brain-baiting story, written by *nouveau romancier* Alain Robbe-Grillet, plays with past, present, future, memory and possibility against the setting of a luxurious country house of long sterile hallways and perfectly sculptured gardens. The performances are detached, almost somnambulistic, while the black-and-white camerawork is both stately and startling, with images which linger in the memory: the frozen fountain; the tiny human figures casting shadows while the manicured bushes do not; and the seemingly endless tracking shots along baroque corridors. The puzzling game Albertazzi continuously plays with matches became the Rubik's cube of its day and the film consolidated Alain Resnais's reputation as a cinematic innovator and philosopher of unique vision.
PUZZLE DRAMA

Pasolini's acclaimed debut Accatone: *Franco Citti as the pitiable anti-hero*

One-Eyed Jacks

141 min.
Director: *Marlon Brando*
Origin: *USA*
Distributor: *Paramount*
Cast: *Marlon Brando, Elisha Cook Jr, Larry Duran, Ben Johnson, Katy Jurado, Karl Malden, Pina Pellicer, Slim Pickens*

Marlon Brando's only film as director, *One-Eyed Jacks*, was also the first time he had taken on the western as an actor. Stanley Kubrick was originally in charge but was replaced after disagreements on character development. Brando is Rio, seeking revenge on his mentor, Dad (Karl Malden reunited with him for the first time since *On the Waterfront*, 1954). Since his betrayal, Dad has turned from bandit to sheriff and family man. Learning of Rio's Oedipal interest in his daughter Louisa (Pina Pellicer in her only US film before committing suicide at the age of 24) and sensing personal danger, Dad administers a public bullwhipping to his surrogate son. Rio rests, recovers and returns to kill Dad with a gun smuggled to him by Louisa, then escapes alone, promising to return for her later. Brando's grand intention "to make a frontal assault on the temple of cliches" sounds pompous, but he gives *One-Eyed Jacks* his usual brooding intensity, while seeming incapable of – or not interested in – delivering a taut narrative. A scheduled two-month shoot turned into six, trebling the original budget, and Paramount insisted on interfering to contrive a happyish ending. They were not rewarded at the box-office. The deliberate approach to characterization and the central love/hate relationship influenced later westerns such as *Pat Garrett and Billy the Kid* (1973), and Brando's inspired choice of Pacific Coast locations made a spectacular departure for a dusty landlocked genre.
REVENGE WESTERN

The Hustler

134 min.
Director: *Robert Rossen*
Origin: *USA*
Distributor: *20th Century-Fox*
Cast: *Michael Constantine, Jackie Gleason, Murray Hamilton, Piper Laurie, Myron McCormick, Paul Newman, George C. Scott*

The legendary pool-house movie *The Hustler*, with a searing script based securely on Walter S. Tevis's novel, scores strongly through electrifying performances from Paul Newman as the young pool hustler "Fast" Eddie Felson and Jackie Gleason as the champion, Minnesota Fats, whom he challenges. In this dark and world-weary story, the streetwise, hard-drinking Felson travels through America fast-talking unsuspecting opponents into high-stake games only to defeat them with what looks like luck. Resolute in his plans to be top dog, Felson heads for New York and tries to fix a clash with the legendary champion from Chicago. The excitement of the game and its hard-bitten characters are thrillingly re-created by director Robert Rossen in a nigh-on-perfect movie, which was considered too arty and downbeat for popular taste in 1961. Cinematographer Eugen Schuftan rightly won an Oscar for his dazzling black-and-white images, conjuring up the seedy, smoky pool-hall backdrop. The impeccable art direction, establishing a believably murky milieu, won a second Oscar. There are several other outstanding performances in the film – especially from Piper Laurie as Felson's boozy floozie and George C. Scott as his promoter. Both were Oscar-nominated, along with Newman and Gleason, but none of them won. Martin Scorsese chalked up a sequel, *The Color of Money*, in 1986, poignantly allowing Newman to re-create the role of Fast Eddie in late middle-age, with Tom Cruise as the young buck. This time Newman, after six previous nominations, finally won the Oscar he had deserved 25 years before.
POOL-ROOM DRAMA

West Side Story

153 min.
Directors: *Robert Wise and Jerome Robbins*
Origin: *USA*
Distributor: *United Artists/ Mirisch/Seven Arts*
Cast: *Richard Beymer* (sung by *Jimmy Bryant), George Chakiris, Rita Moreno, Simon Oakland, Russ Tamblyn, Natalie Wood* (sung by *Marni Nixon*)

The Romeo and Juliet story transferred to the world of teenage gang rumble in Manhattan's Upper West Side, *West Side Story* became one of the most popular musicals in history. Much of the credit must go to Jerome Robbins's spectacular acrobatic choreography, which married jazz dancing and ballet in a truly thrilling way. Robbins, who had conceived the Broadway hit show on which the film was based, was originally hired to direct the entire film, but as his perfectionism pushed up the budget Robert Wise was brought in to direct the non-musical sequences and eventually Robbins was fired. Ironically they won a joint Best Director's statue among the film's ten Oscars. Based on Arthur Laurents's book, the story follows the conflict between two rival gangs: the Puerto Rican Sharks, led by the magnificently feline George Chakiris, and the Jets, who are white and commanded by the likable and cheeky Russ Tamblyn. Caught up in their warfare are the young lovers; Tamblyn's best friend Tony (Richard Beymer) and Chakiris's kid sister Maria (Natalie Wood) and Rita Moreno as Chakiris's fiery girlfriend. The parallels with Shakespeare's play work smoothly and without strain, while allowing the characters to take on a life of their own. The combination of Robbins's choreography and a now-classic score by Leonard Bernstein and Stephen Sondheim provides an unrivalled collection of memorable song and dance numbers: the balletic grace and virility of "The Jet Song" and "Cool"; the flamboyant excitement of "America"; the exuberant "I Feel Pretty"; comedy in "Gee Officer Krupke" and the lyrical love songs, "Tonight" and "Maria".
MUSICAL

1962

Lawrence of Arabia

220 min.
Director: *David Lean*
Origin: *GB*
Distributor: *Horizon/Columbia*
Cast: *José Ferrer, Alec Guinness, Jack Hawkins, Arthur Kennedy, Anthony Quayle, Anthony Quinn, Claude Rains, Peter O'Toole, Omar Sharif, Donald Wolfit*

David Lean's spectacular epic screen biography of T. E. Lawrence won seven Oscars, including Best Picture and Director. Although attacked by some critics as romanticized and trivialized entertainment, the film provides through Robert Bolt's skilful screenplay a clear picture of the complicated politics of Arab unification against the Turks in World War One while still meeting the cinematic need for dramatic conflict and strong characterization. At the centre is the charismatic young Peter O'Toole as Lawrence: blond, blue-eyed and driven by an ultimately self-destructive obsession. He is backed by an outstanding supporting cast, which included Alec Guinness, who two years earlier had played Terence Rattigan's very different view of Lawrence in *Ross* on the London stage, as the leader of the Arab revolt against the Turks. Omar Sharif as the sheik who is Lawrence's chief ally in his unification campaign is introduced in one

of the most memorable and famous shots of the film as a tiny dot on the desert horizon slowly becoming visible as he approaches. Anthony Quinn impresses as tribal leader Auda Abu Tayi, Jack Hawkins gives an effective impersonation of General Allenby; José Ferrer chills as the Turkish bey who takes Lawrence prisoner, while Arthur Kennedy is sincere as the journalist who brings Lawrence's exploits to the public. The film won several deserved technical Oscars, including one for Anne Coates's editing, Freddie Young's shimmering 70mm photography of the sun-drenched desert and Maurice Jarre's memorable score.
BIOGRAPHY/EPIC

Lolita

152 min.
Director: *Stanley Kubrick*
Origin: *GB/USA*
Distributor: *MGM*
Cast: *Diana Decker, Sue Lyon, James Mason, Peter Sellers, Marianne Stone, Shelley Winters*

Stanley Kubrick's *Lolita* is a real cinema curio. As an adaptation of Vladimir Nabokov's controversial novel it could, at first glance, scarcely be more bogus. Originally 12 years old, the schoolgirl object of the hero's perverse attentions is played by a worryingly mature-looking Sue Lyon. Furthermore budgetary restrictions forced the tale's odyssey through open-road America to be shot – at times quite obviously – in 1960s suburban England. But what sounds a recipe for disaster somehow works. For all its intriguing flaws, *Lolita* is a marvellous movie. Treading carefully through the volatile subject matter, Kubrick keeps the theme of sexual lust to a minimum, instead playing the story as a black social satire, a delicious send-up of the hypocritical mores and morals of America's money-eyed, aspirational middle class. But *Lolita* is a supremely cunning movie and by putting a comedic

slant on the taboo topic of child abuse, Kubrick both defuses its tensions and subtly creates a work as warped and surreptitious as the forbidden desires it details. This delicate balance of style and content is cemented by some virtuoso playing, with James Mason seldom better as the urbane, honey-toned, utterly possessed Humbert Humbert who marries into a drab New England home in order to lay his paws on the bubblegum-popping infant in the garden. For her part, Lyon copes well with an awkward role, Shelley Winters is hideously believable as the girl's clinging, voracious mother and Peter Sellers treats us to his full repertoire as the omnipresent Quilty. The result is irresistible: a slyly anarchic morality play.
SOCIAL SATIRE

The Loneliness of the Long Distance Runner

103 min.
Director: *Tony Richardson*
Origin: *GB*
Distributor: *Woodfall/Bryanston/British Lion*
Cast: *James Bolam, Avis Bunnage, Tom Courtenay, Julia Foster, James Fox, Alec McCowen, Michael Redgrave, John Thaw*

Tom Courtenay: *This one will run and run*

More social realism from Tony Richardson and screenwriter Alan Sillitoe (previously partnered on *Saturday Night and Sunday Morning*, 1960), this time borrowing techniques from the French New Wave and turning their attentions to British borstal life. *Chariots of Fire* this is not. Richardson again showed his skill as a talent-spotter, casting Tom Courtenay for his screen debut as the 17-year-old borstal inmate, Colin Smith, riddled with hatred for everything but cross-country running. For his governor (Michael Redgrave) sport equates with rehabilitation; for Smith it is revenge. Failure is his ultimate weapon when, with the big race against a public school all but won, he stops on the line, allowing lesser runners to pass him, a final gesture of defiance to the establishment. Smith's journey to reform school via an unhappy family life, his father's death, joyless joyrides, sex in Skegness and a bakery robbery is told in flashback while he is training for the race. The technique was much criticized but works well alongside an interior monologue that places Smith in the role of victim. The intercutting of the establishment hymn, "Jerusalem", with institutional beatings was so much mimicked that it quickly became a cliché. Sillitoe adapted his own short story, but had to make his main character much more sympathetic for the cinema (starting by giving him a full name, where previously he had been just plain Smith), and Courtenay has a warm vulnerability despite himself. He was rewarded with a British Academy Award for most promising newcomer.
SOCIAL REALIST DRAMA

The Manchurian Candidate

126 min.
Director: *John Frankenheimer*
Origin: *USA*
Distributor: *United Artists*
Cast: *James Gregory, Laurence Harvey, Angela Lansbury, Janet Leigh, John McGiver, Leslie Parrish, Henry Silva, Frank Sinatra*

"Without doubt the finest picture I have ever made," was Frank Sinatra's verdict on *The Manchurian Candidate*. Also marking the creative peak of director John Frankenheimer, the film is a hard-driving, fantastically wrought thriller, tracing the efforts of Korean War captain Marco (Sinatra) to uncover the causes of his haunting nightmares and prevent brainwashed former soldier Raymond Shaw (Laurence Harvey) from being used as a Communist-controlled hitman. But *The Manchurian Candidate* is no ordinary espionage outing. Withdrawn for 20 years due to its uncanny foreshadowing of the Kennedy assassination, it's a nerve-jangling exercise in paranoia that paints both sides of the political spectrum – left and right – as corrupt and redundant, dual engines in the same diabolical machine. Similarly, Frankenheimer puts a hallucinatory spin on an otherwise hard-boiled plotline, best evidenced in Marco's terrifying, cross-cutting dream sequence where innocuous old ladies in flowery hats switch back and forth into uniformed Communist heavies. Harvey is effective as the tortured victim, while Sinatra is hugely impressive in the lead, a beat-up, broken-down hero of the modern era. Both, though, are put in the shade by Angela Lansbury's powerhouse portrayal of Shaw's fanatical mother, pushing for the summit with the help of her puppet son and imbecile husband, the Fascist senator Johnny Iselin (James Gregory). While very much a product of its turbulent times,

The Manchurian Candidate stands up mighty well today. Ferocious, muscular, constantly gripping, it's one of the finest political thrillers ever made.
SPY THRILLER

1963

8½

OTTO E MEZZO   138 min.
Director: *Federico Fellini*
Origin: *Italy*
Distributor: *Cineriz*
Cast: *Anouk Aimée, Guido Alberti, Claudia Cardinale, Rossella Falk, Madeleine Lebeau, Marcello Mastroianni, Sandra Milo, Jean Rougeul, Barbara Steele*

The title comes from Fellini's calculation that his six feature films plus his co-direction of *The White Sheik* and contribution of two episodes to anthology movies totalled seven and a half films and that this semi-autobiographical work was therefore number 8½. Mastroianni plays the Fellini figure, a director suffering from creative block in the preparation of his next movie. Fellini himself described this best foreign film Oscar-winner as "the story of a film director who is trying to pull together the pieces of his life and make sense of them" and it is certainly something in the nature of confession combined with self-analysis, as Mastroianni tries to come to terms with the women of his world, including his wife (Anouk Aimée), his mistress (Sandra Milo) and his star (Claudia Cardinale), while balancing the demands of his work, personified by his producer (Guido Alberti), his intellectually pretentious writer (Jean Rougeul) and a host of other attendant sprites. This he does in a complicated, multi-layered structure through a mixture of surreal dreams about his past and fantasies of his desires. The result is

something of a mixed bag, which at times is reduced to an irritating male menopausal comedy of irresolution touched with *La Dolce Vita*. It is, however, rich in the bizarre and powerful imagery that is a Fellini hallmark, such as the La Saraghina rumba for the benefit of her sexually curious small boy followers and the grotesque procession of cure seekers at the spa. The film also gives a unique insight into the complex and lateral process of creativity as perceived by a great cinematic creative talent.
AUTOBIOGRAPHICAL FANTASY/DRAMA

The Leopard

IL GATTOPARDO   205 min.
Director: *Luchino Visconti*
Origin: *Italy/France/USA*
Distributor: *20th Century-Fox*
Cast: *Claudia Cardinale, Alain Delon, Burt Lancaster, Rina Morelli, Serge Reggian, Paolo Stoppai*

Marxist aristocrat Luchino Visconti's epic saga of Sicily in the 1860s, *The Leopard*, is a hugely ambitious chronicle of social and political revolution, breathtaking in its scope and imagination. In one of his finest performances, Burt Lancaster is majestic as the rigid Sicilian nobleman Don Fabrizio, the Prince of Salina, known as The Leopard, struggling against the tide of change as Italian nationalism gathers force and coming to realize that both he and the old aristocratic order are doomed. Embracing adventure, history lesson, political essay and character study, *The Leopard* is also a popular romance, with the dashing young French star Alain Delon (as Lancaster's nephew Tancredi) and Italy's gorgeous Claudia Cardinale (as the rich merchant's daughter lined up by Lancaster) providing the necessary dash and heady glamour. Adapted from Giuseppe di Lampedusa's novel, *The Leopard* takes the viewer on an elegant and sensual trip through an era on the brink of revolution. It's the kind of intellectual epic Lean or Spielberg could only

aspire to, with its swirling emotional impact, astounding CinemaScope visuals and gorgeous DeLuxe colour. The film is played out in a series of epic set-pieces, topped by the ball sequence finale which lasts an entire hour and is among the cinema's most sustained *tours-de-force*. Originally seen outside Italy in a dubbed and much-cut version, this Cannes Palme d'Or winner was restored to its original glory in 1983 and finally seen by English-speaking audiences the way it was made. Ironically we don't hear Lancaster's real voice in either version.
EPIC/ROMANCE/HISTORY

Tom Jones

129 min.
Director: *Tony Richardson*
Origin: *GB*
Distributor: *Woodfall/United Artists*
Cast: *Diane Cilento, George A. Cooper, George Devine, Edith Evans, Albert Finney, Joan Greenwood, Hugh Griffith, Freda Jackson, Lynn Redgrave, Joyce Redman, David Tomlinson, David Warner, Susannah York*

"Angry young men" Tony Richardson and John Osborne, who had worked together on the first stage production of Osborne's *Look Back in Anger* in 1956, were a surprising team to turn Henry Fielding's sprawling 18th-century novel about a young man's adventures from birth to marriage into this rollicking, bawdy comedy. But their draconian hack and rewrite job on this then little-known work proved to be an enormous critical and box-office success, winning four Oscars, and pushing Fielding's novel into the bestseller lists more than two centuries after it was published. Setting the story against a beautifully detailed and convincing reconstruction of 18th-century England, Richardson and Osborne used every trick available at the time in the screen (and stage) comedy bag – undercranking, titles, stop-motion, Feydeau-style

farce and *Keystone Kops* slapstick – to create a breathtakingly paced, roaringly funny film. They also perceptively picked up on the link between the bawdiness associated with the period and the growing permissiveness of the 1960s, though it was not at this stage necessarily nakedly explicit – one of the funniest and sexiest encounters ever filmed is still the scene of growing lust between fully clothed Albert Finney and Joyce Redman as they stare into each other's eyes while frenziedly demolishing the food on their plates. Finney plays the hero to the lusty, gutsy hilt, Susannah York is his comely but by no means wimpy true love, while Hugh Griffith is memorable among a sterling supporting cast as York's bucolic father.
BAWDY PERIOD COMEDY

Dr No

111 min.
Director: *Terence Young*
Origin: *GB*
Distributor: *United Artists/Eon*
Cast: *Ursula Andress, Sean Connery, Eunice Grayson, John Kitzmiller, Bernard Lee, Jack Lord, Zena Marshall, Lois Maxwell, Joseph Wiseman*

The James Bond films were one of the central myths and media hypes of the 1960s and continue to be so, if to a lesser extent, into the 1990s. If being Bond is enough to ensure fame for life – unless you happen to be unlucky George Lazenby – being the first Bond makes a man immortal. That man was Sean Connery, chosen instead of original author Ian Fleming's preferences of Cary Grant and Noel Coward. The novels were already a success in 1963 when Harry Saltzman and Albert 'Cubby' Broccoli teamed to produce this first Bond pic for United Artists, so you might have expected a sizeable-budget movie. But not so. This was a cost-conscious British film, since no one could guess its potential, and perhaps for that reason, after the big names had said no, the producers decided to reconsider their plans

1964

007 Connery: *Licensed to thrill Ursula Andress*

and go for a young unknown. Never mind that he was a tough, working-class Scotsman playing a suave, middle-class Englishman, he was cheap (reportedly $15,000). This ground-breaking spy caper, after poor reviews and a slow start, took off at the British then American box-offices, boosted by Connery's polished charisma and Ursula Andress's blatant sex appeal. The glossy, absurdist all-action mix of spies, sex, exotic locations, fast cars, silly gadgets, big explosions, sadistic violence, sudden death, rousing megalomaniac villains and breathtaking stunts came as a revelation, and still impresses after all the later lavish refinements and the million and one less successful attempts to rip off the winning formula. Connery played the role seven times until *Never Say Never Again* (1983), as did Roger Moore from *Live and Let Die* (1973) to *A View to a Kill* (1985). He was succeeded by Timothy Dalton for two films before Pierce Brosnan took over in *Goldeneye* (1995).
SPY ADVENTURE

A Hard Day's Night

83 min.
Director: *Richard Lester*
Origin: *GB*
Distributor: *United Artists*
Cast: *Wilfrid Brambell, Deryck Guyler, George Harrison, John Junkin, John Lennon, Paul McCartney, Anna Quayle, Norman Rossington, Victor Spinetti, Ringo Starr*

At a time when rock 'n' roll films were either a revue showcase or a romantic vehicle to promote the star's image, this first Beatles film did something completely different. A pseudo-documentary, which was actually a scripted fiction written by Alun Owen, and shot in black-and-white, it tells the story of 36 hours in the life of the group, from boarding a train to London, accompanied by their manager (Norman Rossington, parodying real-life Svengali Brian Epstein) and Wilfrid Brambell as Paul's reprehensible grandfather with a propensity for "chatting up the birds". The film then follows them through London's swinging nightspots into a television studio, fleeing from frantic fans and so on. Lavishly peppered with the Beatles' hit songs of the time and targeting a youthful audience through the group's enormous popularity and their image as good-humoured deflaters of pompous authority figures, such as in this case Victor Spinetti's self-important television director, the film was virtually thrown together in seven weeks for only half a million dollars to catch the crest of the wave before this new group's popularity waned. As time proved of course producer Walter Shenson need not have been in quite such a rush. The film was a monster hit and the frenetic and anarchic style of Richard Lester's direction, which borrows eclectically from Buster Keaton, the Marx Brothers, Fellini and *cinéma vérité*, was a seminal influence on many trendy London-located films that followed.
MUSICAL/COMEDY

Dr Strangelove

OR HOW I LEARNED TO STOP WORRYING AND LOVE THE BOMB
93 min.
Director: *Stanley Kubrick*
Origin: *GB*
Distributor: *Columbia*
Cast: *Peter Bull, Sterling Hayden, James Earl Jones, Slim Pickens, George C. Scott, Peter Sellers, Keenan Wynn*

Stanley Kubrick's searing satirical attack on mankind's warmongering mentality forsakes none of its incisiveness to accommodate Peter Sellers's three *tour de force* character turns – as a British RAF captain at an American base, the US President (easily the funniest thing in the film) and the eponymous German rocket scientist, sort of a cross between Wernher von Braun on some not very nice drugs and a tea trolley. Then there's George C. Scott as a gung-ho Pentagon general waging war on the Russkies, a deft comic turn balanced by Sterling Hayden's po-faced tough-guy performance as the general who dispatches Yankee bomb-planes on Russia. A darkly comic comment on the stupidity and self-serving nature of politicians and the military, *Dr Strangelove* remains scathingly funny and timelessly relevant due to the clever script and impressive acting. It's also amazing to look at, thanks in part to Gilbert Taylor's startling black-and-white photography but mostly to the breathtaking sets by Ken Adam, the man responsible for the look of the early James Bond films. It was bold of Kubrick, just after the Cuban missile crisis, to make fun of nuclear Armageddon with a deadly-earnest, farcical story of one side or the other blowing the world to bits by atom bomb through absurd accident or plain stupidity. The ending, with Slim Pickens sitting astride the bomb that blasts us all to smithereens to the tune of Vera Lynn's British wartime hit "We'll Meet Again", is particularly dark and dangerous humour. Based on Peter George's book *Red Alert*, it was made at the height of world-holocaust paranoia at the same time as Sidney Lumet's *Fail Safe*, a film with such a similar premise and situations that the *Strangelove* production tried to sue.
BLACK COMEDY

The Umbrellas of Cherbourg

LES PARAPLUIES DE CHERBOURG
90 min.
Director: *Jacques Demy*
Origin: *France/West Germany*
Distributor: *Parc/Madeleine/Beta*
Cast: *Nino Castelnuovo, Jean Champion, Catherine Deneuve, Ellen Farner, Marc Michel, Mireille Perrey, Anne Vernon*

Unlike today's all-song, no-dialogue approach, in 1964 the musical's expected format was big production numbers linked by narrative. But in *The Umbrellas of Cherbourg* every word, even the most banal exchange, is underpinned by Michel Legrand's music. And while director Jacques Demy is paying tribute to the Hollywood musicals that he loved, his film is set far from the glamour of Broadway and Hollywood, in the very Gallic world of provincial middle-class shopkeepers. Geneviève (Catherine Deneuve) works in her mother's umbrella shop. She has a brief affair with Guy (Nino Castelnuovo), a petrol pump attendant who is drafted into the army, before she realizes she is pregnant. She marries a rich diamond merchant and moves to Paris. Years later the now sophisticated Geneviève returns to Cherbourg to find Guy now owns

the garage and has married another girl. In a Hollywood film this would be a tragedy of lost love or a happy ending would be contrived. In Demy's European world there is a suggestion of pragmatism, the triumph of commonsense with a wistful sigh for the romantic foolishness of youth, giving Legrand's hit song "I Will Wait for You" a sense of irony. Demy described *Umbrellas* as "a film in colour and song". It invests mundanity with a poetic realism, and is a visual feast of camera and human movement, marked by the vividly multi-coloured umbrellas of the title and Legrand's rich but never over-lush score. Although the film has the heightened look of the studio set, this was, in reality, created on location in Cherbourg itself by art director Bernard Evein and cinematographer Jean Rabier.
MUSICAL

Roll 'em, roll 'em, roll 'em: Clint Eastwood rides in for a fistful of tobacco

A Fistful of Dollars

PER UN PUGNO DI DOLLARI   94 min.
Director: *Sergio Leone*
Origin: *Italy/Spain/West Germany*
Distributor: *United Artists/Jolly*
Cast: *Mario Brega, Carol Brown, Clint Eastwood, Marianne Koch, Wolfgang Lukschy, Gian Maria Volonté*

Clint Eastwood rides into town – the mysterious Man with No Name (and few words), sporting a scruffy beard, cigar, sombrero and a poncho – and the spaghetti western is born. Clint was 34, still grinding out the hit TV western series *Rawhide* (as trailhand Rowdy Yates), when out of the blue Italian director Sergio Leone invited him to Europe to make a low-budget western with a plot borrowed from Akira Kurosawa's *Yojimbo* (closely enough for the Japanese producers to threaten court action). Leone's plan was to take the western back to the basic violent shoot-'em-up action of the good old days before they had become sophisticated and psychological. Clint took a chance and a trip to Spain for a tiny fistful of dollars ($15,000) and the film was a surprise sensation, helped no doubt by Ennio Morricone's inimitable music. Clint, who's a hired gun playing off one side against another in a gun-war, said later: "I remember I saw *Yojimbo* years ago at a theatre and I said it would make a great western, but no one would have the nerve to make it. Leone and Kurosawa were good visionaries with a great eye for composition. They knew editing and what works." Eastwood teamed with Lee Van Cleef for the lively sequel, *For a Few Dollars More* (1965), then got $250,000 plus a percentage for the final part of the trilogy, *The Good, the Bad and the Ugly* (1966). He returned to America a superstar to make a series of Euro-influenced westerns.
WESTERN

1965

The Sound of Music

172 min.
Director: *Robert Wise*
Origin: *USA*
Distributor: *20th Century-Fox*
Cast: *Julie Andrews, Charmian Carr, Richard Haydn, Anna Lee, Heather Menzies, Marni Nixon, Eleanor Parker, Christopher Plummer, Peggy Wood*

Although derided by intellectuals, *The Sound of Music* remains probably the most popular and best-loved film musical of all time. The final, most fondly remembered of the Richard Rodgers/Oscar Hammerstein collaborations, it was based on a 1959 stage play by Howard Lindsay and Russell Crouse, itself based on the autobiographical *The Von Trapp Family Singers*, by Maria Von Trapp. Oscar-nominated songbird Julie Andrews gives a bravura performance as Salzburg nun Maria, sent, in the late 1930s, as governess to the children of strait-laced widower Captain Von Trapp (Christopher Plummer). The children fall for her, she falls for her boss, they get married and, in a stirring climax, escape over the Alps after Navy officer Von Trapp refuses to serve under Hitler. Filmed against the panoramic backdrop of the Bavarian mountains, it boasts eye-catching scenery, a uniformly excellent cast – including seven children who manage to be cute without being annoying – and precise direction from Robert Wise. The latter employed much the same creative team as he had on *West Side Story* four years previously, and once again cleaned up at the Oscars, himself taking two of the film's five Academy Awards (including for Best Film and Best Director). Jam-packed with hummable tunes – "Do Re Mi", "Climb Ev'ry Mountain", "My Favourite Things", "The Sound of Music" – and carefully worked insights into the rise of Nazism, this glorious entertainment marks a high point of the Hollywood musical.
MUSICAL

1966

Blow Up

110 min.
Director: *Michelangelo Antonioni*
Origin: *GB*
Distributor: *MGM*
Cast: *Jane Birkin, Peter Bowles, John Castle, Julian Chagrin, David Hemmings, Gillian Hills, Sarah Miles, Vanessa Redgrave, Verushka*

Antonioni's first English language film, *Blow Up* proved to be the most successful art film ever made, bringing its director into the commercial arena as young people in particular flocked to see it. The film uses the framework of a

murder mystery with touches of surrealism to examine the nature of reality, illusion and personal perception. David Hemmings plays a photographer at the centre of the chic, hip, swinging 1960s London scene of drugs, fashion and casual sex – a man without real purpose, hiding his weaknesses behind the shield and weapon of his camera. He comes up against an apparent dramatic reality, when he develops some photographs he has taken in the park of two lovers, which appear to show a murder about to be committed. His attempts to solve the mystery bring him up against the illusory nature of his own life, and by implication that of his generation's lifestyle. As a social document the film presents a fashionably nihilistic view of the times, while the mystery element is merely a device for examining the film's philosophical themes, which are emphasized in the powerful visual metaphor of the mime troupe which opens and closes the film. Its true strength lies in Antonioni's skilful translation of complex and abstract ideas into the visual realities of the screen. Hemmings is effectively cast as the passive hero, Vanessa Redgrave suitably enigmatic as the woman in the park, and the film also marks the debut of Jane Birkin as a giggly photographic groupie.
SURREALIST FANTASY THRILLER

1967

Belle de Jour
100 min.
Director: *Luis Buñuel*
Origin: *France/Italy*
Distributor: *Paris Film/Five Film*
Cast: *Pierre Clémenti, Catherine Deneuve, Geneviève Page, Michel Piccoli, Francisco Rabal, Jean Sorel*

Luis Buñuel's surrealist tale of a respectable, middle-class woman

Hooked on being a hooker: *Catherine Deneuve with Geneviève Page*

working in a brothel took the Best Film Award at the 1967 Venice Film Festival, and remains one of cinema's most disturbing studies of sex, death, fetishism and fantasy. Based on a Joseph Kessel novel, it stars Catherine Deneuve as Severine, the frigid wife of a wealthy young surgeon (Jean Sorel). Unable to find sexual fulfilment at home, she spends her afternoons re-enacting sado-masochistic fantasies in a local brothel under the name Belle de Jour. Her marital life is perversely reinvigorated, however, when one of her clients shoots and paralyses her husband, forcing Severine to devote herself wholly to the care of her wheelchair-bound spouse. Buñuel takes a conventionally structured novel and uses it to explore the uncertain line between fantasy and reality, drawing his audience into a complex, absurdist, multi-layered world in which nothing is as it seems. Severine's mental fantasies of physical submission – she frequently imagines herself being gang-raped – are made real with her clients, yet these experiences too are fantasy compared to the reality of her submission to a crippled husband. Like a Russian doll, each apparent certainty gives way to a deeper one as Buñuel endeavours to "search for the truth, as well as the

necessity of abandoning it as soon as you've found it". It is a quintessentially surrealist philosophy, masterfully presented with all Buñuel's usual humour, perversity, inventiveness and irreverence. Disturbing and titillating, *Belle de Jour* remains an anarchic classic of European film.
SURREALIST

Bonnie and Clyde
111 min.
Director: *Arthur Penn*
Origin: *USA*
Distributor: *Warner*
Cast: *Warren Beatty, Faye Dunaway, Gene Hackman, Estelle Parsons, Michael J. Pollard, Denver Pyle, Dub Taylor, Gene Wilder*

Winning two Oscars, for Best Supporting Actress Estelle Parsons and Burnett Guffey's cinematography, this late-1960s take on the 1930s gangster movie revisited and revitalized a genre that had completely disappeared. Though *Bonnie and Clyde* was motivated by its star and producer Warren Beatty, its artistic vision came from director Arthur Penn, and it must be counted as his most important film as well as his most popular and accessible work. Beatty and new star Faye Dunaway play 1930s Texas bank-robber folk-heroes Clyde Barrow and Bonnie Parker,

and Penn sets out to explain these legendary beings as characters swept along against the tide of the Depression – as victims of their situation. He makes these two individuals charismatically attractive and, despite all the blood-letting, we never lose sympathy for them. Indeed, if the piece has any real villains, they are most definitely on the side of the law, and the film's outlaw amorality struck a strong chord with the counter-culture of the late 1960s, helping it to gross $23 million. It was a landmark in the portrayal of screen violence, and the bullet-spattered conclusion was as culturally significant as the finale of *The Wild Bunch* two years later. Though it gives an impression of realism, it is actually heavily stylized, swinging from moments of comic relief to episodes of extreme violence and even passages of dream-like stillness, making it a fascinating reinterpretation of the genre for the 60s modernist generation.
GANGSTER

In the Heat of the Night
109 min.
Director: *Norman Jewison*
Origin: *USA*
Distributor: *United Artists*
Cast: *Quentin Dean, Lee Grant, Warren Oates, Sidney Poitier, William Schallert, Rod Steiger*

Five Oscars including Best Picture, Actor and Writer showered down on this exciting, intelligent and still relevant Deep South thriller, based by writer Sterling Silliphant on John Ball's novel *Heat*. Oscar-winner Rod Steiger is at his rousing best as a racist sheriff mismatched with Sidney Poitier's educated detective on the case of an industrialist's murder in Mississippi. Poitier, arrested on suspicion of murder just because he's black, is eventually persuaded to join Steiger in the inquiry, while Steiger gradually develops from prejudiced redneck to a grudging respecter of Poitier's professional

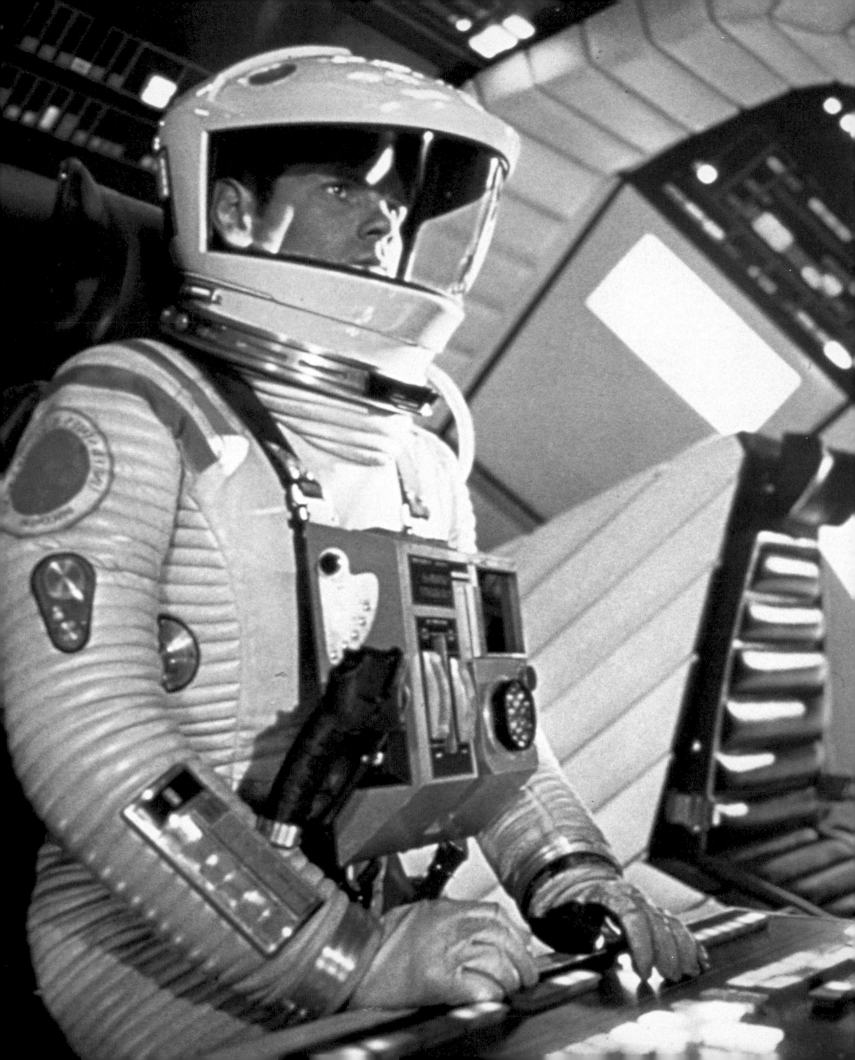

capabilities. These character developments at the heart of the film are persuasively and subtly handled by both the script and the two actors. Against the thriller backdrop, the incendiary race issue is handled with more maturity than in Poitier's other outing that year, *Guess Who's Coming to Dinner*. *In the Heat of the Night*'s popularity may be seen as another small step towards 1960s racial understanding, though it's surprising Poitier wasn't even nominated for an Oscar considering the quality of his performance. This important movie for its day embodies old-fashioned virtues of having a well-carpentered Hollywood production and a humanistic message. It's saved from being dated by its integrity, the punch behind its conviction, its rattling good yarn and its powerhouse acting. There were two sequels with Poitier: *They Call Me MISTER Tibbs!* (1970) and *The Organization* (1971), while Canadian director Norman Jewison, a long-time supporter of liberal political pictures, returned to the theme in *A Soldier's Story* in 1984.
THRILLER

The Graduate

105 min.
Director: *Mike Nichols*
Origin: *USA*
Distributor: *United Artists*
Cast: *Brian Avery, Anne Bancroft, William Daniels, Richard Dreyfuss, Murray Hamilton, Dustin Hoffman, Katharine Ross, Elizabeth Wilson*

Mike Nichols won an Oscar for his deft, freewheeling handling of this poignant, trenchant 1960s classic comedy drama, with boyish-looking Dustin Hoffman grabbing centre-stage in his star-making role as the lost and naive new college graduate Benjamin who returns to his parents' affluent California world that he despises. Just when he can't make up his mind what to do with his future, his parents'

Battles in cyberspace: Hal 9000 turns nasty

married friend Mrs Robinson (Anne Bancroft) makes it up for him by seducing him. This was a time of experiment and liberation, and the first half of the movie is joyously packed with those sentiments, poking fun at a life of commerce ("Benjamin, I have just one thing to say to you – plastics") and the routine of dull marriages. But the second half, with its reactionary plot development in which Hoffman chooses Bancroft's pretty but dull daughter Katharine Ross over the mother, seems boringly conventional and restricting. In fact, the film is remembered almost entirely for the alluringly predatory Bancroft, who turns being a bored, randy housewife into an art form. It's a reflection of Hollywood's conservatism that Bancroft has to pay the price for being sexually predatory, by turning into a hysterical demonic rejected lover, the sort of character that would be played by Glenn Close in the 1980s. Funny and witty though this film is, thanks to Calder Willingham and Buck Henry's razor-sharp script based on the Charles Webb bestseller, its underlying message is basically anti-women and anti-liberation. Yet it's still a real peach of 1960s *Zeitgeist*, and Bancroft is brilliant.
COMEDY DRAMA

1968

2001: A Space Odyssey

141 min.
Director: *Stanley Kubrick*
Origin: *GB*
Distributor: *MGM*
Cast: *Robert Beatty, Keir Dullea, Gary Lockwood, Douglas Rain, Daniel Richter, Leonard Rossiter, William Sylvester*

Stanley Kubrick's sumptuous space epic *2001*, low on plot but high on intensity, marked a watershed in science fiction film-making. Richly complex and introspective, it took four years to complete at a cost of $10 million, most of it lavished on Kubrick's epoch-making, Oscar-winning special effects (one set alone cost $750,000). The meandering plot was based on Arthur C. Clarke's short story, *The Sentinel*, and explores the complex relationship between mankind and his technology, a theme Kubrick had already developed in *Dr Strangelove*. The discovery of a monolithic black slab on the Moon, seemingly left by some higher intelligence, prompts a space mission to Jupiter, a voyage that goes disastrously wrong when malevolent on-board computer Hal 9000 attempts to destroy his astronaut masters (Keir Dullea and Gary Lockwood). Kubrick deliberately sacrifices narrative clarity to visual flair, explaining that "The feel of the experience is the important thing, not the ability to verbalize it". The result is a sometimes unfathomable but nonetheless breathtaking odyssey of human endeavour, crammed with daring images – primitive man discovering weapons; spaceships waltzing through the universe to the strains of "The Blue Danube" – and culminating in a mind-bending climax as one of the astronauts is reborn as a higher being. An oblique homage to Fritz Lang's ground-breaking 1926 sci-fi flick *Metropolis* (which was set in 2000), *2001* provides both a disturbing and a uniquely satisfying cinematic experience.
SCIENCE FICTION

if...

111 min.
Director: *Lindsay Anderson*
Origin: *GB*
Distributor: *Paramount*
Cast: *Arthur Lowe, Malcolm McDowell, Christine Noonan, Robert Swann, Richard Warwick, Mona Washbourne, David Wood*

A relevant, scathing masterwork from British maverick Lindsay Anderson, who asks what if there were a revolution at a public school – in the same year as the May 1968 student riots in Paris. Though filming began fortuitously that March, *if...* had first been dreamt up in 1958 and offered to *Rebel without a Cause* director Nicholas Ray, who felt the material was too British for him to do it justice. Malcolm McDowell, David Wood and Richard Warwick are a trio of dissolute seniors who revolt against the cruelties and humiliations of public school life which Anderson details so convincingly. When the head of house Robert Swann sentences them to a beating for being a "general nuisance" and a bad example to other boys, he triggers a wave of rebellion that ends with the group raining down a hail of bullets on the headmaster, general and parents at the school speech day. Marshalling an acerbic attack on the establishment, Anderson brilliantly bites the hand that feeds him and creates that rarest of creatures – a British film of true originality and vision. He manages a political and social allegory with Brechtian alienating devices, random mix of colour and monochrome filming and intertitles, as well as a homage to Jean Vigo's 1933 *Zéro de Conduite*, and remembers to be darned entertaining too. Though set at an unnamed English public school, it's filmed at Anderson's *alma mater*, Cheltenham – curious that they would give him permission to do this. A controversial winner of the Palme d'Or at Cannes in 1968.
SURREALISM

Rosemary's Baby

136 min.
Director: *Roman Polanski*
Origin: *USA*
Distributor: *Paramount*
Cast: *Ralph Bellamy, Sidney Blackmer, John Cassavetes, Elisha Cook Jr, Angela Dorian, Maurice Evans, Mia Farrow, Ruth Gordon, Charles Grodin, Patsy Kelly*

Rosemary's Baby is horror at its most precise, controlled and unnerving. Roman Polanski shoots like a native New Yorker on his first American assignment, skilfully adapting Ira Levin's novel about Satanism in swinging 1960s Manhattan. Mia Farrow and John Cassavetes play Rosemary and Guy, two bright young things who move into a brooding gothic apartment block where they are pestered by their kill-you-with-kindness old neighbours, Roman and Minnie Castavets (Sidney Blackmer and Oscar-winning Ruth Gordon). But the sudden blossoming of Guy's career is parallelled by Rosemary's increasingly distressing pregnancy, smoothed along by the intrusive attentions of the Castavets and the overbearing Dr Sapirstein (Ralph Bellamy). Alerted to Roman's witchcraft lineage, Rosemary begins to suspect a demonic plot behind her dazed, half-remembered conception. The secret of *Rosemary's Baby*'s chilling power lies in its carefully managed intimacy. The nature of the film's horror is neither outlandish nor escapist, but is played out in the heart of the world's most thriving, super-civilized city. Even

the Castavets' irritating fussiness is not exposed as some cunning disguise. They *are* irritating and they *are* fussy, and they also happen to be devil-worshippers; pure evil in the most humdrum of guises. Ruthlessly prodding at the natural fears of any expectant mother, *Rosemary's Baby* almost casually sets down a world of malevolent, predatory design. It's a personal *tour de force* from Polanski – brilliantly acted, fiendishly well-observed and uniquely unsettling.
HORROR

Weekend
103 min.
Director: *Jean-Luc Godard*
Origin: *France/Italy*
Distributor: *Lira/Comacico/ Copernic/Ascot Cineroid*
Cast: *Juliet Berto, Mireille Darc, Paul Gegauff, Jean-Pierre Kalfon, Valérie Lagrange, Jean-Pierre Léaud, Anne Wiazemsky, Jean Yanne*

Jean-Luc Godard's savage allegorical *tour de force* is a key moment in the development of modernist cinema, and preceded the student

riots of May 1968 by just a few months. A bourgeois couple attempt to visit her parents with murder and a hefty inheritance on their minds. Their trip symbolizes Godard's vision of our historical journey to consumer society hell. A famous bout of first-gear frustration sees them crawl through a lengthy traffic jam of honking, burning and bloodied cars, before the unpleasant couple encounter philosophers, political activists, a beatnik Jesus and Emily Brontë. Finally they are kidnapped by cannibalistic guerrillas and the wife (Mireille Darc) eats the husband (Jean Yanne). Godard disorientates the viewer with neon-caption interruptions designed to confuse rather than enlighten, the characters' awareness that they are in a film, obvious foregrounding of camera technique, and a novel but hard-to-bear interview approach, where psychic Third-World binmen stare out at the camera while others speak their mind from off-screen. There are some hilarious moments: a woman in a blazing car screams in agony for "my Hermes handbag", and later

when offered anything in the world opts for natural blonde hair and a weekend with James Bond, something her husband wants too. *Weekend*'s delight in the degradation of women is less than revolutionary, but the timing of its release in Paris (December 1967) gives it the mythic quality of foresight. Godard ended the film with the caption "La Fin du Cinéma", signalling his extended retreat to the radical fringe.
BLACK COMEDY/SATIRE

1969

Butch Cassidy and the Sundance Kid
112 min
Director: *George Roy Hill*
Origin: *USA*
Distributor: *20th Century-Fox*
Cast: *Jeff Corey, Cloris Leachman, Strother Martin, Paul Newman, Robert Redford, Katharine Ross*

This sexy double-act comedy western yielded four Oscars, launched Robert Redford into superstardom, confirmed Paul Newman's bankability and signalled the beginning of the end of the classic western, as the gun-toting train robbers fumbled and wisecracked their way to huge box-office business: Laurel and Hardy with sex appeal. Loosely based on a true story, *Butch and Sundance* came on the heels of *Bonnie and Clyde*, and firmly established the tradition of unapologetic outlaws as misunderstood good guys. Their sweet-natured humour, as they strive to adapt, and even turn legitimate, is doomed by the realization that, "Dammitall, why is everything we're good at illegal?" The roles were originally offered variously to Steve McQueen, Warren Beatty and Marlon Brando, but Newman as Butch and Redford as Sundance made the film theirs, trading twinkling one-line insults to the bitter

What a **Weekend**!: Jean-Luc Godard pictures a fiery end of the road for civilization

end. Katharine Ross, as the girl they all but share, is memorably serenaded by a bicycling Newman to Burt Bacharach's slushy Oscar-winning song "Raindrops Keep Falling on My Head", and seemed destined for great things, but thereafter assumed a lower profile. Hill gathered Newman and Redford together again for *The Sting* (1973) but, Redford apart, the real beneficiary was Oscar-winning writer William Goldman, who demonstrated he knew just when a non-swimmer should jump off a towering cliff into water ("You stupid fool, the fall'll probably kill you"), and just how to use a freeze-frame ending to hold our heroes in suspended animation, somehow cheating death.
COMEDY/WESTERN

Easy Rider

94 min.
Director: *Dennis Hopper*
Origin: *USA*
Distributor: *Columbia*
Cast: *Luana Anders, Luke Askew, Toni Basil, Karen Black, Peter Fonda, Dennis Hopper, Jack Nicholson, Phil Spector, Robert Walker*

The unrefined essence of hippie America, *Easy Rider* now looks a cinema timepiece, a captivating glance back at a bygone era. A low-budget labour-of-love for director-star Dennis Hopper, the film features Hopper and Peter Fonda as Billy and the enigmatic Captain America, two counter-culture pioneers who set off astride Harley-Davidsons on a drug-financed pilgrimage from Los Angeles to the Mardi Gras in New Orleans. In the course of this cross-country odyssey they encounter hospitable Hispanics, a struggling farming commune and the ever-present representatives of bigoted Middle America. *Easy Rider*'s basic story is pretty vaporous – a loose-limbed, addle-headed state-of-the-nation mumble – but it captured the mood of the time like no other picture, making stars of both Hopper

and a youthful Jack Nicholson, who provided its most detailed performance as boozy Civil Rights lawyer George Hanson. "Hanson is America," Hopper commented. "He's Trapped America, killing itself." Indeed, there's a shamelessly allegorical sweep to all of *Easy Rider* that's oddly disarming in its vitality, a self-belief and utter lack of cynicism. In hindsight, of course, it can be appear naive and indulgent, both in its cod-philosophising content and an eccentric style typified by jarring editing and a prolonged 16mm sequence where Billy and the Captain drop acid in a Louisiana cemetery. "Some of that footage had stains on it," Hopper explained. But while time has itself left some stains on *Easy Rider*, the significance of this immoral counter-culture textbook remains beyond question.
ROAD MOVIE

Le Boucher

THE BUTCHER   94 min.
Director: *Claude Chabrol*
Origin: *France/Italy*
Distributor: *La Boétie/Euro International*
Cast: *Stéphane Audran, Mario Beccaria, Antonio Passalia, Jean Yanne*

Le Boucher demonstrates Claude Chabrol's strengths as a creator of complex, multi-layered characters along with his grasp of the thriller genre. The story is set in a provincial French village whose bourgeois peace and routine are shattered by a murder hunt for a serial killer. The starchy local school-mistress (Stéphane Audran, Chabrol's then-wife) is being wooed by the apparently mild-mannered local shopkeeper of the film's title (Jean Yanne). As her sexuality slowly warms to his advances, she is gradually subject to a more chilling realization – that her suitor is the killer for whom the police are searching. A lifelong admirer of Alfred Hitchcock, Chabrol uses and develops many of the techniques of his mentor, most notably

The schoolmarm and the butcher: *Audran, Yanne*

in the unnerving picnic scene, where Audran and her pupils are disturbed by what at first seem to be drops of rain, but are actually drops of blood dripping from the corpse of the latest victim. The film is otherwise restrained in its use of gore, relying largely for its effect on suspense built through situation, delicate nuances of character and the audience's own expectations, all heightened by the contrast between the lovingly detailed mundanity of everyday provincial life and the horror of the murders. Beautifully photographed by Jean Rabier, *Le Boucher* works perfectly on the pure thriller level, while also being a fascinating addition to Chabrol's on-going cinematic study of psychopathology, obsession and compulsion.
THRILLER

Midnight Cowboy

119 min.
Director: *John Schlesinger*
Origin: *USA*
Distributor: *United Artists*
Cast: *Bob Balaban, Dustin Hoffman, Barnard Hughes, John McGiver, Sylvia Miles, Brenda Vaccaro, Jon Voight*

After the heady hippiness of *Easy Rider* (1969), *Midnight Cowboy* serves up the flipside of the 1960s counter-culture, painting a bleak portrait of a decadent, crumbling, morally-scrambled Manhattan – a place to flee from. For brawny Texan dishwasher Joe Buck (Jon Voight), New York is initially the

promised land. Joe arrives in the city cocksure and confident – certain his sexual prowess among the middle-aged jet-set will earn him a fortune, only to be hamstrung by a complete lack of street-smarts. He gives his first "client" money for her cab fare home and eventually takes up with consumptive, pitiable ne'er-do-well "Ratso" Rizzo (Dustin Hoffman) who dreams of escaping the city for the sunny climes of Florida. Based on the novel by James Leo Herlihy, *Midnight Cowboy* is a compelling odyssey through America's urban underbelly, a stark but touching tale of mismatched losers who hanker for a better life. British director John Schlesinger injects a palpable sense of the Free Cinema qualities of his native industry, lending the picture a notable sense of "kitchen-sink Americana". Fortunately, the film's occasionally over-earnest tone is sparked up by its exuberant style (including a lurid parody of Andy Warhol's Factory clique), relentlessly cheery soundtrack and powerhouse performances. Voight, then a film rookie, gives a splendidly detailed and truthful turn as the half-bright Joe Buck, though centre-stage belongs to Hoffman, masterfully twitchy in a role that could scarcely be further removed from his previous outing as *The Graduate* (1967).
REALIST DRAMA

Once Upon a Time in the West

C'ERA UNA VOLTA IL WEST
165 min.
Director: *Sergio Leone*
Origin: *Italy/USA*
Distributor: *Paramount/Rafan/San Marco*
Cast: *Charles Bronson, Claudia Cardinale, Jack Elam, Gabriele Ferzetti, Henry Fonda, Jason Robards, Lionel Stander, Woody Strode, Keenan Wynn*

Sergio Leone's first film with US backing, *Once Upon a Time in the West*, is a masterpiece of western taciturnity with a wonderful Ennio

Morricone score and one of the longest, most memorable credit sequences in cinema history. Three killers wait for Charles Bronson's train to come in. No one speaks and little happens save for a fly crawling grotesquely across Jack Elam's face, water dripping onto Woody Strode's baldness and the third assassin's excruciating exhibition of knuckle-cracking. The tension is unbearable until Bronson's "Harmonica" makes his spectacular entrance. The sparse plot revolves around the struggle between the violent Old West embodied in bad Frank (Henry Fonda, cannily cast against type) and a newer ruthlessness based on economics, in Gabriele Ferzetti's ugly railway pioneer. Both are after land belonging to a widow (Claudia Cardinale) and are hampered by Bronson's vengeful pursuit of villainous Fonda. Each character is given a distinct musical theme, and Morricone based his composition on the script rather than filmed footage, so Leone directed the actors to move in time to the music rather than the other way around, enhancing his claim that it is a "ballet of the dead... an opera in which the arias are not sung, they are stared". Filmed on location in Spain and Monument

Valley, it's packed with Leone's usual extreme close-ups and great moments of metaphorical imagery such as the smoking gun dissolving into the image of a steam train. Though the original studio-hacked release flopped in the US, *Once Upon a Time in the West* has since been lauded as a western of the first order, and the culmination of Leone's film-making style.
WESTERN

The Conformist

IL CONFORMISTA   115 min.
Director: *Bernardo Bertolucci*
Origin: *Italy*
Distributor: *Mars*
Cast: *Pierre Clémenti, Gastone Moschin, Dominique Sanda, Stefania Sandrelli, Jean-Louis Trintignant*

Bernardo Bertolucci's powerhouse study of one man's psycho-sexual disintegration in 1930s Italy is based on Alberto Moravia's novel about troubled hero Marcello Clerici (Jean-Louis Trintignant) whose life is spent trying to sublimate a childhood sexual encounter with an adult (Pierre Clémenti) by behaving as conventionally as possible; hiding his homosexuality and even volunteering as a spy for the Fascists, for whom he readily com-

mits murder. It's an early display of overwhelming emotions and grand visual style from master director Bertolucci. In one of his key roles, Trintignant chills the soul as the haunted hero dashed down by his ill-advised involvement with the Italian Fascists, while Dominique Sanda is eerily poignant as the seductive wife he pursues for respectability. The weird story, with its European sensibilities and sophisticated mix of adult subject matter, is told in scenes oozing with Art Deco designs and bravura camerawork. Emotionally the film achieves an extraordinary, stifling intensity, though its sexual-political message and views on homosexuality are remarkably ambiguous, appearing more oppressive than liberating. Is it saying "to your own self be true", or does it conclude Clerici's inner-self is simply the result of a childhood "crime"? The overall look of the film, with its Fascist chic, is breathtaking thanks to the outstanding work from two masters of the cinema – cinematographer Vittorio Storaro and set designer Ferdinando Scarfiotti. All in all, a considerable European artwork, now shown in its restored, complete version including the seduction scenes.
CHARACTER STUDY/POLITICAL

1970

Five Easy Pieces

98 min.
Director: *Bob Rafelson*
Origin: *USA*
Distributor: *Columbia*
Cast: *Susan Anspach, Karen Black, Fannie Flagg, Billy Green Bush, Jack Nicholson, Lois Smith*

Despite its small-scale, low-budget nature, Bob Rafelson's *Five Easy Pieces* is an American masterwork, a pure product of the unstable urges and impulses of a new-born nation. At first glance the plot looks rough-

hewn and throwaway. Jack Nicholson plays Bobby Duprea, a check-shirted drifter who toils in the South California oil-fields by day and goes bowling with his "country woman" girlfriend Rayette (Karen Black) by night. But Duprea's existence is an assumed identity. As he heads north to visit his ailing father, the picture suddenly switches gear, probing at the familial ties and refined, intellectual background that Duprea so utterly rejects. After grabbing attention in *Easy Rider* (1969), Nicholson established his belated rise to stardom with *Five Easy Pieces*, carving out his distinctive rebel persona with a series of combative, brilliantly staged setpieces. This is no iconic showboating, though, but a detailed, truthful, supremely handled portrayal the man has seldom equalled since. Even today Nicholson rates his climactic confrontation with his paralysed, inarticulate father as his finest moment as an actor. While sometimes uneven in tone, *Five Easy Pieces* is a coarse-grained treasure, splendidly exploring the culture of the American loner – suspicious of his own intellect and trapped in a suddenly constricting country with nowhere left to roam. At its close, after all the crackling wit and verbal fireworks, there is something desperately sad in the fate of Bobby Duprea, terrified of adult responsibility and chasing his forlorn dream of freedom into the frozen wilds of Alaska.
DRAMA

M*A*S*H

116 min.
Director: *Robert Altman*
Origin: *USA*
Distributor: *20th Century-Fox*
Cast: *René Auberjonois, Roger Bowen, Gary Burghoff, Robert Duvall, Elliott Gould, Sally Kellerman, Jo Ann Pflug, John Schuck, Tom Skerritt, Donald Sutherland, Fred Williamson*

Donald Sutherland as Hawkeye Pierce and Elliott Gould as Trapper John McIntyre are at their comic best as the cynical but big-hearted

Jean-Louis Trintignant: A troubled hero finds it's wrong to conform to the norm in Fascist Italy

boys of the Mobile Army Surgical Hospital (MASH) in director Robert Altman's hilarious, anti-war black farce. Although set in the Korean War, the film's Vietnam parallels and anti-establishment stance touched a chord with audiences worldwide and its success is founded on Ring Lardner Jr's Oscar-winning screenplay. Hollywood maverick Altman carried away the plaudits, and this film, made when he was already 44, is the foundation stone of his glittering career. What made it unusual for its time were its liberal doses of casual bad taste and gore, and the film as a whole shows a level of sophistication matched only by Mike Nichols's *Catch 22*, made the same year. Sally Kellerman, who plays the delightful Hot Lips Houlihan, was Oscarnominated for her performance as the sex-crazed nurse pursued by repressed doctor Robert Duvall, and the performance level throughout the cast is extremely high, but it's the dynamic double act of Sutherland and Gould that forms the film's gravitational centre. Altman had nothing to do with the TV series which assumed a life of its own and ran for 11 years with Alan Alda in the Sutherland role. For the record, *M*A*S*H*'s famous asterisks don't appear on screen in the title but were added later for the poster by a clever publicist.
BLACK COMEDY

1971

Dirty Harry
102 min.
Director: *Don Siegel*
Origin: *USA*
Distributor: *Warner*
Cast: *Clint Eastwood, Harry Guardino, John Larch, Andy Robinson, Reni Santoni, John Vernon*

Arguably Clint Eastwood's best and most famous film, a tough

Dirty Harry Callahan: *Clint Eastwood makes your day*

law-and-order police thriller with Clint in the role he made his own, and will always be identified with, as the maverick San Francisco cop Harry Callahan determined to bring crazed killer Andy Robinson to justice by fair means or foul. The sniper, calling himself Scorpio (based on the real-life Zodiac Killer), is holding the city to $100,000 ransom or he'll carry on the carnage and mayor John Vernon is ready to pay, but Clint won't play. *Diirty Harry* is masterminded by Eastwood's mentor Don Siegel, a master of taut action as director, continually heightening the tension to deliver a fast-paced, exciting thriller with crisp editing, atmospheric locations and an ambiguous message. However, the film's stated dedication leaves little room for ambiguity: "In tribute to the police officers of San Francisco who gave their lives in the line of duty". Back in 1971 that cynical climax with Callahan torturing and eventually despatching the criminal ("Go ahead punk, make my day") seemed extraordinarily controversial and violent; now it's been assimilated into the genre and it's simply the stuff of every cop movie. Contemporary reviews attacked the film for "specious, phony glorification of police and criminal brutality". Ironically the tarnished Dirty Harry became

Clint's most beloved character, and turned him into a megastar. He was persuaded into revisiting Harry in sequels of ever-decreasing quality: *Magnum Force*, *The Enforcer*, *Sudden Impact* and *The Dead Pool*. Even less happily, the movie was also responsible for the vigilante cycle, spawning Charles Bronson's *Death Wish* and its sequels as well as many others.
POLICE THRILLER

Duel
90 min.
Director: *Steven Spielberg*
Origin: *USA*
Distributor: *Universal*
Cast: *Eddie Firestone, Lou Frizzell, Jacqueline Scott, Dennis Weaver*

Steven Spielberg's riveting psychological thriller about lone travelling salesman Dennis Weaver being menaced by a huge smoke-spewing petrol tanker was made for TV but promoted to the big screen by his studio, Universal, who got the young tyro to add an unnecessary 15 minutes of extra footage to make it full cinema-feature length. The almost entirely wordless script sustains its nightmarish idea in terrifying style and it's directed with great brio by the 26-year-old Spielberg, who turned it into a suspense classic and the foundation of his glittering career,

while simultaneously creating one of the most famous TV movies of all time. Weaver is driving in the California backroads when he encounters a 10-ton tanker which he foolishly overtakes and whose sole purpose thereafter seems to be to crush him and his car under its gigantic wheels, endlessly stalking him in a deadly game of cat and mouse on the deserted highway. In this modern-day monster movie, preying on technofear and the terror of an unknown, unseen enemy, the truck's driver is never shown and there's never any explanation of the motivation, following the rule for scare movies – don't show the monster, let the audience imagine it (unless, of course, you've got a zillion-dollar budget for special effects). Effective though Weaver is as the anxiety-ridden hero, this is a director's film – a paragon of pure cinema, in a textbook example of movement, cutting and sustained atmosphere and suspense.
PARANOIA THRILLER

The French Connection
104 min.
Director: *William Friedkin*
Origin: *USA*
Distributor: *20th Century-Fox*
Cast: *Marcel Bozzuffi, Frédéric de Pasquale, Gene Hackman, Tony LoBianco, Fernando Rey, Roy Scheider*

An ultra-tough crime thriller, *The French Connection* portrays an obsessive, streetwise cop who will break any rule to bust an international drugs ring. It was much praised at the time for both its "warts and all" portrayal of the police, led by Gene Hackman as the dedicated and often sadistic "Popeye" Doyle and Roy Scheider as his sidekick, and its realistic portrayal of New York street life, and the film won five Oscars, including Best Film, Best Actor (Hackman) and Best Director (William Friedkin). It is also notable for the scene where the urbane drugs ring leader (Fernando Rey) escapes

from Doyle on a subway train, with an ironic wave to his pursuer, which is followed by a hair-raising car chase under the elevated railway, shot with cameras mounted in the back seat of the car and on the front fenders, which set the agenda for many car chases to follow. *The French Connection* is a thriller of great pace and force, driven by Hackman's faultless performance, though some critics thought it was a run-of-the-mill thriller too much in love with its morally reprehensible anti-hero. The 1975 sequel, *French Connection II*, directed by John Frankenheimer, has Hackman pursuing Rey to Marseilles, where he is force-fed heroin by the gang, resulting in a protracted "cold turkey" sequence. It is superior in its analysis of Doyle's character, though the story is an inferior retread of the original.
CRIME

Klute

114 min.
Director: *Alan J. Pakula*
Origin: *USA*
Distributor: *Warner*
Cast: *Charles Cioffi, Jane Fonda, Rita Gam, Roy Scheider, Jean Stapleton, Donald Sutherland, Dorothy Tristan*

A masterful psychological thriller about the relationship between a small-town policeman (Donald Sutherland), in New York to find his missing best friend, and sophisticated prostitute Bree (Jane Fonda), who is being threatened by a former client. While often scary on the thriller level with a terrific climax which finds Fonda alone in a dark warehouse, pursued by the killer, *Klute*'s real strength lies in the complexities of her characterization, for which she won an Oscar. Though Sutherland has the title role, he is very much her support, sounding-board and the catalyst for the revelation of her inner self. Bree is a woman who feels in control of her life while exercising her profession, as when she coolly glances at her

watch to check the time while in the throes of simulated passion with a client, but is conversely terrified both of the external world and the interior one of her own vulnerability and emotions. This theme, of the sexual politics of control and the contradictions and confusions for the independent woman trying to balance self-sufficiency with emotional commitment, was an enormously attractive one for Fonda to explore, as she has in other films, including to a much lesser extent two subsequent pieces with Pakula: *Comes a Horseman* (1978) and *Rollover* (1981). From Pakula's point of view, though, the film is more strongly related through its *film-noir*ish plot line to his later paranoid thrillers, *The Parallax View* (1974) and *All the President's Men* (1976), which are concerned with the relationship of politics to society rather than sexual politics.
PSYCHOLOGICAL THRILLER

The Last Picture Show

118 min.
Director: *Peter Bogdanovich*
Origin: *USA*
Distributor: *Columbia*
Cast: *Sam Bottoms, Timothy Bottoms, Jeff Bridges, Ellen Burstyn, Cloris Leachman, Cybill Shepherd*

Peter Bogdanovich's *tour de force*, written by the 31-year-old former

film critic with the source novel's author Larry McMurtry, is set in a small Texas town during the 1950s, where sensitive young Timothy Bottoms is having an affair with sad, middle-aged Cloris Leachman, while his cocky high-school jock buddy Jeff Bridges chases golden girl Cybill Shepherd. Perhaps it was unfair that Leachman – as the coach's wife who initiates Bottoms then is ditched by him – and Ben Johnson – as the picture show and pool-room owner – scooped the film's two Oscars instead of the terrific up-and-coming players. But it was also deserved since they both give such astonishing, heartbreaking performances. Sam Bottoms, cast on a visit to see his brother's first day of filming, is also moving as a retarded boy mocked by most of the townsfolk. The title refers to the closing of the town's only movie house, a symbol for Bogdanovich and his movie-going generation of the end of an era of innocence. So strongly does Bogdanovich conjure up the pungent period atmosphere that his film views like a documentary, with its scoreless soundtrack enhanced by the pop tunes of the period, while his cinematographer Robert Surtees films in magical black-and-white. Bogdanovich, whose career suddenly plunged into decline in the 1980s,

poignantly revisited the material for McMurtry's *Texasville* in 1990, though this full-colour reunion of virtually all the original actors was met with bewildering public and critical indifference. You can't go home again.
COMING OF AGE

W.R. – Mysteries of the Organism

W.R. – MYSTERIJE ORGANIZMA
86 min.
Director: *Dusan Makavejev*
Origin: *Yugoslavia/West Germany*
Distributor: *Neoplanta/Telepool*
Cast: *Milena Dravic, Ivica Vidovic*

An intriguing, multi-faceted oddity, Dusan Makavejev's ground-breaking study of sexual mores, made and banned in his native Yugoslavia, set out to define the relationship between political oppression and sexual repression, becoming in the process a *succès de scandale* and gaining widespread notoriety for its upfront sexual explicitness. Based on the theories of maverick German sexologist Wilhelm Reich, *W.R.* is a cinematic collage, comprising elements of documentary, narrative fiction, socio-political analysis and broad surrealism. Divided into two halves, its first section loosely examines the development of Reich's philosophy after his immigration to the USA in 1934. Interviews with relatives, neighbours and students lead into a broader study of American sexuality post-Reich, with some extraordinary backing footage including a porn editor having his penis plaster-casted. Such overt sexual emancipation contrasts with the film's concluding section, a fictional allegory set in Yugoslavia in which a young female worker, Milena (Milena Dravic), embarks on a torrid affair with a touring Russian ice-dancer, Vladimir Ilyich (Ivica Vidovic), who, horrified by the strength of his passion, eventually decapitates Milena with an ice-skate. Tame by today's stan-

Trouble in a Texas town: (left to right) *Jeff Bridges, Sam Bottoms and Timothy Bottoms*

W.R.: Sex and social sermonizing

dards and often misleading about Reich, *W.R.* was nonetheless an important work of post-New Wave cinema, helping to redefine the boundaries of both film structure and content. It never received a theatrical release in the USA (its distribution was limited in many areas to porn cinemas), although Makavejev did prepare a British TV version, modestly using graphics to obscure the erect penis shown in the original.
SURREALIST

1972

Aguirre, Wrath of God

AGUIRRE, DER ZORN GOTTES   95 min.
Director: *Werner Herzog*
Origin: *West Germany*
Distributor: *Hessicher Rundfunk*
Cast: *Ruy Guerra, Klaus Kinski, Del Negro, Cecilia Rivera, Helena Rojo*

A Werner Herzog classic, in which the inimitable German star Klaus Kinski gives one of his world-beating performances as the crazed, possessed Aguirre who leads a breakaway party of Pizarro's Spanish Conquistadors in their 1560 quest for El Dorado, the mythical golden city of Peru, but along the way succumb to the perils of the remote and dangerous jungle. On a realistic level it's the

eye-catching photography of the terrain and the grand, almost theatrical turn of Kinski that marks the film out, but it's also a film with a nightmarish vision and a darkly pessimistic sub-text about man's nature, a modern *Heart of Darkness*. Above all it's a picture that cautious, conservative Hollywood could never have made with all its resources and imagination: it's simply too strange and difficult. Yet Herzog's vision connected with public taste worldwide, at least with the cine-literate, art-house audience. The film is something of a folly, itself shot under the most treacherous of circumstances in the South American jungles and the Peruvian Andes. Easy to see how Herzog must have identified with his beleaguered anti-hero, and it's the immediacy of this that gives a crazed passion to this unique film. Certainly this is the film of a true *auteur*, for no one else could have made it – or would perhaps have wanted to. The end result has greatness thrust upon it, particularly in Kinski's acting and in the climactic bird's-eye image of Aguirre, the lone survivor on a swirling, out-of-control raft; man at the mercy of a chaotic universe.
METAPHORICAL HISTORICAL EPIC

Cabaret

128 min.
Director: *Bob Fosse*
Origin: *USA*
Distributor: *ABC/Allied Artists*
Cast: *Marisa Berenson, Joel Grey, Helmut Griem, Liza Minnelli, Fritz Wepper, Michael York*

To appreciate *Cabaret* fully you have to put to one side the many other incarnations of its story: Christopher Isherwood's original Berlin stories; John van Druten's stage play *I Am a Camera* and Jack Clayton's 1955 film version; and its nearest relative, Kander and Ebb's hit musical on which it is based. Then take it on its own terms and it is a terrific piece of screen musi-

cal entertainment, thoroughly deserving its eight Oscars. Liza Minnelli bears little relationship to Isherwood's uptight, moderately talented English rebel, pathetically struggling to shock. Minnelli's interpretation turns Sally Bowles into a multi-talented star, often, as in the number "Maybe This Time", reminding us of her mother, Judy Garland. Her only excuse for not climbing higher than the Kit Kat club has to be her naive enthusiasm for the attractions of 1920s Berlin's "divine decadence". Director Fosse too often seems fascinated rather than repelled by the sleazy glamour of the period, particularly in his energetically sexual choreography, in the presentation of Joel Grey's exquisitely sly, white-faced Emcee, and in Minnelli and Grey's duet in celebration of "Money". But the film then packs a sinister moral punch as the Nazis turn from laughing-stocks into power figures, in such moments as the "Jewish" punch-line of "If You Could See Her", the chillingly stirring sight of the Hitler youth singing, like angels fated to fall, that "Tomorrow Belongs to Me", and the final panning shot, where the Kit Kat's clientele reflected in the mirror are now all seen to be wearing Nazi uniform and the swastika.
MUSICAL

The Discreet Charm of the Bourgeoisie

LE CHARME DISCRET DE LA BOURGEOISIE   100 min.
Director: *Luis Buñuel*
Origin: *France/Italy/Spain*
Distributor: *Greenwich/20th Century-Fox*
Cast: *Stéphane Audran, Julien Bertheau, Jean-Pierre Cassel, Paul Frankeur, Bulle Ogier, Michel Piccoli, Fernando Rey, Delphine Seyrig*

Buñuel's wickedly subversive surreal comedy is a discreetly well-mannered and elegant attack on the pillars of society – the rich, the military, the police, the church – and, above all, the bourgeoisie which keeps them in place. The story, which isn't a story in the conventional sense, deals with six people in search of dinner. Throughout the film they constantly seek to enjoy this most civilized of repasts and are constantly frustrated in their efforts. They have arrived on the wrong evening; at the restaurant the owner has died and his corpse is on view; there is nothing to drink but water; they are not in a restaurant at all but find themselves on stage with the curtain going up to reveal an angry audience; they are even machine-gunned to death by gangsters before they can eat, though in the next scene they are

Guest who's coming to dinner: Fernando Rey and Delphine Seyrig among the discreetly charming bourgeoisie

alive again and walking in a group along a country road, a recurring image in the film. Are we to believe (as we are sometimes led to) that they are dreaming? Or are they in a comic hell of frustration, paying for such harmless little pastimes as drug-smuggling, torture and fascism, which are revealed to us in the film's third element, in stories narrated by characters outside the circle of friendship? While a corruscatingly funny attack on bourgeois rituals and insecurities, the film also shows a wry affection for its group of six. And why not? Whose fears is Buñuel mocking, after all, if not his and yours and mine?

SURREAL COMEDY

The Godfather

1972 175 min.
Part II 1974 200 min.
Part III 1990 170 min.
Director: *Francis Ford Coppola*
Origin: *USA*
Distributor: *Paramount*
Cast: *Marlon Brando, James Caan, John Cazale, Richard Conte, Robert De Niro, Robert Duvall, Andy Garcia, Diane Keaton, Joe Mantegna, Al Pacino, Talia Shire, Lee Strasberg, Eli Wallach*

Francis Coppola's three-part *Godfather* saga adds up to simply the best gangster movie ever made; a multi-Oscar-winning adaptation of Mario Puzo's bestselling novel about the Mafia which examines with Shakespearean ambition the nature of power and corruption in the microcosm of an Italian-American family. In the first part Marlon Brando carried off the Oscar as the mumbling New York gangland boss Don Vito Corleone. Arguably, though, Al Pacino provides the film's best performance as his reluctant gangster son Michael, who rises to the top of the family on Vito's death, moving chillingly from shy, dubious youngster to calculating planner with a killer instinct. But this is an ensemble of great acting: Diane Keaton as Michael's love Kay Adams, James Caan as the

bullish Sonny and especially Robert Duvall as the quiet adviser Tom Hagen. This irresistible thriller, which also won Best Picture and Script for Coppola and Puzo, is long, complex and compelling, mixing intense, intimate scenes of "family" business with sudden extravagant bursts of violence. The perhaps even more compelling six-Oscar 1974 film is both a prequel and a sequel, with the original cast joined by Oscar-winning Robert De Niro as the young Brando and Lee Strasberg, founder of the Actors' Studio, as a rival Jewish mobster. This is the only sequel to win the Best Picture Oscar, and the only Best Picture sequel that won Best Picture. In 1990 Coppola and Puzo returned to the material for the final word on the mob, centring on Pacino's astonishing turn as the ageing, blank-eyed, irreparably corrupted Michael. It was reputedly the first film to cost more than $100 million, and though flawed stands as a magnificent consummation of the saga. As befits a family saga, Coppola casts his sister Talia Shire in the pivotal role of Pacino's sister, and in *Godfather III*, his daughter Sofia as Pacino's daughter.

GANGSTER

Cries and Whispers

VISKNINGAR OCH RAP   106 min.
Director: *Ingmar Bergman*
Origin: *Sweden*
Distributor: *Svensk Filminstituten*
Cast: *Harriet Andersson, George Arlin, Erland Josephson, Kari Sylwan, Ingrid Thulin, Liv Ullmann*

Ingmar Bergman's searing masterpiece, *Cries and Whispers* is a beautiful but harrowing examination of spiritual emotion and physical pain. In one of the director's greatest films, which packs a devastating emotional impact, the spectre of death visits three sisters in turn-of-the-century Sweden. One of the trio, Harriet Andersson, has terminal cancer and is being cared for by faithful housekeeper Kari Sylwan. Her sisters, the brash, carefree Liv

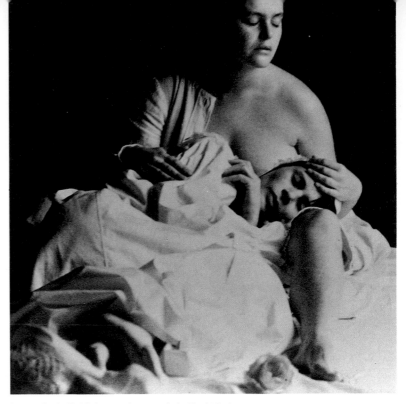

Love and pain: *Kari Sylwan tends cancer victim Harriet Andersson*

Ullmann and the frigid, suicidal Ingrid Thulin, return to the family home to comfort her. As the pair tend to their sister, the loyal servant tries to provide Andersson with spiritual comfort. *Cries and Whispers* finds Bergman's three great female interpreters, Andersson, Ullmann and Thulin at their peak, while the little-known Sylwan is incredibly moving. Breaking the purity of this essentially women's story, another Bergman regular, Erland Josephson, calls in as the doctor. It's a wonderfully crafted, intense and complete film, with a spare, often wordless text contrasting with beautiful rich-coloured photography from Oscar-winning Sven Nykvist. The bracing mix of realism and reaching out to a spiritual dimension adds up to a different kind of essay on death from a famously gloomy director who dealt with it allegorically in the equally memorable *The Seventh Seal*. Bergman stares death steadfastly in the face in this most cathartic and agonizing film and comes up with a highpoint of world cinema. It's almost unbearable to watch, but afterwards you feel a great sense of release and ponder mightily over the words "rest in peace".

SPIRITUAL DRAMA

Deliverance

109 min.
Director: *John Boorman*
Origin: *USA*
Distributor: *Warner*
Cast: *Ned Beatty, Ronny Cox, James Dickey, Bill McKinney, Burt Reynolds, Jon Voight*

John Boorman's thinking-man's adventure film, with a script by James Dickey based on his own first novel, manages to be a parable about nature versus civilization and a study of human instincts for good or evil – to survive, to dominate, to help – while at the same time delivering the genre thrills by brilliantly rendering all the journey's terrors, and so appealing to both smart and popular audiences alike. Burt Reynolds's early career received a big boost from his commanding, archetypal performance as the nasty, gung-ho city slicker who tests his manliness by canoeing down a treacherous Appalachian river along with a trio of Atlanta buddies, played by Ned Beatty (making his screen debut) Jon Voight and Ronny Cox. The river may be treacherous, but they're confronted by scary locals straight out of some horror movie who are even more dangerous. In a perhaps over-schematic

series of characterizations – though they could be defended as archetypes rather than stereotypes – Beatty is the overweight fallguy of the group, who gets picked on by both sides, Cox plays the thinking man, and Voight represents the good-spirited everyman figure who has to save the day. Technically it's beautifully done, with a great atmosphere and tremendous pace produced by sharp editing and eye-catching photography of the river country scenery by top cinematographer Vilmos Zsigmond. It also has the advantage of a catchy score with the "Duelling Banjos" theme that became a pop hit of the day. Its popularity led to a cycle of such films emphasizing the violent exploitation aspects of *Deliverance*. Boorman was criticized for stressing the details of death, maiming and degradation.
ADVENTURE

1973

Badlands
95 min.
Director: *Terrence Malick*
Origin: *USA*
Distributor: *Warner*
Cast: *Ramon Bieri, Warren Oates, Martin Sheen, Sissy Spacek, Alan Vint*

Badlands is the first and finest of only two pictures from errant genius Terrence Malick, a philosophy scholar who brings a unique cold-eyed distance to the fact-based account of Kit (Martin Sheen) and Holly (Sissy Spacek), two psycho-lovers on the run through 1950s USA. Nudged along by a haunting percussive score and Spacek's trippy, pulp-fiction voice-over, this beautifully crafted crime thriller ranks among the decade's brightest pictures. Sheen provides a finely judged turn as the fresh-faced garbage-man who guns down Holly's disapproving dad (a splendidly sleazy Warren Oates)

and spirits his love away to a new life on the road. Kit's frequent shows of violence appear almost casual; in other respects he is courteous, soft-spoken and deferential. Still more chilling is Spacek as Kit's wan, wide-eyed lover – vaguely aware of the wickedness taking place but certain-sure that her "destiny" lies with him. Love – as the pair's tinny transistor informs us – is indeed strange. Kit and Holly are windows through which Malick reveals the moral void in America's wide-open spaces. The gulf between their misplaced mimicry of accepted behaviour and the savagery of their lifestyle indicates a culture turned unreal and divisive. Malick's direction brilliantly emphasizes this disorientating quality, filming with a lyrical poise while keeping his protagonists deliberately unreal and impenetrable. The result is an alien art-work of vivid, slow-burning intensity; a warped overview of America's whitewashed porches and golden prairies that views like a Norman Rockwell painting on acid.
CRIME

Mean Streets
110 min.
Director: *Martin Scorsese*
Origin: *USA*
Distributor: *Taplin-Perry-Scorsese*
Cast: *David Carradine, Cesare Danova, Robert De Niro, Harvey Keitel, David Proval, Amy Robinson, Richard Romanus, Martin Scorsese*

Martin Scorsese's independently made charge through Little Italy announced his arrival as a major, innovative talent, began his great partnership with Robert De Niro, and continued his association with Harvey Keitel following their double debut, *Who's That Knocking at My Door?* (1968). Packed with restlessly energetic camera movement and frenetic dialogue, with violence never far behind, the drama centres around a guilt-ridden Catholic, Charlie (Keitel),

who attempts to take on the responsibility of running a family restaurant while maintaining his friendship with his unruly pal Johnny Boy (De Niro). Charlie is in love with his friend's epileptic sister, Teresa (Amy Robinson), although barely able to express it, and tests his faith by trying to "save" Johnny. But his debt-ridden pal stubbornly refuses to see the light or pay his way, and a violent Scorsese climax is in the offing. Set in the director's own New York backyard, but shot in Los Angeles, Scorsese's third feature uses music to great effect, establishing a distinctive pop-and-violence style, and includes brilliant performances from a nitro-glycerine De Niro and a barely restrained Keitel. Scorsese himself plays the twitchy assassin hired to kill Johnny. The loose, episodic structure at times looks like a work in progress, but although Scorsese has made better it is always when he returns to the same grimy, urban territory he made his own, beginning here. With its in-your-face, machine-gun machismo ("who you callin' a mook?") and excellent characterization, *Mean Streets* is a much-imitated and influential original.
MELODRAMA

1974

Blazing Saddles
93 min.
Director: *Mel Brooks*
Origin: *USA*
Distributor: *Warner*
Cast: *Mel Brooks, Dom DeLuise, David Huddleston, Alex Karras, Harvey Korman, Madeline Kahn, Cleavon Little, Slim Pickens, Gene Wilder*

Mel Brooks's western spoof was his box-office breakthrough film after the cult success of *The Producers* (1968) and is still one of his funniest films, made in the same astonishingly productive

year as his other masterwork *Young Frankenstein*, another movie genre send-up. It showcases the Mel Brooks Academy of Fun at its best, among whom are Cleavon Little as the black sheriff, Gene Wilder as his sidekick, Harvey Korman as crooked lawyer Hedley Lamarr, and Madeline Kahn, who's devastating in a sustained impersonation of Marlene Dietrich as sexy showgirl Lili von Schtupp. And naturally Brooks finds a couple of wild cameos for himself as Governor Lepetomane and the Indian chief. The plot effectively parodies every routine oater you've ever seen, proving that Brooks knows and loves his movies, as the residents of the little town of Rock Ridge find themselves the pathetic victims of the hissable baddie Lamarr and his

Wilder days: *Gene Wilder* (left) *and Cleavon Little*

cronies. But help is at hand in the zany form of former railroad-worker Sheriff Bart and gun-slinger-turned-alcoholic the Waco Kid, who go into action against the prejudice and chicanery threatening law and order. The (sometimes bad-taste) gags are undiscriminating, but they land so thick and fast that it's 93 minutes of non-stop laughs. The baked-bean routine, the assault on an old lady, the horse-punching and, above all, the post-modern ending in the Warner Bros lot all give it edge and class, rocketing it out of the rut of the similar British *Carry On* humour. A big, brash and bawdy comic milestone.
COMEDY

Chinatown

131 min.
Director: *Roman Polanski*
Origin: *USA*
Distributor: *Paramount*
Cast: *Faye Dunaway, John Hillerman, John Huston, Diane Ladd, Perry Lopez, Jack Nicholson, Roman Polanski, Darrell Zwerling*

Director Roman Polanski hit his film-making peak with *Chinatown*, a majestic fable of personal and political corruption in 1930s Los Angeles. Robert Towne may have penned the finely wrought screenplay but the underlying mood is pure Polanski: elegant, elusive and devoid of Hollywood sentiment. Shrewdly revisiting *film noir* country, the picture adopts a hard-boiled narrative to conjure up a saga loaded with allegorical sweep and implication. Polanski shoots in muted, sun-soaked tones, following private-eye Jake Gittes (Jack Nicholson) into the deceitful web of *femme fatale* Evelyn Mulray (Faye Dunaway) and her monstrous, all-powerful father Noah Cross (John Huston). At the heart of *Chinatown* lies a mythic, near-Biblical quality, with its treatment of a city paralysed by drought and the implicit view of Noah Cross as the corrupt king of a blighted land. But in such mythic tales water traditionally serves a healing, life-giving role, whereas *Chinatown*'s water is salted ("bad for the grass"). It is the place where Cross's rival is drowned, while the life it ushers in is ultimately revealed as poisoned and incestuous. What Polanski truly spotlights with this multi-layered spellbinder is the essential nature of American evil, an evil that springs fully formed out of a culture obsessed by wealth and acquisition. In this way, Polanski shows Gittes to be an oddly old-style, outmoded hero, genuinely distressed by the corruption he encounters and shocked by the malevolent aims of Cross, who has diverted the city's dwindling water supply in order to buy himself "the future". One of the 70s' greatest American movies.
THRILLER

The Conversation

113 min.
Director: *Francis Ford Coppola*
Origin: *USA*
Distributor: *Paramount*
Cast: *John Cazale, Robert Duvall, Frederic Forrest, Allen Garfield, Gene Hackman, Cindy Williams*

Arguably Francis Coppola's most satisfying and wholly realized picture, *The Conversation* was a labour of love for the director, riding the crest of a wave after the box-office bonanza of *The Godfather* (1972). Deliberately claustrophobic in tone, the picture traces the efforts of surveillance expert Harry Caul (Gene Hackman) to unravel an initially innocuous exchange between two cutesy lovers (Frederic Forrest, Cindy Williams) for his enigmatic client, the President (an uncredited Robert Duvall). As darker elements begin to be uncovered on the tape, Caul – haunted by Catholic guilt and a tragic previous assignment – begins to fear for the couple's safety and attempts to pick his way through the sludge of half-truths and obscure conversational snatches in the vague hope of redemption. A beautifully wrought essay on the creeping influence of surveillance culture, *The Conversation* gained further significance thanks to its prescient message – released in the US at the heated height of the Watergate scandal. But the film's impact spreads wider than any specific historical incident, mirroring the general decline and disillusion of its 1970s setting. After a series of reined-in shocks, the ending of this cerebral, near-Kafkaesque masterwork packs an almighty punch, with Caul sitting alone in the apartment he has torn apart in fruitless search for a bug, the helpless prisoner of his own technology. A work of mammoth impor-

Bugged out: Gene Hackman

tance, *The Conversation* catches an unhealthy transition time in American history: the point when, reeling from the Vietnam War and the declining boom years of the 1950s and 1960s, this previously expanding culture turned suddenly inward and malignant.
SUSPENSE

The Texas Chainsaw Massacre

83 min.
Director: *Tobe Hooper*
Origin: *USA*
Distributor: *Vortex*
Cast: *Marilyn Burns, Allen Danziger, Gunner Hansen, Ed Neal, Paul A. Partain, William Vail*

The Texas Chainsaw Massacre is the bargain-basement chiller *par excellence*, a drive-in schlock-horror that rejuvenated the genre and shoved it into a grisly new era. Directed at a distance by Tobe Hooper, the film works on one level as a standard stalk 'n' slash pic. Plot is near non-existent. Set in the wild interior of Texas, it turns a jaundiced, aloof eye on a van-load of teens who visit their grandpappy's grave, take aboard a nutty hitchhiker and are finally murdered by a cannibalistic family of out-of-work slaughtermen. With their primitive folk-art – all bones and feathers, formal family dinners and pet hen cramped in a canary cage – this brood are a peculiarly American hybrid of voodoo surrealism and nuclear-family respectability. At its head slumps the ancient, scarcely breathing grandpa, once a legendary slaughterman ("he once killed 60 cattle in five minutes") but the true demon of the pack is the baby – the squealing, oversized Leatherface (Gunner Hansen), his face obscured by a crude patchwork-quilt of human flesh. Equally unnerving is the film's offhand treatment of violence, erupting randomly and without any apparent motive. Contrary to the film's controversial reputation, it boasts little explicit depiction and no dubious glamorization, though this somehow serves to make it even more terrifying – severed from traditional notions of good and evil. At the film's abrupt conclusion, with sole survivor Sally (Marilyn Burns)

Chainsaw reaction: Leatherface (Gunner Hansen) cuts up rough

escaping aboard a pick-up, the camera turns back onto Leatherface's gleeful, chainsaw-whirling dance; an unfathomable, unholy celebration of all the blood-lust urges at the heart of white-trash America.

HORROR

1975

Jaws

124 min

Director: *Steven Spielberg*
Origin: *USA*
Distributor: *Universal*
Cast: *Richard Dreyfuss, Larraine Gary, Carl Gottlieb, Murray Hamilton, Robert Shaw, Roy Scheider*

Steven Spielberg's shark terror-tale brilliantly exploited primal fears of the ocean – to massive financial gain – and shot him into the super-league of Hollywood directors. Despite endless parodies and three inferior sequels, nothing matches Spielberg's dread suspense or John Williams's perfect Oscar-winning score as the coastal resort of Amity Island is besieged by a monstrous Great White. Hydrophobic Police Chief Brody (Roy Scheider) is prevented from closing the beach by the mayor (Murray Hamilton) who is concerned with holiday profits, so Brody turns to a comical brains-and-brawn pairing of marine biologist (Richard Dreyfuss) and salty seadog (Robert Shaw) to see off the monster. The studio wanted Charlton Heston for Brody's part, Jeff Bridges as the scientist and Sterling Hayden for the sailor but 27-year-old Spielberg held out to get his way with the casting. The shark, hydraulically operated by 13 scuba-diving technicians , is wisely kept largely out of sight but firmly in the mind by Spielberg until the finale, though when it's finally seen it looks like an inflatable plastic model. Shot on location in Martha's Vineyard, *Jaws* went way over budget, but became the most financially successful movie ever at the time, setting cross-marketing precedents we're still suffering from today. Some argue it's a Watergate movie about corruption, others that it is a "vagina dentata" movie about the male castration complex, while for critic Pauline Kael it is the movie "Eisenstein might have made if he hadn't intellectualized himself out of reach". Certainly this terrifically sustained exercise in terror was the biggest blessing for the swimming-pool industry since Esther Williams hung up her bathing suit.

SUSPENSE

Nashville

159 min.

Director: *Robert Altman*
Origin: *USA*
Distributor: *Paramount*
Cast: *Ned Beatty, Karen Black, Ronee Blakley, Keith Carradine, Geraldine Chaplin, Henry Gibson, Lily Tomlin*

The unique, undisciplined, sometimes maddening talents of filmmaker Robert Altman found their perfect expression in *Nashville*, a delirious, free-flowing jaunt through the shifting landscape of country-and-western America. Using Joan Tewkesbury's roomy script as a blueprint, the film hurls a loose cover-all canopy over the two-day experiences of no less than 24 principal characters. The movie's catalyst is a music-flavoured political rally held by an unseen presidential candidate who promises "new roots for the nation". Around this central event, Altman sets his protagonists in motion, fashioning a kaleidoscopic cultural overview that builds to the senseless assassination of fading country singer Barbara Jean (Ronee Blakley). Altman's deliberately *laissez-faire* handling blends with improvisatory playing from a star cast (Ned Beatty, Lily Tomlin, Keith Carradine, Karen Black), overlapping dialogue and clever, attention-grabbing cross-cutting between the action. The result is a picture that truly dances to the rhythms of American life, a whirling carousel of coarse parody, deft satire and loving celebration. Stylistically it makes for captivating viewing, yet *Nashville*'s implications are ultimately downbeat, probing at a nation wobbling and unsure of its direction in the wake of Watergate and Vietnam. Its inhabitants look fragile and oddly motiveless, transient inhabitants of a cluttered and dehumanizing environment. Similarly, a film-form that proves liberating can also be unnerving in its headlong, indiscriminate rush. That said, *Nashville* still stands as Altman's peak achievement; a challenging and altogether unique film experience. Watching it is like inhaling pure oxygen.

SATIRICAL DRAMA

Picnic at Hanging Rock

110 min.

Director: *Peter Weir*
Origin: *Australia*
Distributor: *Picnic Productions/Australian Film Corporation*
Cast: *Kirsty Child, Dominic Guard, Vivian Gray, Ann Lambert, Helen Morse, Rachel Roberts, Jacki Weaver*

Picnic at Hanging Rock was in the vanguard of the Australian New Wave. It is one of three films Peter

Magic and menace in the Aussie Outback: Schoolgirls picnic at Hanging Rock

Weir made in his early career while still in Australia, that explore his fascination with the mystic power of a land to which white civilization is a recent and uncomprehending import. Like its precursor *The Cars That Ate Paris* (1974) and subsequent *The Last Wave* (1977), it deals with the disruption of the rational world by the incomprehensible and illogical. The story focuses on a girls' school picnic to the beauty spot of the title on St Valentine's Day, 1900. During the course of a poetically beautiful, sensually hot afternoon that is inexplicably loaded with menace, three of the girls and their teacher disappear, apparently into thin air. Teasingly, the mystery is never solved but the atmosphere of lyrical beauty masking menace and suppressed adolescent sexual hysteria lingers in the memory along with the haunting wood-wind musical theme. Although the beauty of the film and its mystery and intrigue hold the attention for most of its length, the enigmatic lack of resolution is frustrating. The key to the puzzle appears to be emergent sexuality. The Freudian imagery of phallic boulders and narrow passages through rock heightens the sensual power of the natural environment, contrasting it with the strict and stifling English

cultural values of the school, suggesting that the disappearances are a metaphor for the girls' escape from sexual repression into fulfilled womanhood.
MYSTICAL DRAMA

The Rocky Horror Picture Show

100 min.
Director: *Jim Sharman*
Origin: *GB*
Distributor: *20th Century-Fox*
Cast: *Jonathan Adams, Barry Bostwick, Nell Campbell, Tim Curry, Charles Gray, Meat Loaf, Little Nell, Richard O'Brien, Patricia Quinn, Susan Sarandon*

Richard O'Brien's outrageous, gothic masterpiece of high camp and low humour is a madcap mix of vintage B-movie homage, supercharged sensuality, 1970s-style alternative sexuality and fantastic invention. Tim Curry re-creates his long-running London fringe stage performance in the part of a lifetime as divinely deviant Dr Frank N. Furter, a crazy cross-dressing scientist from the planet Transexual in the galaxy of Transylvania. It's the story of an "ordinary" couple of American honeymooners, Brad and Janet (played by Susan Sarandon and Barry Bostwick), who make the terrible mistake of seeking shelter in a storm at Dr Furter's castle on the very special night his "beautiful creature", the Adonis humanoid sex toy Rocky, is to be born. Thrills mix with chills to great songs by O'Brien – "The Time Warp", "Science Fiction Double Feature", "Over at the Frankenstein Place", "Whatever Happened to Saturday Night" and the thumping "Sweet Transvestite". Among the perfectly chosen cast, O'Brien re-creates his stage performance as the rotten butler Riff-Raff, Meat Loaf sings rock 'n' roll, and erstwhile silky James Bond villain Charles Gray is the narrator, in the style of 1950s British B-movie thriller presenter Edgar Lustgarten, and even gets to

join in with "The Time Warp" – "It's just a jump to the left". Perhaps the first audience participation movie: though it flopped on its original release, the film became a late-night hit in London and New York, where young trendies donned the garb of their favourite cast members to join in the routines and mouth the lines. "It's not easy having a good time – why, even smiling makes my face ache!"
HORROR SPOOF

One Flew Over the Cuckoo's Nest

133 min.
Director: *Milos Forman*
Origin: *USA*
Distributor: *United Artists*
Cast: *Danny DeVito, Brad Dourif, Louise Fletcher, Christopher Lloyd, Jack Nicholson, William Redfield, Will Sampson*

Given the high-voltage intensity of his performance, it's astounding to think Jack Nicholson was not first choice to play maverick mental patient Randall McMurphy. James Caan was offered the role but declined, claiming. "all those white walls" put him off. The whole thing didn't sound quite filmic enough. Ken Kesey's classic 1960s novel served as a parable for the conflict between individualism and

mass conformity, using a constrictive Oregon mental ward as the microcosm for contemporary US society. The arrival of McMurphy, a larger-than-life anti-hero, liberates his cowed fellow patients and enrages Big Nurse Ratched (Louise Fletcher), the icy, matriarchal symbol of social order. For the movie, Czech-born director Milos Forman tones down much of the overt symbolism and dumps altogether Kesey's hallucinatory, drug-driven narration. What remains is a stripped-down acting showcase, a heartstopping tale of freedom and rebellion and a heady celebration of pioneering male values in a castrated modern age. Fletcher is stone-faced and terrifying as Ratched while Brad Dourif shines out among a magnificent support cast as the doomed Billy Bibbit. But centre-stage belongs to Nicholson who is on incendiary form as the film's grinning, chaotic, uncompromising engine of liberation. *One Flew Over the Cuckoo's Nest* was that rare beast, a critical and commercial blockbuster. Not since Frank Capra's *It Happened One Night* in 1934 had a picture so swept the board on Oscar night, winning for Best Picture, Director (Forman), Actor (Nicholson), Actress (Fletcher) and script.
DRAMA

Cuckoo's Nest: *Christopher Lloyd* (left) *and Jack Nicholson in a flight from madness*

1976

Network

120 min.
Director: *Sidney Lumet*
Origin: *USA*
Distributor: *MGM*
Cast: *Wesley Addy, Ned Beatty, Robert Duvall, Faye Dunaway, Peter Finch, William Holden, Ken Kercheval, Beatrice Straight*

Sidney Lumet squeezes every drop of drama and satire out of a Paddy Chayefsky script rooted in the writer's love/hate affair with the ruthless, ratings-led world of network television. The only voice of decency in the story is William Holden as the veteran news director labouring to defend serious news values against the predators who see news as a branch of show-business. Faye Dunaway is the carnivorously success-hungry young executive who uses sex as a rung on the ladder to power, and who seduces then ditches Holden according to the needs of her career. The film is, however, dominated by Finch, the over-the-hill newsreader whose world falls apart when he is sacked from the network after 25 years. When he announces he will commit suicide during his last broadcast, his ratings go through the roof, he is given prime time by Dunaway to rant against the ills of the world and becomes a Messianic figure whose battle cry – "I'm mad as hell and I'm not going to take it any more" – becomes a slogan for an embittered and exploited nation. Until, that is, he starts attacking his audience and the network itself. Finch skilfully balances his character between high comedy and the tragedy of madness in a giant performance. Both he and Dunaway won Best Acting Oscars. Also notable are Robert Duvall as the sharklike network chief and Ned Beatty as its manic owner. *Network*

Nasty network: *"Mad as hell and I'm not going to take it any more"*

has been criticized as bilious and overblown, but in the context of the expanding media world of the 1990s with its numerically increased choice of trivia and converse lack of interest in quality programming, it makes essential and horribly relevant viewing.
MEDIA SATIRE

All The President's Men
138 min.
Director: *Alan J. Pakula*
Origin: *USA*
Distributor: *Warner*
Cast: *Murray Abraham, Jane Alexander, Martin Balsam, Meredith Baxter, Ned Beatty, Stephen Collins, Dustin Hoffman, Hal Holbrook, Robert Redford, Jason Robards, Jack Warden*

The scandal of the break-in and bugging of Washington's Watergate Hotel is untangled in a smooth-running, compulsive political thriller based on the book by *Washington Post* journalists Bob Woodward and Carl Bernstein. Revelatory and original though it seemed at the time, *All the President's Men* basically puts a 1970s high gloss on those campaigning thrillers of the 1930s that mostly came from the same studio

as this picture – Warner Bros. But what a gloss, what a story! Robert Redford and Dustin Hoffman turn in charismatic, committed, nervy star turns as the two contrasted campaigning reporters – the sincere WASPish Woodward and the Jewish streetwise Bernstein – who expose corruption during Richard Nixon's presidential term in the White House, a story so big that it eventually brought down the President. In one of the high spots of his career, Alan J. Pakula gives a firework display of skilled, crafted direction that builds the tension in gradual, relentless degrees as the news exposé story of a lifetime unfolds. Jason Robards won a support Oscar as Ben Bradlee, the sceptical newspaper editor eventually won over to the journalists' cause, while there's a notable gallery of eccentric character playing from stalwarts Jack Warden, Martin Balsam, Jane Alexander and particularly Hal Holbrook as the enigmatic informer Deep Throat. These performances rest securely on William Goldman's literate, intelligent, Oscar-winning screenplay, oozing with clarity in the most complex of stories and distilling

all the crucial events into one seamless flow.
POLITICAL THRILLER

Taxi Driver
112 min.
Director: *Martin Scorsese*
Origin: *USA*
Distributor: *Columbia*
Cast: *Peter Boyle, Albert Brooks, Robert De Niro, Jodie Foster, Leonard Harris, Harvey Keitel, Martin Scorsese, Cybill Shepherd*

Martin Scorsese's seminal study in alienation is one of the key works of the 1970s, driven by Paul Schrader's searing script and a powerhouse central turn from Robert De Niro as the Manhattan cabby turned angel-of-vengeance. De Niro's Travis Bickle is a figure sprung fully formed from the most distressing asylum case study; a haunted, emotionally frozen Vietnam vet cast adrift in the asphalt wilderness of New York and projecting his own inner sickness out onto the sleazy subculture flotsam around him. "Someday a real rain will wash all the scum off the streets," he muses. Further unhinged by a fumbled romance and his encounter with child hooker Iris (Jodie Foster), Travis comes to believe he is that "real rain", reinventing himself as a shaven-headed, all-powerful vigilante whose mission it is to purge a corrupt and corrupting world. Aided by Michael Chapman's lurid colour cinematography, Scorsese turns Manhattan into a neon-lit dreamscape through which Bickle's cab glides like some hulking yellow monster. It's a disorientating, upside-down reflection of the western genre's traditional frontier town, menaced by varmint outlaws and awaiting the arrival of the no-nonsense drifter-hero. But the unfortunate Bickle is only a hero in his own unbalanced head, and De Niro's splendidly contained performance conjures him into dark-eyed, mesmerizing life. Around this character,

Scorsese gathers a Pandora's Box-worth of complementary demons: Jodie Foster's spellbinding turn, a bewigged, super-sleazy Harvey Keitel, Bernard Herrmann's nerve-jangling score and the director's

Crazy cabby: *Fare play for Robert De Niro*

own creepy cameo as one of Bickle's more poisonous customers. Many of the films of the 1970s addressed what many regarded as a splintered, collapsing culture. None achieved it with the same visceral, visionary sweep as *Taxi Driver*.
ALIENATION DRAMA

1977

Annie Hall
94 min.
Director: *Woody Allen*
Origin: *USA*
Distributor: *United Artists*
Cast: *Woody Allen, Shelley Duvall, Jeff Goldblum, Carol Kane, Diane Keaton, Tony Roberts, Paul Simon*

The 'Nervous Romance' that brought Woody Allen into the mainstream with its four Oscars and huge box-office success is often hailed as his best film. Certainly it is his first that amounts to much more than a series of comic episodes: take away the gags from *Annie Hall* and you

still have a comedy of considerable sophistication. Evolving from Allen's original attempt to write the more lightweight *Manhattan Murder Mystery* (eventually made in 1993), it is the *Pygmalion*-style story of the relationship between the eponymous Annie (Diane Keaton), an awkward, unconfident nightclub singer, and Alvy (Allen), the neurotic but successful comedian who becomes her mentor. Allen denies that the film is anything more than loosely autobiographical, but the story is strikingly similar to his real-life relationship with Keaton, whose family name is Hall. The script (which Allen wrote with Marshall Brickman) plays on these parallels, blurring the boundaries between the real and imaginary, to produce a fascinating examination of the relationship between life and art. Recounted as a series of freely associated flashbacks, the film brims with great Woody one-liners. Split screens, subtitles and even a few moments of animation are used to daring comic effect, and Alvy/Allen steps out of the action to address the audience. Famously disdainful of the Hollywood system, on the night he was awarded his Oscars for Best Director and Script (with Brickman) Allen remained in New York playing clarinet with his jazz band at Michael's Pub.
ROMANTIC COMEDY

Close Encounters of the Third Kind

135 min.
Director: *Steven Spielberg*
Origin: *USA*
Distributor: *Columbia*
Cast: *Bob Balaban, Melinda Dillon, Richard Dreyfuss, Teri Garr, Cary Guffey, François Truffaut*

A loving hosanna to the glory of the unknown, Steven Spielberg's second blockbuster earned two Oscars, seven other nominations and box-office megabucks, so helping to haul the science fiction genre

out of the doldrums. Scorning cold-war paranoia, Spielberg's aliens come with superior intelligence and without malice. Richard Dreyfuss is ordinary American Roy Neary, whose close encounter on an apparently deserted highway leaves him with a recurring mental image of a mountain. His increasing obsession with it threatens to break up his marriage to Teri Garr, but there is compensation in the very human form of Melinda Dillon, the woman who does understand him. Her infant has been kidnapped by the aliens (borrowed briefly, it turns out), and she joins Neary in a pilgrimage to the mountain that is Devil's Tower, where the UFO has landed. They slip through security to witness scientist Claude Lacombe (played by François Truffaut) communicating with the occupants via John Williams's music (a five-note symphony now almost as famous as Beethoven's 5th). Spielberg's follow-up to *Jaws* (1975) confirmed his Midas touch, and despite going way over budget remains one of the all-time biggest earners. Jack Nicholson was originally envisaged for the part of Neary, but was unavailable, and Dreyfuss as the average Joe in spiritual wonderland seems just right. A Special Edition was released in 1980, shortening the build-up and bringing the encounter even closer, with Neary actually entering the spaceship as a volunteer unable to resist.
SCIENCE FICTION

Saturday Night Fever

119 min.
Director: *John Badham*
Origin: *USA*
Distributor: *Paramount*
Cast: *Joseph Cali, Karen Lynn Gorney, Barry Miller, Bruce Ornstein, Paul Pape, Donna Pescow, John Travolta*

The film that shot John Travolta to stardom, spawned a generation of white-suited disco clones and defined the glitzy face of late-1970s fashion, this is a high-

octane, hip-wiggling romp through the teenage world of downtown Brooklyn. Travolta, in his first film lead, is a charismatic sensation as inarticulate Italian dude Tony Manero, a local boy whose tedious, dead-end existence and miserable home life are made bearable by Saturday nights on the dance floor. Here he meets and falls for elusive Karen Lynn Gorney who, in between superbly choreographed bouts of disco-bumping, shows him there is more to life than hanging around with his mates and having sex in the back of cars. Based on a story by Nik Cohn, *Saturday Night Fever* delivers gritty dialogue, realistic photography, flashy costumes and adrenalin-pumping Bee Gees score that became the anthem for a generation, perfectly capturing

both the disillusionment of daily life and the feverish, drug-like exhilaration of Saturday nights. John Badham's sharp, perceptive direction draws on a number of film genres – romance, dance, social drama – to produce a rip-roaring slice of entertainment and an era-defining insight into a section of late-70s youth culture. A massive contemporary success, it spawned a lumbering 1983 sequel, *Staying Alive* (directed by Sylvester Stallone of all people), and a host of copy-cat, dance-your-way-to-self-discovery movies, including *Fame* (1980), *Flashdance* (1983) and *Dirty Dancing* (1987). None, however, could approach the original, either for intelligence, impact or sheer exuberance.
DANCE DRAMA/MUSICAL

John Travolta and Karen Lynn Gorney: Feverishly boogeying on down

Star Wars

121 min.
Director: *George Lucas*
Origin: *USA*
Distributor: *20th Century-Fox*
Cast: *Kenny Baker, Peter Cushing, Anthony Daniels, Carrie Fisher, Harrison Ford, Alec Guinness, Mark Hamill, James Earl Jones, Dave Prowse*

With its two sequels, *The Empire Strikes Back* (1980) and *Return of The Jedi* (1983), *Star Wars* stands as one of the major myth creations of modern cinema, introducing characters, places and events which, although fictitious, have now entered popular folklore and assumed a reality all of their own. Directed, scripted and produced by George Lucas, and using state-of-the-art special effects (Best Visual Effects was one of its seven Academy Awards), it is the epic tale of Luke Skywalker (Mark Hamill) and his conflict with the Empire, personified by black-clad tyrant Darth Vader (Dave Prowse, with a voice by James Earl Jones). Aided by a mystical power called the Force and an assortment of intergalactic mavericks – space smuggler Han Solo (Harrison Ford), old Jedi warrior Obi-Wan Kenobi (Alec Guinness), cutesy androids R2D2 and C3P0 – Skywalker indulges in a succession of thrilling action sequences as he battles to rescue beautiful Princess Leia (Carrie Fisher) and destroy the Empire's Death Star. His mission is powered along by exuberant performances from a largely unknown cast, an Oscar-winning John Williams score and the remarkable visual effects. Lucas cannily superimposed the qualities of the western and swashbuckler genres on to a novel backdrop, in the process reanimating the whole science fiction movement and setting an unsurpassed standard for all fantasy adventure movies. Awe-inspiring in scale – it was intended, with its two sequels, as the middle trilogy of a nine-film series – and perfect in execution, it remains one of the most successful movies of all time.
SCIENCE FICTION

1978

Eraserhead

90 min.
Director: *David Lynch*
Origin: *USA*
Distributor: *American Film Institute*
Cast: *Jeanne Bates, Allen Joseph, Jack Nance, Laurel Near, Judith Anna Roberts, Charlotte Stewart*

With the help of the American Film Institute for whom he made his influential short *The Grandmother* (1970), David Lynch made his breakthrough both into feature films and on to the international cinema circuit with this extraordinary nightmare art-house horror picture, long a cult favourite among those with a sick mind and a strong stomach. Lynch regular Jack Nance (Pete the Logger in *Twin Peaks*) plays a mindless, braindead automaton, intended as a representative of mankind in general, who moves through an underworld depicting a bizarre mockery of so-called "civilized" city life on earth. In a nod perhaps to *Rosemary's Baby*, his girlfriend, who suffers from cerebral palsy, gives birth to a hideous mutant. Lynch, clearly influenced by the surrealists like Buñuel and Dali, delivers a consistently imaginative mix of non-narrative surrealism and body horror which is easy to admire but harder to like in a film that's both perverse and grotesque, while at the same time infiltrating exquisite touches of visual wit and dark humour. The extraordinary black-and-white images are photographed by David Elmes and Herbert Cardwell and the film's visual textures are extremely beautiful in stark and effective contrast to the nightmarish vision. The movie, which took Lynch five years to complete, found an unexpected admirer in comedian Mel Brooks, who said about Lynch "He's mad, hire him" when Brooksfilms wanted a director for the real-life, Victorian horror story of the hideously deformed John Merrick, *The Elephant Man* (1980).
SURREALIST / HORROR

Jack Nance: *A hair-raising performance*

The Deer Hunter

183 min.
Director: *Michael Cimino*
Origin: *USA*
Distributor: *EMI/Universal*
Cast: *Chuck Aspegren, John Cazale, Robert De Niro, George Dzundza, John Savage, Meryl Streep, Christopher Walken*

The Deer Hunter was a bold gamble since films about Vietnam weren't exactly in vogue in 1978 and little-known director Michael Cimino must have seemed worryingly inexperienced to his backers, Universal and Britain's EMI. His only previous film, the small-scale Clint Eastwood actioner *Thunderbolt and Lightfoot* (1974), was hardly evidence of his ability to handle a three-hour mega-movie with huge budget, large cast, big crowd scenes and one of Hollywood's most idiosyncratic stars – Robert De Niro. Not only was the film's subject – three Pennsylvania steelworker friends going to war – suspect at the box-office, it was to be told with a complex, cross-cutting structure. It was to start sedately and end controversially with the US national anthem. But it's to Cimino's eternal credit that he pulls it off. The controversy over Cimino's claims that the POWs' enforced game of Russian roulette (the film's most sickening sequence) was based on fact brought a glare of publicity that ensured a box-office buzz. As with *Apocalypse Now* (1979), audiences were prepared to wait through the slow segments because they knew exciting, savage moments were coming. Cimino, like Coppola, certainly delivers the goods, successfully bringing together the often bizarre and grandiose elements of his film. De Niro turns in one of his most memorable performances, a crazed-seeming Christopher Walken won an Oscar, while there's more quality acting from John Cazale, John Savage and, in an early role, Oscar-nominated Meryl Streep. The film also won Best Picture Oscar and Cimino Best Director. It all adds up to one of Hollywood's biggest commercial and critical successes.
WAR

1979

Alien

117 min.
Director: *Ridley Scott*
Origin: *GB*
Distributor: *20th Century-Fox*
Cast: *Veronica Cartwright, Ian Holm, John Hurt, Yaphet Kotto, Tom Skerritt, Harry Dean Stanton, Sigourney Weaver*

An unstoppable predator terrorizes a space ship's crew in British director Ridley Scott's chilling modern sci-fi classic *Alien*. In this big-budget version of a 1950s monster-from-space movie, paying homage to a well-established genre, Scott provides a relentless rollercoaster of scares with outstanding photography and Oscar-winning visual effects. Dan O'Bannon's script has similarities to the 1958 B movie *It! The Terror from Beyond Space*, though the plot also has parallels with Agatha Christie's *And Then There Were None*. In keeping with its tradition, the accent is entirely on chills and thrills with no attempt at in-depth individual character development, though the acting is charismatic enough to forge strong and sympathetic archetypes from what, in less capable hands, might only have been stereotypes. Returning to earth from a routine voyage, the slumbering crew of the spacecraft *Nostromo* are woken to investigate distress signals from a nearby planet and discover a repository of mysterious eggs. Crew member John Hurt is suddenly attacked by one of the pods and the crew return him to the ship, not knowing that he has been impregnated with a lethal alien. Tom Skerritt and Harry Dean Stanton lend their usual strong support as the canny captain and the complaining engineer, and Hurt provides the film's most memorable shock when the Thing bursts out of his stomach, but it's Sigourney Weaver's movie. Her spunky first officer Ripley created a new kind of Hollywood action-heroine. A seminal piece of sci-fi design – the visuals sprang from the darkly fascinating visions of the artist H. R. Giger – this film changed the look of the whole genre.

Science fiction / Horror

Apocalypse Now

153 min.
Director: *Francis Ford Coppola*
Origin: *USA*
Distributor: *Omni Zoetrope*
Cast: *Sam Bottoms, Marlon Brando, Robert Duvall, Laurence Fishburne, Harrison Ford, Frederic Forrest, Dennis Hopper, Martin Sheen*

Francis Coppola's epic phantasmagoria drops Conrad's 1899 novel *Heart of Darkness* into the teeming midst of the Vietnam War. It was a project that was to consume its creator throughout the latter half of the 1970s. With a

mushrooming budget, location worries, one star (Marlon Brando) awkward and the other (Martin Sheen) given the last rites after a near-fatal heart attack, *Apocalypse Now* must have looked a doomed folly to all those who worked on it. Instead, in hindsight, this sprawling, visionary fable ranks among the world's most powerful films; a savagely staged voyage through an American dream turned alien, eastern nightmare. *Apocalypse Now* follows army assassin Willard (Sheen) on his mission upriver to "terminate" the command of renegade colonel Kurtz (Brando). Once the darling of the US military, Kurtz has turned "unsound", gone native among the jungle tribesfolk of Cambodia. Given its troubled history, it's amazing that the ingredients in *Apocalypse Now* come together so well. Cinematographer Vittorio Storaro gives the film a lush, otherworldly hue, Coppola directs with unparalleled sweep and spectacle, while the players perform with elan – Sheen all unplugged, residual emotions and Robert Duvall full of steely energy as the demagogic Lt-Col Kilgore. At *Apocalypse Now*'s own heart of darkness sits Brando; shaven-headed and monstrous, emerging from the shadows to whisper unholy words of wisdom. The results are astonishing, pushing *Apocalypse Now* to the summit of film achievement. A mammoth, undiluted, horribly illuminating look at the corrosive effect of war.

War

Mad Max

102 min.
Director: *George Miller*
Origin: *Australia*
Distributor: *Warner*
Cast: *Steve Bisley, Mel Gibson, Hugh Keays-Byrne, Bryce Spence*

Mel Gibson, fetchingly dressed up to the eyeballs in leather accoutrements, heads for stardom in George Miller's smart post-apoca-

A slice of genius: *Woody Allen and Mariel Hemingway in* Manhattan

lypse sci-fi thriller, a thinking person's actioner, driven by a sheer joy in the techniques of the cinema that betrays the director's film-school training and film-buff leanings. Gibson cuts an impressively stoic figure as the damaged hero, an ex-cop called Max Rockatansky, bent on avenging the murder of his wife and child by a gang of psychotic bikers who are terrorizing the countryside. But never mind the plot, it's the style, pace, energy, stunts and grubby leather-punk chic that count. *Mad Max* is a continuous onslaught of violence and machismo in the post-Armageddon desert setting common to a whole range of cheaply made exploiter movies, though most of these have been American, and many of them made by American International Pictures and Roger Corman's New World Pictures. Certainly this Australian film tackles the American cheapie head-on and comes out ahead of most of them. But as an Aussie-speaking film, it was thought to be too hot to handle in America, so the Australian voices were re-dubbed into American. The film flopped in America (though it was a cult hit in Britain) only to be rediscovered when *Mad Max 2: the Road Warrior* (1981) was a hit. It spawned a further sequel, *Mad Max Beyond Thunderdome* (1985) with Tina Turner as Aunty Entity but, more significantly, kick-started a whole sub-genre of dusty road-movie sci-fi.

Science fiction thriller

Manhattan

96 min.
Director: *Woody Allen*
Origin: *USA*
Distributor: *United Artists*
Cast: *Woody Allen, Annie Byrne, Mariel Hemingway, Diane Keaton, Michael Murphy, Meryl Streep*

Woody Allen's glorious black-and-white tribute to his favourite city is arguably his masterwork to date. As usual the story motors on his character's difficult relationships with the women in his life – Diane Keaton, Meryl Streep, and the breathtaking young Mariel Hemingway. Allen gives a great performance as a TV comedy writer, Isaac Davis, who is undergoing a mid-life crisis, ill at ease with himself, his past, his life, his age, his career and his talent, as well as being neurotically unsure about his girlfriend Tracy, beautifully played by the 17-year-old Hemingway, who was Oscar-nominated as Best Supporting Actress. Their age difference becomes a barrier between them as does the arrival of the more worldly Diane Keaton, with whom he also takes up, and to cap it all, Streep, his lesbian former wife, is about to publish an exposé of their marriage. All in all, it's a vintage slice of Allen's comic talent while at the same time there's an abundance of wit and wisdom in the bitter-sweet, partly autobiographical script. It's also an experience in sound and vision: Allen imbues most of his films with a formal beauty, but this is

perhaps his most mesmerizing. There's spectacular monochrome photography on the big Panavision screen (which cries out to be seen in a movie theatre where it looks ravishing) by his regular cameraman Gordon Willis and gorgeous George Gershwin tunes, especially "Rhapsody in Blue", which is accompanied by the most marvellous tour of Manhattan imaginable.
BITTERSWEET COMEDY

1980

Heaven's Gate

219 min.
Director: *Michael Cimino*
Origin: *USA*
Distributor: *United Artists*
Cast: *Jeff Bridges, Joseph Cotten, Brad Dourif, Isabelle Huppert, John Hurt, Kris Kristofferson, Mickey Rourke, Christopher Walken, Sam Waterston*

The movie that bankrupted a studio and whose title became a euphemism for grand follies everywhere, H*eaven's Gate* also sounded the death knell of the western for almost a decade. Its disastrous background is more compelling than the movie itself, and is chronicled in detail in Steven Bach's book, *Final Cut*, written by the then Head of Production after he was fired and what remained of United Artists sold off. The film concerns the Johnson County War of 1892, when cattle barons hired mercenaries to wipe out immigrant settlers in Wyoming, and has been described as the first socialist western. Kris Kristofferson is the marshal trying to uphold order, Christopher Walken a hired gunman, and Isabelle Huppert the prostitute they both share. The title refers to Christ's biblical comment that all but the rich can pass through heaven's gate. It is beautifully shot

but eschews plot in favour of spectacle, including the memorable Harvard Ball (shot at Oxford University, England), the roller-skating celebration and final massacre. Cimino was given enough rope to hang himself and his executives by UA, and the excesses are legendary. His building of towns, and trains, and his search for authenticity through elaborate costumes (even for the 2,500 extras used) racked up a budget of over £35 million. His five-hour version was cut back to three and a half hours, then to two and a half, with little box-office improvement and, despite his explanation that his rush to finish had "clouded my perception of the film", he had to wait five years before being given the opportunity to direct again.
WESTERN

Raging Bull

129 min.
Director: *Martin Scorsese*
Origin: *USA*
Distributor: *United Artists*
Cast: *Nicholas Colasanto, Robert De Niro, Cathy Moriarty, Joe Pesci, Theresa Saldana, Frank Vincent*

Often cited as the finest film of the 1980s, *Raging Bull* is a ferocious feat of writing, acting and direct-

ing – a nimble, razor-sharp biopic that fires penetrating blows into the tortured psyche of its subject – post-war middleweight champ Jake LaMotta (Robert De Niro). Shot in gleaming black-and-white by Martin Scorsese, the picture glides smoothly between LaMotta's time as a lean young scrapper and his later retirement years as a corpulent, washed-up lounge-lizard. Despite its factual base and pungent period atmosphere, this is a Greek-style tragedy of epic proportions. A figure of frustrated, inarticulate energies, LaMotta is eventually laid low by the same values that make him a star, battling against brother Joey (brilliant Joe Pesci) and brutally asserting his shaky machismo against his cold-blooded bride (Cathy Moriarty). Seldom was a Best Actor Oscar more deserved than that awarded to De Niro for providing a gripping interpretation of a character by turns terrifying and pitiable and ballooning 50lbs to play the later sequences. It's a performance that effortlessly holds the viewer transfixed, though Scorsese punctuates these harsh character X-rays with a series of firecracker, fantastically wrought boxing segments (winning another Oscar for editor Thelma

Schoonmaker) and a dreamlike home-movie interlude, eased along by a lilting orchestral score. The result is possibly Scorsese's most intense and self-contained picture, an unrelenting, incandescent feast for the senses. As mumbling LaMotta so aptly puts it – arms outstretched, cigar smouldering – "That's entertainment."
BOXING MELODRAMA

1981

Chariots of Fire

123 min.
Director: *Hugh Hudson*
Origin: *GB*
Distributor: *20th Century-Fox/ Allied Stars/Enigma*
Cast: *Lindsay Anderson, Cheryl Campbell, Ian Charleson, Ben Cross, Brad Davis, Nigel Davenport, Nicholas Farrell, Daniel Gerroll, John Gielgud, Nigel Havers, Ian Holm, Alice Krige, Patrick Magee*

Historically notable for appearing to mark the comeback of the British film to Hollywood, *Chariots of Fire* won a Best Picture Oscar for producer David Puttnam and another for Colin Welland's screenplay. At the awards ceremony, Welland gave voice to his famous jingoistic sentiment that "the British are coming!" The film tells the true story of two contenders in the 1924 Olympics in Paris: devout Scottish Christian Eric Liddell (Ian Charleson), who runs for the glory of his God, and Jewish Cambridge student Harold Abrahams (Ben Cross), who seeks acceptance in an anti-Semitic society. It is tempting to knock the film for its unfashionable patriotism and *Boys' Own*-style moral values, but in the context of its detailed re-creation of a period and its attitudes it succeeds in creating an inspirational feeling, as in the now

Raging Bull: De Niro delivers a knockout turn

oft-parodied lyrical slow-motion sequence of the runners in the surf to the accompaniment of the stirring Vangelis theme. It also manages to make an athletics story appealing in human terms to those who normally loathe sports movies. Apart from the leads, it boasts a fine collection of quality supporting performances and it would be difficult for even the most cynical not to be rooting for Liddell to win in the film's climactic race. In real life, Liddell went on to become a missionary in China and died in a Japanese prisoner-of-war camp, while Abrahams achieved his social ambition, becoming a knighted and venerated elder statesman.
BIOGRAPHY/ATHLETICS DRAMA

An American Werewolf in London

97 min.
Director: *John Landis*
Origin: *USA*
Distributor: *PolyGram/Universal*
Cast: *Jenny Agutter, Griffin Dunne, Brian Glover, Lila Kaye, Rik Mayall, David Naughton, Frank Oz, John Woodvine*

"From the director of *Animal House*, a different kind of animal" ran the advertising slogan for John Landis's film. He'd also directed *Kentucky Fried Movie* (1977) and *The Blues Brothers* (1980) so audiences were probably expecting a horror spoof. Instead they got a modern-day

Howling success:
David Naughton has a hair-raising experience

werewolf chiller – laced with lots of larky humour, it's true, but people should have paid heed to the film's other slogan – "a masterpiece of terror". What's best about the movie is the way Landis is able to craft an old-fashioned horror movie for modern audiences, with humour and state-of-the-art special effects at the service of a scary story. The deceptively jokey start finds two American tourists hiking in the north of England, visiting The Slaughtered Lamb pub, where local yokels Brian Glover, Lila Kaye and even British comic Rik Mayall send up the usual "don't mention the moors" scene. But then the serious horror starts, and when the action moves to London, the terror is made to seem real by its appearance in everyday settings like London Zoo and the Tube. Little-known David Naughton and Griffin Dunne give particularly convincing, naturalistic performances as the tourists, so it's sad they haven't had better acting careers. A major factor in the film's success is Rick Baker's incredible make-up effects for which he won an Oscar. The gruesome transformations from man into werewolf, ushered along

by rousingly appropriate vintage pop songs like "Bad Moon Rising" and "Blue Moon", are nothing short of brilliant and deeply satisfying for all horror buffs.
HORROR

Raiders of the Lost Ark

115 min.
Director: *Steven Spielberg*
Origin: *USA*
Distributor: *Paramount*
Cast: *Karen Allen, Denholm Elliott, Harrison Ford, Paul Freeman, Wolf Kahler, Ronald Lacey, Alfred Molina, John Rhys-Davies*

The comic-book fiction of the 1930s is whipped into dazzling cinematic life by Hollywood wonderkid Steven Spielberg, bouncing back brilliantly after a fumbled stab at comedy in *1941* (1979). *Raiders of the Lost Ark* is entertainment in its purest, most exhilarating form, leading a rollercoaster dash through a yarn spilling over with hidden tunnels, speeding jeeps, leering cartoon Nazis and long-lost magical artefacts. Our intrepid hero is Indiana Jones (Harrison Ford), a soft-spoken, bullwhip-wielding archaeologist, jetting off in search of the Biblical Ark of the Covenant with the help of hard-drinking love interest Madeleine (Karen Allen in a role originally offered to Debra Winger). But, in true storybook fashion, the route to success is littered with danger and Indy, who seems to think little of hanging off submarines or battling crazed swordsmen, must at some

point confront his own overpowering fear of snakes. A mammoth box-office smash that spawned two successful sequels, *Raiders of the Lost Ark* arrived like a breath of fresh air, filling an adventure niche between the flagging James Bond movies and the more adult action-outings of Clint Eastwood and Charles Bronson. Despite a ghoulish horror-movie ending, here was a matinée-style yarn for all ages, simple and uncomplicated yet possessed of enough wry wit and intelligence to hold more fussy adults entranced. For Ford, the movie put the seal on his superstar reputation. "I had no expectation of the level of adulation that would come my way", he later remarked. "I just wanted to make a living with a regular role in a television series".
FANTASY ADVENTURE

1982

Blade Runner

118 min.
Director: *Ridley Scott*
Origin: *USA*
Distributor: *Warner*
Cast: *Harrison Ford, Daryl Hannah, Rutger Hauer, Edward James Olmos, M. Emmet Walsh, Sean Young*

A design classic and one of the best sci-fi films ever made, *Blade Runner* is set in the corporate world of year 2020, when police discover that four lethal androids, known as replicants, have escaped from a space colony to disrupt the humans on earth. Harrison Ford plays Rick Deckard, an embittered ex-cop and expert in distinguishing humans from replicants, who is reluctantly persuaded to accept the task of tracking down and destroying ("retiring") them. The plot, taken from Phillip K Dick's *Do Androids Dream of Electric Sheep?*, is presented in the *film noir* style of the 1940s, featuring a man

Café society: Baltimore boys (left to right) *Kevin Bacon, Mickey Rourke, Daniel Stern and Timothy Daly*

alone in a dark, lonely world beset by evils beyond his control. The cast is impeccable: Sean Young is glacially beautiful as the perfect android who doesn't know she isn't human, Daryl Hannah and Rutger Hauer are hugely impressive as two of the rebel killing machines dreaming of a better life, while Ford is enigmatic, disaffected and certainly doomed. *Blade Runner* had a distinctly chilly reception on its initial release but it established a growing cult reputation throughout the 1980s, and when it was re-presented in the director's cut in 1992, both critics and public hailed it as a genre landmark. The differences between the versions are subtle but considerable, and the later edit has an entirely different atmosphere since Scott ditches Ford's voiceover, adds a new score and a darker, more satisfying, ending.
Science fiction

Diner

110 min.
Director: *Barry Levinson*
Origin: *USA*
Distributor: *MGM*
Cast: *Kevin Bacon, Ellen Barkin, Timothy Daly, Steve Guttenberg, Paul Reiser, Mickey Rourke, Daniel Stern, Michael Tucker*

Five Baltimore youths spend the last days of 1959 thrashing out problems with girls, money and

their future in this quintessential American 1980s coming-of-age tale. Calling-card playing from rising young stars like Mickey Rourke and Ellen Barkin combines with the sharp wit of debut director Barry Levinson to produce a piping-hot concoction, seasoned with honesty and charm. For the five young men (Rourke, Steve Guttenberg, Daniel Stern, Timothy Daly, Kevin Bacon) the local diner is their world – a place to laugh, cry, reminisce and make plans. This is their golden week as they celebrate Christmas and face up to adulthood, which means saying goodbye both to the innocent 1950s and to their traditional meeting place. The plot is easily recognizable as a reworking of the familiar, particularly American rites-of-passage theme previously seen to advantage in *The Last Picture Show* (1971), where the movie house rather than the diner served as the symbol of lost innocence. But *Diner* offers a more personal vision than Peter Bogdanovich's, since the director draws poignantly on his own life story for the glowing nostalgic tale. Levinson's fresh and tasty handling ensured his establishment as a thinking person's *auteur*, a reputation he confirmed when he reworked further chapters of his autobiography into two more Baltimore tales – *Tin Men* (1987) and *Avalon* (1990). It was a rare

feat for a mainstream Hollywood director to come up with a such body of personal work in the more impersonal climate of American movie-making in the 1980s. And *Diner* offers plenty of food for thought.
Coming-of-age / Autobiography

E.T. – The Extra-Terrestrial

115 min.
Director: *Steven Spielberg*
Origin: *USA*
Distributor: *Universal*
Cast: *Drew Barrymore, Peter Coyote, Sean Frye, C. Thomas Howell, Robert MacNaughton, K. C. Martel, Henry Thomas, Dee Wallace*

Spielberg's magical contemporary fairytale *E.T.* became not only the highest-grossing film of all time (now second behind the same director's *Jurassic Park*), but an unparalleled cultural phenomenon, lifting commercial hype to new heights and establishing its crinkly, wide-eyed hero as *the* popular icon of 1980s America. Some critics have scoffed, deriding the film's thin plot-line, one-dimensional characters and lack of intellectual substance, yet it remains a brilliant story brilliantly told, playing, like much of Spielberg's work, upon an elemental human need for wonder, mystery and something beyond the humdrum of daily existence. The Extra-Terrestrial in question, having been inadvertently left on Earth by his companions, is befriended by 10- year-old loner Elliott (Henry Thomas) who, along with sister Gertie (Drew Barrymore) and elder brother Michael (Robert MacNaughton), aids him in his attempts to "phone home". Cue plenty of laughs, tears and a dramatic chase climax as the kids on their bikes outwit the cops and get the alien to a pre-arranged rendezvous with his fellow travellers. Buoyed-up by Oscar-winning music and special effects, and Carlo Rimbaldi's wonderfully life-like alien, this is an endearing, per-

fectly paced science-fiction fable. It's more than possible to see the whole thing as a take on the Gospels – benevolent superior being visits Earth, dies, resurrects and passes once more into the heavens – but such intellectualization is really not necessary. The film stands up perfectly as a simple story masterfully told, appealing to audiences everywhere.
Science fiction

Fanny and Alexander

Fanny och Alexander   197 min.
Director: *Ingmar Bergman*
Origin: *Sweden*
Distributor: *AB Cinematograph*
Cast: *Allan Edwall, Ewa Fröling, Bertil Guve, Erland Josephson, Jan Malmsjö, Gunn Wallgren*

Ingmar Bergman's glorious fairytale of childhood proved the culmination of his decades of self-exploration through cinema – since its release he has never directed another movie. Perhaps there was nothing more to say. At the heart of *Fanny and Alexander* is a beautiful completeness, a perfect merging of modern film techniques with the age-old traditions of the folk-tale, the theatre and a fog of unfathomable mysteries and superstitions. Bergman turns a child's-eye gaze on a magical festive landscape where candles burn at Christmas, statues come to life and the ghosts of the departed mingle freely with the living. Glowing with autobiographical details, the picture zooms in on 10-year-old Alexander (Bertil Guve), spirited from his lush, life-embracing family home when his widowed mother weds the icy Bishop Vergerus (brilliant Jan Malmsjö). Once in the Bishop's cold, forbidding lair, the film narrows its focus further to spotlight the clash between the child's over-active, rebellious imagination and his nemesis's ironclad dogma, a conflict Alexander resolves in a final fiery climax when an androgynous,

247

locked-away lunatic shows the boy "the swift way evil thoughts can go". Evocatively set in 1900s Sweden, *Fanny and Alexander* is a majestic *tour de force*, a magical celebration of the unquenchable power of art and the imagination. Bergman originally filmed the picture for Swedish television in an extended cut running an overpowering 300 minutes, though either version blazes with more ideas than most other films can hold a torch to.
FAMILY SAGA

Gandhi

188 min.
Director: *Richard Attenborough*
Origin: *GB/USA/India*
Distributor: *Columbia*
Cast: *Candice Bergen, Ian Charleson, Edward Fox, John Gielgud, Trevor Howard, Saeed Jaffrey, Ben Kingsley, John Mills, Roshan Seth, Martin Sheen*

Richard Attenborough started to plan a biopic of Gandhi back in the 1960s, before he made his directing debut with *Oh! What a Lovely War* (1969), when he first read Louis Fischer's book on the Indian leader. It's therefore as much a testimony to Attenborough's doggedness as to its subject's unstinting loyalty to his beliefs. The director clearly identifies with the Mahatma's battle against seemingly insurmountable hurdles. *Gandhi* is an old-style epic, made expensively and on a vast canvas, with a cast of British Equity's finest – Edward Fox as General Dyer, John Gielgud as Lord Irwin, Trevor Howard as Judge Broomfield and John Mills as the Viceroy – plus up to 350,000 extras for the breathtaking Delhi funeral sequence. But it's also a sharply focused, microscopic view of one individual from youth as a lawyer in South Africa to old age as India gains its independence from Britain in 1947, propelled along by the Oscar-winning performance of Ben Kingsley in a delicate, magnetic turn which shot him to the front rank after years of British the-

atre and TV work. This eight-Oscar-winner – the most a British film has enjoyed – was attacked, especially at home, for being middle-of-the-road, for fudging Indian religious divisions and for painting the actions of the British in India in too black a light. But it's a thoughtful, intelligent film that addresses notions of faith and hope, and discusses religion and politics in an era when films shun both as box-office poison. In doing so it wooed and wowed an older generation of filmgoers who are usually conspicuous by their absence from movie theatres.
BIOGRAPHICAL EPIC

Tootsie

116 min.
Director: *Sydney Pollack*
Origin: *USA*
Distributor: *Columbia*
Cast: *Dabney Coleman, Geena Davis, Charles Durining, Teri Garr, Dustin Hoffman, Jessica Lange, Bill Murray*

This glorious drag comedy – the best since *Some Like It Hot* – motors on a hilarious, penetrating story about a desperate New York actor (Dustin Hoffman) finding fame, riches and terrible trouble as a female soap opera star. He gets dragged up when, despondent at not being offered work, he discovers that he can land a part on a daytime soap as a woman. The vibrant, serious-minded screenplay, written

Life's a drag: *Dustin Hoffman*

by Larry (*M*A*S*H*) Gelbart and Murray Schisgal, always keeps in focus the underlying issues about sexual politics, feminism and men and women's role-playing ("You have to have a reason why you're doing drag, rather than just have a campy good time", says Gelbart). Happily the script gets the performances it deserves from Oscar-winning Jessica Lange, Teri Garr, Bill Murray and Geena Davis. Sydney Pollack directs with infectious enthusiasm, and also appears in a funny cameo as Hoffman's long-suffering agent. Gelbart says: "*Tootsie* taught me never to work with an actor who's shorter than his Oscar", for the small but perfectly formed Hoffman is almost as famous for striving for perfection as for his acting. They spent a year of almost daily sessions on the script. For Hoffman it was an extension of his *Kramer vs. Kramer* role, only this time he wanted to go the whole way as a man *and* a woman. Their theme is that you're a different man since you've become a woman. It's this serious intent, coupled with Hoffman's unstinting efforts to inhabit a female personality, that underpins the good humour of this dazzling Hollywood comedy.
COMEDY

1983

Rumble Fish

94 min.
Director: *Francis Ford Coppola*
Origin: *USA*
Distributor: *Zoetrope/Universal*
Cast: *Nicolas Cage, Matt Dillon, Dennis Hopper, Diane Lane, Mickey Rourke, Diana Scarwid, Vincent Spano*

After the box-office disaster of *One from the Heart*, Francis Coppola turned his hand to what at first looked a far smaller, less overtly ambitious canvas – two low-budget adaptations of Susie Hinton's pulpy youth novels *The*

Salieri: *Oscar-winning F. Murray Abraham*

Outsiders and *Rumble Fish*. Except that *Rumble Fish*, in its way, is hugely ambitious – a daring filmmaking exercise that owes a major debt to the European art pic. Its deceptively simple tale of mismatched brothers in Smalltown USA is garnished with a flamboyant bag of movie tricks – giddy camera angles, expressionist monochrome imagery and self-consciously poetic, non-naturalistic dialogue. Matt Dillon shot to fame as Rusty James, the half-bright teenager eager to fill the gap left by his legendary hoodlum brother (Mickey Rourke). But Rourke's Motorcycle Boy is a hard act to follow. He's "royalty in exile", a super-charismatic streetgang messiah, old before his time and utterly damned. "Even the most primitive society," lisps Rourke, "has an innate respect for the insane." While *Rumble Fish* is Rusty James's story, detailing his harsh transition to manhood, Coppola stylistically presents the film through the Motorcycle Boy's distorted, colour-blind gaze. But *Rumble Fish* is never art for art's sake. Its claustrophobic style serves a purpose, capturing the inarticulate frustrations of jaded teens trapped in a goldfish bowl where there's no room to grow or develop. Hypnotic, elusive, weirdly illuminating, *Rumble Fish* is Coppola's own favourite work and arguably his last truly great movie.
COMING-OF-AGE

1984

Amadeus

158 min.
Director: *Milos Forman*
Origin: *USA*
Distributor: *Orion/EMI*
Cast: *F. Murray Abraham, Kenny L. Baker, Elizabeth Berridge, Simon Callow, Roy Dotrice, Christine Ebersole, Tom Hulce, Jeffrey Jones, Cynthia Nixon*

Milos Forman's visually stunning screen adaptation of Peter Shaffer's award-winning play won eight Oscars: for Best Picture, Director, Actor, Adapted Screenplay, Art Direction, Sound, Costumes, and Make-up. Oddly, given *Amadeus*'s great visual beauty, Miroslav Ondricek missed out on the cinematography award. Tom Hulce was Academy Award-nominated as the brattish, foul-mouthed Wolfgang Amadeus Mozart, but he was pipped at the post for Best Actor Oscar by little-known F Murray Abraham as 1780s court composer Antonio Salieri, the most renowned musician in Vienna and a favourite of Emperor Joseph ll (a peach of a serious performance from comedic actor Jeffrey Jones). Suddenly there's a threat from an upstart called Mozart, and Salieri is obsessed by his genius while being simultaneously disgusted by his personality. Desperate for revenge on God for making him a mediocrity and bestowing such talent on the wastrel Mozart, Salieri vows to destroy the young composer and hatches the dark plot that will bring about his downfall. Forman casts Simon Callow, who originated the role of Mozart on the London stage, in a consolation prize role as the impresario Emanuel Schikaneder, a tasty snack of a part that Callow turns into a four-course meal, but the film's real *tour de force* comes from Abraham playing Salieri, in flash-back, as a man in his prime and, narrating the story, as an old and withered madman, in a highly detailed and deeply charismatic performance of pyrotechnic brilliance. Add to that a dramatically used musical score which includes some of the best music ever written and what you have is a jewel of modern popular cinema.
COSTUME DRAMA

Heimat

HOMELAND 924 min.
Director: *Edgar Reitz*
Origin: *West Germany*
Distributor: *Reitz/WDR/SFB*
Cast: *Marita Breuer, Peter Harting, Michael Lesch, Johannes Lobewein, Karin Rasenack, Jorg Richter, Dieter Schaad, Rüdiger Weigang*

This epic, 11-part, made-for-television serial, which portrays the history of Germany from 1919 to 1982, won such plaudits when shown at film festivals that it was then given a cinema release, being shown in four parts. Set in a fictional village in the Hunsrück area, where Edgar Reitz was born and brought up, *Heimat* tells its story through the experiences of one family, particularly Maria, born in 1900, and the film's still central point from beginning to end, around which the characters and events revolve. Humane, comic and tragic, it deals with the detail of daily life for ordinary people, which provides the background against which nations and politicians play out their dramas. In the early episodes Reitz uses occasional flashes of colour for emphasis in what is otherwise black-and-white photography, moving into full colour from the early 1950s. It is frequently effective, as in the sequence of the village fete held to celebrate the first year of Hitler's chancellorship: black-and-white except for the chillingly telling red of the swastika banners. The technique was revived to great effect by Spielberg in *Schindler's List* (1993) with the flash of the child's pink coat in an otherwise black-and-white film. The project began with Reitz's desire to rediscover his background by writing down stories of his family and their fellow villagers. Originally planned as a novel, producer Joachim von Mengershausen persuaded Reitz to film it. The whole process from conception to final cut took over five years.
EPIC SAGA

The Terminator

108 min.
Director: *James Cameron*
Origin: *USA*
Distributor: *Hemdale/Orion*
Cast: *Michael Biehn, Linda Hamilton, Lance Henriksen, Dick Miller, Bill Paxton, Rick Rossovich, Arnold Schwarzenegger, Paul Winfield*

Arnold Schwarzenegger finds the role he was born for as a cyborg (part man, part machine) despatched from the 21st century to 1984 Los Angeles to terminate apparently innocuous Linda Hamilton, whose child has a key role to play in the future. But Arnie has to contend with rebel soldier Michael Biehn who's hot on his trail. This was just what 1980s audiences were waiting for: a fast-paced, violent and continuously exciting low-budget sci-fi actioner in which the thrills come non-stop, while the dark high-tech look of the production provides an overlay of quality, adding the most stylish gloss. Basically *The Terminator* is just a 1950s B-movie updated to the 1980s with a high profile through the sheer guts of director James Cameron's nail-biting handling and Arnie's dynamic turn: he proves himself here, and so he has remained, the best and most popular of all the musclemen/gymnasts who have tried their hand at acting. This trailblazer spawned seeming thousands of lesser imitators, and it's tighter and faster than the more grandiose, hugely expensive sequel *Terminator 2: Judgment Day* (1991), which reunited Arnie, Hamilton and Cameron. Part of the first film's real charm is its effective use of the low-budget circumstances – it's powered on invention and imagination rather than merely breathtaking special effects. *The Terminator* is a mighty mouse that roars (on a $6.5 million budget), whereas the second film was a make-or-break blockbuster for its studio Carolco, costing $100 million.
SCIENCE FICTION/ACTION

1985

A Room with a View

115 min.
Director: *James Ivory*
Origin: *GB*
Distributor: *Merchant Ivory*
Cast: *Helena Bonham-Carter, Simon Callow, Daniel Day-Lewis, Judi Dench, Denholm Elliott, Rupert Graves, Rosemary Leach, Julian Sands, Maggie Smith*

It is a curious irony that the finest screen exponents of the manners and sensibilities of Edwardian England should be, respectively, an American director (James Ivory) and an Indian producer (Ismail Merchant) and scriptwriter (Ruth Prawer Jhabvala). Such, however, is the case, and nowhere is their artistry more in evidence than in this delicate tale of a young English girl's sexual and spiritual awakening. Set in 1907 and based, like much of the Merchant/Ivory/Jhabvala team's recent work, on an E.M. Forster novel, *A Room with a View* stars a doll-like Helena Bonham-Carter as repressed debutante Lucy Honeychurch, taken by her meddling aunt Charlotte (Maggie Smith) on a horizon-broadening trip to Florence. There she meets dashing intellectual George Emerson (Julian Sands), renewing the acquaintance back in England and eventually jilting her priggish fiancé Cecil Vyse (Daniel

249

Day-Lewis) in order to marry him. Around this simple love story, Ivory has woven an intricate study of sexual and social mores, laying bare both the charm and hypocrisy of turn-of-the-century English society, and contrasting it with the warmth and simplicity of Mediterranean passions. It is a masterful study of individuals and society, superbly acted, lavishly filmed and hugely successful (especially in a heritage-obsessed America). Jhabvala won an Oscar for Best Adapted Screenplay (it also won in the Costume and Art Direction categories) and a trend was set for tasteful, intelligent English period films that has continued to the present day.
PERIOD ROMANCE

My Life as a Dog

MIT LIV SOM HUND   101 min.
Director: *Lasse Hallström*
Origin: *Sweden*
Distributor: *AB/Svensk Filmindustri*
Cast: *Ing-Marie Carlsson, Anton Glanzelius, Melinda Kinnaman, Anki Liden, Manfred Serner, Tomas von Brömssen*

Lasse Hallström's glowing rites-of-passage tale was a brilliant world-wide success, most notably in the US where it was a double Oscar nominee for Best Direction and Adapted Screenplay, and led to his continuing his career there. Based on Reidar Jonsson's autobiographical novel, it is the story of a 12-year-old boy, Ingemar Johannsson (Anton Glanzelius), who is shunted from town to country in 1950s Sweden, because his terminally ill mother can no longer cope with him, and who shares a name with the real-life Swedish boxer who beat Floyd Patterson for the World Championship in 1959, so providing a triumphantly original ending. Apart from the pugilist, Ingemar particularly identifies with Laika, the lonely dog catapulted into space in a Sputnik by the Soviets and left to die in orbit.

In times of stress Ingemar actually becomes a dog, getting down on his knees and barking. As a survival story this has real child-like integrity. Despite offering a fabulous world of jolly, footballing uncles (Tomas von Brömssen), sexy women anxious to befriend 12-year-olds, matey sporting tomgirls (Melinda Kinnaman), mad roofers and bed-ridden underwear fantasists, it is never so cutesy as to be syrupy. The film came eight years after Hallström's previous international success, *Abba – The Movie* (1977), and was released abroad after winning the Golden Beetle (the Swedish Oscar) for Best Film and Actor (Glanzelius).
RITES-OF-PASSAGE/COMIC DRAMA

1986

Mishima: a Life in Four Chapters

120 min.
Director: *Paul Schrader*
Origin: *USA*
Distributor: *Coppola-Lucas/ Warner*
Cast: *Yasosuke Bando, Toshiyuki Nagashima, Ken Ogata, Kanji Sawada*

Paul Schrader's startling and accomplished film *Mishima* profiles the controversial, prolific Japanese novelist and playwright Yukio Mishima, Tokyo-born author of *Confessions of a Mask, Forbidden Colours* and *The Sailor who Fell from Grace with the Sea*. Mishima,

obsessed with the ethics of traditional Japanese culture as embodied by the samurai, turned his art into action and his life into art by staging a demonstration at an army barracks in 1970 and committing public hara-kiri – ritual suicide – at the age of 45. Though Mishima is arguably Japan's best-known author, for most western cinemagoers Schrader's film is virtually a portrait of an alien, which is its very fascination. He is not afraid to conjure up an uncompromising film about an uncompromising character, tackling its subject as head-on as Mishima did his own concerns. Politically, and especially culturally, Mishima was a reaction-ary – he advocated the return to the most ascetic of Japanese values, even founding his own army – but aesthetically he was a purist, elevating the body to a temple to be worshipped. Schrader gives a clear portrait of his subject's homosexuality, a focus for his aestheticism and way of life. This uniquely successful American artwork is rare in the cinema as a serious attempt to get to the heart of an author's philosophy and essence as a writer, mixing straight biography, pure fantasy and stylized, visually sumptuous interpretations of Mishima's novels. Writers Paul and Leonard Schrader have created a psychological biopic by mixing action and poetry in a fascinating attempt to convey the flavour of an artist who was an extreme expression of an alien culture.
BIOGRAPHY

Top Gun

110 min.
Director: *Tony Scott*
Origin: *USA*
Distributor: *Paramount*
Cast: *Tom Cruise, Anthony Edwards, Val Kilmer, Kelly McGillis, Tim Robbins, Meg Ryan, Tom Skerritt*

Top Gun is a perfect example of the well turned out, slick Hollywood package, aimed at a youth audience, and one that provided its star, Tom Cruise, with an ideal vehicle which shot him to super-stardom as Pete "Maverick" Mitchell, the rebellious, unorthodox pilot accepted into the US navy pilot training programme reserved for the *crème de la crème*. As he battles to live up to his father's memory by becoming the top gun of the corps, he embarks on an affair with his female instructor, bewilderingly called Charlie (Kelly McGillis). The film provided early roles for Meg Ryan, Val Kilmer – as Ice Man, our hero's main rival – and Tim Robbins, though as usual the experienced Tom Skerritt shows his class as the tough flight instructor with a heart of gold. The theme music, Berlin's "Take My Breath Away", became a worldwide number one and gathered the Oscar for Best Song, the film's only award. Britain's Tony Scott, brother of Ridley, directs this prime example of jaw-clenching, gung-ho derring-do like a pop video, giving it all an immediate but phony feel, and the star and director reteamed for the faltering *Days of Thunder* (1990). The magisterial dogfights, captured in Jeffrey Kimball's thrilling aerial photography, are out-and-out the most impressive factor in the movie, though even these have a curiously fake appearance about them, perhaps because they so resemble computer-generated "virtual reality" games. Every now and again, it's startling to realize these war games are actually being staged

Soul of the samurai: Ken Ogata as Mishima

for real. Revealingly *Top Gun* was made with the full help of the US Navy – who were paid over one million dollars – which may go some way to explaining its resemblance to a two-hour recruitment advert. It's one of the last cold-war blockbusters in which Americans are seen blasting Russians with gay abandon, perhaps one of the reasons it appealed so much to the US Department of Defense.
ADVENTURE

Blue Velvet

120 min.
Director: *David Lynch*
Origin: *USA*
Distributor: *De Laurentiis*
Cast: *Laura Dern, Dennis Hopper, Hope Lange, Kyle MacLachlan, Isabella Rossellini, Dean Stockwell*

David Lynch's most provocative and disturbing masterwork so far is a bleak view of the small-town American ideal set in Lumberton USA, a pretty and peaceful place complete with white picket fences and neatly mown lawns. But just under the surface lies a heart of darkness, illustrated by the opening sequence when a neatly mown lawn yields a severed ear. The future *Twin Peaks* star Kyle MacLachlan plays an eager-beaver kind of a kid who falls through the looking glass smack into the underworld of the cinema's craziest mobsters, Dennis Hopper and Dean Stockwell. Laura Dern plays his innocent Girl Friday, and her dark mirror image is Isabella Rossellini as the abused gangster's moll and chanteuse. On the surface *Blue Velvet* operates as a conventional thriller holding true to the rules of the detective story, attending to the genre's traditional thrills, but Lynch is only really interested in the film's parallel existence as a parable of good versus evil and in breaking new boundaries by pushing a mainstream film in the direction of the surreal and psychologically

dangerous. Lynch alienated some audiences who felt he had gone too far and found the film intolerable in its portrayal of brutality towards women and the sheer force of its depiction of personal evil, particularly in the form of the Dennis Hopper character. Hopper, in one of his finest hours, manages to be truly demonic in interpreting a character that hints at self-parody without actually being parodic, a quality that gives him a palpable sense of danger that scorches off the screen.
SURREAL THRILLER

Hannah and Her Sisters

106 min.
Director: *Woody Allen*
Origin: *USA*
Distributor: *Orion*
Cast: *Woody Allen, Michael Caine, Mia Farrow, Carrie Fisher, Barbara Hershey, Maureen O'Sullivan, Max von Sydow, Dianne Wiest*

Woody Allen's move away from purely comic pictures bore glorious fruit with *Hannah and Her Sisters*, a stately, circular saga of family intrigue, played out over two years and structured about a series of Thanksgiving gatherings. Shooting lovingly against his familiar Manhattan backdrop, Allen weaves a spellbinding tale of three mismatched siblings – queenlike Hannah (Mia Farrow),

neurotic Holly (Dianne Wiest) and beautiful Lee (Barbara Hershey). Lee lives with Svengali painter Frederick (Max von Sydow) but is pursued by Hannah's husband Elliott (Oscar-winning Michael Caine), whose forbidden desire threatens to shatter the tranquil surface of this comfortable middle-class environment. Far from the bare-bones gag framework that distinguished Allen's formative efforts, here is a rich, multi-layered work reminiscent of the plays of Chekhov or the cinema of Ingmar Bergman. But *Hannah and Her Sisters* is not all sober, soul-searching drama. Bobbing like a jester throughout the narrative is Woody himself, on sparkling form as hypochondriac TV producer Mickey. Laid low with a suspected brain tumour and terrified of ending up "like the guy in the wool cap who delivers for the florist", Mickey is ultimately saved from despair by a Marx Brothers movie and goes on to experience that rarest of Woody outcomes – a happy ending. It's an affectionate tribute to the comic film pioneers, as well as a touching return compliment. "They say Woody Allen got something from the Marx Brothers," Groucho once commented, back in the 1970s. "He didn't. He's an original. The best. The funniest."
COMEDY

Jean de Florette and Manon des Sources

121 min. and 114 min.
Director: *Claude Berri*
Origin: *France*
Distributor: *Renn Productions*
Cast: *Daniel Auteuil, Gabriel Bacquier, Emmanuelle Béart, Elisabeth Depardieu, Gérard Depardieu, Hippolyte Girardot, Margarita Lozano, Yves Montand*

Rabbit shoot: *Daniel Auteuil and Gérard Depardieu*

Among the most costly, accomplished and universally popular of all French films, *Jean de Florette* and its sequel *Manon des Sources* provide an almost perfect fusion of script, scenery, performance and direction. Costing £11 million, and filmed together over a continuous period of nine months in Southern France, each film was based on one half of Marcel Pagnol's two-part novel *L'Eau des Collines*, an epic saga of greed and retribution in a small Provençal farming community. Gérard Depardieu stars as the eponymous Jean de Florette, a hunchbacked city dweller who moves to Provence with his family after inheriting a small farm. His attempts to start a new life as a farmer, however, are thwarted by self-serving local patriarch César Soubeyran (Yves Montand) who, with his nephew Ugolin (Daniel Auteuil), blocks up Jean's water supply in order to drive him out and buy up his property cheaply, a plot culminating in Jean's tragic death. The second film hops

Three sisters Woody Allen-style: (left to right) *Mia Farrow, Barbara Hershey and Dianne Wiest*

forward ten years, with Jean's daughter, Manon (Emmanuelle Béart), wreaking revenge on Soubeyran and the community that abandoned her father. Director Claude Berri takes us to the very heart of an insular rural society, minutely examining its prejudices, intricacies and loyalties. It is a compelling and brilliantly observed chronicle, supported by triumphant ensemble playing and Bruno Nuytten's dramatic photography. Perfect examples of modern French cinema at its very best, the films attained widespread international acclaim, with *Jean de Florette* winning British Film Academy awards for Best Film, Adapted Screenplay and Supporting Actor (Daniel Auteuil).
DRAMA

Mona Lisa

104 min.
Director: *Neil Jordan*
Origin: *GB*
Distributor: *Handmade*
Cast: *Joe Brown, Michael Caine, Robbie Coltrane, Kate Hardie, Bob Hoskins, Clarke Peters, Cathy Tyson*

Winner of the 1986 Palme d'Or at Cannes, Neil Jordan's taut, *noir*ish thriller provided an eccentric trawl through London's red-light underworld, introducing the themes of

London's underbelly: Bob Hoskins, Cathy Tyson

sexual alienation, fantasy-mongering and duplicity he was later to develop so effectively in *The Crying Game* (1992). It is the story of George (Bob Hoskins), a small-time gangster who, recently released from prison, finds work chauffeuring high-class prostitute Simone (Cathy Tyson). He falls for her, and agrees to help track down her heroin-addicted friend Kathy (Kate Hardie), only to discover that the two women are actually lovers. His fury and devastation are mirrored in the film's frenetic climax, with George abandoning Simone in a blood-spattered hotel room after she has gone berserk and shot gangland pimp Mortwell (Michael Caine). The film's strength lies less with its action sequences than its scorching analysis of romantic illusion. Jordan deftly explores the nature of desire and fantasy, comparing the attitude of a client towards the prostitute with that of George towards Simone, and showing both to be equally illusory. Some of the film's most powerful scenes take us into the nightmarish heart of London's red-light districts, providing images of hopelessness and decay which amply reflect Jordan's assertion that this is "an anti-erotic movie dealing with misplaced passions and emotional devastation." Powerfully scripted (by Jordan and David Leland) and uniformly well acted, it provides an uneasy mix of whimsy and drama, the overall impression being one of darkness, pessimism and abuse.
GANGLAND THRILLER

Platoon

120 min.
Director: *Oliver Stone*
Origin: *USA*
Distributor: *Hemdale*
Cast: *Tom Berenger, Willem Dafoe, Johnny Depp, Kevin Dillon, Richard Edson, John C. McGinley, Francesco Quinn, Charlie Sheen, Forest Whitaker*

Writer/director Oliver Stone was himself a veteran of the Vietnam

Oliver Stone: *The conscience of his generation*

War, and there is more than a hint of spiritual exorcism in this tough, hard-boiled tale of a rookie soldier (Charlie Sheen) struggling to survive in a rag-bag infantry platoon in late 1967. The first, and most effective, instalment in a trilogy exploring the Vietnam experience – *Born on the Fourth of July* (1989) and *Heaven and Earth* (1993) forming the other two parts – this was an uncompromising, no-holds-barred look at the dehumanizing effects of war. Wide-eyed Sheen provides the focus, stumbling from one horror to another and himself becoming brutalized in the process. His character is trapped between the twin extremes of the platoon's joint commanders – humane, drugged-out good guy Willem Dafoe, and vicious redneck bully Tom Berenger – and although he naturally gravitates

towards Dafoe, he is ultimately required to display the same animal savagery as Berenger in order to survive. Stone unflinchingly probes the dark side of America's Vietnam experience, weighing the courage and comradeship of American troops against scenes of rape, drug-taking and extreme brutality towards Vietnamese civilians. The result is an intensely powerful, multi-layered study of men at war less evocative, perhaps, than *Apocalypse Now* (1979), or Kubrick's *Full Metal Jacket* (1987), but tremendously disturbing and effective. Superbly photographed and faultlessly produced, it won four Oscars, including Best Film, Direction, Editing and Sound, following the Oscar gold for *The Deer Hunter* eight years before.
WAR

The Sacrifice

OFFRET   145 min.
Director: *Andrei Tarkovsky*
Origin: *Sweden*
Distributor: *Swedish Film Institute*
Cast: *Allan Edwall, Susan Fleetwood, Gundan Gisladottir, Erland Josephson, Valérie Mairesse, Sven Wolter*

Andrei Tarkovsky won the Special Jury Prize at the Cannes Film Festival in 1986 for this masterful 1980s art-house giant, mixing Russian and Swedish sensibilities for one of his best films. *The Sacrifice* opens with a long, unbroken sequence in which a little boy and his father plant and water a dead tree, an act of innocence and despair combined – a wish for a miracle. The film ends with an even longer, continuous long shot of a house consumed in flames. Tarkovsky is not afraid to do it his way in an age when Hollywood films in short takes and endless quick cuts. The man, a retired actor (Erland Josephson), lives with his alienated wife (Susan Fleetwood) in a far-off coastline house, with only his small son as a confidant. In the midst of their frustrated, meaningless lives the roar of a military aircraft bursts overhead and the vibrations topple a huge glass jar of pure white milk to shatter on the black wooden floor. On the eve of Armageddon, as the start of World War Three is announced on television, the actor offers up to God everything he owns to save the world. His wish is granted, he awakes from a sleep and all has been restored, but he must still make the sacrifice. When he burns down his house he is taken off in an ambulance. The little boy waters the tree, but now it has leaves. *The Sacrifice*, which proved Tarkovsky's last testament since he died the year after its release, is a visionary and deeply affecting parable on the nature of faith and the human condition.
MORALITY

A feast of film-making: *The guests savour* Babette's Feast

1987

Babette's Feast

BABETTES GAESTEBUD   102 min.
Director: *Gabriel Axel*
Origin: *Denmark*
Distributor: *Panorama*
Cast: *Bibi Andersson, Stéphane Audran, Bodil Kjer, Jarl Kulle, Jean-Philippe Lafont, Gudmar Wivesson*

The Oscar for Best Foreign Film went to Gabriel Axel's Danish movie that turns Isak (*Out of Africa*) Dinesen's simple fable into a perfect dish combining character study into human strengths and failings with a poignant tale of regret and reconciliation. This is a splendidly old-style film with all the virtues of classically trained acting and a formal European art-house film-making sensibility. Stéphane Audran plays to the manner born a French refugee befriended by two elderly Danish spinster sisters living an austere and Calvinistic existence in a Jutland coastal village and transforms their dry, barren and joyless lives through the 14 years she spends with them as their cook. Suddenly she wins 10,000 francs in the French lottery and spends it all on preparing the meal to end all meals, a revelatory experience which she bestows on the whole town. Initially reluctant, they are transformed by the experience and we finally learn that she was the Chef de Cuisine at the Café Anglais in Paris. The scenes of the preparation and the consumption of the feast are among the most mouth-watering in the movies, but even more delicious are the human aspects of the situation and, despite the austere setting, the story is a dish for the heart. Perhaps it's a surprising subject for a worldwide cinema hit, but then author Dinesen. looking for a popular story, wrote it as a result of a bet with a friend who correctly judged that the most direct route to the American psyche was through its stomach.
DRAMA

Fatal Attraction

119 min.
Director: *Adrian Lyne*
Origin: *USA*
Distributor: *Paramount*
Cast: *Anne Archer, Glenn Close, Michael Douglas, Ellen Foley, Fred Gwynne, Ellen Hamilton Latzen, J.J. Johnston, Meg Mundy Stuart Pankin*

A social phenomenon in terms of landmark movies, *Fatal Attraction* is a well crafted thriller which became a box-office smash by being in tune with the right-wing moral backlash of the times. It is the story of an extra-marital fling which turns into a nightmare for happily married, comfortably-off lawyer Michael Douglas, who indulges in a weekend of passion with career girl Alex (Glenn Close), while his wife (Anne Archer) is on holiday with the children. He comes unstuck when he gives Alex the brush-off, and she becomes psychotically obsessed with him, growing increasingly unhinged and progressing from nuisance phone calls to physical threats to his family. James Dearden's screenplay, expanded from his own UK short *The Diversion* (1979), is for much of its length a skilful psychological thriller based on the familiar and believable turning terrifyingly unpredictable. His original ending, in which Close commits suicide having first implicated Douglas as her murderer, was rejected after preview audiences called for something more overtly satisfying, resulting in the over-the-top, thrill-a-minute climax incorporating an inappropriately melodramatic lift from Clouzot's *Les Diaboliques* (1954) which considerably cheapens the story and reduces its believability. The film is usually viewed as a Hollywood-style warning against the perils and consequences of promiscuity and an implicit endorsement of family values, with Douglas seen as the foolish but wronged victim of a scheming madwoman. However his and Close's performances also support a contrapuntal point of view of Alex as the real victim of years of being used and discarded by a self-centred and self-obsessed series of chauvinist males. Incidentally, the original version was released as the "Director"s Cut" in 1992, no doubt to Adrian Lyne's considerable satisfaction.
THRILLER/ROMANCE

Wings of Desire

DER HIMMEL ÜBER BERLIN 130 min.
Director: *Wim Wenders*
Origin: *France/West Germany*
Distributor: *Road Movies/Argos/WDR*
Cast: *Curt Bois, Solveig Dommartin, Peter Falk, Bruno Ganz, Otto Sander*

Bruno Ganz: *Winging through Berlin*

A wistful and haunting fantasy about the walls between heaven and earth, fantasy and reality, past and present, *Wings of Desire* is set in a Berlin still divided by a physical wall, which at the time the film was made showed no sign of how soon it would be tumbling. It's not so much a story, more a visual, philosophical meditation. What narration there is deals with two compassionate angels (Bruno Ganz and Otto Sander), dressed in dark, civil service-style suits and sporting ponytail hairdos, who are visible only to children. Their heavenly assignment is to keep an observant eye on the desolate, divided, concrete city of Berlin, listening to the solitary thoughts of its people. Eventually they home in on three of them: an elderly poet (Curt Bois), haunted by memories of the Nazi devastation; an American actor (Peter Falk as him-

self) taking part in a film about that era; and a trapeze artist (Solveig Dommartin), who stirs in Ganz the desire to experience the physicality of the material world, at which point the film's muted black-and-white photography bursts into momentary colour. Shortly afterwards, Ganz checks in his wings, takes on the flesh and goes in search of his love in a now full-colour world. Hypnotically slow and dreamlike, apart from Falk, who brings a self-determining, American energy to the film in deliberate contrast to the melancholy European acceptance of a world which has lost joy and meaning, *Wings of Desire* enjoyed great box-office success for an art movie.

Ganz, Sander, Falk and Dommartin reprised their roles in the sequel, *Faraway So Close* (1993).
FANTASY

Raising Arizona

94 min.
Director: *Joel and Ethan Coen*
Origin: *USA*
Distributor: *Circle Films*
Cast: *Nicolas Cage, Randall "Tex" Cobb, William Forsythe, John Goodman, Holly Hunter, Frances, McDormand, Trey Wilson. M. Emmet Walsh*

Raising Arizona is so crammed with ideas you fear it might explode. Brothers Joel and Ethan Coen (the film's joint writers, producers and directors) have always been a wilfully wacky duo, occasionally undisciplined and sometimes too clever for their own good. But not here. *Raising Arizona* is simply exhilarating; a rollercoaster brainstorming session on the concept of the great American family that finds hamfisted crook "Hi" McDonough (Nicolas Cage) marrying spunky cop Edwina (splendid Holly Hunter) and setting up home in a nearby trailer-park. But broody Edwina is unable to conceive, prompting the pair to

kidnap one of the famed "Arizona quintuplets", the result of the costly fertility treatment administered to the wife of furniture tycoon Nathan Arizona (Trey Wilson). Cautioning the kidnappers to "Watch your butts", Arizona dispatches hell's-angel-of-vengeance Leonard Smalls (Randall "Tex" Cobb) in hot pursuit, setting off a dizzying dash of hectic chases, marauding hounds, convenience store crookery and apocalyptic roadside battles. As Edwina agitatedly observes during one particularly fraught moment: "This ain't family life!". *Raising Arizona*'s satire is exuberantly indiscriminate, poking uproarious fun at all that America holds most dear. The parodied culture it evokes is a world of fumbled aspirations and half-baked values, a land where babies can either be bought or stolen, just like the nappies you fit them into. But the Coens' approach proves more playful than critical with their surrealistic American fairyland rendered almost inviting by the spot-on performances and delirious, freewheeling joy in both writing and handling.
SCREWBALL BLACK COMEDY

Hamfisted crook: *Life's a drag for wannabe dad Nicolas Cage in* Raising Arizona

The Last Emperor

163 min.
Director: *Bernardo Bertolucci*
Origin: *Italy/Hong Kong/GB*
Distributor: *Columbia*
Cast: *Joan Chen, John Lone, Peter O'Toole, Ying Ruocheng, Victor Wong*

Bernardo Bertolucci's monumental biopic of Pu Yi (John Lone), the last ruler of China's Imperial Qing dynasty, provides an extraordinary insight both into one man's spiritual odyssey, and into the secret history of a modern superpower. Told in flashback, *The Last Emperor* is a story that would have been dismissed as ridiculous had it been thought up by Hollywood scriptwriters. Pu Yi is made emperor at the age of three; raised in Peking's Forbidden City; banished by warlords; appointed emperor of Manchuria by the Japanese; imprisoned by the Russians; then returned to China for a further 10 years of imprisonment and re-education before finally ending up as a humble gardener in Peking's Botanical Gardens. This is a remarkable history, and Bertolucci has worked it into a remarkable film, fusing visual extravagance with acute observation as he probes the issues of power, duty, change and self-discovery inherent in his protagonist's tale. Vittorio Storaro's Oscar-winning photography provides not merely a sumptuous *mise-en-scène*, but an essential corollary to Pu Yi's own experiences, with the monumental courtyards, walls, corridors and panoply of the Forbidden City reminding us of both the emperor's absolute power and his virtual imprisonment within his own destiny. Fine performances from a huge cast, especially Lone and Peter O'Toole as Pu Yi's English tutor, are occasionally overshadowed by the film's sheer visual enormity, but that cannot detract from its overall power. A massive contemporary success, it won a breathtaking nine Oscars, including Best Film,

Close encounters with the devil: *Gérard Depardieu and Sandrine Bonnaire*

Direction, Adapted Screenplay, Cinematography, Art Direction, Editing, Costume Design, Original Music and Sound.
HISTORICAL EPIC

Under Satan's Sun

SOUS LE SOLEIL DU SATAN
98 min.
Director: *Maurice Pialat*
Origin: *France*
Distributor: *Erato/Cannon*
Cast: *Alain Artur, Sandrine Bonnaire, Jean-Christophe Bouvet, Yann Dedet, Gérard Depardieu, Maurice Pialat*

Maurice Pialat's unsettling, often brilliant study of Catholicism turned sour was a controversial winner of the Palme d'Or at Cannes in 1987 where it was booed. But Gérard Depardieu impresses as a young doubt-ridden rural priest who becomes passionately troubled about the welfare of one of his parishioners – a wilful girl whose involvement with a local politician and a doctor results in murder. Depardieu's fragile faith is centrally shaken by his encounters with the devil (a chillingly effective Jean-Christophe Bouvet, effortlessly scene-stealing in the film's most striking performance) and the teenage murderess

played by Pialat protégée Sandrine Bonnaire. This intense, unflinchingly bleak drama, adapted from a novel by Georges Bernanos, is stylishly filmed by Pialat, a disciple of Bresson whose austere style he respectfully follows. Pialat also puts in a dramatic acting appearance as Depardieu's disapproving mentor. This is world cinema filmmaking at its most difficult and least ingratiating. Maybe you have to be French or Roman Catholic to understand it fully, but *Under Satan's Sun* is still an important film, worthy of the top Cannes award, especially as an antidote to other wins around that time by

Wild at Heart (1990) or *sex, lies and videotape* (1989), which seem to exist in a different cosmos. Pialat will probably remain a name little-known outside France, though working with Depardieu brought him world attention with *Loulou* (1979) and *Police* (1985). Bonnaire also starred in Pialat's 1984 film *A Nos Amours*.
RELIGION

1988

Women on the Verge of a Nervous Breakdown

MUJERES AL BORDE DE UN ATAQUE DE NERVIOS   88 min.
Director: *Pedro Almodóvar*
Origin: *Spain*
Distributor: *El Deseo/Rank*
Cast: *Antonio Banderas, Maria Barranco, Rossy de Palma, Fernando Guillen, Carmen Maura, Julieta Serrano*

This is the film that established Spanish maverick director Pedro Almodóvar's international reputation – only six years earlier he was working for the country's telephone company. It's a splendid showcase for his favourite star Carmen Maura as a TV actress who's abandoned by her long-time lover after she discovers she's preg-

Spanish steps: *Pedro Almodóvar's satirical tale of middle-class Madrid's sexual mores*

nant. The movie centres on her desperate attempts to find Fernando Guillen, who's been cheating on his wife with her, propelling her into a tangled web of ever wilder events. *Women on the Verge* is a satire of middle-class Madrid mores and a wild screwball farce with a serious feminist text, indulging the director's pronounced taste for the absurd and surreal to the full. A strong current within the comedy is the gay director's camp sensibilities and hardnosed sexual politics. It's subversive but at the same time a mainstream art-house film and the reasons for its success are simple: on the one hand it is wittily funny and on the other Carmen Maura is so strong and appealing in it. In both his earlier and later films (this was his sixth), when Almodóvar pushed harder toward the bizarre and sexually explicit, he left behind sections of his audience and this remains still his biggest popular success. Almodóvar heightens and stylizes the characters' genuine emotions to the level of absurdist melodrama in a conscious nod to 1950s Hollywood

Thou shalt not kill: *Thuggish Miroslaw Baka murders a Warsaw taxi driver*

films like *Magnificent Obsession*, and packages the picture in a pastiche of their artificial surface style with splashes of bright pastel colour. Oscar-nominated as Best Foreign Language Film.
SATIRE

Ten Commandments: A Short Film about Killing
KROTKI FILM O ZABIJANIU   84 min.
Director: *Krzysztof Kieslowski*
Origin: *Poland*
Distributor: *Film Polski/Gala*
Cast: *Miroslaw Baka, Krzysztof Globisz, Jan Tesarz, Zbigniew Zapasiewicz*

Krzysztof Kieslowski's cold, chilling and commanding film, inspired by the fifth commandment, is the deeply troubling story of the senseless killing of a Warsaw taxi driver and the execution of his yobbish young murderer (Miroslaw Baka). The director films using unreal autumnal hues, with a series of disturbing visuals through unsettling tilted shots and jarring jump-edits. It is all astonishingly forceful and alarming: Kieslowski takes care not to glamorize the topic nor to shed tears over either victim, and lingers over both deaths in all their explicitly gruesome particulars as the cabbie's head is repeatedly stoned in and the killer is executed. As drama, it's impossible

not to be moved by this masterly attack on eye-for-an-eye justice, but the film is also important as an example of cinema as propaganda: it's said to have helped sway the Polish government of the day to introduce a five-year moratorium

on capital punishment. This extended feature-length cinema version of *A Short Film about Killing* was the first of Kieslowski's astonishing *Decalogue* cycle of 12 hour-long made-for-TV movies inspired by the Ten Commandments. Naturally, the short TV version was shown as number five in the series. One other film, *A Short Film about Love* (1988), also appeared in a feature-length version. *A Short Film about Killing* won both the Jury Prize and the International Critics' Prize at the 1988 film festival in Cannes, where it caused a furore. The TV series has been shown in cinemas worldwide and made some lists of the best 10 films of the 1980s.
POLEMICAL DRAMA

1989

Batman
126 min.
Director: *Tim Burton*
Origin: *USA*
Distributor: *Warner*
Cast: *Kim Basinger, Michael Gough, Jerry Hall, Pat Hingle, Michael Keaton, Jack Nicholson, Jack Palance, Tracy Walter, Billy Dee Williams, Robert Wuhl*

In the hideously corrupt Gotham City, criminals must face an avenging a caped crusader cracking down on crime. Meanwhile spruce mobster Jack Napier (Jack Nicholson) becomes a patsy for his evil gangland boss (Jack Palance) and undergoes a terrible transformation – emerging as the Joker, a sadistic villain bent on destroying Batman. Comedian Michael Keaton, sombre and dignified, is cast in the straight part of tortured millionaire Bruce Wayne and his alter-ego the caped crusader. He faces his greatest challenge in tangling with the psychotic funster, played for broad humour by serious actor Jack Nicholson in a barn-

No joke: Jack Nicholson, Michael Keaton get to grips

storming *tour de force* that occasionally threatens to overbalance the project but never quite does. Alas, there's no Robin, perhaps because Batman's innocent relationship with the Boy Wonder is now considered ambiguous, so the Dark Knight is given support from the lovely Kim Basinger, though this love interest area turns out to be the film's weak spot. Returning in theme as well as look to the darkness of the Bob Kane *DC Comics* original, *Batman* is a live-action cartoon strip for grown-ups with the merest nod in the direction of a younger audience with Prince's songs. Despite the Oscar for the late Anton Furst's brilliant art direction and much praise for Danny Elfman's thumping score, ultimately it's director Tim Burton's triumph in an ideal realization of his own dark and quirky vision. The public made it the top-grossing film of 1989, and it was even more of a success if you take into account the huge cash-register bonanza for the product spinoffs.
ADVENTURE FANTASY

sex, lies and videotape
101 min.
Director: *Steven Soderbergh*
Origin: *USA*
Distributor: *Outlaw*
Cast: *Steven Brill, Peter Gallagher, Andie MacDowell, Laura San Giacomo, James Spader, Ron Vawter*

An assured and perceptive debut film from its 26-year-old writer/director which, despite its provocative title relies largely on the quiet, literate intimacy of dialogue to tell its story, backed by subtle and well-judged performances from its then virtually unknown four young principal players. Set and filmed in the Louisiana of Soderbergh's upbringing, *sex, lies and videotape* deals with the navel-examining territory more usually associated with California or New York, as it

Cannes hit: *Steven Soderbergh's erotic tangle of* sex, lies and videotape

goes into the problems four "twenty/thirty-somethings" are having with their sex lives, and the lies they tell about themselves. It is all observed, however, with a sophisticated yet sympathetic humour and irony which makes it both intelligent and highly entertaining. Andie MacDowell and Peter Gallagher play a well-off yuppie couple whose marriage is on the rocks. She is prone to chronic anxiety as a cover-up for her feelings of sexual inadequacy. He is having an affair with her far sparkier sister (Laura San Giacomo). The catalyst is a visit from Gallagher's old college friend (James Spader). His problem is impotence, and his bizarre way of conducting relationships is to get his women friends to confess all their secret thoughts and fears to him on videotape. The attraction between him and MacDowell, plus her sister's willingness to reveal all before the video camera, sparks off a series of even more explosive emotional revelations. The film scored a double success at the Cannes Film Festival, winning the Palme d'Or plus Best Actor award for Spader. Soderbergh's screenplay was nominated for an Oscar. But Soderbergh's career continued to mixed reviews with *Kafka* (1991) and *King of the Hill* (1993).
DRAMA/COMEDY

Cinema Paradiso

NUOVO CINEMA PARADISO 122 min.
Director: *Giuseppe Tornatore*
Origin: *Italy/France*
Distributor: *Palace/Films Ariana/ RAI Tre/Forum/Franco/Cristaldi*
Cast: *Salvatore Cascio, Mario Leonardi, Agnese Nano, Philippe Noiret, Jacques Perrin, Leopoldo Trieste*

Winner of a Special Jury Prize at Cannes and an Oscar for Best Foreign Language Film, Giuseppe Tornatore's gentle, poignant meditation on youth, friendship, and the power of cinema is the second-highest-grossing foreign film of all time (behind 1990's *Cyrano de Bergerac*). *Cinema Paradiso* continues to delight audiences with its evocative mix of sentiment, nostalgia and reflections of a bygone age. Related in flashback by Salvatore (Jacques Perrin), a successful film director, it explores the latter's early years in a small Sicilian village and his friendship with Alfredo (Philippe Noiret), the truculent, warm-hearted projectionist at the local Paradiso cinema. The latter acts as mentor to the fatherless young Salvatore (Salvatore Cascio), encouraging his love of film and turning a blind eye when he sneaks into the local priest's weekly censorship previews. "I wanted to make a fantasy about the times when movie-going

was an excitement," says Tornatore, who has captured not only the timeless magic of cinema, but its power to chronicle and reflect the changing face of the world at large. Full of wonderful images – Alfredo collecting the screen kisses that have been edited out by the censor; a helter-skelter trip through the greatest moments of film – this is both a captivating study of the rituals of small-town life and a heartwarming eulogy to the enduring wonders of the imagination. Originally cut to 122 minutes, it was re-released in 1993 with 60 minutes added.
NOSTALGIA

Do the Right Thing

120 min.
Director: *Spike Lee*
Origin: *USA*
Distributor: *40 Acres and a Mule/ UIP*
Cast: *Danny Aiello, Ossie Davis, Ruby Dee, Richard Edson, Giancarlo Esposito, Spike Lee, Bill Nunn, Rosie Perez, John Savage, John Turturro*

Vibrant, hard-hitting and purposeful, *Do the Right Thing* marks the fiery peak of maverick black film-maker Spike Lee. Vividly shot on the graffiti-ized mean streets of Bedford-Stuyvesant, this high-charged urban drama brilliantly lifts the lid on America's simmering pressure-cooker with a keen 24-hour study of a race riot's causes and consequences. Lee casts himself

as Mookie, baseball-capped deliveryman at the "famous pizzeria" owned by Italian-American Sal (Danny Aiello) and his two sons – good-natured Vito (Richard Edson) and bigoted Pino (John Turturro). Angered by a lack of Afro-American "brothers" decorating Sal's "Wall of Fame" celebrity fresco, local upstart Buggin Out (Giancarlo Esposito) marshals a boycott of the pizzeria, triggering off an uprising that spreads like a bushfire, and turns the multi-ethnic community into a war zone. While condemned in conservative quarters as an incitement to racial violence, *Do the Right Thing* is no crass call-to-arms. Lee shows most support for his Afro-American protagonists, but in many ways the movie's most likeable character is Sal, the outmoded but essentially decent and tolerant toiler who unwittingly becomes the focus of racial aggression. Inspired by Public Enemy's driving rap-theme, Lee films as though his life depended on it, spicing the examination with skewed angles and swirling camera motions, and somehow capturing the inherent urgency and volatility of his subject. An engrossing look at what happens when you heat up the melting-pot, *Do the Right Thing* proved one of the 1980s' most provocative and assured pictures. In the light of the 1992 LA riots, it could also be regarded as one of the most worryingly prophetic.
RACE DRAMA

Doing the right thing: *Danny Aiello checks out his pizzeria's "wall of fame"*

Drugstore Cowboy

100 min.
Director: *Gus Van Sant*
Origin: *USA*
Distributor: *Avenue Pictures*
Cast: *William S. Burroughs, Matt Dillon, Heather Graham, James Le Gros, Kelly Lynch, James Remar, Beah Richards, Grace Zabriskie*

Gus Van Sant's ingeniously hip and intelligent look at the junkie culture finds underused Matt Dillon in supreme form, magnificently droll and convincing as Bob, the leader of a crew of addicts who feed their habit by plundering the drugstores and hospitals of the Pacific Northwest. Eventually unnerved by the overdose death of a team-member, Bob elects to "go straight" on the methadone programme, a decision that shocks his wife and partner-in-crime, the beautiful but damned Diane (Kelly Lynch). *Drugstore Cowboy* simply does not hit a bum note. Van Sant films with a flavourful *joie de vivre*, crisply capturing the sights and sounds of its early 1970s setting and draping the tale with a clutch of crackling support turns, most notably from cult-novelist William S. Burroughs as an addict-priest. But where *Drugstore Cowboy* most impresses is in its admirably upfront and objective treatment of drug abuse, right down to its re-creation of the odd-ball rituals and superstitions that govern the junkies' existence. Aided by Dillon's perfectly realized portrayal, Van Sant paints the junkies' lifestyle with honesty and precision – as a transient, instant-gratification culture that carries the constant threat of tragedy. Bob may have ultimately given up a respected position in the criminal subculture to "drill holes in a piece of metal", but in doing so he is somehow saved – freed from the accelerating drive to death that is the junkie's eventual lot. At the end, even broken and barely alive aboard a speeding ambulance, you almost want to cheer for him.
MELODRAMA

A boy named by the Sioux: Kevin Costner is Dances with Wolves

1990

Cyrano de Bergerac

138 min.
Director: *Jean-Paul Rappeneau*
Origin: *France*
Distributor: *Hachette Première*
Cast: *Roland Bertin, Anne Brochet, Gérard Depardieu, Vincent Perez, Josiane Stolerou, Jacques Weber*

Jean-Paul Rappeneau's acclaimed film version of Edmond Rostand's classic play set in 17th-century France enshrines one of Gérard Depardieu's finest performances as the eponymous soldier/ poet whose search for happiness is hindered by his exceptionally large nose. Unable to tell his beautiful cousin Roxanne (Anne Brochet) that he loves her, he agrees to act as an intermediary between her and a handsome young soldier. Depardieu deservedly won the Best Actor award at Cannes for his flamboyant and heartbreaking performance, though he was beaten at the Oscar ceremony by Jeremy Irons for *Reversal of Fortune* (1990).

Some said the voters were influenced when Depardieu's frank press interviews about his teenage years were unearthed. *Cyrano de Bergerac* is a wonderful, costly production, showing 1990s French cinema in a mood of confidence and expansion, prompted by the worldwide success of *Jean de Florette* and *Manon des Sources* (1986). For English-speaking audiences, the problem of translation is perfectly solved as the French couplets are beautifully translated into rhyming sub-titles by Anthony Burgess. José Ferrer won an Oscar in the part in the 1950 American film version and Steve Martin reworked the material as a comedy in the delightful *Roxanne* (1986) with Daryl Hannah. Depardieu parodied the famous balcony scene (filmed imaginatively in a rain downpour) in his own films *Mon Père ce Héros* (1992) and *My Father the Hero* (1994). His Oscar nomination helped turn Depardieu into a name in America, and he consolidated his success with the American-set comedy *Green Card* (1990), his first film in English.
ROMANCE

Dances with Wolves

183 min.
Director: *Kevin Costner*
Origin: *USA*
Distributor: *Tig/Orion*
Cast: *Tantoo Cardinal, Maury Chakin, Kevin Costner, Rodney A. Grant, Graham Greene, Mary McDonnell, Charles Rocket, Floyd Red Crow Westerman*

Kevin Costner's politically correct western, showing the last years of the Sioux through the sympathetic eyes of a member of the race which destroyed them, was a labour of love for its star/director, who fought for years to raise money for the project. Sophisticated critics have mocked the film for the black-and-white naivety of its vision, accusing it of lacking any real insight into Sioux culture, while Costner himself was perceived as being on a bland, boy-scout ego trip. Yet the film won seven Oscars while the Sioux gave it their seal of approval by admitting Costner as a full tribal member. Set against the large canvas of the frontier landscape, *Dances with Wolves* is the story of one man's search for his destiny, with Costner as an old-

style hero – honest, open-minded and courageous, seeking self-knowledge through his relationship with an alien culture he adopts as his own. The depiction of the Sioux as a dignified and warmly humorous people with a complex culture in perfect balance with its environment may be idealistic but is still nearer to the truth than the savage killers and thieves shown in the old-style western. The film boasts scenes of breathtaking spectacle, such as the buffalo stampede, while its life-affirming New Age idealism certainly struck a chord with the large audiences it attracted. It also provided strong roles for previously unknown Native American actors such as Graham Greene and Rodney A. Grant, acting in the Sioux language with subtitles. Costner must have been doing something right.
WESTERN

Goodfellas

146 min.
Director: *Martin Scorsese*
Origin: *USA*
Distributor: *Warner*
Cast: *Lorraine Bracco, Robert De Niro, Samuel L. Jackson, Ray Liotta, Joe Pesci, Catherine Scorsese, Charles Scorsese, Paul Sorvino*

"As far back as I can remember I always wanted to be a gangster." So begins Scorsese's brilliantly rich, energetic and convincing argument for the pleasures of measuring money in inches, murdering while your meatballs stew, and refusing to stand in a line queueing behind anybody. Based on co-screenwriter Nicholas Pileggi's true story, *Wiseguy*, *Goodfellas* is an unapologetic insider's account of mafia foot soldier Henry Hill's (Ray Liotta) progression from wannabe to Witness Protection Program, where he testifies against his partners in crime to save his own skin. Real-life godfather Paul Gotti pronounced it "a government propaganda movie" for portraying informers as heroes, but Scorsese suggests that in Hill's own amoral way he faces a different kind of death by boredom when he goes straight, his only remorse being for the loss of his previously glamorous lifestyle. The film even ends with Sid Vicious's sneering version of "My Way". The first-person voice-over works dazzlingly well alongside a documentary-like structure that concentrates on the ordinary details of an extraordinary way of life, so that moments like the major airport heist are shelved in favour of the lovingly detailed after-mood of celebration and paranoia. Robert De Niro, in his sixth collaboration with Scorsese, is as convincing as ever, but Oscar-winner Joe Pesci is outstanding as the comic psychopath Tommy, and there were five other nominations, including one for Lorraine Bracco's feisty performance as Henry's wife, Karen. Scorsese's parents also enjoyed cameos, as Tommy's doting mother and the hitman specializing in prison tomato sauces.
GANGSTER

Wild at Heart

126 min.
Director: *David Lynch*
Origin: *USA*
Distributor: *PolyGram/Palace*
Cast: *Nicolas Cage, Willem Dafoe, Laura Dern, Diane Ladd, Isabella Rossellini, Harry Dean Stanton*

"The whole world's wild at heart and weird on top," groans languorous Laura Dern during one of the quieter moments of David Lynch's overheated Palme d'Or winner. Yes, indeed. There's something wickedly out of control about *Wild at Heart*, some intoxicating rush to destruction about a film that hurls degenerate lovers Sailor (Nicolas Cage) and Lula (Dern) through a surrealistic American "Oz" – a land inhabited by hitmen, voodoo queens, half-dead road victims, nutty ex-marines and deranged, cockroach-obsessed cousins. Adapted from the pulp novel by Barry Gifford, the plot looks a near-parody of the boy-meets-girl fairytale, with the young couple fleeing west to escape Lula's monstrous, all-powerful mom Marietta (Diane Ladd). But *Wild at Heart* most captivates as an amphetamine-crazed celebration of America's junk culture, from *The Wizard of Oz* to the ballads of Elvis Presley. A controversial winner at Cannes, this postmodern road movie split critics, many of whom saw it as a cynical triumph of style over substance. But despite *Wild at Heart*'s total lack of shade or subtlety, it's impossible to ignore the dazzling wit of Lynch's handling, drawing

Wild things: Nicolas Cage and Laura Dern in filling-station frolics

from an unholy treasure-chest of influences and juggling raucous comedy, po-faced pathos and gruesome ultra-violence to audacious good effect. Fully in keeping with the movie's self-consciously cult appeal, the top cast play to perfection, with Willem Dafoe contributing a real *tour de force* as the gap-fanged, ex-marine Bobby Peru and Ladd obviously relishing her role as the witchlike Marietta. L. Frank Baum was never like this.
ROAD MOVIE

1991

The Silence of the Lambs

118 min.
Director: *Jonathan Demme*
Origin: *USA*
Distributor: *Strong Heart/Orion/Rank*
Cast: *Diane Baker, Roger Corman, Jodie Foster, Scott Glenn, Anthony Heald, Anthony Hopkins, Kasi Lemmons, Ted Levine, Brooke Smith*

Only the third film in history to take the five main Academy Awards for Best Film, Direction, Actor, Actress and Screenplay (the other two were *It Happened One Night* in 1934 and *One Flew Over the Cuckoo's Nest* in 1975), this macabre, spellbinding thriller established a new benchmark for the depiction of horror in mainstream cinema. Although many of its most gruesome scenarios are left to the imagination, issues of cannibalism, mutilation, serial murder and violent sexual deviance are central to its plot, and dealt with in such a way as to make them seem not merely commonplace but, in certain instances, actually acceptable. Based on a Thomas Harris novel, the film revolves around the relationship between rookie FBI agent Clarice Starling (Jodie Foster) and sophisticated psychopath Dr Hannibal "The Cannibal" Lecter (Anthony Hopkins) whom she has

enlisted to help hunt down a brutal serial killer known as Buffalo Bill (Ted Levine). Demme milks the horror for all it's worth, backed up by a searing script (from Oscar-winner Ted Tally) and formidable central performances, particularly from show-stealer Hopkins, who later refused to reprise the role because of its potential to corrupt. The homophobic portrayal of the film's serial killer and sympathetic, quasi-heroic treatment of Lecter aroused huge controversy, yet cannot detract from its overall thrill-value. Intelligent, powerful and deeply disturbing, it also displays some wonderfully macabre wit, finding humour even in an eerie suspense moment when Foster finally rumbles Hopkins's teasing clues: "Your anagrams are showing, doctor."
THRILLER/HORROR

Thelma and Louise

128 min.
Director: *Ridley Scott*
Origin: *USA*
Distributor: *MGM/Pathé*
Cast: *Timothy Carhart, Geena Davis, Harvey Keitel, Michael Madsen, Christopher McDonald, Brad Pitt, Susan Sarandon, Stephen Tobolowsky*

A lipstick-and-headscarves road movie – the first of its kind to be given the feminist makeover. Louise (Susan Sarandon) is the worldly-wise waitress, Thelma (Geena Davis), her girly, housewife foil who together, wishing to go fishing, end up shooting and re-routing along Highway 66. The trouble starts with Thelma's attempted rape at a roadside bar, Louise shooting the assailant dead when his backchat gets out of hand. Panicking that the police won't believe their story, they head for Mexico, avoiding Texas where Louise was raped once before. A good man is hard to find. Brad Pitt, the cute cowboy, liberates Thelma from sexual hang-ups and all of her money, forcing them into a crime spree. Christopher

Greta Scacchi: *Ice-cool girlfriend in sizzling hot sex scenes in* The Player

McDonald is Thelma's sadistic husband, and Michael Madsen Louise's little-better boyfriend. Only Harvey Keitel's sensitive police officer understands what it's like for them but even he can't stop the over-the-top finale, the sisters hurtling into the Freudian symbolism of the Grand Canyon when daddy threatens to take the T-bird away. Several studios passed the script up because its lead roles were both for women, but after Goldie Hawn, Cher and Michelle Pfeiffer were all considered, it was Sarandon and Davis who both earned Oscar nominations (alongside British director Ridley Scott, picture-postcard cinematography and editing), while Callie Khouri won the award for her screenplay. Ultimately the story owes more to Butch and Sundance than a political manifesto, but as an entertaining warning to lecherous truck drivers everywhere its "don't mess" message is clear to all.
ROAD MOVIE

1992

The Player

123 min.
Director: *Robert Altman*
Origin: *USA*
Distributor: *Avenue/Spelling*
Cast: *Vincent D'Onofrio, Peter Gallagher, Whoopi Goldberg, Richard E. Grant, Buck Henry, Lyle Lovett, Tim Robbins, Sydney Pollack, Greta Scacchi, Dean Stockwell, Fred Ward*

A hilarious satire on the lunacies of Hollywood and the insecurities of its power brokers, *The Player* hits its bullseyes with an arrow-sharp accuracy which can be enjoyed even if you miss some of the "in" jokes for film buffs. These include Buck Henry, writer of *The Graduate*, pitching his idea for *Graduate 2* in which bedridden Mrs Robinson moves in with Benjamin and Elaine. This kicks off the remarkable opening tracking sequence which sets the scene by creating a sort of Bayeux Tapestry of cameo incidents in film-executive politics and games-playing. Tim Robbins plays an up-and-coming, kick-anybody-who-is-in-the-way, young executive who murders a writer (Vincent D'Onofrio) and falls for the dead man's ice-cool artist girlfriend (Greta Scacchi). Also involved in the Hollywood kaleidoscope are Peter Gallagher as a carphone-addicted dealmaker; Fred Ward, the vain security chief; Dean Stockwell, a producer who drops celebrity names like executives in less health-conscious times dropped cigar butts; Whoopi Goldberg as an unnervingly smart detective; and Richard E. Grant, a nervous writer desperate to pitch his screenplay. Plus a host of celebrities playing cameos as themselves. The film also features two unusual sizzling sex scenes between Robbins and Scacchi, one of which is purely verbal with them both fully clothed and not even touching, while the other is shot in total close-up, creating its effect through emotional response, without a single flash of full-frontal or any thrashing limbs. *The Player*, Altman's stylish riposte to the system that cannot handle him, earned several Oscar nominations and marked what he describes as his "third comeback". COMEDY/MYSTERY

Basic Instinct

127 min.
Director: *Paul Verhoeven*
Origin: *USA*
Distributor: *Carolco/Guild*
Cast: *Denis Arndt, Michael Douglas, George Dzundza, Leilani Sarelle, Sharon Stone, Jeanne Tripplehorn*

What could have remained a run-of-the-mill cop outing was transformed by director Paul Verhoeven, screenwriter Joe Eszterhas and Sharon Stone's infamous leg-crossing scene into main-stream Hollywood's most super-sleazy, in-your-face, psycho-thriller. Despite its upfront content, *Basic Instinct* knows precisely where it's going, with Eszterhas's record-breaking $3million screenplay punching out a slick whodunnit yarn that has jaded cop Nick Carol (Michael Douglas) investigating a grisly ice-pick sex murder that may or may not have been committed by blonde bombshell Catherine Tramell (Stone). Nominally cast as second-string to Douglas, Stone seized her star-making opportunity as the dynamic Catherine, the bisexual, free-spirited, knickerless novelist who casually sends her police interrogators into a collar-tugging sexual frenzy. Atmospherically set in San Francisco and directed in clean, purposeful strokes by Verhoeven, *Basic Instinct* rang loud bells at the box-office. American screenings were frequently picketed by gay-rights activists incensed by its dubious portrayal of lesbians as deranged, man-hating monsters. They have a point, since *Basic Instinct* seems shrewdly to exploit both male fantasy and male fears, simultaneously painting all its principal female characters as uninhibited sex-machines and possible castrators – deviant, untrustworthy divas that you screw at your peril. But, by aiming so squarely at the cinemagoer's own basest instincts, Verhoeven and co rustle up a steamy, nerve-jangling exercise in 1990s paranoia and one of the most talked-about films of its era. THRILLER

Reservoir Dogs

99 min.
Director: *Quentin Tarantino*
Origin: *USA*
Distributor: *Live America/Rank*
Cast: *Kirk Baltz, Randy Brooks, Steve Buscemi, Harvey Keitel, Michael Madsen, Chris Penn, Tim Roth, Quentin Tarantino, Lawrence Tierney*

Writer-director Quentin Tarantino's heist-gone-wrong pulverizer is one of the most thrilling debuts in cinema history, a canny post-modern "plunder picture" that cannibalizes plot elements from Kubrick's *The Killing* (1956), De Palma's *Casualties of War* (1989), Scorsese's *Mean Streets* (1973) and the flicks of cult film-maker John Woo. An arch film buff who cut his teeth in an LA video store, Tarantino revels in movie paraphernalia and 1990s pop culture flotsam and the fun is infectious. The fractured plot proves a stunning exercise in contained, concentrated viciousness, turning a beady-eye on the disastrous fall-out from a fumbled jewellery heist. Known only by their colour-coded nicknames, the surviving criminals congregate at an abandoned warehouse to examine what went wrong. Obviously relishing Tarantino's tangy dialogue, a top-notch cast play to perfection, with Lawrence Tierney scoring as crime kingpin Joe Cabot and Michael Madsen full of brutish, scary malevolence as "Lee Marvin fan" Mr Blond. The most impressive, though, are old-hand Harvey Keitel as the oddly honourable

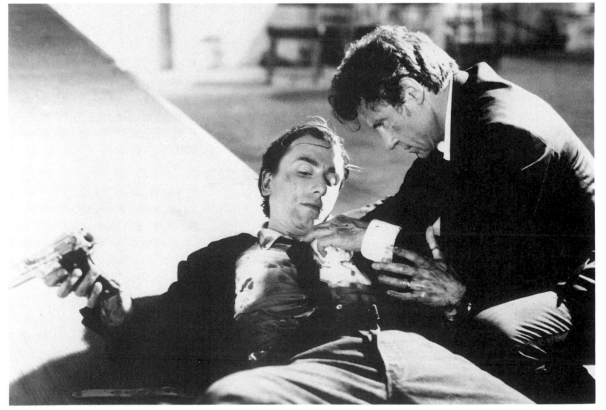

Going to the dogs: The prognosis ain't good for Tim Roth (left) and Harvey Keitel

Mr White and young-gun actor Tim Roth as the gut-shot Mr Orange. Hugely violent but assembled with a giddying wit and energy, *Reservoir Dogs* fires on all cylinders. "What I'm most proud of," Tarantino commented, "is that a cinema-literate viewer can watch it and appreciate it on that level. But if there's a mailman who just wants to watch a good crime thriller... Well, I think I totally give them that too."
CRIME THRILLER

Unforgiven

131 min.
Director: *Clint Eastwood*
Origin: *USA*
Distributor: *Warner*
Cast: *Rod Campbell, Clint Eastwood, Frances Fisher, Morgan Freeman, Gene Hackman, Richard Harris, David Mucci, Saul Rubinek, Anna Thomson, Jaimz Woolvett*

Credited with restoring the dignity of the western genre, *Unforgiven* is actually a supremely intelligent debunking of the entire Wild West cowboy myth. Winner of four Oscars, including two for Eastwood (Best Film and Best Direction), it presents a darkly revisionist view of the dog-days of the gunslinger, rejecting traditional images of heroism and decency and concentrating instead on the filth, cruelty and profound moral ambiguity of the old West. Scripted by David Webb Peoples, it stars Eastwood as William Munny, an ageing gunman turned pig-farmer who, accompanied by old friend Morgan Freeman and impetuous young buck Jaimz Woolvett, undertakes one last contract killing in return for a sizeable reward. His employers are a group of prostitutes, one of whom has been badly mutilated by two clients, and who are unable to find redress from the bullying local sheriff (Oscar-winning Gene Hackman). What at face value looks like a simple good guys/bad guys scenario is lent depth by

Eastwood eyes the shots: *The Oscar-winner dons his director's hat*

superb scripting and direction, emphasizing the complexity of the characters and ambivalence of the situations in which they are involved. The revenge slaying is a sordid, unheroic affair, while Eastwood emerges as brutal, flawed and cold-hearted a character as those he has been employed to assassinate. The performances are faultless, especially from Hackman and dandy gunfighter Richard Harris, but ultimately this is Eastwood's show. Weary, callous and embittered, he delves into the dark side of the cowboy myth to produce one of the most radical, as well as the most satisfying, westerns of modern times.
WESTERN

Wayne's World

95 min.
Director: *Penelope Spheeris*
Origin: *USA*
Distributor: *Paramount*
Cast: *Lara Flynn Boyle, Colleen Camp, Tia Carrere, Dana Carvey, Brian Doyle-Murray, Rob Lowe, Meat Loaf, Mike Myers, Ione Skye*

Comic Mike Myers's scatter-brained, scattergun youth-spoof split viewers fairly equally into fans and phobes, but its overall significance is hard to ignore. A rollicking salute to America's idiot culture, *Wayne's World* evolved from a series of successful skits on the cult TV show *Saturday Night Live*. Series creator Myers plays Wayne, a puckish heavy-metal nerd who, together with his even nerdier pal Garth (a straw-wigged Dana Carvey), runs a public access TV show from the basement of Wayne's folks' home in Aurora, Illinois. For the feature film, Myers hands the directorial reins over to Penelope Spheeris, who helmed the 1981 punk "rockumentary" *The Decline of Western Civilization*. Filming in broad strokes, Spheeris strings a gaggle of gags and gleeful setpieces around a peripheral plot that has our loser heroes chasing 'babes' and falling foul of oily showbiz producer Rob Lowe. Maybe the title of Spheeris's earlier movie was prophetic; many critics saw *Wayne's World* as signalling "the decline of western civilization". But despite its show-off imbecility and daft catchphrases, there's something disarming, engagingly slapdash about this grand show of do-it-yourself amateurism. What really appeals is Myers's remorseless, indiscriminate deconstruction of US culture, with its hoary rock singalongs, direct-to-camera monologues and telegraphed "extreme close-up" and "gratuitous sex scene".

Cobbled together like an exuberant home movie, *Wayne's World* hit a mammoth jackpot at the box-office, making a teen icon of Myers and spawning a more assured and witty sequel in 1993 imaginatively tagged *Wayne's World 2*.
FARCE

1993

Farewell My Concubine

BAWANG BIE JI   170 min.
Director: *Chen Kaige*
Origin: *Hong Kong/China*
Distributor: *Artificial Eye/Tomson*
Cast: *Leslie Cheung, Zhang Fengyi, Gong Li*

Chen Kaige's exquisite, captivating film tells nothing short of the history of 20th-century China through the microcosm of the Peking Opera. *Farewell My Concubine* is both impressively epic and personally intimate, with its triangle drama played out against the events leading to the Cultural Revolution. It opens in 1925 when a delicate, beautiful

Concubine: *Little luck and happiness*

boy is taken in by the All Luck and Happiness opera academy, where he's – reluctantly – trained to take female roles and becomes infatuated with another boy who befriends him. By 1937, on the eve of the Japanese invasion, Cheng Dieyi (Leslie Cheung) is now in love with Duan Xiaolou (Zhang Fengyi) but he becomes betrothed to Juxian (Gong Li), Peking's most desired prostitute. "The love story reflects the transformation of Chinese society itself," says the director, who is most fascinated by Cheng because he "blurs the distinction between theatre and life, male and female. Addicted to his art, he's a tragic figure who only wants to pursue an ideal of beauty, to actually become the concubine he plays." The film comments subtly on male-female roles and the art-life conflict, homing in on telling details of the opera and Chinese life, but its success finally hinges on the trio of heartfelt performances and Kaige's moving handling of the theme of extreme love and total betrayal. Appropriately operatic as it sometimes seems, it's always truthful and emotionally wrenching. It won the Golden Globe for Best Foreign Film and shared the 1993 Cannes Palme d'Or and International Critics' Prize.
ROMANCE/HISTORICAL EPIC

Jurassic Park

126 min.
Director: *Steven Spielberg*
Origin: *USA*
Distributor: *Universal/Amblin*
Cast: *Richard Attenborough, Laura Dern, Martin Ferrero, Jeff Goldblum, Sam Neill, Bob Peck, B. D. Wong*

Steven Spielberg's ultimate monster movie is based on Michael Crichton's 1990 bestselling novel with its ideal film premise that dinosaurs can be genetically engineered using fossil DNA. Spielberg takes over the theme of Crichton's serious-minded book, changing the characters and ditching the scien-

Monster smash: Sam Neill is tyrannized by Tyrannosaurus

tific mumjo-jumbo, and turns it into a good, old-fashioned *King Kong*-style horror movie for 1990s family audiences. He casts fellow director Richard Attenborough, who seems to be thoroughly enjoying himself in his first screen role since 1979 as the mad but wealthy Scottish tycoon John Hammond who unveils the world's first prehistoric theme park on a remote tropical island. Along come awestruck doctors Sam Neill and Laura Dern and wisecracking mathemati-

cian Jeff Goldblum to check it out, but soon the monsters are running amok and they're being tyrannized by the Tyrannosaurus and terrorized by the pterodactyls. The stars of the show are a particularly nasty Tyrannosaurus Rex, who chases our heroes to turn them into a tasty instant snack, and the voracious velociraptors. This state-of-the-art display of cinema magic was the deserved winner of three technical Oscars: for Best Sound, Sound Editing and the breathtaking

Visual Effects. Dinosaurs and DNA suddenly became the flavour of the month and the film an incredible popular success, going on to become the first film to take $1,000 million at the box-office world wide. When Attenborough looked through the script and asked where his death scene from the novel was, Spielberg replied: "Do you want to do the death scene or the sequel?" The world now trembles with anticipation.
FANTASY THRILLER/HORROR

Naked

130 min.
Director: *Mike Leigh*
Origin: *GB*
Distributor: *Thin Man/First Independent*
Cast: *Katrin Cartlidge, Greg Cruttwell, Lesley Sharp, Claire Skinner, David Thewlis, Peter Wight*

Previously noted for his quirky, wryly comic portraits of Little England, writer-director Mike Leigh served up a savage state-of-the-nation address with *Naked*, a boiling-over odyssey through the dingy bedsits and rubbish-strewn streets of 90s inner-city London. The picture's prickly, poisoned anti-hero is tousle-haired Johnny (David Thewlis), fleeing the consequences of a rape in his native Manchester and sheltering at the southern flat of an ex-girlfriend (Lesley Sharp). Through Johnny's distorted, self-loathing gaze, Leigh shows us a society in collapse, a chilly barren landscape where sex and violence seem the only acceptable currency. Unashamedly allegorical in nature, *Naked* is a searing piece of cinema, a film with its roots in the British kitchen-sink school but its head in current clouds of New Ageism and scrambled chaos theorizing. Constructed in improvised gatherings with cast-members, the dialogue crackles with a corrosive wit and energy, reaching its height during Johnny's apocalyptic diatribe inside an abandoned office building. *Naked* is not a flawless movie. Some of its characters – Greg Cruttwell's heartless yuppie in particular – seem annoyingly one-dimensional, and the film's unflinching treatment of violent sex led some viewers to accuse it of misogyny. But as a vision of an urban hell, Leigh's powerhouse picture makes for compulsive entertainment, while as a showcase for the skills of Cannes-award-winning Thewlis it could hardly be better. Acting in a vitriol-spitting, adrenalin-fuelled rush, Thewlis creates in Johnny a British anti-hero to rank with Jimmy Porter and Tom Jones; a doomed and desperate icon for the century's dying years.
SOCIAL REALISM

The Piano

120 min.
Director: *Jane Campion*
Origin: *Australia/France*
Distributor: *Chapman/Ciby 2000*
Cast: *Tungla Baker, Holly Hunter, Harvey Keitel, Genevieve Lemon, Ian Mune, Sam Neill, Anna Paquin, Kerry Walker*

Jane Campion's *tour de force* about love and passion in 19th-century New Zealand was one of the film highlights of 1993, taking the Palme d'Or at Cannes (shared with *Farewell My Concubine*) and winning three Oscars (including one for Campion's screenplay). In development since 1984, it is the story of Ada (Oscar-winner Holly Hunter), a mute Scottish woman dispatched with her nine-year-old daughter (Anna Paquin, winning the Best Supporting Actress Oscar) and her beloved piano to an arranged marriage in New Zealand. On arrival her husband Stewart (Sam Neill) refuses to transport the piano inland, leaving it on a beach where it is salvaged by illiterate neighbour Baines (Harvey Keitel) who then offers Ada the chance to earn it back, key by key, in return for sexual favours. Exquisite performances are augmented by writer/director Campion's mastery of visual symbolism, with sets, scenery and lighting all primed to echo the inner worlds of her characters. Ada's burgeoning love affair with Baines is dramatically reflected in the steamy, tangled primordial mass of jungle they inhabit; while the burnt forest surrounding Stewart's homestead is cruelly indicative of his own emotional barrenness. The piano itself provides Ada with a means of expression and emotional release, and is suggestive both of the constraints of Victorian culture and of the primitive passions inherent in music. At once an uplifting love story and a delicate insight into the sexual mores of a bygone age, this is a rich and poignant screen masterpiece, as complex and resonant as the instrument of its title. Despite all the paludits, however, there were dissenting views of Campion's picture, led by American doyenne critic Pauline Kael, who complained memorably that *The Piano* was crammed with "unexamined feminine smugness."
ROMANCE

Cannes best actor David Thewlis: *A British anti-hero to rank alongside Jimmy Porter*

Beaten to a pulp: *John Travolta (left) and Ving Rhames discuss who is next to suffer some violent discomfort*

1994

Natural Born Killers

134 min.
Director: *Oliver Stone*
Origin: *USA*
Distributor: *Warner*
Cast: *Rodney Dangerfield, Robert Downey Jr, Balthazar Getty, Woody Harrelson, Tommy Lee Jones, Juliette Lewis*

The debate on screen violence reached its angry apogee with this ferocious road movie, a *Badlands*-style serial-killer outing that rides roughshod through the detritus of 1990s popular culture. Even before its release, *Natural Born Killers* was swamped in controversy. Hot-ticket Quentin Tarantino penned the original screenplay, then publicly disowned the picture when he spotted the changes introduced by director Oliver Stone, who turned the film into a savage send-up of the media. Our psycho-lover anti-heroes are meatman Micky (Woody Harrelson) and Mallory (Juliette Lewis), whose orgy of destruction has the nation's youth in an admir-

ing frenzy and whizkid journo Wayne Gayle (Robert Downey Jr) – the brains behind tabloid TV show *American Maniacs* – drooling for an exclusive interview. After allegedly triggering off a spate of copycat crimes, *Natural Born Killers* was initially refused a certificate in Britain, though a censor expressed confusion about where appropriate cuts could be made. "It's like a stick of rock," he observed. "The violence runs right through it." Exactly. The picture is not so much violent in content as it is violent in form. Stone's direction pours out a concentrated mash of multi-media imagery, switching between distorting digital effects, garish back-projections, crazed animated inserts and – in one disturbing instant – a nightmarish spoof sitcom scenario complete with braying, canned laughter. Though *Natural Born Killers* may be ultimately tangled and muddied, unsure precisely what it's criticizing (violence, the media, the media's creation of violence?), its white-hot invention marks this pop-assemblage beast out as a towering film achievement. 21st-century cinema arrived a few years early.
Road movie

Pulp Fiction

153 min.
Director: *Quentin Tarantino*
Origin: *USA*
Distributor: *Miramax*
Cast: *Maria de Madeiros, Samuel L. Jackson, Harvey Keitel, Amanda Plummer, Ving Rhames, Tim Roth, Quentin Tarantino, Uma Thurman, John Travolta, Christopher Walken, Bruce Willis*

Quentin Tarantino's second ultra-violent, dime-store saga, following the cult hit *Reservoir Dogs* (1992), is an anthology story set around Hollywood's criminal culture, focusing in on three intertwining slice-of-low-life narratives constructed in a complex circular structure. Opening and closing his tale in the everyday setting of a diner, where a couple of young thieves (Amanda Plummer, Tim Roth) are casually planning a hold-up, Tarantino draws us into the bizarre lives of a pair of dangerously thick-witted hitmen (John Travolta, Samuel L. Jackson), their mob boss and his sexy, drug-addled wife (Ving Rhames, Uma Thurman), and lastly a double-crossing prizefighter (Bruce Willis) and his absent-minded French

sweetheart (Maria de Madeiros). Tarantino's brilliantly written script, which transforms what he calls "three of the oldest situations in the book", is often unbearably tense and frequently hilarious, pushing as hard as he can in the apparently opposing directions of farce and violence. It's a wry tribute to the pulp literary world of Cornell Woolrich, Jim Thompson and David Goodis, with their lurid stories, dark city settings and world-weary, hard-boiled characters. Weird, reprehensible and remote from most viewers' lives though his characters are, the director is clearly totally wrapped up with them and their milieu, weaving it all together to "organically intertwine the separate stories so in the end you think you've seen one movie, a movie about a community of characters". Tarantino, a proponent of the cathartic nature of screen violence, said he shared the general surprise that his film won the Palme d'Or at Cannes in 1994 because "My films aren't about bringing people together".
Crime

Schindler's List

195 min.
Director: *Steven Spielberg*
Origin: *USA*
Distributor: *Universal/Amblin*
Cast: *Embeth Davidtz, Ralph Fiennes, Caroline Goodall, Ben Kingsley, Liam Neeson*

After three previous nominations, and 20 years of neglect, Hollywood's greatest living storyteller Steven Spielberg finally won his long-overdue Oscar for Best Director for *Schindler's List* (one of its seven Academy Awards, the others being Best Film, Adapted Screenplay, Score, Cinematography, Editing, and Art Direction). This epic three-and-a-quarter-hour essay on the Holocaust saw Spielberg returning

List of Oscars: *Schindler won seven for Spielberg*

to his dormant Jewish roots and confounding those critics who said he was all style and no substance. Filmed in black-and-white and based on Thomas Kenneally's novel *Schindler's Ark*, it tells the true story of German industrialist Oskar Schindler (Liam Neeson). Arriving in Poland in the wake of the German invasion, Schindler quickly establishes a profitable enamelware business using the cheap labour of Jews from the Warsaw Ghetto. What starts as hard-nosed profiteering develops into an obsessive crusade to protect his Jewish employees. The eponymous list of the title held the names of the 1,100 workers Schindler eventually purchased to save from the gas chambers of Auschwitz. While Steven Zaillian's screenplay makes of Schindler something less complex than he was in real life, the emotional and moral impact of the film is still overwhelming. It boasts superb performances from an international cast: Oscar-nominated Neeson, Ralph Fiennes as psychotic SS Commandant Amon Goeth, and Ben Kingsley as Schindler's world-weary Jewish accountant Itzhak Stern. With Janusz Kaminsky's grainy, documentary-style photography – much of it on hand-held camera – and John Williams's haunting violin score (beautifully played by Isaak Perlman), this provides a uniquely uplifting cinematic experience, setting a standard of excellence that Spielberg will struggle to surpass.

EPIC DRAMA/HISTORICAL

Putting the sucker into Hudsucker: Bumpkin nerd Tim Robbins (left) with villainous Paul Newman

The Hudsucker Proxy

111 min.
Director: *Joel and Ethan Coen*
Origin: *USA*
Distributor: *Silver/Warner*
Cast: *Charles Durning, Jennifer Jason Leigh, John Mahoney, Paul Newman, Tim Robbins, Jim True*

Wacky sibling geniuses Joel and Ethan Coen entered the cinema mainstream with this uproarious tale of industrial skulduggery in the boardrooms of 1950s New York. Scripted by both brothers and friend Sam Raimi, and drawing heavily on the whimsical, feel-good styles of Frank Capra and Preston Sturges, it's the story of bumpkin nerd Norville Barnes (Tim Robbins) who unexpectedly finds himself president of blue-chip giant Hudsucker Industries. His sudden rise is engineered by villainous Hudsucker vice-chairman Sidney J. Mussburger (Paul Newman), whose attempts to depress the company's value in order to buy up its shares cheaply are thwarted when Barnes becomes a roaring success. The story of the simple backwoods boy putting one over on the slick city big-shots is hardly original, but director Joel Coen has adapted it to provide both a wonderful homage to 1940s cinema comedy, and a deliciously irreverent take on the whole concept of the American dream. Outlandish sets and cartoon-style characters combine to highlight the surreal, inhuman nature of corporate existence. It's a world gone mad; a monstrous parody of all that America holds most dear – money, power, success – but one, thankfully, in which decency, love and plain stupidity win through in the end. Paul Newman is cigar-chompingly good in one of his rare bad-guy roles, while Jennifer Jason Leigh is a revelation as the fast-talking journalist bitch from hell who first exposes and then falls in love with Barnes. An endearing, intelligent, visually extravagant comedy, it remains the Coen Brothers' finest film to date, despite its surprising lack of commercial success.

COMEDY

Forrest Gump

140 min.
Director: *Robert Zemeckis*
Origin: *USA*
Distributor: *Paramount*
Cast: *Sally Field, Tom Hanks, Gary Sinise, Mykelti Williamson, Robin Wright*

The 1994 box-office and the 1995 Oscar ceremony were both equally dominated by Robert Zemeckis's state-of-the-art version of Winston Groom's novel about a low-IQ everyman (clearly a movie relative of Dustin Hoffman's idiot savant in *Rain Man*) who follows his heart and soul, as well as his mother's daft aphorisms like "simple is as simple does" and "life is like a box of chocolates". This lovingly made film relies heavily on three obviously winning cards in its hand. Firstly, the genuinely likeable Tom Hanks's brio turn as the Southern simpleton who gets to meet Elvis, Kennedy, LBJ, Nixon and Lennon, before coming through Vietnam triumphant, then starting a mass walk across America and founding a powerful corporation. Maybe only Hanks, fresh from his first Oscar on *Philadelphia*, could have made this wet character palatable, indeed so tasty that Hanks went on to be the first Best Actor since Spencer Tracy to win Oscars in successive years. This talented "new man" player seems to defy criticism; his modesty as a performer and human being is a class act and utterly disarming. Second comes the film's amazing special effects in which war-torn Gary Sinise appears to have no legs and Gump talks to the various presidents in virtual-reality trickery of such genius that you can no longer believe anything you see on screen. Zemeckis takes the *Zelig/Dead Man Don't Wear Plaid* idea to its logical conclusion – so far. Third there's the film's controversial philosophizing: its comfortable homespun wisdom, its reinventing of awkward history (particularly Vietnam) and its cosy affirmation of the present as an ideal time. Six Oscars and $350 at the US box-office said Hanks was right when he commented: "One of the great things about the movie is that there is no time that is better than now. The '60s weren't better than now, the '70s sucked, and the '80s weren't any better."

COMEDY/MORALITY FABLE

Movie Genres

When people are deciding which film to watch or which video to rent they decide what kind of film they're in the mood for – comedy, western, horror or whatever. All films can be herded into these genre stables, though many of the best movies are crossbreeds and hybrids. *Bad Day at Black Rock* (1955) is a thriller in a western setting, *Blade Runner* (1982) is a *film noir* disguised as sci-fi, *The Hudsucker Proxy* (1994) is a 1990s pop-video-style pastiche of 1920s German expressionism and 1930s American East Coast screwball (no wonder it baffled a stay-at-home cinema audience!).

Some genres like romance and horror have their roots in an older, pre-cinema, literature-based tradition, others like sci-fi and the western are particular to film. Others again, like the musical, have their roots elsewhere (in opera and operetta and the Broadway show), but have developed their own style through the imagination of a few pioneers and innovators (like Busby Berkeley). Certain actors and directors have become synonymous with certain genres – notably John Ford and Sergio Leone with westerns, Alfred Hitchcock with thrillers and Woody Allen with comedy and Arnold Schwarzenegger with action, though they all occasionally did notable work outside their usual genre. There's a real risk in switching genres, though. The world has never quite forgiven John Wayne for playing the centurion in *The Greatest Story Ever Told* (1965), and declaiming: "Truly this is the Sawn of Gawd".

Adventure:
Swashbucklers and spectacle

The word "adventure" has an exciting ring: a new experience, an exotic venue, something outside the realm of our usual everyday existence. We need it to make life more than just a dreary, humdrum experience. Most of us cannot spend our lives travelling the world looking for adventure, but we can find it vicariously through exciting stories. And one place we find them is in the cinema.

The traditional swashbuckling costume adventure scored megapoints when it came to whisking us off into a more exciting world with glamorous heroes such as Douglas Fairbanks, Tyrone Power and the wickedly wonderful Errol Flynn. History and legend were rich hunting grounds for these stories, a favourite being the tale of Robin Hood. Among those who have had a crack at him have been Douglas Fairbanks Snr (*Robin Hood*, 1922), Richard Todd (*Robin Hood*, 1952), Sean Connery (*Robin and Marian*, 1976), Patrick Bergen (*Robin Hood*, 1991) and Kevin Costner (*Robin Hood: Prince of Thieves*, 1991). But for many Flynn is still the definitive Robin (*The Adventures of Robin Hood*, 1939).

Another rich vein of story material is the mystic East. Rudolph Valentino made his name as the exotic desert chieftain in *The Sheik* (1921) and its sequel, *Son of the Sheik* (1926), both top silent-movie adventures with a splash of romance. About the same time Fairbanks Snr filmed *The Thief of Bagdad* (1924), remade in 1948 by Alexander Korda and in 1978 by Clive Donner, and Tony Curtis in the unlikely but entertaining tale of *The Prince Who*

Exotic adventure: Rudolph Valentino in Son of the Sheik

was a Thief (1951). Special effects wizard Ray Harryhausen has also raided the myth and legend of the East for such movies as *The Golden Voyage of Sinbad* (1973), while pirates and the high seas are another favourite: Burt Lancaster in an atypical Robert Siodmak film *The Crimson Pirate* (1952) and John Derek as *Prince of Pirates* (1953).

True Tales from History

The real history of the loss of the *Bounty* has been mined several times. *In the Wake of the Bounty* (Flynn as Fletcher Christian in his 1932 debut film), two versions of *Mutiny on the Bounty* (1935/1962) and *The Bounty* (1984), in which writer Robert Bolt put the case for Captain Bligh. John Mills's trek to the South Pole as *Scott of the Antarctic* (1948) turned true-life adventure into rich screen material, while war has also proved a ripe source, using both historical fact and fiction: *The Four Feathers* (1929/1939/1976), *Gallipoli* (1981), *The Great Escape* (1963), *The Guns of Navarone* (1961) and *Murphy's War* (1971). The Bible and biblical times have proved another good source of material with films like *Ben-Hur* (1926/1958), *The Ten Commandments* (1923/1956), *Quo Vadis?* (1951/1985), *Spartacus* (1960) and *The Robe* (1953).

Raiding the Bookshelves

A good adventure tale on the page provides a similar escapist function to that on the screen, so the extent to which cinema has raided the bookshelves is hardly surprising. On the swashbuckling side Alexandre Dumas has been a winner: *The Three Musketeers* (1948/1974/1993), plus *The Count of Monte Cristo* (1934/1955/1961/1975) and *The Man in the Iron Mask* (1939/1976). Mark Twain has provided swashbuckling adventure (*The Prince and the Pauper* (1937/1978)) and the all-American adventures of *Tom Sawyer* (1938/1973) and *Huckleberry Finn* in many versions, including an excellent recent one starring Elijah

Wood (1994). The adventure tales of Robert Louis Stevenson were naturals for the movies – the 1950 *Treasure Island* featured Robert Newton as Long John Silver – as was the work of H. Rider Haggard: *King Solomon's Mines* (1937/1950/1977/1985) and *She* (1935/1965).

We explored Africa further with Rudyard Kipling (several versions of *The Jungle Book* including the early 1940 one with Sabu), while Edgar Rice Burroughs's *Tarzan* spawned a whole series of films. Herman Melville took us adventuring in search of a white whale (*Moby Dick* 1930/1956) and Joseph Conrad through the Far East with *Lord Jim* (1965). James Fenimore Cooper told his tale of early American history, *The Last of the Mohicans*, four times on screen (1922/1936/1977/1992).

Sci-fi and Comic-book Heroes

Showman Mike Todd provided the ultimate adventurous journey in *Around the World in 80 Days* (1956), while other Jules Verne tales moved us into the area of science fiction: *Journey to the Centre of the Earth* (1959) and *20,000 Leagues under the Sea* (1954). Raquel Welch and friends took a *Fantastic Voyage* (1966) inside the human body, as did Dennis Quaid in Joe Dante's

clever comedy version *InnerSpace* (1987). The *Star Trek* and *Star Wars* movies conduct their adventures in space, while comic-book hero *Superman* gets about both the heavens and the earth. Other comic-book heroes who have caught the eye of modern film-makers include notably *Batman* (1989/1992/1995), *Flash Gordon* (1980), *Dick Tracy* (1990) and *The Shadow* (1994).

Adventurous Directors

Much of the real-life story of director John Huston reads like the script for an adventure film. Huston was a master of such tales. Apart from *The African Queen* (1951), one of the best adventure-cum-love stories ever made, and *Moby Dick* (1956), his adventure output includes the enthralling *The Treasure of the Sierra Madre* (1948) and a full-blooded version of Kipling's *The Man Who Would Be King* (1975), while fellow master film-maker David Lean gave audiences all the spectacle and adventure they could possibly want in *Lawrence of Arabia* (1962), as did Akira Kurosawa with *Seven Samurai* (1954), the basis for the western *The Magnificent Seven* (1960).

Director John Boorman brought a very individual voice to adventure in *Deliverance* (1972) and *The Emerald Forest* (1985), disturbing tales of modern man versus nature. Fritz Lang's *Die Nibelungen* (1924), a 13th-century saga from his silent film days and acknowledged as one of his masterpieces, while Werner Herzog's *Aguirre, Wrath of God* (1972) and *Fitzcarraldo* (1982) combine art-house values with a sense of high adventure. On the commercial side, Steven Spielberg reinvented the spectacular adventure movie for modern audiences and gave us a new hero with the *Indiana Jones* films.

Spectacular swashbuckler: Burt Lancaster cuts a dashing figure in The Crimson Pirate

(Above) Heroines for the 90s: *Susan Sarandon (left) and Geena Davis as* Thelma and Louise, *a refreshingly original road movie in that the two stars are both women*

Hero for the 80s: *Harrison Ford (left), as Indiana Jones, with Sean Connery as his pappy*

The Modern Action Hero: Killer of True Adventure?

The James Bond movies, which began in 1962 with *Dr No* starring Sean Connery, along with Steve McQueen as *Bullitt* (1968), seemed to mark the birth of the modern action hero, who now in the films of Sylvester Stallone, Arnold Schwarzenegger, Jean-Claude Van Damme and Bruce Willis has largely turned the true adventure and journey genre into tales of violent action. But not totally. *The Rocketeer* (1991) was a recent example of a jolly good rip-roaring adventure, as was the fairy tale of *The Princess Bride* (1987).

And what else is the ever-popular road movie but an adventure? The genre takes us on a trip from the hippy, drug-dazed *Easy Rider* (1969) to *Thelma and Louise* (1991), a rare and highly popular female-centred adventure. *Romancing the Stone* (1984) and *The Jewel of the Nile* (1985), with Kathleen Turner as the action heroine, were true adventures in the traditional sense. On the other hand, just lately the highly original transvestite road movie *The Adventures of Priscilla, Queen of the Desert* (1994) created a whole new sub-genre. So could that be one of the directions in which the adventure movie will move during the twenty-first century, towards true screen sexual equality and a positive new meaning to the word "adventuress"?

Comedies:
Make 'em laugh

Of all the genres, comedy is the most difficult to catch, to sum up and to slot into one all-confining box. Pin it down for examination and its magic is gone. Nobody can ever hope to explain what makes a work "comic" and when they do they generally end up by appearing comic themselves, since comedy's essential role is to debunk authority.

The little tramp:
Charlie Chaplin's
classic creation

In his brilliant 1989 movie *Crimes and Misdemeanors*, writer-director Woody Allen has an obnoxious TV producer (splendidly played by Alan Alda) give his own analysis. "Comedy," states Alda, wagging a finger, "is tragedy plus time." Later in the film there's an even more bewilderingly pompous definition. "If it bends, it's funny," Alda tells us, with the air of one imparting great wisdom. "If it breaks – it isn't." No one knows precisely what comedy is. Its success is elusive and intangible, dependent on an individual's race, sex, cultural background, taste, empathy and buried – or not so buried – neuroses. To put it even more simply: if you laugh at it, it's a comedy.

The Language of Comedy

In the early silent-screen days, comedy was one of the staple languages of cinema. It was more universal than it is today: a set of common, easily identifiable conventions within which the interpreters could develop their own physical actions to articulate emotions that could not be verbally expressed. But, despite appearing raucously simplistic, the works of Charlie Chaplin, Buster Keaton and Harold Lloyd are intricately orchestrated and often devastatingly funny. Pointing to Keaton as the artist "who brought pure physical comedy to its greatest heights", critic James Agee argues that his finest setpieces were textbook examples of "the ideally good gag... which would bring the victim up the ladder by cruelly controlled degrees and leave them drained and exhausted". Selected glances at *The General* (1926) or the hat-buying trip in *Steamboat Bill Jnr* (1928) show exactly what he means.

The arrival of sound revolutionized screen comedy, but what the genre lost in purity it gained in scope. Though most silent-screen clowns floundered in the new medium, strong echoes of their style can be seen in the finely wrought cinema of France's Jacques Tati and – to a lesser extent – in the dexterous wizardry of Steve Martin. With the talkies, verbal confusion came to serve as the wellspring for a new brand of humour. Audiences in the 1930s thrilled to the circus-barker backchat of the Marx Brothers, the fussy misunderstandings of Laurel and Hardy and the curmudgeonly blustering of W. C. Fields. Comedy was still physical, but words and gesture were now-working in tandem.

Comedy as Comment

Wordsmith film-makers, fashioning comedy from behind the camera, rose to prominence and the genre took on a noticeably more satirical edge. Directors like Ernst Lubitsch, Preston Sturges and Jean Renoir aimed delicate barbs at what they saw as the pomposity and hypocrisy of the powers-that-be. To laugh at an institution, be it school, the government, marriage or a funeral, somehows lessens the iron grip that all institutions have on our lives. And, most important of all, don't be fooled by their grins, their pratfalls, their eager-to-please demeanours – comics are dangerous people.

But if comedy is about lampooning institutions and exploding taboos, it begs the question: is there such a thing as a no-go area for comedians, a topic too serious and emotive to be tackled for laughs? Amazingly, all the evidence suggests not. Just think of three of our era's most controversial issues: child abuse, the atom bomb and the Nazi Holocaust. Way back in the early 1960s the first two of these issues were considered fair game by visionary director Stanley Kubrick, who produced the paedophilia-tinged *Lolita* (1962) as an acid comedy of middle-class manners and then translated the threat of nuclear apocalypse into a giddying black farce with *Dr Strangelove* (1963). The Holocaust requires more care. Learning of the full horrors of Hitler's genocidal policies,

W.C. Fields in **The Bank Dick:** *"Anyone who hates small dogs and children can't be all bad"*

the type of comedy mainstream cinema-goers wanted it to be. Word got around and audiences stayed away in droves.

An Enduring Genre

What's more certain is that this is one genre that's been a sure-fire thing throughout movie history. Musicals look to have one dancing-pump in the grave, the western canters in and out of fashion and the crime-thriller is subject to frequent overhauls and reinventions. But comedy is a constant, whether it be Cary Grant's elegant double-takes, Robin Williams's improvised pyrotechnics, Peter Sellers's frantic mimickry or Buster Keaton's soulful, sphinx-like gaze to the camera. And this is a genre deliriously free of rules and conventions. If it bends, it's funny, of course. But if it breaks, if it's broken by artists of timing and talent... well, that can be pretty funny, too.

Chaplin expressed regret at making his World War Two satire *The Great Dictator* (1940), though in more recent years Jewish comic Mel Brooks has dealt broad-based sideswipes at Nazism in *To Be or Not to Be* (1983) and *The Producers* (1968). To hunt for humour in such all-consuming tragedies is in no way an attempt to belittle or trivialize them. The finest social comedy takes the viewer outside a situation, looks at it from completely different angles and finds alternative routes back through a maze of received wisdom.

Of course, great comedy does not have to be so pointedly political. From the sparkling screwballs of the 1930s through to the neuroses-riddled essays of Woody Allen, much of the genre's best work follows a less specific agenda, finding humour in one social microcosm that reflects on the wider world beyond. "Woody Allen makes a movie as if he were lighting 10,000 safety matches to illuminate a city," said fellow comic Gene Wilder. "Each one is a little epiphany; topical, ethnic or political."

Rules to be Broken

But while comedy illuminates the world around us, the genre itself remains defiantly indefinable. It's hard even to say what constitutes a "comedy". 1980s superstar Arnold Schwarzenegger impressed the critics when he moved from effects-laden action hits to comedies like *Twins* (1987) and *Kindergarten Cop* (1991), but many failed to appreciate the tongue-in-cheek approach he brought to even his most vicious, nihilistic films. Who knows? Maybe all of Schwarzenegger's movies are humoresques of one breed or another.

While the term "comedy" provokes specific expectations in the average film-goer, this can be fatally misleading. Howard Hawks's *Bringing Up Baby* (1938), Buñuel's surrealistic *The Discreet Charm of the Bourgeoisie* (1972) and the bawdy Canadian teen pic *Porky's* (1981) hardly seem to hail from the same planet and yet, incredibly, each would be bracketed under the comedy label. Martin Scorsese's *The King of Comedy* (1982) floundered at the box-office because audiences were

fooled by the title and the presence of winsome entertainer Jerry Lewis in the cast-list. *The King of Comedy* is undeniably hilarious, a wickedly subversive satire on the cult of personality, but it wasn't

A comedy? Luis Buñuel's bourgeoise confection

Thrillers:
The suspense is killing me

The thriller is the stuff of all our dreams and nightmares, where we're chased by unknown spies, faceless bogeymen or heartless representations of unbending authority. It's the way we exorcize our fears, allay terrors and purge our psyches of their darkest horrors.

In dreams we do this alone and at random, but in the cinema we can willingly join an audience and do it as a communal, controlled experience. This may be scary – in fact, the scarier the better – but it's ultimately cathartic and comforting as we're introducing an element of control, pattern, organized storylines and art-forms into an unpredictable and pitiless universe.

Gangster thriller: *(left to right) Edmond O'Brien, James Cagney and Virginia Mayo in* White Heat

Hitch

In the same way that the western trail always leads back to a single director – John Ford – the thriller genre too was defined by one man: Alfred Hitchcock. Fifteen years after his death, the word "Hitchcockian" has entered the language while his 50-odd movies

provide a textbook, map reference and starting point for anyone making a thriller. Few directors mined one golden seam so single-mindedly.

There was no thriller literature till Wilkie Collins's *The Woman in White* in the 1860s, but the form struck a chord with the Victorians, and soon there was detective fiction like Conan Doyle's *Sherlock Holmes*, the penny dreadful novelettes, stage grand guignol like *Sweeney Todd, the Demon Barber of Fleet Street*, and real-life cases like the London stalk-and-slasher Jack the Ripper.

Hitchcock, himself a London-born Victorian, was much influenced by all this, and his first true "Hitchcock" film, *The Lodger*

(1926), was a yarn about the Ripper, featuring an innocent, everyman hero fighting to clear his name. *Blackmail* (1928), his next thriller, continued this theme and introduced the idea of a chase sequence in a famous location (London's British Museum). Hitch also enjoyed spy stories like Joseph Conrad's *Secret Agent*, Somerset Maugham's *Ashenden* and John Buchan's *The 39 Steps*. During his British 1930s heyday he filmed all three, and these films are prototypes for his other great films – *The Lady Vanishes* (1938), *Foreign Correspondent* (1940), *Saboteur* (1942) and *North by Northwest* (1959) – influencing in turn the *James Bond* movies and sparking off the whole 1960s spy cycle.

In the 1940s Hitchcock developed another suspense drama type, the character-led study of the criminal mind and the location that breeds it. This kind of film so impressed the 1950s French New Wave that they elevated Hitch to iconic status and paid tribute to his work in films such as Truffaut's *The Bride Wore Black* (1968) and Chabrol's *Le Boucher* (1969). He moved from *Suspicion* (1941), focusing on an archetypal could-a-new-husband-be-a killer plot, to *Shadow of a Doubt* (1943), where kindly uncle Joseph Cotten turns out to be a rotten egg. It's his most literary and perceptive film, where there are few overt thrills but there's a constant tension emanating from shifting character relationships.

Hitch also tried another form, the psychiatric thriller, in *Spellbound* (1945), and throughout the 1950s he became obsessed with

the byways of the criminal mind, as his heroes became more flawed and his villains more understandable. Bit by bit they became one, as suggested by *Strangers on a Train* (1951) when two men agree to swap murders. Although only one of them kills, both are equally guilty in the eyes of the Catholic director. He cunningly used that icon of American goodness, James Stewart, to suggest weakness, wickedness and dangerous obsession in *Rear Window* (1954) and *Vertigo* (1958). Evil is within us all, Hitchcock tells us. We all are guilty.

Hitchcock moved further into the area where the thriller meets the horror film with *Psycho* (1960), where the apparent heroine Janet Leigh is killed because she's stealing her boss's money and the crazed murderer, Anthony Perkins, is forgiven because he loves her. This perverse logic predicates a weird universe where it's dangerous even to have a shower, and it's the enduring appeal of the thriller that we continually want the catharsis, the thrill without real pain.

Angst and Alienation

The thriller may have its roots in the Victorian era, but it's a characteristically modern genre because it expresses existential angst and alienation from one's own society. We're all Norman Bates in *Psycho*. *Film noir* portrays man beset by troubles in a lonely world. In the classic *film noir* we're invited to identify with this alienated central character (such as William Holden in *Sunset Blvd* (1950) or Harrison Ford's Deckard in *Blade Runner*

(1982), an example of the point at which *film noir* spills over into sci-fi). All *noir* characters are on a rollercoaster whose driver is hidden from them, buffeted by a universe they cannot control, swept on by an ever-deteriorating situation, and usually ignorant of the real reasons until it's too late to do anything about them except suffer the consequences. The difference between *noir* and classical drama is that in *noir* motives and structures aren't overt and the universe is utterly mysterious and dark. We the audience exorcize our own alienation by identification with the alienated character. Unlike every other genre, the thriller has never gone out of fashion. It has developed and changed, but always stayed with its basic ingredients. It speaks to

us on a very fundamental, instinctual and gut level. You'd think we'd want to turn away but, as with an accident, we stare despite ourselves. On a physical level the fear induced is very akin to the experience of a ride on a fairground attraction which, considering cinema's roots, is singularly appropriate. But on an intellectual level the thriller's grip is much harder to explain. Why are we fascinated by seeing portrayals of evil and sudden death?

Perhaps it's simply the stuff of classical drama, like Jacobean revenge tragedy or Shakespeare, where the danger is solved, the evil cleared away, the "normality" restored, and we can all get on with our lives feeling happier about a chaotic world we can't do anything to alter. What's odder is

that murder mysteries like Agatha Christie's *Miss Marple* stories are considered lighthearted entertainment to brighten up our lives, like a musical. The very existence of the "comedy thriller" like the 1930s *Thin Man* movies (based on the Dashiell Hammett novels) seems a contradiction in terms.

When the thriller really came of age in the 1940s with *film noir*, and people's sex lives and passions were thrown into the stew with their greed and their pettinesses, great movies emerged. Billy Wilder's *Double Indemnity* (1944), with Barbara Stanwyck giving the most alluring portrait of wickedness as the murderous *femme fatale*, is one of the finest. The odd thing is that it's Stanwyck's sluttish, sleazy evil that's attractive, not Edward G.

Robinson's upright and dogged representation of the law. When the movies followed pulp-fiction thriller writer Raymond Chandler down those hardboiled mean streets in films like *Farewell, My Lovely* (1975), *The Big Sleep* (1946) and *The Long Goodbye* (1973), we were shown on the one hand a flawed, cynical, battered hero and on the other some tremendously engaging portraits of wickedness.

Maybe this is why the thriller continues to exert a powerful draw. We can sin vicariously without ever suffering the consequences. We can enjoy all the vivid, lurid details of all of life's darkest, most terrible things – death, violence, hate, revenge – without a scratch. For, as Hitchcock said on one occasion to his star, Bergman: "It's only a movie, Ingrid."

Classic French gangsters: *Alain Delon (right) is in mortal danger in Jean-Pierre Melville's* The Samourai

Cult and Underground Cinema:

The shock of the new

Ever since the dazzled and panic-stricken audiences of 1896 stared aghast at the ghost train that seemed to be steaming into their very seats, the cinema has always explored the new and the shocking, with successive generations of audiences craving ever more startling experiences and demanding from this magical medium a variety of sensations.

And film-makers at the cutting edge, more than just providing the public with a succession of gimmicks, have long been aware of film's possibilities as a medium for experimentation, exploration and even subversion, from the artistic to the anarchic, from the downright painterly to the political, from the gorgeous to the gut-wrenching.

The surreal thing

The 1930s surrealists formed film's most defined avant garde so far in their use of the medium. Film-makers like Luis Buñuel and artists and poets like Salvador Dali and Jean Cocteau were quick to recognize the potentialities of film to explore the surrealists' ideas of psychological juxtaposition, with their fantastic visual collages and mythological constructions. Even today images such as a human eye apparently being cut with a razor in *Un Chien Andalou* (1928) or Orpheus stepping through the mirror in *Orphée* (1949) still have the power to shock or delight, and instantly to capture the imagination. These early explorations of the fantastic possibilities of film as a medium of challenge, while having to some extent become part of the language of mainstream cinema, continue to influence and inspire experimental film-makers, forming part of the canon of modern film art. Where, for example, would David Lynch have been without the surrealists?

The history of the great movie innovators is twofold. On the one hand you have the definers and refiners of accepted genres, such as Alfred Hitchcock, John Ford, Fritz Lang and Orson Welles. On the other hand you have the rank outsiders, the experimentalists, the challengers of accepted and familiar forms, such as Kenneth Anger, Andy Warhol, Jean Cocteau, Luis Buñuel, Andrei Tarkovsky, Sergei Paradjanov, David Lynch, Derek Jarman and Peter Greenaway.

There is, though, a marked crossover between the two categories and lots of mixing of resources. Hitchcock was fascinated by the surrealists, and their interest in dreams and *amour fou*, and he integrated a famous dream sequence by Salvador Dali in his psycho-romantic thriller *Spellbound* (1945).

Shocking Treatment

Some of the shock is just for sensation, some of it for purposes of artistic advance – and sometimes they can be the same thing. The purpose of shock for the artist is to take the audience by surprise, to disturb the comfortable equilibrium of their expectations – of being shown a lovely picture, of being told a story, of being handed something comfortable and pretty they can admire at arm's length – long enough to have them ask themselves some difficult questions about those expectations, about art, life, their society, who they are, maybe even what it means to be human. This has always been the job of the avant garde in any medium.

Culturally, however, this is no longer the preserve of the left-wing intellectual. The surrealists' fundamental impetus was to challenge the assumptions and cosiness of the bourgeoisie, so it would be ironic if what they saw as a tool for social change had become merely a fashionable entertainment for the middle-class culture vulture. But then this is the "discreet charm of the bourgeoisie": to take everything in your stride and make it safe by embracing it, to turn it into a parlour game. There is little doubt, though, that these films have become a signifier for middle-class culturalism. But then the innovator can't be held responsible for what use others make of his art and, in this case, social history has subverted the subversives. Later generations of innovators, such as

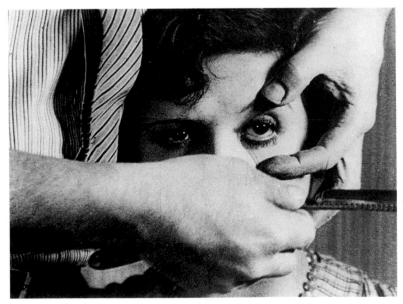

Un Chien Andalou: *Luis Buñuel and Salvador Dali at film-making's cutting edge*

***In the* Flesh**: *Andy Warhol's superstar Joe Dallesandro*

Jarman and Greenaway working in Britain, have operated far more within an accessible imagery and film form, even if the underlying intention was revolutionary.

Foreign Phenomenon

Is "avant garde" a largely non-American phenomenon? Do American films merely borrow and swallow up foreign ideas and film-makers? When the American western died in the late 1960s, the Americans simply imported the avant garde ideas of the spaghetti westerns of Sergio Leone, a true innovator, but also the instigator of what US western film-making became thereafter. Until Kevin Costner, that is, who restored the western to modern popularity by re-conservatizing it and presenting it as even more traditional than tradition – the Reaganite western.

The American horror film, too

looked to Italy for its inspiration in the 1960s and 1970s, though the horror genre is still at the cutting edge of mainstream film-making, for example William Friedkin's *The Exorcist* (1973) and the work of George Romero and Wes Craven. Craven is a genuine innovator with *A Nightmare on Elm Street* (1984). Interesting that its central protagonist and villain, Freddy Krueger, is a creature of dreams. No doubt the surrealists would have approved.

Up to the 1970s, with the international art cinema circuit still in full flow, film-makers within the system, or at least at the side of it, were providing the shock of the new. Werner Herzog, for example, made large-scale, unwieldy narratives that were more like journeys of the soul than movies, long and difficult but with great central images, always tackling questions of man's inner nature and his position in relation to a merciless and implacable universe. Another German innovator, Wim Wenders, produced two extraordinary overviews of Berlin, both before and after the wall came down, in *Wings of Desire* (1987) and *Faraway So Close* (1993) but, while the former was enthusiastically received worldwide, the latter was met with a remarkable chill. Wenders also went to America in 1984 to film what is the ultimate American art movie, *Paris, Texas*, transforming that most traditional of modern American genres, the "road movie", into a highly imaginative, poetic statement, and turning personal drama into something approaching spiritual quest. Finland's Aki Kaurismaki established a place on the world's weird stage with the absurdist *Hamlet Goes Business* (1987) and *I Hired a Contract Killer* (1990), while in Spain Pedro Almodóvar shocked the "moral majority" with his psycho-farces *Tie Me Up! Tie Me Down!* (1989) and *Kika* (1994)

Where To Now?

The shock of the new is now coming more and more from directors operating from within the system such as Quentin Tarantino who, under the cover of familiar forms (the gangster movie genre), is managing to ask some corrosive questions in revolutionary constructions. Neither *Reservoir Dogs* (1992) nor *Pulp Fiction* (1994) is constructed in a traditional way though, for the sake of the box-office returns perhaps, they both give the impression of so being.

At present in western cinema culture there is no true avant garde movement in its original sense. Is this because the public is satisfied or because film-makers are complacent? Maybe it's just that we're all a little bit more frightened. Firstly, films have become so expensive that no one wants to take a chance on financing the unknown and, secondly, the new conservatism is stifling any overtly challenging material in the cinema (and increasingly elsewhere). If the surrealists tried to make *Un Chien Andalou* now, it would almost certainly never reach celluloid.

It is arguable that the place of the innovator is now to be found in the pop video, so a whole new generation of kids is being weaned from an early age on the visual product of surreal subversion. Exciting, huh?

***Derek Jarman's* Sebastiane**: *Shooting at the sharp end of cinema*

Horror:
Be afraid, be very afraid

Like the thriller genre, horror plumbs the depth of our subconscious to expose our hidden fears and suppressed desires. The best horror exploits our most primal nature: our vulnerability at birth, our initial alienation from "adult" society, our terror of the unknown. Despite its reputation as the most downmarket of genres (and to be sure the bulk of its output views like shabby conjuring tricks), horror can be the most potent and resonant of all cinema entertainment.

As with the thriller, the horror movie shifts with the flow of the culture that spawns it, turning a magic mirror on society's tangled influences. With film finding its way as a fledgling art-form, the first outings – 1920's *The Golem*, 1921's *Nosferatu* – drew their inspiration from Gothic fairytale traditions of the previous century. Later horror films like *Frankenstein* (1931) saw the form fully acclimatized to the modern age, often probing at the implications of galloping 20th-century technology for age-old notions of community and individual identity.

While the building-brick conventions of the horror movie – the brooding set-up, the alien threat, the jolting shock – satisfyingly stay the same, the past 50 years have seen subtle but significant changes to the genre's essence. Horror film theorists sum up these shifts by arguing that contemporary horror has moved from a basically secure to a basically insecure or paranoid vision of the modern world. In early horror, the critics claim, the threat or monster is clearly identifiable. It is an alien "other", be it bolt-necked, fanged or furry. Nobody would ever mistake it for "one of us". Similarly,

the picture's ultimately victorious heroes are the authorities, the agents of social order who vanquish the intruder(s) in *The Thing from Another World* (1951) or *The Creature from the Black Lagoon* (1954).

In contrast, the contemporary horror movie is typified by a random viciousness and a lack of clear-cut distinctions between right and wrong, good and evil. Once the heroes of the tale, the authorities – science, the law, the nuclear family – are now revealed to be at best ineffectual, at worst openly destructive.

Psycho Analysis

Critics point to Alfred Hitchcock's seminal killer-chiller *Psycho* (1960) as a milestone along this route from a secure to a paranoid vision. The very narrative form of *Psycho* is enough to make a quivering wreck of the average first-time viewer. Hitchcock forces us into identification with a heroine he suddenly, shockingly has slaughtered, then switches our sympathies on to the timid, mother-fixated Norman Bates (Anthony

Perkins), ultimately the most unreliable of all movie "heroes". But where *Psycho* is most radical is in the way it moves the horror element from something that's outside American society to something that's actually spawned by it and rooted in the family construct – a boy's troubled transition from mothered child to pillar-of-strength adulthood. After *Psycho* the horror movie would never be so clear-cut and easily identified.

The film's influence can be seen in such vintage stalk 'n' slash outings as John Carpenter's *Hallowe'en* (1978) and 1974's *The Texas Chainsaw Massacre*. But *Psycho* was not the only key horror pic of the 1960s. The chilling *Night of the Living Dead* (1968) is a stunning study in dehumanization that turns America's most sacred institutions upside down; an angelic blond-locked child feasts off her mother's corpse and the National Guard, while storming to the rescue, inadvertently gun down the tale's sole reliable hero. Similarly, Roman Polanski's *Rosemary's Baby* (1968) worked so well because it couched its satanic plotline in the bustling normalcy of the present-day, a technique later used to equally devastating effect in *The Wicker Man* (1973) and William Friedkin's *The Exorcist* (1972).

One possible litmus test of the argument that the horror film has shifted from a secure to a paranoid portrayal of the modern world comes when we compare the classic 1954 sci-fi chiller *The Thing from Another World* with John Carpenter's ultra-gruesome 1982

Insanity claws: *Max Schreck's* Nosferatu

remake *The Thing*. Both pictures adopt the same story outline, that of a team of explorers being menaced by a deep-frozen alien at a remote Arctic base. But whereas the original paints the creature as a hulking outer-space behemoth, Carpenter shows the beast as a chameleon-like shape-shifter, first impersonating a bright-eyed husky dog and later the crew members themselves ("Man is the warmest place to hide", ran the poster's tag-line). Because of this, paranoia is rife in the remake and the boundaries around which the film revolves – good and bad, hot and cold, inside and out – soon blur and break down. None of the crew members can trust each other, collaboration is impossible and even the seemingly victorious conclusion is open-ended and faintly suspect. Is the beast still masquerading as one of the two survivors?

The Thing is a prime example of that breed of modern chiller known as the "body horror", best epitomized in the work of horror *auteur* David Cronenberg. This depiction of an unreliable, possibly mutating physical being feeds off our unease over recent breakthroughs in medical science – birth control, cosmetic surgery, mind-

The high-kitsch Hammer horror: Christopher Lee, here in Scars of Dracula, *played the Count in numerous outings*

enhancing drugs and the darker implications of Thalidomide and man-made cancers. On a less tangible level, these new types of chiller can be said to have their roots in a postmodern age where any concept of individual identity is obsolete. The inhabitants of the modern media age, it is argued, are mere free-floating social con-

structs, fired into preconditioned responses by outside stimuli. It is this giddying absence of self that the best horror movies manage to exploit so ruthlessly.

Burn or Ban

Of course, however much truth there may be in the secure-to-paranoid theory, it is inevitably limited, leaning heavily on a handful of ideal texts in order to sketch out a neat but suspiciously tidy overview. The theory conveniently overlooks the decidedly otherworldly tinge of the finest 1920s and 1930s chillers. Similarly, while the received wisdom on 1950s sci-fi movies like *The Thing...* and *Invasion of the Body Snatchers* (1956) is that they were conservative critiques of the dehumanizing effects of communism, others might view them as super-sly assaults on the dehumanizing effects of the McCarthy era's anti-left hysteria. Maybe early horror was a lot more subversive than it's

John Carpenter's The Thing: *The alien as insider*

generally given credit for.

Of all film genres, horror is the field that has traditionally provoked the most intervention from the censors, with pictures frequently singled out for public condemnation and banning. Perhaps the burn-it-or-ban-it brigade are genuinely disgusted by the blood and gore and the dark sides of humanity depicted in horror films. Maybe they genuinely want to protect the public from such shenanigans. But the best horror strikes very deep, dredging up long-submerged fears and anxieties and that can be just a little bit too unsettling for many viewers.

Possibly there are more personal, intimate, closer-to-home reasons why some respectable, upstanding citizens loathe and legislate against the horror film. Perhaps it calls to mind that night, many many years ago, when they awoke in bed, with their parents a thousand miles away down the hall, and the branches at the window-pane looked like a clawed and skeletal hand, trying to get in....

Musicals:
Gotta sing, gotta dance

Surprisingly, the first talkie wasn't a dramatic yarn. It was a musical with little dialogue – Al Jolson's *The Jazz Singer* (1927), in which the Jewish cantor's son now rather embarrassingly gets into blackface to sing what was even then an old song, "My Mammy". It doesn't seem much of a revolution now, but then it was a sensation and a new genre was born (though, in fact, there had previously been silent musicals with scores sent out to cinemas for pianos or orchestras). In the late 1920s the nervous studios were soon vying with one another to bring shows to the screen.

The Jazz Singer was a Warner production and some of the best musicals came from that tough-edged studio, like the snappy, realistically filmed backstage musicals *42nd Street* (1933), *Gold Diggers of 1933*, *Footlight Parade* (1933) and *Dames* (1934) with Dick Powell, Ruby Keeler and Joan Blondell. At least the non-singing parts of the films were realistic; the numbers themselves could hardly be less naturalistic, and another new art-form was born – film choreography.

Bring on the Dancing Girls

The star here was Busby Berkeley, who started swinging the camera around in breathtaking kaleidoscopic patterns, often overhead or underneath shots of chubby chorus girls, and advancing the form by creating self-contained dramatic stories for some of his musical numbers like "Shuffle off to Buffalo". Other routines were simply abstract patterns, with showgirls or pianos or violins treated equally loftily by Berkeley as if they were components of a

moving sculpture.

But the greatest musicals came from the escapist, wholesomely oriented Metro-Goldwyn-Mayer studio, which had the (some believed) ironic motto of "art for art's sake". Certainly MGM's musicals weren't generally perceived as art in their day, except perhaps those of Gene Kelly's latter period – *An American in Paris* (1951) or *Invitation to the Dance* (1956) – but were seen as the most popular of popular entertainments, enshrining the pop music of their day in a kind of long pop video. But now many of the songs have become the standards of the 20th century, we can reassess these hugely popular films for their undoubted artistic merit.

MGM's *Broadway Melody* (1929) was one of the smashes of the early sound era and also the first musical to win an Oscar for Best Picture, and this compendium-style musical, designed to showcase as many performers and numbers as possible, continued to be in vogue throughout the 1930s, with further *Broadway Melodies* in 1936, 1938 and 1940. Although they used the word

Trolley dolly: *Judy Garland singles "The Trolley Song" in* Meet Me in St. Louis

"Broadway" as a glitzy come-on for a Depression-afflicted public, they are their own thing – pure slices of cinema.

A Golden Age

But MGM's golden age of musicals began in 1939, with the evolution of "the Freed Unit" under legendary producer Arthur Freed, starting out with *The Wizard of Oz* (1939) and ending abruptly after the popular and much-Oscared

Gigi in 1958. Freed teamed Mickey Rooney and Judy Garland (*Babes in Arms*, 1939), brought Gene Kelly to MGM (*For Me and My Gal*, 1942), and persuaded Fred Astaire back to the movies (*Easter Parade* (1948), *The Band Wagon* (1953)). Garland is easily the greatest female musical star, with her MGM career running from the Rooney films, via *Oz*, to *The Harvey Girls* (1946), *Meet Me in St Louis* (1944), *In the Good Old Summer Time* (1949) and *Summer*

Stock (1950), though one of her most exciting films was for Warner – *A Star Is Born* (1955) with its electrifying "Born in a Trunk" routine.

MGM made only a handful of pictures with one of the two greatest male musical stars, Fred Astaire, including *Easter Parade* with Garland and his last with his legendary partner Ginger Rogers, *The Barkleys of Broadway* (1949). Fred and Ginger's historic nine-film partnership was forged at the little RKO studios, and their *Top Hat* (1935) and *Swing Time* (1936) are the quintessence of style, glamour and sophistication. All Gene Kelly's great triumphs were at Metro – *Cover Girl* (1944), *Anchors Aweigh* (1945), *The Pirate* (1948), *On the Town* (1949), *Summer Stock* (1950), *Brigadoon* (1954) and everybody's favourite musical, *Singin' in the Rain* (1952), with the genre's most famous dance sequence. MGM also brought together the two top crooners, Bing Crosby and Frank Sinatra, for Cole Porter's *High Society* (1956).

Back to Broadway

Though the musical is an essentially American form, adapted from the European operetta, other countries made musicals, too, with less than cosmic success. Notable exceptions were Jacques Demy's *The Umbrellas of Cherbourg* (1964) and *Young Girls of Rochefort* (1966), and in Britain the 1930s Jessie Matthews musicals (*Evergreen* (1934), *Gangway* (1937)) and the 1960s vehicles for Cliff Richard (*The Young Ones* (1961), *Summer Holiday* (1963)) and the Beatles (*Help!* (1965), *A Hard Day's Night* (1964)).

The nine-Oscar-winning *Gigi* (1958) was simply a conventional filming of a top Broadway show, pointing the way ahead for the survival of musicals after their sell-by date had ended in the mid-1950s. MGM, seeing the writing on the wall, appealed to a new gener-

Guys and Dolls: *Frank Sinatra sings to Vivian Blane in the 50s hit*

ation by switching to Elvis Presley movies.

The 1960s saw a successful run of big Broadway shows on the silver screen, among them *Gypsy* (1962), *West Side Story* (1962), *My Fair Lady* (1964), in which the stage show's star Julie Andrews was unceremoniously dumped for Audrey Hepburn, and *The Sound of Music* (1964) showcasing a personal triumph for the rejected Andrews in one of the most successful film musicals of all time. The same year Julie won an Oscar for Disney's *Mary Poppins* (1964). But just when the musical seemed back in vogue, there was a trio of box-office disasters with ultra-expensive musicals: *Star!* (1968) with Andrews again in a biopic of Gertrude Lawrence; Rex Harrison in *Dr Dolittle* (1967); and even Barbra Streisand in *Hello, Dolly!* (1969), directed by Gene Kelly.

The musical was pronounced dead. But was it? Britain's Ken Russell tried to ape 1930s musicals with his *The Boy Friend* (1971) and filmed the Who's rock opera *Tommy* in 1975. Liza Minnelli, Garland's daughter, scored a huge success in *Cabaret* (1972), winning an Oscar over Diana Ross in *Lady Sings the Blues* (1972), a musical biopic of blues-singer Billie

Holliday. Ross's next attempt in *The Wiz* (1978), an all-black version of *The Wizard of Oz*, flopped despite her and Michael Jackson's presence, though Jackson's best-selling *Thriller* video seemed like a full-scale dance musical. Catering to the nostalgia market, MGM celebrated its 50th birthday with an all-singing, all-dancing compilation of its best moments in *That's Entertainment!* (1974) and scored one of its biggest hits, following it up with *That's Entertainment, Part 2* in 1976 and *That's Entertainment III* in 1994 to mark the studio's 70th anniversary.

John Travolta scored two hits in *Saturday Night Fever* (1977), not strictly a musical but showcasing several hits for the Bee Gees with Travolta dancing up a disco storm, and in *Grease* (1978) with Olivia Newton-John, but when he tried to repeat his *Fever* success with *Staying Alive* (1983) audiences stayed away. Nor would they

buy tickets to the Village People's *Can't Stop the Music* (1980) or Olivia's *Xanadu* (1980), even with Gene Kelly on board. Similarly, Francis Ford Coppola's homages to the musical and music of earlier times, *One from the Heart* (1982) and *The Cotton Club* (1984), weren't appreciated.

On the other hand, Patrick Swayze had a mega-hit with semi-musical *Dirty Dancing* (1987) and Disney cartoons found their way back to favour with Broadway-style tunes in *The Little Mermaid* (1989), *Beauty and the Beast* (1991) and *Aladdin* (1992). Encouraged by their reception, Disney filmed a full-scale original musical, *Newsies* (1992), but it flopped. However, Bette Midler, veteran of *The Rose* (1979) and *For the Boys* (1991), scored a huge popular success on television with a remake of one of Broadway's finest, *Gypsy* (1994), proving this was where the musical's audience now is – at home with a cup of cocoa.

Nastassja Kinski: One from the Heart flopped

Passion and Romance:

Love and pain, and the whole damn thing

It is love that makes the world go round, we are told, and it certainly ensures the continuation of the human species. So it is hardly surprising that tales of romance and passion have been an important part of cinema since its early days. What has changed is how we present them.

The appeal of many romantic stories is in the way they give a sense of destiny and purpose, sometimes even poetry, to our otherwise humdrum relationships. This is certainly true of the great love stories of literature, many of which have found their way to the screen. An obvious example is *Romeo and Juliet*, filmed three times, the best version being Franco Zeffirelli's in 1968 (plus the Nureyev/Fonteyn ballet (1966) and the musical *West Side Story* (1961)). There is a tragic element, too, in the love between Heathcliff and Cathy in *Wuthering Heights* (1939/1970/1992), and that of *Anna Karenina* and Vronsky (Greta Garbo and Fredric March, 1935; Vivien Leigh and Kieron Moore, 1948).

Without his love for Lucie Manette, Sidney Carton (Ronald Colman/Dirk Bogarde) would never have performed his self sacrifice in *A Tale of Two Cities* (1935/1958). The love story of Lara and *Doctor Zhivago* (Julie

Christie and Omar Sharif, 1965) gains another dimension from its entanglement in the historical sweep of revolution and war, as does the explosive and destructive passion of Scarlett O'Hara and Rhett Butler in one of the cinema's favourite romances, *Gone with the Wind* (1939).

And what greater sense of destiny can you have than a love story that reaches across time? – a dramatic device used in fantasies such as *Time after Time* (1979), where Malcolm McDowell as Sherlock Holmes pursues Jack the Ripper into the 20th century and finds love with Mary Steenburgen. Love in the movies even reaches across death itself: Michael Powell's masterly fantasy, *A Matter of Life and Death* (1946), where dying fighter pilot David Niven's heavenly argument for his return to earth rests on love, and *Here Comes Mr Jordan* (1941), remade as *Heaven Can Wait* (1978)

– Robert Montgomery/Warren Beatty returning to earth in a borrowed body and finding true love. There was even a film in which Death itself, played by Fredric March, takes on flesh and falls victim to Cupid's arrow (*Death Takes a Holiday*, 1934).

Although the box-office usually loves a happy ending, it ain't necessarily so when it comes to romance. This is the case in two of the most effective love cinema stories of all time – the beautifully restrained *Brief Encounter* (1945), with the very English Celia Johnson and Trevor Howard conducting their unexpected and overwhelming middle-class love affair through secret meetings at a railway station, and the film which is many people's favourite romance, *Casablanca* (1942), where the cynical Humphrey Bogart character surrenders Ingrid Bergman to higher principle.

Love in Another Genre

Romance often plays a part in films of a different genre. It is usually, though not invariably, at the centre of the musical, while the combination genre of romantic comedy is an audience-puller for

Brief Encounter: *Smoke gets in your eyes*

Blue movie: Béatrice Dalle in the Oscar-nominated Betty Blue

all tastes from screwball to sex farce to thriller and black comedy. But there are also occasions when the love story is the motivating force in a film which is ostensibly something else altogether. David Cronenberg's version of *The Fly* (1986) is as much a touching love story as a sci-fi shocker. On the thriller front, Debra Winger's dilemma in *Betrayed* (1988) is the conflict between her love for a man whom she realizes is a Ku Klux Klan member and her duty as an FBI agent, while Kate Nelligan in *The Eye of the Needle* (1981) has to cope with the fact that the man she loves is a Nazi spy and therefore her enemy.

Sex on the Screen

Sex-appeal and sexual chemistry have of course been part of screen romance from the beginning. Rudolf Valentino made desert sheikhs a byword for it. Garbo and Gilbert had it in spadefuls in *Flesh and the Devil* (1926) and *Queen Christina* (1933), as did Burt Lancaster and Deborah Kerr with their lovemaking on the beach in *From Here to Eternity* (1953) – shockingly explicit for its day. But the changing mores of the 1960s opened the door to far more freedom in terms of how sexual passion could be shown.

British films were in the forefront of the screen sexual revolution with the realistic, working-class-based *Saturday Night and Sunday Morning* (1960) and *A Kind of Loving* (1962), along with Ken Russell's exploration of Lawrentian passion, *Women in Love* (1969). Such films opened the doors to stories which explored sexual attraction, experimentation and obsession, with little or no romantic dressing: *Last Tango in Paris* (1972), *Betty Blue* (1986), *Fatal Attraction* (1987) and *Basic Instinct* (1992). They also made possible a more realistic approach to male/female relationships without the romantic gloss, notably in films like *Carnal Knowledge* (1971) and *Sunday Bloody Sunday* (1971).

A Different Kind of Love

While there has always been a proliferation of films about young love, ranging from *Splendor in the Grass* (1961) to *Mr Wonderful* (1993), older lovers have had their share of the action, too. Ernest Borgnine was touching as *Marty* (1955), the homely butcher courting spinster Betsy Blair; Katharine Hepburn and Rossano Brazzi romanced their way through Venice in *Summertime* (1955); crusty Walter Matthau met hopeless muddler Elaine May in *A New Leaf* (1970); Gene Hackman broke up his marriage at 50 for new love, Ann-Margret, in *Twice in a Lifetime* (1985); and romance flowered late for C. S. Lewis in *Shadowlands* (1993) with Anthony Hopkins.

Less orthodox forms of romance have found screen space, too. The two men and a woman relationships of *Jules et Jim* (1961) and *Cabaret* (1972), for instance, and the once socially unacceptable romance of the young man and older woman. But while Dustin Hoffman's affair with Anne Bancroft in *The Graduate* (1967) is not "the real thing", the relationship between yuppie James Spader and waitress Susan Sarandon in *White Palace* (1990) is more like it. Love between people of different races is featured in Spike Lee's *Jungle Fever* (1991), while Fassbinder combines both unorthodoxies in *Fear Eats the Soul* (1973), the story a 60-year-old cleaning woman and the younger Moorish immigrant she marries.

There are still, however, comparatively few films which look

and Harvey Feinstein in *Torch Song Trilogy* (1988) is certainly a true romance, it is part of a much wider story.

Love Triumphs

Throughout all the changes, however, the fairy-tale, wistful-thinking romance refused to be squeezed off the screen by harsh, everyday reality. In the 1960s and 1970s love in grit and grime shared the screen with the lushness of films like *Un Homme et une Femme* (1966), *Far from the Madding Crowd* (1967), *The Go-Between* (1970) and multi-handkerchief weepies such as *Love Story* (1970) and *The Way We Were* (1973).

In the 1980s *The French Lieutenant's Woman* (1981) and *An Officer and a Gentleman* (1982) counterbalanced more earthy fare,

Love lines: Widower Tom Hanks and son Ross Malinger in Sleepless in Seattle

seriously and sympathetically at the subject of gay romance. *Desert Hearts* (1985) and *Lianna* (1983) are two of the few lesbian love stories; *La Cage aux Folles* (1978) is more comedy than love story; Albert Finney in *A Man of No Importance* (1994) is frustrated in his romantic longings; and though the relationship between Matthew Broderick

while during the 1990s the phony cynicism of *Indecent Proposal* (1993) and the sexual harassment role-reversal of *Disclosure* (1994) can be compared with the success of romances like *When Harry Met Sally* (1989), *Pretty Woman* (1990), *Sleepless in Seattle* (1993) and *Legends of the Fall* (1994). Love, as they say, is here to stay.

Science Fiction:
The shape of things to come

Science fiction is the true mythology of the late 20th century, complete with flawed heroes, impossible quests, fantastical places, great dark villains, unknown and unknowable forces, and monsters emerging from the deep subconscious.

One in the eye: Georges Méliès's A Trip to the Moon

Science fiction as a fully realized genre has its roots in, and takes its main dramatic mechanisms from, the traditions of ancient western mythological drama. At the same time, though, sci-fi connects with modern paranoias, in particular the growing techno-fear of a world ever more dominated by machines, a society ever more dehumanized, a culture that is systematically alienating itself.

It's hard to define the genre exactly because there's an overlap between sci-fi and horror. This is seen especially in the monster movies, those creature-from-space ones, which in some respects fulfil the same function (the raising and vanquishing of cultural and personal demons) but take place in a different setting. However, there are perhaps four basic themes, main currents that run through sci-fi films, making up clearly definable, though frequently overlapping, categories.

First there is the monster from space, the thing prowling the darkness, the fear of the unknown, seen in such films as *Alien* (1979), *It* (1967) and *The Thing* (1951; remade 1982). Then there is the eternal battle between good and evil played out by recognizable archetypes, portrayed notably in the *Star Wars* trilogy, the *Terminator* duo, and *Forbidden Planet* (1956), a futurization of Shakespeare's *The Tempest*. A third category shows man at the mercy of a mysterious and unfriendly world, a victim of his circumstance whose opponents are also victims, an expression of existential angst. Prime examples of this are *Blade Runner* (1982), *1984* (1956; remade 1984) and *Logan's Run* (1976). Finally there's sci-fi as political comment or parable, feeding upon our growing mistrust of the powers that govern us, or of the society that surrounds us. Examples here are *Invasion of the Body Snatchers* (1956), *The Stepford Wives* (1975) and the *Star Trek* septet, which warn respectively of the communist threat ("watch the skies"), growing Fascism within the body politic, depersonalization of society, or of the need to take the enemy seriously even when they seem to be holding out the olive branch.

Literary Sources

Science fiction is maybe the only example of a genre developing alongside, and even influencing and inspiring, its literary source. The two have advanced in tandem – though arguably Mary Shelley did the very first definable sci-fi writing in *Frankenstein*. A perfect example of this cross-fertilization is *2001: A Space Odyssey* (1968). Arthur C. Clarke wrote it as a short story then, after Kubrick filmed it, Clarke turned it into a novel, later writing a second bestseller called *2010,* which Peter Hyams filmed in 1984. On the other hand, Frank Herbert's *Dune* was an international bestseller preceding Lynch's 1984 movie, but Lynch turned it into his own personal vision in line with his experimental *Eraserhead* (1978).

Among the famous sci-fi writers whose works have been eagerly plundered by the cinema are Philip K. Dick (*Blade Runner* (1982) which was based on *Do Androids Dream of Electric Sheep?* and *Total Recall* (1990) taken from *We Can Remember It For You Wholesale*), Walter Tevis (*The Man who Fell to Earth*, 1976) and John Wyndham (*The Day of the Triffids* (1963) and *Village of the Damned* (1960) adapted from *The Midwich Cuckoos*). They have all provided rich seams for moviemakers to mine.

Life Imitates Art

The sci-fi genre has its roots in the purely fantastical – the writings of Jules Verne, Georges Méliès's *A Trip to the Moon* (1902), fairground delight in trickery and using the resources of the cinema to entertain. So it's logical that the overt development of sci-fi has been one of visual style, a trend which is close to the heart of the cinema medium itself.

This style has repeatedly helped to shape the commonplace aesthetics of the day: clothes, furniture, interior design and so on. But more significantly than this, sci-fi has literally predicted reality, though it might arguably be seen as a self-fulfilling prophecy: first you dream it, then you do it. Rockets were first sent to space in the movies with a ten to zero countdown – "we have lift-off". Then years later the American space centre used the same vocabulary to launch real people into the glittering void. Things are only possible once they have been conceived as possibilities, once they have been imagined, and sci-fi is the most visionary and imaginative of genres, one with an inbuilt drive, a fundamental need to embrace ever wider and more fantastic possibilities. As a culture we define ourselves by our mytholo-

gies, so it's little wonder that science fiction should help to shape the future fact.

Aliens and Alienation

On a deeper psychological level sci-fi visuals have mirrored the change in public attitudes to social authority – the rightness of the state, cultural alienation and certainly the general disillusionment and cynicism with government and political dishonesty. Before, it was "us" against the aliens, a clear-cut situation with clean-cut heroes, like the western in space (useful when the western went out of fashion in the 1970s), mirrored in the bland certainties of the script but perhaps even more tellingly in the shiny modernism of sets and props. Gradually, as the edges of the hero, the definition of his or her automatic "rightness", have become more blurred, and the relationship between the protagonist and his or her society has become more uncertain, so too the world of the future has been visualized as less and less clear-cut.

Alien 3: *Exploring the dark side with Sigourney Weaver as First Officer Ripley*

As our image of our cultural selves has tarnished, so too have our heroes and their setting. The mythic future is now portrayed as darker, grubbier and decayed, often barren, desperately post-apocalyptic (as for example in the *Mad Max* trilogy, *Hardware* (1990), *Salute of the Jugger* (1990) and *Cyborg* (1989)), less of a utopia

than a dire possibility. The villains, though, remain pretty constant: they're what they always were in legend. They are phenomena and don't have developed characters. They cannot. They must remain mysterious and only partially comprehended, a product of the shadows.

In the final analysis, science fiction is, like traditional drama, a safe way of exploring our darker selves. Ridley Scott's *Alien* (1979), for example, with its ravaging penile creature, explores and gives vent to some of our darkest cultural fears and taboos, as well as what might be stalking us in the depths of our own subconscious. It serves as a catalyst, a way of dusting out our society's shadowy corners, of exorcizing what we fear most in ourselves. As a genre, sci-fi is a way of coping with our personal helplessness in the face of an unpredictable universe, ameliorating the fact that ultimately, in our real world, we are the aliens, we are the strangers in a strange land and, on the deepest levels, we are strange to ourselves. These legends serve a fundamental, and perhaps increasing, need to locate ourselves outside our fears.

Blade Runner: *Existential angst*

The War Movie:
All noisy on the battlefront

The most traditionally action-packed of all art forms, film lends itself naturally to the portrayal of conflict. Yet as a genre the war movie focuses only on the major confrontations of the 20th century – World Wars One and Two, the Korean War and Vietnam.

The Red Badge of Courage: *World War Two's most decorated soldier Audie Murphy fights the Civil War*

Pictures such as *The Birth of a Nation* (1915), *Waterloo* (1971) or *Gone with the Wind* (1939), which deal specifically with conflicts before 1914, are generally regarded as historical adventures, or epics, or costume actioners, rather than war movies. The scope of the war film is hence exclusively 20th-century; its content, however factually accurate, nonetheless contrived.

Birth of a Genre

The genre was born out of World War One and, since the film industries of most European countries had closed for the duration of hostilities, was developed primarily in America. The first movie truly deserving the title "war film" was

D. W. Griffith's *Hearts of the World* (1918). Although essentially propagandist in tone – hero Robert Harron would rather shoot wife Lillian Gish than let her fall into the hands of the murderous Hun – it was nonetheless the first film fully to acknowledge the horror and heartbreak of war, and established standards of visual realism and narrative scope that were to influence film-makers for many years.

Over the next two decades the war movie came to establish itself as a distinct cinema genre. Valentino's *Four Horsemen of the Apocalypse* (1921) touched on the subject, but a genuine confrontation of the issues involved only

War movie milestone: King Vidor's The Big Parade

began to emerge in works such as William Wellman's *Wings* (1927), first-ever winner of a Best Picture Oscar. Particularly notable from this period, for their humanity, scope and realism, were King Vidor's *The Big Parade* (1925), a poignant study of the effects of trench warfare on an American soldier (John Gilbert); Renoir's *La Grande Illusion* (1937), the story of French prisoners of war; and Lewis Milestone's Oscar-winning *All Quiet on the Western Front* (1930), probably the greatest war film ever made.

World War One continued to provide a focus for films long after the 1930s – Kubrick's *Paths of Glory* (1957), Dalton Trumbo's *Johnny Got His Gun* (1971) and Peter Weir's *Gallipoli* (1981) are among the most evocative of all anti-war tracts – but with the outbreak of World War Two in 1939 filmmakers had a whole new subject to occupy their attention.

World War Two

There have been an inordinate number of films made about World War Two. It is, indeed, the

only conflict in history of which our impressions have been formed almost entirely through cinematic images.

Although most have been traditional gung-ho, wham-bam, action-packed adventures – *The Guns of Navarone* (1961); *The Longest Day* (1962); *The Battle of The Bulge* (1965) – a remarkable number of World War Two pictures have, over the years, balanced the spectacle and excitement of warfare with a sensitive and intelligent study of the moral and human issues.

Once again America was in the forefront of production, kicking off almost as soon as it had entered the war with such classics as William Wyler's *Mrs Miniver* (1942), the multi-Oscar-winning story of a British family coping with the war, Lewis Milestone's *A Walk in the Sun* (1946) about a U.S. patrol in Italy, and John Ford's *They Were Expendable* (1945), about torpedo crews in the Pacific. Other countries have matched the quality, if not the volume, of American World War Two films. *In Which We Serve* (1942), Noel Coward's poignant story of the survivors of

All-star musical: *Richard Attenborough's 1968 treatment of World War One* Oh! What a Lovely War

a torpedoed destroyer, co-directed by David Lean, was one of the best British war films ever made, although *The Dam Busters* (1955), *The Bridge on the River Kwai* (1957) and *A Bridge Too Far* (1977) were also notable. From Italy came Rossellini's neo-realist masterpieces *Rome, Open City* (1945), about the Italian Resistance, and *Paisà* (1946), six interwoven stories about the country's liberation, while France produced, among others, René Clément's Oscar-winning *Jeux Interdits* (1952), about the macabre games played by two children in occupied France. Germany, too, has probed deeply and pessimistically into the issues raised by the war, and with films such as Bernhard Wicki's *The Bridge* (1959), about a group of conscripted German schoolboys, and Wolfgang Petersen's U-boat epic *Das Boot* (1981), created some of cinema's most effective studies of the futility of battle, all the more poignant because they came from the losing side.

The unparalleled extent of World War Two ensured that it

would be the dominant war-film subject for the next 30 years. The Korean War (1950–51) inspired a handful of tolerable actioners such as *The Bridges at Toko-Ri* (1954), and two mini-masterpieces – Lewis Milestone's tough-talking adventure *Pork Chop Hill* (1959), and Robert Altman's free-wheeling, spaced-out anti-establishment black comedy *M*A*S*H* (1970). It never left a significant mark on the

war genre, however, possibly because its scope was so limited.

The Vietnam Cycle

An entirely new dimension was added to the genre during the 1970s and 1980s, however, as Hollywood began to explore the disaster of the Vietnam War. This was particularly fascinating because it was the first combat-war of the 20th century in which America had been on the losing side, and that sense of loss pervades every film that has been made on the subject. It was also a war without apparent moral purpose, and one in which extreme savagery was practised not just by the enemy, but by American troops as well. As a result of this films about Vietnam display not merely a darkness, ambiguity and strong anti-war sentiment, but something entirely new – self-loathing.

The two acknowledged masterpieces of the Vietnam War film genre are Michael Cimino's *The Deer Hunter* (1978), the story of three recently drafted Pennsylvania steelworkers, and Francis Ford Coppola's *Apocalypse Now* (1979), a brooding, psychedelic reworking of Joseph Conrad's novel *Heart of Darkness*. Both concentrate less on battle and more on the effect it has on those involved, providing a

bitter, tortured and deeply pessimistic look at the American psyche during the country's darkest hour. Also notable have been Ted Post's *Go Tell the Spartans* (1978), Hal Ashby's *Coming Home* (1978), Stanley Kubrick's *Full Metal Jacket* (1987) and a searing trilogy of films from Oliver Stone – *Platoon* (1986), *Born on the Fourth of July* (1989) and *Heaven and Earth* (1993). The Vietnam cycle has radically shifted the emphasis of the war film, bringing a new introspection and psychological complexity to the genre. The enemy is no longer merely, or mainly, an exterior one facing you on the battleground, but something from within ourselves.

This in itself is not new – European cinema has always tended to dwell on the psychological implications of war, as indeed have American films such as *The Best Years of Our Lives* (1946) and *Twelve O'Clock High* (1950). What is new is that the inner turmoil of the combatants appears to be in the process of replacing the outer turmoil of battle as the key focus of the genre in mainstream cinema. Whether this is a brief aberration or the future of the war film remains to be seen, but it has certainly made for some of the most effective movies of the last two decades.

Leading the troops: *John Wayne in* The Green Berets

The Western:
Call of the wild

More than any other screen genre the western is synonymous with the American film industry. It's no coincidence that the first true narrative movie made in America – Edwin S. Porter's *The Great Train Robbery* (1903) – was a western, nor that the first universally popular American film star – Gilbert "Broncho Billy" Anderson – made his reputation in cowboy pictures. From the outset the western has been both the defining genre of US cinema, and America's unique contribution to the world of film.

What actually constitutes a western? After all, there is little immediate similarity between a contemporary drama such as Martin Ritt's *Hud* (1962) and the 1930s musical antics of Gene Autry – yet they belong, broadly speaking, within the same bracket.

The definition is partly geographical – westerns are set in the west of America, trans-Mississippi. Location is by no means exclusive, however – King Vidor's *Northwest Passage* (1940) and John Ford's *Drums along the Mohawk* (1939) both take place in eastern America; while Sam Peckinpah's *The Wild Bunch* (1969) was set in Mexico and Anthony Mann's *The Far Country* (1954) in the Yukon.

A more specific definition comes with appearance – from *The Great Train Robbery* (1903) to Clint Eastwood's *Unforgiven* (1992), from Burt Lancaster's *The Kentuckian* (1955), set in the 1820s, to Peckinpah's *Junior Bonner* (1972), set in the 1970s, there is a particular look that marks a film out as a western – the sweeping frontier landscape, the isolated homestead, the clothes, the guns, the horses, the rural setting.

Whatever the date or context, the "western look" is immediately recognizable.

Likewise there is a demonstrable "western attitude" – a toughness, solitude and self-sufficiency of character that suggest not merely a hero, but a western hero. Roy Rogers, James Stewart, Clint Eastwood and Tom Mix all played very different roles in very different films, yet possessed, to varying degrees, a unifying spirit.

Above all else, the western formula is rooted in conflict – between man and man; man and savage; man and nature; civilization and wilderness; farmer and industrialist.

The B-Western

Since 1903 there have been over 7,000 westerns made, not including the many thousands of episodes of western TV series. The vast bulk of these films have been series, or B-westerns – short, dependable, formulaic adventures starring the likes of Broncho Billy Anderson in the 1910s, Tom Mix, Tim McCoy, Art Acord, Hoot Gibson and Ken Maynard in the 1920s, Gene Autry in the 1930s and Roy Rogers – "The King of the Cowboys" – in the 1940s.

Until the mid-1950s the B-westerns constituted a quarter of Hollywood's total output, a figure unmatched by any other film genre. They were cheap to make – (the 1930s *Lone Star* westerns, starring John Wayne, cost $5,000 each) – hugely popular and launched the careers of countless actors and directors (Sam Peckinpah, John Wayne, Raoul Walsh, John Ford and Clint Eastwood to name but a few). For more than 40 years they kept scores of independent companies afloat and provided the bread-and-butter income with which the major Hollywood studios financed their more weighty projects. It would be no exaggeration to say that the golden age of the American movie industry was substantially based upon the income generated by the B-western.

More than just a lucrative money-spinner, however, the western was a eulogy to, and chronicle of, the past-fading values of the old American frontier world. Vestiges of the Old West were still present during the early days of cinema. Frank James, Geronimo, Pat Garrett, Buffalo Bill Cody, Wyatt Earp – characters later immortalized on film – were all still alive during the medium's infancy. John Ford would later claim the gunfight at the OK Corral in *My Darling Clementine* (1946) was based on a real-life conversation with Earp; and, when the latter died in 1929, his coffin was carried by William S. Hart and Tom Mix, the two greatest western stars of the day. Hart himself had first-hand experience of the Old West, as did a number of other key western figures including Raoul Walsh and Tim McCoy.

Saving the day: *Tom Mix is the hero in the original 1932 version of* Destry Rides Again

The A-Western

The feature-length, or A-western, developed specifically from a desire both to chronicle more accurately the disappearing world of the western frontier and to preserve something of its essence and majesty. New cinematic techniques were developed to capture the scale and grandeur of that frontier – two-strip Technicolor, widescreen, CinemaScope and Cinerama were all invented for western films – and in the hands of directors such as John Ford, Howard Hawks and Raoul Walsh the genre was raised to the level of high art.

Although the 1910s, 1920s and 1930s all produced classic A-westerns – notably Cecil B. De Mille's *Squaw Man* (1914), the first-ever feature western, James Cruze's *The Covered Wagon* (1923), John Ford's *The Iron Horse* (1924) and Wesley Ruggles's *Cimarron* (1930), the first western to win an Academy Award for Best Picture (Costner's *Dances With Wolves* in 1990 and Eastwood's *Unforgiven* in 1992 are the only others to have done so) – the epic western reached its apogee in the 1940s and 1950s, an era ushered in by Ford's masterful *Stagecoach* (1939).

This was the period when the western achieved not merely a grandeur of appearance, but a new social, emotional and psychological depth. Howard Hawks's *The Outlaw* (1943) introduced to the genre a previously unseen element of sex and salaciousness; William A. Wellman's *The Ox-Bow Incident* (1943) painted the frontier, for the first time, as a morally dark, unheroic place; while Walsh's *Pursued* (1947) presented a profound, multi-layered study of psychology and motive. The 1950s brought, among others, Delmer Daves' *Broken Arrow* (1950), a landmark in Hollywood's treatment of the Indian; Henry King's elegiac *The Gunfighter* (1950); Fred Zinnemann's *High Noon* (1952); and Ford's disturbing *The Searchers* (1956).

From the outset the genre has spoken volumes about not only America's past, but also its present, projecting national hopes, aspira-

tions and values back on to a quasi-mythical bygone age. Thus John Ford's *The Iron Horse* (1924) captured the industrial optimism of the Roaring Twenties; Gene Autry's ten cowboy commandments perfectly enshrined the values of the average 1930s mid-west American male;

duce notable works – *Butch Cassidy and the Sundance Kid* (1969) was one of the most popular westerns of all time and saved the Fox studio from bankruptcy, while Don Siegel's *The Beguiled* (1970), Sydney Pollack's *Jeremiah Johnson* (1972) and Clint Eastwood's *The Outlaw Josey Wales*

(1980), a $35 million flop that bankrupted United Artists.

The successes of Kevin Costner's *Dances with Wolves* (1990) and Clint Eastwood's *Unforgiven* (1993), however, suggest that pessimism is premature. As early as 1911 critics were forecasting the

One good man standing alone: Gary Cooper epitomized the character in numerous roles, such as here in High Noon

John Ford's *The Searchers* (1956) evoked the paranoid cynicism of the Cold War; and the 1960s films of Sam Peckinpah and Sergio Leone mirrored an increasingly violent, lawless world.

Although the period since the late 1950s has continued to pro-

(1976) were all, in their way, minor masterpieces – the genre has, nonetheless, been in decline for the last three decades. The final B-film series had been made in 1954 and the feature western was officially declared dead with Michael Cimino's underrated *Heaven's Gate*

end of the genre, but it has always demonstrated a remarkable resilience and capacity for reinvention. It is doubtful whether the western will ever again reach the popular heights of the 1930s, 1940s and 1950s, but it looks to have some mileage in it yet.

Academy Awards

Just in case you didn't know, the Oscar is properly called an Academy Award statuette, won at each April's awards ceremony in Los Angeles.

The films, actors and personnel are all nominated for work that must have been premiered in America before December 31 the previous year. The first ceremony was in 1928, supporting actor Oscars began only in 1936 and foreign film Oscars started (initially as special awards) in 1947.

Oscar is just a little over a foot tall, made of gold-plated metal, designed by MGM art director Cedric Gibbons, and sculpted by George Stanley.

The story goes that Bette Davis once said: "It reminds me of my uncle Oscar", a remark recorded by one of the gossip columnists, though there are various versions of this story attributed to different people. And though it was just a chance overheard remark, the word Oscar entered the public consciousness from 1931 and both the words Oscar and Academy Award are now carefully protected by copyright.

The Oscars began in 1928 and have continued annually since with no gap for the war. The show is seen on worldwide television by an audience of nearly a billion, and Bob Hope, the most regular and famous presenter, hosted it on 20 occasions, though Johnny Carson was a regular in the 1980s and Billy Crystal in the 1990s.

Best Picture

1927–28	*Wings*
1928–29	*Broadway Melody*
1929–30	*All Quiet on the Western Front*
1930–31	*Cimarron*
1931–32	*Grand Hotel*
1932–33	*Cavalcade*
1934	*It Happened One Night*
1935	*Mutiny on the Bounty*
1936	*The Great Ziegfeld*
1937	*The Life of Emil Zola*
1938	*You Can't Take It with You*
1939	*Gone with the Wind*
1940	*Rebecca*
1941	*How Green was My Valley*
1942	*Mrs Miniver*
1943	*Casablanca*
1944	*Going My Way*
1945	*The Lost Weekend*
1946	*The Best Years of Our Lives*
1947	*Gentleman's Agreement*
1948	*Hamlet*
1949	*All the King's Men*
1950	*All About Eve*
1951	*An American in Paris*
1952	*The Greatest Show on Earth*
1953	*From Here to Eternity*
1954	*On the Waterfront*
1955	*Marty*
1956	*Around the World in 80 Days*
1957	*The Bridge on the River Kwai*
1958	*Gigi*
1959	*Ben-Hur*
1960	*The Apartment*
1961	*West Side Story*
1962	*Lawrence of Arabia*
1963	*Tom Jones*
1964	*My Fair Lady*
1965	*The Sound of Music*
1966	*A Man for All Seasons*
1967	*In the Heat of the Night*
1968	*Oliver!*
1969	*Midnight Cowboy*
1970	*Patton: Lust for Glory*
1971	*The French Connection*
1972	*The Godfather*
1973	*The Sting*
1974	*The Godfather, Part II*
1975	*One Flew Over the Cuckoo's Nest*
1976	*Rocky*
1977	*Annie Hall*
1978	*The Deer Hunter*
1979	*Kramer vs Kramer*
1980	*Ordinary People*
1981	*Chariots of Fire*
1982	*Gandhi*
1983	*Terms of Endearment*
1984	*Amadeus*
1985	*Out of Africa*
1986	*Platoon*
1987	*The Last Emperor*
1988	*Rain Man*
1989	*Driving Miss Daisy*
1990	*Dances with Wolves*
1991	*The Silence of the Lambs*
1992	*Unforgiven*
1993	*Schindler's List*
1994	*Forrest Gump*

Sweeping the board

Ben-Hur (1959) is the all-time Academy Award champion, scooping most Oscars to date at 11, with *West Side Story* (1961) close behind at 10. *All About Eve* (1950) holds the record for most Oscar nominations at 14, though it won six, while *Forrest Gump* (1994) also took six after 13 nominations.

Rebecca: *Best Picture win for Alfred Hitchcock in 1940*

Best Actor

1927–28	**Emil Jannings** *The Last Command / The Way of All Flesh*
1928–29	**Warner Baxter** *In Old California*
1929–30	**George Arliss** *Disraeli*
1930–31	**Lionel Barrymore** *A Free Soul*
1931–32	**Wallace Beery** *The Champ /* **Fredric March** *Dr Jekyll and Mr Hyde*
1932–33	**Charles Laughton** *The Private Life of Henry VIII*
1934	**Clark Gable** *It Happened One Night*
1935	**Victor McLagen** *The Informer*
1936	**Paul Muni** *The Story of Louis Pasteur*
1937	**Spencer Tracy** *Captains Courageous*
1938	**Spencer Tracy** *Boys Town*
1939	**Robert Donat** *Goodbye, Mr Chips*

1940 **James Stewart**
The Philadelphia Story
1941 **Gary Cooper**
Sergeant York
1942 **James Cagney**
Yankee Doodle Dandy
1943 **Paul Lukas**
Watch on the Rhine
1944 **Bing Crosby**
Going My Way
1945 **Ray Milland**
The Lost Weekend
1946 **Fredric March**
The Best Years of Our Lives
1947 **Ronald Colman**
A Double Life
1948 **Laurence Olivier**
Hamlet
1949 **Broderick Crawford**
All The King's Men
1950 **Jose Ferrer**
Cyrano de Bergerac
1951 **Humphrey Bogart**
The African Queen
1952 **Gary Cooper**
High Noon
1953 **William Holden**
Stalag 17

A useful door stopper

Clark Gable, The King of Hollywood, received three nominations for the Best Actor Academy Award, winning only once, for *It Happened One Night* (1934). His acceptance speech is one of the shortest on record for a major Oscar – just two words: "Thank you." He was a hot favourite to carry off the Best Actor statuette again in 1939 for his performance as Rhett Butler in *Gone with the Wind*, but the award went instead to Robert Donat for *Goodbye Mr Chips*. In a fit of pique, Gable gave his original Oscar to the son of his wife Carole Lombard's secretary, telling the boy to "prop open his lavatory door with it".

1954 **Marlon Brando**
On the Waterfront
1955 **Ernnest Borgnine**
Marty
1956 **Yul Brynner**
The King and I

1957 **Alec Guinness**
The Bridge on the River Kwai
1958 **David Niven**
Separate Tables
1959 **Charlton Heston**
Ben-Hur
1960 **Burt Lancaster**
Elmer Gantry

Playing it for laughs

One of the most popular recipients ever of a Best Actor Academy Award was David Niven, who won in 1958 for *Separate Tables*. As he went up to receive his award, he stumbled on the steps to the stage, explaining during his acceptance speech that he had done so because he was so loaded down with good luck charms. However, he paused after the word "loaded", thereby, in his own words, "establishing myself as the first self-confessed drunk to win the Academy Award". He brought the house down again some years later when, while hosting the awards, he was confronted by a streaker named Bob Opel. "Isn't it fascinating," he ad-libbed to several million TV viewers, "that probably the only laugh this man will ever get in his life is by stripping off his clothes and showing his shortcomings."

1961 **Maximilian Schell**
Judgment at Nuremberg
1962 **Gregory Peck**
To Kill a Mockingbird
1963 **Sidney Poitier**
Lilies of the Field
1964 **Rex Harrison**
My Fair lady
1965 **Lee Marvin**
Cat Ballou
1966 **Paul Scofield**
A Man for All Seasons
1967 **Rod Steiger**
In the Heat of the Night
1968 **Cliff Robertson**
Charly
1969 **John Wayne**
True Grit
1970 **George C. Scott**
Patton: Lust for Glory
1971 **Gene Hackman**
The French Connection

A non-competitive sport

The first Oscar-winner ever to turn down an award was actor George C. Scott, voted Best Actor in 1970 for his performance as U.S. General George Patton, the controversial World War Two commander of the Seventh Army in Italy, in *Patton: Lust for Glory* (1970). Scott declared at the time: "Life isn't a race. And because it's not a race I don't consider myself in competition with my fellow actors for awards or recognition. That is why I have rejected the Oscar and nomination for playing Patton."

1972 **Marlon Brando**
The Godfather
1973 **Jack Lemmon**
Save the Tiger
1974 **Art Carney**
Harry and Tonto
1975 **Jack Nicholson**
One Flew Over the Cuckoo's Nest

Acceptance by proxy

Two years after George C. Scott turned down his Best Actor Academy Award for *Patton* (1970), Marlon Brando did the same, although in more spectacular fashion, for his performance in the title role of *The Godfather* (1972). Brando had already received one Best Actor Academy Award, for *On the Waterfront* (1954), but refused to attend the 1972 ceremony, sending a proxy named Sacheen Littlefeather to refuse the award in his place. Dressed in traditional Native American garb, Littlefeather announced to a bewildered audience: "I am Apache, and I am President of the National Native American Affirmative Image Committee. I'm representing Marlon Brando this evening and he has asked me to tell you that he very regretfully cannot accept this very generous award. And the reasons for this are the treatment of American Indians today by the film industry and in television re-runs." Later in the same ceremony presenter Clint Eastwood quipped that perhaps the Best Picture Award should be dedicated to "all the cowboys shot in John Ford westerns over the years".

1976 **Peter Finch**
Network
1977 **Richard Dreyfuss**
The Goodbye Girl
1978 **Jon Voight**
Coming Home
1979 **Dustin Hoffman**
Kramer vs Kramer
1980 **Robert De Niro**
Raging Bull
1981 **Henry Fonda**
On Golden Pond
1982 **Ben Kingsley**
Gandhi

An Oscar he could refuse: Marlon Brando in The Godfather (1972)

1987 **Michael Douglas**
Wall Street
1988 **Dustin Hoffman**
Rain Man
1989 **Daniel Day-Lewis**
My Left Foot
1990 **Jeremy Irons**
Reversal of Fortune

1983 **Robert Duvall**
Tender Mercies
1984 **F. Murray Abraham**
Amadeus
1985 **William Hurt**
Kiss of the Spider Woman
1986 **Paul Newman**
The Color of Money

1991 **Anthony Hopkins**
The Silence of the Lambs
1992 **Al Pacino**
Scent of a Woman
1993 **Tom Hanks**
Philadelphia
1994 **Tom Hanks**
Forrest Gump

Best Actress

1927–28 **Janet Gaynor**
*Seventh Heaven /
Street Angel / Sunrise*

1928–29 **Mary Pickford**
Coquette

1929–30 **Norma Shearer**
The Divorcee

1930–31 **Mary Dressler**
Min and Bill

1931–32 **Helen Hayes**
*The Sin of Madelon
Claudet*

1932–33 **Katharine Hepburn**
Morning Glory

1934 **Claudette Colbert**
It Happened One Night

1935 **Bette Davis**
Dangerous

1936 **Luise Rainer**
The Great Ziegfeld

1937 **Luise Rainer**
The Good Earth

1938 **Bette Davis**
Jezebel

1939 **Vivien Leigh**
Gone with the Wind

1940 **Ginger Rogers**
Kitty Foyle

1941 **Joan Fontaine**
Suspicion

1942 **Greer Garson**
Mrs Miniver

1943 **Jennifer Jones**
The Song of Bernadette

1944 **Ingrid Bergman**
Gaslight

1945 **Joan Crawford**
Mildred Pierce

1946 **Olivia de Havilland**
To Each His Own

1947 **Loretta Young**
The Farmer's Daughter

1948 **Jane Wyman**
Johnny Belinda

1949 **Olivia de Havilland**
The Heiress

1950 **Judy Holliday**
Born Yesterday

1951 **Vivien Leigh**
*A Streetcar Named
Desire*

1952 **Shirley Booth**
*Come Back, Little
Sheba*

1953 **Audrey Hepburn**
Roman Holiday

1954 **Grace Kelly**
The Country Girl

1955 **Anna Magnani**
The Rose Tattoo

1956 **Ingrid Bergman**
Anastasia

1957 **Joanne Woodward**
The Three Faces of Eve

1958 **Susan Hayward**
I Want To Live!

1959 **Simone Signoret**
Room at the Top

1960 **Elizabeth Taylor**
Butterfield 8

1961 **Sophia Loren**
Two Women

1962 **Anne Bancroft**
The Miracle Worker

1963 **Patricia Neal**
Hud

1964 **Julie Andrews**
Mary Poppins

1965 **Julie Christie**
Darling

1966 **Elizabeth Taylor**
*Who's Afraid of
Virginia Woolf?*

1971 **Jane Fonda**
Klute

1972 **Liza Minnelli**
Cabaret

In her prime: Maggie Smith in The Prime of Miss Jean Brodie (1969)

How *not* to win an Oscar

Elizabeth Taylor didn't show up at the 1966 Oscars to collect her best actress statuette for *Who's Afraid of Virginia Woolf?*, saying oddly that Richard Burton was in Paris, scared of flying himself and refused to let her fly solo. Afterwards Taylor was annoyed that Burton had lost on his fifth best actor nomination and wouldn't receive her award, though she finally accepted it from Lord Louis Mountbatten at the British awards ceremony when she also took the British Film Academy's best foreign actress statue. Taylor didn't receive another Oscar and Burton never won after seven tries.

1967 **Katharine Hepburn**
*Guess Who's Coming
to Dinner*

1968 **Katharine Hepburn**
The Lion in Winter /
Barbra Streisand
Funny Girl

1973 **Glenda Jackson**
A Touch of Class

1974 **Ellen Burstyn**
*Alice Doesn't Live
Here Anymore*

1975 **Louise Fletcher**
*One Flew Over the
Cuckoo's Nest*

How to win an Oscar

An actress can be funny and kooky like 1968's *Funny Girl* winner Barbra Streisand's comment to her Oscar ("Hello gorgeous ... gee whiz it's some kind of a wild feeling sitting there tonight"). She can be modest and thrilled like 1984's *Places in the Heart* winner Sally Field ("I wanted more than anything to have you respect me ... I can't deny the fact you like me, right now you really like me!"). Or she can be actressy and excited like 1983's *Terms of Endearment* winner Shirley MacLaine ("I'm going to cry because this show has been as long as my career ... I deserve this!")

1969 **Maggie Smith**
*The Prime of Miss Jean
Brodie*

1970 **Glenda Jackson**
Women in Love

1976 **Faye Dunaway**
Network

1977 **Diane Keaton**
Annie Hall

1978 **Jane Fonda**
Coming Home

1979 **Sally Field**
Norma Rae

1980 **Sissy Spacek**
*Coal Miner's
Daughter*

1981 **Katharine Hepburn**
On Golden Pond

1982 **Meryl Streep**
Sophie's Choice

1983 **Shirley MacLaine**
Terms of Endearment

1984 **Sally Field**
Places in the Heart

1985 **Geraldine Page**
The Trip to Bountiful

1986 **Marlee Matlin**
*Children of a Lesser
God*

1987 **Cher**
Moonstruck

1988 **Jodie Foster**
The Accused

1989 **Jessica Tandy**
Driving Miss Daisy

1990 **Kathy Bates**
Misery

1991 **Jodie Foster**
*The Silence of the
Lambs*

1992 **Emma Thompson**
Howards End

1993 **Holly Hunter**
The Piano

1994 **Jessica Lange**
Blue Sky

Best Supporting Actor

1936 **Walter Brennan**
Come and Get It

1937 **Joseph Schildkraut**
*The Life of Emile
Zola*

1938 **Walter Brennan**
Kentucky

1939 **Thomas Mitchell**
Stagecoach

1940 **Walter Brennan**
The Westerner

1941 **Donald Crisp**
*How Green Was My
Valley*

1942 **Van Heflin**
Johnny Eager

1943 **Charles Coburn**
The More the Merrier

1944 **Barry Fitzgerald**
Going My Way

1945 **James Dunne**
*A Tree Grows in
Brooklyn*

1946 **Harold Russell**
*The Best Years of our
Lives*

1947 **Edmund Gwenn**
Miracle on 34th Street

1948 **Walter Huston**
*The Treasure of the
Sierra Madre*

1949 **Dean Jagger**
Twelve O'Clock High

1950 **George Sanders**
All About Eve

1951 **Karl Malden**
A Streetcar Named Desire
1952 **Anthony Quinn**
Viva Zapata
1953 **Frank Sinatra**
From Here to Eternity
1954 **Edmond O'Brien**
The Barefoot Contessa
1955 **Jack Lemmon**
Mister Roberts
1956 **Anthony Quinn**
Lust for Life
1957 **Red Buttons**
Sayonara
1958 **Burl Ives**
The Big Country
1959 **Hugh Griffith**
Ben-Hur
1960 **Peter Ustinov**
Spartacus
1961 **George Chakiris**
West Side Story
1962 **Ed Begley**
Sweet Bird of Youth
1963 **Melvyn Douglas**
Hud
1963 **Peter Ustinov**
Topkapi
1965 **Martin Balsam**
A Thousand Clowns
1966 **Walter Matthau**
The Fortune Cookie
1967 **George Kennedy**
Cool Hand Luke
1968 **Jack Albertson**
The Subject Was Roses
1969 **Gig Young**
They Shoot Horses, Don't They?
1970 **John Mills**
Ryan's Daughter
1971 **Ben Johnson**
The Last Picture Show
1972 **Joel Grey**
Cabaret
1973 **John Houseman**
The Paper Chase
1974 **Robert De Niro**
The Godfather, Part II
1975 **George Burns**
The Sunshine Boys
1976 **Jason Robards**
All the President's Men
1977 **Jason Robards**
Julia
1978 **Christopher Walken**
The Deer Hunter
1979 **Melvyn Douglas**
Being There
1980 **Timothy Hutton**
Ordinary People

1981 **John Gielgud**
Arthur
1982 **Louis Gossett Jnr**
An Officer and a Gentleman
1983 **Jack Nicholson**
Terms of Endearment
1984 **Haing S. Ngor**
The Killing Fields
1985 **Don Ameche**
Cocoon
1986 **Michael Caine**
Hannah and Her Sisters
1987 **Sean Connery**
The Untouchables
1988 **Kevin Kline**
A Fish Called Wanda
1989 **Denzel Washington**
Glory
1990 **Joe Pesci**
Goodfellas
1991 **Jack Palance**
City Slickers
1992 **Gene Hackman**
Unforgiven
1993 **Tommy Lee Jones**
The Fugitive
1994 **Martin Landau**
Ed Wood

Best Supporting Actress

1936 **Gale Sondergaard**
Anthony Adverse
1937 **Alice Brady**
In Old Chicago
1938 **Fay Bainter**
Jezebel
1939 **Hattie McDaniel**
Gone with the Wind
1940 **Jane Darwell**
The Grapes of Wrath
1941 **Mary Astor**
The Great Lie
1942 **Teresa Wright**
Mrs Miniver
1943 **Katina Paxinou**
For Whom the Bell Tolls
1944 **Ethel Barrymore**
None but the Lonely Heart
1945 **Anne Revere**
National Velvet
1946 **Anne Baxter**
The Razor's Edge
1947 **Celeste Holm**
Gentleman's Agreement
1948 **Claire Trevor**
Key Largo

1949 **Mercedes McCambridge**
All the King's Men
1950 **Josephine Hull**
Harvey
1951 **Kim Hunter**
A Streetcar Named Desire
1952 **Gloria Grahame**
The Bad and the Beautiful
1953 **Donna Reed**
From Here to Eternity
1954 **Eva Marie Saint**
On the Waterfront
1955 **Jo Van Fleet**
East of Eden
1956 **Dorothy Malone**
Written on the Wind
1957 **Miyoshi Umeki**
Sayonara
1958 **Wendy Hiller**
Separate Tables
1959 **Shelley Winters**
The Diary of Anne Frank
1960 **Shirley Jones**
Elmer Gantry
1961 **Rita Moreno**
West Side Story
1962 **Patty Duke**
The Miracle Worker
1963 **Margaret Rutherford**
The VIPs
1964 **Lila Kedrova**
Zorba the Greek
1965 **Shelley Winters**
A Patch of Blue
1966 **Sandy Dennis**
Who's Afraid of Virginia Woolf?

1967 **Estelle Parsons**
Bonnie and Clyde
1968 **Ruth Gordon**
Rosemary's Baby
1969 **Goldie Hawn**
Cactus Flower
1970 **Helen Hayes**
Airport
1971 **Cloris Leachman**
The Last Picture Show
1972 **Eileen Heckart**
Butterflies Are Free
1973 **Taum O'Neal**
Paper Moon
1974 **Ingrid Bergman**
Murder on the Orient Express
1975 **Lee Grant**
Shampoo
1976 **Beatrice Straight**
Network
1977 **Vanessa Redgrave**
Julia
1978 **Maggie Smith**
California Suite
1979 **Meryl Streep**
Kramer vs Kramer
1980 **Mary Steenburgen**
Melvin and Howard
1981 **Maureen Stapleton**
Reds
1982 **Jessica Lange**
Tootsie
1983 **Linda Hunt**
The Year of Living Dangerously
1984 **Peggy Ashcroft**
A Passage to India
1985 **Anjelica Huston**
Prizzi's Honor

1986 **Dianne Wiest**
Hannah and Her Sisters
1987 **Olympia Dukakis**
Moonstruck
1988 **Geena Davis**
The Accidental Tourist
1989 **Brenda Fricker**
My Left Foot
1990 **Whoopi Goldberg**
Ghost
1991 **Mercedes Ruehl**
The Fisher King
1992 **Marisa Tomei**
My Cousin Vinny
1993 **Anna Paquin**
The Piano
1994 **Dianne Wiest**
Bullets Over Broadway

Best Director

1927–28 **Frank Borzage**
Seventh Heaven
1928–29 **Frank Lloyd**
The Divine Lady
1929–30 **Lewis Milestone**
All Quiet on the Western Front
1930–31 **Norman Taurog**
Skippy
1931–32 **Frank Borzage**
Bad Girl
1932–33 **Frank Lloyd**
Cavalcade
1934 **Frank Capra**
It Happened One Night

The Grapes of Wrath: *Jane Darwell won the 1940 Best Supporting Actress Award playing Ma Joad*

1935 **John Ford**
The Informer

1936 **Frank Capra**
Mr Deeds Goes to Town

1937 **Leo McCarey**
The Awful Truth

1938 **Frank Capra**
You Can't Take It with You

1939 **Victor Fleming**
Gone with the Wind

1940 **John Ford**
The Grapes of Wrath

1941 **John Ford**
How Green Was My Valley

1942 **William Wyler**
Mrs Miniver

1943 **Michael Curtiz**
Casablanca

1944 **Leo McCarey**
Going My Way

1945 **Billy Wilder**
The Lost Weekend

1946 **William Wyler**
The Best Years of Our Lives

1947 **Elia Kazan**
Gentleman's Agreement

1948 **John Huston**
Treasure of the Sierra Madre

1949 **Joseph L. Mankiewicz**
A Letter to Three Wives

1950 **Joseph L. Mankiewicz**
All About Eve

1951 **George Stevens**
A Place in the Sun

1952 **John Ford**
The Quiet Man

1953 **Fred Zinnemann**
From Here to Eternity

1954 **Elia Kazan**
On the Waterfront

1955 **Delbert Mann**
Marty

1956 **George Stevens**
Giant

1957 **David Lean**
The Bridge on the River Kwai

1958 **Vincente Minnelli**
Gigi

1959 **William Wyler**
Ben-Hur

1960 **Billy Wilder**
The Apartment

1961 **Robert Wise & Jerome Robbins**
West Side Story

1962 **David Lean**
Lawrence of Arabia

1963 **Tony Richardson**
Tom Jones

1964 **George Cukor**
My Fair Lady

1965 **Robert Wise**
The Sound of Music

1966 **Fred Zinnemann**
A Man for All Seasons

1967 **Mike Nichols**
The Graduate

1968 **Carol Reed**
Oliver!

1969 **John Schlesinger**
Midnight Cowboy

1970 **Franklin J. Schaffner**
Patton

1971 **William Friedkin**
The French Connection

1972 **Bob Fosse**
Cabaret

1973 **George Roy Hill**
The Sting

1974 **Francis Coppola**
The Godfather, Part II

1975 **Milos Forman**
One Flew over the Cuckoo's Nest

1976 **John G. Avildsen**
Rocky

1977 **Woody Allen**
Annie Hall

1978 **Michael Cimino**
The Deer Hunter

1979 **Robert Benton**
Kramer vs Kramer

1980 **Robert Redford**
Ordinary People

1981 **Warren Beatty**
Reds

1982 **Sir Richard Attenborough**
Gandhi

1983 **James L. Brooks**
Terms of Endearment

1984 **Milos Forman**
Amadeus

1985 **Sydney Pollack**
Out of Africa

1986 **Oliver Stone**
Platoon

1987 **Bernardo Bertolucci**
The Last Emperor

1988 **Barry Levinson**
Rain Man

1989 **Oliver Stone**
Born on the Fourth of July

1990 **Kevin Costner**
Dances with Wolves

1991 **Jonathan Demme**
The Silence of the Lambs

1992 **Clint Eastwood**
Unforgiven

1993 **Steven Spielberg**
Schindler's List

1994 **Robert Zemeckis**
Forrest Gump

Best Foreign Film

1947 *Shoe Shine* (Italy)
1948 *Monsieur Vincent* (France)
1949 *The Bicycle Thief* (Italy)
1950 *The Walls of Malapaga* (France/Italy)
1951 *Rashomon* (Japan)
1952 *Forbidden Games* (France)
1953 No award
1954 *Gate of Hell* (Japan)
1955 *Samurai* (Japan)

1956 *La Strada* (Italy)
1957 *The Nights of Cabiria* (Italy)
1958 *Mon Oncle* (France)
1959 *Black Orpheus* (France)
1960 *The Virgin Spring* (Sweden)
1961 *Through a Glass Darkly* (Sweden)
1962 *Sundays and Sybele* (France)
1963 *8 1/2* (Italy)
1964 *Yesterday, Today and Tomorrow* (Italy)
1965 *The Shop on Main Street* (Czechoslovakia)
1966 *A Man and a Woman* (France)
1967 *Closely Observed Trains* (Czechoslovakia)
1968 *War and Peace* (Russia)
1969 *Z* (France)
1970 *Investigation of a Citizen Above Suspicion* (Italy)
1971 *The Garden of the Finzi-Continis* (Italy)
1972 *The Discreet Charm of the Bourgeoisie* (France)
1973 *Day for Night* (France)
1974 *Amarcord* (Italy)
1975 *Dersu Uzala* (Japan)

1976 *Black and White in Colour* (Ivory Coast/France)
1977 *Madame Rosa* (France)
1978 *Get Out Your Handkerchiefs* (France)
1979 *The Tin Drum* (Germany)
1980 *Moscow Doesn't Believe in Tears* (Russia)
1981 *Mephisto* (Hungary)
1982 *To Begin Again* (Spain)
1983 *Fanny and Alexander* (Sweden)
1984 *Dangerous Moves* (Switzerland)
1985 *The Official Story* (Argentina)
1986 *The Assault* (Netherlands)
1987 *Babette's Feast* (Denmark)
1988 *Pelle the Conqueror* (Denmark)
1989 *Cinema Paradiso* (Italy)
1990 *Journey of Hope* (Switzerland)
1991 *Mediterraneo* (Italy)
1992 *Indochine* (France)
1993 *Belle Epoque* (Spain)
1994 *Burnt by the Sun* (Russia)

Cabaret: *Minnelli and Gray, two of eight Oscars won*

Cannes Film Festival

The Cannes Film Festival, held each May, started as a showcase of world film-art – which frightened the Americans enough to stop them sending any of their "product" unless it was especially "arty". Although American stars like Robert Mitchum came to Cannes in the 1950s, the beach was more likely to be occupied by the likes of Brigitte Bardot or topless starlets. But in the 1970s a trickle of Hollywood mainstream movies gave way to a flood, and by the 1990s and the "Hollywoodization" of Cannes had taken place: it became another marketplace, a corporate showcase for stars seeking publicity.

Now Sylvester Stallone, Madonna and Arnold Schwarzenegger will be prized guests at Cannes, rubbing shoulders with the likes of Akira Kurosawa, Wim Wenders or Catherine Deneuve.

Film festivals have mushroomed across the world as publicity binges for movies, a long version of the "junkets" film companies hold for journalists to meet their stars and peddle stories about their wares. Though Berlin, Moscow, Toronto, London, Tokyo, Edinburgh, New York, Sundance and others may have their claims, Cannes takes the award for top film festival. Begun in 1939, but interrupted by the war, Cannes now seems to offer a prize for virtually every film it shows, but here's a year-by-year rundown of the only one that really counts – the Golden Palm or Palme D'Or.

Best Film

1946 *The Lost Weekend / Battle of the Rails / Maria Candelaria / Rome Open City / La Symphonie Pastorale*
1947 No award
1948 No award
1949 *The Third Man*
1950 No award
1951 *Miracle in Milan / Miss Julie*
1952 *Othello / White Mane / Two Cents Worth of Hope*
1953 *Wages of Fear*
1954 *Gate of Hell*
1955 *Marty*
1956 *The Silent World*
1957 *Friendly Persuasion*
1958 *The Cranes are Flying*
1959 *Black Orpheus*
1960 *La Dolce Vita*
1961 *Viridiana / The Long Absence*

1962 *La Parole Donnée*
1963 *The Leopard*
1964 *The Umbrellas of Cherbourg*
1965 *The Knack and How to Get It*
1966 *A Man and a Woman / The Birds, the Bees and the Italians*
1967 *Blow Up / Dutchman*
1968 No award
1969 *If...*
1970 *M*A*S*H*
1971 *The Go-Between*
1972 *The Mattei Affair / The Working Class Go to Heaven*
1973 *Scarecrow*
1974 *The Conversation*
1975 *Chronicle of the Burning Years*
1976 *Taxi Driver*
1977 *Padre Padrone*
1978 *The Tree of Wooden Clogs*
1979 *Apocalypse Now / The*

Tin Drum
1980 *All That Jazz / Kagemusha*
1981 *Man of Iron*
1982 *Missing, Yol*
1983 *The Ballad of Narayama*
1984 *Paris, Texas*
1985 *Dance with a Stranger / When Father Was Away on Business*
1986 *The Mission*
1987 *Under Satan's Sun*
1988 *Pelle the Conqueror*
1989 *sex, lies and videotape*
1990 *Wild at Heart /* OVERSEAS PRIZE: *Three Women with Man Trouble*
1991 *Barton Fink*
1992 *The Best Intentions / My New Gun*
1993 *Farewell My Concubine / The Piano*
1994 *Pulp Fiction*

M*A*S*H*: *Donald Sutherland as Hawkeye in Robert Altman's 1970 smash*

Index

Page numbers in **bold** refer to main features.

Index

Index